中國現代小說戲劇一千五百種

謝泳、蔡登山　編

「中國現代文學史稀見史料」前言

謝泳

　　這裡搜集的有關中國現代文學史研究的三種史料並不特別難見，但在事實和經驗中，它們的使用率並不高，有鑒於此，我和登山兄想到把它們集中重印出來，供從事中國現代文學史研究的學者使用。

《中國現代小說戲劇一千五百種》

　　第一本是英文《中國現代小說戲劇一千五百種》（*1500 Modern Chinese Novels & Plays*）。

　　本書是一九四八年輔仁大學印刷的，嚴格說不是正式出版物，所以可能流通不廣。夏志清寫《中國現代小說史》的時候，在前言裡專門提到宋淇送他的這本書非常有用。這本書的作者，通常都認為是善秉仁。關於此書的編輯情況是這樣的：當時「普愛堂出版社」計劃出版一套叢書，共有五個系列，第一個系列是「文藝批評叢書」，共有四本書，其中三本與中國新文學相關，一本是《文藝月旦》（甲集，原名《說部甄評》），一本是《中國現代小說戲劇一千五百種》，還有一本是《新文學運動史》。《中國現代小說戲劇一千五百種》由三部分組成：

　　第一部分是蘇雪林寫的「中國當代小說和戲劇」（Present Day Fiction & Drama In China）。

　　第二部分是趙燕聲寫的「作者小傳」（Short Biographies Of Authors）。

　　第三部分是善秉仁寫的「中國現代小說戲劇一千五百種」。

　　本書印刷的時間是一九四八年，大體上可以看成中國現代文學結束期的一個總結，作為一本工具性的書，因為是總結當代小說和戲劇以及相關的作家問題，它提供的材料準確性較高。特別是善秉仁編著的《中國現代小說戲劇一千五百種》，主要是一個書目提要，雖然有作者的評價，如認為適合成年人、不適合任何人或者乾脆認為是壞書等，但這些評價現在看來並不是沒有價值，我們可以從他的評價中發現原書的意義，就是完全否定性的評價，對文學史研究來說也不是毫無意義。比如當時張愛玲出了三本書，分別是《傳奇》《流言》和《紅玫瑰》（原名如此），提要中都列出了。認為《流言》適於所有的人閱讀，而對《紅玫瑰》是否定的，建議不要推薦給任何人；對《傳奇》則認為雖然愛情故事比較危險和灰色，不合適推薦給任何人閱讀，但同時認為，小說敘述非常自由和具有現代風格，優美的敘述引人入勝且非常有趣。另外，本書對《圍城》的評價也不高。

本書的編纂有非常明確的宗教背景，前言開始就說明是向外國公眾介紹中國當代文學，但同時也有保護青年、反對危險和有害的閱讀。作為中國早期一本比較完善的現代文學研究著作，本書的價值可以說是相當高的，除了它豐富和準確的資料性外，蘇雪林的論文也有很重要的學術史意義。它基本梳理清了中國現代小說和戲劇的發展脈絡，而且評價比較客觀。她對魯迅在中國現代小說史上的開創性地位有正面的評價，對老舍、巴金的文學地位也有較高評價。對新興的都市文學作家群、鄉土作家群、北方作家群等等，都有專章敘述，中國現代文學史上有地位的小說家和劇作家基本都注意到了。本書敘述中國當代小說，蘇雪林第一個提到的就是魯迅，她說無論什麼時候提到中國當代小說，我們都必須承認魯迅的先鋒地位，這個見識體現了很遠大的文學史眼光。

《文藝月旦‧甲集》

第二本是善秉仁的《說部甄評》。

本書原是用法文寫的一本書，後來譯成中文，名為《文藝月旦‧甲集》，一九四七年六月初版，署景明譯，燕聲補傳。書前有一篇四萬餘字的〈導言〉，其中第三部分「現代中國小說的分析」，多有對中國現代文學的評價。本書除了善秉仁的〈導言〉外，還有趙燕聲編纂的「書評」和「作家小傳」，這些早期史料，對中國現代文學研究很有幫助，特別是其中一些史料線索很寶貴，比如善秉仁在《文藝月旦》的導言最後中提到：「文寶峰神父的《中國新文學運動史》業已出版。一種《中法對照新文學辭典》已經編出，將作為『文藝批評叢書』的第三冊，第四冊又將是一批《文藝月旦》的續集。」

《新文學運動史》

第三本是文寶峰的《新文學運動史》（*Histoire de La Litterature chinoise modern by H.Van Boven Peiping*）

我最早是從常風先生那裡聽到這本書的。我查了一下印在《中國現代小說戲劇一千五百種》封面上的廣告目錄，提示英文正在計劃中，而法文本已經印出。本書列為「文藝批評叢書」的第二種。

常風先生在世的時候，我有時候去和他聊天，他常常告訴我一些上世紀三十年代文壇的舊事，有很多還是一般文學史中不太注意的。文寶峰（H.Van Boven）這個名字，我就是從他那裡聽到的。記得他還問過我，中國現代文學界對這個人有沒有研究，我說我不清楚。他說這個人對中國現代文學很有興趣，寫過一本《中國現代文學史》。聽常風先生說，文寶峰是比利時人。一九四四年春間，他曾和常風一起去看過周作人。常風先生後來寫了〈記周作人〉一文，交我在《黃河》雜誌發表，文章最後一段就寫這個經歷。他特別提到「見了文寶峰我才知道他們的教會一直在綏遠一帶傳教，因此他會說綏遠方言。文寶峰跟我交談是英文與漢語並用，他喜歡中國新文學，被日本侵略軍關進集中營後，他繼續閱讀新文學作品和有關書籍，我也把我手頭對他有用的書借給他。過了三四個月，文寶峰就開始用法文寫《中國現代文學史》，一九四四年七月底他已寫完。一九四五年日本帝國主義投降後不久文寶峰到我家找我，他告訴我說他們的教會領導認為他思想左傾要他回比利時，他在離開中國之前很希望能拜訪一次周作人。與文寶峰接觸近一年，我發現他對周作人和魯迅都很崇拜。」[1]

---

[1]　常風：《逝水集》（瀋陽：遼寧教育出版社，一九九五年），頁一〇六。

　　梁實秋在〈憶李長之〉一文中曾說：「照片中的善司鐸面部模糊不可辨識，我想不起他的風貌，不過我知道天主教神父中很多飽學之士，喜與文人往來。」[2]

　　梁實秋這篇回憶李長之的文章，就是由常風先生寄了一張一九四八年他們在一起吃飯時的合影照片引起的，這張照片上有當時北平懷仁學會的善秉仁，文寶峰當時可能也在這個機關服務。這張照片非常有名，主要是當時「京派」重要作家都出席了，此後他們大概再沒有這樣集中過，梁實秋此後也再沒有回過北平。記得好多年前，子善兄曾托我向常風先生複製過這張照片，我幫他辦了此事，還就此事給《老照片》寫過一篇短文。

　　文寶峰（H.Van Boven）是比利時人，曾在綏遠、北京一帶傳教，喜歡中國新文學，一九四四年，被日本侵略軍關進集中營後，他繼續閱讀新文學作品和有關書籍，用法文完成了《新文學運動史》（*Histoire de La Litterature chinoise moderne*），一九四六年作為「文藝批評叢書」的一種，由北平普愛堂印行。此書中國國家圖書館現在可以找到，希望以後能翻譯出來供研究者使用。關於文寶峰其人，我後來還在臺灣大學古偉瀛教授編輯的一本關於傳教士的名錄中見到了相關的介紹，印象中他後來到了日本傳教，二〇〇三年在日本姬鹿城去世。

　　《新文學運動史》正文共有十五章，除序言和導論外，分別是：

一、桐城派對新文學的影響

二、譯文和最早的文言論文

三、新文體的開始和白話小說的意義

四、最早的轉型小說──譯作和原創作品

五、新文學革命：

　　（一）文字解放運動

　　（二）重要人物胡適和陳獨秀

　　（三）反對和批評

　　（四）對胡適和陳獨秀作品的評價

　　（五）新潮

---

[2]　《梁實秋懷人叢錄》（北京：中國廣播電視出版社，一九八九年），頁三一八。

趙燕聲在〈現代中國文學研究書目〉一文中認為「西文的中國新文學史，此書現在是唯一本。內容偏重社團史料，作家傳記；敍事截止於一九三三、一九三四左右。錯誤的地方很多。」[3]

在以往中國現代文學史編纂史研究中，還沒有注意到這部著述。因為它完成於上世紀四十年代中期，大體是中國現代文學史的完整歷史，是一部非常有意義的著述。我們從它的目錄中可以看出，文寶峰敍述中國現代文學史的眼光很關注新文學和中國傳統文學的關係，特別是對轉型時期翻譯作品對新文學的影響有重要論述。本書的影印出版，對開拓中國現代文學史研究視野很有幫助，同時也促使學界用新眼光打量中國現代文學編纂史。由於文寶峰對周氏兄弟的新文學史地位評價很高，本書對魯迅研究、周作人研究的啓示意義也是顯而易見的。雖然作者有明顯的宗教背景，但他在評價新文學史的時候，還是保持了非常獨特的眼光。文寶峰在序言中，特別表達了對常風先生的感激之情，認為是常風先生幫助他完成了這部著作，文寶峰說，在集中營修改此書的漫長歲月裡，常風先生審看了他的稿子並給他帶來必要的信息和原始資料。

希望這三種史料的影印出版能推動中國現代文學史研究的發展。上世紀六十年代中期，香港龍門書局曾翻印過《中國現代小說戲劇一千五百種》，但大陸一般研究者也不易

---

[3]　《文潮》第五卷六期，民國三十七年。

見到，其它兩種就更少聽說了。現在秀威資訊科技出版公司將三種史料一併同時推出，對於加強兩岸中國現代文學研究的交流有非常重要的意義。至於另外一種《中法對照新文學辭典》，目前我們還沒有找到，希望以後能有機會發現並貢獻給研究者。

謝泳

二○一○年九月三十日於廈門大學人文學院

SCHEUT EDITIONS

1500 MODERN CHINESE NOVELS & PLAYS

BY

JOS. SCHYNS (善秉仁)

& OTHERS

PRESENT DAY FICTION & DRAMA IN CHINA

BY

SU HSUEH-LIN (蘇雪林)

SHORT BIOGRAPHIES OF AUTHORS

BY

CHAO YEN-SHENG (趙燕聲)

PEIPING 1948

———◆———

Sole Distributors: Catholic University Press, Peiping-China.

SCHEUT EDITIONS

ERIES I-CRITICAL AND LITERARY STUDIES-VOL. III

1500 MODERN CHINESE NOVELS & PLAYS

SCHEUT EDITIONS

1500 MODERN CHINESE NOVELS & PLAYS

BY

JOS. SCHYNS (善秉仁)

& OTHERS

PRESENT DAY FICTION & DRAMA IN CHINA

BY

SU HSUEH-LIN (蘇雪林)

SHORT BIOGRAPHIES OF AUTHORS

BY

CHAO YEN-SHENG (趙燕聲)

PEIPING 1948

Sole Distributors: Catholic University Press, Peiping-China.

中　國　印

Printed in China

Yu Lien Press, Peiping

FOREWORD.

In publishing this book, we are pursuing two distinctive aims, which are, to protect young people against the danger of pernicious reading, and to introduce modern Chinese literature to the foreign public.

Certain "freethinkers" without religion or conscience may shrug their shoulders when turning the leaves of this book; nevertheless, by irony of fate, they might be the first to consult it if their own children's spiritual welfare should be at stake.

These pages are meant, above all, for educators and head of families, who have a sense of their own responsibilities. We are far from arrogating to ourselves the right to set ourselves up for censors. All we wish to do is to fulfil our duty as educators.

Our second aim, for the achievement of which we have spared no effort, is to give the public at large a knowledge and an appreciation of modern Chinese literature. There can be no real understanding and recognizing of the true value of a people, without taking the trouble to study the works of their thinkers and the tastes of their reading public.

Ancient Chinese literature is fairly well known, and there is no lack of documentation on it. This, however, is not the case with contemporary literature, and we look in vain for serious comprehensive studies on the subject. Apart from a few elementary articles, we can find but a few rare studies by the Rev. Fathers *Monsterleet, O. Brière* (S.J.)[1] and H. *Van Boven* (C.I.C.M.)[2] They are of a serious nature, and those wishing to go deeper into the matter, will find thorough, though not complete information in these works.

There are also Chinese studies on the subject, but as far as they are known to us, they cannot satisfy foreign critics entirely. They often lack coherence and are not sufficiently impartial in their study of literature, in general, and modern literary movements, in particular.

---

[1] Cf. "Collectanea Comm. Synodalis", 1942, pp. 578 ff., and 1944, pp. 175 ff. "Bulletin de l'Aurore", 1942, pp. 577 ff. and 1944, pp. 429 ff.

[2] "Histoire de la littérature chinoise moderne" (History of Modern Chinese Literature) by Henri Van Boven. Published in "Scheut Editions", 1946, in Peiping (out of print).

I

There is no pretension, on our part, that the present work will fill the gap. Publishing, in this volume, a summary of modern literature and a certain number of short biographical sketches, as well as reviews of 1500 novels and plays, we are merely giving a general survey. We hope, however, that the book as a whole may be of service to sinologists as material for more comprehensive, more critical, and more profound studies.[3]

We must point out especially that our book reviews do not aim at presenting a critique from the literary point of view. We believe, however, that a perusal of the book will enable the experienced reader to form an opinion on the literary value of quite a number of authors, although it may be an opinion deriving from the general impression made by the tenor of the whole book, rather than from a judgement based on analysis. It may be repeated that, taken separately, our reviews do not aim at literary criticism.

Some of our Chinese friends who are well versed in literature, were rather shocked to see us honour several authors without literary value whatsoever, by citing their works. To them we reply, that wishing, above all, to moralise, we do not review books because of their literary value, but because they are read by the public. We have nevertheless yielded to a pressing demand by a talented writer, and discarded a certain number of reviews dealing with the works of authors who are too plainly of mediocre, or low calibre.[4]

Readers who know our French or Chinese publications may be surprised not to find in this survey, at the head of each review, the signs indicating into which category we have classified the book in question. This omission has been made on purpose. The said signs, and their explanation, appear at the end of this volume where a list is given of all the reviewed books, together with the indications of their value from the moral point of view. Those of our readers who use this book only for practical reference, will find there all the information they are looking for.

It can hardly be supposed that we alone have read all the books that are reviewed here. In fact, only about half of them have passed through our hands, whereas a considerable number of collaborators have been in charge of reading the other half. Our readers may nevertheless be assured that all those concerned have carried out their task most conscientiously. The books in question being written in a foreign language, and moreover in one that is very difficult to understand, we have not the least pretension to being infallible, and we are ready to revise our judgments, should there be any critics kind enough to offer us better ones. It will be noticed, moreover, that certain judgments in this book differ from those published in the French edition, as we have altered them after an exchange of views with qualified readers.

---

3 A part of the present work (600 reviews) has been published in French, under the title "Romans à lire et Romans à proscrire" (Novels to read and novels to proscribe"), in "Scheut Editions", 1946 (at present out of print), and in Chinese, under the title "文藝月旦", "Scheut Editions", 1947, Peiping.

4 Such as 金小春, 冷眼生, 遯隱, 評花主人, 思瑛館主, 捉刀人, 王雪倩, 于水如, 月明樓主 默厂主人, etc. whose works are pervers and at times even pornographic.

We are not free from expectation of reproaches from some readers, who will say: "Your survey is incomplete", or, "the book I have in hand, is not included". We are aware of such omissions which, however, are excusable, considering the enormous amount of work involved in a task of this kind. If God grant us life and the necessary perseverence, we hope to publish another volume in the not too distant future, which will supplement this work.

We also often hear two contradictory objections. We are told, "You are too severe", or else, "you are much too indulgent"! To both we can only reply: we do our best. We have taken to heart the moral health of youth, and this is our criterion and what has guided us in our task. It may, however, be repeated that there is no finality in our judgments.

Another objection must be mentioned that comes very often from well-meaning people. They say that it is due to our survey that "the attention of young people is drawn to bad books". But in the big cities, young people have access to easier and cheaper means of information than this work concerning the kind of literature alluded to. And it is quite unnecessary to dwell upon the strong reasons that render such a survey indispensable for educators. It suffices to repeat a pronouncement of the Sovereign Pontiff who is the highest moral authority in the world: "They are to be praised . . . all these educational works that make it their task to signal, . . . by special publications, . . . to parents and educators, the moral and religious dangers . . . insinuated by certain books. . . " (H. H. Pius XI, Encyclical on Christian Education of Youth).

We conclude our Foreword with the pleasant duty of thanking our many collaborators.

First of all, we wish to express our gratitude to Mrs. *Su Hsüeh-lin* (蘇雪林) a famous Catholic writer, and professor of literature at Wu-han University.[5] Our readers will judge for themselves of the opportuneness and value of the Introduction she has written for this volume. In the survey she gives us of modern authors and their works, she has omitted the important place she herself occupies in modern literature. We know her publications. They reveal artistic refinement, polished style and nobility of sentiment. In justice to her, we cannot refrain from recognizing the enviable position she holds among modern writers, and the undeniably beneficient influence she exercises on youth.[5]

We also extend our warmest thanks to Mr. *Chao Yen-sheng* (趙燕聲) of the Centre Franco-Chinois, who is an indefatigable and conscientious worker, and we wish him every success for the future. His biographical sketches will be greatly appreciated by lovers of literature.

Special thanks are due to Miss *Shu-ping Kuai* (蒯淑平), a graduate of Oxford University, and at present a professor at the National Peking University. To her valuable collaboration and useful advice we render all the appreciation that is due.

---

5 Cf. Biogr. No. 141.

Finally, we wish to mention the many reviewers of books who have helped to produce this work. Knowing the tediousness of their task, we are all the more grateful for what they have done. Of the lay collaborators, we may mention especially the *Viscountess de Kermadec* and Dr. *Li Ming-sheng* (李銘琛). As to the clerical collaborators, their great number makes it impossible to mention them all. It would, however, be unjust on our part, not to make special mention, among the Jesuit, Franciscan and Scheut reviewers, of the Rev. Fathers *Hofbauer, Potveer* and *Jos. Hemeryck*[6]

In conclusion, we may add that it is our earnest wish that the present work may in some way contribute towards the moral reconstruction of the youth of China, and promote understanding of the people in whose midst we live.

Peiping, St. Joseph's Day, March 19, 1948.

Jos. Schyns (善秉仁)
Verbiest Academy
2, Niu P'aitze Hutung
(20) Peiping
懷 仁 學 會
北平牛排子胡同二號

---

6 His was the lion's part.

PRESENT DAY FICTION AND DRAMA IN CHINA

By

Su Hsüeh-lin (蘇雪林)

PRESENT DAY FICTION AND DRAMA IN CHINA

INTRODUCTION

The Chinese have always considered novels and plays as the trifling play-things of art, that cannot be compared in dignity with the orthodox efforts of literature, among which they have no place. Taking for instance, the Index of the 四庫全書 , we observe that it includes no novels written in the vernacular, or *pei-hua*. Although novelists are grouped as a class in the Tzŭ-pu, or category of scholars and philosophers, the works that are included are limited to notes, souvenirs, and sketches written in refined *wen-yen*, or literary style full of classical allusions; and although lyrics and songs are included as a separate item in the category of pure literature, they are restricted to those of real poetic value, while vernacular plays of the Yuan Dynasty and romances, that were recited or acted to popular audiences in the Ming and Ch'ing Dynasties, find no place in such exalted company.

But towards the end of the Ch'ing Dynasty, we were so rough-handled by western nations that our extreme self-satisfaction began to dwindle, and we began to be aware of merits in the civilization of the "barbarious", who had thrust themselves upon our notice. What we imitated in the beginning was only the material side of western civilization, but gradually we began to realize that the spiritual side of western culture was also well worth our notice, and we began to study their political theories, social systems and moral and ethical principles. But we took little heed of their literature, because as a nation founded on letters, we could be confident that even though we might not have attained to as high a level in other aspects as foreign nations, at least with regard to literature, no one could surpass us.

Then at the end of the Ch'ing Dynasty, a change of attitude was indicated in the person of *Lin Shu* (林紓) who, with the assistance of collaborators familiar with foreign languages translated over fifty European novels into classical Chinese; and although many of these were of the second or third order, nevertheless quite a number were literary masterpieces. He claimed that the construction and word-ing of the works of Sir Walter Scott and Charles Dickens might be compared to that of *Ssu-ma Ch'ien* (司馬遷) and *Pan Ku* (班固). But this may be considered as a sensational argument made to promote the popular consideration of European literature, so that the value of his own translations would be enhanced. He need not necessarily have been sincere and the litterati of the old school, naturally subscribed still less to this point of view.

Liang Ch'i-ch'ao (梁啓超) thought highly of the novel, and wrote "The

Function of the Novel in the Government of the Masses'', (小說與群治之關係) in which he maintained that if a people are to be reformed, the novels of the nation must first be instilled with a new spirit. Nevertheless he did not consider the novel as a proper form of literature, but only as a means of propaganda among the common people. He also turned his attention to Chinese plays. He attempted two plays including "The Romance of New Rome" (新羅馬傳奇) at the period when he was publishing the "New People" (新民叢報). In it yellow-haired, green-eyed westerners were forcibly fitted into the parts of the traditional Chinese opera, and while the ideas expressed were those of the 19th century of the West, what was actually sung was the traditional form of the Chinese drama of the fifteenth and sixteenth centuries; so that although the actual phrasing may not have lacked refinement of beauty, the general impression created was extremely bizarre. For this reason neither of these two plays were carried further than the beginning, and never reached completion.

Also, during the first years of the Republic, there appeared two dramatic societies, "The Spring Willow Society" (春柳社) and the "Chin Hua T'uan" (進化團), that wrote and produced a number of plays in the vernacular, but owing to the strength of the traditional drama, they met with no support and soon disappeared. The remnants of these two societies, in order to earn a livelihood, were reduced to acting in the old plays, and the new form of drama that they had promoted declined into the *"Wen Ming Hsi"*, the so-called "fashionable" new drama or "reformed plays", that gasped out, a painful existence in Shanghai and Peking. Being no less decadent than the traditional form, they soon lost the confidence of the people.

The novel and the drama were not promoted to a recognized status as literature, until the time of the May 4th Student Movement.[1] Owing to the growing impetus of popular demand, and to the enthusiastic promotion of certain scholars with advanced ideas, such as *Ch'en Tu-hsiu* (陳獨秀) and *Hu Shih* (胡適) the vernacular took the place of the classical language that had been traditional for thousands of years, and the novel and the drama which, until now had had no recognized status, not only forced their way into the closed circle of literature, but even became two of its most important forms.

Owing to the limits of this preface, no detailed analyses will be made of aspects of the literary revolution in Modern China, such as the growth and development of the new vernacular style, or the arguments for and against it. Nor will mention be made of contemporary poetry, essays, articles and sketches, and literary criticism etc., which are not directly connected with the subject. Only a birds' eye view will be taken of the birth and development of the novel and the drama since the May 4th Student Movement until now.

The writers and writings, dealt with in this preface, have not been selected according to any rigid rule, for the New Literature has only thirty years of life to its credit, and is in consequence pitiably poor in accomplishment. There would be very little left to talk about, if a rigid selection were made.

_____

(1) May 4th 1919.

The arrangement of the material is based upon the groups into which the various writers fall, which may not be a satisfactory method of dealing with living writers owing to possibilities of fluctuations and developments in their subject-matter and style. But some such method has been necessary, for if the subject had been taken as a whole without division into groups, the result could not have been anything but loose and confused.

CONTEMPORARY CHINESE FICTION

Lu Hsün (魯迅)

Whenever contemporary Chinese fiction is mentioned, we must recognise *Lu Hsün* (魯迅) as the first pioneer. Although his most valuable contribution has been concentrated in only two collections, "Cries" (吶喊) and "Hesitation" (傍徨), yet it is enough to assure him the foremost and most honourable place in modern Chinese literature. When his "Diary of a Madman" (狂人日記) was publised in the seventh year of the Republic (1918) in the "New Youth Magazine" (新青年), its form, subject matter, and atmosphere, down to the ideas it expressed, were so extraordinary and startling that it gave a very great stimulation to the youth of the time, making them discard the old bottles of their mental processes and adopt new forms in which to express their ideas. Then, "The True Story of Ah Q" was published in the Literary Supplement of the Ch'en Pao (晨報). The hero was only a jobless vagabond of the countryside of Shao-hsing yet he represented the deeply-rooted failings of the ordinary member of society in China. The style was so lively, gay, witty and entertaining that readers were overcome by it.

Besides the above, the best of the short stories included in these two collections may be said to be the following, "Storm" (風波) "Homeside" (故鄉) "Festival Play" (社戲), "K'ung Yi-chi" (孔乙己), "Benediction" (祝福) and "A Piece of Soap" (肥皂). In these he shows himself expert in portraying the countryside, and as most of his characters were taken from a village of the Shao-hsing district of which he was a native, they were all the more vivid, and convincing.

Before his death, another publication, "Old Tales Retold" (故事新編) appeared, which was a collection of short stories adapted from Chinese history. It was, however, only a flippant representation of his subject matter indicating a probable decline of his powers.

In estimating Lu Hsün, we ought also to lay emphasis on his shorter articles in which he records his reminiscences. They do not differ in either technique or attitude from his short stories, that is to say, he is original in both, and in both, his style is concise and powerful and inimitable in the profundity of his thougts with its many implications.

Lu Hsün's pen has been compared to a surgeon's lancet, but whereas a surgeon operates on the human body, his subject is the soul of man. Without any concession to human feelings he scoops out the secrets from our innermost depths and the weaknesses we have tried our best to conceal. He considers that mankind as a whole is evil, the individual members of which are selfish, and even if there are a few that are comparatively good, they are only hypocritical Pharisees.

He subjects the self-satisfied to a minute scruting, and reveals the corruptness of their motives, and often he does not mind demolishing one with the effluvia of the pen and catching one in the undertow of his meaning, thus revealing his countenance of a typical "Shao-hsing schemer."

It is difficult to find real generosity, amiability or true altruism in his stories or other articles, but easy to detect in them a cold fierceness in which every word is like a vicious curse, and every phrase a diabolic grin of mockery.

Due to the defects of his early environment combined with his own special gifts, Lu Hsün may be considered as having become a sadist, for one finds in both his thought and feeling thoroughly unhealthy elements, echoing the diseased mind of modern China.

For political reasons he has been idolized by leftist elements and raised to the golden throne of literature as the leading thinker and great literary master of present times. When he died in the Autumn of the 25th year of the Republic (1936), lively propaganda was made on his behalf in literary circles throughout the country, and if all the exaggerated eulogies of him were collected they would amount to millions of words. The ignorant and hypnotized youth of the country considered the neurotic man, who was an able writer but of unsound "Weltanschauung," the great sage of the Orient, and the worship accorded him was no less than that given by the men of letters of the past to the great and accomplished Master, Confucius.

With those whom Lu Hsün considered as opposing his opinions, he used what he called a strategy of "beseiging and suppressing", or "driving the fox to bag", which meant that he called upon his friends and fellows to join the hunt which would not cease until the victim was utterly demolished. He also used another species of attack which was to hang onto his victim without letting go, a tactic resembling that of a bulldog, and the years would pass while he was thus employed without his realizing it. Other ways of opposing his literary enemies were to wake up stories, spread rumours, strike from behind, take them unawares, and the employment of such vicious measures was carried to the extreme. It was natural that he was called by his enemies a "literary bandit".

The Chinese Communists realized that utilized for political purposes these methods of Lu Hsün were very efficient. Therefore these same methods. adopted by the Communists for there propaganda in literary circles, had immediate effect, so that nearly all the younger writers were either intimidated or bought over to their camp and became members of their rank and file. And as for the writers of longer experience and greater distinction, they also were either intimidated into subscribing to the Communist tenets, or, with an apologetic attitude towards them, were allowed to maintain a precarious independence, so that there was no one left with the courage to make an open stand against them. Thus the whole literary movement in China became a monopoly of the Communists.

It now becomes clear that the writers and their works mentioned in the following pages will form nothing but a review of leftist literature.

After the late Sino-Japanese War, the Communists extended their control from pure literature to the wider field of culture as a whole, and they, together with Lu Hsün whom they had adopted as their mouthpiece, must take a responsibility for the present deplorable state of public opinion in which casuistry reigns supreme, so that black may be taken for white and white for black, an attitude that leads to endless argument.

Culture is the name we give to the outward manifestation of both the soul and mind of a nation for their proper functioning which depend upon a healthy union, but it seems that China at the moment is suffering from split personality, a sad condition which cannot fail to bring about much misery. And when a nation has been loosed from its moorings, the danger of the influence of a leader of unsound mental capacity cannot be over-exaggerated, as for instance in the example of Hitler, who through his dictatorship reduced the German nation almost to annihilation. Now in the case of Lu Hsün, what the result will be of following in the footsteps of this late writer, who suffered from severe persecution complex, is fearful to contemplate.

Disciples of Lu Hsün

Among those whose style and subject matter have been influenced by Lu Hsün, the earliest were Wang Lu-yen (王魯彥) Hsü Ch'in-wen, (許欽文) Feng Wen-ping (馮文炳) and Li Chin-ming (黎錦明).

Wang Lu-yen (王魯彥)

Over twenty years ago Wang Lu-yen was already praised by Shen Yen-ping (沈雁冰) (now known as Mao Tun (茅盾), as a creator of types. Among his publications are "Yellow Gold" (黃金) and "Pumelos" (柚子), in which he excels in description of the psychology and way of life of peasant and petit bourgeois in the country. His works have the atmosphere of his native town of Ningpo, and the temperament of the people there is well-presented even to their habit of prevarication, all which brings one in mind of Lu Hsün. His stories are full of sentiment, gloom and mystic depression, so that with a little more emphasis they would be in the style of Edgar Allan Poe. He is however, a child of the materialistic age and at the same time a naive realist of the peasant type, so that mysticism with him cannot be carried very far. His craftsmanship, however is practiced and his wording concise. Unfortunately he died in Kueilin in the latter years of the war. Otherwise he would have made an incalculable contribution to the new literary movement.

Hsü Ch'in-wen (許欽文)

Hsü Ch'in-wen is a prolific writer. He has published over ten collections of short stories. When his first book, "Birthplace" (故鄉) appeared, Lu Hsün said: "In describing country life, the author is not as proficient as myself, but in the portrayal of psychology of the young, I am not his equal." Moreover, in one of his own short stories, Lu Hsün has explained that it is after the style of Hsü Ch'in-wen. Since such a well-established writer as Lu Hsün has paid this author the compliment of imitation, his works will naturally repay our perusal.

Hsü Ch'in-wen's most interesting stories are those with a love theme, depicting the psychology of the young in the transitionary period immediately after the May 4th Student Uprising, of which the "Troubles of Mr. Chao" (趙先生的煩惱) is a good example.

Feng Wen-ping (馮文炳). Nom-de-plume, *Fei Ming.* (廢名)

The first publication of this author, "Tale of a Bamboo Grove" (竹林的故事) is also his best. He gives a deep feeling of the countryside. He has also absorbed much Russian influence and that of the literature of the smaller countries of Europe. He indulges chiefly in the depicting of the life of ordinary people, giving an effect like that of some Russian writers in which tears are shimmering beneath their smiles. He is naturally attracted to the style of K'ung Yi-chi (孔乙己) by Lu Hsün, one of the Na Han (吶喊) collection, which has cast its influence over more than one story from his pen.

His later productions, however published under the nom-de-plume of Fei Ming, have not the value of his earlier work. The "Peach Orchard" (桃園), "The Bridge" (橋), "The Life of Mr. Mo-hsü-yu" (莫須有先生傳) are ambiguous attempts that do not contain the directness of his earlier work.

Li Chin-ming (黎錦明)

This author is in his element depicting the tribal customs of the natives of southwestern Hunan, west of the River Hsiang. His style is more robust than that of Wang Lu-yen and Hsü Ch'in-wen, and he has the forcible and daring spirit of a Hunanese.

Among his works the most important are "The Miracle of Young Master Ma" (馬大少爺的奇蹟) and "A Suicide" (一個自殺者).

His works fall into two different groups, those that are worth reading and those that may be ignored without much loss.

Later Disciples of Lu Hsün

Peng Fang-ts'ao (彭芳草)

As a prose writer, Peng Fang-ts'ao is in the direct descent from Lu Hsün, especially in the criticism of social abuses, and he has imitated Lu Hsün's style so successfully that his work is difficult to distinguish from the Master's. He has made no really original contribution, his thought being merely an echo of Lu Hsün's.

His chief work may be found in "Let Him Be" (管他呢), "Bad Luck" (厄運) and "Song of Fading Flowers". (落花曲)

Kao Ch'ang-hung (高長虹) and *Kao Ko* (高歌)

Kao Ch'ang-hung and his younger brother, Kao Ko, were also faithful followers of Lu Hsün, but separated from the Master in his later years, when they established the literary society, "Storm and Stress" (狂飆社) which began a new literary movement. They still remained very much under Lu Hsün's influence.

A great number of miscellaneous works may be ascribed to Ch'ang-hung, while the central piece of Kao Ko's accomplishment is "Men Like Beasts" (野獸樣的人們).

At this juncture two writers of the name of Wong may be mentioned who at one time enjoyed a fair amount of popularity, but who have not persisted in their literary career.

Among the works of *Wong Ching-hsi*, (汪敬熙) "A Snowy Night" (雪夜) should be noticed. It is a collection of nine stories which include "Daughter Cuts Wood" (砍柴的女兒) and "The Donkey of the Cripple, Wang-erh" (瘸子王二的驢), in which the style is natural and unforced like that of Wang Lu-yen and Fei Ming.

The other Wong, *Wong Ching-chih* (汪靜之) was one of the new poets of the May 4th Student Movement. "Jesus' Command" (耶穌的吩咐), "Father and Daughter" (父與女) and "Ts'ui Ying and her Husband" (翠英及其夫) are the best-known of his works. The last contains a profound study of a peasant woman, and an extremely moving picture of the difficulties of the peasants in the country.

The Literary Society (文學研究會)

The "Literary Society" had its rise from the May 4th Student Movement and many of its members were famous writers of fiction.

Yeh Shao-chün (葉紹鈞)

In the early days, Yeh Shao-chün published seven or eight collections of short stories, such as "Coldness" (隔膜), "Without Satiety" (未厭), "Footsteps" (脚步), "In the City" (城中), "Under the Level" (線下), and "Fire" (火災). He was also the author of a well-known novel "Ni Huan-chih" (倪煥之).

In his early days he was very much under the influence of Dostoievsky, and was fond of choosing his characters from the oppressed with the object of leading his readers to see beauty in filth and sordidness. But he himself was often overcome by the actual abuses of society that he observed, so that in many instances he emphasises the darker side of life. Nevertheless we are so attracted by the purity of his style that we often overlook the depressing qualities of his subject matter.

Hsü Ti-shan (許地山) — Original nom-de-plume *Lo hua-sheng.* (落華生)

His chief works are "Spider in a Net" (綴網勞蛛) and "Spring Peach" (春桃).

In his early works we find his pages full of descriptions of the customs and life of the Malays and other inhabitants of the tropical countries of the South, his chief aim being to create an exotic atmosphere, which he achieves with great vividness. Later he imitated the exaggerated simplicity of the old traditional style to such an extent that a feeling of immobility was produced in his own work which became more retrogressive than progressive.

Wang T'ung-chao (王統照)

His chief works are ''Night of Spring Rain'' (春雨之夜) and ''Mountain Rain'' (山雨).

His early works are raw efforts, in which the material has not passed sufficiently through the furnace of the mind. They are, moreover too long, and not well enough sustained. ''Mountain Rain'' alone is a masterpiece consisting of over 200,000 words, having for its theme the bankruptcy of the villages of North China.

Hsieh Liu-yi (謝六逸)

Hsieh Liu-yi obtained his higher education in Japan. Upon his return he devoted himself to promoting interest in Japanese literature. He specializes in children's stories which he has published in nine issues. From his collected works the following may be selected for special mention: ''Foam'' (水沫), ''Mother'' (母親) and ''The Crime of Fan Chi'' (范集的犯罪).

Cheng Chên-to (鄭振鐸)

Under the penname of Kuo Yuan-hsing (郭源新) this author published ''The Catching of the Fire-snatcher'' (取火者之逮捕), based upon the story of Prometheus, in which he expressed his own ideas upon class struggle, and the style of which is refreshing.

Mention should also be made of ''Kuei Kung's Pond'' (桂公塘), a historical tale written by a practised hand.

Mao Tun (茅盾)

The greatest writer of the ''Literary Society'' however must be acknowledged to be Mao Tun (茅盾). His longer works include ''Disillusion'' (幻滅), ''Uncertainty'' (動搖), and ''Search'' (追求), a trilogy eventually issued under the general title of ''Eclipse'' (蝕); also ''The Rainbow'' (虹), ''The Road'' (路), ''Three Men On the Road'' (三人行) ''Midnight'' (子夜). Among his short stories mention should be made of ''Wild Roses'' (野薔薇) and ''Silkworms'' (春蠶).

Mao Tun is an artist who reveals to us the spirit of the age. The ''Eclipse'' trilogy, has as its background the Nationalist Army's Campaign of the Fifteenth Year of the Republic (1926), and we are carried with it until the establishment of Nanking as the national capital. Using a technique of scientific analysis, he examines social phenomena and the mental processes of people of all classes in a period of change and disorder.

The subject of ''Midnight'' is the collapse of national economy in China when the country is caught between the aggression of foreign imperialism on one hand, and the disorder created by the struggle of the war-lords on the other, with the inevitable result of speculation taking the place of honest trade.

"Silkworms" (春蠶), "Ling's Shop" (林家的舖子) and "Harvest" (秋收) are about the bankruptcy of the peasants and the trade depression suffered by the merchants in the city.

During the war, Mao Tun wrote the first part of "Red Autumn Leaves" (霜葉紅似二月花) laid in a complicated background, the second part of which, unfortunately, has never appeared.

"Each Man's Trade" (走上崗位) tells of the removal of factories into the interior during the war, and how everyone made a contribution to the war efforts each in his own way.

Mao Tun is a leftist writer with a wide influence. There is not a simple book that falls from his pen that does not promote class struggle in some way. He is vast in conception and brings both power and talent to the execution of his original plan. His sole aim is to depict "actual historical manifestations", which, more clearly defined, is his pet theory of the eventual collapse of the capitalist system, and the inevitable triumph of Communism.

Unfortunately, all to many of the writers of the new literary movement in China were influenced by those political ideas.

The eventual split on a worldwide scale has not yet manifested itself, but we in China have already felt its effects for over ten years of bloodshed and misery, which have never been as concentrated as at the present moment, and for which advocates of the Communist way of thinking, such as Mao Tun have to accept their share of responsibility. As an artist, however, Mao Tun may be considered a literary giant and a leader of the present literary movement, although by the past he allowed Lu Hsün to appropriate the literary palms of the age, and now is ready to recede before the genius of Kuo Mo-jo (郭沫若), a personal effacement which cannot but call forth our admiration.

An Independent Writer of Considerable Stature: Pa Chin (巴金)

Outside the circle of the "Literary Society," another contemporary writer who should be considered, and whose reputation and accomplishment is no inferior to Mao Tun, is Pa Chin (巴金). He was influenced in his earlier years by anarchism, and a nihilistic atmosphere is to be found in most of his works. Since anarchism denies all principles and rules, and all authority aiming at reducing all mankind to the same dead level, it is the active destructive force of the communistic ideal, and naturally leads to nihilism. This attitude is most clearly indicated in Pa Chin's first work, "Destruction" (滅亡). The chief character in this novel, Tu Ta-hsin (杜大心), reminds one of Shevyrev, the hero of Artsybashev's work, "The Working Man". He also resembles another of Artsybashev's character, Sanine.

Pa Chin also is known to promote the philosophy of Hate. His Hate, however, is born of Love. He is full of an impetus enthusiasm which refuses to submit to the yoke of restraint, and causes his characters to be egoistic and romantic. His enthusiasm, moreover, makes his style like a waterfall which overwhelms us in a sudden rush.

Before the war the chief works from his pen were "Destruction" (滅亡), "A Voyage" (海行), "Sea Dream" (海底夢), "Glory" (光明), "Vengeance" (復仇), "Home" (家) and the trilogy, "Love" (愛情三步曲). Since the war he has published "Spring" (春), "Autumn" (秋), "Fire" (火), "Garden of Leisure" (憩園), "Cold Night" (寒夜) etc.

Pa Chin together with Shen Ts'ung-wen (沈從文) and Chang Tzu-p'ing (張資平) have been called prolific writers. But with Pa Chin, at least, although his work is produced at a terrific rate, it does not have the air of being carelessly written.

The Creative Association (創造社)

Another group that has had as much influence as the "Literary Society", is the "Creative Association" (創造社), of whom the best-known members are Kuo Mo-jo (郭沫若), Yü Ta-fu (郁達夫), and Chang Tzu-p'ing (張資平).

Kuo Mo-jo (郭沫若)

Kuo Mo-jo is above all, a poet. But his interests are wide, and we have fiction, plays, and essays from his pen. His other work, however, does not have the value of his poetry. In his stories he uses one of Lu Hsün's collections "Old Tales Retold" (故事新編) as his model, producing in this way tales such as "Last Day of a Tyrant" (一個昏君的末日), "Meng-tzu Repudiates His Wife" (孟子休妻), and "Confucius is Hungry" (孔子絕糧). In these attempts he is a little too smart, and lacks the wit of Lu Hsün. His souvenirs and the events of his own life are given in his autobiographical books "Black Cat" (黑貓) and "Olives" (橄欖). But the impression obtained from these works is that they are rather crude, youthful efforts.

Yü Ta-fu and Chang Tzu-p'ing, however, are the real novelists of the "Creative Association", although their work cannot claim real literary merit, yet it appeared at just the right juncture when the public was ready to welcome fiction in the new style and therefore it justifies by its popularity a careful review.

Yü Ta-fu (郁達夫)

In the year 1921, Yü Ta-fu brought out a collection "Sinking" or "Decadence" (沉淪) which was attacked energetically by literary circles in Shanghai, but it was fortunate enough to obtain the support of Chou Tso-jen (周作人) who then was the foremost critic in China, and who recommended it not to the general public, but as reading for the initiated. After the approval of Chou Tso-jen, it was easy sailing for the author who found himself famous overnight.

A number of works followed. "Cold Ashes" (寒灰) "Chicken's Ribs" (鷄肋), "The Past", (過去) "Trivia " (畸零), and "Old Broom-" (敝帚) which were collections of short stories. The following novels were also published, "Lost Sheep" (迷羊), and "Weak Woman" (她是一個弱女子).

Yü Ta-fu's works are on a single subject: sex. It is to be expected, therefore, that they betray the restlessness of unsatisfied desire, and the abnormalities of an erotic imagination. His characters being a reflexion of himself rather than of the society in which he moves, they do not appeal to a wide sympathy. He can be accused of egotism, sentimentality, and decadence. And his favourable themes are poverty, the miseries of being out of work, despair, discontenty, pessimism and disease. His characters indulge in opium, alcohol, gambling, robbery and are the habitués of low dives and brothels. He has no idea of how to construct a plot, so that he produces mere fragmentary sketches of his own life. His style is barren and crude, fit only to portray the ugly sides of his own character and life. As, however, he draws no veil over even the most intimate phases of his own behavior, he satisfies the adolescent craving for sensation of the reading public, upon which his popularity is based.

He can claim two ardent followers, *Wang Yi-Jen* (王以仁) author of "Lone Swan" (孤雁), and *Yeh Ting-lo* (葉鼎洛), author of "Story of a Stranger" (他鄉人語), "Double Shadow" (雙影), and Crows" (烏鴉), who are both actually better writers than himself.

Chang Tzu-p'ing (張資平)

The other novelist of the "Creative Association", Chang Tzu-p'ing (張資平) is known as a writer of triangular and quadrangular love stories. Since the beginning of his literary career in 1922, he has published the following novels: "Alluvial Fossils" (冲積期的化石), "Eventual Joy" (最後的幸福), "Lyra's Daughter" (天孫之女) and "God's Children" (上帝的兒女們); and the following collections of short stories: "Focus of Love" (雪之除夕), "Snowy New Year's Eve (愛的焦點) etc. etc. to the number of about thirty volumes, which are all on the same subject of love with only one or two exceptions. Moreover, his love affairs never proceed smoothly, being always involved in triangular or multiple complications. His characters resemble those of Yü Ta-fu; all of them are diseased in mind and body, and especially the heroines. Also, like Yü Ta-fu, his works reflect the unenviable aspects of his own character. He is moreover, narrow-minded, has no restraint, and specialises in the portrayal of the restlessness of male desire. So much similarity of theme in his prolific production actually gives rise to a feeling of monotony. A single novel of his is enough to represent the rest and he is, in consequence nothing but a "popular writer".

Before the appearance of Chang Tzu-p'ing, the public had already been subjected to the efforts of *P'ing-chiang-pu-hsiao-sheng* (平江不肖生) who had written, "Romance in Japan" (留東外史) and "Wandering Adventures" (江湖奇俠傳); of *Hsü Cheng-ya* (徐枕亞) who wrote "Soul of Yü-li (玉梨魂), and "The Sad Tale of Hsüeh Hung" (雪鴻淚史); of *Li Han-ch'iu* (李涵秋), author of "Full Tide at Kuang-ling" (廣陵潮); of *Chou Shou-chüan* (周瘦鵑) leader of the "Saturday Weekly" group (禮拜六派). And after the appearance of Chang Tzu-p'ing, the limelight of popularity has been directed on *Chang Hen-shui* (張恨水), author of "Funny Affair" (啼笑因緣) and "Romance of the Imperial City" (春明外史)

These authors all unite in the old style, whereas Chang Tzu-p'ing considers himself a serious writer of the new style. Actually, however, he panders to the most vulgar instincts of the reading public, stimulating their neurotic curiosity, and is fit only to entertain the leisure hours of the money-making class. The result must, nevertheless, be thoroughly satisfactory to himself, for he has acquired both fame and prosperity, partly through engaging a number of "ghost-writers" whose work is published under his name.

Before the war he was often alluded to as the leader of the frivolous "Shanghai literary group", and called a "trader in novels". During the war he joined the Japanese puppet government at Nanking, and has since fallen under the odium of being arrested as a "cultural collaborator" despised by the whole country.

Ch'eng Fang-wu (成仿吾)

Ch'eng Fang-wu (成仿吾) is also a pillar of the "Creative Association". He has to his credit, "Vagabond", (流浪), a collection of short stories which is about his own experiences. He is, however, better known as the only theorist and critic of the Association.

Minor Members of the Creative Association

Minor members taking part in the activities of the Association may be mentioned in passing as for instance: *Yeh Ling-feng* (葉靈鳳), who obtained his early training as a student of the Shanghai College of Fine Arts, and who designed the covers of the publications of the society. He is the author of "Collected Stories of Ling-feng" and "Nü-wo-shih's Heirs" (女媧氏的餘孽). *Chou Ch'uan-p'ing* (周全平) is the author of "A Smile in a Dream" (夢裡的微笑), and "Sorrows Upstairs" (樓頭的煩惱). *Hua Han* (華漢) is the author of "Energy" (活力), "Two of the Fair Sex" (兩個女性), and "The Sorrows of the Tenth Aunt" (十姑的悲愁). *P'an Han-nien* (潘漢年) who is the younger brother of the well-known Communist, P'an Chih-nien (潘梓年), is the author of "Divorce" (離婚), "Miss Man-ying" (曼英姑娘), and "The Secret of Love" (愛的秘密). *Cheng Po-ch'i* (鄭伯奇) is the author of "General K'uan Ch'eng-tzu" (寬城子大將). Like many members of the association in question, he is a returned student from Japan. He is, moreover, one of its most active members.

Still other members that should be mentioned are *T'eng Ku* (滕固), *Chin Man-ch'eng* (金滿成) *Huang Chung* (華中), *Shao Hsün-mei* (邵洵美), *Chang Yi-p'ing* (章衣萍) and *Sun Hsi-chen* (孫席珍). These writers are all hypnotised by the power of carnal love, and liable to forget the sobering facts of hard reality, so that they are generally known as the "decadents". They may be grouped together as the disciples of Yü Ta-fu, although in technique they are far superior.

The Sun Society (太陽社)

A literary group allied with the "Creative Association" was the "Sun Society" (太陽社), whose chief member was *Chiang Kuang-tz'u* (蔣光慈), also known as Chiang Kuang-ch'ih (蔣光赤), who had been a student in Soviet Russia. He was the editor of the "Sun Monthly" (太陽月刊) and of the "Pioneer" (拓荒者) and other periodicals. He was a promoter of proletarian literature which has also been styled "the literature of the new upward trend". (新興文學).

Besides articles of passing interest, he has to his credit an enormous mass of work including novels, poems, essays, and translations from Soviet literature. Among his novels, the following may be mentioned: "A Young Vagabond" (少年飄泊者), "On the Yalu River" (鴨綠江上) "The Short Trouser Party" (短褲黨), "Chü-feng", (菊芬), "Country Sacrifice" (野祭) and "Sorrows of Li-sha" (麗沙的哀怨).

His style is both crude and violent, without any artistic flavour, but as an advocate of revolutionary theories, he has attained to great popularity among the youth of the nation.

Ch'ien Hsing-ts'un (錢杏邨) was a co-editor of the "Sun Monthly" with Chiang Kuang-tz'u, and was also a promoter of proletarian literature, of which he styled himself a critic. Both these writers were Lu Hsün's literary enemies in the beginning, and incurred the rancour of the latter, who, however, changed his attitude when he observed the direction of the new literary tendency, and to meet the wishes of his younger readers, came to a compromise, through which act he was able to acquire the literary palms of the time.

The first attack leveled against Lu Hsün by Ch'ien Hsing-ts'un was embodied in "Post Ah Q Era" (死去了阿Q時代), whose appearance cannot be ignored by those interested in literary gossip. Ch'ien Hsing-ts'un's chief contribution lies in criticism and drama, although he also wrote a well-known novel, "The Graveyard". (義塚).

Other members of the "Sun Society" were: *Yang Ts'un-jen* (楊邨人), author of "Lost" (失踪), and "Wild Waves" (狂瀾); *Hung Ling-fei* (洪靈菲), author of "Return" (歸家), "Transition" (轉變), and "Exile" (流亡); *Kung Ping-lu* (龔冰盧) author of "Before Dawn" (黎明之前), a story with Tsingtao as the background and dealing with the life of factory workers there, and "Coalminer" (炭礦夫) which is a vivid record convincingly told, as the author himself had been a coalminer at one time. It is a good demonstration of the theory current that proletarian literature should be written by the proletarians themselves.

The stories of *Meng Ch'ao* (孟超) were also published in the "Sun Monthly". They were constructed upon the theory of the "Conflict of Opposites", which was a dramatic way of describing the struggle going on in the soul of the youth of the nation, between revolutionary aspirations and selfish desires to satisfy their amorous cravings. As this theme was a vital one, his work attained to great popularity. But he also suffered from the failings of the members of the "Sun Society", chief of which was an over-heated enthusiasm that was like wild fire in its lack of discipline, and which was not free of unreflecting anger and vilifications directed against those who did not agree with them. But as their opinions were so forcibly expressed, the members of the "Sun Society" contributed not a little to the proletarian literature of the time.

Two other members that must be mentioned are *Chao P'ing-fu* (趙平復) who wrote under the pen-name of *Jou Shih* (柔石), and *Hu Yeh-p'in.* (胡也頻).

Jou Shih was author of the "Death of the Ancient Régime" (舊時代之死) and "Hope" (希望). He was not only a contributor to the new literary movement but a practical communist who was arrested by the National Government in 1931, and together with Hu Yeh-p'in (胡也頻) *Li Wei-sheng* (李偉森), *Yin Fu* (殷夫) and the authoress, *Feng Keng* (馮鏗), was condemned to death, and executed.

Hu Yeh-p'in was the husband of the famous communist woman writer Ting Ling (丁玲). He has to his credit, "Live Pearls" (活珠子), "Three disunited Fellows" (三個不統一的人物), "The Holy Disciple" (聖徒), and "Going to Moscow" (到莫斯科去).

A New Group

Now a few writers will be dealt with who have been connected more or less with the literary societies already mentioned, and who will well repay our attention as they form a new group by themselves of those authors who have enjoyed considerable influence in recent years.

Shen Ts'ung-wen (沈從文)

Shen Ts'ung-wen has been enthusiastically welcomed ever since the first appearance of his writings in the fifteenth or sixteenth year of the Republic (1916 or 1917). About sixty volumes have come from his pen, including such well-known works as "After Joining the Army" (入伍之後), "Moonlight Views" (月下小景), and "Border City" (邊城). His themes are varied, his work may be roughly classified under the following: heading, army life, customs and usages of the native tribes of South China, social novels, tales based upon buddhist legends, and children's stories.

In describing the Miao tribes of the South, he brings out the freedom of their environment in which they live and love without the restraints to which we have become used, and this together with the description of the grand and lovely scenery of the borders of Hunan and Kueichow which acquires a mystic and lyrical beauty under the magic of his pen, opens endless vistas of escape to us who have become numbed and exhausted under the yoke of civilisation.

This author claims for himself that his style is lucid and simple, but it must be admitted that he often indulges in complications with no central idea. Although he has not enjoyed the benefits of higher education, and cannot be said to be well-read, his imagination is so rich, and his power of association so strong, that he can fill a canvas with his own fancies, making water to flow from dry rocks. He writes prodigiously with an intuitive faculty that catches sentiment while still in flight, and before the results of his observation have settled in his mind, they are produced in a natural flow not subject to conscious planning. Occasionally he adds grotesque details not based upon observation in order to increase the interest of the readers, which produces a feeling of frivolity, and vagueness.

Shen Ts'ung-wen has been the editor of the Literary Supplement of the "Ta-Kung Pao" (大公報文藝副刊) whose contributors reside mainly in Peiping, from which fact has arisen their self-styled appellation of the "Peking Group". The terms "Peking Group" and "Shanghai Group" rose originally from the different camps into which the actors of the old Chinese opera were divided. The "Peking Group" emphasised singing and acting technique, in which they preserved the traditional excellencies of grace and precision, while the "Shanghai Group" was well-known for mechanical devices of theatrical production, and sketching a play to an incredible number of acts, full of hustle and movement, (e.g. "Prince into Civet Cat" (狸貓換太子), through which the applause of the audience was stimulated by rather disreputable methods, and in which the form of the traditional opera disappeared completely.

These terms, however, are not entirely applicable to the new literary movement. For a number of highly talented and creative writers, as for instance *Mu Shih-ying* (穆時英), became known as members of the "Shanghai Group" from the mere fact that they lived in Shanghai and that heterogeneous city formed the background of their writings. This was unfortunate for their reputation, as a natural prejudice rose in people's minds when the "Shanghai Croup" was mentioned.

On the other hand, although the "Peking Group" under the leadership of Shen Ts'ung-wen cannot be said to have lived up entirely to its ideals, it has nevertheless a distinct character of its own, which can be discovered by turning the pages of the pre-war issues of the Literary Supplement of the "Ta Kung Pao," and that special character bears throughout the impress of Shen Ts'ung-wen himself. His chief henchmen may be said to be *Li Kuang-t'ien* (李廣田), *Ho Ch'i-fang* (何其芳), *Pien Chih-ling* (卞之琳), *Hsiao Ch'ien* (蕭乾), and *Ch'ang Feng* (常風). And the younger writers that appear in the "Literary Review" (文學雜誌) edited by *Chu Kuang-ch'ien* (朱光潛), such as *Ling P'u* (林蒲) and *Wang Ts'eng-ch'i* (王曾祺) are also influenced by Shen Ts'ung-wen.

Lao Shê (老舍)

Lao Shê is the chief humorous writer of modern China. His early works, however typified by "The Philosophy of Old Chang" (老張的哲學), and "Chao Tzu-yueh" (趙子曰), although entertaining and amusing, are apt to degenerate into prevaricating triviality. And "The City of Cats" (貓城記) is also a failure. Only "The Two Mas" (二馬), "Divorce" (離婚) "Rickshaw Boy" (駱駝祥子), and "The Adventures of Niu T'ien-Ts'u" (牛天賜傳) are to be recommended.

During the latter years of the war, Lao Shê planned a vast effort with the title "Four Generations in One House" (四世同堂), of which only a part has

appeared, but judging by what has already been published it will be a comprehensive work of great value.

Alone among present day writers in China, Lao Shê is full of national
feeling, and shows his distaste for the leftist writers who glibly subserve to
proletarian and red influences. Indications of his attitude may be seen already
in the "Two Mas" and "Divorce", but his national sentiments are expressed
more fully in "The City of Cats". He, however, has the intelligence to recognise
the strength of the left wing, and realizing that it is unwise to stir their animosity,
he has been able to escape a direct attack.

At the beginning of the war he was the central member of the "Literary
League" (文協). His original aim was to bring about peace between the opposite
groups of leftist and rightist writers, but the former being greatly in the majority
he became beseiged by them, resulting in a leftist tendency in himself.

In the fact of present day materialism, his thought appears conservative.
He, for instance, lays special emphasis upon character building, and his attitude
is sound towards such questions as feminism and divorce. Full of humour, he is
sometimes cynical, but his cynicism is not cold and does not wound like that of
Lu Hsün. On the contrary, he is warm and generous. There is not a single bene-
volent character in Lu Hsün, while Lao Shê's creations are so sympathetic, that
sometimes they have the air of not having been poured into the modern world,
but of being old-fashioned romantic heros and heroines.

Chang T'ien-yi (張天翼)

The author who is the most similar to Lao Shê is Chang T'ien-yi. Because
of his fluent manipulation of northern dialect, and his natural wit of humour,
Lao Shê's cloak may be said to have fallen upon him. Chang T'ien-yi's "Journal
of Hell" (鬼土日記) reminds one of "The City of Cats" by Lao Shê, both being
satires of the decadent aspects of Chinese society. Chang T'ien-yi's technique
is many-sided, but he generally seizes upon a few simple and strong themes with
which to frame his story, omitting unnecessary details. With such virtues of
construction, the readers interest is sustained to the end. Nevertheless like Lao
Shê, in spite of the width of his outlook, he is often guilty of sinking into a rather
prevaricating and trivial manner, which is also the chief failing of his imitator,
Wan Ti-ho (萬迪鶴) who carries it to an even further extreme, and for this
reason, is hardly worth mentioning in such august company

Shih Chih-ts'un (施蟄存)

Shih Chih-ts'un is a comparatively late but brillant arrival in the literary
field, but from the artistic point of view, he is far inferior to many of the pioneers
of the new literary movement. He is stylist, creator of psychological novels,
and sensationalist. all at the same time, but he excells mainly in psycho-analysis.
He has produced a great mass of fiction consisting of both novels and short
stories, in which he has employed modern psycho-analytical methods in the exposing of his characters, as for instance in "The General's Head" (將軍的頭)
which is a vivid portrayal of the struggle of a dual personality full of sex com-
plexes. His style is fine and artistic reminding one of *Li Shang-ying* (李商隱) and

Li Ho (李賀) of the T'ang Dynasty. In writing chiefly from the aesthetic point of view, he is unique at the time when other methods are engrossing the attention of young writers, for this reason alone he is worthy of our attention. But he is by no means to be considered an aesthete in an "Ivory Tower", as he can also obtain an effect by sketching a few broad lines, and he also shows an interest in the poorer and oppressed classes.

His most powerful works may be said to be "The Ghoul" (夜叉), "Black Magic" (魔道), and "The Haunted House" (凶宅) which are full of a mystic and terrible atmosphere that startle the reader into seeing ghosts and devils, and which resemble very much the tales of Edgar Allen Poe. Later he began imitating the pure and concise style of the classical writers of fiction, in which he is much more successful than Hsü·Ti-shan (許地山). At a time of wide-spread proletarian literature such an experiment has an air of impressive originality.

Shortly before the war Shih Chih-ts'un was editor of "L'Ere Contemporaine" (現代) in which he demanded freedom for literary men in their choice of subject, maintaining that he was neither leftist nor rightist, but "a third kind of writer" (第三種人). As, however, the leftist wing will not allow of any other principles than their own, how can they be induced to tolerate "a third kind of writer"? It was inevitable that Shih Chih-ts'un should become an object of their virulent attack resulting in his being precipitated into a hapless condition of uncertainty, and a number of magazines of literary value that had maintained a precarious independence from the proletarian movement including his own, "L'Ere Contemporaine", were forced to cease publication.

A Minor Group

A group of writers whose articles may often be seen in contemporary publications are *Tu Heng* (杜衡), *Tai Wang-shu* (戴望舒), *Chin Yi* (靳以), *Mu Shih-ying* (穆時英), *Liu Na-o* (劉吶鷗).

Tu Heng's chief works are "Homesick" (懷鄉集) and "Whirlpool" (漩渦裡外).

Tai Wang-shu is chiefly a poet but also a short story writer.

Chin Yi's chief works are: "Blue Flowers" (青的花) "Wormeaten" (蟲蝕) and "Ferryman" (渡家). As Chin Yi comes from the Northeast, his work contains descriptions of conditions in the former so-called puppet state of Manchukuo.

Mu Shih-ying however, is the chief writer of the above group. Like Shih Chih-ts'un, his talent is many-sided. He goes from one extreme to the other, turning from very finely chiseled work to adventure stories full of life and action. In the latter category is "North Pole and South Pole" (南北極), in which the characters are all pirates, bandits, kidnappers, gangsters, and such like gentlemen who evade the law. Their deeds fill his pages with a fierce and lawless atmosphere that is extremely stimulating. At the other extreme are "The Graveyard" (公墓) and "Platinum Statues" (白金女體塑像), which are surprising productions coming from the same hand as "North Pole and South Pole". In them the life and soul of big cities such as Shanghai is portrayed in graceful and refreshing language of which the individual sentences are of complex structure and many-faceted meaning, resulting in a general effect similar to that of cubism.

Mu Shih-ying is our most successful exponent of the "New-Sensationalism", and in the vanguard of writers of "City-Literature" (都市文學), and in this he may be compared with Paul Morand, Sinclair Lewis and the Japanese Writers 橫光利一 and 喼口大學

He has furthermore, a great admiration for *Liu Na-o's* "Views of the City" (都市風景線), and these two writers have had much influence upon each other. Their fate, also, has been similar in that they both joined the "puppet organization" after the fall of Shanghai during the late Sino-Japanese war. Mu Shih-ying was assassinated soon after, while the whereabout of Liu Na-o are still unknown.

Another writer of "City-Literature" is *Huang Cheng-hsia* (黃震遐) author of "Destruction of Greater Shanghai" (大上海的毀滅). He has great imaginative power and considerable talent in the description of city life.

Devotees of "City-Literature"

Before the rise of Mu Shih-ying, a number of writers in Shanghai had already advocated the promotion of "City Literature". We are reminded in this connection of *Chang Jo-ku* (張若谷), *Fu Yen-ch'ang* (傅彥長) (朱應鵬), *Chu Yin-p'eng* (朱應鵬), and *Tseng Hsü-po* (曾虛白).

Chang Jo-ku is a Catholic, a graduate of the Law School of Aurora University. He specialises in the writing of familiar essays. Among his longer efforts is "The Bohemians" (波希米的人們), in which he gives a picture of literary gentry and anecdotes about them. This work, however, has not enjoyed much measure of success. But as an old resident of Shanghai, he is familiar with all the ins and outs of that city, and so deserves our consideration as a promoter of "City Literature".

Tseng Hsü-po (曾虛白) is the son of Tseng Meng-p'u (曾孟樸) a famous writer of the later years of the Ch'ing Dynasty, who under the pen-name of "The Sick Man of the Far East" (東亞病夫) attained to fame with his novel of "Flower of the Flesh" (孽海花). In 1928, father and son established the Cheng Mei Shan Publishing House (眞善美書店) in Shanghai, through which they courted the new literary movement. Tseng Meng-p'u has to his credit an autobiographical work "Lu Nan-zu" (魯男子) while his son, Hsü-po, has written "Sister Tê" (德妹), "Devil's Cave" (魔窟), and "Secret Flame" (潛熾的心).

In addition there is *Hsü Wei-nan* (徐蔚南), a one-time schoolmate of Chang Jo-ku, who is a talented writer of the present day. He evinces a light and pleasant touch in "Travel-weary" (奔波), and "City Dwellers" (都市的男女), which in addition, are powerful works.

Hsü Hsia-ts'un (徐霞村) has written "Citizens of an Old Country" (古國的人們) and "Life in Paris" (巴黎生活) which conveys the exotic atmosphere of a foreign country, although it cannot be considered as a formal novel. He, together with Chang Jo-ku, Fu Yen-ch'ang, the two Tsengs, and Hsü Wei-nan may be taken as a group, under the leadership of Tseng Meng-p'u whose age gave him a natural right to that position, who, moreover, was versed in the French language, and introduced many French classics to the Chinese public through the medium of his publishing house. He came, therefore, to be looked upon as the leader of all the younger writers who had come under the influence of French literature.

In this connection two writers who obtained their higher education in France may be mentioned. *Li Chi-jen* (李劼人) has introduced Flaubert and Daudet to the Chinese reading public, and is the author of an original work, "Sympathy" (同情); while *Li Ch'ing-ya* (李青崖) has translated Maupassant into Chinese, and written an original novel, "Shanghai" (上海), which in diction and plot resembles his favourite author, Maupassant.

Lo Hei-chih (羅黑芷) is a Hunan co-provincial of Li Ch'ing-ya who has written "A Spring Day" (春日), and "Intoxication" (醉裡), which, according to popular estimation is well-constructed, concentrated, and well-chiseled work. *Mu Mu-t'ien* (穆木天) is also a French scholar. He has translated much of Balzac and written a number of original stories and essays.

Back to City Literature

Hsü Yü (徐訏)

Another writer should be reviewed here, whose works are seen on all the bookstalls of Shanghai. He is no other than the famous Hsü Yü of "Demoniacal inspiration" (鬼才), who has attained to a fair measure of notoriety in literary circles. He also is a city-child, born and brought up in the metropolis of Shanghai. He has never known any other kind of milieu. His senses are dazzled by jazz-music, fox-trotting, cocktails, Egyptian tobacco, eight-cylinder limousine, ladies' fashions, skyscrapers and the glare of neon lights. Being familiar with the sights, the sounds, the odours, and the texture of the big city, he can convey them to his readers.

He is also a poet whose work combines a far a-way romantic feeling with the sensational indulgence of his novels, a mixture that explains the attractiveness of his work to the smart modern ladies and gentlemen of the big towns.

"Demon Love" (鬼戀) attained to great popularity both in Shanghai and the interior during the war. As all his works are light and entertaining, Hsü Yü can distract our leisure hours of rest after meals. He has been a main contributor to the following magazines: "West Wind" (西風雜誌) "People's World" (人間世), "Wind of the Universe" (宇宙風), but from the literary point of view he cannot be given a very high position.

Women Writers

In the period since the May 4th. Student Uprising until the present day, a good many women writers have appeared. The most famous is without doubt *Hsieh Ping-hsin* (謝冰心) who belonged to the "Ch'en Pao" Literary Supplement group, and since has become an important member of the "Literary Society". She is known for her philosophy of love, an antithesis to Pachin's philosophy of hate, and in this she may be considered a successor to Tolstoi, and Tagore. She has, moreover, translated a number of Tagore's poems. In her original work, emphasis is laid upon the love of mother and child which is the central theme of "Superman" (超人) a work that appeared soon after the May 4th. Student Uprising. The style of this book is fresh, lovely, and rich in poetic feeling. Although it has an obviously feminine quality, it must nevertheless be classed as a masterpiece.

"Letters to My Young Readers" (寄小讀者) is a collection of letters that were written while Ping-hsin was still a student in America, and may be recommended as good reading for children.

Huang Lu-yin (黃廬隱) is a contemporary of Ping-hsin who also appeared for the first time after the Student Uprising. Her earlier works of fiction consisted of "Friend by the Sea" (海濱故人), "Mental Tides" (靈海潮汐), and "An Ivory Ring" (象牙戒指), in which her special characteristics of flowing diction and enthusiasm are well illustrated, and which have a special appeal for girl students.

Before her death she joined the nationalistic youth party and began the writing of "Flame" (火燄), built around the anti-Japanese activities of the 19th Route Army. Unfortunately, before the completion of this work, she died in childbirth.

Ch'en Heng-tsê (陳衡哲) was a student in America, contemporary with Hu Shih. Her collection "Little Raindrops" (小雨點) is actually composed of essays which may however also be considered as short stories. We have also from her a long novel written during the war, depicting the conditions and abuses then current, such as widespread corruption, speculation, and hoarding among the officials and merchants which practices intensified the suffering of the intellectual class.

Feng Yuan-chün (馮沅君) under the pen-name of *Kan Nü-shih* (淦女士) has written short story collections, "Chüan-shih" (卷葹), and "Burnt-out Ashes" (刧灰) in which she describes the warming love of women in a fervent and frank fashion. Even though her work appeared after the traditional restrictions to which women were subjected had already been partially dissolved, yet her bold and intrepid spirit is startling in its intensity. Another of her works, "Traces of Spring" (春痕) is composed of fifty letters, supposed to have been written by a girl to her lover, in which is recorded the development of a love affair during several months from its incipient beginning to the engagement of the principals. As the authoress is well-versed in the old traditional literature, traces of its diction naturally find their way into her work, and some of her short stories are composed almost entirely of the five character line in exactly the same style as the shorter letters of the famous writers of the Ming and Ch'ing dynasties.

Ch'en Hsüeh-chao (陳學昭) has written "Dream of the South Wind" (南風的夢), "Memories of Paris" (憶巴黎), "Ts'un-ts'ao Hsing" (寸草心) which are collections of sketches and essays. She and Ting Ling (丁玲) are at the moment both within the red area.

Lu Ching-ch'ing (陸晶清) is the author of "Plain Letters" (素箋), written to ten men who have meant something in her life, but from whom she has become separated. These letters are extremely convincing and entertaining, and may be considered either as narrative prose or as fiction, their chief quality being an originality of form entirely of the invention of this author. She has also written a novel which appeared as a serial in the "Ho-P'ing Jê-pao" (和平日報), which has as its theme the conditions in Chungking during the war years. Her attitude toward the art of writing being severe and serious, she does not take up her pen lightly.

Ch'en Ch'eng-ying (陳沅櫻), the wife of Liang Tsung-tai (梁宗岱) published the following before the war: "A Certain Young Woman" (某少女) "End of Night" (夜闌), "After the Wedding Feast" (喜筵之後), and "One of the Fair Sex" (女性). Her characteristics are delicacy and vividness.

Ling Shu-hua (凌叔華), wife of Ch'en Hsi-ying (陳西瀅) is the author of "Temple of Flowers" (花之寺) "Two Little Brothers" (小哥倆), and "Women" (女人), which are all collections of short stories. Ling Shu-hua has often been compared with Katherine Mansfield, and it is true that she has consciously modeled her style on the English authoress, and she is as fond as Katherine Mansfield of subtle psychological studies, in which half the meaning remains unrevealed to the casual eye.

Ting Ling (丁玲), the famous communist woman writer, attracted the attention of startled readers when she published "Meng K'o" (夢珂) and other tales in the "Short Story Magazine" (小說月報). Her other works are: "In the Dark" (在黑暗中), "Diary of a Suicide" (自殺日記), "A Woman" (一個女人) "Wei-hu" (韋護), "Water" (水), and "The Mother" (母親).

"In the Dark" deals with the abnormal psychology of a lower middle class woman. It is nihilistic in atmosphere, and full of romantic sensibilities that demonstrate an uncomfortable "maladie de fin de siècle".

The communist sympathies of the authoress were already manifest in "Shanghai I" and "Shanghai II" (上海之一，上海之二). But she did not limit her characters to peasants and workmen until the appearance of "Water" (水) in 1933, when she became an exponent of the "literature of the masses". Her style is powerful and sonorous, practiced, and precise, and she often attracts the readers' attention with a remarkable originality of phrase. She is a friend of Shen Ts'ung-wen (沈從文) by whom she has been influenced, but her writing has stronger qualities, being more carefully constructed, and impregnated with a masculine vigour. She remains moreover, closer to reality.

Hsieh Ping-ying (謝冰瑩) became famous with the publication of ''Diary of A Woman Soldier'' (從軍日記) which has been re-named subsequently as ''Autobiography of a Woman Soldier'' (一個女兵的自傳). Among her other works are: ''In the Firing Line'' (在火線上), and ''The Plum Maiden'' (梅子姑娘) in which she shows a raw enthusiasm full of vigour. She is welcomed by those seeking for new sensations, as her main theme is life on the battlefield.

Lu Hsiao-man (陸小曼) was the wife of *Hsü Chih-mou* (徐志摩). She brought out a play, ''The Pien-K'un Ridge'' (卞昆岡) in collaboration with her husband, and ''Love Letters'' (愛眉小札) consisting of letters between herself and her husband, in which the style is fresh and graceful. As a city dweller, her observation of city life is thorough, and she often brings out unexpected aspects which give her pages a feeling of originality, as may be demonstrated in ''Imperial Hotel'' (皇家飯店) which has appeared recently in the ''Anonymous Miscellany'' (無題集).

Lo Hung (羅洪), the wife of the writer *Chu Wen* (朱雯) is also a short story writer of considerable merit. Her chief works are: ''First Moon'' (春王正月) ''Lonely Island'' (孤島時代), and ''The Devil's Shadow'' (鬼影). The texture of her writing is strong and closely woven, coming from a generous character not easily subdued.

Su Ch'ing (蘇青), originally named Feng Ho-yi (馮和儀), published many articles before the war in the light of humourous pages of magazines, such as ''Wind of the Universe'' (字宙風). Among them were: ''Swelling Wave'' (濤). and ''Ten Years of Marriage'' (結婚十年). She writes boldly of the mentality and sexual life of women, stimulating to sensation-seekers, but her frankness is exaggerated, frequently descending to an obscenity that detracts from the value of her story.

Feng Feng-tzu (封鳳子) was already known before the war, for her first attempt at a novel, ''Dumb Sing-song Girl'' (無聲的歌女) which has a closely-woven plot, and which is clearly and beautifully told with a literary flavour. Her work may be compared with what she says herself in the ''Portrait'' (畫像), ''Her eyes were originally luminous and bright, but now are covered with a mist of melancholy. She gazes into the far distance......as though ignoring the many people around her, and even her own existence.''

We now come to a Catholic writer, *Chang Hsiu-ya* (張秀亞), who although she has not yet become accepted as a writer of the new literary movement, has given indications of talent in the few volumes already published. As Catholic literature in China is still in its early stage, and can boast of very few exponents, we pin our hope to this young pioneer whose contributions may not be ignored.

Hsiao Hung (蕭紅) is from the Northeast and did not come to China proper until after the Manchurian Incident in 1931. She became famous after being sponsored by Lu Hsün. She is also known as an intimate friend of the writer, Hsiao Chün (蕭軍) and later, of Tuan-mu Hung-liang (端木蕻良). She died during the war, in Hongkong.

"The Field of Life and Death" (生死場) is representative of her work, in which the scene is laid in a village near Harbin shortly after the Manchurian Incident. In it a peasant man and his wife are depicted, with their sorrows of separation and joys of meeting again, together with the awakening of their patriotic perceptions shaken into activity by the Japanese invasion. Another of her works is "Cries from the Wild" (曠野的呼喊). Hsiao Hung's work is generally considered more powerful than that of Hsiao Chün.

Lo Shu (羅淑) the wife of Ma Tsung-jung (馬宗融) is no longer alive but is remembered for "Widow with a Living Husband" (生人妻), which is a profond and careful analysis of the psychology of a woman who has been forced to re-marry while the husband is still alive.

Yü-Ju (郁茹) is a protegée of Mao Tun. During the war, she wrote "Love From Afar" (遙遠的愛) which depicts a new type of woman who sacrifices personal love of home and family for the greater love of country and the nation as a whole. This book, when it was brought out in Chungking, attained to an immediate popularity.

Kê Ch'in (葛琴), the wife of Chin Ch'üan-ling (荊荃麟) has written a novel, "Mad" (狂), and a collection, "Short Stories of Kê Ch'in" (葛琴創作集).

We also have An E (安娥) wife of the famous playwright T'ien Han (田漢) and Tzü-kang (子岡) wife of Hsü Yin (徐盈), who is a well-known journalist. They have both written many articles and stories for contemporary publications but their work has not yet been issued under separate cover.

Later Writers

We shall now review the writers of the period beginning from just before the war to the present day, taking them in their natural order, dealing first with those who appeared first.

Contributors to the Literary Supplement of the "Ta-Kung Pao"

The most obvious group to come under observation is composed of the contributors to the Literary Supplement to the "Ta-Kung Pao" (大公報文藝副刊) shortly before the war, prominent among whom is Hsiao Ch'ien (蕭乾). He is a great friend of Shen Ts'ung-wen and succeeded to the latter as the literary editor of the "Ta-Kung Pao". During the war he was attached to the London School of Oriental Studies. He has to his credit "Dream Valley" (夢之谷), and lately has brought out a large volume entitled "Living Records" (人生探訪) which consists of his articles published in the "Ta-Kung Pao" while he was a correspondent on special assignments in both China and abroad. This book has enjoyed a great deal of popularity.

The second of this group is *Li Kuang-T'ien* (李廣田) who was with the United Universities in K'un-ming. He excells as a writer of familiar essays and sketches. Among his short stories: "Crock of Gold" (金罈子) should be mentioned, and since the end of the war, he has published a novel, "Attraction" (引力) whose original technique has called forth much praise.

Hsü Yin (徐盈) is known for character studies and has published "At the Front and Behind the Lines" (前後方). Among his collections of short stories are "Facing West" (向西部), and "Between the Hans and the Barbarians" (漢夷之間), in which the people and the lands of the Western borders are described.

A Group of Veteran Writers

There is also a group of veteran writers whose work during the war is important.

Ch'en Ch'üan (陳銓) is a returned student from Germany who has been a professor at the National Wuhan University. His first novel "Asking Heaven" (天問) appeared in the first decade of the new literary movement. And during the war, he published another novel, "Storm" (狂飇).

Hsü Chung-nien (徐仲年) is a returned student from France, who is a professor at the National Central University. He has specialised in introducing Victor Hugo to the Chinese reading public. During the war, he wrote "Double-tailed Scorpion" (雙尾蝎), and recently has published a novel, "Fiery Lotus" (火中蓮).

Wang P'ing-ling (王平陵) is editor of the "Literary Monthly" (文藝月刊) and the writer of "Gifts" (送禮), and "Autumn Colours by the Lake" (湖濱秋色)
Ts'ui Wan-ch'iu (崔萬秋) is a returned student from Japan, and before the war introduced Japanese literature into China in large quantities. During the war, he wrote "The Second Age" (第二代) which gives a description of the living conditions of inhabitants of the big cities during the early years of the war. He has also to his credit "New Road" (新路).

Tsang K'o-chia (臧克家) is a famous poet who has become a novelist since the end of the war, whose "Red Sign" (掛紅) has obtained much praise

Hsiung Fo-hsi (熊佛西) is a well-known playwright, who during the war published a novel "The Iron Anchor" (鐵苗) in his magazine "Literary Works" (文學創作). In this book we are given a picture of a group of young people who participated actively in the war, and the conditions of the front and behind the lines are reflected in its pages which are full of pathetic love stories and brave deeds, so vividly told that they open to us a vista of the world of the future.

The treatment of the subject is refreshing and original, and we are not surprised that it is the work of an experienced writer.

Another of the works of this author is "Iron Flower" (鐵花) which may be considered a sequel of "Iron Anchor".

Specialists in Peasant Life

Immediately before the war several new writers appeared who may be termed representatives of the group of young writers who specialise in peasant life. They are Sha Ting (沙汀), Hsü Chuan-p'eng (徐轉篷), Wei Chin-chih (魏金枝), Wu Tsu-hsiang (吳組湘), and Ai Wu (艾蕪), of whom the two latter are the most prominent.

Sha Ting (沙汀) published "Paths Beyond the Law" (法律外的航線) before the war, which contains fine writing, but in which it is difficult to discover a central theme. His characters are only types in which there is not much individualization. During the war the two following novels appeared: "Prospecting for Gold" (陶金) and "Caged Beasts" (困獸), a novelette "Forcing the Pass" (闖關), and a collection of short stories, "Roars" (呼嚎), in which his creative powers attained to their apex. His characters are the familiar figures of Szechuan villages, such as members of secret societies, the chiefs of village groups, village elders, and primary school teachers. Dialect gives local colour to his work, but he rarely overcomes his weakness of generalisation. Alone of all his works "Prospecting for Gold" (陶金) gives a really convincing picture of the conditions in gold mines in Szechuan, for which he made considerable preparations by living for a period the kind of life he described.

Hsü Chuan-p'eng (徐轉篷) together with *Ho Chia-huai* (何家槐) have given us descriptions of the countryside of Kiangsu and Chekiang. The latter, however, ceased his literary activities before the war, while Hsü has continued to give us occasional products from his pen, which however, are superficial in character, indicating a lack of practical experience on the part of the author.

Yao P'eng-tzu (姚蓬子) and *Tai Wang-shu* (戴望舒) are both symbolic poets. Yao has latterly joined the ranks of proletarian writers. Before the war, he was fond of describing peasant life, but he was unable to present his theme convincingly. He has written the collections, "Pictures of this World" (浮世畫) and "Silhouette" (剪影集), but has shown an inclination to give up short stories for essays and articles.

Wei Chin-chih (魏金枝) produced "White Signaler" (白旗手) before the war, in which army life is depicted. He has also written "Wet Nurse" (奶媽), which is an unconvincing picture of village life.

Wu Tsu-hsiang (吳組湘) is one of the most prominent of modern writers. Although his works did not appear until the immediate years before the war, he has obtained recognition as a writer of great power, and in his description of peasant life surpasses the older writers, Lu Hsün, Mao Tun, Yeh Shao-chün, and Wang Lu-yen.

When his lengthy short story "One Thousand and Eight Hundred Piculs" appeared in the "Literary Quarterly" (文學季刊), the eyes of his readers were suddenly opened to its extraordinary merit. And the applause of the critics was called forth by such stories as "Dusk" (黃昏) and "Peace on Earth" (天下太平) that came out in his "Western Willow Collection" (西柳集). In these tales, he takes us into the dead villages of the country, and shows us the miserable conditions they are in, as the result of the agressive economic policy of foreign nations. There we can see "living corpses walking about, crying, wailing, and groaning, in the last throes of despair."

During the war this author produced a novel, "The Duck Bill Fall" (鴨嘴澇), which was the name he gave to a hamlet in the mountains. This book has been re-named subsequently "Mountain Torrent" (山洪). In it he gives a picture of a small village in Anhwei, on the south bank of the Yangtze which is inhabited by hill rustics. Fire and slaughter are abroad, but the country people are at first indifferent to the war until it comes to their very gates. When they are aroused, however, each contributes what he has, either in money or services, towards the war effort. The convincing quality of the picture derives from the fact that the author himself was a native of this village, and is therefore thoroughly familiar with its dialect and peculiar customs, which are reproduced with aptness and vividness. Under his magic wand, his characters talk and move as in real life, with possibly that heightened vitality that stamps his work as a masterpiece.

Ai Wu (艾蕪) was already known before the war, but his most important works all appeared during the war years. Chief among them are the following: collections of short stories, "Childhood" (童年) "Native Place" (故鄉), and "Wasteland" (荒地); the novelettes, "Spring Days" (春天) and "River Voyage" (江上行); and the novels, "Harvest" (秋收), and "Fertile Field" (豐饒的原野). His most representative work is "Harvest" in which he gives an account of the co-operation between the army and the people during the war. This book has been dramatised by Ch'en Po-ch'en (陳白塵). Ai Wu lacks Wu Tsu-hsiang's genius and power, but his observation is finer, and his simple tales of the countryside have special appeal of their own. He comes of peasant stock, and has not enjoyed the advantages of wide education. It has even been rumoured that he has earned his living as a "boy". We have, therefore, to be grateful for the rise of the new vernacular literature, which has exalted one of such humble origins to take his rightful place in the ranks of modern writers.

Ou Yang-shan (歐陽山) whose original pen-name was Lo-hsi (羅西) is a Cantonese. He had already produced some dozen works before the war, including "Poor Faded Roses" (玫瑰殘了), and "T'ao-chün's Lover" (桃君的情人), but has produced very little since.

Wang Hsi-yen (王西彥), judging by the similarity in names, is apt to be mistaken for a brother of Wang Lu-yen (王魯彥), but in actual fact, they are unrelated. His style, however, resembles Wang Lu-yen's in purity and precision. It is simple, suggestive, and powerful. One of his longer works is "Village

Lovers'' (村野戀人), in which he brings out the essence of the war, and the social changes in the country during that period. He is author also of two collections, "An Old House" (古屋) and "Country Friend" (鄉下朋友).

Hsü Chieh (徐傑) had produced much before the war, and is known also as a writer of country life who together with Wang Lu-yen (王魯彥) and Fei Ming (廢名) are in the direct descent from Lu Hsün. His prewar works are: "Sad Mist" (慘霧), "Late Spring" (暮春) "Cocoanuts and Oranges" (椰子與榴槤) "The Crater" (火山口), and "Drifting" (飄浮). Subsequently he has written "After Victory" (勝利以後), which appeared after an interim of some years.

Both *Nieh Kan-nu* (聶紺弩) and *Ou Yang-shan* (歐陽山) owe something to Lu Hsün. The former excells particularly in satirical sketches on social subjects. During the war he was co-editor of the "Chiu-Wang Daily" (救亡日報) with Hsia Yen (夏衍), and concurrently editor of its literary supplement. His collection of short stories "On the Road" (在路上) is realistic and vividly told, and has been praised by the left wing as having the power to shake the consciousness of the age, and therefore worthy to be ranked as a masterpiece.

Shih T'o (師陀) wrote originally under the pen-name of *Lu-Fen* (盧焚), under which he became known as an essayist. Among his attempts at fiction are: "Marriage" (結婚), and "Story of the Orchard" (果城園記), which are simple tales full of sentiment.

Li Ni (麗尼) is the pen-name of Kuo An-jen (郭安仁), a native of Hupeh. He has been influenced by Pa Chin (巴金). He has also translated many of the works of Tchekov, Turgenev and André Gide.

The Northeast Group

Another group of young writers is widely known as the "Northeast Group". They share the same experience in having come to China proper after the Manchurian Incident, and in having been sponsored by Lu Hsün, so it was natural that they should have become his pack of hounds ready to raise a hue and cry on his behalf. Also it was natural that they should turn into reinforcements for the left wing.

The best-known of this group are Hsiao Chün (蕭軍), also known as Liu Chün (劉軍) and alternately as T'ien Chün (田軍), Hsiao Hung (蕭紅), Tuan-mu Hung-liang (端木蕻良), Li Huei-ying (李輝英), Lo Feng (羅烽) and Shu Ch'ün (舒群). Apart from Tuan-mu Hung-liang, the members of this group are not remarkable for scholarship. Judging by their writings, they must keep the printers busy carving special characters that no one has ever seen before. Their diction is defective, their sentence-structure is faulty, and their thought is illogical in the extreme.

They, however, have their place, for having suffered from the combined oppression of the Japanese and the puppet government of Manchoukuo, they are particularly equipped to remind us of the unhappy conditions that have prevailed in the Northeast. Besides which, their political sympathies being those of the majority of contemporary writers, in a very short time, they have become the favoured darlings of the literary world.

The most representative work of *Hsiao Chün* (蕭軍) is "Village In August" (八月的鄉村), in which is given a vivid and powerful picture of how the villagers of the Northeast resisted the invasion of the Japanese after the Manchurian Incident. Other works from his pen that have appeared subsequently are: "Sheep" (羊), "On the River" (江上), "A Tale of Green Leaves" (綠葉的故事), and "The Third Generation" (第三代).

It has been claimed that "Village In August", by which he became known, was revised by Lu Hsün before publication, and belief in this has been enhanced by the weakness of his work since the death of the great Master. The extra-ordinary number of errors, grammatical and otherwise, in his later work makes them difficult to read. But as he is a strong leftist supporter, his works have been translated in bulk into Russian, so that this youthful writer of very low calibre has attained to an international reputation. From this fact we can see that support of the left wing is a short cut to literary fame, and we cannot be surprised if this easy path has a fatal attraction for young people with literary aspirations. This is only one proof of the formidable success of the communist policy toward cultural activities.

Tuan-mu Hung-liang (端木蕻良) is the most successful of the "Northeast Group". Whether describing nature or inanimate objects such as the furniture in a room, his work is careful and accurate like the *Kung-pi style* (工筆) of meticulous craftsmanship of certain Chinese paintings. He is also fond of antithesis and poetic repetitions to such an extent that his prose presents an over-elaborated effect. It goes without saying that he has absorbed much classical literature, but as he is young and has a very lively imagination, he is no slavish imitator, and sometimes is unexpectedly original. Among his works are short pieces such as "The Feng-ling Ferry" (風陵渡), "The Grassy Plain of the Khorch'ins" (科爾沁旗草原) and "Resentment" (憎恨). His longer works are: "The Great River" (大江), and "The Sea of the Great Land". (大地的海).

Li Huei-ying (李輝英) has to his credit "On the Amur River" (松花江上) which is a story of the resistance to the Japanese in the Northeast. Being a native of the Northeast himself, he is familiar with the conditions in Inner Mongolia. During the war, he wrote a successful short story entitled, "Shih Lao-yao" (石老么), in which the hero is a nomad herdsman who resists the Japanese.

Lo Feng (羅烽) is a native of Dairen, and has written a collection, "Five Years of Short-Story Writing" (小說五年)

Shu Ch'ün (舒羣) brought out during the war "The Further Shore", (海的彼岸) which is a short story about Korea.

Lo Pin-chi (駱賓基) was already known before the war, and since that time has been a prolific writer. We have from him the following long novels: "The Blue Tumen" (圖門江) in which the native people of the mountains of Kirin are depicted, and "On the Frontier" (邊陲線上) which is the story of the resistance to the Japanese in the Northeast. He has also written a novelette. "A

Strong-willed Man'' (一個倔強的人), which is a story describing the guerrilla activities of the peasants near Shanghai during the anti-Japanese resistance, and the following collections of short stories, ''Spring in the Northward Garden'' (北望園的春天), and ''Chaos'' (混沌). Lo Pin-chi is an active communist, and after the outlawing by our government of the communist party has been arrested.

Chang Huang (張煌) is a returned student from Japan who during the war published a magazine in Kueilin, called ''The Creative Monthly'' (創作月刊). His favorite theme is the Northeast, and he is known especially for descriptions of the brutal behaviour of the Japanese military, and the activities of the underground movement of resistance. His most representative work however is ''Floral Wedding'' (花嫁), which is a story that has Peiping as the background, and is romantic in the extreme. He has also produced the short collections: ''Pardon'' (饒恕) and ''The Vanity of Worldly Glory'' (浮華篇). As he is well under thirty, we may still expect much good work from this author.

Sun Ling (孫陵) was co-editor in Kueilin, during the war, with Chang Huang (張煌) of the periodical ''Free China'' (自由中國). The reputations of these two young authors have grown up together. Sun Ling's chief work, ''Wind and Snow'' (大風雪) is of the oppressed people of Harbin during the war. ''Breaking the Seige'' (突圍記) is a record of the battles of Hsiangyang and Fanch'eng in Hupeh during the war.

Neither Sun Ling nor Chang Huang were known before the war. Both may be included in the ''Northeast Group'', but unlike other members of this circle, they are too young to have been under the personal influence of Lu Hsün.

Creators of a Really New Literature

A new group will now be introduced, composed of writers of different ages. They can, however, be classified together as their works have not appeared until comparatively late, after the outbreak of the war. They are, of course, all of leftist sympathies, and even those who do not subscribe wholly to Communist tenets, are at least, leftist in tendency; otherwise, they would never be accorded the acclaim of the new literary movement. Being a large group, their individual achievement is unequal in standard, but taken as a whole, they are freer from the restraints of the old tradition than the writers of the May 4th. Student Movement. They have a fresher outlook, and are more supple in the manipulation of their material. And their work may be considered the nearest approach until now of Dr. Hu Shih's idea of a really ''New Literature''.

Yao Hsüeh-yin (姚雪垠)

Yao Hsüeh-yin (姚雪垠) should be the first of this group to be reviewed. He is a native of Anhwei, and immediately, at the outbreak of the war, he joined the army, and was engaged in guerrilla activites. It follows naturally, that his work is full of descriptions of the war. His first short story ''Half a Cart-load of Straw Missing'' (差半車麥稭) which appeared in the ''Literary Battlefield''

(文藝陣地) attracted immediate attention, and is still considered the best war story that has yet been produced. His novelette "Niu Ch'üan-tê and Red Radish" (牛全德與紅蘿蔔), is about the antagonism between a second-in-command of a company of guerrillas, named Niu Ch'üan-tê and a soldier of peasant origin whose nickname is "Red Radish". Their personal animosity is dissolved under danger, and turns into comradeship, so that in the end, one saves the life of the other. The description of Niu Ch'üan-tê is realistic and not exaggerated. We are clearly shown his regeneration from a rascally fellow, with no feeling of responsibility, into one who risks his own life to save another man. His character is convincing, and we believe in his individual existence, so that he is not just the traditional adventurer of the old Chinese legends. Such individualistic treatment may be considered an advance in technique.

Another book of this author, "When Flowers Burgeon" (春暖花開的時候), consists of stories of the men and women with the guerrilla forces. "Warrior Love" (戎馬戀) is the love story of a young officer and a nurse. "Long Night" (長夜) is about the terrible conditions in villages of North China, and tells of the deeds of the stout fellows whose home is in the woods. "Hymn of New Life" (新生頌) is of the growth and development of war orphans in the present age. The above four are all long novels.

With these works Yao Hsüeh-yin has become one of the foremost of contemporary writers. He does not fall into the error of purely objective writers of dry factual recording; neither is his work as indefinite and devoid of meaning as that of most romantic writers. He takes a middle path and confines a romantic spirit within the rigid control of a severe and serious technique. The result is clear, pure writing that is very readable.

Having once served in the Chinese national army, he has become the butt of a vitriolic attack on the part of *Hu Feng* (胡風), a communist writer who undoubtedly is aggrieved at Yao Hsüeh-yin's enviable reputation. To this Yao has replied, partly with a reputation of Hu's argument, and partly with a claim that he should receive better consideration as he himself is not devoid of leftist sympathies. Hu Feng, however, is of such uncompromising character, that once he has sentenced a man with his pen, he will admit of no question of his act. Should the poor victim try to protect himself, he will commit him to the death penalty; that is, harry him to death with his virulent pen. Even among the ranks of communist writers who, as a rule, are easily aroused, he is an exception, recognising no other rule than his personal likes and dislikes. This perhaps may be taken as an example of the famous communistic slogans of "democracy" and "freedom of thought and expression"

Minor Writers of the War

The war brought forth a number of young writers: the following are a few.

Tung P'ing (東平) was an active member of the army who died on the battlefield. His writing comes of his own practical experience in the war of resistance against Japan. He has written a collection of short stories "Company Seven" (第七連).

Liu Pei-yü (劉白羽) and *Chou Er-fu* (周而復) both write about the Red Army. It would appear from their works that they have been with the Eighth Route Army for a long time. Liu has written "Happiness" (幸福) and "The Sun" (太陽).

Yeh I-ch'ün's (葉以群) "Tales of the New People" (新人的故事) is mostly about the life of soldiers in the Northeast.

Wu Hsi-ju (吳奚如), it would appear, is an army officer. At the beginning of the war, he published a short story "Captain Hsiao" (蕭連長) which is very well-written (the writer does not know whether he has brought out any other work).

Ku Ssu-fan (谷斯範) has written a novel divided up in the old traditional style, entitled "New Water Margin" (新水滸), in which he tells us of the deeds of the bandits on the shores of T'ai-hu against the invading Japanese. His style is realistic, powerful, and vivid. He may be put in the same category as Chang Hen-shui (張恨水), with this further proviso, that it is difficult to believe that he could have given us such powerful and convincing descriptions of bandit life if he himself had not had practical experience of it.

Younger Writers of the Present Day

The following is a group of promising writers of the present day.

Pi Yeh (碧野) is a native of Ssuchuan and a very prolific writer. His work indicates that he is a great traveller, for at one moment he is telling us of the great plain of Ulanbulang in Mongolia, at the next moment of the fishermen of the South Seas. He turns with lightening rapidity from the villages of North China to those of Kuangtung, from the battle-scarred youth of China struggling amid a rain of bullets to the peaceful but weary raft punters of western Ssuchuan. He tells us of all this in clear, flowing language, which nevertheless does not lack power. Being still youthful, he may be said still to be at the beginning of his career, yet can already boast of seven considerable works of fiction: "Fertile Land" (肥沃的土地), "Love of Wind and Sand" (風砂之戀), "Spring Without Wind" (沒有風的春天), "Blue Sea" (湛藍的海), "Slaves Flowers and Fruit" (奴隸的花果), "Yellow Tide" (黃泛), and "Far Away" (遠方), all of which are novels or novelettes of fair length.

Lu Ling (路翎) wrote "Hungry Kuo Su-ô" (饑餓的郭素娥) during the war, which was immediately taken up by the leftist section of the literary world. Since then we have from this author the following works: "Courtship" (求愛), "Blessing of Springtide" (青春的祝福), and "The Children of a Wealthy Man" (財主的兒女們). Lu Ling is a workman who has not finished middle school, but he has given indications of marked literary talent. He excels in exposing human nature, analysing life, and his understanding of psychology is profound. *Liu Hsi-wei* (劉西渭) also known as *Li Chien-wu* (李健吾) has said of Lu Ling's

"Hungry Kuo Su-ô": "I have felt a violent force in Lu Ling. The whirlpools and waves of great lakes and rivers are not free from sand and grit to which may be compared the work of the great master Emile Zola who attracts us because of his enthusiasm, not his logic. . . . I have also felt a crude force in him, but his crudity does not take away from his power. . . sometimes it enhances it when the two are properly combined so that we feel a whirlwind swirling in our heads".

Lu Ling is especially popular in Shanghai, where the critics have paid him particular attention.

T'ien T'ao (田濤) has written a lengthy work "Tides" (潮) about the war-work of a group of young people of both sexes. This book has been well-received. He has also written another novel "Fertile Ground" (沃土) which is about the conditions of life of ordinary people in North China who are opposed by the officials and the army. A short story, "Hope" (希望) has also come from his pen.

Feng Ts'un (豐村) is a new but influential writer of present literary circles. He has written a collection, "Anxious Years". (煩惱的年代)

The Newest Group

We have also a group of writers whose fame cannot yet be compared with those already mentioned. As, however, they are still writing, their future is in their own hands.

Mei Ling (梅林) has written "Madness" (瘋狂), on the theme of present day frustration, and a collection of short stories, "Infancy" (嬰).

Chin Yu-ling (荊有麟) and *Chin Ch'üan-ling* (荊荃麟) are generally considered as brothers. The former has written, "The Spy's Wife" (間諜夫人), which is full of romantic sentiments, while the latter has written "The Inn" (宿店).

Ssu-ma Wen-sên (司馬文森) has written a great deal of fiction, both novels and short stories, but his work is not easy to find in the interior of China, being under a ban owing to its communist colouring. One of his works, however, was published in Kueilin, "The Opium Season". (烟苗季).

Ch'eng Tsao-shih (程造時) has written "Underground" (地下) and "Virgin Soil" (沃野). The latter is a novel of about a hundred thousand characters but of no particular interest.

Chiang Mu-liang (蔣牧良) is of peasant origin, and it naturally follows that he lays emphasis upon peasant life. He had already written a great deal before the war, but was not widely known until the publication of "Night Work" (夜工) during the war.

Ai Ming-chih (艾明之) has written the short story, "When Starving" (饑餓的時候) and a novel "Night in the Misty Town" which is about the disappointment of those who had taken an active part in the war when faced with the ignominious peace.

Ch'ien Chung-shu (錢鍾書) has written a novel, ''The Beseiged City'' (圍城) in a very original manner which gives value of his writing.

Feng Chih (馮至) has written a historical tale, ''Wu Tzü-hsü'' (伍子胥), which has obtained the favour of the critics, and is without doubt a poetic piece of writing.

Sung Ling (宋霖) has written ''Sandbank'' (灘) which is worth reading, for the subject it deals with — the struggle of the factories in the interior during the difficult conditions imposed by the war.

The Anonymous One (無名氏)

At the end a word may be said about a writer who in many ways may be compared with Hsü Yü (徐訏) and whose works are to be seen on the Shanghai bookstalls. Originally known as *P'u Ning* (卜寧), his present pen-name is *''the Anonymous One''* (無名氏). His works did not appear until the second half of the war. But from what he has written, may be seen that he is greatly influenced by the younger Dumas, and he is as prolific as Hsü Yü. His chief works are ''A Million Years Ago'' (一百萬年以前), ''Sea Beauty'' (海艷), ''Russian Love'' (露西亞之戀), ''City Gate On Fire'' (火燒的都門) ''The Dragon's Cave'' (龍窟) ''Landscape of the North Pole'' (北極風景畫) ''Woman in the Tower'' (塔裡的女人), and ''Beasts, Beasts, Beasts'' (野獸 野獸 野獸). As his stories do not deal with the burning questions of the day, such as the problems of factory workers, peasants, and of the oppressed classes in general, and he does not indulge in the familiar communist attitude of hatred of the present, with hope only for the future, he cannot be considered a serious writer, and is in consequence fit only to entertain the leisured bourgeois over their tea tables.

CONTEMPORARY CHINESE DRAMA

Foreword

We shall now discuss the dramatic works that have been produced during the new literary movement. When language reform became one of the great problems of the time after the May 4th. Student Movement, it was also felt that the Chinese drama needed to be modernised. ''Aspects of Reform of the Chinese Drama'' by Fu Ssu-nien (傅斯年的戲劇改良各面觀), ''A Personal View of the Reform of the Chinese Drama'' by Ou-yang Yü ch'ien (歐陽予倩的予之戲劇改良觀) and ''Literary Evolution and Reform of Drama'' by Hu Shih (胡適文學進化觀念與戲劇改良) all attacked severely the old traditional Chinese drama. These works' were all destructive. Hu Shih, however, through his article, ''Ibsenism'' (易卜生主義) and a comedy ''Lifes' Great Affair'' i. e. Marriage (終身大事), written in the vernacular after the manner of foreign plays, sounded a constructive vote, after which problem plays in the modern manner became popular in China. Ibsen's ''Ghosts'', and ''Doll's House'' was acted with great success in Chinese schools, and Bernard Shaw's ''Mrs. Warren's Profession'' also was staged in Shanghai.

Early Pioneers

Ch'en Ta-pei (陳大悲) was an early pioneer in promoting modern plays on the Chinese stage. He introduced ''aesthetic plays'' hoping that they would take the place of the so-called ''fashionable new drama'' (文明戲), and in this he obtained enthusiastic support from *P'u Po-ying* ｜蒲伯英). Neither, however, had any profound knowledge of modern dramatic art. All their plays were adaptations or copies of western or Japanese models, and as these were used as vehicles of the burning social problems brought into light by the Student Movement, they contained a great deal of didactic dialogue, and were not constructed according to the rules of dramatic harmony. They employed dramatic or rather melodramatic devices, which were the same as those of the ''fashionable new drama'' that they sought to reform, so these plays are also full of suicides, threats, blackmail, shooting, unexpected revelations and confessions, through which it was hoped to stimulate the interest of the audience.

Two other dramatists who became active at this time were Ou-yang Yü Ch'ien and Hsiung Fu-hsi (熊佛西).

Ou-yang Yü Ch'ien (歐陽予倩) began his dramatic career as a member of the ''Spring Willow Dramatic Society'' (春柳社). Afterwards he turned his attention to the traditional drama and became known as a singer of "virtuous lady" rôles (青衣). The plays that he wrote himself are entertaining but are set in the same mould as the "fashionable new drama", with the exception of "P'an Chin-lien" (潘金蓮) which has undoubted merit.

Hsiung Fu-hsi (熊佛西) is a writer of comedies, specializing in those with a satirical twist, such as his "Western Chuang-yuan" (洋狀元) and "The Trumpet" (喇叭). He also indulges in farces, such as "The Artist" (藝術家). These plays enjoyed a momentary success, but have no permanent value. His later work that was produced immediately before and after the outbreak of the war, are a great improvement. "Sai Chin-hua" (賽金花) and "Yuan Shih-k'ai" (袁世凱) have chances of enduring longer than his early work.

Kuo Mo-jo's (郭沫若) "Three Revolutionary Women" (三個叛逆的女性) is a trilogy of three famous women of ancient times, Wang Chao-chün (王昭君) Cho Wen-chün (卓文君), and Nieh Ying (聶嫈). These plays are loosely constructed, and full of vulgar language. The historical characters are mere mouth-pieces through which the writer expresses his own ideas and opinions, so that they do not act, but give lectures to the audience. These attempts, therefore, cannot be considered as historical plays. They have to be termed didactic plays or mere propaganda.

During the war this author wrote "Ch'ü Yuan" (屈原) "Kao Chien-li" (高漸離), "The Tiger Tally" (虎符), "Poem from a Prison House" (南冠草) and "The Peacock's Gall-bladder" (孔雀胆), all based upon historical tales. These plays all suffer from Kuo Mo-jo's chief defect, in that they are loosely constructed. In "Ch'ü Yuan" the great father of Chinese poetry is made to symbolize the author himself, and therefore the legendary figure of Ch'ü Yuan is brought rather too much down to earth. "The Peacock's Gall-bladder", however, is very popular as it is lively with characters, is large in conception, and necessitates gorgeous costumes in its representation. Nevertheless the hero, Tuan Kung (段功), who in the original story, is a warrior, is made into a fool who is easily deceived, and the plot turns upon simple machinery provided by poison and murder. This gives point to the opinion of the critics that, although Kuo Mo-jo attempted a drama on a big canvas in the style of Shakespeare, he has only succeeded in producing a common melodrama.

Another important member of the "Creative Association" (創造社), who might be mentioned in passing was the poet *Wang Tu-ch'ing* (王獨清). In both poetry and drama, but especially in the latter, he is a slavish imitator of Kuo Mo-jo. He claims for himself that "The Death of Yang Kuei fei" (楊貴妃之死) and "Tiao Ch'an" (貂蟬) are historical plays, but they are fit company for Kuo Mo-jo's "Three Revolutionary Women", being in no way superior to that raw attempt.

Playwrights of the "Contemporary Review"

The playwrights of the "Contemporary Review" (現代評論) were Ting Hsi-lin (丁西林), Yuan Ch'ang-ying (袁昌英), and Hsü Chih-mo (徐志摩).

Ting Hsi-ling has produced the "One Act Plays of Ting Hsi-ling" (丁西林獨幕劇), which has been criticised by Ch'en Hsi-ying (陳西瀅), "The plots of these plays are extremely economical, and the dialogue is fluent and witty, . . . the characters . . . are full of life and have opinions of their own, but their ways of thought are not those of the Chinese of the present day. They are inhabitants of an ideal world . . . It is possible that after thousands of years we shall come up to their level. Intellectually they are far superior to us, and emotionally they have been sifted thought thousands of years of civilization more than we have, so that their feelings have become thoroughly rational." In proof that this criticism is just the following plays may be cited: "The Hornet" (一隻馬蜂), "Blind in One Eye" (瞎了一隻眼), "Miaofengshan" (妙峰山), and "When the Mistress Returns" (等太太回來的時候).

Yuan Ch'ang-ying (袁昌英) has written "The Peacock Flies Southeast" (孔雀東南飛) and other plays, which contains six pieces of creative writing. The title piece is based upon the ancient Chinese narrative poem of that name, which has inspired more than one modern dramatist. Among their efforts, that of Yuan Ch'ang-ying may be said to be the most successful, and his differs from the other modern conceptions of this story in making the Lady Chiao (焦母) (mother of the hero) into the main character instead of Lan-chih (蘭芝), the hero's wife. We are given here a thoroughly modern treatment of the old story, where the Lady Chiao's resentment of her daughter-in-law is explained according to Freudian theory, and her unhappiness at the partial alienation of her son's affections after his marriage is represented in a very moving manner; while the conflict of personality between her and her daughter-in-law is extremely dramatic.

Before the war, Yuan Ch'ang-ying had already written five or six plays such as "Laughter" (笑), and "Night of Spring Thunder" (春雷之夜), but they have not been issued in collected form .

During the war she produced "Horses at a Waterhole by the Great Wall" (飲馬長城窟), which is a five-act play. It cannot, however, be considered as anything more than propaganda.

The poet, *Hsü Chih-mo* (徐志摩), brought out before his early death, "The Pien K'un Ridge" (卞昆岡) in collaboration with his wife, *Lu Hsiao-man* (陸小曼). According to Yü Shang-yuan (余上沅), it has the atmosphere of a modern Italian play. He says, "We can see in modern Italian plays a close connection with poetry. They reveal the mystic secret of life and express them in burning language. It would seem that the present writer has not been able to avoid the influence of such works as "Chimera" and "La Città morte". . . Hsü Chih-mo is a poet, which fact reveals itself in every turn of "the Pien K'un Ridge", in the neatness of his diction, in the spontaneity of his rhythm, in the richness of his imagination and in his choice of characters."

Yü Shang-yuan (余上沅) himself was not a member of the "Contemporary Review" group, but the style of his writings resembles that of the contributors to this periodical. When he was a student at Carnegie University, Pittsburgh, he made a special study of Western drama. He has translated many famous

European plays, and of his own original work we may cite, ''Shang-yuan's Plays Vol. I'' (上沅劇本甲集), which includes three plays, ''Return Home'' (回家) ''The Statue'' (塑像), and ''Mutiny'' (兵變), of which ''The Statue'' has the most complicated and well-planned plot. Unfortunately it is rather stiff and lacking in natural development.

Ku I-ch'iao (顧一樵) also, who was not strictly of the ''Contemporary Review' group, although he had affiliation with them, has taken a stand against the left wing, and may be considered to be a nationalist writer. He has to his credit ''Yueh Fei and Other Plays'' (岳飛及其他), which is a collection of four plays, ''Yueh Fei'' (岳飛), ''Chin K'o'' (荊軻), ''Hsiang Yü'' (項羽) and ''Su Wu'' (蘇武). In these he has attempted to display the qualities of four great heroes through which our national feeling should be aroused, but unfortunately he has not had sufficient art to fulfil his conception.

Another Pioneer

Hsiang P'ei-liang (向培良) was one of the chief members of ''The Storm and Stress Society'' (狂飈社), and organised the dramatic section of that association, as well as an opera company. He took the two organizations that he had organised on a tour of South China, reaching as far as Amoy. Through this he became a promoter of national drama giving indications of being a strong nationalist. He wrote the following: ''Melancholy Plays'' (沉悶的戲劇), ''The City of Death'' (死城), and ''Unfaithful Love'' (不忠實的愛).

A Group of Successful Playwrights

There are also several playwrights who cannot be classified with any special group, but the success of their work demands our attention.

Yang Yin-sheng (楊蔭深) has written ''Rocks and Reeds'' (磐石與蒲葦) which is another play based upon ''The Peacock Flies Southeast''. In it he describes vividly the love between the hero, Chiao Chung-ch'ing (焦仲卿) and the heroine, Liu Lan-chih (劉蘭芝), and the ill-will between the two mothers.

Another play of this author is ''A Gust of Wind'' (一陣狂風) in three acts, which is based upon the popular love story of Liang Shan-po and Chu Ying-t'ai (梁山伯與祝英台).

Ku Chung-yi (顧仲彝) is a promoter of amateur plays in schools. He believes that the reform of Chinese drama should begin in the schools. Before the war he embarked upon a plan to write ten plays suitable for acting in schools, within the short period of three years. ''Liu San-yeh'' (劉三爺) is one of these ten, in which we are given a good portrait of a chivalrous northern gentleman. It is so well done that all who see it receive a strong and lasting impression.

His other plays are based upon foreign sources: ''All Victorious'' (皆大勝利), ''Seven Boddhisatvas'' (七尊菩薩), ''Outsider'' (門外漢) ''My Darling''

(我愛) and "Dawn" (天亮了). His adaptations, however, are so thorough, that in both form and spirit they are completely Chinese.

Yuan Mu-chih (袁牧之) has written "Cupid's Arrow" (愛神的箭), "Ling-ling" (玲玲), and "Play with Two Actors" (兩個角色演的戲).

Hou Yao (侯曜) 's first publication "Resurrection of the Rose" (復活的玫瑰) is on free love, and may be considered a bomb thrown at the old Confucian teaching of strict family relations. "Tears From the Mountains and Rivers" (山河淚) is on the Korean independence movement, and a cry in defence of all the oppressed nations of the earth. This author has also written "The Rock Is Nodding" (頑石點頭), and "Spring Birthday" (春的生日).

Huang Pei-wei (黃白薇), a woman playwright, has written "Ling-li" (琳麗). which is a romantic treatment of a love theme. The attitude she takes is "Art for Art's sake". Ch'en Hsi-ying (陳西瀅) considered it so highly that he ranked it immediately after his choice of the ten most creative masterpieces of modern Chinese literature; through this opinion the authoress attained to immediate fame. It is much to be doubted, however, whether this play deserved much high praise, and the subsequent work of this writer, "Forcing a Passage Out of the Ghost Tower" (打出幽靈塔) is even inferior to her early work.

Chief Playwrights of the New Literary Movement

We should now deal with those playwrights who have been most active and popular in the new literary movement, and whose work rises in merit above the mass of the new literature, and whose contribution to it, therefore, deserves our notice.

T'ien Han (田漢)

The first to be reviewed in this section is "T'ien Han" (田漢), who is an artistic writer of considerable talent. When the new literary movement started with the May 4th. Student Uprising, he was already known, and since then has been able to maintain an enviable reputation. Before the war, he already had to his credit five or six volumes of plays and at the present moment there is no indication of any decline in his creative powers.

According to his own confession, his literary history has passed through three stages. In the first he believed in "Art for Art's sake", during which period he produced "Tragedy On the Lake" (湖上的悲劇) and "Death of a Famous Actor". The characters in these plays are dreamy and illusive, living in a beautiful poetic world far removed from reality.

A transition to the second stage when the playwright became a promoter of social reform may be seen in "Night Talk in Soochow (蘇州夜話), "Views of a Riverside Village" (江村小景), "Night of the Tiger Hunt" (獲虎之夜), "Hospital Ward No. 5" (第五號病室), and "New Year's Eve Dinner" (年夜飯). These plays are on the evils brought on by civil war, against forced marriages arranged by parents, and the oppression of the poorer classes.

In the third state, T'ien Han's communist sympathies became more marked. "The Death of Ku Chen-hung" (顧正紅之死), "Comrades in Battle" (戰友), "Moonlight Sonata of 1932" (一九三二年的月光曲), and "Seven Women in a Storm" (暴風雨中的七個女性) are representative of his third period, in which he attacks capitalism, and agitates for class struggle.

T'ien Han's plays have the power of infecting the audience with his ideas. It has been said that when "Tragedy On the Lake" was produced in Canton, it caused a number of suicides of unhappy lovers. His plays on social abuses are also agitating in the extreme and, as means of communistic propaganda, may be classed in importance and power with the novels of Mao Tun. The construction of his plots is carefully worked, and even small details are appropriately selected, bearing out the truth of Tu Fu's (杜甫) words that the best art is where

> "The beautiful lady irons out
> the stitches and seams left by the tailor."

He is a master of all kinds of dialogue, sometimes logical and strictly on the subject, sometimes humourous, sometimes serious, stimulating, emotional, tragic, poetic, and eloquent. His chief fault however, is the inclusion of long passages of didactic exortation.

"Autumn Song" (秋聲賦), which appeared in the first years of the war, has been recommended by Hung Sheng (洪深) as one of the ten representative works depicting the war effort.

During the war T'ien Han tried his hand at adapting old Chinese plays for the modern stage, keeping the traditional form and dialogue as much as possible. His works in this style include "Fisherman's Song" (江漢漁歌) and "New Warriors of Both Sexes" (新兒女英雄傳). And recently "Wu Ts'ê-t'ien" (武則天) has appeared in the pages of the "Ta-Kung Pao".

T'ien Han has also invented a kind of play which has come to be known as "drama of a new type", of which his "Parade of Fair Women" (麗人行) is an example."

His technique is realistic, but his fundamentally romantic spirit has led him to forsake original work, in which he excels, to questionable experiments at reforming the Chinese traditional drama. Apart from refining the diction of the old plays, he has not improved them in any way, and has latterly restricted his genius to the old worn-out mould. His adaptations cannot be called successful, for on the whole, there is nothing in them to merit preference over the original form of the traditional plays that have come down to us. His experiments in this direction are, therefore, a warning to those who are too keen on effecting so-called "modern improvements."

Hung Sheng (洪深)

Hung Sheng follows naturally upon T'ien Han (田漢), for they have often been called the "twin jade ornaments" of modern drama. Before the war, Hung Sheng wrote, "Tragedy of the Poor" (貧民慘劇), "King Chao of Hades" (趙閻王),

"Wu K'uei-ch'iao" (五奎橋), and "Fragrant New Rice" (香稻米); during the war, he wrote "Pao Tê-hsing" (包得行), "Warriors of the Air" (飛將軍), followed by "Women! Women!" (女人，女人), "The Cock Crows! Travellers, Look At the Weather" (鷄鳴早看天), and "White and Yellow" (黃白丹青).

Hung Sheng's chief virtue lies in the careful construction of his plots. He had been a student of porcelain manufacture in Ohio State University for three years, when friends persuaded him to enter Harvard University to study the dramatic art. According to his own estimation of himself, "My three years of apprenticeship to porcelain manufacture has made my method of writing plays rigid and stiff. When I frame a play it is as though I was constructing a porcelain kiln. I have to gather together all the threads of my conception, and lay each one methodically in its place". Since this is his method, it will not be expected that Hung Sheng's works give the impression of being gusts of inspiration. They are, in fact, the result of careful craftsmanship. He never flies, but walks step by step upon the earth.

Hung Sheng also excels in the manipulation of plays needing a large cast. "King Chao of Hades" is an exception from the rest of his work, for it contains few characters. "Wu K'uei-ch'iao", however, necessitates a cast of twenty to thirty people, and "Fragrant New Rice" needs even more. His characters nevertheless, are so carefully conceived that each one is sufficiently individualised to hold the attention of the audience. Never for a moment does he lose control, for each character also contributes to the general effect.

He brings out the finer aspects of his characters, as for instance in "King Chao of Hades", where their soldierly bearing and speech are extremely convincing. And in "Wu K'uei-ch'iao" and "Fragrant New Rice", we are led by imperceptible methods to hate the landlords and degenerate gentry depicted in them. We despise their subtle minds that are able to meet all contingencies, and their pacification of the poor labourers with the arts of persuasion, so that the latter are tricked into obedience. This is indeed the method referred to in the Chinese phrases "to hide a knife in a smile", and "to kill without shedding blood". Pastmaster of this art is Squire Chou in "Wu K'uei-ch'iao".

There is a former student of Hung Sheng's who should be considered in this connection, *Ma Yen-hsiang* (馬彥祥), who is the author of the play, "The Traitor, Wang Ching-wei" (國賊汪精衛).

Ts'ao Yü (曹禺)

Ts'ao Yü (pen-name of *Wan Chia-pao* (萬家寶) rose to fame just before the beginning of the war. With his rare genius and his power of expression, he has become the spokesman of the modern age. Upon his appearance T'ien Han was paled into insignificance, and Hung Sheng took to his heels.

"Thunderstorm" (雷雨), "Sunrise" (日出) and "The Wild" (原野) form a trilogy. The two first were acted in the leading cities of China before the war, and were applauded wherever they were seen.

Ts'ao Yü's art has been influenced by that of other countries. He is not only indebted to Tchekoy, but also to the example of Greek tragedy. In "Thunderstorm'', for instance, when he presents to us the obstacles to progress embodied in the old feudal conception of society, and the decadence of the traditional family system, he obtains an effect of a tragic struggle between the paltry efforts of Humanity with Fate.

In ''Sunrise'' he predicts the imminent collapse of society dominated by outmoded capitalism. He brings out its licentiousness, corruption, decadence, deceit, and tyranny in strong, straightforward terms. ''The Wild'' is a story of vengeance taken by a farmer. It is so tragic and moving that it stuns with its vital power.

Ts'ao Yü's technique is undoubtedly of the highest order, but the complication of his characters, incidents, and dialogue is so great that the audience has to strain after his meaning to such an extent that it is left exhausted and panting behind. ''Thunderstorm'' for example, easily contains material for three or four normal plays, and from this fact its complication of detail may easily be imagined.

''Peking Man'' (北京人) and ''Metamorphosis'' (蛻變) appeared during the war. The former depicts the dissolution of an old-fashioned family, where the descendants all live under the same roof, and the rise of a new spirit is also indicated. In this play the family of Tseng Hao (曾皓) represents the old culture of China, and the ''Peking Man'' symbolises Communism. The ideas expressed are the same as those of the usual leftist sympathiser. Ts'ao Yü is convinced of the imminent dissolution of the old order of things in China, and that the only salvation of the country lies in Communism.

''Metamorphosis'' is a propaganda play of the war which depicts the process in which a military hospital is reorganised from a corrupt into an efficient institution. The main characters, Dr. Ting and Commissioner Liang, are very convincingly portrayed, and are intended to be models for those concerned with the war effort.

Li Chien-wu (李健吾)

Li Chien-wu in technique may be considered the direct antithesis of Ts'ao Yü. Whereas Ts'ao Yü's plays are all extremely complicated, Li Chien-wu's are constructed on a few simple, broad lines. His dialogue is all in pure Peking dialect. The effect that he gives is natural and self-possessed, polished, yet vigorous. He uses an extreme economy of words in which not a single one is either misplaced or superfluous. He does not give the immediate stimulous of Ts'ao Yü, as his power is hidden beneath a smooth surface, but those who perceive his meaning will recognise that his art is the result of a mind braced to its highest tension.

His pre-war productions were ''This is Only Spring'' (這不過是春天), ''To Take as a Model'' (以身作則), ''The Mother's Dream'' (母親的夢), ''Liang Yün-ta'' (梁允達) etc. And during the war he published ''Day With No Night'' (不夜天) under the pen-name of Hsi Wei (西渭), and the following under his own name: ''Yuan Shih-k'ai'' (袁世凱) and ''A-shih-na'' (阿史那), which is the story of Othello personified by a military leader of the T'ang Dynasty.

Plays and Playwrights Since the Outbreak of the Sino-Japa-nese War.

Let us now pass under review the development of drama in China since the beginning of the late war. A leftist writer has said that, in his opinion, the contemporary drama has passed through four stages in recent years, the most glorious of which is the period of the war. There is a great deal of truth in this, for the progress made by other forms of writing although perceptible, cannot be compared with the immense strides made by the drama. The explanation for this is easy to find, lying in the conviction of educated people in the power of the drama to stimulate and direct public opinion, and consequently in its aptness as an instrument for the salvation of the nation. Besides which, diversion was needed badly by those imprisoned in the interior during the war; therefore all kinds of entertainment were heartily welcomed, whether opera in the old traditional style, modern plays of dialogue in the vernacular, music, or the cinema. The theatres were full regardless of the price of the tickets. Thus plays such as those of Shakespeare, which were ignored before the war owing to the cost of production, could now be presented to enthusiastic audiences. And men who had written other forms of literature before the war, all tried their hand at drama, while new dramatists were given a heaven-sent chance to show their talent.

Immediately before the war, the new literary movement had promoted "the literature of national defence", which naturally brought forth "the drama of national defence". We thus have plays such as those of *Yu Ching* (尤兢) and *Chang Min* (章泯), who present to us the activities of the volunteer army in the Northeast.

Soon after war broke out, both Peiping and Shanghai fell into the hands of the enemy, and the playwrights followed the general trek into the interior. With the assistance and encouragement of the government, ten companies were formed under the name of "Resistance Dramatic Groups". They went everywhere, acting to soldiers, peasants, and all sorts of people both in the country and in the towns, giving birth to a large number of patriotic "street plays", and "people's plays" such as "Lay Down Your Whip" (放下你的鞭子), "Where Can One Run To?" (往那裡逃). "The Road" (路), and "Sweeping With Bullets" (掃射), which were the most popular of their repertoire. "Warriors of the Air" (飛將軍), "Eight Hundred Brave Men" (八百壯士), and "Above all the Fatherland" (國家至上) are also plays of intense patriotic feeling.

In the Spring of 1941, a survey was made of the plays current at that time. They amounted to a hundred and twenty. They deal with every imaginable subject: the combined struggle of the people and the army against the invaders, recruiting for the army, underground activities of the resistance, the infamous conduct of the enemy and their puppet government, the progress of the resistance, the activities of the enemy's spies, and the punishment of speculators. The irrational aspects of society were thus laid bare, corrupt and inefficient officials also came in for their share of criticism, and the decadence of the traditional Confucian family system is also exposed. Purely historical plays were also presented, but more often, a historical theme was made to veil a burning question of the day.

These plays were acted amid much acclaim in the towns, and were also acted by the dramatic societies of the universities. They were also sold in printed form on the stalls of every bookstore, and passed from hand to hand among numberless readers. Thus interest in the drama rose to hitherto undreamed of heights, and this period of the war may be considered the "Golden Age" of Chinese Drama.

The dramatists who began their career at this time, or shortly before, will now be considered in the following pages.

Hsia Yen (夏衍)

Hsia Yen is the pen-name of Shen Tuan-hsien (沈端先), who is a contemporary of Mao Tun (茅盾), but his work did not appear until shortly before the war, when he published "Sai Chin-hua" (賽金花), which like Tseng Meng-pu's (曾孟樸) work, is about the famous courtisan who enjoyed an international reputation at the time of the Boxer Rebellion. The style which is concentrated and polished, and the characterization which is steady and consistent in conception, stamp this play as coming from an experienced writer. The dialogue also is carefully conceived, reminding one at once of the conversation of educated people of that time. For these reasons, it is not to be wondered that the play became an immediate success, attracting a great deal of attention, and the author obtained much praise.

During the war, Hsia Yen's talents developed to their apex with the appearance of "Within One Year" also named "On Earth and In the Sky" (一年間　又名：天上人間), which tells of the exploits of members of the Chinese Air Force during a year of the war, and the problems encountered by their families. This play is so realistically treated, being sketched in a few bold lines with all extraneous detail omitted, that it may be said to have created a new fashion in the dramatic representation of the war.

"The City of Sorrows" (愁城記) is a comprehensive survey of the different aspects of life in Shanghai after the Japanese occupation, and "Fortress of the Heart" (心防) has for theme the mental resistance and refusal of educators to submit to the Japanese after occupation. The latter has been included by Hung Sheng (洪深) as one of the ten representative war plays selected by him. "Fascist Infection" has a bacteriologist for hero, and tells of the adventures he went through as a refugee of the war. "Home On the Water" is of the nostalgia for home and of war refugees who have been forced to go inland. The cold tone of this play has precluded it from being often acted. "Luxuriant Grass" (離離草) is of the people of the Chia-mu-ssu (佳木斯) district in the Northeast, and of how they helped the volunteer army in resistance to a forced emigration insisted upon by the Japanese invaders. "Fragrant Grass to the Horizon" is on the contradictions to be found in love, marriage and the home.

Hsia Yen has also collaborated with Sung Chih-ti (宋之的) and Yü Ling (于伶) to produce "Soldiers in The Undergrowth" (草木皆兵) which is about the underground resistance in Shanghai during the war and the reprisals taken by the enemy. This play, being well-constructed and lively, has become very popular and is often acted.

The general impression of Hsia Yen's plays is rather bald. Under a smooth surface however, he hides great emotional power which he expends on themes of high moral tone, which are not devoid of many very human touches.

Yang Han-sheng (陽翰笙)

Yang Han-sheng is the pen-name of *Ou-yang Hua-han* (歐陽華漢). He is the Hua Han who became known as a writer of the second period of the "Creative Society" (創造社). Before the war, he brought out a collection under the general title of "Ground Spring" (地泉), composed of three plays: "Far In" (深入), "Change" (轉變) and "Regeneration" (復興), which are also known as the "Three Plays of Hua Han." (華漢三部曲).

Yang Han-sheng is another playwright whose talents were stimulated to great exertions by the war. Being a native of Szechuan, he is familiar with the conditions on the Tibetan frontier which he has depicted in "Wind and Cloud Over the Frontier" (塞上風雲). In this play, the complications caused by a love affair between Chinese and Mongols are made to symbolise the racial antagonisms of the two peoples which are as oil and water. Another element is also brought in. The artifices of Japanese spies are exposed. They are represented as being so unscrupulous that they will even utilize the disguise of a lama, if thereby they can obtain a hold over the people, and in some instances, they have remained undiscovered for over ten years. In the play, the rivals eventually sink their differences after the death of the coveted "Flower of the Desert", and they combine their energies to oppose the common enemy. The play is thus constructed on a few bold lines which succeed in conveying a powerful story.

Yang Han-sheng is also familiar with the activities of the members of the famous secret societies of Szechuan. "Heros of the Tall Grasses" (草莽英雄) is on this subject. The heroine is "Shih-san Mei" (時三妹) a feminine member of a secret society at the end of the Ch'ing Dynasty. The organization of these secret societies is thoroughly known to the author who is familiar with their slightest detail, as demonstrated in the above play.

"The Death of Li Hsiu-ch'eng" (李秀成之死) and "The Spring and Autumn Annals of the Heavenly Empire" (天國春秋) are both on the T'ai-p'ing Rebellion. The heroine of the latter is Fu Shan-hsiang (傅善祥) a woman who passed first in the highest official examinations conducted by the rebels. And the story is woven around the triangular love affair in which she and Hung Hsüan-chiao (洪宣嬌), wife of the "Western Prince", were rivals for the affections of Yang Hsiu-ch'ing (楊秀清), the "Eastern Prince", an affair which eventually became the greatest internal feud of the T'ai-p'ings. The play of emotions is so vivaciously represented that this piece has obtained an enthusiastic ovation wherever it has been presented. Together with "Wind and Cloud over the Frontier" it is the most representative work of Yang Han-sheng.

Of "the Death of Li Hsiu-ch'eng" the writer has himself commented: "I have tried to remind people of the fall of our capital in 1937 into the hands of the Japanese invader through depicting the seige of Nanking under the T'ai-pings''. This point of view which considers the T'ai-p'ings as national heros concurs with that of Sun Yat-sen, the father of the Republic. But from the fact of taking Li Hsiu-ch'eng (李秀成) a robber and a rebel as the hero, and from the general atmosphere of the play, it is easy to see that the writer had in mind, not Nanking, but the fall of Jui-chin (瑞金) in Kiangsi, the first red capital from which the Communists were evicted by national troops. From this we can gather the comprehensiveness of communist propaganda which never forgets its message under any circumstances or at any time.

A Word On Communist Propaganda

Now it will be remembered that at the beginning of the war the Communists made a declaration that they would co-operate with the National Government in a joint resistance to the enemy. In actual fact, however, the Chinese Communists have never carried out their promises. On the contrary, they took advantage of the situation to extend their own power. Cultured circles also organised themselves into the ''National Literary League'' (全國文藝協會) which had the declared purpose of including literary men of all shades of opinion in the great work of national salvation. Nevertheless the feuds and quarrels of different sections did not cease, and leftist writers continued to spread communist theories either openly or in veiled fashion. And the plays of Yang Hansheng are only one example of this kind of propaganda.

A Ying (阿英)

A-Ying is the pen-name of *Ch'ien Hsing-ts'un* (錢杏邨), a veteran writer of the ''Sun Society'' (太陽社). He is known for having written under a number of pseudonymous, and for having dealt with a wide range of subjects. Not only is he a playwright but also a critic and a specialist on the history of the Southern Mings and of the latter part of the Ch'ing Dynasty. He is also known for his familiarity with folk literature and the old-style tales chanted to a musical accompaniment.

A-Ying has been a resident of Shanghai for many years. The following are his most representative works: ''Oriols Everywhere'' (羣鶯亂舞), ''Wind and Rain in The City'' (滿城風雨), ''Five Sisters'' (五姊妹), ''The Peach Fountain'' (桃花源), ''Shanghai Night'' (夜上海), ''Spring Wind and Autumn Rain'' (春風秋雨), ''City of No Night'' (不夜城).

Under the pen-name of Wei Ju-huei (魏如晦) he has brought out several historical plays: ''Heroes of a Country By the Sea'' (海國英雄), ''Lament For The Fall of the Mings'' (明末遺恨), ''Hung Hsüan-chiao'' (洪宣嬌) and ''Yang Ê'' (陽娥傳). In these plays, A-Ying shows a familiar acquaintance with the history of the Ming and Ch'ing Dynasties, and therefore is able to present his work in a convincing manner.

Sung Chih-ti (宋之的)

Sung Chih-ti produced a very immature work before the war entitled "Wu Tsê-t'ien" (武則天), which, however, has been revised by another hand. Soon after the outbreak of the war, he collaborated with fifteen other writers, including Chang Min (章泯) and A-Ying (阿英), to bring out the play "Marco Polo Bridge" (蘆溝橋). And shortly after appeared his individual publication of "Self-Defence Corps" (自衞隊) also entitled "The Glory of the People" (民族光榮), both of which plays are on the national resistance to the Japanese invaders.

Sung Chih-ti made marked progress in technique after joining the trek inland from the coast cities that had fallen to the enemy, and in collaboration with Lao Shê (老舍), wrote "Above All the Fatherland" (國家至上) which has been included by Hung Sheng in his "Ten most representative plays of the war", and which has often been compared by the critics to the "Metamorphosis" (蛻變) of Ts'ao Yü (曹禺). The hero is a teacher of boxing, "Master Chang", who brings about cooperation between the pure Chinese and the Mohammedans in his home district in the Northwest, through the welding of his moral influence. It has been said that the new literature has given birth to two successful prototypes of the Chinese peasant, Lu Hsün's "Ah Q" who represents the journeyman labourer of the South, and Sung Chih-ti's creation, "Master Chang" who represents the small owner-farmer of the North.

Another of Sung's plays is "The Whip" (鞭), also entitled, "Misty Chungking" (霧重慶), is which the disorderly conditions and the muddy impurities of society in Chungking were laid bare. This work has been compared in both matter and style with Lao Shê's "Sad Mist" (殘霧). Subsequently, "Punishment" (刑) appeared having as its theme the progress made in the war of resistance.

Later, to commemorate the fortieth birthday of the celebrated producer Ying Yün-wei (應雲衞), Sung Chih-ti, together with Hsia Yen (夏衍) and Yü Ling (于玲) brought out a review of contemporary drama (戲劇春秋), containing anecdotes of the theatre world since its inauguration with the so-called "Culture Drama". This work may be said to be an extremely moving account of an agitated period.

Sung Chih-ti was one of the three authors (the other two being Hsia Yen and Yü Ling) who wrote "Soldiers in the Undergrowth" (草木皆兵), which has already been reviewed as one of Hsia Yen's works.

Still another of his plays is "Cries from The Mother Country" (祖國在呼喚) in which he describes the return of the cultured classes, who had sought refuge in Hongkong, to the mother country when they flocked into the interior during the latter part of the war.

Ou-yang Yü-chien (歐陽予倩)

Ou-yang Yü-ch'ien is a veteran playwright and reformer of the Chinese stage, for long before the May 4th. Student Movement, he had already suggested changes in the old traditional opera, and promoted plays which contained natural dialogue in the vernacular. Although his own plays were only examples of the "Culture Drama" (文明戲), he was a progressive influence, as he was able to keep abreast with the new literary movement of his time. In the years before the war he combined the duties of a manager of an old-style opera company with constant investigation into the activities of the promoters of the new drama.

Long before the war he had produced "P'an Chin-lien" (潘金蓮) which had already been mentioned in these pages. "The Shrew" (潑婦) and "Return Home" (回家) are also plays in the vernacular.

Together with T'ien Han (田漢) he has thrown himself enthusiastically into the work of reforming the old drama. And discovering an actress of talent in Kueilin, he wrote a play especially for her entitled, "Liang Hung-yü" (梁紅玉), built around the story of Liang Hung-yü, wife of Han Shih-chung (韓世忠), general of the Southern Sung Dynasty. When she beat a drum on Mt. Chin, the soldiers responded and drove out the invading Mongols. This play has enjoyed great popularity and may be considered a most successful adaptation of an old drama.

Of Ou-yang Yü-ch'ien's original work, "Prince Li Hsiu-ch'eng" (忠王李秀成) should be cited. The treatment of this play is entirely different from Yang Han-sheng's "Death of Li Hsiu-ch'eng", although the central figure in both is the same T'ai-p'ing hero. Its power to stir the audience is greater than Yang Han-sheng's effort, and it is generally considered a better play.

Wu Tsu-kuang (吳祖光)

Wu Tsu-kuang has been secretary of the "National School of Dramatics" (國立戲劇學校). His plays began to be known during the war. He has written "Wen T'ien-hsiang" (文天祥), also named, "Song of the Everlasting Spirit" (正氣歌) based upon the life of the great national hero of the end of the Sung Dynasty. Since the Kuomintang has given the stamp of official approval to the promotion of "National Culture" (本位文化), figures, such as Wen T'ien-hsiang of the Sung Dynasty and Shih K'o-fa (史可法) of the Ming Dynasty have often been taken as the heros of books produced by those in line with government policy. But historical themes are notoriously complicated and difficult to adapt for current consumption. Cheng Chen-to (鄭振鐸) has for instance, built a story around Wên T'ien-hsiang entitled "Kuei-kung's Pond" (桂公塘), which cannot be considered a successful attempt, and the same difficulties have to be overcome by anyone wishing to dramatise the history of such a historical figure. Wu Tsu-kuang's play, however, is carefully planned throughout, and the chorus, introduced by him in the beginning, consisting of two bands of singers, one in white and the other in black, chanting the famous "Song of the Everlasting Spirit" (正氣歌) is extremely effective.

Wu Tsu-kuang's first work was probably "The Phoenix City" (鳳凰城) on the theme of the resistance of the guerillas in the Northeast to the Japanese. The hero is a famous guerilla leader Chao T'ung (趙侗). This play has been acted successfully a number of times, but has lost in popularity since the slaying of the real Chao T'ung by the Communists.

Since Wu Tsu-kuang is a dramatist of great talent, he has been the butt of leftist efforts to bring him within the communist fold, and he has not succeeded

In keeping his opinions free from the continual pressure that is brought to bear upon him.

His most successful play is "Return on a Stormy Night" (風雨夜歸人), which is about the adventures of actors and actresses with Peking as a background, and in which the central figure is an actress. As, however, a great deal of the dialogue is exceedingly leftist in tendency, it was prohibited from the stage during the war.

Another of his works, "Wanderings of the Young" (少年遊), is of the discovery of the underground activities of a group of students in Peiping, and their adventures when they are forced to seek refuge in the interior. "The Cowherd and the Weaving Maid" (牛郎織女) is a play based upon an old Chinese legend. "Laying Devils" (捉鬼傳), written after the end of the war, is a famous satire of this author.

Yang Ts'un-pin (楊村彬)

Yang Ts'un-pin is a professor of old standing in the National School for Drama (國立戲劇學校). He has also had experience as a director of cinema films. In his own writing, he is known for his clever manipulation of scenes requiring many actors, especially in historical plays, as for instance, in "Ch'in Liang-yü" (秦良玉) of which the heroine is the well-known woman warrior of the end of the Ming Dynasty. His particular powers are however, displayed to even better advantage in "Intimate History of the Imperial Palace of the Ch'ings" (清宮外史) which is a trilogy of three plays depicting the struggle for power between the Empress Dowager, Ts'i Hsi, and the Emperor Kuang-hsü. The first play of the trilogy, "Kuang-hsü Reigns" (光緒親政記), is generally considered the best, and there we find such familiar historical characters as Li Hung-chang, Wong T'ung-ho, K'o Lien-ts'ai and Li Lien-ying (李鴻章, 翁同龢, 寇蓮材, 李蓮英). This piece is a successful example not only of a historical play but of the "Palace Plays" that in China have attained to a separate classification. It necessitates a complicated production, the costuming and scenery contributing a great deal to its success. The dialogue also is extremely convincing, reminding one of the elegant and cultured conversation of that time, and from this point of view is a distinct advance on the Yuan Dynasty plays of similar nature, where court officials are sometimes made to speak like peasants. The only flaw of this trilogy is that the writer has not completely mastered the complicated manners of the palace, and therefore occasionally his characters lack the dignity to be expected from those brought up in the rigid discipline of court etiquette.

Yuan Chün (袁俊)

Yuang Chün is the pen-name of Chang Chün-hsiang (張駿祥). He is one of the first Chinese students to have specialised in dramatics in America. It may be said that his dramatic theory is better than his practice as a stage producer, and that in turn is superior to his talent as a playwright. A number of plays, however, have come from his pen: "Cape of Good Hope" (好望角), "President Liner" (美國總統號), "Tale of a Mountain City" (山城故事), "Tale of a Frontier City" (邊城故事), and "Model for Ten Thousand Generations" (萬世師表).

"Tale of a Frontier City" is one of the propaganda plays to which the war gave birth. It is built around the need of the government for gold to purchase foreign exchange. The attempts of the government to mine gold in the eastern borders of Szechuan meet with many difficulties, such as primitive methods and equipment, and the disorderly conduct of the landowners, native residents, and the aboriginal tribes of that district. The situation is saved when a young director is appointed. He proves to be exceedingly capable, just and honest, and not afraid of responsibility. He leaves no stone unturned to persuade all the different classes of people, who have been creating trouble, to co-operate with the government, and he induces them to use the new modern equipment that has been provided, with the result that the gold mine becomes a flourishing business, contributing a great deal towards the war effort. This director is an ideal character born of the imagination of the playwright, and may be classed in the same caterory as "Commissioner Liang" in Ts'ao Yü's "Metamorphosis". Of course it cannot be said that such government servants do not exist, nevertheless their idealization has been attacked severely by leftist writers who have said of "Metamorphosis": "We do not disclaim the existence of such men as Commissioner Liang and Dr. Ting — such men may even be quite common — but what kind of government is needed for men of such calibre to maintain their position? Favourable conditions are needed for them to be able to rise above their difficulties and to dispell corruption and not be swallowed up by it. On this point the author is silent." A criticism similar to the above has been levelled against "Tale of a Frontier City."

The other propaganda play from Yuan Chün is "Model for Ten Thousand Generations" (萬世師表). It is of the good work done by educators under the harassing conditions of the war, in which they struggled, oppressed by great personal privation. The central figure of this play is also idealised, for he is a model teacher whose story is very moving. But as people of his stamp are more frequently encountered in educational circles than in government offices, he may be said to be fairly convincingly presented. And this play is, in consequence, suitable for acting in schools.

Ch'en Pei-ch'en (陳白塵)

Ch'en Pei-ch'en is a professional writer who concentrates entirely on plays. His career began before the war with "Stormy Night" (風雨之夜), and "Return" (歸來), but he is chiefly known for his productiveness during the war. He excels in keeping strictly to his theme, and amid much movement there is always order in his "mise en scène". His plays are either comedies or farces, and the best is generally considered to be "The Devils Cave" (魔窟), also called "The Dance of the Devils" (群魔亂舞). The story is built around a group of rascals in a certain district near Shanghai, who are delighted at the Japanese occupation, which gives them an opportunity to join the puppet government. During the war, this play enjoyed great popularity and was acclaimed a masterpiece, but it may not have such enduring qualities as "Harvest" (秋收), also by this author, and sometimes known under the titles of "Gold All Over the Ground" (大地黃金) and "Autumn in the Fields" (陌上秋). This play has been listed by Hung Sheng as one of the ten representative plays of the war. It is full of delicate and pleasing touches in depicting the co-operation of the army with the farmers in the gathering of their harvest.

"Wartime Men and Women" (亂世男女) has many points of similarity with "Sad Mist" (殘霧) by Lao Shê. They are both about the disorderly conditions in the interior during the war.

"Wedding March" (結婚進行曲) revised by the author from his earlier work "An Unmarried Couple" (未婚夫婦), is an extremely entertaining comedy warranted to fill the house with laughter wherever it is presented. "Spring Returns to the Land" (大地回春) is of a manufacturer, who at the cost of much effort, succeeds in moving his factory inland where it continues to produce necessary articles for the war effort. On the very first day that the factory is ready to re-open again, it is bombed by enemy planes. Not only is part of the building destroyed but the manufacturer himself loses a leg. He is not discouraged however, but continues his work heroically until the factory is in good running condition. His determination and patriotism are very striking in contrast with the self-indulgence of his grown-up children who continue to engage in selfish love affairs, and who have not sufficient will-power to stand the strain of privation. When the factory has been restored and the machines begin to rumble again, the brave manager leaps up from his bed of sickness and lets out a hearty cheer "Long Live China!" The sun is then breaking through the mists of dawn, and soon is shining brightly upon a hopeful future. This stage effect never fails to rouse the audience to enthusiastic applause.

"S.S. Victory" (勝利號) written during the war was the author's conception of what should happen when the final victory arrived and the refugees in the interior were free to return to their homes. The three acts of the play, all take place in the saloon of a ship, which the government is employing to return war-workers to their homes. The best cabins have been given to them, and there we see them gathered: a university professor with a big rent in his trousers, crippled soldiers, workmen, foremen, and office workers. The ship begins to move, the scenery shifts behind the portholes, and from this agglomeration of humanity, natural complications arise. The play is farcical in nature, but under the amusing situations lies much sober meaning, for this piece was written when war conditions were becoming stringent, the inflation was gaining great impetus, and people were feeling the strain to such an extent that they had only one hope: that the war would soon come to an end, and they would be able to return home. The immense popularity of this play may therefore be explained in its fulfilling the wish psychology of the audience at the time it was produced. "The Chart of Official Promotion" (陞官圖) as indicated by its title is a satire on officialdom, in which exaggeration and caricature is freely employed. "The Last Days of Shih Ta-k'ai" (石達開的末路) also named "Big Ferry River" (大渡河) belongs to the same category as "The Death of Li Hsiu-ch'eng" by Yang Han-sheng and "Prince Li Hsiu-ch'eng" by Ou-yang Yü-ch'ien, being another play with the background of the T'ai-p'ing Rebellion. "The Oil Peddlar" (賣油郎) also named "Love on the Precipice" (懸崖之戀) has appeared recently. It has as its theme the love story of a rich merchant and a music student laid in the background of Chungking during the war and just after.

Yü Ling (于伶)

Yü Ling wrote before the war under the pen-name of Yu Chin (尤兢). His life is obscure but it seems that he has been brought up in the theatre. He adopted the pseudonym of Yü Ling during the Japanese occupation to avoid the notice of the occupation authorities in Shanghai, having already attained to some reputation under his former name.

As Yu Chin, he has written "Cup of Night Radiance" (夜光杯), which is a story of patriotism overcoming family scruples. This play was very popular at one time.

"Women's Hostel" (女子公寓) is a problem play on the question of employment for women, in which all the characters, numbering fourteen, are female. "Flowers Weep" (花濺淚) is a collection of both laughter-provoking and tear-provoking scenes of Shanghai. "Shanghai By Night" (夜上海), which is one of the ten representative plays of the war selected by Hung Shêng, is of the rivalries and struggles in the night life and underground activities of Shanghai. "Long Night Journey" (長夜行) is of the struggle of a middle school teacher during the war.

Yü Ling's masterpiece is "Apricot Blossom and Spring Rain in the South" (杏花春雨江南). It is of the aftermath of the war in the former occupied area south of the Yangtze. A change of attitude in the landowners there is brought about by the end of the war. As the technique of this play is extremely sound, it has won praise from the critics.

A few historical plays have also come from Yü Ling's pen such as "Heros of the Ming Dynasty" (大明英烈傳).

Shen Fu (沈浮)

Shen Fu is a writer of farces, as for instance, "Full of Money" (金玉滿堂), which is about a Szechuanese family that makes a fortune through war-profiteering, but when their dubious activities are brought under government notice, and they are subjected to restriction, ruin rapidly follows. "Twenty-four Hours in Chungking" (重慶二十四小時) has as its theme the life of deprivation led by those in the interior during the war. "Small Man's Fantasia" (小人物狂想曲) is built around the story of the hero Ma Lung (馬龍), who is fighting at the front at the beginning of the war, but after being wounded is invalided out of the army. He then goes of Chungking with an old schoolmate and both find refuge with the principal of the school they once attended. There Ma Lung is unhappy and tries to drown his sorrows in wine. His friend however, saves him from this state, partly through persuasion and partly through bringing the wife and daughter of Ma Lung from Peiping. After their arrival Ma Lung gradually leads a saner existence. He concentrates his energies on a musical composition he has in mind, which he calls "The Small Man's Fantasia". In it he tries to express all his hopes in final victory, but when it is presented to his patron, the principal of the school, it draws forth a criticism that it is too amorpheous a creation. Ma Lung revises the whole composition, and in the end attains to a substantial success. Around this central theme is woven a love intrigue, and another character of considerable importance is a schoolmate of the hero, who has made a fortune through war-profiteering, got tired of his wife, and plans to murder his teacher who has always treated him with the utmost benevolence, all of which adds more interest than complication to the plot.

Some Younger Playwrights

Hsü Ch'ang-ling (徐昌霖) is an able young dramatist whose career has begun only recently, since the end of the war. His power of characterization is considerable, and he may be placed in the same class as Shen Fu as a realist. He has to his credit "Under Chungking Eaves" (重慶屋簷下), in which the intellectuals are presented in contrast with the merchants, and the admirable qualities of honest people are shown up in contrast with those who wish only to take advantage of the war. "Golden Tide" (黃金潮) is of the sudden rise in the price of gold, with its subsequent effects upon prices of commodities in general. "Mitkyna Storm" (密支那風雲) is of the Burma campaign.

Chang Min (章泯) attained to sudden fame at the beginning of the war through a three act play, "Our Native Home" (我們的故鄉), and "Laughter in the Dark" (黑暗中的笑聲). Both are about the destruction in the countryside wrought by the Japanese invaders, and of the popular resistance against them. Being on such popular subjects, they have been well-received. Another of Chang Min's plays is "Battle" (戰鬥). A criticism that may be levelled against him is that his work suffers from loose construction. He begins with great enthusiasm, but does not know how to control the development to a logical conclusion.

Chou Yen (周彥) has had experience in promoting drama among the peasants of Tinghsien from where the "1000 character movement" originated. He is often alluded to in connection with Hsiung Fo-hsi (熊佛西). We have from him "The Peach Blossom Fan" (桃花扇) and "Hate Behind the Crimson Door" (朱門怨), the latter of which is of the decadent behaviour of an old family.

Shu Yin (舒湮) is known for historical plays of which the best known are, "Tung Hsiao-wan" (董小宛) and "Ch'en Yuan-yuan" (陳圓圓).

The above two writers may be said to be successful in this "genre". An ample knowledge of our old history is obviously necessary for the successful composition of either historical novels or plays. Scholars of the old school, however, who have this knowledge, seldom condescend to produce a piece for pure entertainment, while those who write in the new style are rarely possessed of much scholarship. In this unfortunate impasse we are lucky to have at least two rising young playwrights who can present us with our old history dressed in a popular form, without too much deviation from classical tradition.

The following should be briefly noted:

Hsien Ch'ün (洗群) for a very interesting play, "Song of Drifting Petals" (飛花曲); *Yao Su-feng"* (姚蘇鳳) for "When the Maid is Married" (之子于歸); *Lu Chüeh-wu"* (魯覺吾) for "Ten Thousand Ounces of Yellow Gold" (黃金萬兩),

"*Yi-ch'ün*" (以群) for "Four Sisters" (四姊妹); *Wang Chen-chih* (王震之) for "Captain of Banditti" (流寇) which has been listed by Hung Sheng as one of his ten representative plays of the war; and *P'an Chieh-nung* (潘孑農) and *Hung Mo* (洪謨), for their play, "Nepotic Skirts" (裙帶風) which satirises one of the chief abuses of officialdom.

Kuomintang Playwrights

A few Kuomintang playwrights will now be mentioned.

Wang P'ing-ling (王平陵) has written "Death of an Actress" (女優之死), and "Love is Blind" (情盲), of which the former is well-known to the public.

Chang Tao-fan (張道藩) has written "Ti Ssu-niang" (狄四娘) and other plays based upon foreign originals.

Wang Chin-shan (王進珊) has written "More Glorious Than Sun Or Moon" (日月爭光), in which the hero is Ch'en Ch'i-mei (陳其美), one of the founders of the Kuomintang, and the spirit in which the drama is revealed is patriotic and moving.

Hu Shao-hsüen (胡紹軒) is an innovator of new forms. At the beginning of the war he produced "To Be A Soldier" (當兵去) which may be considered the pioneer of the "Street Plays" that flourished during the War. It introduced a new technique; for being acted informally in the street, there was no sharp division between actors and audience. The drama unfolds naturally as though actually happening before the eyes of the spectators, and therefore has great power to rouse those who see it.

Another play of Hu Shao-hsüen's that should be noticed is "We Will Not Be Slaves" (我們不作亡國奴). In this a device is used to impress the moral upon the minds of the audience. The prologue takes the form of one of the actors commencing a speech which is interrupted by the blowing of a whistle, which is a sign for the actual play to begin. Throughout the rest of the play, acting alternates with lecturing, and members of the company intermingle with the audience. Hu Shao-hsüen has given a name to this kind of technique, calling it "synthetic propaganda play."

This kind of technique has also been employed by T'ien Han (田漢) in "Parade of Fair Women" (麗人行), and it is difficult to say whether he adopted it consciously from Hu Shao-hsüen, or whether the two playwrights developed the same technique independently.

Another of Hu Shao-hsüen's works is "After Sorrow Come Happy Days" (否極泰來) based upon "China's Destiny" by the Generalissimo Chiang Kai-shek. This play is valuable for its educational content.

Ch'en Ch'üan (陳銓) has written "Wild Roses" (野玫瑰), "Blue Butter-flies" (藍蝴蝶), "The Ring of Gold" (金指環). The first is a combination of a love theme with a detective story with everything happening in the house of a traitor. As it is intensely romantic, well-constructed, and the dialogue is poetic, it is a favourite with theatre-goers. The traitor is Wang K'o-min (王克敏), and as the writer is versed in Nietzsche's philosophy, he makes his chief character a power-crazy politician. It is to be expected, however, that since the writer is a member of the Kuomintang, his work does not find favour with the leftist elements of the literary world. And a severe attack was launched in the supplement of the "Shih-shih Hsing Pao" (時事新報), "Clear Light" (青光) by Ch'en Pai-ch'en (陳白塵) under the title, "Sugar-coated Poison" (糖衣的毒藥), in which the author of "Wild Roses" was held up to castigation for being too traitor-conscious . . . that is to say, for having an unhealthy intimacy with the psychology of traitors. Hung Sheng and Hsia Yen joined in the fight against Ch'en Ch'üan, beseiging him with heavy disapproval.

Summary

The plays that have been produced since the outbreak of Sino-Japanese hostilities may be classified roughly into the following:

1) A large number of war plays; 2) historical plays such as "The Peacock's Gall Bladder" and "Ch'en Yuan-yuan"; 3) plays based upon old Chinese romances such as "The Dream of the Red Chamber" among which may be mentioned, "Dream of the Red Chamber" (紅樓夢) by Tuan-mu Hung-liang, (端木蕻良) "Oppressive Thunder" (鬱雷) by Chu T'ung (朱彤), and "Beneath the Cold Moon" (冷月葬詩魂) by Chao Ch'ing-ko (趙清閣); 4) plays adapted from foreign originals such as, "The Ring of Gold" (金指環) by Ch'en Ch'üan (陳銓), and "Resurrection" by T'ien Han and Hsia Yen.

STORM AND STRESS

The boiling up of ideas in present-day China has been briefly surveyed in the foregoing pages. The whole of what has come to be known as the "modern literary movement" is confused, just as the political history of China of the past few decades is confused. Heterogeneous forces have been working upon us, pulling us in different directions, and the results have not always been happy. Often no solutions of our problems are possible because they are too vast. Yet at least, a number of writers have forced their problems courageously, some few of whom have been mentioned in passing as having made a name in the new form of fiction and drama, which now prevails among the younger generation in China.

The difficulties that have had to be faced, and which are still present in greater or lesser degree, may be illustrated by the natural division of the "literary movement" into two parts. Until the formation of the League of Left Wing Writers in 1930, the battle that was fought was chiefly a linguistic one. No popular literature was possible as long as the old classical style was enthroned as the secret code of a favoured few. The revolution would have been meaningless, if there had been no parallel "literary revolution" extending an intellectual franchise to the classes who were learning the rudiments of reading and writing in the newly-established schools. The tremendous task had to be undertaken of creating a new language to express the wealth of ideas that had been suddenly cast upon the nation.

Since 1930, however, ideology has been stressed more than linguistic problems, so that we have a period of revolutionary literature. The cautious will deplore the extremist demonstrations of this period, but admiration cannot be withheld from writers who take pride in a merciless self-analysis of both personal and national weakness, who persist indomitably in the assertion of individual rights, who do not shrink from the hardships and vicissitudes of life, and who, moreover, continue writing with no hope of pecuniary gain, for it is almost unknown in China for a writer to be able to live by his pen.

To our foreign friends, this last fact cannot be over-emphasised. In a predominatingly agricultural country, where the peasantry have been ruined by a succession of civil wars, where industry is meagre and unorganized, and communications either disrupted or non-existent, all intellectual life is a luxury. Nevertheless it is a luxury that will be indulged in at all costs. A devotion to literature

is in the very air we breathe. It is the most persistent part of the Confucian tradition that endures after we have cast its shackles to the four winds.

Few of our present-day writers, however, are so engrossed in personal idiosyncrasies as in social reform. The popularity of Ibsen in China is explained by this fact, and Bernard Shaw would have as large a following if his peculiarly English jokes were not beyond the comprehension of an average Chinese audience. Marriage is an ever-present problem in a country where the right to choose one's own partner for life has won a grundging recognition from only a small educated minority. The emancipation of women from her age-old subjection, and of children from tyrannical parental authority, the claim of the masses to free education, of workers to a share in the government — these Victorian problems form a strange pattern intertwined with the exaltation of free-love, anarchist ravings, and per-verse hackings at the source of law and order, the government itself.

Modern Chinese writers deserve all the adjectives that have been levelled against them. They are atheistic, materialistic, positivistic, rationalistic, nihilistic, agnostic, sadist, a skeptical, free-thinking, unhallowed crowd. But they write from the sheer love of writing, or because they are impelled by a burning desire for the betterment of humanity. Their idealism is instinctive and unconscious, their solutions are often violently impractical, and the dignity of restraint sometimes is sadly lacking.

But out of the jostling of this roaring, screaming, and gesticulating mob, out of its very incoherence, out of its suffering, which should be considered not as the dying agonies of an old culture but as the birth pangs of a new civilization, something worthwhile may be born.

THE END

SHORT BIOGRAPHIES OF AUTHORS

by

Chao Yen-shêng（趙燕聲）

NOTE

The system for transliterating names of persons, places, and titles of books is the one devised by Thomas F. Wade for his Peking Syllabary of 1859, and slightly revised by Herbert A. Giles for his Chinese-English Dictionary of 1912. The only exceptions are the names of provinces and the more important cities, for which the Post Office spelling is used. The letters T. and H. which appear beside some of the Chinese names indicate that the characters following them are the courtesy names (Tzŭ 字) and the literary names (Hao 號) respectively of the person in question. All the works marked with* are reviewed in this volume.

SHORT BIOGRAPHIES OF AUTHORS

1. Ai Wu 艾 蕪.

Novelist, short-story writer, and essayist. Born in Szechwan. He is an intimate friend of Sha Ting 沙汀, the novelist. He cultivated the habit of reading fiction in his boyhood. The first novel he read was *San Kuo Yen I* 三國演義 (Romance of the Three Kingdoms). While studying in the First Normal School of Chengtu 成都第一師範學校, shortly after the famous May Fourth Movement, he began to read the Chinese translations of the works of C. Dickens and L. Tolstoy. After four years of normal school study, he left his family in 1925, and began a wandering life. From Szechwan he went to Yunnan, and later proceeded to Burma. In Rangoon, by the pressure of financial difficulties, he wrote his first short story, entitled *Lao Han Jên* 老憨人 (A Foolish Fellow), which was published in the *Rangoon Daily News* 仰光日報, in the winter of 1927, and earned twenty rupees for the author. He then wrote twenty or thirty short stories in succession. But they were all unsuccessful experiments. His first success was the *Jên Shêng Chê Hsüeh Ti I K'o* 人生哲學的一課 (One Lesson of the Philosophy of Life), a short story written after his settlement at Shanghai, and published in the *Wên Hsüeh Yüeh Pao* 文學月報 (Literary Monthly).

During the Sino-Japanese War, he lived in Kweilin, where he was in charge of the Kweilin Branch of the "National Writers' Anti-Aggression Association" 中華全國文藝界抗敵協會, and published his writings in the Association's publication *K'ang Chan Wên I* 抗戰文藝 (Wartime Literature). He returned to Shanghai in the summer of 1947. His newest work *Wo Ti Ch'ing Nien Shih Tai* 我的青年時代 (My Youth), was published in the magazine *Wên I Fu Hsing* 文藝復興 (Renaissance), from September of 1947 on.

Being a novelist, he writes about China's southwest. He is the author of the following works: *P'iao Po Tsa Chi* 漂泊雜記 (Sketches on My Wandering Life, 1934, 生活); *Nan Hsing Chi* 南行記 * (Travels in the South, a record of the author's wandering life, 1935, 文化生活出版社); *Nan Kuo Chih Yeh* 南國之夜 (Night Scene in South China, collection of short stories, 1935, 良友); *Yeh Ching* 夜景* (Night Scene, collection of short stories, 1936, 文化生活出版社); *Chiang Shang Hsing* 江上行 (Travels on the River, a novel, 1943, 新羣出版社); *Ch'iu Shou* 秋收 (Harvest, collection of short stories, 1944, 讀書出版社); *Fêng Jao Ti Yuan Yeh* 豐饒的原野 (The Fertile Wilderness, a novel, 1946, 自强出版社); *Wo Ti Lü Pan* 我的旅伴 (My Companion, a novel, 1946, 華夏); *Wên Hsüeh Shou Ts'ê* 文學手冊 (Literary Studies, 1946, 生活); *Ch'un T'ien* 春天 * (Spring, 良友); *Pa Chiao Ku* 芭蕉谷* (collection of short stories, 商務); etc.

3

2. Chang Fang-hsü 章方叙.

Also named 章依, T. 正候. He is better known under the pen-name of Chin I 靳以. His other pen-name is 陳湄.

Novelist, and short-story writer. He graduated from the Department of Commerce of Fuhtan University 復旦大學, Shanghai. While in school he had no interest at all in the curriculum and the professors, but applied himself to the reading of literary works. Later, he published short stories in the *Hsien Tai Yüeh K'an* 現代月刊, and other major literary magazines. When he won fame as a writer, he edited the *Wên Hsüeh Chi K'an* 文學季刊 (Literary Quarterly) at Peiping, in collaboration with Chêng Chên-to 鄭振鐸 and a few others. Later, he founded the *Wên Chi Yüeh K'an* 文季月刊, a literary monthly, together with Pa Chin 巴金, a well-known novelist. In 1937, he published another monthly magazine *Wên Ts'ung Yüeh K'an* 文叢月刊, at Shanghai. With the outbreak of the Sino-Japanese War, he went to Canton, where he continued the publication of *Wên Ts'ung*. After the fall of Canton, he moved to Chungking, where he was appointed professor at Fuhtan University, and editor of the literary supplement of the newspaper *Kuo Min Hsin Wên* 國民新聞. During his three years' sojourn in Chungking, he completed his masterpiece *Ch'ien Hsi* 前夕 (On the Eve), a long novel of nearly half million words. Later, he went to Fukien, and taught in a normal school for two years. He then returned to Chungking, and resumed his post in Fuhtan. After the Victory over Japan, he returned to Shanghai, where he teaches in Fuhtan, and edits the *Sunday Literature* of *Ta Kung Pao* 大公報星期文藝.

Works: 聖型 (collection of short stories, 1933, 現代); 羣鴉 * (collection of short stories, 1934, 新中國) 蟲蝕 * (collection of short stories, 1934, 良友); 青的花 * (collection of short stories, 1934, 生活); 珠落集 * (collection of short stories, 1935, 文化生活出版社); 渡家 * (collection of short stories, 1935, 文化生活出版社); 秋花 * (a novel, 1936, 文化生活出版社); 黄沙 * (collection of short stories, 1936, 文化生活出版社); 殘陽 * (collection of short stories, 1936, 開明); 貓與短簡 * (collection of essays, 1937, 開明); 洪流 (collection of short stories, 1942, 文化生活出版社) 紅燭 (collection of essays, 1942, 文化生活出版社); 衆神 (collection of short stories, 1944, 文化生活出版社); 血與火花* (collection of essays, 1946, 萬葉); 春草 (a novel, 1946, 文化生活出版社); 人世百圖 (collection of essays); 遙遠的城 (collection of short stories); 馬橋小集 (collection of essays); 沈默的果實 (collection of essays); 遠天的冰雪 * (collection of short stories, 文化生活出版社); etc.

3. Chang Hên-shui 張恨水.

(1895 —   )

Novelist, and journalist. Born in Ch'ienshan 潛山, Anhwei. He served for many years as reporter in various newspapers. Later, he became the director and editor-in-chief of the Newspaper *Jên Pao* 人報 at Nanking. During the Sino-Japanese War he held the position of manager and editor-in-chief of *Hsin Min*

Pao 新民報 at Chungking. After the Victory over Japan, he returned to Peiping and resumed his post of manager of *Hsin Min Pao*.

Chang Hên-shui is a prolific writer. Up to 1946, he had written one hundred and six novels, of which fifty were put into book form. His *T'i Hsiao Yin Yuan* 啼笑姻緣,* *Chin Fên Shih Chia* 金粉世家,* *Man Chiang Hung* 滿江紅 * are popular novels for the home, and have been adapted for films.

4. Chang Hsiu-ya 張秀亞.

Pen-name: 陳藍. Novelist, and short-story writer. Born in Tsanghsien, Hopei. She first graduated from Tientsin Normal College for Women 天津女子師範學校 Before the Sino-Japanese War she published her short stories in the literary supplement of *Ta Kung Pao* 大公報, edited by Hsiao Ch'ien 蕭乾. Later she collected these narratives into one volume, entitled *Tsai Ta Lung Ho P'an* 在大龍河畔* (On the Bank of Ta Lung River, 1936, 天津海風出版社). In 1938, she attended Fu Jên University 輔仁大學 at Peiping to study Western literature, and became a Catholic. During these four years she wrote many poems, essays, and two novels: *Hsing Fu Ti Ch'üan Yuan* 幸福的泉源* (The Fountain of Happiness, 1941, 山東兗州保祿印書舘), and *Kuei I* 皈依 * (Conversion, 1941, 山東兗州保祿印書舘) After her graduation in 1942, she went to Chungking, where she edited the literary supplement of *I Shih Pao* 益世報 and married Yü Li-po 于犖伯, the younger brother of Archbishop Paul Yü Pin 于斌. In Chungking she published two new works: *K'o Lo Tso Nü Shên* 珂羅佐女神, and *Pei Fang Ti Ku Shih* 北方的故事 (Story of the North), both of which won fame. After the Victory over Japan, she returned to Peiping, where she teaches English in Fu Jên University.

5. Chang I-p'ing 章衣萍.

(1902 —   )

Courtesy name of 章鴻熙, but he is noted for this name instead of the original. Essayist, poet, and short-story writer. Born in Chiki, Anhwei. He graduated from the National University of Peking 北京大學. In Nov., 1924, together with Lu Hsün 魯迅, and Chou Tso-jên 周作人, he founded the magazine *Yü Ssŭ* 語絲, in which he published most of his writings. In 1926, he published one volume of love letters, entitled *Ch'ing Shu I Shu* 情書一束* (北新), which was received with tremendous enthusiasm by the Chinese youth, and has been translated into Russian. In 1927, he married Miss Wu Shu-t'ien 吳曙天, authoress of *Tuan P'ien Ti Hui I* 斷片的囘憶 (Reminiscences), and *Luan Ai Jih Chi San Chung* 戀愛日記三種 (天馬). Later, he taught in the Chinan University 暨南大學 at Shanghai.

Works: *Shên Shih* 深誓 (Oath, 1925, collection of poems. This book appeared a second time under the title *Chung Shu Chi* 種樹集, in an enlarged edition); *Chên Shang Sui Pi* 枕上隨筆* (Sketches Written in Bed, 1931, 北新, con-sists of short amusing sketches concerned with famous people); *Ch'uang Hsia Sui Pi* 窗下隨筆 * (Sketches Written below the Window, 北新); *K'an Yüeh Lou Tz'ŭ* 看月樓詞 (collection of Tz'ŭ 詞, 1932, 女子書店); *I P'ing Shu Hsin* 衣萍書信 (Letters, 1932, 北新); *Sui Pi San Chung* 隨筆三種 (Three Sketches, containing 枕上隨筆 窗下隨筆, and 風中隨筆, 1934, 現代); *Hsiu Tz'ŭ Hsüeh Chiang Hua* 修辭學講話 (Rhetoric, 1934, 天馬); *I P'ing Wên Ts'un* 衣萍文存 (Collected Works, 2 volumes, 1933-35, 樂華); *Yu Ch'ing* 友情* (Friendship, a novel, 現代); *I Chên Jih Chi* 倚枕日記 (Diary, 北新); *Ku Miao Chi* 古廟集 (Old Temple, collection of essays, 北新); *Hsiao Chiao Niang* 小嬌娘 (黎明); *Ch'ing Shu Erh Shu* 情書二束 * (Love Letters, second series, 樂華); *Ch'iu Fêng Chi* 秋風集 (Autumn Wind, col-lection of essays, 春光); *T'an Nü Jên* 談女人 (On Women, collection of essays, 北新); *T'ao Sê Ti I Shang* 桃色的衣裳 (北新); *Ch'ing Nien Chi* 青年集 (Youth, 良友); *Ying Hua Chi* 櫻花集 * (1929, 北新); etc. Translation: 少女日記 * (trans-lated in collaboration with T'ieh Min 鐵民, 2 volumes, 1927, 北新).

6. Chang K'o-piao 章克標.

Pen-name: 豈凡. Essayist. Born in Haining, Chekiang. He received his advanced education in Japan and France. Upon returning to China, he became an editor of the Kaiming Book Co. 開明書店, Shanghai. In January, 1926, he edited the monthly magazine *I Pan* 一般 (The Masses), published by Kaiming. The contributors were: Fêng Tzŭ-k'ai 豐子愷, Liu Hsün-yü 劉薰宇, Hsia Mien-tsun 夏丏尊, Chu Kuang-ch'ien 朱光潛. Chiang Shao-yuan 江紹原, Ho Yü-p'o 賀玉波, Lou Chien-nan 樓建南, etc. In 1933, he edited the literary fortnightly *Shih Tai* 時代 (Times).

Works: 開明文學辭典 (1932, 開明); 文壇登龍術 (1933); 風涼話 (collection of essays, 開明); 文學入門 (開明); 銀蛇*; etc.

Translations: 水上 (*Sur l'Eau* by G. de Maupassant, 1928, 開明); 菊池寬集 (Works of Kan Kikuchi, 1929, 開明); 谷崎潤一郎集 (Works of Junichiro Tanizaki, 1929, 開明); 夏目漱石集 (Works of Soseki Natsume, 1932, 開明); 日本戲曲集 (Japanese plays, 1934, 中華); etc.

7. Chang Min 章 泯.

Playwright. Before the Sino-Japanese War, he had written some "Na-tional-Defence" plays 國防戲劇, concerning the volunteer corps of the Northeast Provinces. During the War, he lived in Chungking, and edited the famous magazine *Wên I Chên Ti* 文藝陣地 (Literary Field), together with Mao Tun 茅盾, the well-known novelist and literary critic, in which he published a great many dramatic articles.

He wrote these plays: 我們的故鄉 * (in 3 acts); 黑暗的笑聲 (in 4 acts); 棄兒; 戰鬥; 夜 * (1947, 大東); etc.

8. Chang Nai-ying 張廼瑩.

(1911-1942)

Pen-name: 蕭紅. Novelist, and short-story writer. Born in a landlord's family in Hulan, Heilungkiang. She received but little formal school education. Her wandering career commenced at the year when she just finished her second grade in the junior middle school. In 1932, she met Hsiao Chün 蕭軍 (pen-name of T'ien Chün 田軍 the author of *Village in August*), at Harbin, who became her husband later. In 1933, they wrote a book together, entitled *Po Shê* 跋涉 (To Travel), and organized a dramatic troupe. But by the pressure of bad circumstances, they could not stay there long, and went to Tsingtao, where she completed her first novel *Shêng Ssŭ Ch'ang* 生死場 (Life and Death), which was published by the "Slave Society" 奴隸社, in 1935, when they arrived Shanghai. Its theme being the unhappy lot of some farmers. Prefaced by Lu Hsün 魯迅. It brought immediately fame for the author. Her later works were published mostly in the magazines *Chung Hsüeh Shêng* 中學生 (Juvenile Student), *Wên Hsüeh* 文學 (Literature), *T'ai Pai* 太白, etc. After the outbreak of the Sino-Japanese War, she went to Wuchang, then to Chungking to recuperate her health. In the spring of 1940, she went to Hongkong, where she died in January, 22, 1942.

Works: *K'uang Yeh Ti Hu Han* 曠野的呼喊* (Cry in the Wilderness, collection of short stories, 1940, 上海雜誌公司) *Ma Po Lo* 馬伯樂 (a novel); *Hu Lan Ho Chuan* 呼蘭河傳 (The History of Hu Lan River, a novel); *Niu Ch'ê Shang* 牛車上* (collection of short stories, 文化生活出版社); *Hui I Lu Hsün Hsien Shêng* 回憶魯迅先生 (Recollections on Mr. Lu Hsün, 1940, Chungking, 中外出版社); etc.

Her friend Lo Pin-chi 駱賓基 wrote a biography of her, entitled *Hsiao Hung Hsiao Chuan* 蕭紅小傳, published in 1947.

9. Chang Tao-fan 張道藩.

(1897 —   )

Playwright. Born in Panhsien, Kweichow. He graduated from the Department of Fine Arts (Slade School), University College, University of London. While in England, he served as the head of the Assembly of the London Branch of the Kuomintang, 1923. After his return to China in 1926, he was appointed secretary of the Department of Agriculture and Labor of the Kwangtung Provincial Government. In 1928, he became the chief secretary of the Municipal Government of Nanking. In 1930, he occupied the position of dean of the National Tsingtao University. And in 1931, he became a member of the Chekiang Provincial Government and concurrently Commissioner of Education. Shortly after, he was transferred to Nanking as Vice-Director of the Organization Department. After acting as Minister of Information for ten years, from 1932 to 1942, he became the Chairman of the Central Cultural Movement Committee, a position which he has been holding still.

He wrote two plays: *Ti Ssŭ Niang* 狄四娘 and *Tzŭ Chiu* 自救* (in four acts, 1935, 正中). Translations: 近代歐洲繪畫 (*Recent European Art* by W. G. Constable); 蜜月旅行 (正中); etc.

10.　Chang T'ien-i　張天翼．

Pen-names: 老傽, 哈迷蚩, 鐵池翰 , etc.

Novelist, and short-story writer. Born in Hunan. His works were published mostly in the *Wên Hsüeh Yüeh Pao* 文學月報 (Literary Monthly), *Hsien Tai* 現代 (Modern Times), and the monthly magazine *Wên Hsüeh* 文學 (Literature). He lectured once on the history of contemporary Chinese literature at Chinan University 暨南大學, Shanghai. In the early years of the Sino-Japanese War, he taught in Changsha. With the fall of Changsha, the consumptive author went to Chungking, then to Chengtu, where he lived until now, recovering his health gradually.

Works: 從空虛到現實 (1931, 聯合); 小彼得 (1931, 湖風); 一年 * (1933, 良友); 蜜蜂* (1933, 現代); 移行 * (1934, 良友); 反攻 (1934, 生活); 團圓 (1935, 文化生活出版社); 速寫三篇 (1943, 文化生活出版社); 談人物描寫 (1947, 作家書屋) 追 * (1947, 開明); 鬼土日記 (正午); 華威先生; 新生 ; 清明時節 ; 好兄弟* (文化生活出版社); 在城市里 * (1937, 良友); 同鄉們 * (1939, 文化生活出版社) 洋涇濱奇俠* (1936, 新鐘); 齒輪 (神州國光社); etc.

11.　Chang T'ing-ch'ien　張廷謙．

(1903 — 　　)

T. 矛塵. Pen-names: 川島 倖塵, etc. Novelist. Born in Shaohsing, Chekiang. After his graduation from the National University of Peking 北京大學, he edited the magazine *Yü Ssŭ* 語絲, in the winter of 1924, together with his natives Chou Shu-jên 周樹人 (better known under his pen-name Lu Hsün 魯迅) and Chou Tso-jên 周作人. In 1931, he became the secreatry to the Chancellor of the National University of Peking; and in 1936, lecturer of the Department of Literature and History of the Women's College of Arts and Science of National Peipiing University 北平大學女子文理學院. During the Sino-Japanese War, he was the secretary of the National Southwest Associated University 西南聯合大學 in Kunming. He wrote *Yüeh Yeh* 月夜* (1924, 北大新潮社), a novel.

12.　Chang Tsün-hsiang　張駿祥．

(1910 — 　　)

Pen-name: 袁俊. Playwright. Born in Chenhai, Chekiang. After his graduation from the Department of Western Languages and Literature of the National Tsinghua University 清華大學, he became an assistant in his alma mater.

Two years later he went to the United States to study dramatic art in Yale University, where he received his M. A. degree. Upon returning to China in 1937, he was appointed a professor at the National Academy of Dramatic Arts 國立戲劇專科學校. He married Miss Pai Yang 白楊, a famous actress, at Chungking. He is now a director of the Central Motion Picture Co. 中央電影攝製廠 of Shang-hai.

He wrote the following plays: 小城故事 * (1941, 文化生活出版社); 邊城故事 * (1941, 文化生活出版社); 山城故事 * (1943, 文化生活出版社); 美國總總號 (1943, 文化生活出版社); 萬世師表 * (1946, 文化生活出版社); 邊鄉日記 etc.

Translations: 審判日 (by E. Rice, 1946, 萬葉); 富貴浮雲* （世界）; etc.

13. Chang Tzŭ-p'ing 張資平.

(1895 —   )

Novelist, and short-story writer. Born in Meihsien, Kwangtung. He cultivated the habit of reading fiction in his childhood. At the age of 10, he read *Hsi Yu* 西遊, *Shuo Yüeh* 說岳, *Fên Chuang Lou* 粉粧樓, *Hsüeh Jên Kuei Chêng Tung* 薛仁貴征東, and *Lo T'ung S'ao Pei* 羅通掃北 At the age of 11, he read *Tsai Shêng Yuan* 再生緣 which caused him to nearly forget his dinner and sleep for a few days. Later, he read *T'ien Yü Hua* 天雨花, *Hung Lou Mêng* 紅樓夢 (The Dream of the Red Chamber), *Hua Yüeh Hên* 月花痕 (The Indication of Moon and Flower), *Chin Ku Ch'i Kuan* 今古奇觀 (Strange Stories Old and New), *P'in Hua Pao Chien* 品花寶鑑, *Shui Hu* 水滸 (All Men Are Brothers), and *Hsiao Wu I* 小五義. At 12 or 13, he himself tried to write chivalrous and love romances imitating the books mentioned above. At 17, he began to read the Chinese translations of Western novels, rendered by Lin Ch'in-nan 林琴南. This was his first contact with Western literature. But his knowledge of literature was acquired from the teachers of English and French in his high school studies at Japan.

After finishing his course in geology at the Imperial University, Tokyo, he returned to China in 1922, and organized the "Creative Society" 創造社 at Shanghai, together with Kuo Mo-jo 郭沫若, Ch'êng Fang-wu 成仿吾, and Yü Ta-fu 郁達夫. In 1926, he was appointed professor of mineralogy at the National Normal University of Wuchang (now Wuhan University 武漢大學). He returned to Shanghai in 1928, where he taught literature at Chinan University 暨南大學, and Great China University 大夏大學, and directed the "Creative Society". He founded, at the same year, a book-store, "Lo Ch'ün Shu Tien" 樂羣書店, and published a literary monthly *Lo Ch'ün Yüeh K'an* 樂羣月刊. It closed a few months later. He then established another book-store "Huan Ch'iu T'u Shu Kung Ssu" 環球圖書公司, which too was short-lived. From then on he was engaged in writing at Shanghai.

During the Sino-Japanese War, he joined the puppet régime of Wang Ching-wei 汪精衞. After the Victory over Japan, he escaped to Formosa, but returned soon to Shanghai. He was accused, in June, 1947, for collaborating with the enemy. He is now still on trial.

Creative works: 沖積期化石 * (1922, 泰東); 愛之焦點 (1923, 泰東); 飛絮* (1926, 現代); 不平衡的偶力 (1926, 商務); 苔莉 * (1927, 光華); 梅嶺之春 (1928, 光華) 最後的幸福 (1928,現代); 愛力圈外 (1929, 樂華); 長途 (1929, 南強); 愛之渦流 (1930, 光華); 紅霧 (1930, 樂華); 跳躍着的人們 * (1930, 文藝); 天孫之女 (1930, 文藝); 上帝的兒女們 * (1931, 樂華); 脫了軌道的星球 (1931, 現代); 北極圈裡的王國 (1931,現代); 羣星亂飛 * (1931, 光華); 柘榴花 (1931, 樂羣); 明珠與黑炭* (1932, 光明) 雪的除夕 (商務) 青春 (現代) 麚欄 (樂羣); 戀愛錯綜* (文藝); 十字架上 (明月) 素描種種 (光明) 植樹節 (教育社); 資平小說集 (樂羣) etc.

Critical works: 歐洲文藝史大綱 (現代); 普羅文藝論 (創造社出版部); etc.

He translated several books from Japanese: 草叢中 (樂羣); 平叺風波 (樂羣) 襯衣 (光華); 某女人的犯罪 (樂羣); 壓迫 (新宇宙); 空虛 (新宇宙); 文藝新論 (現代); etc.

His autobiography, *Tzǔ P'ing*, *Tzǔ Chuan* 資平自傳, was published in 1934, by the 第一出版社. And the essays on him were collected by Shih Ping-hui 史秉慧, in his *Chang Tzǔ P'ing P'ing Chuan* 張資平評傳, published in 1933, by 現代書局.

14. Chang Tz'ŭ-hsi 張次溪.

(1908 —   )

Original name: 張仲銳, also named 張江裁, T. 次溪. Pen-name 燕歸來簃主人.

Novelist, and scholar. Born in Tungkun, Kwangtung. He graduated from the K'ung Chiao University 孔教大學. Later, he served as an editor of the Department of History of the National Academy of Peiping 北平研究院, and often published his writings in the magazine *Peiping* 北平, issued by this Academy. He is known for his study of Chinese drama and the social life in Peiping.

Work: 靈飛集* (1939, 北京印刷廠).

15. Chao Chia-pi 趙家璧.

Literary critic, and translator. Born in Kiangsu. His interest in literature was aroused at the age of 13, after reading the Chinese translation of Lewis Carroll's *Alice in Wonderland*, rendered by Dr. Chao Yuan-jên 趙元任. After graduating from the Department of Western Languages and Literature of Kwang Hua University 光華大學, Shanghai, he became an editor of the Liang Yu Publishing Co. 良友圖書公司 at the same city. He was the editor-in-chief of the famous *Chung Kuo Hsin Wên Hsüeh Ta Hsi* 中國新文學大系 (Great Series of New Chinese Literature, 10 volumes, 1935-36, 良友). This compilation, by reclaiming and setting into order the achievements of the first decade (1917-1926) of the new vernacular literature, is a valuable and praiseworthy work. The editor of each ·of the volumes contributes a long introduction, surveying his particular field in a comprehensive manner. He was also the editor of the anthology *Erh Shih Jên So Hsüan Tuan P'ien Chia Tso Ch*i 二十人所選短篇佳 作集, (Best Short Stories Selected by Twenty Persons, contains more than 50 representative short stories of 1936, 良友, 1936).

Works: 半日遊程 (1934, 良友); 今日歐美小說之動向 (良友); etc. Translations: 新傳統 * (1936, 良友); 月亮下去了 (1946, 晨光); etc.

16. Chao Ching-shên 趙景深.

(1902 —)

T. 旭初. Pen-names· 卜朦朧, 冷眼, 陶明志, 博菫, 露明女士 鄒蕭, 鄒嘯, 鮑芹村, 露明, etc.

Short-story writer, essayist, poet, literary critic and historian. Born in Ipin, Szechwan. He received but little school education. It was through his hard and constant self-study that he acquired all the necessary knowledge about literature, and won the fame of literary critic and historian. He had taught in various middle schools and colleges, such as Sung Yun Middle School 嶽雲中學, First Normal School of Changsha 長沙第一師範, Fuhtan University 復旦大學, China Institute 中國公學, Shanghai University 上海大學, University of Fine Arts 藝術大學. Besides his teaching career, he worked for some time in the Editorial Bureau of the Kaiming Book Co. 開明書店, and then became the editor-in-chief of Pei Hsin Book Co. 北新書局. He held this post until the outbreak of the Sino-Japanese War. During the early years of the War, he stayed in Shanghai; later, he went to the free district of Anhwei Province. After the Victory over Japan, he returned to Shanghai. He is now a professor at Fuhtan University, Experimental Dramatic School 上海市立實驗戲劇學校, and editor-in-chief of Pei Hsin Book Co.

Before the War, he edited the *Wên Hsüeh Chou Pao* 文學週報 (Literary Weekly), the *Hsien Tai Wên Hsüeh* 現代文學 (Contemporary Literature), and the *Ch'ing Nien Chieh* 青年界 (Youth), at Shanghai. He edits now the *T'ung Su Wên Hsüeh* 通俗文學, a weekly supplement of *Ta Wan Pao* 大晚報; *Su Wên Hsüeh* 俗文學, a weekly supplement of *Chung Yang Jih Pao* 中央日報, and the *Ch'ing Nien Chieh.*

Chao Ching-shên is a prolific writer. He wrote these creative works: 荷花 (collection of poems, 1928, 開明); 栀子花球 (collection of short stories, 1928, 北新); 小妹 * (collection of essays, 1933, 北新)· 瑣憶集 (collection of essays, 1936, 北新); 海上集 (collection of essays, 1946, 北新); etc.

His works on criticism and history of literature are: 童話概要 (1927, 北新); 中國文學小史 (1928, 光華); 作品與作家 (1929, 北新); 童話學 ABC (1929, 世界); 童話論集 (1929, 開明); 一九二九年的世界文學 (1930, 神州國光社); 一九三〇年的 世界文學 (1931, 神州國光社); 一九三一年的世界文學 (1932, 亞細亞); 文學概論 (1932, 世界); 現代世界文學 (1932, 現代); 小說原理 (1932, 商務), 文學概論講話

(1933, 北新)；郁達夫論 (1933, 北新)；文藝論集 (1933, 廣益)；世界文學史綱 (written in collaboration with 李菊休, 1933, 亞細亞)；文學講話 (1936, 中國文化 服務社)；中國文學史新編 (1936, 北新)；讀曲隨筆 (1936, 北新)；文人剪影* (1936, 北新)；小說閒話 (1937, 北新)；大鼓研究 (1937, 商務)；彈詞考證 1938, 商務)；銀字集 (1946, 北新)；文人印象 (1946, 北新)；文學常識 (1946, 永祥印書舘)；中國文法講話 (1946)；小說論叢 (1947)；現代文學雜論(光明)；現代世界文壇鳥瞰；俄國三大文豪(亞細 亞)；小說學；民間故事研究；民間故事叢話；etc.

Translations：羅亭 (*Rodin* by I. S. Turgenev, 1928, 商務)；月的話 (*What the Moon Saw* by H. C. Andersen, 1929, 開明)；柴霍甫短篇傑作集 (Complete Short Stories of A. Chekhov, eight volumes, 1930, 開明)；蘆管 (Short Stories of A. Pushkin, G. de Maupassant, O. Wilde, and others, 1930, 神州國光社)；柳下 (Selected Translations from the *Fairy Tales* by H. C. Andersen, 1933, 開明)；皇帝的新衣 (*Emperor's New Clothes* by H. C. Andersen, 開明)；格列姆童話集 (*Fairy Tales* by J. L. Grimm, 崇文)；etc.

17. Chao P'ing-fu 趙平復.

(1901 — 1931)

Pen-name: 柔石. Novelist, short-story writer, and playwright. Born in a poor family in Ninghai, Chekiang. He began his study at the age of 10. In 1917, he entered the Normal School at Hangchow 杭州師範學校, While still a student, he joined the literary society "Hangchow Ch'ên Kuang Shê" 杭州晨光社. After graduating, he became a teacher, and wrote fiction and criticism in his leisure. In 1923, he attended the National University of Peking 北京大學. Two years later, he returned South again, and taught in the Chen Hai Middle School 鎮海中學. Striken with consumption, he left his job. In 1926, he was appointed the chief of the Bureau of Education in Chen Hai. In 1928, he went to Shanghai, and entered the literary world. He contributed to *Yü Ssŭ* 語絲, a leading magazine of that time. In 1930, he joined the "China League of Left Writers" in which he held an important position. In the same year he represented the League to attend the Meeting of Chinese Soviet District Delegates 全國蘇維埃區域代表大會. On Dec. 17, 1931, he was arrested together with some left authors, and put to death on Feb. 7, the same year.

Works: 人間的喜劇 (collection of plays)；舊時代的死 (a novel in two volumes, 北新)；希望* (containing twenty-eight short stories, 1929, 商務)；二月* 三姊妹；etc.

Translations：浮士德與城 (*Faust and the City* by A. Lunacharsky, 1930, 神州國光社)；and the works of M. Gorky and other Russian writers.

18. Chao Tsung-lien 趙宗濂.

(1914 — 1943)

Pen-name: 蘆沙. Short-story writer. Born in Jihchao, Shantung. He studied for some time in the Department of History of the National University of Peking 國立北京大學. After the outbreak of the Sino-Japanese War in 1937, he was transferred to Fu Jên University 輔仁大學 of Peiping. After his graduation there he attended the post-graduate class of the same university to continue his historical studies. Later, he worked in the Museum of Oriental Ethnology of Fu Jên University, and edited the magazine *Fu Jên Wên Yuan* 輔仁文苑 (Fu Jên Literary Garden). He died in the autumn of 1943 at Peiping. His only collection of short stories *Tsai Ts'ao Yuan Shang* 在草原上* was published in 1940 by the above-mentioned magazine.

19. Ch'ên Ch'üan 陳 銓.

(1905 —   )

T. 濤西. Novelist, and playwright. Born in Fushun, Szechwan. After his graduation from the Department of Western Languages and Literature of the National Tsinghua University 清華大學, he went to the United States, where he entered Oberlin College, and received B.A. and M.A. degrees. He then went to Germany to continue his literary studies. Upon returning to China, he was appointed professor at the College of Arts and Letters of Wuhan University 武漢大學; later, he taught German in Tsinghua University. During the Sino-Japanese War he was a professor at the Central Political Institute 中央政治學校 in Chungking. He is now in Shanghai.

Works: 天問 (1928, 新月); 革命前的一幕 * (1934, 良友); 徬徨中的冷靜* (1935, 商務); 死灰 * (1935, 天津大公報館); 再見冷荇 (1947, 大東); 歸鴻 (1947, 大東); 從叔本華到尼采 (1946, 大東); 狂飆 (正中); 野玫瑰* (商務); 藍蛺蝶; etc.

20. Ch'ên Hsiang-ho 陳翔鶴.

Short-story writer. Born in Chengtu, Szechwan. He contributed first to the literary quarterly *Ch'ien Ts'ao* 淺草季刊 of Shanghai. In the autumn of 1925. he organized the society "Ch'ên Chung Shê" 沉鐘社 (a name borrowed from Hauptmann's *Die Versunkene Glocke*), at Peiping, together with Fêng Chih 馮至, Yang Hui 楊晦, and Ch'ên Wei-mo 陳煒謨, and published, on October 10, the same year, the *Ch'ên Chung Weekly* 沉鐘週刊, which suspended publication after its tenth issue. Between 1926 and 1927, they edited a fortnightly to succeed the weekly, under the same title. It published 12 numbers altogether. In 1927, he published his collection of short stories, entitled *Pu An Ting Ti Ling Hun* 不安定的靈魂 (Uneasy Soul, 北新). In the autumn of 1932, collaborating with Lin Ju-chi 林如稷 the former editor of *Ch'ien Ts'ao*, they published again the *Ch'ên Chung Fortnightly*, which ceased publication half a year later. In 1937, he published another collection of short stories, called *Tu Shên Chê* 獨身者 * (中華)

During the Sino-Japanese War, he lived in his native place, Chengtu, where he was in charge of the Chengtu Branch of the "National Writers' Anti-Aggression Association" 中華全國文藝界抗敵協會 for many years, and published one volume of short stories, entitled *Ying Chao Li San* 鷹爪李三. He teaches now in several middle schools at Chengtu.

21. Ch'ên Kuo-fu 陳果夫.

(1892 —   )

Courtesy name of 陳祖燾, but he is noted for this name instead of the original. Short-story writer, and playwright. Born in Wuhing, Chekiang. After receiving his preliminary education from the Ming Teh School, Changsha, and the Chekiang School, Nanking, he entered the Military Primary School of Chekiang 浙江陸軍小學堂, in 1908, and was promoted to the Military Middle School at Nanking 南京陸軍中學堂 in 1911. After graduating there, he took up his advanced studies in Japan. Upon returning to China, he was appointed an instructor in the Whampoa Military Academy 黃浦軍官學校. In 1927, he became the chief of the Organization Department of the Central Party Headquarters, and was promoted to the Vice-President of the Control Yuan at the next year. In 1933, he was appointed chairman of the Kiangsu Provincial Government. He is now a member of the Nationalist Government.

Works: *Hao Lin Ko Chi* 鶴林歌集 (collection of poems); *Ch'uang Lien Chi* 窗帘集 * (Window-Blind, collection of short stories, 黎明); *Kuo Fu Hsiao Shuo Chi* 果夫小說集 (Short Stories of Ch'ên Kuo-fu, 現代); *Yin Shui Wei Shêng Chi Ch'i T'a* 飲水衞生及其他 (collection of plays); *Hsiao I Ssu Chi* 小意思集 (collection of essays, 1947, 正中); etc.

22. Ch'ên Mien 陳 綿.

(1901 —   )

T. 伯旱. Playwright, and translator. Born in Minhow, Fukien. He received his B.A. degree from the National University of Peking 北京大學, and Ph. D. from the Université de Paris. He was once an assistant of the Ecole des Langues Orientales Vivantes of France, and lecturer in the Université de Paris. Upon returning to China, he was appointed lecturer of the Department of Foreign Languages and Literature of the National University of Peking, and professor at the Université Franco-Chinoise 中法大學 at the same city. During the Sino-Japanese War, he lived in Peiping, and taught French in the Teachers' College for Women 女師學院, and the College of Fine Arts. 藝術專科學校.

Ch'ên Mien is a famous director of plays. Under his direction many Chinese and foreign plays were staged by the "China Travelling Dramatic Troupe" 中國旅行劇團 before the War.

He wrote two plays: 候光 (1943, 中國公論社); and 牛夜 * (1944, 華北文化書局).

Translations: 昂朶馬格 (*Andromaque* by J.B. Racine, 1936, 商務); 熙德 (*Le Cid* by P. Corneille, 1936, 商務); 復活 (*La Résurrection* by H. Bataille, 1937,

商務）; 牛大王 (*Bluff* by G. Delance, 1937, 商務）; 茶花女劇本 (*La Dame aux Camélias* by A. Dumas fils, 1937, 商務).

23. Ch'ên Pai-ch'ên 陳白塵．

Pen-name: 墨沙．Playwright, novelist, and short-story writer. Born in Yencheng, Kiangsu. After finishing his middle school studies, he entered the Nan Kuo (Li Midi) College of Arts 南國藝術學院, founded by the veteran dramatist T'ien Han 田漢. From then on he never ceased his dramatic activities until present. He taught once in the Dramatic School directed by Hsiung Fo-hsi 熊佛西‘ and worked in many dramatic groups. After the outbreak of the Sino-Japanese War, 1937, he led the "Shanghai Stars Dramatic Troupe" 上海影人劇團 to give performances of propagandist plays in the Interior. Later, he became a professor at the National Academy of Dramatic Arts 國立戲劇學校 in Chungking. Between 1944 and 1945, he was the editor of the literary supplement of the *West China Evening Paper* 華西晚報, at Chengtu. He lives now in Shanghai, and is a member of the Standing Committee of the "Chinese Writers' Federaton" 中華全國文藝協會．

Works: 曼陀羅集 (The Mandâra, collection of short stories, 1936, 文化生活出版社）; 石達開的末路 (The Last Days of Shih Ta-k'ai, 1936, 生活．A four-act historical drama, portraying the last days of Shih Ta-k'ai, one of the ablest leaders of the T'ai-P'ing Rebellion, When he was surrounded by Ch'ing forces in Szechwan. This book appeared a second time under the title 大渡河*, 1946, 羣益出版社）; 泥腿子 (Soiled Legs, 良友, 1936, a novel. The story of a villager drafted from home to dig a canal, his dishonesty and consequent troubles); 風雨之夜 (Stormy Night, collection of short stories, 大東）; 歸來 (collection of short stories); 小魏的江山* (collection of short stories, 1937, 文化生活出版社）; 亂世男女* (A three-act drama, 1940, 上海雜誌公司）; 漢奸 (Traitor, a play, 1940, 華中圖書公司）; 勝利號 (A three-act play); 太平天國* (T'ai-P'ing-T'ien-Kuo, 生活）; 秋收 (Harvest, also named 大地黃金, or 陌上秋）; 歲寒圖; 後方小喜劇*; 陞官圖* (A play, 羣益出版社）; 新官上任 (also called 魔窟, or 群魔亂舞）; 結婚進行曲* (A play, in 5 acts, 作家書屋）; 茶葉棒子* (collection of short stories, 1947, 開明）; 賣油郎* (a play, 1947); etc.

24. Ch'ên Shên-yen 陳慎言．

(1892 —   )

Novelist. Born in Minhow, Fukien. After his graduation from the Naval College 海軍學校, he became secretary of the Ministry of Navy, and later secretary of the Ministry of Communications. He wrote more than fifty novels, published mostly in various newspapers. He is now in Peiping.

25. Ch'ên Wei-mo 陳煒謨.

Short-story writer. He contributed first to the literary quarterly *Ch'ien Ts'ao* 淺草季刊 of Shanghai. In the autumn of 1925, he organized the society "Ch'ên Chung Shê 沉鐘社, (a name borrowed from Hauptmann's *Die Versunkene Glocke*), at Peiping. Together with Fêng Chih 馮至, Yang Hui 楊悔, and Ch'ên Hsiang-ho 陳翔鶴, they published, on October 10, the same year, the *Ch'ên Chung Weekly* 沉鐘週刊, which suspended publication after its tenth issue. Between 1926 and 1927, they edited a fortnightly to succeed the weekly, under the same title. It published 12 numbers altogether. In 1927, he published his collection of short stories, entitled *Lu Pien* 爐邊* (Fireside, 北新). In the autumn of 1932, collaborating with Lin Ju-chi, the former editor of *Ch'ien Ts'ao,* they published again the *Ch'ên Chung Fortnightly,* which ceased publication half a year later.

26. Ch'ên Ying 陳　瑛.

Pen-names: 沉櫻, 小鈴, 沉櫻女士, 非兆, 陳塵英, 陳因, 陳沉櫻, etc.

Short-story writer. She is the author of the following works: 夜闌 (containing seven short stories, 1929, 光華）；喜筵之後 (containing nine short stories, 1929, 北新)；某少女 (a novel composed of fifty-eight letters, 北新)；女性* (1934, 生活)；一個女作家 * (1935, 北新); etc.

Most of her stories deal with the love and marriage life of young people. She is skillful in technique and refined in language. Above all, there is subtle and exact analysis of women's psychology in her works.

She married Ma Yen-hsiang 馬彥祥, a well-known dramatist. During the Sino-Japanese War, she was a refugee in the Interior, and wrote but little. After the Victory over Japan she returned to Shanghai, and taught in the Experimental Dramatic School 上海市立實驗戲劇學校. She translated many short essays, but did not produce much original work. She is working in the Fuhtan University 復旦大學 at present, and publishes now and then some short essays in different literary magazines.

27. Chêng Chên-to 鄭振鐸.

(1898 —　　　)

T. 西諦. Pen-names: 郭源新, 賓芬, C.T., 文基, etc. Literary critic and historian, essayist, short-story writer, and translator. Born in Changlo 長樂 Fukien. After graduating from the National University of Communications 交通大學, Peiping, he served as an editor for many years in the Commercial Press of Shanghai. It was he who founded the first magazine for children *Erh T'ung Shih Chieh* 兒童世界 (Children's World) in China. After the famous May Fourth Movement, he established the "Society of Literary Research" 文學研究會 at Peiping, in collaboration with Chou Tso-jên 周作人, Mao Tun 茅盾, and many other leading writers of that time. Later, he edited the *Hsiao Shuo Yüeh Pao* 小說月報 (The Short Story Magazine) for nearly ten years. He had travelled in Europe and published one volume of diary of this voyage when he came back, entitled *Ou Hsing Jih Chi* 歐行日記 * (1934, 良友). He then taught in Chinan University 暨南大學, Yenching University 燕京大學, and Tsinghua University 清華大學. Before the Sino-Japanese War, he edited several major literary magazines in Peiping and Shanghai, such as *Wên Hsüeh Chi K'an* 文學季刊 (Literary Quarterly), *Wên Hsüeh* 文學 (Literature), and *Shih Chieh Wên K'u* 世界文庫 (Anthology of World Literature).

In the winter of 1937, when Shanghai fell into the hands of Japanese troops, he was the dean of the College of Arts and Letters of the National Chinan University there; he held this post for four years until the Pearl Harbour Incident of Demember, 8, 1941. He then lived in complete seclusion in Shanghai until the Victory. He is now the editor of the literary monthly *Wên I Fu Hsing* 文藝復興 (Renaissance) at Shanghai.

His works on criticism and history of literature are: 文學大綱 (4 volumes, 1926, 商務); 中國文學史 (4 volumes, 1932, 樸社); 俄國文學史略 (1924, 商務); 痀僂集 (1934, 生活); 短劍集 (1935, 文化生活出版社); 中國文學論集 (2 volumes, 1934, 開明); 中國俗文學史 (1938, 商務); etc.

Creative works: 山中雜記 (1927, 開明); 家庭的故事 * (1931, 開明); 取火者的逮捕 * (1934, 生活); 桂公塘 * (1937, 商務); 三年* (藝光); 海燕 * (1932, 新中國); 戀愛的故事 (商務); etc.

Translations: 貧非罪 (*Poverty is no crime* by A.N. Ostrovsky, 1922, 商務); 飛鳥集 (*The Strayed Birds* by R. Tagore, 1922, 商務); 沙寧 (*Sanine* by M. Artzybashev, 1932, 商務); 高加索民間故事 (by A. Dirr, 1928, 商務); 俄國短篇小說譯叢 (1938, 商務); 灰色馬 (*The Pale Horse*, by V. Ropshin, 商務); 卡拉馬助夫 (*Karamazov* by F. Dostoesvky, 生活); 太戈爾戲曲集 (商務); 太戈爾詩 (商務); etc.

28. Chêng Po-ch'i 鄭伯奇.

Pen-names: 何大白, 東山, 鄭君平, 泳濤, etc. Playwright, short-story writer, and literary critic. Born in Shensi. He finished his literary studies in the Imperial University, Kyoto, Japan. Upon returning to China, he joined the famous "Creative Society" 創造社, and held an important position in it. After the suspension of the said Society in 1928, he founded a publishing house at Shanghai, called "Wên Hsien Shu Fang" 文獻書房, which closed a few months later. During the Sino-Japanese War, he lived in Chungking.

He started his literary career by writing critical articles, which were published in *Hsüeh Têng* 學燈, a literary supplement of the newspaper *Shih Shih Hsin Pao* 時事新報, and the magazine *Shao Nien Chung Kuo* 少年中國 (The Journal of the Young China Association). His first short story, *Tsui Ch'u Ti I K'o* 最初的一課 (First Lesson) was published in the first number of the *Ch'uang Tsao Chi K'an* 創造季刊 (Creation Quarterly), August, 1922. And he began to write plays in 1927, which were published in the *Ch'uang Tsao Yüeh K'an* 創造月刊 (Creation Monthly).

Works: 抗爭 (Struggle, containing 3 plays, 1928); 打火機 * (The Automatic Cigarette Lighter and Other Stories, 1936, 良友); 帝國的榮光 (a novel); 軌道 (a three-act play, 啓智); 兩棲集 * (1937, 良友); 寬城子大將 (良友); etc.

Translation: 魯森堡之一夜 (*Une Nuit au Luxemburg* by R. de Gourmant, 泰東).

29. Chiang Kuang-tz'u 蔣光慈.

(1901 — 1931)

Original name: 蔣光赤. Pen-names: 伯川, 陳倩華, 華西理, 華希理, 華希祖, 華維素, 維素, 魏敦夫 , etc.

Novelist, and poet. Born in Hwokiu, Anhwei. He received his advanced education in U.S.S.R., where he wrote one volume of verse, entitled *Hsin Mêng* 新夢 (New Dream, 1925, 上海書店). Upon returning to China, he produced three more collections of poems: *Ai Chung Kuo* 哀中國 (Lament for China, 1925, 新青年社); *Hsiang Ch'ing* 鄉情 (Pining for Home, 1928); and *K'u Su* 哭訴 (1929). In 1926, he began to publish his novels in the *Ch'uang Tsao Yüeh K'an* 創造月刊 (Creation Monthly), edited by the "Creative Society" 創造社 and endeavoured to introduce Russian literature to China. His article *Shih Yüen Ko Ming Yü O Kuo Wên Hsüeh* 十月革命與俄國文學 (The October Revolution and Russian Literature) appeared in the *Ch'uang Tsao Yüeh K'an*, no. 3, 4, 7, and 8, 1926-1927, has attracted great attention at that time. And his early novels, such as *Shao Nien P'iao Po Chê* 少年飄泊者 (1925, 亞東); *Ya Lü Chiang Shang* 鴨綠江上 (1927, 亞東); *Yeh Chi* 野祭 (1927, 創造社); *Chü Fên* 菊芬 (appeared in the *Ch'uang Tsao Yüeh K'an*, no. 10, 1927); were enthusiastically received by the Chinese youth.

Before 1927, he joined the Communist Régime in Wuhan 武漢 , Hupeh. After the split between Kuomintang and Communists, he went to Shanghai, where he founded a book-store "Ch'un Yeh Shu Tien" 春野書店 in collaboration with Ch'ien Hsing-ts'un 錢杏邨 and Yang Ts'un-jên 楊邨人, and published the *T'ai Yang Yüeh K'an* 太陽月刊 (The Sun Monthly) on January 1, 1928, to promote proletarian literature. It was ordered to cease publication by the National Government in August of the same year. Then, in 1929, he edited another literary monthly *Hsin Liu Yüeh Pao* 新流月報 (New Current), published by the Hsien Tai Book Co. 現代書局. It too was short-lived. Later he went to Japan, where he produced one volume of essays, entitled *I Hsiang Yü Ku Kuo* 異鄉與故國 (Foreign Country and Fatherland, 1930, 現代). On his return to China, the spring of 1930, he edited, again for the Hsien Tai Book Co., a literary magazine *T'o Huang Chê* 拓荒者. It published five numbers altogether. He died of consumption in August of 1931, in Shanghai, at the age of 31.

Besides the above-mentioned works, he wrote the following novels: 短袴黨 (1928); 最後的微笑 (1929, 現代); 麗莎的哀怨 (1929, 現代); 衝出雲圍的月亮 (1930, 北新); 三對愛人兒 * (1932, 月明書店); 田野的風 (also called 咆哮了的大地, 1932, 湖風); 失業以後 (北新); etc. We have a collection of his essays 紀念碑. He wrote, in collaboration with Ch'ü Ch'iu-pai 瞿秋白, a book on Russian literature, entitled 俄羅斯文學 (1927, 創造社).

Translations: 一週間 (*The Week* by Y.N. Libedinsky); 愛的分野 (*The New Commandant* by P. Romanov, 亞東); 冬天的春笑 (Selected Short Stories of Soviet Union); etc.

30. Chiang Mu-liang 蔣牧良.

Novelist, and short-story writer. He wrote the following works: *Han* 旱 (The Drought, 1936, 良友. It is a story of the break-up of rural villages under the combined pressure of drought and human ravages); *T'i Sha* 銻砂 (Antimony Ores, collection of short stories, 1936, 文化生活出版社); *Yeh Kung* 夜工 * (a novel written during the War); *Ch'iang Hsing Chün* 強行軍 (collection of short stories, 開明); etc.

31. Chiang Ping-chih 蔣冰之.

(1907 —)

Also named 蔣煒. She is better known under the pen-name of Ting Ling 丁玲. Her other pen-names are: 丁冰之, 冰姿, 何交, 雪貞, 彬之, 彬芷, 賓芷, 叢喧, L.L., etc.

Novelist, and short-story writer. Born in Liling, Hunan. Her father died when she was still a little girl. She began her study at Changteh, where she spent her childhood with her mother. At the age of 17, she entered the Sung Yun Middle School 嶽雲中學 of Changsha. Without graduating she went to Peiping by herself with the aim of entering the National University of Peking 北京大學, "Cradle of the Chinese Literary Renaissance". She arrived in Peiping in 1924, but found she could not enter the University immediately. She lived in the Western Hills surrounded by a group of enthusiastic young literati and students of art. It was there she met Hu Yeh-p'in 胡也頻, who later became her husband. And she also became acquainted with Shên Ts'ung-wên 沈從文. Later, they founded many enterprizes.

In 1926, she began to publish her short stories in the *Hsiao Shuo Yüeh Pao* 小說月報 (The Short Story Magazine). They were received with tremendous enthusiasm, and critics began to say that Ting Ling might even replace Miss Hsieh Ping-hsin 謝冰心 as China's greatest authoress. Later, she collected these narratives into one volume, entitled *Tsai Hei An Chung* 在黑暗中 * (In the Darkness, 1928, 開明).

In 1928, she went to Shanghai and in collaboration with her husband,

Hu Yeh-p'in, and Shên Ts'ung-wên, she edited the *Hung Yü Hei* 紅與黑 (Red and Black), a literary supplement of the newspaper *Chung Yang Jih Pao* 中央日報, and published two literary magazines, the *Jên Chien Yüeh K'an* 人間月刊, and *Hung Hei Yüeh K'an* 紅黑月刊, both of which had but a short life.

In 1930, she joined the "China League of Left Writers" 中國左翼作家聯盟, and edited the organization's publication *Pei Tou* 北斗 (Great Dipper), in which she published her most distinguished work *Shui* 水 (Flood, 1933, 新中國). The magazine was suppressed very soon.

On May 14, 1933, Ting Ling was arrested in Shanghai by the authorities, together with P'an Tzŭ-nien 潘梓年, and was set free a year later. She then proceeded to Peiping and thence to Sian where she remained in hiding until it was possible to enter the Communist areas where she is residing now.

Works: 自殺日記 (1929, 光華); 一個女人* (1930, 中華); 韋護* (1930, 大江); 法網 (1931, 良友); 一個人的誕生 (1931, 新月); 夜會 (1933, 現代); 母親* (1933, 良友); 意外集* (1936, 良友); 一顆未出膛的槍彈 (1946, 上海知識出版社); 我在霞村的時候; 丁玲代表作*; etc.

Shên Ts'ung-Wên, her intimate friend, wrote an biography of Ting Ling, entitled *Chi Ting Ling* 記丁玲 (vol. 1, 1934, 良友; vol. 2, 1940, 良友) And the essays on Ting Ling were collected by Chang Pai-hsüeh 張白雪, in his *Ting Ling P'ing Lun* 丁玲評論 (1934, 春光); and by Chang Wei-fu 張惟夫, in his *Kuan Yü Ting Ling* 關於丁玲 (1933).

32. Chien Hsien-ai 蹇先艾.

(1906 —   )

T. 蕭然; pen-name: 錢九. Essayist, poet, and short-story writer. Born in Tsunyi, Kweichow. After finishing his economics course at the College of Law of the National Peiping University 北平大學法學院, he served as the head of the Sung P'o Library 松坡圖書舘 at the same city. Later, he taught Chinese in different middle schools. During the War, he lived in Kweiyang where he was in charge of the Kweiyang Branch of the "National Writers' Anti-Aggression Association" 中華全國文藝界抗敵協會, and edited the *Pi Lei* 筆壘, a literary supplement of *Kweichow Daily Post* 貴州日報.

In 1922, while still studying in the Middle School of the National Normal University of Peiping 師大附中, he organized a literary society, "Hsi Shê" 曦社, together with his schoolmates Chu Ta-nan 朱大柟, and T'êng Ch'in-hua 滕沁華, and published the magazine *Chio Huo* 嚼火. Later he contributed to the literary supplement of *Ch'ên Pao* 晨報副刊, and the poetry magazine *Shih K'an* 詩刊, both of which were edited by the late poet Hsü Chih-mo 徐志摩. Before 1930, he wrote poems under the influence of Hsü. As a short-story writer, he is adept in description of rural life. And in his essays, he writes about natural scenery and social conditions in a simple and direct style.

Works: *Chiu Chia* 酒家 * (The Tavern, collection of short stories, 1934, 新中國); *Huan Hsiang Chi* 還鄉集 (Return of the Native and Other Stories, 1934, 中華); *Ch'ou Ch'u Chi* 躊躇集 (What To Do and Other Stories, 1936, 良友); *Ch'êng Hsia Chi* 城下集 (Under the City Wall, collection of essays, 1936, 開明); *Yen Ti Ku Shih* 鹽故的事 (The Story of Salt, collection of short stories, 1937, 文化生活出版社); *I Wei Ying Hsiung* 一位英雄 (A Hero, collection of short stories, 北新); *Chao Wu* 朝霧 (Morning Fog, collection of short stories, 北新); etc.

33. Ch'ien Chung-shu 錢鍾書.

T. 默存 . Pen-name: 中書君 . Essayist, and novelist. Born in Wusih, Kiangsu. Son of Ch'ien Chi-po 錢基博 , a famous scholar. After graduating from the Department of Western Languages and Literature of the National Tsing-hua University 清華大學 , he taught in the Kwang Hua University 光華大學 Shanghai. Later, he was sent on a Boxer Indemnity Scholarship to England, where he studied English literature in Oxford University. Upon returning to China, he published his writings in the magazines *Hsüeh Wên Yüeh K'an* 學文月刊 (edited by Yeh Kung-ch'ao 葉公超), *Tsing Hua Chou K'an* 清華週刊 , *Wên Hsüeh Tsa Chih* 文學雜誌 (Literary Magazine, edited by Chu Kuang-ch'ien 朱光潛), etc. After the outbreak of the Sino-Japanese War, he went to the Interior, but returned to Shanghai later. He then lectured in the Aurora College for Women 震旦女子文理學院 . After the Victory over Japan, he became the editor of the magazine *Philobiblon* (Quarterly Review of Chinese Publications, in English), published by the National Central Library of Nanking 南京國立中央圖書館 .

Works: *Hsieh Tsai Jên Shêng Pien Shang* 寫在人生邊上. (collection of essays, 1941, 開明); *Jên Shou Kuei* 人獸鬼 (Men, Beasts and Ghosts, collection of short stories, 1946, 開明); *Wei Ch'êng* 圍城* (a novel, 1946, 晨光); etc.

34. Ch'ien Hsing-ts'un 錢杏邨.

Pen-names: 阿英, 方英, 阮无名, 亞魯, 島田, 徐衍存, 張若英, 張鳳吾, 寒生, 黃華. 錢謙吾. 魏如晦 , etc.

Literary critic, playwright, novelist, essayist, and poet. Born in Anhwei. He became famous through his severe criticism of Lu Hsün 魯迅 , published in the *T'ai Yang Yüeh K'an* 太陽月刊 (The Sun Monthly) in 1928. Later, he wrote many articles on various authors like Kuo Mo-jo 郭沫若 . Yü Ta-fu 郁達夫 , Chiang Kuang-tz'ŭ 蔣光慈. Chang Tzu-p'ing 張資平 , Hsü Chih-mo 徐志摩 , Mao Tun 茅盾, etc. In 1930 he collected these articles into two volumes, entitled *Hsien Tai Chung Kuo Wên Hsüeh Tso Chia* 現代中國文學作家 (Contemporary Chinese Authors), published by T'ai Tung Book Co. 泰東書局 .

His other critical works are: 創作與生活(良友); 安特列夫評傳 (1931. 文藝); 現代中國文學論 (合衆社); 文學與社會傾向 (泰東); 文藝批評集 (1930, 神州國光社); 作品論; 力的文藝 (1929 泰東); 現代中國女作家; 現代十六家小品 (1935, 光明); 怎樣研究新興文學 (1930, 南強); 中國新文壇祕錄 (1933, 南強); 小說閒談 (1936, 良友)

中國新文學運動史資料 (1934, 光明); 中國新文學大系史料索引 (1936, 良友); etc. The last two works are indispensable references for studying contemporary Chinese literature.

His works on the history of Chinese literature are: 晚清小說史 (1937, 商務); 彈詞小說評考 (1937, 中華); etc.

Besides critical works, he has written many dramas, novels, poems, and essays. Of his dramatic works we have: 洪宣嬌* (1941, 國民); 群鶯亂飛*; 滿城風雨; 五姊妹*; 桃花源*; 夜上海; 春風秋雨; 不夜城*; and four historical dramas on the latter part of the Ming Dynasty: 海國英雄; 楊娥傳; 明末遺恨; 碧血花*. Of his novels we have: 義塚; 一條鞭痕; 餓人與飢鷹; 革命的故事; etc. The collections of his poems are: 荒土; 暴風雨的前夜 etc. And the collections of his essays are: 夜航集; 海市集; etc.

His criticism, as well as his creative works, are all propaganda of the revolutionary thought of the proletariate. In his critical works he criticized only the thought of the author; and the characters whom he depicted in his creative works were mostly the oppressed workmen and poor people.

Before 1927, he joined the Communist Régime in Wuhan 武漢, Hupeh. After the split between Kuomintang and Communists, he went to Shanghai; in collaboration with Yang Ts'un-jên 楊邨人, and Chiang Kuang-tz'ǔ, he established a book-store, "Ch'un Yeh Shu Tien" 春野書店, and published the *T'ai Yang Yüeh K'an*, its contributors were: Wang I-chung 王藝鐘, Hsü Hsün-lei 徐迅雷, Hung Ling-fei 洪靈菲, Lin Po-hsiu 林伯修, Lou Chien-nan 樓建南, Chu Hsiu-hsia 祝秀俠, Tai P'ing-wan 戴平萬, etc. In August, 1928, the *T'ai Yang Yüeh K'an* was ordered to cease publication by the National Government.

In 1930, he joined the "China League of Left Writers" 中國左翼作家聯盟 and edited a magazine *Hai Fêng Chou Pao* 海風週報 (The Sea Wind Weekly).

He was once the dean of the College of Arts and Letters in Tat'ung University 大同大學, and concurrently the chairman of the Department of Chinese Literature.

In the early years of the Sino-Japanese War, he stayed in the International Settlement in Shanghai, and devoted himself to the writing of historical dramas, and edited a magazine, *Wên Hsüan* 文選 (Reader's Digest). After the Pearl Harbour Incident of Dec. 8, 1941, he left Shanghai secretly, and since then we have no knowledge of his whereabouts.

35. Chin Man-ch'êng 金滿成.

Pen-name: 小江平. Short-story writer. Born in Meishan, Szechwan. He received his advanced education in France. Upon returning to China, he joined the literary society "Huan Shê" 幻社, organized by Yeh Ling-fêng 葉靈鳳, and P'an Han-nien 潘漢年, and contributed to the magazines *Huan Chou* 幻洲, and *Ko Pi* 戈壁, published by the said society. Later, he edited the literary supplement of the newspaper *Hsin Min Pao* 新民報 in Nanking. In 1930, he married Miss Ch'ên Huan-nung 陳幻儂, a student of Fuhtan University 復旦大學, in Shanghai. During the Sino-Japanese War, he lived in Chungking, where he edited for some time the literary supplement of the newspaper *Hsin Shu Jih Pao* 新蜀日報. He was a member of the "National Writers' Anti-Aggression Association" 中華全國文藝界抗敵協會, and often published his translation of French literature in the Association's publication *K'ang Chan Wên I* 抗戰文藝 (The Wartime Literature). Later, in consequence of an attack of eburnation, he stopped his literary career, and entered the business world.

Works: 林娟娟 (collection of short stories, 1928, 現代); 我的女朋友們 (collection of short stories, 1927, 光華); 愛與血 (collection of short stories, 1928, 現代); 女孩兒們 (collection of short stories, 1929, 樂華); 友人之妻 (collection of short stories, 1931, 光華); 愛慾 (1931, 光華); 花柳病春 * (現代); etc.

Translations: 友人之書 (*Le Livre de Mon Ami* by A. France, 1927, 北新); 紅百合 (*Le Lys Rouge* by A. France, 現代); 女性的風格 (*L'Ecole des Femmes* by A. Gide, 1947, 作家書屋); etc.

36. Chou Ch'üan-p'ing 周全平.

Pen-names: 霆聲, 駱駝, etc. Short-story writer, essayist, and literary critic. Born in Ihing, Kiangsu. He was a student of Kuo Mo-jo 郭沫若. At first he worked in the Evans Book Co. In 1926, he joined the famous "Creative Society" 創造社, and edited the Association's publication *Hung Shui* 洪水 (Flood). Later, he went to Manchuria to cultivate the virgin lands for a few years. When the proletarian literary movement sprang up in Shanghai, he returned to the South to participate, and founded a bookstore "Hsin Hsing Shu Tien" 新興書店 at Nanking, and published a magazine *Ch'u Pan Yüeh K'an* 出版月刊 to spread the news of publication. These undertakings were suspended with his departure from Nanking.

The collections of his short-stories are: 夢裏的微笑 * (1925, 光華); 苦笑 (1927, 光華); 樓頭的煩惱 (1930, 光華); 他的懺悔 * (1935, 大新); 箬船 (光華); 煩惱的網; etc. We have a collection of his essays 殘兵 (1929, 現代). And he wrote a book on the principle of literary criticism, entitled 文藝批評淺說 (1935, 商務)

37. Chou Hsin-hua 周信華.
(1906 —)

Novelist. A native of Ninghsien, Chekiang, he was born in Paoting, Hopei. In 1909, he went to the South, and lived in Shanghai. In 1921, he entered the St. Vincent's Minor Seminary of Ninghsien, and was promoted in 1926 to the St. Paul's Major Seminary at the same place. In 1931, he was ordained priest, and taught in St. Vincent's, his alma mater. In 1945, he returned to the North to recuperate. He is now working in the Institvtvm S. Thomae of Peiping.

38. Chou I-pai 周貽白.

Playwright. He wrote several books on the history of Chinese drama. They are: *Chung Kuo Hsi Chü Shih Lüeh* 中國戲劇史略 (商務); *Chung Kuo Chü Ch'ang Shih* 中國劇場史 (商務); *Chung Kuo Hsi Chü Hsiao Shih* 中國戲劇小史 (1946, 永祥印書館). He is also the author of the following plays: *Wang Shu I Hên* 亡蜀遺恨 * (in 4 acts, 1946, 潮鋒出版社); *Lü Ch'uang Hung Lei* 綠窗紅淚 (世界); *Chin Ssǔ Ch'iao* 金絲雀* (Canary, 世界); *Yang Kuan San Tieh* 陽關三叠 * (世界); *Lien Huan Chi* 連環計* (世界); *Pei Ti Wang* 北地王 * (1940 潮鋒); *Hua Mu Lan* 花木蘭 * (1941, 開明); etc.

39. Chou Shu-jên 周樹人.

(1881 — 1936)

T. 豫才. He is mostly known under the pen-name of 魯迅. His other pen-names are: 丁萌, 丁璫, 之達, 干, 子明, 元艮, 不堂. 尤剛, 巴人, 公汗, 史癖, 冬華, 白在宣, 令飛, 自樹, 吳謙, 谷, 迅行, 何丹仁, 何家幹, 余銘, 長庚, 周揚, 佩韋, 洛文, 前犢, 某生者, 風子者, 風聲, 家幹, 唐俟, 旅隼, 神飛, 索士, 桃椎, 荀繼, 許廣昇, 雪之, 略文, 符靈, 游光, 越客, 隋洛文, 幹, 慶明, 葦索, 敬一尊, 遠, 楮冠, 鄧當世, 孺牛, 豐之餘, 羅撫, 欒廷石, L.S., R.S., etc.

Short-story writer, essayist, and scholar. Born of a well-to-do country-scholar's house at Shaohsing, Chekiang, on August 3, 1881. At the age of 13, a great adversity befell his family, throwing him into poverty and disgrace. His father died when he was 16. The financial circumstances of the family became so bad that he could not even afford to pay his tuition fee. At the age of 18, he went to Nanking, where he attended the Naval School 水師學堂. About half a year later he was transferred to the Mining and Railway School 礦路學堂 to study mining. Following his graduation there, he was sent on a government scholarship to take up advanced study in Japan. After graduating from a preparatory school in Tokyo, he went to the Medical College of Sendai instead of entering a mining school, in viewing that medicine had done a great part in making Japan to become a modern power. But he soon changed his mind. For after the outbreak of the Russo-Japanese War, a couple of years later, he suddenly thought that China needed new literature as badly as medicine. He then abandoned his medical training, and went back to Tokyo to start the magazine *Hsin Shêng* 新生 (New Life). But it was a complete failure.

Upon returning to China in 1909, he became a teacher of chemistry and physiology at the Normal School of Hangchow 杭州兩級師範學堂. In 1911, he was appointed the dean of studies of the Shaohsing Middle School 紹興中學堂. After the occupation of Shaohsing by the Revolutionary troops in October that year, he was named principal of the Normal School in the same city. The next year, in 1912, when the Republican Government was established in Nanking, he was invited by Ts'ai Yuan-p'ei 蔡元培, the Minister of Education, to take a post in the Ministry. In 1913, following the move of the Government, Lu Hsün went to Peiping, where, in addition to the works in the Ministry of Education, he became concurrently professor of Chinese literature at the National University of Peking 北京大學, the National Normal University 師範大學, and the National Normal University for Women 女子師範大學.

Since the April of 1918, a year before the famous May Fourth Movement, Lu Hsün began to write short stories; the first of which was *K'uang Jên Jih Chi* 狂人日記 (The Diary of a Mad Man), appeared in the magazine *Hsin Ch'ing Nien* 新青年 (New Youth), vol. 4, no. 5, May of the same year, under the pen-name Lu Hsün. It was an immediate success. The theme of the story is a fierce attack against the oppressive old Chinese tradition. And in December of 1921, he published his most famous work *A Q Chêng Chuan* 阿Q正傳 * (The True Story of Ah Q) in the literary supplement of *Ch'ên Pao* 晨報, under the pen-name of Pa Jên 巴人. It has been translated into thirteen different languages. From 1918 to 1925, he wrote 26 short stories altogether, which he collected into two volumes, entitled *Nan Han* 吶喊 * (The Cries, 1923, 北新), and *P'ang Huang* 徬徨 * (Hesitation, 1926, 北新).

In 1925, a strike occured in the National Normal University for Women, in which Lu Hsün, a professor of the school, stood on the side of the students. The result was that he lost his post in the Ministry of Education. He left Peiping in 1926 with the general exodus of radical professors, and arrived at Amoy, where he became professor of Chinese literature in the Amoy University 廈門大學, at the invitation of Lin Yü-t'ang 林語堂. A few months later, he proceeded to Canton, where he was appointed the dean of the College of Arts and Letters of the Sun Yat-sen University 中山大學. But he did not remain here long either. In 1927, he went to Shanghai and launched a fierce dispute with the "Creative Society" 創造社, and the "Sun Society" 太陽社, over the issue of revolutionary literature. In 1928, he founded the literary monthly *Pên Liu* 奔流, in collaboration with Yü Ta-fu 郁達夫, the novelist. It published 17 numbers altogether. In the spring of 1930, he joined the "China League of Left Writers' 中國左翼作家聯盟, and edited *Mêng Ya* 萌芽, a literary monthly, which was banned by the authorities half a year later. Since then he devoted himself to translation and writing short commentaries. He died of tuberculosis on October 19, 1936, at Shanghai.

Collections of short stories: 吶喊*；徬徨*；故事新編 * (1936, 文化生活出版社).

Collections of essays: 熱風 (1925, 北新)；華蓋集 (1926, 北新)；華蓋集續編 (1927, 北新)；而已集 (1927, 北新)；三閒集 (1929, 北新)； 二心集 (1931, 北新)；偽自由書 (1933, 北新)； 南腔北調集 (1933, 北新)； 准談風月 (1933, 北新)； 花邊文學 (1934, 北新)；且介亭雜文 (two volumes, 1934 - 35)；且介亭雜文末集.

Collections of letters: 兩地書 (in collaboration with 許廣平, 1933, 北新)；魯迅書簡 (1946, 魯迅紀念委員會).

Literary Studies: 中國小說史略 (1923, 北新); 小說舊聞鈔 (1926, 北新); 唐宋傳奇集 * (1928, 北新); 古小說鈎沉; 會稽郡故書集; 嵇康集; 漢文學史綱要 .

Miscellanies: 墳; 野草; 集外集; 集外集拾遺 .

Translations: 月界旅行 (*Voyage à la Lune* by J. Verne, 1903); 地底旅行 (*Voyage au Centre de la Terre* by J. Verne, 1903); 域外小說集 (1909); 現代日本小說譯叢 (1921); 工人綏惠略夫 (*The Workingman Shevyrev* by M. Artzybashev, 1921, 北新); 現代日本小說集 (1922); 一個青年的夢 (by S. Mushakoji, 1922, 商務); 愛羅先珂童話集 (by V. Eroshenko, 1922, 商務); 桃色的雲 (by V. Eroshenko, 1923, 北京新潮社); 苦悶的象徵 (by H. Kuriyagawa, 1924, 北新); 出了象牙之塔 (by H. Kuriyagawa, 1926, 北新); 思想, 山水, 人物 (by Y. Tsurumi, 1928, 北新); 小約翰 (*De Kleine Johannes* by F. van Eden, 1928, 北新); 近代美術思潮論 (1929); 藝術論 (*Ob Iskusstwe* by A. V. Lunacharsky, 1929, 大江); 現代新興文學的諸問題 (1929); 壁下譯叢 (1929); 藝術論 (by Plechanow, 1930, 光華); 文學與批評 (by A. V. Lunacharsky, 1930); 文藝政策 (1930); 十月 (*October* by H. Jokovlev, 1930); 毀滅 (*Razgrom* by A. A. Fadeev, 1931, 三閒) 小彼得 (1931); 藥用植物 (1931); 豎琴 (1933, 良友); 一天的工作 (1933, 良友); 山民牧唱 (1935); 錶 (*Die Uhr* by L. Panteleew, 1935, 生活); 俄羅斯的童話 (1935); 死魂靈 (*The Dead Souls* by N. V. Gogol, 1935, 文化生活出版社); 壞孩子和別的奇聞 (1936); 譯叢補 .

Many books and essays have been written about him, the important ones are: 關于魯迅及其著作 (compiled by 臺靜農, 1926, 未名社); 魯迅在廣東 (compiled by 鍾敬文, 1927, 北新); 魯迅論 (compiled by 李何林, 1930, 北新); 魯迅批判 (written by 李長之, 1935, 北新); 魯迅先生二三事 (written by 孫伏園, 1945, 作家書屋); 回憶魯迅先生 (written by 蕭紅, 1946); 魯迅傳 (by T. Oda, and translated by 范泉, 1946, 開明); 亡友魯迅印象記 (written by 許壽裳, 1947, 峨嵋出版社); 民元前的魯迅先生 (written by 王冶秋, 1947, 峨嵋出版社); 人民文豪魯迅 (written by 平心, 1947, 心聲閣); 魯迅回憶 (written by 荊有麟, 1947, 上海雜誌公司); etc.

40. Chou Tso-jên 周作人 .

(1885 —   )

T. 啓明 . Pen-names: 知堂, 智堂, 藥堂, 苦雨老人, 苦雨翁, 苦茶, 豈明, 苦雨, 子榮, 山叔, 王遐壽, 不知, 仲密, 何曾亮, 知, 周逴, 槃山, 茶蘼, 豈, 淳于, 粥尊, 萍雲, 開明, 凱明, 尊, 憶明, 樟, 獨應, 難明, 難知, 藥, 藥廬, 儅敬, etc.

Essayist. Born in Shaohsing, Chekiang. He is the younger brother of Chou Shu-jên 周樹人 (better known under his pen-name Lu Hsün 魯迅 . After reading the Chinese Classics at home, he attended the Naval School at Nanking 江南水師學堂, when he was 17. Five years later he was sent on a government scholarship to take up advanced study in Japan. Upon returning to China in 1911, he was appointed superintendent of the Bureau of Education of Chekiang Provincial Government. Half a year later he became a teacher of the Chekiang Provincial Fourth Middle School 浙江省立第四中學 He held this post for four years, and went to Peiping in 1917, where he served as professor of literature at the National University of Peking 北京大學; later he taught at Yenching University 燕京大學, Women's College of Arts and Science of the National Peiping

University 北平大學女子文理學院 , and the Université Franco-Chinoise 中法大學,

During the Sino-Japanese War he became the Chancellor of the Japanese-sponsored University of Peking, and at the same time the Minister of Education in the puppet government of North China. After the Victory over Japan, he was sentenced to ten years' imprisonment by the Supreme Court at Nanking.

The collections of his essays are: 雨天的書 (1926, 北新); 自己的園地 (1927, 北新); 談龍集 (1927, 北新); 澤瀉集 (1927, 北新); 永日集 (1929, 北新); 藝術與生活 * (1931, 群益); 看雲集 (1932, 北新); 談虎集 (1934, 北新); 夜讀抄 * (1934, 北新); 苦茶隨筆 * (1935, 北新); 風雨談 * (1936, 北新); 苦竹雜記 * (1936, 良友); 瓜豆集 * (1937, 宇宙風社); 藥味集 * (1942, 新民印書館); 秉燭談 (1944, 新民印書館); 秉燭後談 * (1944, 新民印書館); 書房一角 (1944, 新民印書館); 藥堂雜文 (1944, 新民印書館); etc.

The collection of his poems is entitled 過去的生命 * (1922, 北新).

His critical works are: 歐洲文學史 (1918, 商務); 中國新文學 的源流 (1932, 北平人文); 兒童文學 (北新); etc.

Translations: 域外小說集 (1909); 點滴 * (1920, 北京大學出版部); 現代小說譯叢 (1922, 商務); 兩條血痕 (1927, 開明); 瑪加爾的夢 (Makar's Dream by V. I. Korolenko, 1927, 北新); 冥土旅行 (1927, 北新); 空大鼓 (1928, 開明); 黃薔薇 (A Sérea Rozsa by Jókai Mór, 1931, 商務); 希臘擬曲 (1934, 商務); 現代日本小說集 (商務); 狂言十番 (北新); 炭畫 (北新); 匈奴奇士錄 (Egy az Isten! by Jókai Mór, 商務); 陀螺 (北新); etc.

The essays on Chou Tso-jên were collected by T'ao Ming-chih 陶明志 (pen-name of 趙景深), in his *Chou Tso Jên Lun* 周作人論 (1934, 北新).

41. Chou Yü-ying 周毓英.

Pen-names: 玉道, 鄭菊華, etc. Novelist, and literary critic. Born in Ihing, Kiangsu. He was an editor of the Lo Ch'ün Book Store 樂群書店 in 1928. His writings were published mostly in the following magazines: *Hung Shui* 洪水 (Flood), edited by the "Creative Society" 創造社; *Huan Chou* 幻洲 , edited by Yeh Ling-fêng 葉靈鳳 and P'an Han-nien 潘漢年; and *Lo Ch'ün Yüeh K'an* 樂群月刊, edited by Chang Tzŭ-p'ing 張資平. He produced three volumes of novels *Hsiang Ts'un* 鄉村 * (Village, 1934, 民族書局); *Tsui Hou Shêng Li* 最後勝利 (The Final Victory); and *Tsai Lao Chung* 在牢中 (In Prison); and one volume of criticism *Hsin Hsing Wên I Lun Chi* 新興文藝論集 (Essays on the Revolutionary Literature, 1930, 上海勝利書局).

42. Chu Chao-lo 朱肇洛.

Pen-name: 蕭人. Literary and dramatic critic. He studied first Western languages and literature, and then Chinese literature in Yenching University 燕京大學. During the Sino-Japanese War, he taught in the Department of Chinese

Literature of Fu Jên University 輔仁大學 of Peiping. After the Victory over Japan, he edited the literary supplement of the Newspaper *Ching Shih Jih Pao* 經世日報 at the same city. He compiled 戲劇論集 (1931, 北平文化學社); 近代獨幕劇選 * (1941, 北平文化學社).

43. Chu Hsiang 朱　湘.

(1904 — 1933)

T. 子沅. Poet. Born in Taihu, Anhwei. After his graduation from the National Tsinghua University 清華大學 of Peiping, he went to the United States, where he studied Western literature in Laurence University, and later in the University of Chicago. Upon returning to China in 1930, he was appointed the chairman of the Department of Western Languages and Literature of Anhwei University 安徽大學 in Hwaining. In the summer of 1932 he resigned, and returned to Shanghai. After living a wandering life for a year and half, he drowned himself in the Yangtse River, on December 5, 1933.

While still a university student, he began to write poetry in the spoken language. They were published mostly in the *Wên I Tsa Chih* 文藝雜誌 (Literary Magazine, edited by Liu Ya-tzǔ 柳亞子), *Hsiao Shuo Yüeh Pao* 小說月報 (The Short Story Magazine, published by the "Society of Literary Research" 文學研究會, of which Chu Hsiang was an important member), and the literary supplement of *Ch'ên Pao* 晨報副刊. His chef-d'oeuvre *Wang Chiao* 王嬌, a long poem of more than 900 lines, was enthusiastically received by the young literati. The first collection of his poems, entitled *Hsia T'ien* 夏天 (Summer), was published in 1925, by the Commercial Press. And in 1927, he produced his second volume *Ts'ao Mang Chi* 草莽集 (開明). His third volume of verse, *Shih Mên Chi* 石門集 *, was published posthumously in 1934, also by the Commercial Press.

In addition to the above-mentioned works, he also wrote: *Chung Shu Chi* 中書集 (collection of essays, 1934, 生活); *Yung Yên Chi* 永言集 (collection of essays, 1936, 時代); *Hai Wai Chi Ni Chün* 海外寄霓君 * (collection of letters, 1934, 北新).

Besides being a novelist, he is also known as a critic. As a writer of poetry, he is qualified to criticize writings in that field. He wrote these critical works: *P'ing Hsü Chün Chih Mo Chih Shih* 評徐君志摩之詩 (On the Poetry of Hsü Chih-mo); *P'ing Wên Chün I To Chih Shih* 評聞君一多之詩 (On the Poetry of Wên I-to), both of which were published in the *Hsiao Shuo Yüeh Pao;* and *Wên Hsüeh Hsien T'an* 文學閒談 (Causerie on Literature, 1934, 世界).

Translations: 英國近代短篇小說集 (Contemporary English Short Stories, 北新); 路曼尼亞民歌一斑 (*The Songs of Dambovita* by Miss E. Vacarescu, 商務); 番石榴集 (1936, 商務).

44. Chu Kuang-ch'ien 朱光潛 ·

(1898 —   )

T. 孟實. Aesthete, and literary critic. Born in Tungcheng, Anhwei. He studied first in the Wuchang Higher Normal School 武昌高等師範, and was then transferred to Hongkong University. After finishing his literary course there, he went to Europe, where he studied literature and philosophy for eight years, and received M.A. degree from Edinburgh University, England, and Ph. D. degree from Strassburg University, France. Upon returning to China, he was appointed lecturer at the China Institute of Woosung 吳淞中國公學, and later at the National Tsinghua University 清華大學. From 1935 on, he served as a professor at the National University of Peking 北京大學, and concurrently lecturer at the Women's College of Arts and Science of the National Peiping University 北平大學女子文理學院. After the outbreak of the Sino-Japanese War, he went to Szechwan, where he was appointed dean of the College of Arts ans Letters of Szechwan University 四川大學. Later he became the rector and concurrently the chairman of the Department of Western Languages and Literature of Wuhan University 武漢大學. After the Victory over Japan, he returned to Peiping, and functions as the chairman of the Department of Western Languages and Literature of the National University of Peking, and editor of the *Wên Hsüeh Tsa Chih* 文學雜誌 (Literary Magazine), published by the Commercial Press.

His *Wên I Hsin Li Hsüeh* 文藝心理學 (Psychology of Art, 1936, 開明), based on Croce's theory of aesthetics, is a learned psychological study of art. His *Mêng Shih Wên Ch'ao* 孟實文鈔 * (Collected essays, 1936, 良友, later changed its name to *Wo Yü Wên Hsüeh* 我與文學, Literature and I, 1946, 開明), though more popular in nature, are to be found equally penetrating discussions. During the War, he published another distinguished work, entitled *Shih Lun* 詩論 (On Poetry, 1943, Chungking, 國民圖書出版社), which had won a prize given by the Ministry of Education. His new treatises on literature were collected in his *T'an Wên Hsüeh* 談文學 (Chats on Literature, 1946, 開明).

Works: *T'an Mei* 談美 (On Beauty, 1932, 開明); *Kei Ch'ing Nien Ti Shih Erh Fêng Hsin* 給青年的十二封信 (Twelfe Letters Written to Young Readers, 1931, 開明); *Pien T'ai Hsin Li Hsüeh P'ai Pieh* 變態心理學派別 (Different Schools of Abnormal Psychology, 1930, 開明); *Pien T'ai Hsin Li Hsüeh* 變態心理學 (Abnormal Psychology, 1933, 商務); *T'an Hsiu Yang* 談修養 (1946, 中周出版社).

45. Chu Ping-sun 朱炳蓀 ·

Novelist. She graduated from Yenching University 燕京大學. In 1946, she married Hu Chung-ching 胡鍾京, the head of the Foreign Office of the Eleventh War Zone. She wrote *Hui Ming* 晦明 * (1939, 和平印書局), a novel.

46. Chu Tzŭ-ch'ing 朱自清 .

(1899 —　　　)

T. 佩弦 . Essayist, poet, and short-story writer. A native of Shaohsing, Chekiang, he was born in Kiangtu, Kiangsu. While still a student in the National University of Peking 北京大學 , he began to contribute to the magazines *Hsin Ch'ao* 新潮 (New Tide), and *Hsin Chung Kuo* 新中國 (New China). After finishing his course in philosophy there, he taught Chinese in various middle schools and normal schools in different places. In 1923, he travelled in Europe, and published one volume of notes on his voyage when he came back, entitled *Ou Yu Tsa Chi* 歐遊雜記 (1934, 開明). Later, he became a professor at the Women's College of Arts and Science of the National Peiping University 北平大學 女子文理學院 , and the National Normal University 師範大學 at Peiping. Before the Sino-Japanese War, he was the chairman of the Department of Chinese Literature of Tsinghua University 清華大學 . In the War years, he lived in Kunming, where he served as the chairman of the Department of Chinese Literature of the National Southwest Associated University 西南聯合大學 . After the Victory over Japan, he returned to Peiping, and resumed his post in Tsinghua. He publishes sometimes his new writings in different magazines and newspapers.

Works: *Hsüeh Chao* 雪朝 (collection of poems, 1922, 商務); *Tsung Chi* 踪跡 (Track, collection of poems and essays, 1924, 亞東); *Pei Ying* 背影 * (collection of essays, 1929, 開明); *Ni Wo* 你我 * (You and I, collection of essays, 1936, 商務); *Lun Tun Tsa Chi* 倫敦雜記 (Notes on London, 開明); *Kuo Wên Chiao Hsüeh* 國文教學 (How to Teach Chinese, written in collaboration with Yeh Shao-Chün, 葉紹鈞, 開明); *Shih Yen Chih Pien* 詩言志辨 (開明); *Ching Tien Ch'ang T'an* 經典常談 (Talks on Chinese Classics, 1945, Shanghai, 國民圖書出版社); etc.

47. Chu Wên 朱雯 .

Pen-name: 王墳 . Short-story writer, and essayist. Husband of Lo Hung 羅洪, a well-known authoress. He graduated from the Tungwu University 東吳大學 at Soochow. He edited once a literary magazine *Pai Hua* 白華 . During the Sino-Japanese War, he was in the Interior, and returned to Shanghai after the Victory.

Works: *Luan Jên Shu Chien* 戀人書簡 (Love-Letters, written in collaboration with Lo Hung, 樂華); *Ch'u Luan Ch'ing Shu Chi* 初戀情書集 (Letters of First Love, 現代); *Tang Tai Wên Fa* 當代文法 (Modern Grammar, 1934, 中學生); *Yü Yüeh Chieh* 逾越節 * (1939, 文化生活出版社); etc.

Translations: 愛國者 (*Patriot* by P.S. Buck); 地下火 ; etc.

48 Ch'u Hsüeh-sung 褚雪松.

(1900 —   )

Pen-names: 一痀女士, 疢儂, 張問鵑, 褚問鵑, 問鵑 , etc.

Novelist. Born in Chiahsing 嘉興 , Chekiang. After graduating from the Soochow Girls' Normal School 蘇州女子師範學校 , She taught once in the Tatung Girls' Normal School 大同女子師範 , Shansi. She married Chang Ching-shêng 張競生 , a professor of the National University of Peking 北京大學, but divorced later.

Works: 陪審員 (1929, 光華); 小江平遊滬記 * (1932, 新明); etc.

49. Fang Ching 方 敬.

Essayist, and poet. Born in Szechwan. After graduating from the Department of Western Languages and Literature of the National University of Peking 北京大學, he taught English in different middle schools for many years. In 1940, he went to Kunming, then to Kweilin, the center of publication during the War. There he inaugurated a publishing house, called "Kung Tso Shê" 工作社 (Working Society). With the fall of Kweilin, he went to Kweiyang, where he was appointed a lecturer of the Department of Western Languages and Literature of Kweichow University 貴州大學 , and concurrently the editor of *Chên Ti* 陣地 a literary supplement of the Newspaper *Ta Kang Pao* 大剛報. He is now still teaching in the Kweichow University.

Works: *Fêng Ch'ên Chi* 風塵集 * (collection of essays)-; *Pao Hu Sê* 保護色 (Protective Color, collection of essays); *Hsing Yin Ti Ko* 行吟的歌 (collection of poems); *Shêng Yin* 聲音 (Sound, collection of poems); *Yü Ching* 雨景 (collection of poems and essays, 1942, 文化生活出版社); etc.

Translations: 家庭幸福 (*Family Happiness* by L. Tolstoy, 1946, 文化生活出版社); 聖誕歡歌 (*Christmas Carol* by C. Dickens); etc.

50. Fang Hsin 芳 信.

Novelist, Short-story writer, and playwright. He edited once a literary magazine *Lü* 綠 (Green), in collaboration with Chu Wei-chi 朱維基 and Lin Wei-yin 林微音 .

Works: *Hsüeh Wên* 血吻 (a play, 1928 光華); *Ch'un Wan* 春蔓 (a novel, 光華); *Ch'iu Chih Mêng* 秋之夢 (collection of short stories, 光華); *Lo Man Lo Lan P'ing Chuan* 羅曼羅蘭評傳 (A Critical Study of Romain Rolland, 1947, 永祥); etc.

Translations: 海鷗 (*Sea-mew* by A. Chekhov, 世界); 萬尼亞舅舅 (*Uncle Vania* by A. Chekhov, 世界); 欽差大臣 (*The Reviser* by N. N. V. Gogol, 世界) ; 新婚交響曲 (by V. Katayev, 世界); 下層 (*The Lower Depths* by M. Gorky, 世界); 大雷雨 (*Storm* by A. Ostrovsky, 世界); 大學教授 (by L. Andreyev, 世界);

黑暗之勢力 (*The Power of Darkness* by L. Tolstoy, 世界); 櫻桃園 (*Cherry Orchard* by A. Chekhov, 世界); 少校夫人 (世界); etc.

51. Fang Nai-ho 方奈何.

(1909 —   )

Novelist and journalist. Born in Peiping. He graduated from the Department of Political Science and Economics of the North-China University 華北大學 Peiping. Before the Marco Polo Bridge Incident, he was a reporter in his native city. During the Sino-Japanese War, he went to the Interior, and held the position of editor-in-chief of *Hsin Min Pao* 新民報, and *I Shih Pao* 益世報, in Chungking and Chengtu, and concurrently served as one of the directors of the "Association of Social Service" 中國社會服務事業協進會. After the Victory over Japan he returned to Peiping and resumed his post as editor-in-chief of *Hsin Min Pao*. He is the author of *Ch'un Fêng Yang Liu* 春風楊柳,* a novel.

52. Fêng Chi-jên 封季壬.

Pen-names: 鳳子, 禾子. Novelist, short-story writer, and essayist. Born in Kwangsi. After graduating from the Department of Chinese Literature of Fuhtan University 復旦大學, she became the editor of the magazine *Nü Tzŭ Yüeh K'an* 女子月刊 (Women's Monthly), published by the Women's Book Store 女子書店 in succession of Pai Wei 白薇, a famous authoress. Later, she travelled in Japan. During the Sino-Japanese War, she was in the Interior, and once edited the literary supplement of *Chung Yang Jih Pao* 中央日報. After the Victory over Japan, she returned to Shanghai, where she edits the monthly magazine *Jên Shih Chien* 人世間 (This Human World).

Works: *Wu Shêng Ti Ko Nü* 無聲的歌女 (The Silent Songstress, a novel, 1946, 正言出版社); *Pa Nien* 八年* (Eight Years, collection of short stories and essays); *Wu T'ai Man Pu* 舞台漫步 (collection of sketches); etc.

Besides being a famous writer, Fêng is also an actress of fame.

53. Fêng Chih 馮至.

Poet, and essayist. He is a returned student from Germany. He contributed first to the literary quarterly *Ch'ien Ts'ao* 淺草季刊 of Shanghai. In the autumn of 1925, he organized the society "Ch'ên Chung Shê" 沉鐘社 (a name borrowed from Hauptmann's *Die Versunkene Glocke*) at Peiping, together with Ch'ên Hsiang-ho 陳翔鶴, Yang Hui 楊晦, and Ch'ên Wei-mo 陳煒謨, and published the *Ch'ên Chung Weekly* 沉鐘週刊, on October 10, the same year, which suspended publication after its tenth issue. Between 1926 and 1927, they edited a fortnightly to succeed the weekly, under the same title. It published 12 numbers altogether. In 1927, he published his first collection of essays, entitled *Tso Jih Chih Ko* 昨日之歌 (Song of Yesterday, 北新); and in 1929, he produced his second volume, entitled *Pei Yu Chi Ch'i T'a* 北遊及其他 (Travels in the North and Other Essays, Peiping, Ch'ên Chung Shê). In the autumn of 1932, collaborating with Lin Ju-chi 林如稷 , the former editor of *Ch'ien Ts'ao,* they published again the *Ch'ên Chung Fortnightly*, which ceased publication half a year later.

During the Sino-Japanese War, he lived in Kunming, where he taught in the National Southwest Associated University 西南聯合大學 . After the Victory over Japan, he returned to Peiping, and is now a professor of the National University of Peking 北京大學 .

Besides the works mentioned above, he also wrote: *Shan Shui* 山水 (collection of essays, 1943, Chungking); *Wu Tzŭ Hsü* 伍子胥 * (a novel, 1946, 文化生活出版社); *Shih Ssŭ Hang Shih* 十四行詩 (Sonnets); etc.

He translated 給一個青年詩人的十封信 (by R. M. Rilke, 商務); etc.

54. Fêng Ho-i 馮和儀 .

Pen-name: 蘇青 . Novelist. She edited the magazine *T'ien Ti* 天地 at Shanghai during Japanese occupation. Her novel *Chieh Hun Shih Nien* 結婚十年 * was quite popular during those few years. She wrote also *T'ao* 濤 *; *Wan Chin Chi* 浣錦集 ;* etc.

55. Fêng Shu-lan 馮淑蘭 .

(1902 —   )

T. 德馥, 沅君 . Pen-names: 淦女士, 易安, 大琦 , etc.

Short-story writer and scholar. Born in Tangho, Honan. She is a younger sister of the well-known philosopher, Fêng Yu-lan 馮友蘭. After graduating from the post-graduate class of the National University of Peking 北京大學, and of the National Normal University 師範大學 at the same city, she taught in various universities and colleges. In 1929, she married Lu K'an-ju 陸侃如 , a scholar, in Shanghai. During the Sino-Japanese War, she was a professor at different universities in Yunnan. She lectures now in Shantung University 山東大學 , Tsingtao.

In 1924, she began to publish her short stories, *Lü Hsing* 旅行 (Travel), and *Ko Chüeh* 隔絕 (Separation), in the weekly magazine *Ch'uang Tsao Chou Pao* 創造週報 , under the pen-name of Kan Nü Shih 淦女士 (Miss Kan). The bold exposition of the women's psychology of their love life won her nation-wide fame during those few years. She was the author of three collections of short stories: 卷葹 * (1926, 北新); 春痕 (1926, 北新); and 劫灰* (1929, 北新).

In recent years she turned to the study of ancient Chinese drama, and produced no creative works.

In collaboration with her husband Lu K'an-ju, she wrote a history of Chinese poetry, entitled *Chung Kuo Shih Shih* 中國詩史 .

56. Fêng Tzŭ-k'ai 豐子愷 .

(1898 —   )

Essayist and artist. Born in Shihmen, Chekiang. His father died when he was quite young, and left ten children to the mother who brought them up with great care. Fêng Tzŭ-k'ai began to study in a private school at the age of 10, and attended a primary school at 13. When 17 years old, he went to Hangchow, where he entered the First Normal School 杭州第一師範 . His interest in painting and music was firstly aroused at that time by his teacher of fine arts, Li Shu-t'ung 李叔同 (later he became a monk, H. 大慈山僧，弘一法師). Graduated at 22, he married Miss Hsü Li-min 徐力民 In the same year his friend Wu Mêng-fei 吳夢非 and Liu Chih-p'ing 劉質平 founded a school of fine arts in Nanking, he was appointed a teacher. At the age of 24, he went to Tokyo to study painting and music. One year later he came back, and taught fine arts in the Ch'un Hui Middle School of Shangyü 上虞春暉中學 , Chekiang, for three years. In his spare time, he devoted himself to the reading of world literary masterpieces and books on art. At the age of 28, he served as a tutor of fine arts in the Li Ta Institute 立達學園 of Shanghai, and concurrently teacher of painting, music, and aesthetics in Shanghai University 上海大學 , Fuhtan Middle School 復旦中學 , Ch'êng Chung Middle School 澄衷中學 , and Sung Chiang Girls' Middle School 松江女子中學 , Later he joined the Editorial Bureau of the Kaiming Book Co. 開明書店 . His mother's death, which occured when he was 33, brought on him heavy grief; since then he resigned all his jobs, and sought seclusion in a humble house in Chiahsing 嘉興 , a city near his birth place Shihmen, and applied himself to writing and drawing, from which he wished to procure his repose of mind. Two years later, his studio "Yuan Yuan T'ang" 緣緣堂 was built in his native town, in which he lived until the outbreak of the Sino-Japanese War. He then went to Yishan 宜山. Kwangsi, to teach aesthetics and literature in the Chekiang University 浙江大學 , Later he left for Tsunyi, Kweichow, and then to Chungking, where he was appointed professor at the National Academy of Fine Arts 國立藝專 ; but one year later he resigned. After the Victory over Japan, he returned to Hangchow, where he lived until now, making his living by painting and writing.

Fêng Tzŭ-k'ai is an artist of highest rank in China. The collections of his paintings are: 阿 Q 漫畫; 護生畫集 (開明); 子愷畫集 (1927, 開明); 子愷漫畫集 (1929, 開明); 光明畫集 (1931, 蘇州弘化社); 子愷漫畫全集 (1946, 開明); 又生畫集 (1947, 開明); etc.

He is also noted as a man of letters. His literary works were published mostly in the magazines *Hsiao Shuo Yüeh Pao* 小說月報 (The Short Story Magazine), *Wên Hsüeh Chou Pao* 文學週報 (The Literary Weekly), and *I Pan* 一般 (The Masses). The collections of his essays are: 子愷小品集 (開明); 中學生小品

(開明); 隨筆二十篇 (1934, 天馬); 車箱社會 * (1935, 良友); 緣緣堂隨筆 * (1937, 開明); 緣緣堂再筆 (開明); 率眞集 ;* etc.

He translated: 初戀 * (*First Love* by I. Turgenev, 1931, 開明); 自殺俱樂部 (*Suicide Club* by R. L. Stevenson, 1932, 開明); 苦悶的象徵 (by H. Kuriyagawa); 孩子們的音樂 (by Y. Tanabe, 1928, 開明); 生活與音樂 (by Y. Tanabe 1929, 大江); 現代藝術十二講 (by B. Ueda, 1929, 開明); 音樂的聽法 (by N. Kadoma, 1930, 大江); 藝術概論 (by H. Kuroda, 1934, 開明); etc.

He wrote the following works on art: 音樂的常識 (1925, 亞東); 音樂入門 (1926, 開明); 中文名歌五十曲 (in collaboration with 裘夢痕, 1927, 開明); 西洋美術史 (1928, 開明); 構圖法 ABC (1929, 世界); 谷訶 (Van Gogh) 生活 (1929, 世界); 近世 十大音樂家 (1930, 開明); 音樂初步 (1930, 北新); 世界大音樂家與名曲 (1931, 亞東); 西洋名畫巡禮 (1931, 開明); 藝術敎育 (1932, 大東); 西洋音樂楔子 (1932, 開明); 開明 音樂講義 (1934, 開明); 藝術趣味 (1934, 開明); 開明圖畫講義 (1934, 開明); 現代藝術 綱要 (1934, 中華); 繪畫與文學 (1934, 開明); 藝術論集 (1935, 中華); 藝術叢話 (1935, 良友); 繪畫概說 (1935, 亞細亞); 藝術漫談 (1936, 人間); 少年美術故事 (1937, 開明); 洋琴彈奏法 (開明); etc.

57. Fêng Wên-ping   馮文炳

(1901 —   )

Pen-name: 廢名 . Born in Hwangmei, Hupei. At first he was a teacher in a primary school in Wuchang. In 1922, he entered the preparatory class of the National University of Peking 北京大學, two years later he became a freshman in the Department of English Literature in the same university. After his graduation in 1929, he was appointed lecturer of the Department of Chinese Literature in his alma mater. During the Sino-Japanese War, he returned to his native town to teach in primary and middle schools. After the Victory over Japan he returned to Peiping, and now is teaching again in the National University of Peking. He sometimes publishes his new writings in the literary supplement of *Ta Kung Pao* 大公報, and the *Wên Hsüeh Tsa Chih* 文學雜誌 (The Literary Magazine) published by the Commercial Press.

The literary activity of Fei Ming before the Marco Polo Bridge Incident may be divided into several periods. During the first period (1922 - 1923) he published his writings in the *Nu Li Chou Pao* 努力週報 (The Endeavour Weekly). Later he collected these narratives into one volume, which he called *Chu Lin Ti Ku Shih* 竹林的故事 (Tales of the Bamboo-grove, 1925, 北新). The second period (1924 - 1930) during which he published his writings in the magazine *Yü Ssŭ* 語絲, we have his *Ch'iao* 橋 * (The Bridge) as a representative work. During the third period (1930 - 1931) he was connected with the magazine *Lo T'o Ts'ao* 駱駝草 , his main work was *Mo Hsü Yu Hsien Shêng Chuan* 莫須有先生傳 (The Biography of Mr. Would — Be, 1932). In the fourth period (1932 - 1935) he contributed to the magazine *Jên Chien Shih* 人間世 (This Human World). His principal work was *Tu Lun Yü* 讀論語 (On Reading the Analects of Confucius). In the fifth period (1936 - 1937) he wrote many essays for the *Ming Chu* 明珠

a literary supplement of the newspaper *Shih Chieh Jih Pao* 世界日報.

Besides the above-mentioned works, he wrote *Tao Yuan* 桃園* (The Peach-orchard, 1928, 開明); *Shui P'ien* 水邊* (collection of poems); etc.

58. Fu Tung-hua 傅東華.

(1895 —   )

Original name: 傅則黃 , T. 凍藹. Pen-names: 伍實，陸若水，etc.

Literary critic, and translator. Born in Kinhwa, Chekiang. After finishing his engineering course at Nanyang University 南洋大學 Shanghai, he threw himself immediately into the literary world, and became famous through his translation of critical works. He was an important figure of the "Society of Literary Research" 文學研究會. Before the Sino-Japanese War, he taught in the National Normal University of Peiping 北平師範大學, China University 中國大學, Pingmin University 平民 大學 at Peiping, China Institute at Woosung 吳淞中國公學, Shanghai University 上海大學, and the Sun Yat-sen University 中山大學 at Canton. During the War, he was a professor at Chinan University 暨南大學, and Fuhtan University 復旦大學 at Shanghai.

Works: *Wên Hsüeh Ch'ang Shih* 文學常識 (Common Sense of Literature, 1927, 商務); *Shih Ko Yuan Li ABC* 詩歌原理 ABC (Principles of Poetry, 1928, 世界); *Wên I P'i P'ing ABC* 文藝批評 ABC (Principles of Literary Criticism, 1928, 世界); *Li Pai Yü Tu Fu* 李白與杜甫 (Biography of Li Pai and Tu Fu, two most important poets of the T'ang Dynasty, 商務); *Li Ch'ing-chao* 李清照 (Bio-graphy of Li Ch'ing-chao, a famous authoress of the Sung Dynasty, 1934 商務)；*Shan Hu T'ao Chi* 山胡桃集 * (Wild Walnuts, collection of critical and miscel-laneous essays, 1935, 生活); etc.

Translations: 近世文學批評 (*A Modern Book of Criticism* by L. Lewisohn, 1928, 商務) ；文學之社會學的批評 (*Newer Spirit: Sociological Criticism of Literature* by V. Calverton, 1930, 華通); 社會的文學批評論 (Social *Criticism of Literature*, by G. Bucy, 商務); 詩之研究 (*A Study of Poetry* by B. Perry, 1933, 商務); 詩學 (*Poetica* by Aristotle, 1933, 商務); 比較文學史 (*A History of Com-parative Literature* by F. Lolière, 1931, 商務); 美學原理 (*Aesthetics* by B. Croce, 1934, 商務); 文學概說 (by T. W. Hunt, 1935, 商務); 我們的世界 (Van Loon's *Geography*, 1933, 新生活); 眞妮姑娘 (*Jennie Gerhardt* by T. Dreiser, 1935, 中華); 化外人 (1936, 商務); etc.

59. Ho Ch'i-fang 何其芳.

(1911 —   )

Poet, and essayist. Born in Szechwan, where he remained with his family until his fifteenth year, receiving a strict classical education. When he was under ten years of age, he was made to recite the *Four Books* 四書, the *Shih Ching* 詩經

(Book of Poetry), and *Shu Ching* 書經, from beginning to end. And he continued to study classical prose and poetry, Confucius, and Chuang Tzŭ 莊子, ever since, deriving considerable benifit from that early discipline. In 1931, he entered the National University of Peking 北京大學 to study philosophy. His first book, *Hua Mêng Lu* 畫夢錄 (Recollections of Dreamland, 1936, 文化生活出版社), has won the *Ta Kung Pao* 大公報 literary prize as the best essays of 1936. In the same year, he published his first collection of poems, entitled *Han Yuan Chi* 漢園集 (商務), written in collaboration with his schoolmates Pien Chih-lin 卞之琳, and Li Kuang-t'ien 李廣田 "Han Yuan" is the name of a street where their alma mater, the National University of Peking, is located. During the Sino-Japanese War, he went to Chengtu, then to Yenan, the former Red capital, where he taught in the Lu Hsün Institute of Arts 魯迅藝術學院, and was in charge of the Yenan Branch of the "National Writer's Anti-Aggression Association" 中華全國文藝界抗敵協會, and edited the Association's publication *Ta Chung Wên I* 大衆文藝 (Mass Literature).

In addition to the works mentioned above, he wrote: *K'o I Chi* 刻意集 * (collection of poems and essays, 1938, 文化生活出版社), *Huan Hsiang Jih Chi* 還鄉日記 * (collection of essays, 1939, 良友); *Yeh Ko* 夜歌 (Night-Songs, collection of poems, 1945, 詩文學社); *Hsing Huo Chi* 星火集 (collection of essays, 1946, 群益出版社); *Yü Yen* 預言 (Prophecy, collection of poems, 1947, 文化生活出版社); etc.

60. Ho Chia-huai 何家槐.

Pen-name: 先河. Short-story writer. Born in Iwu, Chekiang. He is the author of the following collections of short-stories: 竹布衫 (1933, 黎明); 曖昧* (1933, 良友); 懷舊集 (1935, 天馬); 寒夜集 * (1937, 北新); etc.

During the Sino-Japanese War, he was a refugee in the Interior. He wandered through many places, but he never ceased writing. He has contributed to the *Wên I Yüeh K'an* 文藝月刊 (Literary Monthly), published by the "Chinese Literary Society of Chungking" 重慶中國文藝社 , and the *Wên I Shêng Huo* 文藝生活 (Literary Life), edited by Ssù-Ma Wên-sên 司馬文森. In 1941, he produced a volume of essays entitled *Mao Yen Chi* 冒烟集, published by the Wên Hsien Publishing Co. 文献出版社, Kweilin.

Now he teaches in a middle school in his native place, and sometimes publishes his new writings in different literary magazines in Shanghai.

61. Ho Ku-t'ien 何穀天.

Pen-names: 周文, 王鋼, etc. Short-story writer. After ten years' study under a private tutor, he entered a government school. But on account of financial difficulties, he left it two years later, and went to Sikang where he attended a military academy, and later became a copyist in a certain government office. It was shortly after the Shanghai Incident of January 28, 1932, when he settled himself at Shanghai, that he began to write his first short story *Hsüeh Ti* 雪地 (Snow Field), in which he depicted the life of soldiers of Sikang of whom he was quite accustomed.

During the Sino-Japanese War, he lived in Yenan, the former Red capital, where he was in charge of the Yenan Branch of the "National Writers' Anti-Aggression Association" 中華全國文藝界抗敵協會, and edited the magazine *Ta Chung Wên I* 大衆文藝 (Mass Literature), together with Ting Ling 丁玲, and Liu Pai-yü 劉白羽 .

Works: *Fên* 分 * (Divided, collection of short stories, 1935, 文化生活出版社); *Fu Tzǔ Chih Chien* 父子之間 (Father and Son, collection of short stories, 1935, 良友); *To Ch'an Chi* 多產集* (A Prolific Collection, collection of short stories, 1936, 文化生活出版社); *Yen Miao Chi* 烟苗季 *; *Chou Wên Tuan P'ien Hsiao Shuo Chi* 周文短篇小説集 (Short Stories of Chou Wên, one of his pen-names, 開明); *Ai* 愛 (Love, collection of short stories, 開明); *Tsai Pai Sen Chên* 在白森鎭 (1940, 良友復興); etc.

62. Hsia Mien-tsun 夏丏尊.

(1885 — 1946)

Essayist and literary critic. Born in Shangyü, Chekiang. He was a Hsiu-ts'ai 秀才 of the Ch'ing Dynasty. On account of financial difficulties he did not finish his study in any school, native or foreign, although he had stayed in Japan for about two years. It was through his own constant and unwearied efforts in self-study that he had acquired all the necessary knowledge about literature and foreign language. He was one of the leading figures of the famous May Fourth Movement in 1919, when he was a teacher in the First Normal School of Chekiang 浙江省立第一師範學校 . Later, he taught Chinese in the First Normal School of Hunan 湖南省立第一師範學校 , Ch'un Hui Middle School 春暉中學 of Shangyü, and Chinan University 暨南大學 of Shanghai. In collaboration with his friends K'uang Hu-shêng 匡互生 , Liu Hsün-yü 劉薰宇 , Fêng Tzǔ-k'ai 豐子愷 and others, he founded the Li Ta Institute 立達學園 in Shanghai. He was among the group of literary friends that laid the foundation of the Kaiming Book Co. 開明書店 which have done considerable work in the enhancement and development of Chinese culture. Special contribution has been in the line of producing novels by first class writers as well as the monthy magazine *Chung Hsüeh Shêng* 中學生 (The Juvenile Student), which has won the nation-wide popularity among the student class and of which he was one of the editors and chief contributors. From 1926 on, he worked in the Kaiming Editorial Bureau until the outbreak of the Sino-Japanese War. Then he lived a secluded life in extreme poverty at Shanghai. In the winter of 1943, he was kept in detention on the accusation of "being impure in thought" by the Japanese gendarmes in Shanghai for a period of three weeks. After the Victory over Japan, he resumed his post in Kaiming. Since then he had symptoms of tuberculosis and with his health going gradually from bad to worse, he died on the night of the 23rd of April, 1946, at the age of 61.

Works: 生活與文學 (北新); 現代世界文學大綱 (神州國光社); 文章講話 (in collaboration with Yeh Shao-chün 葉紹鈞 開明); 文章作法 (in collaboration with Liu Hsün-yü, 1926, 開明); 文藝論 ABC (1930, 世界); 文心* (in collaboration with Yeh Shao-chün 葉紹鈞, 1934, 開明); 平屋雜文 * (1935, 開明), etc.

Translations: 社會主義與進化論 (by M. Takatsu, translated in collaboration with Li Chi-chên 李繼楨, 1922, 商務); 棉被 (by K. Tayama, 1927, 商務); 愛的教育 (*Cuore* by Edmonde de Amicis, 1927, 開明); 近代的戀愛觀 (by H. Kuriyagawa, 1928, 開明); 近代日本小說集 (1928, 開明); 續愛的教育 (*Igiene del-l'amore* by P. Mantegazza, 1931, 開明); 蒲團 (by K. Tayama, 開明); 芥川龍之介集 (*Works of Ryunosuke Akutagawa*, translated in collaboration with Lu Hsün 魯迅 and others, 開明); etc.

63. Hsiang K'ui 向達.

T. 覺然. Pen--names: 平江不肖生, 不肖生, etc.
He was a forerunner of the School of Chivalrous Novels 劍俠小說 of China. His novel *Chiang Hu Ch'i Hsia Chuan* 江湖奇俠傳 was one of the most favorite books among the juvenile readers, and has been adapted by the Star Motion Picture Co. 明星影片公司 for a film.

64. Hsiang P'ei-liang 向培良.

(1901 —)

Pen-name: 鄉下人. Playwright, short-story writer, and novelist. Born in Kienyang, Hunan. He contributed at first to the magazines *Mang Yuan* 莽原 and *Wei Ming* 未名, published by the "Unnamed Association" 未名社. Later, in collaboration with his friends Kao Ch'ang-hung 高長虹 and Kao Ch'ang-chiang 高長江, he organized the "Storm and Stress Society" 狂飇社, publishing the weekly magazine *K'uang Piao* 狂飇 (Storm and Stress) on one hand, and starting a dramatic group on the other. After Separating from the Kao brothers, he led a troupe "Tzu Ko Chü Tui" 紫歌劇隊 staging in Amoy and other places. After-wards, he participated in the Nationalistic Literary Movement 民族主義文學運動 to promote nationalistic drama. He was the editor of the monthly magazine *Ch'ing Ch'un Yüeh K'an* 青春月刊 (The Youth), but it was short-lived. His early works were published also in the *Hsiao Shuo Yüeh Pao* 小說月報 (The Short Story Magazine) and *Pei Hsin Pan Yüeh K'an* 北新半月刊, besides the magazines mentioned above.

During the Sino-Japanese War he toured with a wandering troupe "Nu Ch'ao Chü T'uan" 怒潮劇團 in the Interior. He lives now in Shanghai, and publishes sometimes his new writings in different magazines.

He is the author of 飄渺的夢 (collection of short stories, 1926, 北新); 我離開十字街頭 * (a novel, 1927, 光華); and several collections of plays: 不忠實的愛情 (1929, 啟智); 光明的戲劇 (1929, 光華); 繼母 (北新); 死城 (泰東); 沉悶的戲劇 (光華); etc.

Besides his creative works, he is also known for his dramatic criticism, of which we may mention 中國戲劇概評 (泰東); 紫歌劇集, 導演概論, 戲劇導演術 (世界).

65. Hsiao Ch'ien 蕭 乾.

Short-story writer, and reporter. Born in Peiping. His literary career commenced after he began contributing to the literary supplement of *Ta Kung Pao* 大公報 (edited by Shên Ts'ung-wên 沈從文), while he was still a student at Yenching University 燕京大學. In 1935, after graduatiing from the Department of Journalism of Yenching, he took the editorship of the literary supplement of *Ta Kung Pao* in succession of Shên, and served concurrently as a travelling reporter of the same paper. He travelled extensively in Shantung, Kiangsu, and Yunnan. From 1939 on, he served as a special correspondent of *Ta Kung Pao* in London, and taught in the University of London. In 1946, he returned to China. He is now a professor at Fuhtan University 復旦大學, Shanghai, and concurrently the editor of the literary supplement of *Ta Kung Pao*.

Works: *Shu P'ing Yen Chiu* 書評研究 (A Study of Book Review, 1935, 商務); *Li Hsia Chi* 籬下集 * (Under Other's Shelter and Other Stories, 1936, 商務); *Li Tzu* 栗子 (Chestnuts, collection of short stories, 1936, 商務); *Mêng Chih Ku* 夢之谷 * (a novel which tells the story of a school teacher, who fell in love with a girl. He failed owing to lack of money, 1938, 文化生活出版社); *Hsiao Shu Yeh* 小樹葉 (Little Leaf, 1936, 商務); *Lo Jih* 落日 (The Setting Sun, 1936, 良友); *Chien Wên* 見聞 (1939, 桂林烽火社); *Hui Chin* 灰燼 (1939, 文化生活出版社); *Nan Tê Ti Mu Ch'iu* 南德的暮秋 (Late Autumn of South Germany, 1946, 文化生活出版社); *Jên Shêng Ts'ai Fang* 人生探訪 (1947, 文化生活出版社); *China but not Cathay* (in English, 1943, Forest Hills, Transatlantic Arts); *Spinners of Silk* (in English); *Etching of a Tormented Age* (in English); *A Harp of Thousand Strings* (in English); etc.

66. Hsieh Jên-p'u 謝人堡.

Original name: 謝仁甫. Novelist. Born in Mukden. He graduated from Fu Jên University 輔仁大學, Peiping, in 1940. He wrote the following novels: 葡萄園 * (1942, 唯一書店); 寒山夜雨 * (1944, 勵力出版社); 春滿園 * (1944, 馬德增書店); 月夜三重奏 * (1944, 馬德增書店); 逐流之歌 (1944); etc.

67. Hsieh Liu-i 謝六逸．

(1906 — 1945)

T. 宏徒，H. 無堂．Pen-name：中牛．

Born in Kweiyang, Kweichow. He graduated from the Waseda University, Japan. Upon returning to China, he held the following positions: an editor of the Commercial Press, chairman of the Department of Literature of China Institute 中國公學 of Woosung, professor of National Chinan University, 暨南大學, chairman of the Department of Chinese Literature and concurrently chairman of the Department of Journalism of Fuhtan University 復旦大學, editor of the newspaper *Li Pao* 立報 editor of *Erh T'ung Wên Hsüeh* 兒童文學 (Children's Literature), a monthly magazine published by Chung Hwa Book Co. 中華書局．

After the outbreak of the Sino-Japanese War, he returned to his native place Kweiyang, where he taught in the College of Arts and Letters of Great China University 大夏大學, and edited the literary supplement of the newspaper *Chung Yang Jih Pao* 中央日報．Before his death, which occured on August 11, 1945, he was in charge of the Kweiyang branch of the "National Writers' Anti-Aggression Association" 中華全國文藝界抗敵協會．

Being a member of the "Society of Literary Research" 文學研究會, he published his works in the Association's publication *Hsiao Shuo Yüeh Pao* 小說月報 (The Short Story Magazine). At first, he introduced Japanese literature, and then turned, in his late years, to the study of fairy-tales and journalism.

Creative works: 范某的犯罪 (1929, 現代)；水沫集 (1929, 世界)；茶話集 (1931, 新中國)；母親 (北新)；清明節 (北新)；接吻 (大江)；紅棗 (聯合)；鸚鵡 (聯合)；慧星 (中華)；etc.

Critical works: 西洋小說發達史 (1923, 商務)；日本文學 (1927, 開明)；日本文學史 (1929, 北新)；世界文學 (1935, 世界)；兒童文學 (1935, 中華)；文藝思潮史 (北新)；近代文學與社會改造 (商務)；歐美文學史畧 (大江)；小說概論 (大江)；農民文學 (世界)；神話學 ABC (世界)；etc.

Translations: 伊利亞特故事 (The Story of Iliad, 1929, 開明)；近代日本小品文選 (1929, 大江)；志賀直哉集 (Works of N. Shiga, 1935, 中華)；文藝與性愛 (by T. Matsumura, 開明)；etc.

68. Hsieh Ping-ying 謝冰瑩．

(1908 —　　)

Orininal name: 謝鳴岡，T. 鳳寶．She changed her name to 謝彬, when she became a university student. Pen-names：冰瑩, 冰瑩女士, 芷英 蘭如, 紫英, 鄉鮑姥, 林娜, 格雷, 瑛, 南芷, 劉澄, 無畏, 碧雲, 小兵 etc.

Novelist, short-story writer, and essayist. Born in Sinhua, Hunan. After her graduation from the Hunan Provincial First Normal School for Women 湖南省立第一女子師範學校 at Changsha, in 1926, she joined the Revolutionary Army during the Northern Expedition. At the same year she entered the Central Military and Political Academy 中央軍事政治學校, where she graduated in 1927. Based on her personal experience in the troops, she wrote a book, entitled *Ts'ung Chün Jih Chi* 從軍日記* (Diary of an Amazon, 1926, 光明), published in the newspaper *Chung Yang Jih Pao* 中央日報, under the pen-name of Ping Ying 冰瑩. It was translated into English by Lin Yü-t'ang 林語堂, and published at the same time in the same paper. Later on it was translated into French, German, Japanese, Russian, and Esperanto.

In 1928, she entered the National Normal University for Women 女子師範大學, at Peiping, to study Chinese literature. She left it, however, in 1931 without graduation and stayed in Japan for a short time. Upon returning to China, she taught Chinese in various middle schools at Peiping, Hunan, Fukien, and Kwangsi. In 1935, she visited Japan again, where she entered Waseda University 早稻田大學 to study Western literature with Mr. Hisao Honma 本間久雄.

After the outbreak of the Sino-Japanese War, she organized, in August of 1937, a War Area Service Corps for the women of Hunan. She went to Chungking in December of the same year to recuperate her health, where she became the editor of 血潮, the literary supplement of the daily paper *Hsin Min Pao*. In the spring of 1938, she went to the front at Hsüchow, and served as a field reporter, and concurrently secretary at the Headquarters of the Fifth War Zone. She returned to Chungking in the autumn of the same year, and became an editor at the Ministry of Education. She went to Sian in 1940, where she edited a literary monthly *Huang Ho* 黃河 (Yellow River) for three years. From 1943 on, she taught at Chengtu.

After the Victory over Japan, she proceeded to Hankow, where she edited the literary supplement of the newspaper *Ho P'ing Jih Pao* 和平日報. Later she came to Peiping, and functions as lecturer of contemporary Chinese literature at National Normal College 師範學院, and concurrently editor of the literary monthly *Wên I Yü Shêng Huo* 文藝與生活 (Literature and Life).

She wrote the following works: 前路 (collection of short stories, 1932, 光明); 麓山集 (collection of essays, 1932, 光明); 青年王國材 (a novel, 1933, 開華); 青年書信 (北新); 湖南的風 (collection of essays, 1936, 北新); 一個女兵的自傳* (autobiography, vol. 1. 1936, 良友); 在火線上 (collection of short stories 1937, 生活); 新從軍日記 (1937, 天馬); 軍中隨筆 (1937, 救亡日報); 戰士的手 (1937, 獨立出版社); 第五戰區巡禮 (1938, 廣西日報社); 日軍的暴行 (1938, 仿古書店); 鍾進士殺鬼 (1938, 藍田); 梅子姑娘 (1940, 新中國文化出版社); 寫給青年作家的信 (1940, 大東); 姊姊 (1943, 藍田書報合作社); 冰瑩抗戰文選集 (1940, 大東); 一個女兵的自傳 (autobiography, vol. 2, 1946, 紅藍出版社北平分社); 生日 (collection of essays, 1946, 北新); 在日本獄中 (1942, 西安華北新聞社); 冰瑩創作選 (仿古); etc.

69. Hsieh Wan-ying 謝婉瑩.

(1902 —   )

She is better known under the pen-name of 冰心. Her other pen-name is 男士.

Short-story writer, poet, and essayist. Born into a family of official rank and fine traditions in Minhow, Fukien. She spent her childhood in Yentai (Cheefoo), Shantung, where the beautiful scenery of the sea made a deep impression upon her young mind, and which was not unfrequently reflected in her works later on.

She cultivated the habit of reading fiction in her childhood. At the age of 11, she finished the *Shuo Pu Ts'ung Shu* 說部叢書; *Hsi Yu Chi* 西遊記; *Shui Hu Chuan* 水滸傳 (All Men Are Brothers); *T'ien Yü Hua* 天雨花; *Tsai Shêng Yuan* 再生緣; *Erh Nü Ying Hsiung Chuan* 兒女英雄傳; *Shuo Yüeh* 說岳; *Tung Chou Lieh Kuo Chih* 東周列國志; *Hung Lou Mêng* 紅樓夢 (The Dream of the Red Chamber); and *Fêng Shên Yen I* 封神演義.

After studying for a little while in a girls' normal school at her native place, she entered the Pei Man Girls' Middle School 貝滿女中 at Peiping, in 1914. After graduation there she became a student of Yenching University 燕京大學. It was during the famous May Fourth Movement that she began to write propagandist articles in Pai Hua (spoken language), and published in the literary supplement of *Ch'ên Pao* 晨報副刊, edited by her cousin Liu Fang-yuan 劉放園, under her real name Hsieh Wan-ying. Later she read numerous Chinese translations of the works of Dewey, Russell, Tagore, and Tolstoy which appeared in the magazines *Hsin Ch'ao* 新潮 (New Tide), *Hsin Ch'ing Nien* 新青年 (New Youth), and *Kai Tsao* 改造 (Reformation). Her interest in literature being thus aroused, she wrote a short story entitled *Liang Ko Chia T'ing* 兩個家庭 (Two Families), which was published, three days later, in the literary supplement of *Ch'ên Pao*, under the pen-name of Ping Hsin 冰心. From then on she wrote many short stories and essays which were published mostly in the literary supplement of *Ch'ên Pao*, and the famous *Hsiao Shuo Yüeh Pao* 小說月報 (The Stort Story Magazine), published by the "Society of Literary Research" 文學研究會, of which she was a member.

Graduated from Yenching University, in 1923, she went to the United States immediately, where she entered Wellesley College, and received her M.A. degree in 1926. Upon returning to China, she was appointed professor of literature at her alma mater. She married Professor Wu Wên-tsao 吳文藻 a sociologist, in 1929, at Peiping. She held the post in Yenching until the outbreak of the Sino-Japanese War.

In the War years, she lived in Peipei, near Chungking, and became a Member of the People's Political Council. After the Victory over Japan, she returned to Peiping, and then proceeded to Japan.

The complete works of Ping Hsin were published between 1932 and 1933, by Pei Hsin Book Co. 北新書局, in three volumes entitled *Ping Hsin Hsiao Shuo Chi* 冰心小說集 * (Short Stories of Ping Hsin); *Ping Hsin Shih Chi* 冰心詩集*

(Poems of Ping Hsin); and *Ping Hsin San Wên Chi* 冰心散文集 (Essays of Ping Hsin). During the War she wrote *Kuan Yü Nü Jên* 關於女人 (About Women, 1943, 重慶天地出版社), and *Hsü Chi Hsiao Tu Chê* 續寄小讀者 (Additional Letters to Young Readers).

The essays on Ping Hsin were collected by Li Hsi-t'ung 李希同 in his *Ping Hsin Lun* 冰心論 (1932, 北新).

70. Hsiung Fo-hsi 熊佛西.

(1900 —   )

Original name: 熊福禧. Playwright. Born in Fengcheng, Kiangsi. During the Chinese Revolution, 1911, his father brought him to Hankow, where he finished his study in primary and middle school. In 1919, he attended the Yenching University 燕京大學 at Peiping to study education and literature. His love of the theater was revealed very early. While still a university student, he engaged in the promotion of new drama. After graduating from Yenching in 1923, he went to the United States at the same year to study dramatic arts in the postgraduate class of Columbia University, and received his M.A. degree in 1926. Upon returning to China, he was appointed the chairman of the Department of Dramatic Arts of the National Peiping University 國立北平大學, and lecturer at his alma mater. In 1932, he became director of the rural theater of Tinghsien, Hopei, under the auspices of the Chinese National Associatin of the Mass Education Movement 中華平民教育促進會. After the Marco Polo Bridge Incident in 1937, he went to Hankow with the Association, then to Changsha. When the Association suspended its activity, he and his troupe of players called the "Farmers' Enemy-Resisting Dramatic Corps" 農民抗敵劇團 went to Chengtu, where they gave a series of performances which drew tens of thousands of people. In view of the success of this dramatic corps, the Szechwan Provincial Government established the Szechwan Provincial College of Dramatic Arts 四川省立戲劇學校 and asked Mr. Hsiung to be its president. He accepted the offer and the "Farmers' Enemy-Resisting Dramatic Corps" was incorporated into the College. Later, he became the head of the "Central Youth Dramatic Club" 中央青年劇社 of the San Min Chu I Youth Corps. In 1942, he went to Kweilin, where he founded two literary magazines *Tang Tai Wên Hsüeh* 當代文學 (Contemporary Literature) and *Wên Hsüeh Ch'uang Tso* 文學創作 (Literary Creation). After the Victory over Japan, he returned to Shanghai where he serves as the president of the Experimental Dramatic School 上海市立實驗戲劇學校.

Hsiung Fo-hsi is one of the pioneers of the new dramatic movement in China. He wrote plays when he was still a middle school student. His *Hsin Wên Chi Chê* 新聞記者 (The Reporter) and *Ch'ing Ch'un Ti Pei Chü* 青春的悲劇 (The Tragedy of Youth) dated as early as 1919. Since then he has been putting out new plays every year. His important works are collected into four volumes which he called *Hsiung Fo Hsi Hsi Chü Chi* 熊佛西戲劇集 * (The Dramatic Works of Hsiung Fo-hsi), published from 1930 to 1932 by the Commercial Press. During the Sino-Japanese War, he wrote a play *Yuan Shih-k'ai* 袁世凱, which was banned. He then stopped writing dramatic works, composed only some fiction, short essays, and notes of travels. His novel, *T'ieh Miao* 鐵苗,* was published in 1946, by the Hua Hua Book Co. 華華書店, Shanghai.

Besides his plays, he is also known for his dramatic criticism, of which we may mention *Fo Hsi Lun Chü* 佛西論劇 (Hsiung Fo-hsi's Essays on Drama, 1928, 北平樸社), and *Hsieh Chü Yuan Li* 寫劇原理 (Principles of Play-Writing). He was also the editor of the leading dramatic magazine *Hsi Chü Yü Wên I* 戲劇與文藝 (Drama and Literature) before the War.

71. Hsü Chieh 許 傑.

(1900 —   )

Original name: 許竹君, T. 漢三, 士仁. Pen-name: 張子三.

Short-story writer. Born in Taichow, Chekiang. He graduated from the Imperial University, Tokyo, Japan. Upon returning to China, he joined the famous "Society of Literary Research" 文學研究會, and published his early works in the Association's publication *Hsiao Shuo Yüeh Pao* 小說月報 (The Short Story Magazine). Later, he travelled in the Malay Archipelago, where he edited for some time the newspaper *I Ch'ün Pao* 益羣報, and composed many sketches on the experiences of his journey, which he collected into one volume, entitled *Yeh Tzŭ Yü Liu Lien* 椰子與榴槤 (1930, 現代). Later he became professor at the Hsin Hua University of Fine Arts 新華藝術大學, Shanghai; Sun Yat-sen University 中山大學, Canton; Chinan University 暨南大學, Shanghai; and editor-in-chief of the newspaper *Kuo Min Hsin Wên* 國民新聞, Canton. During the Sino-Japanese War, he went to the Interior, and wrote short stories for the famous magazine *Wên I Chên Ti* 文藝陣地 (Literary Field), edited by Mao Tun 茅盾. He is now in Shanghai, and publishes sometimes his new writings in different literary magazines.

He is the author of the following collections of short stories: 慘霧* (1925, 光華); 慘霧* (1926, 商務); 飄浮 (1926, 上海出版合作社); 劚匪 (1929, 明日); 火山口 (1930, 樂華); 別扭集 (1947, 開明); 勝利以後 (1947, 黃河出版社); etc.

His critical works are: 新興文藝短論 (明日書店); 明日的文學; etc.

72. Hsü Chih-mo 徐志摩.

(1896 — 1931)

Pen-names: 南湖, 詩哲, etc.

Poet. Born in Haining, Chekiang. He studied at first in Hu Kiang University 滬江大學, and was transferred then to the National University of Peking 北京大學. After his graduation there he went to the United States to study banking in Columbia University, where he received his M.A. degree. He then went to England, where he studied Economics and Political Science in Cambridge University, and received another master's degree. Born a poet, he wrote many poems in his spare time. He was one of the pioneers in modern Chinese poetry. He proved not only that modern poems can be different from the old, but also that they can be great in themselves. He broke completely away from tradition. Upon returning to China in 1922, he was appointed professor at the National University of Peking, National Tsinghua University 清華大學 , and P'ing Min University 平民大學 . In 1924, when the Indian poet R. Tagore came to visit China, he served as interpreter. Later he re-visited Europe. On his return to China, he edited the literary supplement of the newspaper *Ch'ên Pao* 晨報 at Peiping. In 1927, he went to the South, and taught in Kwang Hua University 光華大學, Great China University 大夏大學 at Shanghai, and National Central University 中央大學 at Nanking. In 1928, he organized a literary society "Hsin Yüeh Shê" 新月社 (Crescent), with Hu Shih 胡適 , Liang Shih-ch'iu 梁實秋 , Wên I-to 聞一多 , and Lo Lung-chi 羅隆基 and published the *Hsin Yüeh Yüeh K'an* 新月月刊 (Crescent Monthly) as its organ. He married at first Miss Chang Ling-i 張令儀 , the younger sister of the famous politician Chang Chün-mai 張君勤 , but divorced later on. He then married Lu Hsiao-man 陸小曼 , a painter and writer, who wrote 卞昆崗 ,* a play, (1928, 新月) with her busband.

He was killed, in August of 1931, in an aeroplane crash near Tsinan, Shantung, at the age of 36.

The collections of Hsü Chih-mo's poems are: *Fei Lêng Ts'ui Ti I Yeh* 翡冷翠的一夜 (A Florentine Night, 1927, 新月); *Chih Mo Ti Shih* 志摩的詩 (Poetic Works of Hsü Chih-mo, 1928, 新月); and *Mêng Hu Chi* 猛虎集 (Tiger, 1931, 新月) The collections of his essays are: *Pa Li Ti Lin Chao* 巴黎的鱗爪* (Souvenirs of Paris, 1927, 新月); *Tzü P'ou* 自剖 * (Self-Analysis, 1928, 新月); and *Lo Yeh* 落葉* (Those Fallen Leaves, 北新). He wrote one novel called *Ch'iu* 秋 (Autumn, 1931 商務).

He translated 曼殊斐爾小說集 (Short Stories by K. Mansfield, 1927, 北新); 瑪麗瑪麗 (*Mary Mary* by J. Stephens, 1927, 北新); 贛弟德 (*Candide* by F.M.A. Voltaire, 1927, 北新); 渦堤孩 (*Undine* by F.H.K. de La Motte-Fouqué, 1931, 商務); etc.

His love-letters and diaries were collected by his wife Lu Hsiao-man, and published under the title *Ai Mei Hsiao Cha* 愛眉小札 * (1936, 良友), and *Chih Mo Jih Chi* 志摩日記* (1947, 晨光) respectively.

73. Hsü Ch'in-wên 許欽文 .

(1897 —　　　)

Pen-names: 田耳. 湖山客 , etc. Novelist, and short-story writer. Born of a wealthy family in Shaohsing, Chekiang. After the Chinese Revolution the family became bankrupt, thus he left his native city and worked as clerk and teacher in primary and middle schools in different places. Later, he went to Peiping. Urged by his friend Sun Fu-yuan 孫伏園 , the editor of the literary supplement of *Ch'ên Pao* 晨報 , he wrote a short story *Li Ku Hsiang* 離故鄉 (Leave the Native), which was his first effort, but brought fame to our author after publication. Thus started his literary career. His writings were published mostly in the *Hsiao Shuo Yüen Pao* 小說月報 (The Short Story Magazine), *Yü Ssŭ* 語絲 , and the literary supplement of *Ch'ên Pao*. Gradually he became acquainted with Lu Hsün 魯迅 , the most famous writer of that time. He often submitted his fiction to the latter for criticism. Lu Hsün highly praised them by saying that in describing the youth's psychology, Hsü Ch'in-wên was even better than himself. His early works, such as *Ku Hsiang* 故鄉 (Native Place, 1926, 北新) and *Chao Hsien Shêng Ti Fan Nao* 趙先生底煩惱 * (The Sorrow of Mr. Chao, 1926, 北新) found an eager acceptance among the Chinese youth. But afterwards he did not produce any noticeable works, except some short essays and sketches. Later, he went to Hangchow, where he taught in a middle school until the outbreak of the Sino-Japanese War. He then went to the Interior. He is now professor at the Union University 協和大學 at Foochow, and publishes sometimes his new writings in different literary magazines of Shanghai

Besides the above-mentioned works, he also wrote the following fiction: 回家 * (a novel, 1926, 北新); 鼻涕阿二 * (a novel, 1927, 北新); 兩條裙子 (a novel, 1934, 北新); 西湖之月 (a novel, 北新); 毛線襪 * (collection of short stories, 1927, 北新); 幻象的殘象 * (collection of short stories, 1928, 北新); 沒有共事 (collection of short stories, 1928, 北新); 彷彿如此 * (collection of short stories, 1928, 北新); 蝴蝶* (collection of short stories, 1928, 北新); 一罎酒 * (collection of short stories, 1930, 北新); etc.

His critical works are: 寫給青年創作家 (文藝社); 創作三步法 (1933, 開明); etc.

His autobiography entitled *Ch'in Wên Tzŭ Chuan* 欽文自傳 , was published in 1936, by the 上海時代圖書公司 .

74. Hsü Hsü 徐訏 .

Novelist. He was the co-editor of the humorous magazines *Lun Yü* 論語 (The Analects), and *Jên Chien Shih* 人間世 (This Human World), both founded by Lin Yü-t'ang 林語堂. Later, he edited, at Shanghai, the *Yü Chou Fêng* 宇宙風, another humorous magazine, in collaboration with Lin Han-lu 林憾廬 , the elder brother of Lin Yü-t'ang. After the outbreak of the Sino-Japanese War, he went to Hongkong, where he continued to publish the *Yü Chou Fêng*. After living for a long time at Kweilin, he went to the United States, and returned to China in 1946. His chef-d'oeuvre is *Fêng Hsiao Hsiao* 風蕭蕭 ,* a novel which appeared first in the newspaper *Sao Tang Pao* 掃蕩報 at Chungking. Besides this, he wrote 荒謬的英法海峽 *; 吉布賽的誘惑 *; 海外的情調 *; 一家 *; 精神病患者的哀歌 *; 費宮人 *; 何洛甫之死 *; 生與死 *; 月光曲 *; 母親的肖像 *; 孤島的微笑 *; 春韮錄 *; 鬼戀 *; etc.

75. Hsü Ti-shan 許地山.

(1893 — 1941)

Original name: 許贊堃, T. 地山. Pen-name: 落華生. Short-story writer, and scholar. Born in Lungki, Fukien. After graduating from Yenching University 燕京大學 in 1923, he went to the United States at the same year together with Miss Ping Hsin 冰心, and Liang Shih-ch'iu 梁實秋. After receiving his M.A. degree from Columbia University, he went to England, where he obtained his B.A. degree from Oxford University. Upon returning to China in 1926, he was appointed professor at Yenching University, Tsinghua University 清華大學, and the National University of Peking 北京大學. After the Mukden Incident of September 18, 1931, he went to Hongkong, where he taught in the Hongkong University 香港大學. He died there after an attack of heart disease on August 4, 1941.

Hsü Ti-shan was a pioneer of the new literary movement of China. While a student in university, he engaged in writing short stories and poems, and joined the "Society of Literary Research" 文學研究會. Later he turned to the study of philology and Indian culture.

The collections of his short stories are: 無法投遞之郵件 (1928, 北平文化學社); 解放者 * (1933, 北平星雲堂); 綴網撈珠 (商務); etc.

The collection of his poems is entitled 空山靈雨 .*

In addition to his creative works, he wrote 語體文法大綱 (Outline Grammar of Spoken Language, 1923, 中華); 道教史 (A History of Taoism, 1934, 商務); 印度文學 (Indian Literature); etc. And he translated 孟加拉民間故事 (Folk-Tales of Bengal).

76. Hsü Wei-nan 徐蔚南.

Pen-name: 澤人. Short-story writer, and translator. Born in Wuhsien, Kiangsu. Once he taught Chinese literature in the National Chekiang University 浙江大學. Later, he served as an editor of the World Book Co. 世界書局, Shanghai. He made himself known by his translation of French and Belgian literary works, among which we may mention: 她的一生 (Une Vie by G. de Maupassant, 世界); 女優泰綺思 (Thaïs by A. France, 1929, 世界); 茂娜凡娜 (Monna Vanna by M. Maeterlinck, 1930, 開明); 法國名家小說選 (French Short Stories, 開明).

He wrote the following works: Pên P'o 奔波 (collection of short stories, 北新); Tu Shih Ti Nan Nü 都市的男女; Lung Shan Mêng Hên 龍山夢痕 (Notes of his visit to Shaohsing, written in collaboration with Wang Shih-ying 王世穎, 1927, 開明); I Shu Chê Hsüeh 藝術哲學 (Philosophy of Art, 1929, 世界); Yin Tu T'ung Hua Chi 印度童話集 (Indian Fables, 1932, 世界); Shui Mien T'ao Hua 水面桃花 (1933, 黎明); Shang Hai Mien Pu 上海棉布 (1936, 中華); Ku Hsiu K'ao 顧繡考 (1936, 中華); 乍浦遊簡 * (1937, 開明); etc.

He lives now in Shanghai.

77. Hu Shan-yuan 胡山源.

Playwright. Born in Kiangyin, Kiangsu. In the spring of 1923, he organized a literary society "Muse" 彌灑社 at Shanghai, together with Ch'ên Tê-chêng 陳德徵, Ch'ien Chiang-ch'un 錢江春, Chao Tsu-k'ang 趙祖康, and T'ang Ming-shih 唐鳴時, and published a monthly magazine under the same title. It published six numbers altogether. He was the editor of the following newspapers and magazines: *Ch'ing Nien Chou Pao* 青年週報 (Youth's Weekly, published by the World Book Co. 世界書局); *Tao Pao* 導報; *Hung Ch'a* 紅茶 (Red Tea); *Tzŭ Yu T'an* 自由談 (Free Talk, a literary supplement of the newspaper *Shên Pao* 申報); and *Wen I Shih Chieh* 文藝世界 (Literary World). Once he taught ancient Chinese drama in Chih Kiang University 之江大學.

Works: *Hung* 虹.* (Rainbow, 1940, 中華); *Fêng Ch'ên San Hsia* 風塵三俠 (1927, 商務); *Yu Mo Pi Chi* 幽默筆記 (1935, 世界); *Yu Mo Shih Hua* 幽默詩話; *Kiangyin I Min Pieh Chuan* 江陰義民別傳; *Kiating I Min Pieh Chuan* 嘉定義民別傳; *Yangchow I Min Pieh Chuan* 揚州義民別傳; *Ta Kuei* 打鬼 (世界); etc.

He translated 一個西方人眼中的日本與日本人 (*Japan, an Attempt at Interpretation* by L. Hearn, 1930, 商務); 人人是堯舜 (世界); etc.

78. Hu Shih 胡適.

(1891 —   )

Original name 胡洪騂, T. 適之, or 嗣穈. Pen-names: 天風, 希彊, 期自勝生. 藏暉, 鐵兒, H.S.C., Q.V., etc.

Literary critic, poet, playwright, and translator. Born at Chiki, Anhwei. He is the son of an elderly scholar and a young country-woman, who was left a widow at 23. "My mother's greatest gift", he writes, "was forbearance", and to her, as well as to the memory of his father, he owes much. Herself illiterate, she set him at a very tender age to follow up the lessons which his father had given him. Remaining in the village school for 9 years, he read and memorized the books which had made the core of Chinese education for so many centuries. They are: the *Four Books* 四書, the *Five Classics* 五經, etc. Early in his 13th year, he went to Shanghai for higher education. During his six years' stay in Shanghai, he studied at the Ch'êng Chung Middle School 澄衷中學, and the China Institute of Woosung 吳淞中國公學. Financial difficulty compelled him to support himself by teaching and by editing a revolutionary magazine *Fên Tou* 奮鬥 (Struggle), at Shanghai, which was published in the vernacular. At the age of 18, he obtained one of the Boxer Indemnity Scholarships and sailed for America, where he first studied agriculture at Cornell University. But he soon changed his mind, and was transferred to the College of Arts and Science at the same university, where he devoted himself to English literature, political science, and philosophy. He was elected to the Phi Beta Kappa Society in 1913, and was awarded the Hiram Corson Prize for his essay on Robert Browning in 1914. After his graduation in 1914, he continued his study in philosophy and was given a graduate scholarship at the Sage School of Philosophy in Cornell University.

In 1915, he went to Columbia University, where he spent two years, and wrote his doctoral dissertation on *The Development of Logical Method in Ancient China.* It was during these two years that he gradually developed his ideas of a radical reform in Chinese literature, these ideas were afterwards formulated into an article entitled *Wên Hsüeh Kai Liang Ch'u I* 文學改良芻議 (Suggestions for the Reform of Chinese Literature), which was published in the famous magazine *Hsin Ch'ing Nien* 新青年 (New Youth), vol. 2, no. 5, January, 1917. This article formed the first manifesto of the "Literary Revolution", and its historical place was only superseded by another article of his, entitled *Chien Shê Ti Wên Hsüeh Ko Ming Lun* 建設的文學革命論 (A Constructive Revolution in Chinese Literature), published in *Hsin Ch'ing Nien*, vol. 4, no. 4, April, 1918.

Upon returning to China in 1917, he was appointed a professor of philosophy at the National University of Peking 北京大學, the so called "Cradle of the Chinese Literary Revolution". In 1922, he became the chairman of the Department of English Literature at the same university. And in January, the same year, he organized and edited a weekly in Peiping, entitled *Nu Li* 努力 (Endeavor). He spent 1923 at Hangchow to recuperate his health, and returned to Peiping in 1924, and again taught at the National University of Peking. In 1925, he was invited by the British Government to serve on the Advisory Committee on the British China Indemnity; he went to England in 1926, and revisited America in 1927. From 1927 to 1930, he was a resident in Shanghai, where he served for two years as the President of the China Institute of Woosung, 1928-30. During these years, he published a series of articles criticizing the defects of the Nationalist Government; these articles brought him much criticism from Kuomintang quarters. They were collected later in a volume under the title *Jên Ch'üan Lun Chi* 人權論集 (Essays on Human Rights, 新月). He returned to Peiping in 1931, and was appointed the dean of the College of Arts and Letters of the National University of Peking. From the September of 1938 on, he served as the Chinese Ambassador to U.S.A. He returned to China in 1946, and functions now as the Chancellor of the National University of Peking.

Hu Shih was the first Chinese poet to devote himself to writing poetry exclusively in the spoken language. He has published over a hundred poems in the vernacular language, which he collected into one volume entitled *Ch'ang Shih Chi* 嘗試集 (Experimental Poems, 1920, 亞東).

In addition to the works mentioned above, he also wrote: *Chung Kuo Chê Hsüeh Shih Ta Kang* 中國哲學史大綱 (Outline History of Chinese Philosophy, Vol. 1, 1919, 商務); *Pai Hua Wên Hsüeh Shih* 白話文學史 (History of Vernacular Literature, Vol. 1, 1928, 新月); *San Shih Nien Lai Shih Chieh Chê Hsüeh Shih* 三十年來世界哲學史 (World Philosophy in Recent Thirty Years, 1925, Shanghai, 世界圖書館); *Tai Tung Yuan Ti Chê Hsüeh* 戴東原的哲學 (The Philosophy of Tai Chên 戴震, 1927, 商務); *Hu Shih Wên Ts'un* 胡適文存 (Collected Essays, in three series, 12 volumes in toto, first series, 1920; second series, 1924; and third series, 1930; all published by 亞東); *Tz'ŭ Hsüan* 詞選 (Selection of Tz'ŭ, 1932, 商務); *Hu Shih Lun Hsüeh Chin Chu* 胡適論學近著 (Recent Essays on Learned Subjects, 1935, 商務); *Ssŭ Shih Tzŭ Shu* 四十自述 (Forty Years: An Autobiography, 亞東); *Chang Shih Chai Hsien Shêng Nien P'u* 章實齋先生年譜 (Bio-

graphy of Chang Hsüeh-ch'êng 章學誠, 1922 商務); *Ts'ang Hui Shih Cha Chi*
藏暉室劄記 (Diaries and Sketches, 4 volumes, 1939, 亞東); *Chinas' Own Critics*
(in English, written in collaboration with Lin Yü-t'ang 林語堂, 1931, Peiping,
China United Press,); *The Chinese Renaissance* (in English, 1934, Chicago, The
University of Chicago Press); etc.

79. Hu Yeh-p'in 胡也頻.

(1904 — 1931)

Original name: 胡崇軒, but he is known by his courtesy name 也頻 instead
of the original. Pen-names: 沉默, 何一平, 紅笑, etc.

Short-story writer and playwright. Born in Minhow, Fukien. He was the
husband of the most famous left authoress Ting Ling 丁玲. He attended at first
the Preparatory Naval School 海軍預備學校 in Yentai 烟台 (Cheefoo), Shantung.
In 1920, with the suspension of that school, he went to Peiping. About in 1926,
he edited the *Min Chung Wên I* 民衆文藝 (Mass Literature), a weekly supplement
of the newspaper *Ching Pao* 京報; and thus became acquainted with one of its
contributors Shên Ts'ung-wên 沈從文. They became intimate friends, and later
on founded many enterprizes together.

His early works were published mostly in the magazine *Yü Ssŭ* 語絲, and
the literary supplement of *Ching Pao* and *Ch'ên Pao* 晨報. Later, he went to
Shanghai, where, in collaboration with Shên Ts'ung-wên and Ting Ling, he edited
the *Hung Yü Hei* 紅與黑 (The Red and the Black), a literary supplement of the
newspaper *Chung Yang Jih Pao* 中央日報, and published two magazines, the
Jên Chien Yüeh K'an 人間月刊 and *Hung Hei Yüeh K'an* 紅黑月刊, both of
which had but a short life. He then went to Shantung to teach in the Shantung
Provincial Senior School 山東省立高級中學, but three months later he returned
to Shanghai, and participated in the socialist revolution. In January, 1931, he
was arrested, together with some other left writers, and was put to death on
February 7, the same year.

After his death, Shên Ts'ung-wên, his intimate friend, wrote a biography
of him, entitled *Chi Hu Yeh-p'in* 記胡也頻 (About Hu Yeh-p'in, 1933, 光華).

Works: 聖徒* (collection of short stories 1927, 新月); 詩稿 (1928, 現代);
往何處去 (collection of short stories, 1928, 第一線書店); 鬼與人心 (collection of four
plays, 1928, 開明); 別人的幸福 (collection of five plays, 1929, 華通); 到莫斯科去
(a novel, 1929, 光華); 三個不統一的人物 (collection of short stories, 1929, 現代); 一
個寫實的悲劇 (1930, 中華); 四星期 (collection of short stories, 1931, 華通); 活珠
子 (collection of short stories); 光明在我們前面 (a novel); 也頻小說集 (1936, 大光);
etc.

80. Hu Yun-i 胡雲翼.

Pen-names: 北海, 胡南翔, 拜蘋女士, etc.

Short-story writer and literary historian. Born in Hunan. In the spring of 1925, collaborating with Liu Ta-chieh 劉大杰. he founded a literary society "I Lin Shê" 藝林社 in Wuchang, and published a magazine *I Lin* 藝林, which suspended publication in the winter of the same year. For many years he was a teacher of Chinese in various middle schools in Hunan. During the Sino-Japanese War, he joined the army in Fukien.

The collections of his short stories are: 西冷橋畔* (北新); 愛與愁 (亞細亞); 中秋月 (1928, 中華); etc.

His works on the history of Chinese literature are: 唐代的戰爭與文學 (1927, 商務); 宋詞研究 (1929, 中華); 詞學 (1930, 世界); 中國文學史 (1933, 北新); 中國詞史大綱 (1933, 北新); 詞選 ABC (1934, 北新); 唐詩研究 (1934, 商務); 宋詩研究 (1934, 商務); etc.

81. Huang Chung-su 黃仲蘇.

Short-story writer, and literary critic. Born in Shucheng, Anhwei. He received his B.A. degree from University of Illinois in the United States, and M.A. degree from the Université de Paris. Upon returning to China, he was appointed professor of Western literature at the National Normal University at Wuchang 武昌師範大學, and the National Southeast University 東南大學. After serving for some time as the secretary of the Shanghai Municipal Government, and of the Ministry of Foreign Affairs, he became the Chinese Consul to Melbourne in 1931.

Being a member of the "Young China Association" 少年中國學會, he published his works in the Association's organ *Shao Nien Chung Kuo* 少年中國 (The Journal of the Young China Association). His works were also published in the *Ch'uang Tsao Chou Pao* 創造週報 (Creation Weekly), and *Tung Fang Tsa Chih* 東方雜誌 (Oriental Magazine).

He wrote the following collections of short stories: *Ch'ou Ch'ang* 惆悵 (Sorrow, 1929, 中華); *Yin Yüeh Chih Lei* 音樂之淚* (1934, 商務); *T'an Hsin* 譚心 (光華); *Ch'ên Chi* 陳迹* (1940, 中華); etc.

His critical works are: *Lang Sung Fa* 朗誦法 (How to Read Aloud. It studies rhythm in old Chinese literature: the peculiarities of the language, the formation of the rhythmic "tune", punctuation, types of rhythm. 1936, 開明); *Chin Tai Fa Lan Hsi Wên Hsüeh Ta Kang* 近代法蘭西文學大綱 (Outline of Modern French Literature, 1932, 中華); etc.

82. Huang Lu-yin 黃廬隱.

(1898 — 1934)

Original name: 黃英. Novelist, and short-story writer. Born in Minhou, Fukien. Her father died in Hunan when she was 8. The family then moved to Peiping; where she attended the Mu Chên Institute 慕貞學院. Later she completed her education in the Department of Chinese Literature of the National

Normal University for Women 女子師範大學 . She then taught Chinese in various middle schools. Born with a revolutionary spirit, she opposed strongly throughout her life the fetters of old Chinese tradition. She broke the engagement with her fiancé Lin and married Kuo Mêng-liang 郭夢良 , a socialist who had already married. Two years later, Kuo died. She then married, in 1930, Li Wei-chien 李唯建 a young student of the National Tsinghua University 清華大學 , who won fame as a poet. After four happy years she died on May 6, 1934, of childbirth.

Huang Lu-yin was a member of the "Society of Literary Research" 文學研究會 . Her works were published mostly in one of the Association's publications, *Hsiao Shuo Yüeh Pao* 小說月報 (The Short Story Magazine). Her first effort *Hai Pin Ku Jên* 海濱故人 published in 1925 by the Commercial Press, was the autobiography of her early life. Thenceforth she wrote 曼麗 * (collection of short stories, 1927, 北平文化學社); 歸雁 (collection of short stories, 1930, 神州國光社); 靈海潮汐 * (a novel, 1931, 開明); 玫瑰的刺 * (collection of short stories, 1933, 中華); 女人的心 (1933, 上海四社出版部); 象牙戒指 * (a novel, 1934, 商務); 或人的悲哀 ; etc.

The collection of her essays was published posthumously in 1936 by Pei Hsin Book Co. 北新書局 under the title 東京小品 . Her love-letters, written in collaboration with Li Wei-chien, were collected into 雲鷗情書集 * (1931, 神州國光社)

She wrote an autobiography, entitled 廬隱自傳 * (1934, 第一出版社).

83. Huang Su-ju 黃素如 .

Pen-names: 白薇, 白薇女士, 紫紅, 楚洪 , Zero, etc.

Playwright, and novelist. Born in Hunan. Wife of Yang Sao 楊騷 , a well-known writer also. While studying her biological course in the Girls' Higher Normal School of Tokyo, Japan, she met T'ien Han 田漢 , a pioneer of the new dramatic movement, who opened the literary world to her with the plays of Ibsen. After reading the works of Shakespeare, Maeterlinck, Strindberg, and Hauptmann, she tried to write herself. Her first effort was *Su Wên* 蘇斐 , a play in three acts, which was performed by herself in Japan.

Upon returning to China in 1926, she settled in Canton, and devoted herself completely to writing. In the same year, she published *Lin Li* 琳麗, (商務), a three-act play. Her later works were published mostly in the magazines *Yü Ssŭ* 語絲, *Hsiao Shuo Yüeh Pao* 小說月報 , and *Pên Liu* 奔流 . During the Sino-Japanese War, she worked in the Third Department of the Ministry of Political Training.

Besides the works mentioned above, she also wrote: *Cha Tan Yü Chêng Niao* 炸彈與征鳥 (a novel, 1930, 北新); *Tso Yeh* 昨夜 (Last Night, written in collaboration with her husband Yang Sao, 1934, 南強); *Ta Ch'u Yu Ling T'a* 打出幽靈塔 * (collection of plays, 湖風); *Ai Wang* 愛網 (a novel); *Pei Chü Shêng Ya* 悲劇生涯 (a Tragic Life, an autobiography written in the form of a story, 1936, 生活); etc.

84. Huang Tso-lin 黃佐臨.

Playwright. He is now the chairman of the Department of Modern Drama in the Experimental Dramatic School of Shanghai. He wrote the following plays: *Ch'u Nü Ti Hsin* 處女的心 (Virgin's Heart); *Liang Shang Ch'ün Tzu* 樑上君子 (A Thief, 世界); *Huang Tao Ying Hsiung* 荒島英雄* (A Hero in a Deserted Island, 世界); etc.

85. Hung Ling-fei 洪靈菲.

Pen-names: 李鐵郎. 韓仲鵠, etc.

Novelist and short-story writer. Born in Kwangtung. He contributed first to the left magazine *T'ai Yang Yüeh K'an* 太陽月刊, edited by Ch'ien Hsing-ts'un 錢杏邨 and Chiang Kuang-tz'ǔ 蔣光慈. In 1930, he joined the "China League of Left writers" in which he held an important position. Later, he founded the "Hsiao Shan Book Store" 曉山書店, and published a monthly magazine *Wuo Mên Yüh K'an* 我們月刊, which was shortly ordered by the authorities to cease publication.

He is the author of the novels: 流亡* (1928, 現代); and 轉變 (1928, 亞東); collections of short stories: 歸家 (1929, 現代); and 氣力出賣者. He translated 地下室手記 (*Letters from the Underworld* by F. Dostoevsky, 1931, 湖風); and 賭徒 (*The Gambler* by F. Dostoevsky, 1933, 湖風).

86. Hung Mo 洪謨.

Playwright. He is a member of the "Shanghai Dramatic Arts Troupe" 上海劇藝社. He wrote the following plays: *Ho Ti Kuang Lin* 闔第光臨 (世界); *Ch'ün Tai Fêng* 裙帶風 (written in collaboration with P'an Chieh-nung 潘孑農 1947, 作家書室); etc.

87. Hung Shên 洪深.

(1893 —   )

T. 伯駿, 淺哉. Playwright. Born in Wuchin 武進, Kiangsu. He was one of the pioneers of the new dramatic movement of China. Many well-known contemporary dramatists, like Ma Yen-hsiang 馬彥祥. Fêng Tzǔ 鳳子. are his students.

After graduating from the National Tsinghua University 清華大學, he went to the United States to study dramatic arts, and received his M.A. degree from the Harvard University. Upon returning to China, he held the following positions: professor of dramatic arts in Great China University 大夏大學 Shanghai; chairman of the Department of Foreign Languages and Literature of Chinan University 暨南大學, professor of English literature and dramatic arts in Fuhtan University 復旦大學, and professor at Tsingtao University 青島大學 of Shantung.

For many years he worked for the promotion of new drama. He organized at first the "Dramatic Association" 戲劇協社 with Ying Yun-wei 應雲衞, and led the "Dramatic Club of Fuhtan University" 復旦劇社 to stage in many places. Owing to his leftist leaning in thought, he was arrested for several times by the authorities. Thenceforth he stopped his dramatic activity, and worked in the Star Motion Picture Co. 明星影片公司 at Shanghai. He visited Hollywood, and on his return, produced the first sound film in China.

During the early years of the Sino-Japanese War, he led a dramatic troupe to give performances of propagandist plays in different villages in the Interior. When the Third Department of the Ministry of Political Training was established, he was appointed the director of the dramatic branch. Later he became a member of the Committee for the Promotion of Cultural Activities, and organized the Instructive Dramatic Corps" 教導劇團 for the Ministry of Political Training. Although busy with the dramatic activities throughout the War years, he never left his academic career. He taught at first in the Sun Yat-sen University 中山大學, then in the Kiangsu College of Dramatic Arts 江蘇劇專, Social Education Institute of Pishan 璧山社教學院, and Fuhtan University in Peipei 北碚 near Chungking. After the Victory over Japan, he returned to Shanghai, where he functions as professor at the Fuhtan University, and chairman of the Department of Motion Picture of the Experimental Dramatic School 上海市立實驗戲劇學校.

His dramatic works written before the War are 洪深戲劇集* (1932, 現代); 王奎橋 * (1933, 現代); and some short plays collected in the *Series of the Dramatic Association* 戲劇協社叢刊. During the War, he wrote 女人女人 *; 鷄鳴早看天; 飛將軍; 米; 鶴頂紅; 包得行 (1940, 上海雜誌公司); 黃白丹青; etc.

His critical works on drama and motion picture are 洪深戲劇論文集 (1934, 天馬); 電影術語辭典 (1935, 天馬); 電影戲劇表演術 (1935, 生活); 電影戲劇的編劇方法 (1935, 正中); 戲劇的念辭與朗誦; 導演的基本技術 ; etc. The last two works are composed in the War time.

88. Hung Wei-fa 洪爲法.

(1900 —)

Short-story writer, essayist, and literary critic. Born in Yangchow, Kiangsu. After graduating from the Department of Chinese Literature of the National Normal University of Wuchang 武昌師範大學, he taught Chinese in various middle schools and normal schools at different places In September, 1925, he edited the magazine *Hung Shui* 洪水 (Flood), published fortnightly by the "Creative Society 創造社, together with Chou Ch'üan-p'ing 周全平, and others.

Works: *Chüeh Chü Lun* 絕句論 (On the Four-Line Poems, 1934, 商務); *Lü Shih Lun* 律詩論 (On the Lü, or Eight-Line Poems, 1936, 商務); *Kuo Wên*

Hsüeh Hsi Fa 國文學習法 (How to Study Chinese 1933, 亞細亞); *Chuan Chi Wên Hsüan* 傳記文選 (Selection of Biographical Literature, 1935, 北新); *Wei Fa Hsiao P'in Chi* 爲法小品集* (collection of essays, 1936, 北新); *Lien Tzŭ Chi* 蓮子集 (Lotus, collection of poems, 北新); *Tai E* 獃鵝 (Stupid Goose, collection of short stries, 文華); *Ch'ang Kuei* 長跪 (光華); *Wên Jên Ku Shih Hsüan* 文人故事選 (Selected Stories of Writers); *Chung Kuo Wên Jên Ku Shih Chiang Hua* 中國文人故事講話 (Tales of Chinese Writers); etc.

89. Kêng Yü-hsi 耿郁溪.

T. 曉隄, pen-name: 耿小的. Novelist. He graduated from the National Normal University of Peiping 北平師範大學. His novels appeared mostly in the newspapers *Hsiao Shih Pao* 實報, *Hsin Pei Ching Pao* 新北京報, and *Hsin Min Pao* 新民報 of Peiping, under the Japanese occupation.

90. Ko Ch'in 葛 琴.

Pen-name: 柯琴. Novelist, and short-story writer. Wife of Ching Ch'üan-lin 荊荃麟, another novelist who wrote *Su Tien* 宿店.

During the Sino-Japanese War, she was in Kweilin, and published her works in the magazine *Wên I Shêng Huo* 文藝生活 (Literary Life), edited by Ssŭ-Ma Wên-sên 司馬文森.

Works: *I Ko Pei P'o Hai Ti Nü Jên* 一個被迫害的女人 (1946, 中華); *Fan* 犯 (a novel, 1947, 耕耘出版社); *Ko Ch'in Ch'uang Tso Chi* 葛琴創作集 (collection of short stories); etc.

91. Ku Chung-i 顧仲彝.

(1904 ——   )

Courtesy name of 顧德隆; but he is known for this name instead of his original. Pen-name: 焚玉.

Playwright. Born in Chiahsing, Chekiang. He finished his literary course in the National Southeast University 國立東南大學. In 1924, he joined the famous "Society of Literary Research" 文學研究會. He was once an editor of the Commercial Press. Later, he became professor at the Chinan University 暨南大學, Fuhtan University 復旦大學, and Franco-Chinese Academy of Dramatic Arts 中法劇藝學校. In September, 1929, corporating with Ou-Yang Yü-Ch'ien 歐陽予倩 the veteran dramatist, he edited the dramatic monthly *Hsi Chü Tsa Chih* 戲劇雜誌, which held an important position in the Chinese new dramatic movement.

Not long ago he was the president of the Experimental Dramatic School at Shanghai 上海市立實驗戲劇學校 . In February, 1947, he resigned on account of his bad health, and was succeeded by Hsiung Fo-hsi 熊佛西 , a well-known dramatist.

Works: 同胞姊妹* (1928, 新月); 劉三爺 (1931, 開明); 劇場 (1937, 商務); 重見光明* (1944, 世界); 八仙外傳* (1945, 世界); 嫦娥* (1945, 永祥); 文學概論 (1947, 永祥); 三千金*; 新婦*; 野火花*; 上海男女*; 黃金迷*; 人之初*; 大地之愛; 衣冠禽獸*; etc.

Translations: 相鼠有皮 (*The Skin Game* by J. Galsworthy, 1927, 商務); 美利堅小說史 (by J. Finnemore, 1927, 商梅); 梅蘿香* (*Just a Woman* by E. Walter, 1927, 開明); 威尼斯商人 (*The Merchant of Venice* by W. Shakespeare, 1930, 新月); 哈代短篇小說選 (Short Stories of Thomas Hardy, 1930, 開明); 富於想像 的婦人 (*Imaginative Woman* by T. Hardy, 1933, 黎明); 殉情* (*Kabale und Liebe* by J.C.F. von Schiller, 1940, 光明); 水仙花* (an adaptation of *Jane Eyre* by C. Bronte, 1943, 光明); etc.

92. Ku Chün-chêng 顧均正 .

Essayist, and translator. He became known by his scientific essays written in popular form. He is now the editor of the magazines *Chung Hsüeh Shêng* 中學生 (Juvenile Student), and *Ying Wên Yüeh K'an* 英文月刊 (English Monthly), both published by the Kaiming Book Co. 開明書店 .

Works: *K'o Hsüeh Ch'ü Wei* 科學趣味 (開明); *K'o Hsüeh Ti Ching I* 科學的驚異 (開明); *Tien Tzǔ Ku Niang* 電子姑娘 (開明); *Tsai Pei Chi Ti Tsia* 在北極底下 ;* etc.

Translations: 風先生和雨太太 (*Le Monsieur Vent et la Madame Pluie* by P. Musset, 1927, 開明); 寶島 (*Treasure Island* by R.L. Stevenson, 1930, 開明); 化學奇談 (*The Wonder Book of Chemistry* by J.H. Fabre, 1932, 開明); 水蓮花 (by H.C. Anderson, 1932, 開明); 魯濱孫飄流記 (*Robinson Crusoe* by D. Defoe, 開明); 烏拉波拉故事集 (開明); 任何人之科學 (開明); etc.

93. Ku Ming-tao 顧明道 .

Novelist. Born in Wuhsien, Kiangsu. He died at the age of about fifty. He spent the greater part of his life in Shanghai, where he published most of his novels in the newspaper *Hsin Wên Pao* 新聞報 .

94. K'ung Ling-ching 孔另境 .

(1904 —   )

Pen-name: 東方曦 . Essayist. Born in Tunghsiang, Chekiang. Brother-in-law of Mao Tun 茅盾, the novelist. He graduated, in 1927, from Shanghai University 上海大學. After the outbreak of the Sino-Japanese War, he stayed in the International Settlement in Shanghai, and founded a dramatic school, in which he trained a number of distinguished actors. He also edited a series of plays for the World Book Co. 世界書局, called *Chü Pên Ts'ung K'an* 劇本叢刊. He is the editor of the magazine *Hsin Wên Hsüeh* 新文學 (New Literature) from 1946 on.

Works: *Chung Kuo Hsiao Shuo Shih Liao* 中國小說史料 (Collected Notes on Chinese Novels, 1936, 中華); *Yung Yuan Chi* 庸園集 (1946, 永祥印書舘); *Ch'ing Nien Hsieh Tso Chiang Hua* 青年寫作講話 (1946, 永祥印書館); *Ch'iu Ch'uang Chi* 秋窗集 ;* *Li T'ai-pai* 李太白 * (a play, 世界); *Ch'ên Hsiang Chi* 沉箱記 * (a play, 世界); *Ch'un Ch'iu Yuan* 春秋怨 * (a play, 世界); *Fêng Huan Ch'ao* 鳳還巢 * (a play, 世界); *Ku Huo* 蠱惑 * (a play, 世界); etc.

He compiled *Hsien Tai Tso Chia Shu Chien* 現代作家書簡 (Selected Letters of Contemporary Writers, 1936, 生活).

95.　Kuo An-jên　郭安仁.

Pen-name: 麗尼. Essayist, and translator. Before the Sino-Japanese War, he established the "Cultural Life Publishing Co." 文化生活出版社, at Shanghai, together with Pa Chin 巴金, Chin I 靳以, and others. During the War, he lived in Szechwan, where he worked in the Board of Military Training. After the Victory over Japan he returned to Nanking, and served as a secretary in the Ministry of National Defence.

Works: *Huang Hun Chih Hsien* 黃昏之獻 (collection of essays, 1935, 文化生活出版社); *Chiang Chih Ko* 江之歌 (collection of short stories, 1935, 天馬); *Ying Chih Ko* 鷹之歌 (The Eagle's Song, collection of essays, 1936, 文化生活出版社); *Pai Yeh* 白夜 * (collection of essays, 1937, 文化生活出版社; *Yin Ying* 陰影 (新時代); etc.

Translations: 貴族之家 (*A House of Gentlefolk* by I.S. Turgenev, 1937, 文化生活出版社); 前夜 (*On the Eve* by I.S. Turgenev, 1939, 文化生活出版社); 田園交響樂 (*La Symphonie Pastorale* by A. Gide 1935, 文化生活出版社); 海鷗 (*The Sea-Mew* by A. Chekhov, 1946, 文化生活出版社); 伊凡諾夫 (*Ivanov* by A. Chekhov, 1946, 文化生活出版社); 萬尼亞舅舅 (*Uncle Vania* by A. Chekhov, 1946, 文化生活出版社); 俄國文學史 (*Russian Literature: Ideals and Realities* by P. Kropotkin, 重慶); 天藍的生活; 蘇瓦洛夫元帥 ; etc.

96.　Kuo Mo-jo　郭沫若.

(1892 ―　　)

Original name: 郭開貞, H. 鼎堂. Pen-names: 坎人, 易坎人, 麥克昂, 愛牟, 石沱, 杜衍, 杜術, 杜荷, 谷人, 佐藤貞吉, 滕子丈夫, etc.

Novelist, short-story writer, playwright, poet, literary critic, and scholar. Born in Loshan, Szechwan. After being educated in a provincial middle school in Chengtu, he studied medicine in Japan, and graduated from Kyushu Imperial University. While studying in Japan, he wrote many poems which he collected in one volume, entitled *Nü Shên* 女神 (Goddess), published in 1921 by the T'ai Tung Book Co. 泰東書局. Upon returning to China in 1921, he became an editor of T'ai Tung. In 1922, together with his friends Yü Ta-fu 郁達夫, Chang Tzŭ-p'ing 張資平, and Ch'êng Fang-wu 成仿吾, he organized the "Creative Society" 創造社 in Shanghai, which turned out to be one of the most influential literary associations in the history of modern Chinese literature. They published the *Ch'uang Tsao Chi K'an* 創造季刊 (Creation Quarterly) on May 1, 1922, the *Ch'uang Tsao Chou Pao* 創造週報 (Creation Weekly) on May 13, 1923, and the *Ch'uang Tsao Jih* 創造日 (Creation Daily) on July 21, the same year. In 1924, in consequence of financial difficulties and a quarrel with the publisher, all of the three magazine suspended publication. Kuo Mo-jo then went to Canton, in 1925, where he was appointed the dean of the College of Arts and Letters of the Sun Yat-sen University 中山大學. During the Northern Expedition in 1926, he served as the vice-director of the Political Training Department of the Revolutionary Army Headquarters. When the split of the Kuomintang and the Communists came, in 1927, he returned to Shanghai, where he devoted himself to the promotion of proletarian literature. When the situation became intolerable for left wingers, he escaped to Japan, and devoted himself to the study of ancient Chinese history. He stayed there until the outbreak of the Sino-Japanese War. He then returned to China and served as the head of the Third Department of the Ministry of Political Training, later, chairman of the Committee for the Promotion of Cultural Activities. On November 16, 1941, on the occasion of his 50th birthday, a large meeting was held in Chungking to pay tribute to him, under the auspices of the "National Writers' Anti-Aggression Association" 中華全國文藝界抗敵協會. He visited U.S.S.R. in 1945, and attended the Political Consultative Conference as non-party delegate in January, 1946. He is now in Hongkong, and publishes often his new writings in various magazines.

Kuo Mo-jo is a prolific writer. He wrote novels, short stories, plays, poems, essays, critical works, and books on archaeology, social problems, and political science.

Works: 落葉 * (a novel, 1928, 創造社出版部); 塔 * (collection of short stories, 光華); 橄欖 (collection of short stories, 1926, 現代); 女神及叛逆的女性 (collection of plays, 光華); 沫若詩集 * (collection of poems, 現代); 文藝論集 (collection of critical essays, 1925, 光華); 水平線下 * (collection of essays, 現代); 歸去來*; 蘇聯紀遊*; etc.

Translations: 少年維特之煩惱 (*Die Lieden des Jungen Werther* by J.W. von Goethe, 1928, 創造社出版部); 屠場 (*The Jungle* by U. *Sinclair*, 1929, 南強); 煤油 (*Oil* by U. Sinclair, 1930, 光華); 石炭王 (*King Coal* by U. Sinclair, 1930, 樂群); 茵夢湖 (*Immensee* by T. Storm, 1930, 光華); 新時代 (*The Virgin Soil* by I.S. Turgenev, 商務); 戰爭與和平 (*War and Peace* by L. Tolstoy, 新文藝); 法網

(*Justice* by J. Galsworthy, 1927, 創造社); 銀匣 (*The Silver Box* by J. Galsworthy, 1929, 現代); 浮士德 (*Faust* by J.W. von Goethe, 1932, 現代); 約翰沁孤戲曲集 (*Plays of J. Synge*, 商務); 沫若譯詩集 (創造社出版部); 魯拜集; (*Rubaiyat* of Omar Khayyam by Fitzgerald, 1928, 泰東); 德國詩選 (*German Poems*, 1928, 創造社出版部); 雪萊詩選 (*Selected Poems of P.B. Shelley*, 泰東); 新俄詩選; etc.

After the Victory over Japan, he brought his works together into *Kuo Mo-jo Wên Chi* 郭沫若文集 (Collected Works of Kuo Mo-jo), published by the Ch'ün I Publishing Co. 群益出版社 of Shanghai. The first series contains ten volumes: (1) 十批判書 (2) 青銅時代, (3) 屈原研究, (4) 棠棣之花 *, (5) 屈原 ,* (6) 虎符 (7) 筑 ,* (8) 南冠草,* (9) 孔雀胆,* (10) 波. The second series is in print now.

Autobiographical works: 我的幼年 * (1931, 光華); 黑貓 * (1932, 現代); 創造十年 * (1932, 現代); 反正前後 * (1932, 現代); 北伐途次 (1936, 文化生活出版社); 創造十年續編 (1946, 北新); etc.

The essays written about him were gathered in 郭沫若論 (edited by Huang Jên-ying 黃人影, 1934, 光華), and 郭沫若評傳 (edited by Li Lin 李霖, 1932, 現代).

97. Li Chieh-jên 李 劼人.

Novelist, and translator. Born in Szechwan. He was a member of the "Young China Association" 少年中國學會. During the War, he lived in Chengtu, where he was in charge of the Chengtu Branch of the "National Writers' Anti-Aggression Association" 中華全國文藝界抗敵協會.

Works: *Pao Fêng Yü Ch'ien* 暴風雨前 * (1940, 中華); *Ssŭ Shui Wei Lan* 死水微瀾 (a novel, 1936, 中華); *T'ung Ch'ing* 同情 (Sympathy, a novel, 中華); etc. Translations: 薩郎波 (*Salammbo* by G. Flaubert, 1931, 商務); 婦人書簡 (*Lettres de Femmes* by M. Prévost, 1924, 中華); 小物件 (*Le Petit Chose* by A. Daudet; 1922, 中華); 達哈士孔的拂拂 (*Tartarin de Tarascon* by A. Daudet, 1924, 中華); 馬丹波娃利 (*Madame Bovary* by G. Flaubert, 1925, 中華); 人心 (*Notre Coeur*, by G. de Maupassant, 1935, 中華); 女郎愛里沙 (*La Fille Eliza*, by E. de Goncourt, 1934, 中華); 文明人 (*Les Civilisés* by C. Farrèr, 1934, 中華); 靭都亞納 (*Batouala* by R. Maran, 1928, 北新); etc.

98. Li Chien-wu 李健吾.

  (1906 —)

Pen-name: 劉西渭.

Playwright, short-story writer, and literary critic. Born in Anyi, Shansi. After graduating from the Department of Western Languages and Literature of National Tsinghua University 清華大學, he became an assistant in his alma mater. A few years later, he went to Paris to continue his study. Upon returning to China he was appointed professor at the National Chinan University 暨南大學

and Franco-Chinese Academy of Dramatic Arts 中法劇藝學校 , in Shanghai. During the Sino-Japanese War he stayed in Shanghai, and devoted himself to writing plays and translating the novels of Flaubert. He was once arrested by the Japanese gendarmes. After the Victory over Japan, he functions as professor at the Experimental Dramatic School of Shanghai, 上海市立實驗戲劇學校 and edits the literary monthly *Wên I Fu Hsing* 文藝復興 with Chêng Chên-to 鄭振鐸 .

His dramatic works published by the Wên Hua Shêng Huo Shê 文化生活社 of Shanghai are: (1) 這不過是春天 ,* (2) 以身作則 ,* (3) 母親的夢 ,* (4) 新學究. (5) 黃花 ,* (6) 秋 ,* (7) 撒謊世家 , and single book was published by the Life Book Co 生活書店 , entitled 梁允達 * (1934).

The collections of his short stories are: 西山之雲 * (1928, 北新); 罐子* (1931, 開明); 心病 (1933, 開明); 使命 ; etc.

The collection of his essays is called 希伯先生 .*

His critical works are: 福樓拜評傳 (1935, 商務); 咀華集 (1936, 文化生活出版社); 咀華二集 (1941, 文化生活出版社); etc.

Translations: 委曲求全 (*She Stoops to Compromise* by Wang Wên-hsien, 1932, 北平人文); 福樓拜短篇小說集 (*Trois Contes* by G. Flaubert, 1936, 商務); 聖安東的誘惑 (*Le Tentation de Saint Antoine* by G. Flaubert, 1937, 生活); 艷陽天 (an adaptation of *Mariage de Figaro* by Beaumarchais); 愛與死的搏鬥 (*Le Jeu de l'Amour et de la Mort* by Romain Rolland, 1939, 文化生活出版社); 花信風* (*Fernande* by V. Sardou, 1944, 世界); 風流債 * (*Séraphine* by V. Sardou, 世界); 喜相逢 * (*Fédora* by V. Sardou, 1944, 世界); etc.

99. Li Chin-ming 黎錦明 ·

·(1906 —   )

Pen-name: 黎君亮 ·

Short-story writer, novelist, and literary critic. Born in Siangtan, Hunan. He was the younger brother of Li Chin-hsi 黎錦熙 , a well-known philologist. While studying in middle school he was noted for painting and wished himself to be a painter. He attended, in consequence, a school of fine arts in Peiping to study the arts of design. Two years later, when he found that there was no development for him in this subject, he was transferred to a university, where he began to love Western literature, and try to write short stories. His first success was *Ssŭ Chi* 四季 (Four Seasons), a short story appeared in the famous literary magazine *Hsiao Shuo Yüeh Pao* 小說月報 (The Short Story Magazine) in 1925. From then on he contributed to various magazines such as *Yü Ssŭ* 語絲 , *Tung Fang Tsa Chih* 東方雜誌 (The Oriental Magazine), *Wên Hsüeh Chou Pao* 文學週報 (Literary Weekly), *Hung Shui* 洪水 (Flood). Later, he joined the "Creative Society" 創造社 . He lectured once on literary criticism and contemporary literature in Hopei University 河北大學 ·

The collections of his short stories are: 烈火 (1926, 開明); 塵影 (1927, 開明); 破壘集 (1927, 開明); 馬大少爺的奇蹟 (1928, 現代); 瓊昭 (1929, 北新); 戰烟 (1933, 天馬); 失去的風情 (1933, 現代); 獻身者 (1933, 北平星雲堂); 夜遊人 (1936, 北新); 大街的角落 * (1936, 北新); 霾 (良友); etc.

His novels are: 一個自殺者 (光華); 蹈海 (亞細亞); etc.

He wrote two volumes of critical works: 新文藝批評談話 (1933, 人文); and 文藝批評淺說 (1934, 北新).

100. Li Fei-kan 李芾甘.

(1905 —   )

He is better known under the pen-name of Pa Chin 巴金. His other pen-names are: 王文慧, 巴比, 余一, 余三, 余五, 余七, 歐陽鏡蓉, etc.

Novelist, short-story writer, essayist, and publisher. He was born in a large family at Chengtu, Szechwan. He lost his mother at the age of 10, and his father died when he was 13. Sorrow has then cut deeply into his young heart. He left Chengtu at 19, and arrived Nanking, where he entered the Middle School affiliated with the Southeast University 東南附中. Three years later, in 1926, he went to Paris to study biology. But he soon changed his mind, and began his literary studies. It was one year after his arrival at Paris that he started to write a novel entitled *Mieh Wang* 滅亡* (Destruction, 1929, 開明) which was published in the famous *Hsiao Shuo Yüeh Pao* 小說月報 (The Short Story Magazine), 1929, and won immediately great fame. Upon returning to China in 1929, he devoted himself to writing and translation in Shanghai. In 1932, he travelled in North China, and later in Japan. In the spring of 1934, he became a co-editor of the most distinguished literary magazine *Wên Hsüeh Chi K'an* 文季月刊 (Literary Quarterly) at Peiping. After a quarrel with Li Ch'ang-chih 李長之, one of the editors, Pa Chin left Peiping in the winter of 1935, and arrived Shanghai, where he founded the Cultural Life Publishing Co. 文化生活出版社, and published a literary monthly *Wên Chi Yüeh K'an* 文季月刊 in collaboration with Chin I 靳以, the novelist. During the Sino-Japanese War, he lived in Kweilin, and never ceased to write. After the Victory over Japan, he returned to Shanghai, there he engages now in writing.

He wrote the following works: 死去的太陽 (a novel, 1931, 新中國); 復仇 (collection of short stories, 1931, 新中國); 光明 * (collection of short stories, 新中國); 海底夢 * (a novel, 1932, 新中國); 春天裡的秋天 * (a novel, 1932, 開明); 沙丁* (a novel, 1932, 開明); 新生 * (a novel, 1932, 開明); 電椅 (collection of short stories, 1932, 新中國); 神鬼人 (collection of short stories, 1935, 文化生活出版社); 海行雜記 * (collection of essays, 1935, 開明); 點滴 * (collection of essays, 1935, 開明); 愛情三部曲 * (containing 霧, 雨, 電, three novels, 1936, 良友); 生之懺悔 (1936, 商務); 髮的故事 * (1936); 雪 * (a novel, 1936, 文化生活出版社); 小人小事* (1945, 文化生活出版社); 短簡 * (collection of essays, 1938, 良友); 旅途隨筆 (1940, 開明); 憶* (collection of essays); 憩園 * (a novel, 1944, 文化生活出版社); 寒夜 * (a novel,

1946, 晨光); 第四病室* (a novel, 1946, 晨光); 懷念 (collection of essays, 1947, 開明); 激流三部曲* (containing 家, 春, 秋, three novels, 開明); 火* (a novel in three volumes); 還魂草; 巴金代表作*(1940); 巴金選集* (1936, 萬象書屋); etc.

Translations: 秋天裏的春天 (開明); 屠格涅夫散文詩 (*Poems in Prose* by I.S. Turgenev, 文化生活出版社); 草原故事 (*In the Steppe* by M. Gorky, 生活); 父與子 (*Father and Sons* by I.S. Turgenev, 文化生活出版社); 處女地 (*Virgin Soil* by I.S. Turgenev, 文化生活出版社); 遲開的薔薇; etc.

101. Li Hsün-fêng 李薰風·

Novelist. He spent the greater part of his life in Peiping, where he published his novels in the newspapers *Hsiao Shih Pao* 小實報 , *Hsin Pei Ching Pao* 新北京報. He is now still in Peiping.

102. Li Hui-ying 李輝英·

Original name: 李連萃. Pen-names: 西村, 李東離, etc. Novelist, and short-story writer. Born in Manchuria. He studied once in the China Institute of Woosung 中國公學. His first success was his novel *Wan Pao Shan* 萬寶山, During the Sino-Japanese War, he lived in the Interior. In 1939, he was sent by the "National Writers' Anti-Aggression Association" 中華全國文藝界抗敵協會 to visit the front, together with some other young writers, and produced a long report when he came to Chungking, entitled *Chün Min Chih Chien* 軍民之間 (Between Soldiers and People, 上海雜誌公司).

Works: *Jên Chien Chi* 人間集* (collection of short stories 1937, 北新); *Fêng Nien* 豐年 (A Year of Plenty, collection of short stories, 1935, 中華); *Tsai Shêng Chi* 再生集* (Rebirth, collection of essays, 1936, 新鐘); *Sung Hua Chiang Shang* 松花江上 (On the Sung Hua River, a novel, 1945, 建國); etc.

103. Li Kuang-t'ien 李廣田·

(1907 —   )

Pen-name: 黎地. Poet, essayist, short-story writer, novelist, and literary critic. Born of a family of farmers in Tsitung, Shantung. He was brought up amid rural surroundings. He graduated from the Department of Western Languages and Literature of the National University of Peking 北京大學. In 1936, he published one volume of verse, entitled *Han Yuan Chi* 漢園集(商務, "Han Yuan" is the name of a street where his alma mater, the National University of Peking is located), together with his schoolmates Ho Ch'i-fang 何其芳, and Pien Chih-lin 卞之琳. Besides being a pastoral poet, he is also a distinguished essayist. The collections of his essays, published before the Sino-Japanese War, were two altogether, they are: *Hua Lang Chi* 畫廊集 * (The Picture Gallery, 1936, 商務); and *Yin Hu Chi* 銀狐集 (The Silver Fox, 1936, 文化生活出版社).

During the War, he lived in Kunming, where he taught in the National Southwest Associated University 西南聯合大學. He completed a novel, entitled *Yin Li* 引力 (Attraction), and wrote many critical articles which he collected into two volumes entitled *Shih Ti I Shu* 詩的藝術 (The Art of Poetry 1944, 開明), and *Wên Hsüeh Chih Yeh* 文學枝葉 (Branches and Leaves of Literature, 1948, 智益). And his new essays are collected into *Kuan Mu Chi* 灌木集 (開明), and *Jih Pien Sui Pi* 日邊隨筆 (1948, 文化生活出版社)

His collection of short stories is entitled *Chin T'an Tzŭ* 金罈子 (Golden Jar, 1946, 文化生活出版社).

After the Victory over Japan, he returned to Tientsin, where he joined the staff of Nankai University 南開大學. From the autumn of 1947 on, he served as professor at Tsinghua University 清華大學 at Peiping, and publishes often his new writings in different magazines and newspapers.

104. Li Lieh-wên 黎烈文.

Pen-names: 李維克, 林取, 達六, 達五 , etc.

Essayist, publisher, and translator. Born in Liuyang, Hunan. After studying in Japan and France for six years, he returned to China in 1932. He then became the editor of *Tzŭ Yu T'an* 自由談 (Free Talk), a literary supplement of the newspaper *Shên Pao* 申報, Shanghai, and he joined the "Society of Literary Research" 文學研究會. Later he published a literary magazine *Chung Liu* 中流, at Shanghai, which had a large circulation before the Sino-Japanese War.

During the War, he originated a publishing house, called "Kai Chin Ch'u Pan Shê" 改進出版社 at Yungan, Fukien, and edited the magazine *Hsien Tai Wên I* 現代文藝 (Contemporary Literature), together with Wang Hsi-yen 王西彥. After the Victory over Japan, he went to Formosa, where he became the vice-president of the newspaper *Hsin Shêng Pao* 新生報, and concurrently editor of its literary supplement *Hai Fêng* 海風 (Sea Wind).

Works: *Chou Chung* 舟中 (In a Ship, collection of short stories, 泰東); *Ch'ung Kao Ti Mu Hsing* 崇高的母性 * * (collection of essays); etc. Translations: 河童 (by R. Akutagawa, 1928, 商務); 妒誤 (*Le Feu Qui Reprend Mal* by J.J. Bernard, 1933, 商務); 紅蘿蔔鬚 (*Poil de Carotte* by R. Renard, 1934, 生活); 企鵝鳥 (*L'Ile des Pingouins* by A. France, 1935, 商務); 醫學的勝利 (*Le Triomphe de la Médecine* by J. Romains, 1933, 商務); 箄爾和哲安 (*Pierre et Jean* by G. de Maupassant, 1936, 商務); 冰島漁夫 (*Pêcheurs d'Islande* by Pierre Loti, 1936, 生活); 法國短篇小說集 (French Short Stories, 1936, 商務); 第三帝國的兵士; 最高勳章; 偉大的命運; 伊爾的美神 (*La Vénus d'Ille* by P. Mérimée, 1948, 文化生活出版社); etc.

His wife Hsü Yüeh-hua 許粵華, (better known under her pen-name 雨田), is also a famous writer, who edited the magazine *Hsien Tai Erh T'ung* 現代兒童 (Contemporary Children), in the War years.

105. Liang Shih-ch'iu 梁實秋.

(1902 —   )

Original name: 梁治華. Pen-names: 秋郎, 希臘人. Literary critic, and translator. Born in Hangchow, Chekiang. After graduating from the National Tsinghua University 清華大學, he went to America, where he entered Harvard University, and received his M.A. degree. Upon returning to China, he taught English literature in different universities, such as: National Southeast University 東南大學, Kwang Hua University 光華大學, Chinan University 暨南大學, Fuhtan University 復旦大學, China Institute 中國公學, National Shantung University 山東大學, etc. Before the Sino-Japanese War, he was the chairman of the Department of Western Languages and Literature of the National University of Peking 北京大學. Besides his academic career, he was once editor of the literary supplement of the newspaper *Shih Shih Hsin Pao* 時事新報, Shanghai.

During the War, he was a member of the People's Political Council in the Interior, and editor of the literary supplement of the newspaper *Chung Yang Jih Pao* 中央日報. He worked once in the National Institute of Compilation and Translation 國立編譯館, and lectured on Shakespeare's plays in the National Academy of Dramatic Arts 國立劇專. After the Victory over Japan, he returned to Peiping, and functions as a professor of English literature at the National Teachers' College 國立北平師範學院.

Works: *Lang Man Ti Yü Ku Tien Ti* 浪漫的與古典的 (Romantic and Classic, collection of critical essays, 1927, 新月); *Wên Hsüeh Ti Chi Lü* 文學的紀律 (Discipline of Literature, 1928, 新月); *Ma Jên Ti I Shu* 罵人的藝術 (1931, 新月); *P'ien Chien Chi* 偏見集 * (Prejudices, collection of critical essays, 1934, 正中); *Wên I P'i P'ing Lun* 文藝批評論 (Literary Criticism, 1934, 中華); *Yüeh Han Sun* 約翰孫 (Samuel Johnson, 1934, 商務); etc.

Translations: 潘彼得 (by G.M. Barrie, 1929, 開明); 織工馬南傳 (*Silas Marner* by George Eliot, 1932, 新月); 阿伯拉與哀綠綺思的情書 (*Abelard et Héloïse*, 新月); 西塞羅文錄 (*De Senectute de Amictia* by Cicero, 商務); 挪威短篇小說 (商務); 威尼斯商人 (*The Merchant of Venice* by W. Shakespeare, 1936, 商務); 馬克白 (*Macbeth* by W. Shakespeare, 1936, 商務); 李爾王 (*King Lear* by W. Shakespeare, 1936, 商務); 如願 (*As You Like It* by W. Shakespeare, 1936, 商務); 丹麥王子哈姆雷特的悲劇 (*Hamlet* by W. Shakespeare, 1936, 商務); 奧賽羅 (*Othello* by W. Shakespeare, 1936, 商務); 暴風雨 (*The Tempest* by W. Shakespeare, 1936, 商務); 第十二夜 (*Twelfth Night* by W. Shakespeare, 1936, 商務); etc.

106. Lin Yü-t'ang 林語堂.

(1895 —   )

Original name: 林玉堂. Pen-names: 毛驢, 宰予, 宰我, 豈青, 薩天師, etc.

Essayist, novelist, and critic. Born in Lungki, Fukien. He attended St. John's University of Shanghai in 1911, and graduated in 1916. He then taught English in the National Tsinghua University 清華大學 at Peiping for three years. In 1919, he went to the United States where he studied philology in the post-graduate department at Harvard University, and received his M.A. degree in 1921. He continued his philological studies in the University of Leipzig, where he received his Ph. D. in 1923. Upon returning to China, he became professor of English philology at National University of Peking 北京大學, 1923-1926; chairman of the English Department of the National Normal University for Women 國立女子師範大學 at Peiping, in 1926. He left Peiping in 1926 with the general exodus of radical professors, and arrived Amoy, where he was appointed the dean of the College of Arts and Letters of Amoy University 廈門大學. In 1927, he joined the Wuhan Government, and served as the secretary of the Ministry of Foreign Affairs. After the success of the Nationalist Revolution, he left politics and devoted himself exclusively to writing. He joined the Academia Sinica 中央研究院 (National Research Academy) in 1930 as foreign language editor and research fellow in philology.

At first he was a contributor of the *Yü Ssü* 語絲 Magazine (1924-1930), edited by Lu Hsün 魯迅 and his younger brother Chou Tso-jên 周作人. In 1932, he founded the humorous fortnightly *Lun Yü* 論語 (The Analects) at Shanghai, which won him the fame of the "Master of Humor" 幽默大師. In the spring of 1934, he edited the *Jên Chien Shih* 人間世 (This Human World), published by the Liang Yu Book Co. 良友圖書公司, a magazine devoted to the promotion of the familiar style, which suspended publication in the spring of 1935. He then published, in collaboration with Huang Chia-yin 黃嘉音 and Huang Chia-tê 黃嘉德, the *Hsi Fêng* 西風 (West Wind), a magazine devoted to the translation of Western essays. During the Sino-Japanese War, he served for some time as an attaché of the Chinese Embassy in the United States. Later he devoted himself completely in writing.

He wrote the following works in English: *My Country and My People** (1936, N.Y., Reynal & Hitchcock); *Confucius Saw Nancy* (1937, Shanghai, Commercial Press); *The Importance of Living* (1937, N.Y., J. Day); *The Birth of a New China* (1939); *Moment in Peking** (1940, N.Y., J. Day); *With Love and Irony* (1941, N.Y., J. Day); *A Leaf in the Storm* (1942, N.Y., J. Day); *Wisdom of China and India* (1942); *Between Tears and Laughter* (1943, N.Y., J. Day); *The Vigil of a Nation* (1945, N.Y., J. Day); *The Gay Genius: The Life and Times of Su Tungpo* (1947, N.Y., J. Day); etc.

His works in Chinese are: 剪拂集 * (1928, 北新); 大荒集 (1934, 生活); 我的話 (two volumes, 1934-1936, 時代圖書公司); 錦秀集* (1941, 朔風); 女子與知識 (北新); 幽默小品集* (朔風); etc.

107. Ling Shu-hua 凌淑華·

Pen-name: 素心, 素華

Short-story writer. Born in Kwangtung. After her graduation from Yen-ching University 燕京大學, she married Professor Ch'ên Yuan 陳源 (T. 西瀅, H. 通伯), the editor of the periodical *Hsien Tai P'ing Lun* 現代評論 (Contemporary Review), in which she published her first short story *Chiu Hou* 酒後 (After Drinking) in 1925, which immediately won great fame. Her later short stories appeared mostly in the *Hsin Yüeh Yüeh K'an* 新月月刊 (The Crescent Monthly), and in the literary supplement of *Ch'ên Pao* 晨報副刊, besides the *Hsien Tai P'ing Lun*. Later, she collected these narratives into three volumes, entitled *Hua Chih Ssŭ* 花之寺* (Temple of Flowers, 1928, 新月); *Nü Jên* 女人* (Women, 1930, 商務); and *Hsiao Hai* 小孩 (Children, 商務). From 1930 on, she did not produce much. The characteristic of her stories is the vivid description of the life and psychology of wealthy and educated women.

During the Sino-Japanese War, she was in the Interior. After the Victory over Japan she returned to Shanghai from where she went to London to join her husband.

108. Liu Chih-lien 劉植蓮·

Pen-name: 雷妍. Novelist. After graduating from the Women's College of Arts and Science of the National Peiping University 北平大學女子文理學院 she taught in the Mu Chên Middle School for Girls 慕貞女子中學 in Peiping. Her novels 良田* (1943, 大華印書局), and 白馬的騎者 (1944, 新民印書館) appeared during the Japanese occupation.

109. Liu Fu 劉 復·

(1889 — 1934)

Original name: 劉壽彭 , T. 半農 , H. 曲庵. Pen-names: 伴儂, 含星, 海, 寒星 , etc.

Poet and philologist. Born in Kiangyin, Kiangsu. At the age of 29 he went to Europe, and lived in England and France for six years. He received his Ph. D. from the Université de Paris. Upon returning to China, he was appointed professor of the Department of Chinese Literature of the National University of Peking 北京大學, and concurrently instructor of the post-graduate class of Chinese Department of the same university; and later chairman of the Department of Chinese Literature of the Université Franco-Chinoise 中法大學, dean of the Women's College of Arts and Science of the National Peiping University 北平大學女子文理學院 , director of studies of Fu Jên University 輔仁大學. He edited for some time the literary supplement of the newspaper *Shih Chieh Jih Pao* 世界日報. In 1934, he died at Peiping after a tour in Suiyuan province to study the dialect.

His two volumes of poems, *Yang Pien Chi* 揚鞭集 (1926, 北新), and *Wa Fu Chi* 瓦釜集 (1926, 北新) won him fame as a leading poet during the early years of the Chinese new literary movement, and did a great part in the promotion of the Pai Hua (spoken language) poetry. During his late years, he engaged in the movement of the unification of Chinese national language.

In addition to his poetical works, he also wrote essays, which were collected into *Pan Nung Tsa Wên* 半農雜文 (Essays of Liu Pan-nung, 2 volumes), published posthumously by the Liang Yu Book Co. 良友圖書公司, 1934-1935.

He compiled *Ch'u Ch'i Pai Hua Shih Kao* 初期白話詩稿 (1933, 北平星雲堂), an anthology of the Pai Hua poetry of the early years.

Translations: 茶花女劇本 (*La Dame aux Camélias* by A. Dumas Fils, 1926, 北新), and 法國短篇小說集 (French Short Stories, 1927, 北新).

110. Liu Pai-yü 劉白羽.

Short-story writer. In his stories, he describes the life of the Communist soldiers. During the Sino-Japanese War, he was in Yenan, the former Red capital, where he was in charge of the Yenan branch of the "National Writers' Anti-Aggression Association" 中華全國文藝界抗敵協會 and edited the magazine *Ta Chung Wên I* 大衆文藝 (Mass Literature), together with Chou Wên 周文, Ting Ling 丁玲, and others.

Works: *Hsing Fu* 幸福 (Happiness, containing six short stories); *Ts'ao Yuan Shang* 草原上 (On the Steppe, collection of short stories, 文化生活出版社) *T'ai Yang* 太陽 (The Sun); *Wu T'ai Shan Hsia* 五台山下 (At the Root of Wu T'ai Mountain); etc.

111. Liu Ta-chieh 劉大杰.

(1904 —   )

Pen-names: 修士, 湘君, etc.

Short-story writer, and literary critic. Born in Yoyang, Hunan. He graduated from the National Wuchang University 國立武昌大學, where he studied with Yü Ta-fu 郁達夫. a well-known novelist. Through the latter's recommendation, he published his first short story *T'ao Lin Ssŭ* 桃林寺 (Temple in the Peach-Grove) in the literary supplement of *Ch'ên Pao* 晨報副刊, and thus started his literary career. Later, urged by Kuo Mo-jo 郭沫若, he went to Japan, where he attended the post-graduate class of the Waseda University 早稻田大學. Upon returning to China, he taught at first in the Wuhsi Middle School 無錫中學, and then in Anhwei University 安徽大學. Fuhtan University 復旦大學. He was once the chairman of the Department of Chinese Literature of Amoy University 廈門大學, He edited for some time the *Hsien Tai Hsüeh Shêng* 現代學生 (The Modern

Student), published by the Tatung Book Co 大東書局. In the spring of 1925, collaborating with Hu Yun-i 胡雲翼, he organized a literary society "I Lin Shê" 藝林社 in Wuchang, and published a magazine *I Lin* 藝林, which suspended publication in the winter of the same year. He is now a professor at Chinan University 暨南大學, Shanghai.

The collections of his short stories are: 支那女兒 * (1928, 北新), 盲詩人 (1929, 啓智); 昨日之花 * (1929, 北新); 寒鴉集 * (1929, 啓智); 山水小品集 (1934, 北新); 三兒苦學記 * (1935, 北新); 渺茫的西北風 * (北新); 她病了; 一個不幸的女子 (啓智); 秋雁集 ;* etc.

He wrote these critical works: 德國文學概論 (1928, 北新); 易卜生研究 (1928, 商務); 托爾斯泰 (1933, 商務); 德國文學大綱; 表現主義文學論; etc.

Translations: 高加索的囚人 (*A Prisoner of the Caucasus* by L. Tolstoy, 1930, 中華); 兩朋友 (*Punin and Baburin* by I.S. Turgenev, 1931, 亞東) 苦戀 (*Frau Bertha Garlan* by A. Schnitzler, 1932, 中華); 東西文學評論 (1934, 中華); 俄國小說集 (*A Collection of Russian Short Stories*, 1934, 中華); 野性的呼喚 (*The Call of the Wild* by J. London, 1935, 中華); 戀愛病患者 (by K. Kikuchi, 北新); 三人 (*Three of Them* by M. Gorky); 白癡 (*The Idiot* by F. Dostoevsky); etc.

112. Liu Ta-pai 劉大白.

(1880 — 1932)

Original name: 劉清裔, T. 大白, H. 白屋. Pen-name: 漢冑.

Poet and literary critic. Born in Shaohsing, Chekiang. He was a Chü-jen 舉人 of Ch'ing Dynasty. During the early years of the Republic, he edited a magazine *Yü Yü Ch'un Ch'iu* 禹域春秋 in his native place. Later, he travelled in Japan. He was the chairman of the Department of Chinese Literature of Fuhtan University 復旦大學, Shanghai; secretary at the Bureau of Education of Chekiang Provincial Government; chief secretary at the National Chekiang University 浙江大學; and finallly vice-minister of the Ministry of Education of the National Government.

Being a poet of the early years of the new literary movement, he wrote the following collections of poems: 舊夢 (1924, 商務); 郵吻 (1926, 開明); 賣布謠 (1929, 開明); 丁寧 (1929, 開明); 再造 (1929, 開明); 秋之淚 (1930, 開明); 白屋遺詩七種 (1935, 開明); etc.

His collection of short stories is called 故事的罈子* (1934, 黎明).

His criticisms on poetry we have 舊詩新話 (1928, 開明); 白屋說詩 (1929, 大江); etc.

His letters were collected by Hsü Wei-nan 徐蔚南, and published, after his death, in 1932, by the World Book Co. 世界書局, under the title 白屋書信.

113. Liu Yun-jo 劉雲若.

Novelist. Born in Tientsin. His novels were published in various daily papers of Tientsin and Peiping. He is now in Tientsin, where he engages in writing novels.

114. Lo Hei-chih 羅黑芷.

(? — 1927)

Original name: 羅象陶, T. 晉思, H. 黑芷, or 黑子. Essayist and short-story writer. Born in Changsha, Hunan. He graduated from the Keioo University of Japan. Upon returning to China, he became an editor of the Commercial Press, and a member of the famous "Society of Literary Research" 文學研究會. He died in 1927 in his native place, and left only three volumes of works: 牽牛花 (collection of essays, 1926, 長沙北門書屋); 醉里 * (collection of short stories, 1927, 商務); and 春日 (collection of short stories, 1928 開明).

115. Lo Hung 羅 洪.

Pen-name: 虹. Novelist, and short-story writer. Wife of Chu Wên 朱雯 (pen-name: 王墳), a novelist also. During the Sino-Japanese War, she was in Kweilin. After the Victory over Japan, she returned to Shanghai, where she lives until now.

Works: *Ch'un Wang Chêng Yüeh* 春王正月* (1936, 良友); *Chê Shih Tai* 這時代 (This Age, 1946, 正言出版社); *Erh T'ung Chieh* 兒童節 (Children's Day, collection of short stories, 1946, 文化生活出版社); *Huo Lu* 活路 * (1945, 萬葉); etc.

116. Lo K'ai-lan 羅皚嵐.

Original name: 羅正暲. Pen-names: 溜子, 山風大郎, etc.

Novelist, and short-story writer. He graduated from the Department of Western Languages and Literature of the National Tsnghua University 清華大學 He is an intimate friend of Lo Nien-shêng 羅念生, Chu Hsiang 朱湘, and Liu Wu-chi 柳無忌. All of the three persons are graduates of Tsinghua.

His first novel. *K'u Kuo* 苦果* (Bitter Fruit), was published in 1925, in the newspaper *Ta Kung Pao* 大公報, Tientsin. It won fame for the author.

Works: 六月裡的杜鵑 (collection of short stories, 1926, 現代); 招姐 (collection of short stories, 光華); 創 * (a novel, 1939, 東亞印書局); etc.

117. Lo Shu 羅 淑.

(? — 1938)

Original name: 羅世彌. Short-story writer, and essayist. In 1929, she married Ma Tsung-jung 馬宗融, a famous writer. After the outbreak of the Sino-Japanese War, she, together with her husband and children, left Shanghai and went to Chengtu, where she died in the spring of 1938, after giving birth to a child, and left three volumes of works. They are: *Shêng Jên Ch'i* 生人妻* (collection of short-stories, 1938, 文化生活出版社); *Ti Shang Ti I Chio* 地上的一角 (One Corner on the Earth, 1941, 文化生活出版社); and *Yü Erh Ao* 魚兒坳 (collection of essays and short stores, 1941, 文化生活出版社).

118. Miao Ch'ung-ch'ün 繆崇羣.

(? — 1945)

Pen-name: 終一. Essayist, and short-story writer. In 1931, he edited a literary magazine in Nanking. The next year he went to Peiping, where he married in the same year. After the death of his wife, which occured in 1935, he returned to Shanghai. During the Sino-Japanese War, he went to Kweilin, then to Chungking. He died on January 18, 1945, at the Kiangsu Hospital, Chungking, and left eight volumes of works and translations. They are: *Hsi Lu Chi* 晞露集* (collection of essays, 1933, 北平星雲堂); *Chi Chien K'ang Jên* 寄健康人 (良友); *Kuei K'o Yü Niao* 歸客與鳥 (collection of short stories, 1935, 正中); *Fei Hsü Chi* 廢墟集 (文化生活出版社); *Hsia Ch'ung Chi* 夏蟲集 (collection of essays, 文化生活出版社); *Shih P'ing Sui Pi* 石屏隨筆 (collection of essays, 1942, 文化生活出版社); *Chüan Chüan Ts'ao* 眷眷草 (文化生活出版社); and *Hsien Tai Jih Pên Hsiao P'in Wên* 現代日本小品文 (Contemporary Japanese Essays, translated from Japanese, 中華).

His friend Pa Chin 巴金 compiled his posthumous essays into *Pei Hsia Sui Pi* 碑下隨筆.

119. Mu Shih-ying 穆時英.

(1912 — 1939)

Pen-names: 伐揚, 匿名子 , etc.

Short-story writer. Born in Shanghai, where he completed his education in the Department of Chinese Literature of Kwang Hua University 光華大學. While still a student, he started to write fiction. His first short story *Hei Hsüan Fêng* 黑旋風 was published in the *Hsin Wên I Yüeh K'an* 新文藝月刊 (The New Literature Monthly), edited by Shih Chê-ts'un 施蟄存 ; and through the latter's recommendation, his second short story *Nan Pei Chi* 南北極 appeared in the *Hsiao*

Shuo Yüeh Pao 小說月報. His first collection of short stories, entitled *Nan Pei Chi*,* published in 1932 by the Hu Fêng Book Co. 湖風書局, won him the reputation of genius. Later he became a co-editor of the literary magazine *Hsien Tai* 現代 (Modern Times). In 1939, he joined the puppet régime of Wang Ching-wei 汪精衞, and served as the chief editor of the newspaper *Kuo Min Jih Pao* 國民日報, under the latter's auspices. He was assassinated by the under-ground workers at Shanghai in the same year.

Works: 室閑少佐 (a novel, 1932, 良友); 公墓 (1933, 現代); 白金的女體塑像 (containing eight short stories 1934, 現代); 聖處女的感情 (collection of short stories, 1935, 良友); 上海的狐步舞 (良友); 被當作消遣品的男子 (良友); 黑牡丹 (1934, 良友); 中國行進 (良友); etc.

120. Ni I-tê 倪貽德.

Short-story writer and artist. Born in Hangchow, Chekiang. He completed his advanced education in Japan. Upon returning to China, he joined the famous "Creative Society" 創造社. He was also noted as painter. He taught, before the Sino-Japanese War, in Canton College of Fine Arts 廣州市立美術專科學校 Shanghai College of Fine Arts 上海美術專門學校, Wuchang College of Fine Arts 武昌藝術專門學校, and in the War years, in Shanghai College of Fine Arts.

His works were published mostly in the literary supplement of *Ch'ên Pao* 晨報副刊 and the *Creation Monthly* 創造月刊. The collections of his short stories are: 玄武湖之秋 (1924); 殘春 (1928, 北新); 百合集* (1929, 北新); 東海之濱; etc.

He wrote these works on art: 水彩畫概論 (1929, 光華); 藝術漫談 (1930, 光華); 西洋畫概論 (1933, 現代); 現代繪畫概觀 (1934, 商務); 畫人行脚* (1934, 良友); 高中美術教本 (1934, 北新); etc.

Translation: 現代繪畫概論 (by U. Toyama, 1934, 開明).

121. Nieh Kan-nu 聶紺弩.

Pen-names: 紺弩, 耳耶, etc.

Short-story writer, and essayist. His literary career commenced as an editor of the newspaper *Nan Yang Hua Pao* 南洋華報. Later he entered the Whampoa Military Academy 黃浦軍官學校 as a cadet. In 1942, he founded a newspaper *Chiu Wang Jih Pao* 救亡日報 at Kweilin, in collaboration with Hsia Yen 夏衍, the dramatist, and edited its literary supplement by himself. He was once a professor at the Lu Hsün Institute of Arts 魯迅藝術學院 in Yenan, the former Red capital.

Works: *Hsieh Hou* 邂逅 (1935, 天馬); *Li Shih Ti Ao Mi* 歷史的奧秘 (The Secrecy of History, collection of essays, 1941, 桂林文獻出版社); *Shê Yü T'a* 蛇與塔 (Snake and Pagoda, collection of essays, 1941, 桂林文獻出版社); *Tsai Lu Shang* 在路上 (On the Road, collection of short stories); etc.

122. Ou-Yang Yü-ch'ien 歐陽予倩.

(1887 —   )

Playwright and actor. Born in Liuyang, Hunan. He went to Japan in 1919. There, after seeing a play performance by the Ch'un Liu Shê 春柳社, he became so much interested in dramatic art that he joined the society. His first acting experience was in a minor role in a play based upon the novel *Uncle Tom's Cabin*. While in Tokyo, Ou-Yang also began to learn the classical Peking drama of which he became later a professional actor. As a female impersonator, he was well received by the public. There was a saying current at that time: "In the North, there is Mei Lan-fang 梅蘭芳; and in the South, there is Ou-Yang". And he was invited by the late Chang Ch'ien 張謇, the last Chuang-yuan 狀元 of Ch'ing Dynasty, to direct a dramatic school at Nantung, Kiangsu. The school was known as Ling Kung Hsüeh Shê 伶工學社 (School for Actors). The purpose of the school was to effect the necessary reforms needed in the Peking drama. Ever since then Ou-Yang has been deeply interested in the movement for adapting Peking drama to present-days needs.

In 1923, he joined the Shanghai Dramatic Association 上海戲劇協社, organized by Ku Chien-ch'ên 谷劍塵, and earned reputation by playing himself the principal role of his first piece *P'o Fu* 潑婦 (1928, 商務). In 1927, he was in charge of the National Theatre 國民劇場 in Nanking. In 1928, he collaborated with T'ien Han 田漢 in the establishment of the Nan Kuo (Le Midi) Institute of Arts 南國藝術學校 to promote the dramatic education. In 1929, he became the director of the Kwangtung Institute of Dramatic Studies 廣東戲劇研究所 and editor of the *Hsi Chü Tsa Chih* 戲劇雜誌 (Dramatic Magazine). He took part in the Revolution of Fukien in 1933, and became the superintendent and head of the play-writing department of the Star Motion Picture Co. 明星影片公司 of Shanghai in 1936.

In the early years of the Sino-Japanese War, he went to Hongkong, where he founded the "China Arts Dramatic Troupe" 中國藝術劇團. The troupe had a number of experienced actors and actresses. Their performances were enthusiastically received by the Hongkong theatre-goers. Later he went to Kweilin, where he directed the Kwangsi School of Dramatic Art 廣西劇專, and was in charge of the Kweilin Branch of the "National Writers' Anti-Aggression Association" 中華全國文藝界抗敵協會

Ou-Yang Yü-ch'ien devoted nearly thirty years of his life to the promotion of modern drama in China. He was esteemed by the young dramatists, and has been advisor to many dramatic societies. His famous article *Yü Chih Hsi Chü Kai Liang Kuan* 予之戲劇改良觀 (Reform of Drama As I See), published in *Hsin Ch'ing Nien* 新青年 (New Youth Magazine), vol. 5, no. 4 (October 15, 1918), was one of the most influential essays in the history of Chinese new dramatic movement. Later he wrote many dramatic articles which he collected into one volume entitled *Yü Ch'ien Lun Chü* 予倩論劇 (Essays on Drama by Ou-Yang Yü-ch'ien, 泰東), and his experience on stage was recorded in *Tzŭ Wo Yen Chü I Lai* 自我演劇以來 (1933, 神州國光社). Besides the works mentioned above, he wrote

回家以後 (1928, 商務); 潘金蓮 * (published in the *Hsin Yüeh Tsa Chih* 新月雜誌 in 1928), and many short pieces appeared in the *Hsi Chü Tsa Chih*. During the War he wrote many historical dramas to awaken the patriotism among Chinese masses in the face of Japanese invasion. Among which we may mention: 忠王 李秀成; 木蘭從軍; 桃花扇; 梁紅玉.

After the Victory over Japan he returned to Shanghai from Kweilin.

123. P'an Han-nien 潘漢年.

Pen-names: 天長, 愛仙, 潑皮, 潑皮男士, etc.

Short-story writer. Born in Yihsing, Kiangsu. He was the younger brother of P'an Tzu-nien 潘梓年, a well-known writer. He joined at first the famous "Creative Society" 創造社, and then organized a literary group "Huan Shê" 幻社, with Yeh Ling-fêng 葉靈鳳, and published a literary fortnightly *Huan Chou* 幻洲 in 1926. The contributors were Chin Man-ch'êng 金滿城, Yen Liang-ts'ai 嚴良才, T'êng Kang 滕剛, etc. It was a very popular magazine among the young readers. But owing to its leftist leaning in thought, it was ordered to cease publication by the authorities. They then published another periodical *Go Bi* 戈壁 which was too short-lived.

Works: 離婚 * (1928, 光華); 曼瑛姑娘; 犧牲者; etc.

124. P'an Hsü-tsu 潘序祖.

Pen-name: 予且. Novelist, short-story writer, and essayist. Before the Sino-Japanese War, he was an editor of the Chung Hwa Book Co. 中華書局, and teacher of history in the Kwang Hua Middle School 光華中學, Shanghai. During the Sino-Japanese War, he stayed in Shanghai, and published his writings in the periodical *Tsa Chih* 雜誌 (Miscellany).

Works: 小菊 (a novel); 雞冠集 * (1934, 四社出版部) 兩間房 * (1937, 中華); 予且短篇小說集 (1943, 上海太平洋書局); 妻的藝術; 如意珠; etc.

125. P'an Kuang-tan 潘光旦.

(1898 —   )

Original name: 潘保同, T. 仲昂. A famous eugenist. Born in Paoshan, Kiangsu. After graduating from Tsinghua University 清華大學, he went to America, where he studied philosophy at Columbia University, and received his Ph. D. degree. Upon returning to China, he was appointed the director of studies of the National University of Political Science at Woosung 吳淞國立政治大學. Later he became the dean of the College of Arts and Letters of Kwang Hua University 光華大學, and editor of the *Hsüeh Têng* 學燈, a literary supplement of the newspaper *Shih Shih Hsin Pao* 時事新報, Shanghai. He then founded the Crescent Book Co. 新月書店 at the same city, which has done a great part in the development of new Chinese literary movement. Before the Sino-Japanese War, he was a professor at Tsinghua. During the War years, he taught at the National Southwest Associated University 西南聯合大學 at Kunming. After the Victory over Japan, he returned to Peiping, and is now the Director of library of Tsinghua University.

Works: *Jên Wên Shih Kuan* 人文史觀 (1927, 商務); *Fêng Hsiao Ch'ing* 馮小青 * (1928, 新月); *Chung Kuo Chih Chia T'ing Wên T'i* 中國之家庭問題 (1928, 新月); *Tu Shu Wên T'i* 讀書問題 (1930, 新月); *Yu Shêng Kai Lun* 優生概論 (新月); *Jih Pên Tê I Chih Min Tsu Hsing Chih Pi Chiao Yen Chiu* 日本德意志民族性之比較研究 (新月); *Jên Wên Shêng Wu Hsüeh Lun Ts'ung* 人文生物學論叢 (新月); *Hsüan Ch'uan Pu Shih Ko Ming* 宣傳不是革命 ; etc.

Translation: 自然陶汰與中華民族性 (*The Character of Races*, 1929, 新月).

126. P'an Shih 潘 式.

T. 伯鷹, H. 髡公. Pen-names: 髡工, 孤雲, 雲, 悲慧, etc.

Novelist. Before the Sino-Japanes War, he published his novels *Jên Hai Wei Lan* 人海微瀾 and *Yin Hsing* 隱刑 * in the newspaper *Ta Kung Pao* at Tientsin. During the War, he lived in Chungking, and wrote but little. After the Victory over Japan, he wrote a new novel for the newspaper *Ching Shih Jih Pao* 經世日報 at Peiping, entitled *Hai Wang Hsing Li Hsien Chi* 海王星歷險記. He is now in Shanghai.

Works: 殘羽 * (1933, 天津書局); 情海生波 * (1942, 京津出版社); 生還* (1937, 天津大公報館); etc.

127. P'êng Chia-huang 彭家煌.

(1900 — 1933)

Also named 彭介黃, H. 韞松. Pen-name: 彭芳草.

Short-story writer. Born in Siangyin, Hunan. He collaborated once with Li Shih-ts'in 李石岑, a famous philosopher, in editing the magazines *Chiao Yü Tsa Chih* 教育雜誌 (Education Magazine), and *Min To Tsa Chih* 民鐸雜誌. In 1933, he was arrested by the authorities on the charge of instigating revolt, but was set free after finding him innocent. He died not long after he gained liberty.

Works: 慫恿 (1927, 開明); 茶杯裏的風波 (1928, 現代); 皮克的情書 (1928, 現代); 管他呢 * (1928, 北新); 平淡的事 (1929, 大東); 寒夜 (1930, 神州國光社); 厄運 (1930, 神州國光社); 落花曲 (1931, 現代); 喜訊 * (1933, 現代); 出路 (1934, 大東); etc.

128. Pi Huan-wu   畢奐午.

Essayist and poet. He is a student of Wang Hsi-chêng 王西徵, and Kao T'ao 高滔, both of whom are well-known writers. His interest in literature revealed itself very early. While still studying in a middle school, he began to contribute. His writings were published in these magazines: *Wên Hsüeh Chi K'an* 文學季刊, *Shui Hsing* 水星, and *Wên Chi Yüeh K'an* 文季月刊; and the literary supplement of the newspaper *Ta Kung Pao* 大公報. During the Sino-Japanese War, he lived in complete seclusion in Peiping. After the Victory over Japan, he works in the College of Agriculture of Tsinghua University 清華大學.

Works: *Chüeh Chin Chi* 掘金記* (Digging for Gold, collection of poems and essays, 1936, 文化生活出版社); *Yü Hsi* 雨夕 (Rainy Night, collection of essays, 1939, 文化生活出版社); etc.

129. Shên Ch'i-yü   沈起予.

(1904 —   )

Pen-name: 綺雨. Novelist, and short-story writer. Born in Szechwan. He studied for some time in the Department of Philosophy, Imperial University, Tokyo. Upon returning to China, he participated in the literary movement launched by the "Creative Society" 創造社, in which he held an important position. In 1936, when the "Asscciation of Chinese Authors" 中國交藝家協會 was established in Shanghai, he was chosen as one of the directors. In the same year, he edited the *Kuang Ming* 光明 magazine in collaboration with Hung Shên 洪深, the dramatist. He was once a professor at Kwang Hua University 光華大學. During the Sino-Japanese War, he lived in Chungking, and was a member of the "National Writers' Anti-Aggression Association" 中華全國文藝界抗敵協會.

Works: 殘碑* (1935, 良友); 火線內 (1935, 良友); 飛露; 出發之前; 怎樣閱讀文藝作品 (1936, 生活); etc. Translations: 兩個野蠻人的戀愛 (*Atala* by Chateaubriand); 酒塲 (*L'Assommoir* by Emile Zola, 1936, 中華); 狼 (by Romain Rolland); 藝術科學論 (*La Littérature à la Lumière du Matérialisme Historique* by M. Ickowicz, 1931, 現代); 歐洲文學發達史 (*Statji Po Zapadnoewropeiskoj Literature* by F. M. Friche, 1931, 現代); etc.

130. Shên Sung-ch'üan   沈松泉.

Pen-name: 沈川. Short-story writer and poet. Born in Wuhsien, Kiangsu. He first published his works in the *Ch'uang Tsao Jih* 創造日, edited by the "Creative Society" 創造社. Later, he established the "Kuang Hua" Book Co. 光華書局 with Chang Ching-lu 張靜廬 and others. His collections of short stories are: 死灰* (1927, 光華); 少女與婦人* (1928, 光華); 醉吻 (光華); etc.

131. Shên Ts'ung-wên 沈從文.

(1902 —   )

Pen-names: 小兵, 懋琳, 休芸芸, 甲辰, 璇若, 紅黑舊人, 芸芸, 岳煥, 季蕤, 若琳, 上官碧, 窄而霉齋主人, etc.

Novelist, and short-story writer. Born in Fêng Huang Ch'êng 鳳凰城, west Hunan, where he spent his early life. It is a remote place, where Chinese people live together with the Miao Tribe. He was quite familiar with the life of the latter. Later he not unfrequently adopted member of this tribe as the characters of his stories.

His grandfather, father, and brothers were all officers in the army. He also enlisted when he was very young. With the army he wandered several years in the provinces of Szechwan, Hunan, Hupeh, and Kweichow. Later, he decided to resume his studies. Having arrived in Peiping he began to contribute to different newspapers in order to earn his living. He became the intimate friend of Hu Yeh-p'in 胡也頻 and his wife Ting Ling 丁玲, both unkwown in the literary world at that time, but important authors some years later. They afterwards founded many enterprizes together.

Not long after his arrival at Peiping, he met Dr. Hu Shih, the leader of the new literary movement of China, and submitted his novels to the latter for criticism. Mr. Hu highly praised them. Through the latter's recommendation, Shên Ts'ung-wên's novels were accepted by the major magazines. Gradually, he became acquainted with Yü Ta-fu 郁達夫, Hsü Chih-mo 徐志摩, Ch'ên Yuan 陳源 and other leading men of letters of that time. His works were published mostly in the literary supplement of the newspaper Ch'ên Pao 晨報, and Hsien Tai P'ing Lun 現代評論 ; afterwards in the Hsiao Shuo Yüeh Pao 小說月報 and Hsin Yüeh 新月 (The Crescent) magazine.

In 1928, he went to Shanghai and there in collaboration with his friends, Hu Yeh-p'in, and Ting Ling, he edited the Hung Yü Hei 紅與黑 (The Red and the Black), a literary supplement of the newspaper Chung Yang Jih Pao 中央日報 and published two magazines, the Jên Chien Yüeh K'an 人間月刊 and Hung Hei Yüeh K'an 紅黑月刊, both of which had but a short life.

In 1929, he taught in the China Institute of Woosung 吳淞中國公學, and in 1931 was appointed professor at the National Wuhan University 國立武漢大學 and then at Tsingtao University, Shantung 山東省立青島大學. From 1934, he edited the literary supplement of the newspaper Ta Kung Pao 大公報.

In the War years, he taught in the National Southwest Associated University 西南聯合大學, in Kunming. After the Victory over Japan he returned to Peiping, and is now a professor at the National University of Peking 北京大學, and editor of the literary supplement of the newspaper I Shih Pao 益世報 of Tientsin.

Shên Ts'ung-wên is a prolific writer. Within ten years he has written more than fifty novels and collections of short stories, of which the important ones are: 鴨子* (1927, 北新); 蜜柑 (1927, 新月); 入伍後 (1928, 北新); 老實人 (1928, 現代);

阿麗思中國遊記 * (1928, 新月); 十四夜間 (1929, 開明); 神巫之愛 (1929, 光華); 沈從文甲集 (1930, 神州國光社); 旅店及其他 * (1930, 中華); 從文子集 (1931, 新月); 石子船 * (1931, 中華); 舊夢 (1931, 商務); 虎雛 (1932, 新中國); 一個女劇員的生活 (1932, 大東); 都市一婦女 (1932, 新中國); 泥塗 (1932, 北平星雲堂); 沫沫集 (1934, 大東); 游目集 (1934, 大東); 如蕤集 * (1934, 生活); 邊城 (1934, 生活); 浮世輯 (1935, 良友); 八駿圖 * (1935, 文化生活出版社); 新與舊 * (1936, 良友); 從文小說習作選 (1936, 良友); 從文小說集 (1936, 大光); 沈從文選集 * (1936, 萬象); 月下小景; 湘行散記; 主婦集; 湘西; 春燈集; 黑鳳集; 雲南看雲集; 鳳子; etc.

Besides being a novelist he is also known for his literary criticism. His early critical works like *Lun Chung Kuo Ti Ch'uang Tso Hsiao Shuo* 論中國的創作小說 (On Chinese Creative Novels), *Lun Wang Ching-chih Hui Ti Fêng* 論汪靜之蕙的風 (On *Hui Ti Fêng* of Wang Ching-chih); *Lun Chu Hsiang Ti Shih* 論朱湘的詩 (On the Poetry of Chu Hsiang), *Lun Chiao Chü-yin Ti Shih* 論蕉菊隱的詩 (On the Poetry of Chiao Chü-yin), published in the *Wên I Yüeh K'an* 文藝月刊 (The Literary Monthly) display his keen perception, and are considered to be valuable works in the Chinese literary world.

His biographical works are: *Ts'ung-wên Tzŭ Chuan* 從文自傳 (The Autobiography of Shên Ts'ung-wên, 1934, 上海第一出版社); *Chi Hu Yeh-p'in* 記胡也頻 * (The Life of Hu Yeh-p'in, 1933, 光華); and *Chi Ting Ling* 記丁玲 * (The Life of Ting Ling, vol. 1, 1934, 良友; vol. 2, 1940, 良友).

132. Shên Tuan-hsien 沈端先.

    (1900 —   )

    Pen-names: 夏衍, 丁一之, 丁謙吾, 宰白, 席耐芳, 崔若沁, 黃子布, 蔡叔聲, 羅子揚 羅浮, etc.

Playwright. Born in a small family of landowners in Hangchow, Chekiang. There he graduated in 1919 from a technical school. He then went to Japan to take up his advanced study, and graduated from the Kyushu Engineering School in 1925. He joined the Northern Expedition of the Revolutionary Army in 1927, and thenceforth gave himself solely to writing. He edited once a monthly magazine *I Shu Yüeh K'an* 藝術月刊. After the outbreak of the Sino-Japanese War, he launched the newspaper *Chiu Wang Jih Pao* 救亡日報, at Shanghai, together with Kuo Mo-jo 郭沫若. With the fall of Shanghai, he went to Hongkong, where he edited a monthly magazine *Kêng Yun* 耕耘, together with Tai Wang-shu 戴望舒, Yeh Ch'ien-yü 葉淺予, Chang Kuang-yü 張光宇, and others. In 1942, he arrived in Chungking. After the Victory over Japan, he returned to Shanghai, and founded a newspaper *Chien Kuo Jih Pao* 建國日報 there. It was ordered to suspend publication after issuing its twelfth number. In September, 1946, he arrived in Hongkong from Shanghai.

Shên Tuan-hsien is a versatile writer, he writes plays, novels, essays, and critical articles. But playwriting is his main interest. Of his plays, *Sai Chin Hua* 賽金花 (1936, 生活) deals with the patriotic activities of Sai Chin Hua, a sing-song girl friend of General Waldersee, during the Boxer times. *I Nien Chien* 一年間 (Within One Year, also called *T'ien Shang Jên Chien* 天上人間, 生活) concerns the first year of the War. *Shang Hai Wu Yen Hsia* 上海屋簷下* (Under Shanghai Roofs) describes the poverty and misery of the common people in Shanghai even before the outbreak of War. *Fa Hsi Ssŭ Hsi Chün* 法西斯細菌* (The Fascist Bacillus 開明) is the story of a Japanese-trained Chinese physician who brought his Japanese wife back to China and had to bear the insults which his countrymen flung against his wife and his child, and the violence of the invaders, who destroyed his life's work in bacteriological research. *Ch'ou Ch'êng Chi* 愁城記* (City of Sorrow 開明) portrays the dangerous life of progressive writers in Japanese-occupied Shanghai. *Shui Hsiang Yin* 水鄉吟 (1946, 群益出版社) depicts the nostalgia of the people who went to the Interior from the Occupied Areas. *Hsin Fang* 心防* (Heart Defence 開明) describes the teachers' patriotic activities in the Japanese-occupied places. *Li Li Ts'ao* 離離草 tells about the anti-Japanese volunteer corps in Kiamusze. *Fang Ts'ao T'ien Ya* 芳草天涯 describes love, marriage, and family life. *Ts'ao Mu Chieh Ping* 草木皆兵, written in collaboration with Sung Chih-ti 宋之的, and Yü Ling 于伶, depicts the under-ground workers in Shanghai.

Shên Tuan-hsien also collaborated with Sung Chih-ti and Yü Ling in writing *Hsi Chü Ch'un Ch'iu* 戲劇春秋 (Birth Struggles of the Modern Drama).

Translations: 歐洲近代文藝思潮論(by H. Honma, 1929, 開明); 犧牲 (by S. Fujimori, 1929, 北新); 初春的風 (Japanese short stories, 1929, 大江); 敗北 (Japanese short stories, 1930, 神州國光社); 平林泰子集 (works of T. Hirabayashi, 1933, 現代); 有島武郎集 (works of T. Arishima, 1935, 中華); 奸細 (by M. Gorky, 北新); 地獄 (by Y. Kaneko); 在施療室 (by T. Hirabayashi, 水沫); 沈醉的太陽 (*Pjjanoe Solnz* by F. Gladkov, translated in collaboration with others, 現代); 母親 (*Mother*, by M. Gorky, 2 volumes, 大江); 戀愛之路 (*Wege Zu Liebe* by A. Kollontay, 開明); 復活 * (*Resurrection* by L. Tolstoy, 美學出版社); etc.

133. Shên Yen-ping 沈雁冰.

(1896 —   )

Original name: 沈德鴻. He is better known under the pen-name of Mao Tun 茅盾. His other pen-names are: 方璧, 方璧, 止敬, 毛臙, 玄, 玄珠, 未名, 丙生, 矛盾, 吉卜西, 朱璟, 沈餘, 形天, 何典, 東方未明, 郎損, 逃墨舘主, 惕若, 終葵, 雁冰, 蒲, 蒲牢, 德洪, M.D., etc.

Novelist, short-story writer, playwright, and literary critic. Born of a large family in Tunghiang, Chekiang. His father, being a scholar, has given him a sound education during his childhood. At the age of 18, Mao Tun graduated from the An Ting Middle School 安定中學 of Hangchow. He then attended the preparatory class of the National University of Peking 北京大學. Three years later, on account of financial difficulties, he served as a proof-reader for the Commercial Press. In 1921, collaborating with Chêng Chên-to 鄭振鐸, Chou-Tso-jên 周作人, Hsü Ti-shan 許地山 (better known under his pen-name Lo Hua Shêng 落華生), Wang T'ung-chao 王統照, Yeh Shao-chün 葉紹鈞, and a few others, he founded the "Society of Literary Research" 文學研究會 in Peiping, which turned to be one of the most important literary societies in the history of contemporary Chinese literature. And Mao Tun was appointed, from January of 1921 on, the editor of one of the Association's publications *Hsiao Shuo Yüeh Pao* 小說月報 (The Short Story Magazine). Since then he published many literary articles and translations of Western literary works. In 1924, he resigned the editorship of the *Hsiao Shuo Yüeh Pao*, and engaged in the revolutionary work at Shanghai. During the Northern Expedition in 1926, he served as the Publicity Assistant of the Political Training Department, and editor-in-chief of the newspaper *Min Kuo Jih Pao* 民國日報 of Wuhan. After the split between Kuomintang and Communists in 1927, he went to Kuling, Kiangsi, to recuperate his health. He returned to Shanghai in August of the same year, where he devoted himself to the writing of novels. The result was his most famous trilogy of *Huan Mieh* 幻滅* (Disillusion, 1927, 商務) *Tung Yao* 動搖 * (Agitation, 1927, 開明), and *Chui Ch'iu* 追求* (Pursuit, 1928, 開明), later he collected them into one volume entitled *Shih* 蝕 (The Eclipse), published by Kaiming Book Co. 開明書店 . The three stories described the restlessness of Chinese youth in the revolutionary period, and won him the nationwide fame as one of the foremost novelists of China. In 1928, he travelled in Japan, where he wrote a long thesis *Ts'ung Ku Ling Tao Tung Ching* 從牯嶺到東京 (From Kuling to Tokyo) to show his attitude toward revolutionary literature, and has caused a fierce literary battle. He was one of the founders of the "China League of Left Writers" 中國左翼作家聯盟, established at Shanghai in 1930. From 1929 to 1932, he produced three novels: *Hung* 虹* (The Rainbow, 1929, 開明); *San Jên Hsing* 三人行 * (Three Persons, 1931, 開明); and *Lu* 路* (Road, 1932, 光華); and two collections of short stories: *Yeh Ch'iang Wei* 野薔薇* (Wild Roses, 1929, 大江書舖); and *Su Máng* 宿莽 * (1931, 大江書舖). In 1933, he published another novel *Tzŭ Yeh* 子夜* (Midnight, 開明), describing the crisis of Chinese industry, which was considered by critics as an epoch-making production of contmporary Chinese literature. Later, he wrote: *Ch'un Ts'an* 春蠶* (Silkworm, 1933, 開明); *Hua Hsia Tzŭ* 話匣子* (Chatterbox, collection of essays, 1934, 良友); *Mao Tun Tuan P'ien Hsiao Shuo Chi* 茅盾短篇小說集 (Collected Short Stories of Mao Tun, 1934, 開明); *Ku Hsiang Tsa Chi* 故鄉雜集 (Sketches of Native Place, 1934, 今代); *P'ao Mo* 泡沫* (Froth, collection of short stories, 1935, 生活); *Su Hsieh Yü Sui Pi* 速寫與隨筆* (Sketches and Notes, 1935, 開明); *To Chio Kuan Hsi* 多角關係 * (Polygonal Relations, a novel, first published in the *Wên Hsüeh Yüeh Pao* 文學月報 in 1935, describing the financial panic at the end of 1934, 1936, 生活); *Yen Yun Chi* 烟雲集* (Smoke and Cloud, 1937, 良友); *Yin Hsiang Kan Hsiang Hui I* 印象感想回憶*; etc.

He wrote these critical works: *Ou Chou Liu Ta Wên Hsüeh Chia* 歐洲六大文學家 (Six Great European Writers, 1929, 世界); *Hsien Tai Wên I Tsa Lun* 現代文藝雜論 (Notes on Contemporary Literature, 1929, 世界); *Hsi Yang Wên Hsüeh T'ung Lun* 西洋文學通論 (Outline of Western Literature, 1930, 世界); *Tso Chia Lun* 作家論 (Criticism on Some Writers, 1936, 文學出版社); *Ou Chou Ta Chan Yü Wên Hsüch* 歐洲大戰與文學 (European War and Literature, 開明); *Hsi Yang Wên Hsüeh* 西洋文學 (Western Literature, 世界); *Chin Tai Wên Hsüeh Mien Mien Kuan* 近代文學面面觀 (A Bird's-Eye View of Contemporary Literature, 世界); *Chin Tai Wên Hsüeh ABC* 近代文學 ABC (ABC of Contemporary Literature, 世界); *Hsiao Shuo Yen Chiu ABC* 小說研究 ABC (ABC of Fiction Study, 世界); etc.

Translations: 雪人 (1929, 開明); 文憑 (*With a Diploma and the Whirlwind* by V. I. Nemirovitch-Dantchenko, 1932, 現代); 世界文學名著 (Selected Translations of World Masterpieces, 1936, 開明); 阿富汗的戀歌 (Lovesongs of Afghanistan); 倍那文德戲曲集; 太戈爾短篇小說集 (Selected Short Stories of R. Tagore); etc.

Like so many of his literary friends, the author left Shanghai in the winter of 1937. He arrived in Hongkong, where he edited the *Yen Lin* 言林 a literary supplement of the newspaper *Li Pao* 立報, and the *Wên I Chên Ti* 文藝陣地 (Literary Field) a monthly magazine published by the Life Book Co. 生活書店 of Canton. With the fall of Hongkong, he went to Kweilin, then to Chungking. He lived for some time in Sinkiang, where he was appointed the dean of the College of Arts and Letters of Sinkiang University, and member of the Standing Committee of the Sino-Soviet Cultural Relations Association, Sinkiang Branch. Upon returning to Chungking, he became a member of the Committee for the Promotion of Cultural Activities of the Ministry of Political Training. He held this post until 1945. During the Sino-Japanese War he wrote *Shuang Yeh Hung Ssû Erh Yüeh Hua* 霜葉紅似二月花 (Frosty Leaves Are as Red as Flowers in the Second Moon, a novel depicting the influence of Chinese traditional ideas on modern youth, 1943, Kweilin, 華夏書店), *Fu Shih* 腐蝕 (a novel), *Chieh Hou Shih I* 劫後拾遺 (生活書店), *Ti I Chieh Tuan Ti Ku Shih* 第一階段的故事 * (Stories of the First Stage of War, describing the conditions of Shanghai during the first stage of the Sino-Japanese hostilities, 1945, Shanghai, 亞洲圖書社) *Ch'ing Ming Ch'ien Hou* 清明前後 (Around the Ch'ing Ming Festival, a play depicting the life of the speculative merchants of Chungking in War time).

After the Victory over Japan, he returned to Shanghai, where he edited the literary magazine *Wên Lien* 文聯 (Literary Union), published by the Yung Hsiang Press 永祥印書館 On December 15, 1946, he set out on a journey to U.S.S.R. where he gave lectures on Chinese literature. He is now engaging in writing at Hongkong.

The essays written about him were collected by 黃人影 into *Mao Tun Lun* 茅盾論(光華); and by 伏志英 into *Mao Tun P'ing Chuan* 茅盾評傳 (1932, 現代)

134. Shih Chê-ts'un 施蟄存.

(1903 —)

Original name: 施青萍 T. 安華, H. 劈尼. Pen-names: 江兼霞 (It is also the pen-name of 戴克崇) 李萬鶴, etc.

Short-story writer. Born in Hangchow, Chekiang. As a student in the middle school, he learned to love poetry. After reading the poetry of the T'ang and Sung Dynasties, he himself tried to write poems in the old form. In 1920, the *Ch'ang Shih Chi* 嘗試集 (The Experimental Poems) of Dr. Hu Shih 胡適 made its appearence; he read them and was not pleased. He considered that

Dr. Hu simply liberated poetry from the fetters of conventional form, but established no new form. By the time of the publication of *Nü Shên* 女神 (The Goddess) by Kuo Mo-jo 郭沫若 in 1921, the new poetry seemed to begin finding its own way, which was as he expected. He then wrote many new poems and published in the *Chüeh Wu* 覺悟, a literary supplement of the newspaper *Min Kuo Jih Pao* 民國日報, edited by Shao Li-tzŭ 邵力子. At that time the renewed *Hsiao Shuo Yüeh Pao* 小說月報 (The Short Story Magazine) published many Chinese translations of Russian novels. His interest in fiction being thus aroused, he wrote several short stories. But there were no periodicals which would accept them except the *Chüeh Wu*.

Having finished his study in middle schools, he entered the Chih Kiang University 之江大學, and was then transferred in turn to Shanghai University 上海大學, Tat'ung University 大同大學, and finally to the Université l'Aurore 震旦大學 in Shanghai. He spent five or six years reading numerous Western novels and poems, during which he published several poems in the *Hsien Tai P'ing Lun* 現代評論 (The Contemporary Review), a leading magazine of that time.

With Tai Wang-shu 戴望舒 and Tu Hêng 杜衡 he edited a periodical *Ying Lo Hsün K'an* 瓔珞旬刊; it published altogether only four numbers. It was in this magazine that he published his short stories *Ch'un Têng* 春燈 and *Chou Fu Jên* 周夫人, which attracted no attention at all. After his novel *Chüan Tzŭ* 絹子 appeared in the *Hsiao Shuo Yüeh Pao*, the name of Shih Chê-ts'un began to be known in the literary world.

After his graduation from the university he returned to his native town, Hangchow, to teach in a middle school. At that time his friends Tai Wang-shu and Liu Na-ou 劉吶鷗 established a book-store "Ti I Hsien Shu Tien" 第一線書店 in Shanghai, and edited a literary magazine *Wu Kuei Lieh Ch'ê* 無軌列車, in which he published many of his works. Later, the "Ti I Hsien Shu Tien" changed its name to "Shui Mo Shu Tien" 水沫書店. It was this book-store which published his first collection of short stories, entitled *Shang Yuan Têng* 上元燈* in 1928. This book immediately brought him fame.

In 1929, co-operating with Tai Wang-shu, Tu Hêng, Liu Na-ou and Yang Ts'un-jên 楊邨人, he edited a literary magazine *Hsin Wên I Yüeh K'an* 新文藝月刊 (The New Literature Monthly) to succeed the *Wu Kuei Lieh Ch'ê*. During that year, the movement of proletarian literature reached its highest development. Many writers participated in it; and our author, together with the *Hsin Wên I Yüeh K'an*, also turned in that direction. The two short stories *A Hsiu* 阿秀 and *Hua* 花 are his only contribution to proletarian literature; as he soon became conscious of the fact that there was no future for him in that field, he turned away from it.

He then adopted Freudism and began writing psychological novels: *Pa Li Ta Hsi Yuan* 巴黎大戲院 and *Mo Tao* 魔道, published in the *Hsiao Shuo Yüeh Pao* led many to consider him a "neo-sensationalist".

We may reduce his later fiction to three classes. The first is the historical novel, as *Chiang Chün Ti T'ou* 將軍的頭 (1933, 新中國); The second deals with abnormal psychology, as *Mei Yü Chih Hsi* 梅雨之夕 (1933, 新中國). The last is narrative of personal affairs and analysis of women's psychology, as *Shan Nü Jên Ti Hsing P'in* 善女人的行品 * (1933, 良友).

In May, 1932, he edited a literary magazine *Hsien Tai Yüeh K'an* 現代月刊 (The Modern Times), published monthly by the Hsien Tai Book Co. The contributors were all famous men of letters of that period, like Tai Wang-shu, Tu Hêng, Chên Hsüeh-fan 陳雪帆, Ou-Yang Yü-ch'ien 歐陽予倩, Mao Tun 茅盾, Wang Lu-yen 王魯彥, Pa Chin 巴金, Yeh Shao-chün 葉紹鈞, Lao Shê 老舍, Li Chin-fa 李金髮, Chang T'ien-i 張天翼, Yeh Ling-fêng 葉靈鳳, Mu Shih-Ying 穆時英, etc. This magazine held a prominent place throughout those few years. Later, he edited the *Wên I Fêng Ching* 文藝風景 (Literary Scenary), published monthly by the Kuang Hua Book Co. 光華書局; its contributors were almost identical with the authors contributing to *Hsien Tai Yüeh K'an*. It published only two numbers. Then he edited the *Wên Fan Hsiao P'in* 文飯小品, published twice per month by the Shanghai Magazine Co. 上海雜誌公司. It too was short-lived.

During the Sino-Japanese War he worked for some time with the Catholic Truth Society of Hongkong, translating a book, 轉變. Later he went to the unoccupied area of Anhwei province. In January, 1946, he returned to Shanghai, and later went to Hsüchow, where he functioned as teacher in the Kiangsu Institute 江蘇學院. He is now a professor at the Chinan University 暨南大學, Shanghai, and sometimes publishes his new writings in different literary magazines.

Works: 李師師 (良友); 無相庵小品; 雲絮詞 (printed by the author); 娟子姑娘 (亞細亞); 燈下集 * (1937, 開明); 小珍集* (1936, 良友); 待旦集; etc.

Translations: 婦心三部曲 (*Frau Bertha, Frau Beate, Fräulein Else* by A. Schnitzler, 1931, 神州國光社); 今日之藝術 (*Art Now* by Herbert Reed, 1935, 商務); 波蘭短篇小說集 (1937, 商務); 捷克短篇小說集 (商務); 匈加利短篇小說集 (商務); etc.

135. Shih P'ing-mei 石評梅.

(1902 — 1928)

Original name: 石汝璧. Pen-name: 評梅女士 · Short-story writer. Born in Pingan 平安, Shansi. After graduating from the Shansi Provincial Girls' Normal School 山西省立女子師範學校, she entered the Higher Normal School for Women 女子高等師範 at Peiping, and graduated in 1923. She then became the Principal of the Girls' Middle School affiliated with the National Normal University of Peiping 師大女附中, and concurrently teacher of Chinese and physical exercise at the same school. Before her death, which occured in 1928, she was a lecturer of the National Normal University of Peiping, and editor of the magazine *Fu Nü Chou K'an* 婦女週刊 (Women's Weekly). She left two volumes of short stories: *T'ao Yü* 濤語* (1932, 北新); and *Ou Jan Ts'ao* 偶然草 (文化書局).

136. Shih Yen 史 岩.

Original name: 史濟行 . Pen-names: 彳亍，天行，岩，華嚴一丐，齊衍，etc.

Novelist and art critic. His literary creations are: 模型女 (a novel, 1927, 光華)；蠶蛻集 * (collection of short stories, 1929, 廣益). He wrote these works on art: 東洋美術史 (1936, 商務)；現代家庭裝飾 (1933, 大東)；繪畫之理論與實際 (1935, 商務).

137. Shu Ch'ing-ch'un 舒慶春.

(1897 —)

T. 舍予. He is better known under the pen-name of Lao Shê 老舍. Novelist, short-story writer, playwright, and poet. He won wide attention in the United States with the appearance in English of one of his novels *Ricksha Boy* (Chinese name being *Lo T'o Hsiang Tzŭ* 駱駝祥子, Shanghai, Cultural Life Publishing Co. 文化生活出版社，1937), translated by Evan King, published in New York, 1945.

Shu Ch'ing-ch'un is of Manchu descent. He was born at Peiping in December 1897. Since the author rarely writes or talks about himself, little is known about his early life. All we know is that he studied at a provincial normal school where he later taught, and that he also attended the National University of Peking 北京大學, during which time he wrote short stories. Whether he received a degree from the university is unknown. He devoted several years to teaching until he accepted an opportunity to go to Oxford University to study education.

In London, he became acquainted with the late Professor Hsü Ti-shan 許地山 (better known under his pen-name Lo Hua Shêng 落華生), a well-known scholar and short-story writer. Through the latter's recommendation, Shu Ching-ch'un's first novel *Lao Chang Ti Chê Hsüeh* 老張的哲學* (The Philosophy of Old Chang, 1932, 商務) was published in 1926 in the most distinguished literary magazine *Hsiao Shuo Yüeh Pao* 小說月報 (The Short Story Magazine). It was an immediate success.

Upon returning to China, he was appointed professor at the National University of Peking 北京大學, and then at Tsingtao University 青島大學; later, he became the dean of the College of Arts and Letters of Cheeloo University 齊魯大學, Shantung. Within a few years he published seven novels besides the *Lao Chang Ti Chê Hsüeh*: *Erh Ma* 二馬* (The Messrs. Ma, 1932, 商務); *Chao Tzŭ Yüeh* 趙子曰* (Mr. Chao Said, 1933, 商務); *Li Hun* 離婚* (Divorce, 1933, 良友)；*Mao Ch'êng Chi* 貓城記* (The City of Cats, 1933, 現代); *Hsiao P'o Ti Shêng Jih* 小坡的生日* (The Birthday of Hsiao P'o, 1934, 生活); *Niu T'ien Tz'ŭ Chuan* 牛天賜傳* (Biography of Niu T'ien-tz'ŭ, 1935, 人間書屋); and *Wên Po Shih* 文博士*. And he also produced several collections of short stories: *Kan Chi* 趕集* (1934); *Ying Hai Chi* 櫻海集* (five short stories written in Tsingtao, 1935, 人間

書屋); *Ko Tsao Chi* 蛤藻集 * (Shells and Sea-Weeds, containing seven short stories, 1936, 開明); 老字號 * etc.

After the Marco Polo Bridge Incident of July, 1937, he left North China and went to Hankow. When the "National Writers' Anti-Aggression Association" 中華全國文藝界抗敵協會 was organzied there on March 27, 1938, he became the president, and by repeated re-election, has retained that position. During the War, in addition to pursuing his literary work, he was active in the organization and direction of Chinese writers in the cause of their country. Under his auspices the association sent young writers to homes and the front, and to the enemy's rear to visit Chinese soldiers and write of their experiences. The resulting stories, sketches, poems, plays, and critical articles were published in the organization's publication *K'ang Chan Wên I* 抗戰文藝 (Wartime Literature). Shu Ch'ing-ch'un himself travelled in the Northwest and produced a long narrative poem *Chien Pei P'ien* 劍北篇 (North of Chienmenkuan), of nearly forty thousand words, describing his journey to Sian and Lanchow; and a four-act play *Kuo Chia Chih Shang* 國家至上 * (The State Comes First), written in collaboration with Sung Chih-ti 宋之的, a young dramatist, portrays a stubborn Moslem who is finally convinced that to win the War he must discard racial and religious prejudices and coöperate with his fellow Chinese of other faiths. He composed several plays during the War besides the one mentioned above: *Ts'an Wu* 殘霧 (The Fog) is his first effort, and then *Mien Tzŭ Wên T'i* 面子問題 (The Problem of Face); *T'ao Li Ch'un Fêng* 桃李春風 (written in collaboration with Chao Ch'ing-ko 趙清閣, an authoress); *Chang Tzŭ Chung* 張自忠 (in four acts dealing with the heroic deeds of General Chang Tzŭ-chung); *Kuei Ch'ü Lai Hsi* 歸去來兮 * (Go Back, in five acts, 1943, 作家書屋). His novel *Huo Tsang* 火葬 * (Cremation, printed in the Literary Vanguard), depicted the guerrillas incinerated in their own villages when they refused to surrender. He also wrote short stories which he collected into *Huo Ch'ê Chi* 火車集 (1940, 上海雜誌公司); *Tung Hai Pa Shan Chi* 東海巴山集 *; *P'in Hsüeh Chi* 貧血集; etc.

After the Victory over Japan he published the first two volumes of his longest novel entitled, *Ssŭ Shih T'ung T'ang* 四世同堂 * (Four Generations Live Together, 1946, 晨光), which depicts the miserable life of Chinese masses of Peiping under Japanese occupation. It is considered to be the greatest Chinese production within the last ten years.

His newest short stories were collected into *Wei Shên Chi* 微神集 (1947, 晨光).

He was invited by the State Department for a year's stay in the United States under the Department's cultural coöperation program. He left Shanghai in March, 1946, and arrived at San Francisco in April.

His experience in writing is recorded in his *Lao Niu P'o Ch'ê* 老牛破車 *, published in 1937.

138. Shu Yin 舒湮.

Playwright. He is noted especially for his historical plays such as *Tung Hsiao Yuan* 董小宛* (光明); and *Ch'ên Yuan Yuan* 陳圓圓. In the early years of the Sino-Japanese War, he edited the ''Modern Dramatic Series'' 現代戲劇叢書 for the Kuang Ming Book Co. 光明書店, Shanghai.

Works: *Yên Chü I Shu Chiang Hua* 劇演藝術講話 (光明); *Ching Chung Pao Kuo* 精忠報國* (1944, 光明); *Lang T'ao Sha* 浪淘沙* (1946, 萬葉); etc.

Translations: 中國的再生 (by O. Erdberg, translated in collaboration with Pai Yü 柏雨. 1936, 金湯); 世界名劇精選* (Famous World Plays, 2 volumes, 1939, 光明); etc.

139. So Fei 索非.

Pen-name: A. A. Essayist, and short-story writer. From 1927 on, he worked in the Kaiming Book Co. 開明書店 for nearly 20 years. He had a thorough knowledge of medicine, thus he wrote many stories in the field of medicine for young readers. Later, he collected them into 5 volumes entitled *Chi Ping T'u Shu Kuan* 疾病圖書館 (Library of Diseases 開明); *Hai Tzŭ Mên Ti Tsai Nan* 孩子們的災難 (The Misfortunes of Children 開明); *Jên Yü Ch'ung Ti Po Tao* 人與蟲的搏鬥 (The Struggle between Man and Insects, 開明); *Jên T'i K'ô Hsüeh T'an Hsieh* 人體科學談屑 (Talks on Human Body, 開明); *Chan Shih Chiu Hu* 戰時救護, (開明). In addition to his scientific writings, he wrote also literary works, of which we may mention: *Lung T'ao Chi* 茏套集* (1946, 萬葉); *Shan Nü Jên* 善女人 (A Kind Woman); Ch'i 氣 (Anger); *K'u Ch'ü* 苦趣 (collection of essays, 1927, 開明); *Yü Chung Chi* 獄中記 (In a Prison, collection of essays, 1927, 開明); *Ch'iu Jên Chih Shu* 囚人之書 (Letters from a Prisoner, collection of essays, 開明); etc. He is also a scholar of Esperanto, on which he wrote *Shih Chieh Yü Ju Mên* 世界語入門 (How to Learn Esperanto, 開明).

140. Su Man-shu 蘇曼殊.

(1873 — 1918)

Novelist, poet, and essayist. He was of Japanese descent. After the death of his father he was adapted by a certain Mr. Su 蘇, a merchant of Kwantung, thus he changed his sur-name to Su, and named himself Hsüan-ying 玄瑛 Man-shu was his religious name when later he became a monk. He knew English and French, and was specialized in the Buddhist Canons. Besides, he was also known as a painter. He died at the age of 35, leaving many poems, essays, and novels, which were collected into *Su Man Shu Ch'üan Chi* 蘇曼殊全集 (The Complete Works of Su Man-shu), 5 volumes, compiled by Liu Ya-tzu 柳亞子, and published by the Pei Hsin Book Co. 北新書局, 1928-1931. His autobiographical novel *Tuan*

Hung Ling Yen Chi 斷鴻零雁記 was translated into English by George Kin Leung under the title *Lone Swan*, published by the Commercial Press, Shanghai.

141. Su Mei 蘇 梅.

(1897 —   )

Original name: 蘇小梅, T. 雪林· Pen-names: 綠漪, 靈芬, 天嬰, 老梅, etc.

Novelist, short-story writer, essayist, and scholar. Born in Taiping, Anhwei. She became a Catholic in 1924. After her graduation from the National Normal University for Women 女子師範大學, Peiping, in 1921, she went to France, where she studied fine arts in the Université d'Outre-mer de Lyon. Upon returning to China in 1925, she was appointed professor of Chinese literature at Hu Kiang University 滬江大學 of Shanghai, Tung Wu University 東吳大學 of Soochow, and Anhwei University 安徽大學. From 1931 on, she served as professor at Wuhan University 武漢大學.

During the Sino-Japanese War, she lived in Loshan, Szechwan, to where the Wuhan University moved. In spite of her ill health, she never ceased to write. After the Victory over Japan, she returned to Wuchang, still holds the position at Wuhan University.

Up to 1947, she wrote 11 volumes altogether. They are: 李義山戀愛事蹟考 (Treatise on the Romantic Life of Li I-shan, a famous poet of T'ang Dynasty, 1927, 北新); 綠天* (Green Sky, collection of short stories, 1928, 北新); 棘心* (Bitter Heart, an autobiographical novel, 1929, 北新); 蠹魚的生活 (literary studies, 1929, 眞美善); 唐詩概論 (Poetry of the T'ang Dynasty, 1934, 商務); 屠龍集 (collection of short stories, 1941,· 商務); 南明忠烈傳 (Biographies of the Loyalists in the End of Ming Dynasty 1941, Chungking); 鳩那羅的眼睛 (collection of plays, 1946, 商務); 遼金元文學 (Literature of Liao, Chin, and Yuan, 1934, 商務); 青鳥集 (literary studies); and 蟬蛻集 (1945, 商務).

142. Sun Chia-jui 孫嘉瑞.

Pen-name: 梅娘. Novelist. She was known by her novels 魚*, 蟹*, 第二代, etc., all published in Peiping during the Japanese occupation.

143. Sun Fu-hsi 孫福熙.

(1898 —   )

T. 春苔. Pen-names: 丁一, 壽明齋, etc. Essayist. Born in Shaohsing, Chekiang. He is a younger brother of Sun Fu-yuan 孫伏園, a well-known writer. He graduated from the College of Fine Arts at Lyon, France. Upon returning to

China, he became a professor at the National Academy of Fine Arts 國立藝專, Hangchow, and editor-in-chief of a monthly magazine *I Fêng Yüeh K'an* 藝風月刊. In 1932, he edited the *Hsiao Kung Hsien* 小貢獻 (Little Contribution), a literary supplement of the newspaper *Chung Hua Jih Pao* 中華日報. Later he settled down at Westlake, Chekiang, and devoted himself completely in writing. During the Sino-Japanese War, he went to Yunnan where he taught in different schools. After the Victory over Japan, he edited for a short time the literary supplement of the evening paper *I Shih Pao* 益世報晚刊, at Nanking. He is now at Shanghai.

Works: *Ch'un Ch'ên* 春城 (開明); *Pei Ching Hu* 北京乎 (開明); *Kuei Hang* 歸航 (開明); *Shan Yeh To Shih* 山野掇拾* (開明); *San Hu Yu Chi* 三湖遊記 (開明); etc.

144. Sun Hsi-chên   孫席珍.

(1906 —   )

Courtesy name of 孫彭, but he is noted for this name instead of the original. Pen-names: 鄒宏道，織雲女士, etc.

Novelist, and literary critic. Born in Shaohsing, Chekiang. His career started as proof-reader for the newspaper *Ch'ên Pao* 晨報. In 1931, through the recommendation of Chao Ching-shên 趙景深, he became a teacher in the Loyang Normal School 洛陽師範 Honan. Later he taught Chinese and Western literature in different universities at Peiping, such as: National Normal University 師範大學, Min Kuo University 民國大學, China University 中國大學, and the Women's College of Arts and Science of the National Peiping University 北平大學女子文理學院. In January, 1935, he was arrested by the authorities in Peiping on charges of radicalism.

His interest in literature revealed itself very early. While still a child, he began to write. He contributed first to the literary supplement of *Ch'ên Pao*, and the *Shih K'an* 詩刊 (Poetry Magazine), edited by Yeh Shao-chün 葉紹鈞, and Liu Yen-ling 劉延陵. He became famous through the publication of his trilogy: *Chan Ch'ang Shang* 戰場上 (The Field of War), *Chan Chêng Chung* 戰爭中 (War), and *Chan Hou* 戰後 (After War). Besides these he has published six novels: Chin *Pien* 金鞭 (Golden Whip); *Tao Ta Lien Ch'ü* 到大連去 (To Talien, 春潮); *Hua Huan* 花環 (The Ring of Flowers, 亞細亞); *Fêng Hsien Ku Niang* 鳳仙姑娘 (Miss Fêng Hsien, 現代); *Nü Jên Ti Hsin* 女人的心 (Heart of Woman); and *Yeh Chiao Chiao* 夜皎皎. His critical works are *Hsin K'o Lai P'ing Chuan* 辛克萊評傳 (A Critical Study of Upton Sinclair, 神州國光社); *Hsüeh Lai Shêng Huo* 雪萊生活 (Life of Shelley, 世界); *Mo Po Sang Ti Shêng Huo* 莫泊桑的生活 (Life of Maupassant, 世界); *Kao Erh Chi P'ing Chuan* 高爾基評傳 (Critical Study of Gorky); *Chin Tai Wên I Ssŭ Ch'ao* 近代文藝思潮 (Modern Western Literature, 人文); etc.
    Translations: 英國文學研究 (*Interpretations of Literature* by L. Hearn, 現代); 東印度故事 (East Indian Tales, 亞細亞); etc.

145. Sun Ta-k'o 孫大珂.

Pen-name: 石靈. Novelist, and playwright. He is praised especially for his stories of rural life. Besides, he wrote also some popular stories for the uneducated people. His dramatic works are: *T'ao Hua Mêng* 桃花夢 (a play in five acts, its original title is *Tang T'a Mên Mêng Hsing Ti Shih Hou* 當他們夢醒的時候, When They Awoke, 世界); *Wo Mên Fang K'ai En Yuan* 我們放開恩怨 (a one-act play); *Wang Fei Hsin Chi* 枉費心機* (1941, 光明); etc. He is the author of a novel, called *Pu Huang Chê* 捕蝗者* (The Grasshopper-Catcher, 1935, 中華). Translation: 鮑志遠 (by Ibsen, published in the magazine *Wên I Hsin Ch'ao* 文藝新潮).

146. Sung Chih-ti 宋之的.

(1914 —   )

Playwright. Born of a family of farmers in Hopei. His family wanted him to become a railway engineer, so the boy went to work with an uncle on the Peiping-Suiyuan railway. The rapid pace of political events in 1927 turned him toward books of social implication. He was influenced by such writers as Tolstoy, Dostoevsky, Balzac, and Lu Hsün 魯迅. In 1928, after the railway explosion that killed Chang Tso-lin 張作霖, the Manchurian war lord, Sung Chih-ti took part in an anti-imperialist, anti-Japanese school play. The Mukden Incident of September 18, 1931, terminated his college career midway. With many other students, he joined the National Salvation Movement. Their patriotic, propagandist plays frequently involved him with the police in the days when China was appeasing Japan. The outbreak of the Sino-Japanese War in July, 1937, started Sung Chih-ti on his playwriting career, and he later toured Western China with a troupe staging his own and other modern plays.

Before the War, he had published a historical drama, entitled *Wu Tsê-t'ien* 武則天, describing the life of an empress of the T'ang Dynasty. After the outbreak of the Sino-Japanese War, corporating with A Ying 阿英, Chang Min 章泯 and 13 other playwrights, he wrote *Lu Kou Ch'iao* 蘆溝橋 which depicts the Marco Polo Bridge Incident of July, 1937. He then collaborated with Ch'ên Pai-ch'ên 陳白塵 in adapting Schiller's *Wilhelm Tell* into *Min Tsu Wan Sui* 民族萬歲 (Long Live China), which was enthusiastically received by the public when it was performed in Hankow, Yichang, Chungking, and Chengtu, during the early year of the War. His *Tzu Wei Tui* 自衛隊 (Self-Defence Corps, also named *Min Tsu Kuang Jung* 民族光榮 Glory of the Nation, in 4 acts) depicts the guerrillas. *Fa* 罰 (Punishment) concerns a young magistrate who takes the place of a corrupt old official. *Wu Ch'ung Ch'ing* 霧重慶 (Foggy Chungking, also named *Pien* 鞭, Whip, 1940, 生活 in 4 acts) describes the backwash of the War's initial wave of patriotism. *Tsu Kuo Ti Hu Shêng* 祖國的呼聲 (Fatherland Calling) tells a physician who remains behind in Occupied China to give medical aid to his fellow countrymen, until finally he is forced to admit that the Japanese yoke makes an objective stand impossible, and he slips through the lines to Unoccupied

China. *Kuo Chia Chih Shang* 國家至上 (The State Comes First), written in collaboration with Lao Shê, portrays a stubborn Moslem who was finally convinced that to win the War he must discard racial and religious prejudices and coöperate with his fellow Chinese of other faiths.

In 1939, he was sent by the "National Writers' Anti-Aggression Association" 中華全國文藝界抗敵協會 to pay visit to the Chinese soldiers at the front, and produced a play, entitled *K'ai Ko* 凱歌* (Victory, 1946, 上海書局), when he came back. He then edited the magazine *Wên I Chên Ti* 文藝陣地 (Literary Field), in collaboration with Mao Tun 茅盾, in Chungking. After the Victory over Japan, he went to Lini, Shantung.

In addition to the works mentioned above, he also wrote: *Hsi Chü Ch'un Ch'iu* 戲劇春秋 (Birth Struggles of the Modern Play, written in collaboration with Hsia Yen and Yü Ling 于伶); *Ts'ao Mu Chieh Ping* 草木皆兵 (a play, written in collaboration with Hsia Yen and Yü Ling); *Ch'un Han* 春寒* (Coldness of Spring, a play in 5 acts); etc.

147. Sung Ch'un-fang 宋春舫.

(1891 —   ?)

Playwright. Born in Wuhing, Chekiang. At the age of 13, he received the degree of Hsiu-Ts'ai 秀才 under the Ch'ing Dynasty. After graduating from St. John's University, Shanghai, he went to Switzerland to study social and political science at Geneva University, where he graduated with M.A. degree. Upon returning to China, he was appointed lecturer on modern languages at St. John's University, 1916-17. He taught French at Tsinghua University 清華大學 in 1918, and at the National University of Peking 北京大學 from 1918 to 1920. Later he travelled in Europe to study postwar social conditions and literary tendencies in 1920, and there he also served as secretary of the Chinese Delegation to the Peace Conference at Paris. On his return, he became a professor of French literature at Tung Wu University 東吳大學, Shanghai, and then the director of library of the National Tsingtao University 青島大學, and concurrently councillor of the Municipal Government of Tsingtao.

Works: *Parcourant le Monde en Flammes* (in French, 1917, Shanghai, Presse Orientale); *Sung Ch'un-fang Lun Chü* 宋春舫論劇 (Essays on Drama, vol. 1, 1923, 商務; vol. 2, 1936, 生活); *Wu Li Wu Chung* 五里霧中 (What's It All About? A comedy in three acts, 1936, 生活); *I Fu Hsi Shên* 一幅喜神 (a play, 新月); etc.

148. Tai K'o-ch'ung 戴克崇.

(1907 —   )

Pen-names: 杜衡, 蘇汶, 蘇文, 文木, 白冷, 老頭兒, 李今, 江兼霞 (It is also the pen-name of Shih Chê-ts'un 施蟄存); etc.

Novelist, and short-story writer. Born in Kiangsu. He graduated from the Université l'Aurore, where he cultivated friendship with his school-mates Tai Wang-shu 戴望舒, and Shih Chê-ts'un. Later, they founded many enterprizes.

In his boyhood he read only the classical prose of the T'ung Ch'êng School 桐城派. At the age of 17, he left his native place and arrived Shanghai, where he happened to read Ch'ên Lun 沉淪 (Downfall), a novel by Yü Ta-fu 郁達夫, and the Chinese translations of Ibsen's plays. Stimulated by what he read, he himself tried to write fiction and plays, which were all unsuccessful experiments.

At the age of 20, his first collection of short stories entitled Shih Liu Hua 石榴花 was published by the book-store "Ti I Hsien Shu Tien" 第一線書店, founded by Tai Wang-shu and Liu Na-ou 劉吶鷗. Later, collaborating with Tai Wang-shu, he edited two literary magazines Ying Lo 瓔珞 and Wu Kuei Lieh Ch'ê 無軌列車, both of which were short-lived. In 1927, he returned to his native place, where he translated 道連格雷畫像 (The Picture of Dorian Gray by O. Wilde, 1928, 金屋書店), and 黛絲 (Thaïs by A. France, 1928, 開明). And at the same year, through the recommendation of Tai Wang-shu, he began to publish his short stories in the famous Hsiao Shuo Yüeh Pao 小說月報 (The Short Story Magazine), edited by Yeh Shao-chün 葉紹鈞.

In 1929, when the progress of the proletarian literature reached its highest development, Tai K'o-ch'ung also turned to that direction. He wrote two short stories Hei Kua Fu Chieh 黑寡婦街 (The Street of the Black Widow), and Chi Ch'i Ch'ên Mo Ti Shih Hou 機器沉默的時候 (When Machine is Silent), published in the Wu Kuei Lieh Ch'ê, under the pen-name of Su Wên 蘇汶, which were his only contribution to proletarian literature.

In 1929, co-operating wih Tai Wang-shu, Shih Chê-ts'un, Liu Na-ou, and Yang Ts'un-jên 楊邨人, he edited a literary monthly Hsin Wên I Yüeh K'an 新文藝月刊 to succeed the Wu Kuei Lieh Ch'ê. In 1932, at the invitation of Shih Chê-ts'un, he became a co-editor of the literary monthly Hsien Tai 現代 (Modern Times). And he launched, at the same year, a fierce literary quarrel with the left writers about the freedom in literary creation. These articles were collected in his Wên I Tzǔ Yu Lun Pien Chi 文藝自由論辯集 (1933, 現代).

After the outbreak of the Sino-Japanese War, he went to Hongkong and became a Catholic. With the fall of Hongkong, he proceeded to Szechwan, where he served as the editor-in-chief of the South Press 南方印書館, and the editor-in-chief of the newspaper Chung Yang Jih Pao 中央日報.

Works: 懷鄉集* (collection of short stories, 1933, 現代); 叛徒 (a novel, 1936, 今代); 漩渦裏外* (a novel, 1937, 良友); etc.

Translations: 結婚集 (Married by A. Strindberg, 1929, 光華); 哨兵 (Sentry by B. Prus, 1930, 光華); 統治者 (by T. Hardy, 1937, 商務); etc.

149. T'ai Ching-nung 臺靜農.

(1902 —   )

Short-story writer. Born in Hwokiu, Anhwei. He graduated from the National University of Peking 北京大學. Later, he taught in the Fu Jên University 輔仁大學 Peiping. During the Sino-Japanese War, he lectured in the National Fuhtan University 復旦大學 at Peipei 北碚, near Chungking.

After the Victory over Japan, he went to Formosa, where he was appointed the chairman of the Department of Chinese Literature of the National University of Formosa 台灣大學.

T'ai Ching-nung was one of the founders of the "Anonymous Society" 未名社, and his short stories were published mostly in the association's publications: *Mang Yuan* 莽原, and *Wei Ming* 未名 Later, he collected these narratives into two volumes, entitled *Ti Chih Tzŭ* 地之子* (The Children of Earth, 1928, 未名社); and *Chien T'a Chê* 建塔者 (The Pagoda Builder, 1930, 未名社). He compiled *Kuan Yü Lu Hsün Chi Ch'i Chu Tso* 關於魯迅及其著作 (Lu Hsün: Life and Works, 1926, 未名社); and *Huai Nan Min Ko Chi* 淮南民歌集 (Folksongs of the South of Huai River).

150. T'ang T'ao 唐弢.

(1913 —   )

Pen-names: 風子, 晦庵, etc. Essayist. Born in Chenhai, Chekiang. He contributed first to the *Tzŭ Yu T'an* 自由談 (Free Talk), a literary supplement of *Shên Pao* 申報, edited by Li Lieh-wen 黎烈文, a returned student from France. During the Sino-Japanese War, he stayed in Shanghai, and edited the magazine *Wên I Chieh* 文藝界 (Literary World). In Septemter, 1946, he edited the weekly magazine *Chou Pao* 周報 at Shanghai, together with K'o Ling 柯靈 (pen-name of Kao Chi-lin 高季琳), the essayist and playwright. It had but a short life. He then became the editor of *Pi Hui* 筆會, a literary supplement of the newspaper *Wên Hui Pao* 文匯報, Shanghai.

Works: *Wên Chang Hsiu Yang* 文章修養 (1939, 文化生活出版社); *Tuan Ch'ang Shu* 短長書 (collection of essays, 1947, 南國出版社); *T'ou Ying Chi* 投影集 (collection of essays, 文化生活出版社); *Hai T'ien Chi* 海天集* (1936, 新鍾); etc.

151. T'ien Chün 田軍.

Pen-name: 蕭軍. Novelist, and short-story writer. He is known to the American readers by his novel *Village in August* (Chinese title being *Pa Yüeh Ti Hsiang Ts'un* 八月的鄉村 1936, 容光), translated into English by Evan King, and published in New York in 1942.

Born in Manchuria, he left his native place after the Mukden Incident of September 18, 1931, and went to Shanghai together with his wife Hsiao Hung

蕭紅, also a famous novelist. Both won fame by their narrative of the life of Chinese masses in Manchuria under Japanese occupation.

During the early years of the Sino-Japanese War, he edited the literary supplement of the newspaper *Hsin Min Pao* 新民報 in Chengtu. Later he went to Yenan, the former Red capital. He is now still working with the Communists.

Works: *Yang* 羊 (Sheep, collection of short stories, 1935, 文化生活出版社); *Chiang Shang* 江上* (On the River, collection of short stories, 1936, 文化生活出版社); *Lü Yeh Ti Ku Shih* 綠葉的故事 (Story of a Green Leaf, collection of essays, 1936, 文化生活出版社); *Ti San Tai* 第三代 (The Third Generation, a novel, 1937, 文化生活出版社); *Shih Yüeh Shih Wu Jih* 十月十五日* (October the Fifteenth, collection of essays, 文化生活出版社); etc.

152. T'ien Han 田 漢.

      (1898 —   )

    T. 壽昌. Pen-names: 伯鴻, 明高, 春夫, 張堃, 陳瑜, 漢仙, 漱人, 鐵端章, etc.

Dramatist. Born in Changsha, Hunan, on March 12, 1898. He entered, in 1911, the Changsha Normal School 長沙師範學校 After his graduation there, he went to Japan, where he studied in the Superior Normal School of Tokyo. Upon returning to China, he took part in the "Creative Society" 創造社, organized by Kuo Mo-jo 郭沫若, Chang Tzu-p'ing 張資平, Yü Ta-fu 郁達夫, and Ch'êng Fang-wu 成仿吾. But he soon separated from the group after a dispute with Ch'êng Fang-wu, and founded the society "Nan Kuo" (Le Midi) 南國社, in collaboration with his wife I Sou-yü 易漱瑜, to promote the new dramatic movement. He published a fortnightly, under the same name *Le Midi*, which suspended after its fourth issue. After working for a little while in the New Youth Motion Picture Co. 新少年影片公司, he became professor at Shanghai University of Fine Arts 上海藝術大學. Later he founded a college of fine arts, still in the name "Le Midi" 南國藝術學院, at Shanghai, in collaboration with Hsü Pei-hung 徐悲鴻, and a few others. He taught dramatic arts in Chinan University 暨南大學, Great China University 大夏大學, and Fuhtan University 復旦大學. And he served for some time as an editor in the Chung Hwa Book Co. 中華書局.

In 1938, he joined the Ministry of Political Training, and served as the director of the Bureau of Fine Arts of the Third Department. Later he devoted himself to the promotion of the movement for the adaptation of Peking drama to modern needs. A troupe of dramatic workers under his leadership toured the northwestern provinces, during the Sino-Japanese War, giving performances of modern Peking dramas; everywhere they went with much success. He is now in Shanghai.

He wrote the following dramatic works: 新桃花扇, 咖啡店之一夜, 環球璘與薔薇, 獲虎之夜, 午飯之前, 暴風雨中的七個女性, 薔薇之路, 南歸, 一致, 蘇州夜話, 湖上悲劇，名優之死，生之意志，古潭里的聲音，火之跳舞，孫中山之死，第五號病室，卡門，三個摩登女性，母性之光，到民間去，etc. T'ien Han's collected works, entitled *T'ien Han Hsi Chü Chi* 田漢戲劇集 *, 5 volumes, were published between 1930 and 1933, by the Hsien Tai Book Co. 現代書局.

During the War he wrote: 麗人行*，秋聲賦，江漢漁歌，情探，武松與潘金蓮，etc.

The collections of his essays are: 田漢散文集 (1936, 今代); and 銀色的夢 (良友). And he wrote one volume on the principles of literature, entitled 文學概論 (1927, 中華).

Translations: 哈夢雷特 (*Hamlet* by W. Shakespeare, 1930, 中華); 羅密歐與朱麗葉 (*Romeo and Juliet* by W. Shakespeare, 1930, 中華); 戲劇檻論 (by K. Kishida, 1933, 中華); 復活 (*Resurrection* by L. Tolstoy, 1936, 上海雜誌公司); 霣泰棋兒之死 (*La Mort de Tintagiles* by M. Maeterlinck, 現代); 圍着棺的人們 (by U. Akita, 亞東); 父歸 (by K. Kikuchi); 沙樂美 (*Salomé* by O. Wilde); 日本現代劇三種 (東南); 日本現代劇選 (中華); etc.

153. T'ien T'ao 田 濤.

Novelist, and short-story writer. He wrote the following works: *Huang* 荒* (Dearth, collection of short stories, 1940, 文化生活出版社); *Chan Ti Chien Chi* 戰地剪集 (Sketches Written in the Battlefield, 1940, Chungking, 正中); *Yen* 熖* (Flame, a novel, 1946, Peiping, 大道出版社); *Hsi Wang* 希望* (Hope, collection of short stories, 1946, 萬葉); *Ch'ao* 潮 (Tide, a novel, 1946, 建國); *Wo T'u* 沃土 (Fertile Land, a novel, 1947, 文化生活出版社).

154. Ting Hsi-lin 丁西林.

(1893 —   )

Original name: 丁燮林. T. 巽甫. Playwright. Born in Taihing, Kiangsu. He completed his advanced education in England, where he received M. Sc. degree from Birmingham University. Upon returning to China, he was appointed professor of physics at the National University of Peking 北京大學, and then at the National Central University of Nanking 中央大學. From 1928 on, he served as the director of the Research Institute of Physics in the Academia Sinica. In 1945, he was invited by the Soviet Government to attend the celebration of the 220th anniversary of the Soviet Academy of Sciences in Moscow and Leningrad. He is now a professor of physics at Shantung University 山東大學, Tsingtao.

Works: *I Chih Ma Fêng* 一隻螞蜂 (A Hornet, 1925, 新月 It contains three pieces: *Chiu Hou* 酒後 *Ch'in Ai Ti Chang Fu* 親愛的丈夫, and *I Chih Ma Fêng*); *Hsi Lin Tu Mu Chü* 西林獨幕劇* (One-act Plays of Ting Hsi-lin, 1925, 新月); *Miao Fêng Shan* 妙峰山* (1945, 文化生活出版社); etc.

155. Tsang K'o-chia 臧克家.

(1910 —   )

Poet, and short-story writer. Born in Chucheng, Shantung. After graduating from a normal school, he joined the Revolutionary Army during the Northern Expedition, 1927. He left politics after the success of the Revolutionists, and entered the Shantung University 山東大學 at Tsingtao, where he graduated in 1933. He then taught in various middle schools of Shantung. During the Sino-Japanese War, he went to Changsha, where he edited the magazine *K'ang Chan Wên I* 抗戰文藝 (Wartime Literature). Later he proceeded to Chungking, and never ceased writing. After the Victory over Japan, he returned to Shanghai, and edited the monthly magazine *Wên Hsün* 文訊 (Literary News), published by the Wên T'ung Book Co. 文通書局. Its contributors are: Kuo Mo-jo 郭沫若, Mao Tun 茅盾, Yeh Shao-chün 葉紹鈞, T'ang T'ao 唐弢, Yuan Shui-p'ai 袁水拍, Fang Ching 方敬, Li Chien-wu 李健吾, etc.

Being a poet, Tsang K'o-chia is realistic in his approach but did not despise beauty in form. In a way, his poems best reflects the spirit of our times. He attempted to lead a movement for simplicity and clarity in opposition to an abstruse symbolist school initiated by Li Chin-fa 李金髮 and followed by Tai Wang-shu 戴望舒.

Works: *Tsui E Ti Hei Shou* 罪惡的黑手 (The Black Hand of Sin, collection of poems, 1934, 生活); *Lo Yin* 烙印 (collection of poems, 1934, 開明); *Yun Ho* 運河 (The Canal, collection of poems, 1936, 文化生活出版社); *Tzŭ Chi Ti Hsieh Chao* 自己的寫照 (Self-portraiture, a long poem of one thousand lines, 1936, 生活); *Huai Shang Yin* 淮上吟 (a long poem, 1941, 上海雜誌公司); *Ku Shu Ti Hua To* 古樹的花朵 (a long poem of five thousand lines, Chungking); *Ni Nao Chi* 泥淖集 (collection of poems, 生活); *Ts'ung Chün Hsing* 從軍行 (collection of poems, 生活); *Shêng Ming Ti Ling Tu* 生命的零度 (collection of poems); *Ni T'u Ti Ko* 泥土的歌 (collection of poems); *Kan Ch'ing Ti Yeh Ma* 感情的野馬 (a long poem, 1946, 建國); *Pao Pei Erh* 寶貝兒* (collection of poems, 1946, 萬葉); *Wo Ti Shih Shêng Huo* 我的詩生活 (My Poetic Life, 1947, 讀書出版社); *Kua Hung* 掛紅 (collection of short stories, 1947, 讀書出版社); *Yung Pao* 擁抱 (Embrace, collection of short stories, 1947, 上海寰星出版社); etc.

156. Ts'ao Chih-lin 曹之林.

Also named 曹京平. He is better known under the pen-name of Tuan Mu Hung Liang 端木蕻良. Novelist, and short-story writer. He first aroused the attention of the public by his short stories *Hsüeh Yeh* 雪夜 (Snowy Night), and *Lu Tzŭ Hu Ti Yu Yü* 鷺鷥湖的憂鬱 (Sorrow of the Lu Tzŭ Lake), appeared in the monthly magazine *Wên Hsüeh* 文學 (Literature), which were highly praised by Mao Tun 茅盾, the famous novelist and literary critic. During the Sino-Japanese War, he was very active in Kweilin. He lives now in Hankow, and publishes sometimes his new writings in the literary magazine *Wên I Ch'un Ch'iu* 文藝春秋 of Shanghai.

Works: 科爾沁旗草原* (1939, 開明)；風陵渡 (1940, 上海雜誌公司)；憎恨* (1946, 文化生活出版社)；新都花絮 (1946, 知識出版社)；大江 (1947, 晨光)；etc.

157. Ts'ao Wei-fêng 曹未風.

Translator. He translated the completed works of Shakespeare into Chinese. They were published during the Sino-Japanese War at Kweichow by the Wên T'ung Book Co. 交通書局. After the Victory over Japan, ten of them were reprinted by the Interculture Inc. 文化合作公司 of Shanghai. They are: 1. 仲夏夜的夢 (*A Midsummer - Night's Dream*); 2. 安東尼及柏婁薤 (*Antony and Cleopatra*); 3. 如願 (*As You Like It*); 4. 李耳王 (*King Lear*); 5. 馬克白斯 (*Macbeth*); 6. 微尼斯商人 (*The Merchant of Venice*); 7. 漢姆萊特 (*Hamlet*); 8. 暴風雨 (*Tempest*); 9. 羅米歐與朱麗棄 (*Romeo and Juliet*); and 凡隆納的二紳士 (*Two Gentlemen of Verona*).

158. Tsêng Chin-k'o 曾今可.

Pen-names: 君荷, 金凱荷, etc.

Poet, novelist, and short-story writer. He contributed first to the magazines *Yü Ssŭ* 語絲, and *Malaya* 馬來亞. In 1931, he edited a literary monthly *Hsin Shih Tai* 新時代 (New Times) at Shanghai, published by the Hsin Shih Tai Book Co. 新時代書局. The contributors are: Pa Chin 巴金 Ch'ên Ying 沈櫻 Ku Chung-i 顧仲彝, and a few others. He is now a professor at the National University of Formosa, 台灣大學, and concurrently serves as the chief editor of the Chêng Fêng Publishing Co. 正風出版社.

Works: 愛的逃避 (containing six short stories, 1931, 新時代)；訣絕之書 (collection of short stories, 1932, 新時代)；死 (a novel, 1932, 新時代)；小鳥集 (1933, 新時代)；一個商人與賊* (1933, 新時代)；玲玲的日記 (1933, 兒童書局)；法公園之夜 (馬來亞)；兩顆星 (新時代)；愛的三部曲 (collection of poems, 馬來亞)；etc.

159. Tsêng P'u 曾樸.

(1871 — 1935)

T. 太樸, 孟樸, 小木, H. 籀齋. Pen-name: 東亞病夫.

Novelist, and miscellaneous writer. Born in Changshu, Kiangsu. He was a Chü-jên 舉人 of the late Ch'ing dynasty. After living an official career for many years, he retired from the political world and founded a book-store "Chên Mei Shan Shu Tien" 眞美善書店 at Shanghai with his son, Tsêng Hsü-pai 曾虛白, a novelist.

Tsêng P'u was a prolific writer. His complete works, published by the above-mentioned bookstore, contain six volumes of poems, two volumes of essays, five volumes of sketches, one play, and two novels. His fame chiefly rests on his fiction *Nieh Hai Hua* 孽海花, and *Lu Nan Tzŭ* 魯男子*. They are considered to be the best novels at the end of the Ch'ing dynasty.

Translations: 呂克蘭斯鮑夏 (*Lucrèce Borgia* by V. Hugo, 1927, 眞美善), 呂伯蘭 (*Ruy Blas* by V. Hugo, 1927, 眞美善); 歐那尼 (*Hernani* by V. Hugo, 1927, 眞美善); 死與肉 (*Aphrodite* by P. Louiys, 1927, 眞美善); 項日樂 (*Angelo* by V. Hugo, 景山); 夫人學堂 (*L'Ecole des Femmes* by Molière, 景山); etc.

160. Tuan K'o-ch'ing 段可情.

Poet, and short-story writer. Born in Szechwan. After finishing his middle school studies, he went to Japan, from thence he proceeded to Europe, where he studied Western literature for four years. He then lived in U.S.S.R. about one year to study literary criticism. Upon returning to China, he published his works in the *Creation Monthly* 創造月刊 edited by the "Creative Society" 創造社

Works: *Tu Chüan Hua* 杜鵑花* (containing six short stories, 1934, 現代); *Pa Li Chih Ch'un* 巴黎之春 (The Spring of Paris); etc.

Translations: 死 (*Der Tod* by A. Schnitzler, 現代); 新春 (by H. Heine); etc.

161. Wan Chia-pao 萬家寶.

(1905 —   )

T. 小石. He is better known under the pen-name of Ts'ao Yü 曹禺.

Playwright. Born in Tsienkiang, Hupeh. Between 1926 and 1930, he was a member of the "Nankai Dramatic Club" 南開劇社, and translated some modern European plays into Chinese. He graduated from the Departmant of Western Languages and Literature of the National Tsinghua University 清華大學 in 1934. At the same year, he published his first play *Lei Yü* 雷雨* (Thunder and Rain, 1936, 文化生活出版社) in the second issue of the famous *Wên Hsüeh Chi K'an* 文學季刊 , (Literary Quarterly). Like lightning, the play created a sensation in the twinkling of an eye. and the author was hailed by the reading public, as well as the theater-goers, like the thunder that ensued. The English translation, rendered by Mr. Yao Hsin-nung 姚莘農, was published in *T'ien Hsia Monthly*, vol. 3-4, 1936-1937. His second play *Jih Ch'u* 日出* (The Sun Comes Up, 1936, 文化生活出版社) won the *Ta Kung Pao* Literary Prize 大公報文學獎金 for the best play in 1936. And in 1937, he produced his third work *Yuan Yeh* 原野* (Wilderness, 文化生活出版社). The three plays formed the "Trilogy of Ts'ao Yü".

After teaching for a short time in the Tientsin Normal College for Women 天津女子師範學院 , he was appointed the principal of the National Academy of Dramatic Arts 國立劇專 at Nanking. In 1937, he taught at the National Tsinghua University. When the Sino-Japanese War broke out, he went to the Interior with many of his friends in the August of the same year, and became soon the principal of the National Academy of Dramatic Arts at Chungking.

During the War, he wrote *Pei Ching Jên* 北京人* (Peking Man); *T'o Pien* 蛻變*; *Chia* 家* (Family, an adaptation of Pa Chin's novel 家); *Chêng Tsai Hsiang* 正在想 (文化生活出版社); and *Hei Tzŭ Erh Shih Pa* 黑字二十八 (in collaboration with Sung Chih-ti 宋之的), and translated 柔密歐與幽麗葉 (*Romeo and Juliet* by W. Shakespeare).

Ts'ao Yü is a playwright of international fame. After the Victory over Japan, he was invited by the State Department for a year's stay in the United States. He left Shanghai in March, 1946, and arrived America in April. He functions now as professor at the Experimental Dramatic School of Shanghai 上海市立實驗戲劇學校 His newest production *Ch'iao* 橋 (Bridge) was published in the literary monthly *Wên I Fu Hsing* 文藝復興 (Renaissance), edited by Li Chien-wu 李健吾 and Chêng Chên-to 鄭振鐸.

162. Wan Ti-ho 萬迪鶴.

Short-story writer, and novelist. He became known in 1934. His first collection of short stories, entitled *Huo Tsang* 火葬* (Cremation), was published in 1935, by the Liang Yu Publishing Co. 良友圖書公司. *Cremation*, from which the collection gets its name, is a story of the farmers' resistance against oppression. In 1936, he produced his second volume, enitled *Ta Shêng P'ien* 達生篇 (A Worker's Life and Other Stories, 文化生活出版社). During the Sino-Japanese War, he was in the Interior, where he published his writings in the magazine *K'ang Chan Wên I* 抗戰文藝 (Wartime Literature). His novel, *Chung Kuo Ta Hsüeh Shêng Jih Chi* 中國大學生日記 (Diary of a Chinese University Student), was published in the War years by the Life Book Co. 生活書店.

163. Wang Ch'ang-chien 王長簡.

Pen-names: 蘆焚, 師陀 etc. Novelist, short-story writer, and essayist. He received no school education. All the knowledge about literature he acquired through constant self-study. As a fiction writer, he is adept in the description of Chinese rural life. His *Ku* 谷 (The Valley, 1936, 文化生活出版社) won the *Ta Kung Pao* 大公報 literary prize as the best short story of 1936. Works: *Huang Hua T'ai* 黃花苔* (collection of essays, 1937, 良友); *Shang Hai Shou Cha* 上海手札 (collection of essays, 1941, 文化生活出版社); *Ma Lan* 馬蘭 (a novel, 1942, 文化生活出版社); *Kuo Ch'êng Yuan Chi* 果城園記 (1946, 上海書店); *Chieh Hun* 結婚 (Marriage, a novel, 1947, 晨光); *K'an Jên Chi* 看人集* (collection of essays, 1947, 開明); *Chiang Hu Chi* 江湖集* (collection of essays, 1947, 開明); *Yeh Tien* 夜店 (a four-act play, based on Gorky's *Night at an Inn*, written in collaboration with K'o Ling 柯靈, 1947, 上海出版公司); *Li Mên Shih Chi* 里門拾記* (collection of short stories, 文化生活出版社); *Yeh Niao Chi* 野鳥集 (Wild Bird, collection of short stories, 文化生活出版社); etc.

164. Wang Chung-hsien 汪仲賢.

Pen-name: 優遊.

Playwright of the early years of Chinese new literary movement. In 1921, together with Ch'ên Ta-pei 陳大悲, P'u Po-ying 蒲伯英, Ou-Yang Yü-ch'ien 歐陽予倩, Sung Ch'un-fang 宋春舫, and Hsü Pan-mei 徐半梅, he organized the "Mass Dramatic Association" 民衆戲劇社 in Shanghai, and published a monthly magazine *Hsi Chü* 戲劇 (Drama) in the May of that year, which suspended publication in April, 1922. Then, collaborating with the same dramatists mentioned above, he inaugarated the "New China Dramatic Union" 新中華戲劇協社 in Shanghai, and continued to promote the new dramatic movement. His play *Hao Erh Tzŭ* 好兒子 (Good Son), staged in Shanghai, in 1924, was enthusiastically received by the theatre-goers. He wrote also *Nao Jên Ch'un Sê* 惱人春色 * (Spring Fret, 萬象), and many articles published in the *Hsi Chü* and other literary magazines.

165. Wang Hsiang-ch'ên 王向辰.

Pen-name: 老向. Short-story writer and essayist. Like his friend Lao Shê 老舍, he is also known for writing in the Peking dialect and humorous style. In addition to fiction, he also wrote many popular works for the uneducated people. Before the Sino-Japanese War, he published most of his writings in the popular, humorous fortnightly *Lun Yü* 論語. *Jên Chien Shih* 人間世, and *Yü Chou Fêng* 宇宙風, all three of which were edited by Lin Yü-t'ang 林語堂 In the autumn of 1938, he went to Szechwan, where he worked in the National Institute of Compilation and Translation 國立編譯舘 of the Ministry of Education until the Victory. He then went to Formosa to promote the national language movement. He is now in Nanking.

Works: 庶務日記 * (1934, 上海時代圖書公司); 黃土泥 * (1936, 人間書屋); 全家財 (宇宙風社); etc.

166. Wang I-jên 王以仁.

T. 盟鷗. Short-story writer, and poet. Born in Taichow, Chekiang. Being a member of the "Society of Literary Research" 文學研究會, he published his works in the Association's publication *Hsiao Shuo Yüeh Pao* 小說月報 (The Short Story Magazine), and also in the magazines *Ch'uang Tsao Chou Pao* 創造週報 and *Hung Shui* 洪水 (Flood), edited by the "Creative Society" 創造社. In 1926, Wan I-jên disappeared after an unhappey love affair, and till pressent, we do not know where he is. He left two volumes of works: *Ku Yen* 孤雁* (Lone Swan, collection of short stories, 1926, 商務); and *Huan Mieh* 幻滅 (Disillusion, edited by his intimate friend Hsü Chieh 許傑).

167. Wang Jên-shu 王任叔．

T. 碧珊. Pen-names： 趙冷，屈軼，巴人，etc.

Short-story writer, and novelist. Born in Fenghwa, Chekiang. He served as a teacher for many years. His early short stories were published in the *Hsiao Shuo Yüeh Pao* 小說月報 (The Short Story Magazine), one of the publications of the "Society of Literary Research" 文學研究會． Thus he soon joined this Association, and took part in the dispute between the said Association and the "Creative Society" 創造社 about revolutionary literature. Later, he collected these articles into one volume which he called *Ko Ming Wên Hsüeh Lun Wên Chi* 革命文學論文集． Afterwards, he contributed to the literary supplement of *Ch'ên Pao* 晨報副刊, edited by Sun Fu-yuan 孫伏園． He was once the editor of a fortnightly magazine *Shan Yü* 山雨, but it attracted no attention, and suspended publication very soon. His later short stories appeared mostly in the *Shên Pao Yüeh K'an* 申報月刊, *Hsin Shêng Chou K'an* 新生週刊, and *Wên Hsüeh* 文學 (Literature).

During the early years of the Sino-Japanese War, he stayed in Shanghai, where he edited the *Tzŭ Yu T'an* 自由談 a literary supplement of the newspaper *Shên Pao*. In August, 1941, he arrived Singapore, where he became a teacher in Nan Ch'iao Normal School 南僑師範學校, and published his writings in the literary supplement of the newspaper *Nan Yang Shang Pao* 南洋商報, and the magazine *Min Ch'ao* 民潮, edited by the poet Yang Sao 楊騷． When the War come to Malay Peninsula he organized many anti-Japanese associations there. After the fall of Malay, he went to Sumatra, where he continued his cultural underground works against Japan, and was once in danger of death. He is now still in Sumatra.

Works: 監獄 (collection of short stories, 1927, 光華)；殉* (collection of short stories, 1929, 泰東)；捉鬼篇* (1936, 新城)；常識以下 (1936 多樣社)；阿貴流浪記 (a novel, 光華)；在沒落中 (collection of short stories, 光華)；證章 (1936, 文學出版社)；兩代的愛* (a play in 5 acts, 1947, 海燕)；etc.

168. Wang Lu-yen 王魯彥．

(? — 1945)

Also named 王忘我. Pen-names： 王魯顏，魯彥，etc.

Novelist, and short-story writer. Born in a merchant's family in Chênhai 鎮海, Chekiang. He received only middle school education in Ninghsien. It was through his own constant and unwearied efforts in self-study for many years that he acquired all the necessary knowledge about literature. He was a well-known scholar of Esperanto, from which he translated a great many fiction of various small nations.

Before the Nationalist Revolution of 1927, he taught in Changsha, where he produced his first effort *Yu Tzŭ* 柚子 (Shaddock), a short story, published later in the famous *Hsiao Shuo Yüeh Pao* 小說月報 (The Short Story Magazine), which brought immediately fame to our author. He then contributed to the literary supplement of *Ch'ên Pao* 晨報副刊, and the *Yü Ssŭ* 語絲 Magazine. Mao Tun 茅盾, the famous novelist and literary critic, in his article *Wang Lu Yen Lun* 王魯彥論 (On Wang Lu-yen), published in the *Hsiao Shuo Yüeh Pao*, vol. 18, praised him as the typical writer of China.

Later he joined the "Society of Literary Research" 文學研究會, and published successively two collections of short stories: *Huang Chin* 黃金* (Gold, 1928, 新生命), and *T'ung Nien Ti Pei Ai* 童年的悲哀 (The Sorrow of Childhood, 1931, 亞東). In 1930, he became a teacher of the Chi Mei Normal School 集美師範學校 of Tungan, Fukien; then in Li Ming Middle School 黎明中學, Ch'üanchow, in the same province. He disagreed with the school authorities, and resigned his post. From then on he taught in various schools in Fukien and Shensi. In 1936, he returned to Shanghai, and devoted himself to the writing of *Yeh Huo* 野火* (1937, 良友), a novel.

After the outbreak of the Sino-Japanese War, he went to his native place, Chênhai, then to Hankow. When the "Esperanto Association of China" 中國世界 語協會 was inaugarated there on June 26, 1938. He and twenty other scholars were elected to serve on th Executive Council. Later, he went to Kweilin, where he edited the *Wên I Tsa Chih* 文藝雜誌 (Literary Magazine), which had a large circulation in the Interior. He died of consumption in 1945 at Kweilin.

Wang Lu-yen was a prolific writer. During his rather short life-time, he wrote and translated more than thirty volumes of novels and collections of short stories, but most of them are out of print now. His important collections of short stories are: 柚子* (1926, 北新); 屋頂下* (containing seven short stories, 1934, 現代); 小小的心* (containing seven short stories, 1934, 天馬); 驢子和騾子* (1935, 生活); 雀鼠集* (1935, 文化生活出版社); 河邊* (containing six short stories, 1936, 良友); 王魯彥短篇小說集 (開明).

Besides *Yeh Huo*, he also wrote the novel 鄉下 (1936, 文學出版社). The collections of his essays are: 旅人的心 (1937, 文化生活出版社); and 王魯彥散文集 (1947, 開明).

Translations: 猶太小說集 (1927, 開明); 顯克微茲小說集 (*Noveloj* by H. Sienkiewicz, 1928, 北新); 世界短篇小說集 (1929, 亞東); 苦海 (*La Fundo de l'mizero* by W. Sierotzwesky, 1929, 亞東); 在世界的盡頭 (1930, 神州國光社); 懺悔 (*Konfeso* by M. Pogacic, 1931, 亞東); 肖像 (*The Portrait* by N. V. Gogol, 亞東); 波蘭小說集; 花束 ; etc.

169. Wang P'ing-ling 王平陵

Poet, short-story writer, and essayist. Born in Liyang, Kiangsu. He is a famous Kuomintang writer. In 1930, he promoted the movement of Nationalist Literature 民族主義文學, together with Shih Chê-ts'un 施蟄存, Fu Yen-ch'ang 傅彥長, Huang Chên-hsia 黃震遐, and a few others. During the Sino-Japanese

War, he worked in the Ministry of Education at Chungking, and edited the magazine *Wên I Yüeh K'an* 文藝月刊 (Literary Monthly), in collaboration with Sha Yen 沙雁.

Works: *Shih Tzǔ Hou* 獅子吼 (Roar of Lion, collection of poems, 南京); *Mei Hsüeh Kang Yao* 美學綱要 (Outline of Aesthetics, 泰東); *Ch'i Tai* 期待 (Awaiting, collection of short stories, 正中); *Tung Fang Ti T'an Lun Pao* 東方的坦倫堡 (1940, Chungking, 正中); *Fu Ch'an P'in* 副產品 (collection of poems and essays, 1946, 商務); *Chiao Ch'uan* 嬌喘* (1946, 百新); *Hu Pin Ch'iu Sê* 湖濱秋色 (collection of short stories, 1947, 商務); etc.

170. Wang Tu-ch'ing 王獨清.

(1898 — 1940)

Poet, playwright, and short-story writer. Born in Changan, Shensi. He studied fine arts in France. Upon returning to China, he joined the "Creative Society" 創造社, organized by Kuo Mo-jo 郭沫若, Chang Tzǔ-p'ing 張資平, Ch'êng Fang-wu 成仿吾, and Yü Ta-fu 郁達夫, and held an important position in it. In 1925, he became the dean of the College of Arts and Letters of Sun Yat-sen University 中山大學 at Canton, and director of the "Creative Society". After the suspension of the said Association, he became the director of studies of the Shanghai University of Fine Arts 上海藝術大學, and editor of the monthly magazine *Chan K'ai* 展開. He died on August 31, 1940.

Works: *Shêng Mu Hsiang Ch'ien* 聖母像前 (collection of poems, 1926, 光華); *Wei Ni Shih* 威尼市 (collection of poems, 1927, 創造社); *Tuan Lien* 煅煉 (collection of poems, 光華); *Ssǔ Ch'ien* 死前 (Before Death, collection of poems, 1927, 創造社); *Ling Luan Ts'ao* 零亂草 (collection of poems, 樂華); *Tu Ch'ing Shih Hsüan* 獨清詩選 (Selected Poems of Wang Tu-ch'ing, 新教育社); *Tiao Ch'an* 貂嬋 (a historial play, 樂華); *Yang Kuei Fei Chih Ssǔ* 楊貴妃之死 (The Death of Yang Kuei Fei, a historial play, 1927, 創造社); *Ch'ien Hou* 前後 (collection of letters, 樂華); *Ch'ang An Ch'êng Chung Ti Shao Nien* 長安城中的少年 (A Youth of Changan, autobiography, 光華); *Wo Tsai Ou Chou Ti Shêng Huo* 我在歐洲的生活 (My Life in Europe, 良友); *An Yun* 晤雲 (Dark Cloud, collection of short stories, 光明); etc.

Translations: 新生 (*La Vita Nuova* by A. Dante, 光明); 獨清譯詩集(現代); etc.

171. Wang T'ung-chao 王統照.

T. 劍三. Pen-names: 提西, 縈者, 鍰山, etc.

Novelist, short-story writer, playwright, poet, and essayist. Born 111 Chucheng, Shantung. He graduated from the China University 中國大學. While still a student, he published his novels, *I Yeh* 一葉 * (One Leaf, 1922, 商務), and *Huang Hun* 黃昏 (Evening, 1925, 商務), in the famous *Hsiao Shuo Yüeh Pao* 小說月報 (The Short Story Magazine). They attracted great attention in the literary cycle. Later, he joined the "Society of Literary Research" 文學研究會, in which he held an important position. In 1924, when the Indian poet R. Tagore came to visit China, he served as interpreter. He travelled in Europe and published one volume of notes on his journey when he came back to China, entitled *Ou Yu Tsa Chi* 歐遊雜記 (Notes on the Travel in Europe, 開明).

He was the editor of the *Wên Hsüeh Hsün K'an* 文學旬刊, a literary supplement of *Ch'ên Pao* 晨報; co-editor of the *Hsiao Shuo Yüeh Pao*, *Wên Hsüeh Chou Pao* 文學週報, and *Yü Ssŭ* 語絲. In 1936, he became the editor of the monthly magazine *Wên Hsüeh* 文學 (Literature), in succession of Fu Tung-hua 傅東華. He is now a professor of Shantung University, Tsingtao.

Works: 秋實 (a novel); 春花 * (a novel 1936, 良友); 春雨之夜 * (collection of short stories, 1924, 商務); 霜痕 (collection of short stories, 1931, 新中國); 王統照短篇小說集 (collected short stories of Wang T'ung-chao, 開明); 死後的勝利 (a play, 1925, 商務); 片雲集 * (collection of essays, 1934, 生活); 青紗帳 * (collection of essays, 1936, 生活); 童心 (collection of poems, 1925, 商務); 夜行集 * (collection of poems, 1936, 生活); 山雨 * (collection of poems, 開明); 江南曲 (collection of poems, 文化生活出版社); 華亭鶴 (collection of poems, 文化生活出版社); 這時代 (collection of poems); 王統照選集 * (1936, 萬象書屋); 去來今 * (1940, 文化生活出版社); 銀龍集 (文化生活出版社); 北國之春 (1931, 神州國光社); etc.

172. Wang Wên-hsien 王文顯.

(1886 —   )

T. 力山. Playwright. Born in Kunshan, Kiangsu. After receiving his B. A. degree from the University of London, he returned to China in 1915. In 1921, he became the director of studies of Tsinghua University 清華大學, and acting Chancellor at the same year. From 1925 on, he served as the chairman of the Department of Western Languages and Literature of Tsinghua, and concurrently lecturer at the National University of Peking 北京大學, National Normal University 師範大學, and Fu Jên University 輔仁大學 at Peiping.

Works: *She Stoops to Compromise* (a play, written in English and rendered into Chinese by his student Li Chien-wu 李健吾, under the title 委曲求全, 人文); *Mêng Li Ching Hua* 夢裡京華 * (a play, 世界); etc.

173. Wang Yü-ch'i 王余杞.

Novelist. Born in Tzeliutsing, Szechwan. His first novel *Hsi Fên Fei* 惜分飛 (Departure), published in 1928, by the Ch'un Ch'ao Book Co. 春潮書局, was highly praised by the late Yü Ta-fu 郁達夫, the novelist and critic. Later, he published two novels, *Fu Ch'ên* 浮沉 (Swim and Sink, 1933, 北平星雲堂); and *P'êng Yu Yü Ti Jên* 朋友與敵人 (Friend and Enemy, 1933, 天津現代社會月刊社) in succession.

During the Sino-Japanese War he served as a reporter in his native place. After the Victory over Japan, he went to the North, and is now secretary in the Tientsin Municipal Government. He publishes sometimes his new writings in *Ta Kung Pao* 大公報 and *I Shih Pao* 益世報 of the same city.

174. Wei Chin-chih 魏金枝.

Short-story writer. He is noted for his vivid description of rural life in China. His works were published mostly in the magazines *Pên Liu* 奔流, and *Mêng Ya* 萌芽, both edited by Lu Hsün 魯迅

The collections of his short-stories are: 七封書信的自傳 * (1928, 人間書屋); 奶媽 (1930, 現代); 白旗手 * (1933, 現代); etc.

He is now the editor of the monthly magazine *Wên T'an* 文壇 (Literary World) in Shanghai, and publishes often his new writings in various literary magazines.

175. Wên Kuo-hsin 聞國新.

Short-story writer. Born in Shaohsing, Chekiang. After his graduation from the College of Law and Commerce of the National Peiping University 北平大學法商學院, he taught Chinese in the Wên Ch'üan Middle School 溫泉中學 Peiping. During the Sino-Japanese War, he served for some time as a judge in Anhwei Province and later devoted himself in writing at Peiping.

Between 1925 and 1926, he contributed to the literary supplement of *Ch'ên Pao* 晨報副刊, edited by the late poet Hsü Chih-mo 徐志摩. His later works were published mostly in the magazines *Yü Ssŭ* 語絲, *Wên Hsüeh Chi K'an* 文學季刊, *T'ai Pao* 太白, and the *Mei Jih Wên I* 每日文藝 (Daily Literature), a literary supplement of the newspaper *Hua Pei Jih Pao* 華北日報.

The collections of his short stories are: 生之細流 (北平文化學社); 蓉蓉 * (1943, 華北文化書局); 落花時節 * (1944, 新民印書館); etc.

176. Wu Hsi-ju 吳奚如.

Pen-name: 奚如. Novelist, and short-story writer. He learned to love literature at the year 1928. The first book which he read with enthusiasm was *Fathers and Sons* of I. Turgenev. His interest in fiction being thus aroused, he continued to read the works of M. Gorky, F. Gladkov, S. A. Serafimovitch,

A. Neverov, and other Russian writers. He wrote the following works: *Yeh Po* 葉伯 (collection of short stories, 1935, 天馬); *Ch'an Hui* 懺悔* (Repentance, a novel, 1936, 良友. It tells the story of a man who murdered his brother for the sake of family property, and how later, with tears in his eyes, he walked to meet his death at the gallows); *Hsiao Wu Chi* 小巫集 (collection of short stories, 1936, 文化生活出版社); *Pei Chien Chê Ti Ling Hun* 卑賤者的靈魂 (containing five short stories 1948, 潮鋒出版社); etc.

177. Wu Jên-chih 吳仞之.

Playwright. He is now the director of studies of the Experimental Dramatic School of Shanghai 上海市立實驗戲劇學校. He wrote *Chuan Wên Chi* 賺吻記*, a play, published by the World Book Co. 世界書局.

178. Wu T'ien 吳 天.

Playwright. He is now a professor of the Experimental Dramatic School of Shanghai 上海市立實驗戲劇學校. He wrote the following plays: *Chia* 家 (Home, an adaptation of Pa Chin's novel, *Chia*); *Tzŭ Yeh* 子夜* (Midnight, 1946, 永祥); *Hung Lou Mêng* 紅樓夢* (The Dream of Red Chamber, 1946, 永祥); *Ch'un Kuei Ho Ch'u* 春歸何處 (1948, 潮鋒出版社) *Ch'un Lei* 春雷* (開明); etc.

179. Wu Tsu-hsiang 吳組湘.

Original name: 吳祖襄.

Novelist, and short-story writer. Born in Chinghsien, Anhwei. He guaduated from the Department of Chinese Literature of the National Tsinghua University 清華大學 While still a student, he published a short story *I Ch'ien Pa Pai Tan* 一千八百擔 (1800 Piculs of Rice) in the famous *Wên Hsüeh Chi K'an* 文學季刊 (Literary Quarterly), it won unanimous approval throughout the literary world of China. Since then he wrote many short stories which he collected into two volumes, entitled *Hsi Liu Chi* 西柳集* (1934, 生活); and *Fan Yü Chi* 飯餘集* (1935, 文生化活出版社).

During the Sino-Japanese War he was in the Interior. Being a member of the "National Writers' Anti-Aggression Association" 中華全國文藝界抗敵協會, he published sometimes his new writings in the organization's publication *K'ang Chan Wên I* 抗戰文藝 (Wartime Literature). Among those productions the novel *Ya Tsui Lao* 鴨嘴澇 (1940, later he changed its name to *Shan Hung* 山洪) is considered to be the most successful.

In September, 1946, he went to the United States as the secretary of General Fêng Yü-hsiang 馮玉祥.

180. Wu Tsu-kuang 吳祖光.

(1917 —   )

Playwright. Born in Wutsin, Kiangsu. He graduated from the Université Franco-Chinoise of Peiping. During the Sino-Japanese War, he worked in the National Academy of Dramatic Arts 國立劇專 at Chungking. After the Victory over Japan, he returned to Shanghai. He is now the editor of a monthly magazine *Ch'ing Ming* 清明, and the literary supplement of *Hsin Min Pao* 新民報.

He wrote the following plays: *Chêng Ch'i Ko* 正氣歌* (also named *Wên T'ien Hsiang* 文天祥. 開明); *Fêng Hsüeh Yeh Kuei Jên* 風雪夜歸人 (開明); *Shao Nien Yu* 少年遊* (開明); *Fêng Huang Ch'êng* 鳳凰城 (生活); *Cho Kuei Chuan* 捉鬼傳* (開明); *Niu Lang Chih Nü* 牛郎織女* (開明); *Ch'ang E Pên Yüeh* 嫦娥奔月 (開明); *Lin Ch'ung Yeh Pên* 林沖夜奔 (開明); etc.

The collection of his essays is entitled *Hou T'ai P'êng Yu* 後台朋友 (1946, 上海出版公司).

181. Yang Chên-shêng 楊振聲

(1891 —   )

T. 今甫. Novelist. Born in Penglai, Shantung. After his graduation from the National University of Peking 北京大學. he went to the United States, where he attended Harvard University, and then Columbia University. Upon returning to China, he was appointed professor of literature at his alma mater, later at Wuchang University 武昌大學, Sun Yat-sen University 中山大學 at Canton, and Yenching University 燕京大學 at Peiping. He was once the dean of the College of Arts and Letters and concurrently chairman of the Department of Chinese Literature of the National Tsinghua University 清華大學, Peiping. Before the Sino-Japanese War he was the Chancellor of the National Cheeloo University 齊魯大學 at Shantung. In the War years, he served as professor of Chinese Literature and concurrently chief secretary of the National Southwest Associated University 西南聯合大學 Kunming. After the Victory over Japan, he returned to Peiping, and functions as chairman of the Department of Chinese Literature of the National University of Peking, and editor of the *Wên I Chou K'an* 文藝週刊 a weekly supplement of the newspaper *Ching Shih Jih Pao* 經世日報.

In 1921, while still a student of the National University of Peking, he started to contribute to the *Hsin Ch'ao* 新潮 (New Tide), a leading magazine at that time. In December of 1924, he published his novel *Yü Chün* 玉君 * (1925, 樸社) in the *Hsien Tai P'ing Lun* 現代評論 (Contemporary Review). It is on this book that his fame as a novelist chiefly rests.

182. Yang I 楊 儀.

(1907 —)

Pen-names: 歐陽山，羅西, etc. Novelist and short-story writer. Born of a poor family at Canton. While still a child he wandered with his parents in different places and kept contact with persons belonging to various societies. He started his literary career in 1924, when he published his first short story *Ti I Yeh* 第一夜 (First Night) in the *Hsüeh Shêng Tsa Chih* 學生雜誌 (The Student's Magazine). His first collection of short stories *Mei Kuei Ts'an Liao* 玫瑰殘了 appeared in 1927, published by Kuang Hua Book Co. 光華書局. Since then he wrote many novels and short stories among which we may mention 桃君的情人 (1928, 光華)；愛的奔流 (1928, 光華)；你去吧* (1928, 光華)；蓮蓉月 (1928, 現代)；蜜絲紅 (1929, 光華)；七年忌* (1935, 生活)；生底煩憂 (1936, 文化生活出版社)；飢寒人* (1937, 北新)；流浪人的筆跡 （光華）；竹尺和鐵鎚 （正午）；人生的夢（正午）；人生底路 （正午）；光明 (1932 南京拔堤書局)；鐘手 （南京拔堤書局）；再會罷黑貓 （北新）；流奔之愛* (1943, 啓東); etc.

The collections of his essays and poems are: 雜碎集，世界走得這樣慢 (正午); etc.

In September, 1932, he organized the "Canton Literary Society" 廣州文藝社 and published the *Kuang Chou Wên I Chou‧ K'an* 廣州文藝週刊 (Canton Literary Weekly), which suspended publication in the following year.

In 1939, he went to Chungking, where he joined the "National Writers' Anti-Aggression Association" 中華全國文藝界抗敵協會 and often published his fiction in one of the organization's publications *K'ang Chan Wên I* 抗戰文藝 (Wartime Literature), and other literary magazines such as *Wên I Chên Ti* 文藝陣地 (Literary Field) of which he was one of the editors, and *Tan Hua* 彈花, edited by Chao Ch'ing-ko 趙清閣.

183. Yang Kang 楊 剛.

(1909 —)

Novelist, and reporter. Born in Kiangling, Hupeh. She is the younger sister of Yang Ch'ao 楊潮 (better known under his pen-name Yang Tsao 羊棗), a famous army reporter. After graduating from Yenching University 燕京大學 she worked in *Ta Kung Pao* 大公報 for many years. She is now a special correspondent in the United States of the said newspaper.

Works: *Huan Hsiu Wai Chuan* 桓秀外傳* (a novel, 1942, 文化生活出版社); *Kung Sun Yang* 公孫鞅* (1941 文化生活出版社); etc.

184. Yang Sao 楊 騷.

Poet, and playwright. Born in Fukien. Husband of Pai Wei 白薇 (pen-name of Huang Su-ju 黃素如), a famous authoress. During the Sino-Japanese

War, he lived in Chungking, and published many poems in the magazine *K'ang Chan Wên I* 抗戰文藝 (Wartime Literature). In 1939, he joined the "Writers' War Area Service Corps" 作家戰地服務團, directed by the "National Writers' Anti-Aggression Association" 中華全國文藝界抗敵協會, to visit Chinese soldiers at the front.

Works: *Mi Ch'u* 迷雛 (a play, 1928, 北新); *T'a Ti T'ien Shih* 他的天使* (a play, 1929, 北新); *Chi I Chih Tu* 記憶之都* (1937, 商務); *Hsin Ch'ü* 心曲 (collection of poems, 北新); *Shou Nan Chê Ti Tuan Ch'ü* 受難者的短曲 (collection of poems, 1929, 開明); *Ch'un Ti Kan Shang* 春的感傷 (開明); *Hsi I Lao Pan Yü Shih Jên* 洗衣老板與詩人 (開明); *Tso Yeh* 昨夜 (Last Night, written in collaboration with Pai Wei); *Hsien Tai Tien Ying Lun* 現代電影論 (On the Motion-Picture of To-day, 1933, 申報館); etc.

Translations: 癡人之愛 (by J. Tanizaki, 北新); 沒錢的猶太人 (*Jews Without Money* by M. Gold, 1930, 南強); 十月 (*October*, A. Yakovlev, 南強); 鐵流 (*Sheleznyi Potok* by S. A. Serafimovitch, 南強); 赤戀; etc.

185. Yang Ts'un-pin 楊村彬.

Playwright. He was a professor at the National Academy of Dramatic Arts 國立劇專 for many years, and once a director of a certain motion picture co. His *Ch'ing Kung Wai Shih* 清宮外史* (Romance of the Ch'ing Dynasty, 1946, 國訊), a play, won him nation-wide fame. Besides this, he wrote also *Ch'in Liang Yü* 秦良玉, an historical play.

186. Yang T'ung-fang 楊同芳.

He is better known under the pen-names of Sha Ting 沙汀 His other pen-names are: 仲俊, 晚紫, etc.

Novelist, and short-story writer. Born in Szechwan. He once studied in the First Normal School of Chengtu 成都第一師範學校.

Being a novelist, he is noted for the use of the pithy vernacular of south-west China. He is the author of the following works: 法律外的航線 (collection of short stories, 1932, 辛墾); 土餅* (collection of short stories, 1936, 文化生活出版社); 航線 (1937, 文化生活出版社); 苦難* (collection of short stories, 1937, 文化生活出版社); 闖關 (1946, 新羣出版社); 獸道 (1946, 羣益出版社); 播種者 (1946, 華夏); 淘金記 (novel, 1946, 文化生活出版社); etc.

He is now professor of the Ch'êng Ming College of Arts and Letters 誠明文學院, Shanghai, and often publishes his new writings in different literary magazines.

187. Yang Yin-shên 楊蔭深.

Novelist, playwright, and literary critic. He wrote the following works: *P'an Shih Yü P'u Wei* 磐石與蒲葦 (Rock and Rush, a play, an adaptation of *K'ung Ch'iao Tung Nan Fei* 孔雀東南飛, the longest ancient poem of China, 1927, 光華); *I Chên K'uang Fêng* 一陣狂風 (A Gale of Wind, a three-act play, dealing with the popular story about Liang Shan-po 梁山泊 and Chu Ying-t'ai 祝英台 1926, 光華); *Shao Nien Ying Hsiung* 少年英雄* (1933, 開明); *Man Na* 曼娜 (a novel composed of 62 love-letters, 現代); *K'u Yü Hsiao* 哭與笑 (Tear and Laughter, a novel, 現代); *Chung Kuo Min Chien Wên Hsüeh Kai Shuo* 中國民間文學概說 (Chinese Popular Literature, 1930, 華通); *Wu Tai Wên Hsüeh* 五代文學 (Chinese Literature during the Five Dynasties, 1935, 商務); *Li Hou Chu* 李後主 (The Life of Li Yü 李煜 of the Southern T'ang Dynasty, 1935, 商務); *Chung Kuo Wên Jên Ku Shih* 中國文人故事 (Stories of Famous Chinese Authors, 1936, 中華); *Kao Shih Yü Ts'ên Ts'an* 高適與岑參 (Two Poets of the T'ang Dynasty, 1936, 商務); *Wang Wei Yü Mêng Hao Jan* 王維與孟浩然 (A Comparative Study of Two T'ang Poets, 1936, 商務): etc.

188. Yao K'o 姚 克.

Also named Yao Hsin-nung 姚莘農. Playwright. He translated *Lei Yü* 雷雨 (Thunder and Rain) of Ts'ao Yü 曹禺 into English, published in the *T'ien Hsia Monthly*, vol. 3, no. 3 (October, 1936) to vol. 4, no. 2 (February, 1937). In 1940, he went to Moscow to join the celebration of the Dramatic Festival, and travelled in Europe and America. Upon returning to China, he taught at a certain university at Shanghai, and published a great many dramatic articles in different magazines, such as *Wên I Chieh* 文藝界, edited by T'ang T'ao 唐弢; *Chêng Yen Pao* 正言報: *Hsiao Chü Ch'ang* 小劇場; etc.

He wrote the following plays: *Ch'ing Kung Yuan* 清宮怨* (世界); *Ch'u Pa Wang* 楚霸王* (世界); *Yin Hai Ts'ang Sang* 銀海滄桑* (世界); *Mei Jên Chi* 美人計* (世界); etc.

189. Yao Pêng-tzǔ 姚蓬子.

Original name: 姚方仁; later he changed it into 姚杉尊. Pen-names: 丁愛. 小瑩, 姚夢生, 慕容梓, etc.

Short-story writer, and poet. Born in Shaohsing, Chekiang. He was an important figure of the "China League of Left Writers" 中國左翼作家聯盟 In 1931, he edited the *Wên I Shêng Huo* 文藝生活 (Literary Life) at Shanghai, published by the Union Book Co. 聯合書局; and in 1932, he founded the *Wên Hsüeh Yüeh Pao* 文學月報 (Literary Monthly), in collaboration with Chou Ch'i-ying 周起應, published by Kuang Hua Book Co. 光華書局.

During the Sino-Japanese War he established a publishing house "Authors' Bookstore" 作家書屋 in Chungking.   Being a member of the Standing Committee of the "National Writers' Anti-Aggression Association" 中華全國文藝界抗敵協會, he edited the organization's publication *K'ang Chan Wên I* 抗戰文藝 (The Wartime Literature) together with Lao Shê 老舍, the novelist.

After the Victory over Japan he moved his "Authors' Bookstore" to Shanghai.

The collections of his short stories are: 剪影集 * (1933, 良友); 浮世畫 (1932, 良友); etc.

The collections of his poems we have: 銀鈴 (建設圖書館); 蓬子詩鈔; etc.

He has translated 結婚集 (*Married* by A. Strindberg 1929, 光華); 小天使 (*Little Angel and Other Stories* by L. Andreyev, 1929, 光華); 婦人之夢 (*Le Songe d'une Femme* by R. de Gourmont, 1930, 光華); 處女的心 (*Un Coeur Virginal* by R. de Gourmont, 1927, 北新); 沒有櫻花 (*No Cherry Blossom* by P. Romanov, 1930, 光華); 我的童年 (*My Childhood* by M. Gorky, 光華); 愛情與麵包 (*Love and Bread* by A. Strindberg, 1947, 作家書屋); etc.

190. Yeh Ling-fêng 葉靈鳳.

Original name: 葉蘊璞.   Pen-names: 佐木華, 雨品巫, 亞靈, 秦靜聞, 疊華, etc.

Novelist, short-story writer, and essayist.   Born in Nanking.   He studied once in the Shanghai College of Fine Arts 上海藝術大學.   He drew and painted almost all the covers of the publications of the "Creative Society" 創造社, of which he was a member.   His early works were published in the Association's publication *Hung Shui* 洪水.   In 1926, he organized a literary society "Huan Shê" 幻社 with P'an Han-nien 潘漢年 and published the *Huan Chou* 幻洲, a fortnightly magazine.   Owing to its leftist leaning in thought, it was ordered to suspend publication by the authorities.   They then published another periodical *Go Bi* 戈璧, but it too was short-lived.   Later he edited a literary monthly *Hsien Tai Hsiao Shuo* 現代小説 (Modern Fiction), published by the Hsien Tai Book Co. 現代書局.   The first number appeared in January, 1928, and suspended publication in March, 1930.   It was an important magazine in the proletarian literary movement.   The contributors were: Ch'ien Hsing-ts'un 錢杏邨 (better known under his pen-name A Ying 阿英), Lo K'ai-lan 羅鐀嵐, Hsiang P'ei-liang 向培良, Hung Ling-fei 洪靈菲, Tai P'ing-wan 戴平萬, Lou Chien-nan 樓建南, P'an Han-nien 潘漢年, Yeh Ting-lo 葉鼎洛, Hsü Chieh 許傑, etc.

During the Sino-Japanese War he lived in Hongkong, where he edited the *Yen Lin* 言林, a literary supplement of the newspaper *Li Pao* 立報.   He is now the editor of the literary supplement of the newspaper *Kuo Min Jih Pao* 國民日報, and a weekly magazine *Wan Jên Chou K'an* 萬人週刊 in Hongkong.

Works: 女媧氏的遺孽 (1927, 光華); 菊子夫人 (1927, 光華); 鳩綠媚* (1928, 光華); 處女的夢* (1929, 現代); 紅的天使 (1930, 現代); 永久的女性 (1936, 良友); 未完成的懺悔錄 (1936, 今代); 天竹 (現代); 白蕖雜記; etc.

Translations: 新俄短篇小說集 (Collection of Russian Short Stories, 1928, 光華); 蒙地加羅 (*Monte Carlo* by H. Sienkiewicz, 光華); 白利與露西 (*Pierre et Luce* by R. Rolland, 現代); 九月的玫瑰; etc.

191. Yeh Shao-chün 葉紹鈞.

. (1893 —   )

T. 聖陶. Pen-names: 秉丞, 柳山, 桂山, 郢, 郢生, 華秉丞, etc.

Short-story writer, novelist, and fable writer. Born in Wuhsien, Kiangsu. He received only middle school education, but he acquired a wide knowledge of literature through self-study. He taught for ten years in various primary schools, thus later on he not unfrequently adopted teachers' life as the theme of his stories. After 1921, he taught at different middle schools and universities in Shanghai. Being a member of "Society of Literary Research" 文學研究會, he edited for some time the Association's publication *Hsiao Shuo Yüeh Pao* 小說月報 (The Short Story Magazine). He was also the editor of the *Fu Nü Tsa Chih* 婦女雜誌 (Women's Magazine), published by the Commercial Press, and co-editor of of the poetry magazine *Shih* 詩. published by the Chung Hwa Book Co. 中華書局. Later, he joined the Editorial Bureau of the Kaiming Book Co. 開明書店, and edited the *Chung Hsüch Shêng* 中學生 (Juvenile Student) in collaboration with Hsia Mien-tsun 夏丏尊 and Fêng Tzù-k'ai 豐子愷. He also published his writings in the magazines *Wên Hsüeh Chou Pao* 文學週報. *Pei Tou* 北斗, *Wên Hsüeh Yüeh Pao* 文學月報, and *Wên I Shêng Huo* 文藝生活.

In 1938, he lectured at the National Wuhan University 武漢大學 in Loshan, Szechwan. Since 1940, he lived in Chengtu, where he worked in the Kaiming Book Co. until the Victory. He is now an editor of Kaiming at Shanghai.

Works: 隔膜* (collection of short stories, 1922, 商務); 劍鞘 (collection of essays, written in collaboration with 兪平伯, 1924, 樸社); 城中* (collection of short stories, 1926, 開明); 未厭集 (collection of short stories, 1929, 商務); 倪煥之 (a novel, 1930, 開明); 文心 (in collaboration with 夏丏尊, 1934, 開明); 火災* (collection of short stories, 商務); 線下* (collection of short stories, 商務); 平常的故事 (collection of short stories); 一個青年 (collection of short stories); 腳步集 (collection of short stories, 新中國); 懇親會 (collection of plays); 稻草人* (fable, 商務); 古代英雄的石像* (fable), 牧羊兒 (fable); 作文論 (開明); 文章講話 (in collaboration with 夏丏尊, 開明); 國文教學 (in collaboration with 朱自清. 開明); 西川集 (開明); 未厭居習作* (開明); 四三集* (1936, 良友); etc.

192. Yeh Tzŭ 葉　紫.

Novelist, and short-story writer. Born in Hunan. At first he edited a monthly magazine at Shanghai, but it was short-lived. His first success, *Fêng Shou* 豐收 (Harvest), containing six short stories, was fervently praised by Lu Hsün 魯迅. He then wrote a novel, entitled *Hsing* 星* (Stars), published in 1936, by the Cultural Life Publishing Co. 文化生活出版社. In the final years of the Sino-Japanese War, he died in Hunan.

193. Yü Ling 于　伶.

Pen-name: 尤兢. Playwright. Born in Yihing, Kiangsu. He graduated from a normal school of Soochow. Before the Sino-Japanese War, he wrote many "National Defence" plays, depicting the activities of the volunteer corps in Manchuria under Japanese occupation. During the early years of the War, he stayed in the International Settlement of Shanghai, and devoted himself to playwriting. Later, he went to the Interior. As a member of the "National Writers' Anti-Aggression Association" 中華全國文藝界抗敵協會 , he published his new writings in the Association's publication *K'ang Chan Wên I* 抗戰文藝 (Wartime Literature).

He wrote the following plays: *Su Chiao Chiao* 蘇矮矮 (1940, 上海雜誌公司); *Ta Ming Ying Lieh Chuan* 大明英烈傳* (1941, 上海雜誌公司); *Yeh Shanghai* 夜上海 (The Night of Shanghai); *Ch'ang Yeh Hsing* 長夜行*; *Yeh Kuang Pei* 夜光怀*; *Nü Tzŭ Kung Yü* 女子公寓*; *Hua Chien Lei* 花濺淚; *Ch'ing Hai I Yun* 情海疑雲; *Nü Erh Kuo* 女兒國 (The Country of Girls); *Hsing Hua Ch'un Yü Chiang Nan* 杏花春雨江南; *Wu Ming Shih* 無名氏 ; etc.

194. Yü P'ing-po 俞平伯.

(1899 —　　　)

Original name: 俞銘衡. Pen-name: 屈齋. Essayist, poet and literary critic. Born in a family of scholars at Tehching 德清. Chekiang. His great grandfather Yü Ch'ü-yuan 俞曲園, was one of the finest classical scholars of the Ch'ing Dynasty. He graduated from the National University of Peking 北京大學 . In the first flush of Pai Hua experiment, he published three outstanding volumes of verse, entitled *Tung Yeh* 冬夜 (Winter Night, 1921. 亞東); *Hsi Huan* 西還 (Return from the West, 1924, 亞東); and *I* 憶 (Recollections, 樸社). He is a learned and discriminating critic. His long thesis on *Hung Lou Mêng* 紅樓夢 (The Dream of the Red Chamber), entitled *Hung Lou Mêng Pien* 紅樓夢辨 (1923, 亞東), is an important study of that famous novel. Besides, he is also a leading authority on ancient Chinese poetry and Tz'ŭ 詞, on which he wrote *Tu Shih Cha Chi* 讀詩札記 (Notes on Reading the *Book of Poetry*, 1934, 人文); and *Tu Tz'ŭ Ou Tê* 讀詞偶得 (Notes on Reading the Tz'ŭ 1934, 開明).

At first he taught Chinese literature at Yenching University 燕京大學 , and then at the National University of Peking 北京大學 , and Tsinghua University 清華大學 . During the Sino-Japanese War he stayed at Peiping, and lectured on Chinese literature at the China University 中國大學 . After the Victory over Japan, he resumed his post at the National University of Peking.

Works: *Chien Ch'iao* 劍鞘 (collection of essays, written in collaboration with Yeh Shao-chün, 1924, 霜楓社); *Tsa Pan Erh* 雜拌兒* (collection of essays, in two volumes, 1933, 開明); *Yen Chih Ts'ao* 燕知草 (collection of essays, 開明); *Yen Chiao Chi* 燕郊集* (Essays Written in a Suburb of Peiping, 1936, 良友); *Ku Huai Mêng Yü* 古槐夢遇 (collection of essays, 1936, 世界); etc.

195. Yü Shang-yuan 余上沅 .

(1897 —   )

Pen-name: 舶客 . Playwright. Born in Kiangling, Hupeh. After graduating from the National University of Peking 北京大學 he went to the United States, where he studied dramatic arts at Carnegie University and Columbia University. Upon returning to China, he lectured on drama at the National Academy of Fine Arts 國立藝術專科學校, of Peiping, National Southeast University 東南大學 , and Kwang Hua University 光華大學 at Shanghai. Later, he became the manager of the Crescent Book Co. 新月書店 , and the editor of the *Crescent Monthly* 新月月刊. Before the Sino-Japanese War, he was a lecturer of English literature at the National University of Peking. In the recent years, he served as the president of the National Academy of Dramatic Arts 國立戲劇專科學校 .

Works: *Kuo Chü Yun Tung* 國劇運動 (National Drama Movement, 1927, 新月); *Hsi Chü Lun Chi* 戲劇論集 (Essays on Drama, 1927, 北新); *Shang Yuan Chü Pên Chia Chi* 上沅劇本甲集* (Dramas of Yü Shang-yüan. Series I, 1934, 商務. Containing three pieces of plays); etc.

Translations: 可欽佩的克萊敦 (*The Admirable Crichton* by J. M. Barrie, 1930, 新月); 長生訣 (by Capek Karel, 北新); etc.

196. Yü Ta-fu 郁達夫 .

(1896 — 1945)

Courtesy name of 郁文, but he is noted for this name instead of the original. Novelist, short-story writer, and literary critic. Born in Fuyang, Chekiang. When studying in primary school, he was rated among the best pupils in the matter of good character. He worked hard at his lessons, and when at leisure, he read only historical classics and poetry of the T'ang Dynasty. As to the stories written by the Saturday School 禮拜六派, or Western romances translated by Lin Ch'in-nan 林琴南 , he read none at all until he graduated from primary school. From then on, however, he began devouring novels, the first two being *Hung Lou Mêng* 紅樓夢 (The Dream of the Red Chamber), and *Shui Hu Chuan* 水滸傳 (All Men Are Brothers).

After summer vacations, he found two novels is a second-hand book-shop, one *Hsi Hu Chia Hua* 西湖佳話 (Romance of the West Lake), the other *Hua Yüeh Hên* 花月痕 (The Indication of Moon and Flower). They were the first novels he read after spontaneous research. It was then the second year of the last Manchu emperor, and he was studying in Hangchow in a middle school. The next year the Revolution started in Wuchang. When autumn came, all government schools were closed. So he had to transfer to a missionary school. But at that time academic grades of missionary schools were much lower than those of the government. So he had leisure for outside reading. Among the books he read, *T'ao Hua Shan* 桃花扇 (Peach Fan), and *Yen Tzŭ Chien* 燕子箋 (Swallow Letter) were his favorite dramas.

That same year he went to Japan to study. In spite of heavy assignments in his school there, he happened to read English translations of Turgenev's *First Love* and *Spring Tide*. From then on, he began to acquaint himself with Western literature: from Turgenev to Tolstoy, Dostoevsky, Gorky and Chekhov. And from Russian he was led to study German literature. As a result, he almost gave up his school work and stayed in his boarding house reading novels. In his four years of high school, he completed about 1000 novels and short stories by Russian, German, English, Japanese, and French authors. In 1921, when he was studying in the Imperial University, Tokyo, he began to write short stories, which he collected into a volume called *Ch'ên Lun* 沉淪 (Downfall, 1921, 泰東).

Upon returning to China in 1922, he founded the "Creative Society" 創造社 at Shanghai, together with Kuo Mo-jo 郭沫若, Chang Tzŭ-p'ing 張資平, and Ch'êng Fang-wu 成仿吾. In 1923, he went to Peiping, where he taught literature in the National University of Peking 北京大學. In 1925, he lectured at Wuchang University 武昌大學, near Hankow. And a year later he returned to his native place because of the death of his son. Later, he became professor of literature at Sun Yat-sen University 中山大學 of Canton. From 1926 on, he stayed in Shanghai, where he devoted himself to writing, and directed the "Creative Society". In 1927, he taught in Shanghai College of Law 上海法科大學. Later, he became a champion of revolutionary literature at the persuasion of his lover Miss Wang Yang-hsia 王映霞 and of his friend Ch'ien Hsing-ts'un 錢杏邨 (better known under his pen-name A Ying 阿英), a proletarian critic. In 1928, he edited the literary monthly *Pên Liu* 奔流 in collaboration with Lu Hsün 魯迅. And in 1929, he edited the *Ta Chung Wên I* 大衆文藝 (Mass Literature) to promote proletarian literature. In 1930, he joined the "China League of Left Writers". But Yü Ta-fu was too romantic and emotional for a revolutionary life, so he soon retired from that field, and lived, from 1930 on, with Miss Wang at the West Lake of Hangchow.

Before the Sino-Japanese War, he was counsellor to the Fukien Provincial Government. He arrived Singapore in the end of 1938, where he became the editor-in-chief of the newspaper *Hsing Chou Jih Pao* 星州日報. After the Pearl Harbour Incident of 1941, he escaped to Sumatra, where he changed his name to Chao Lien 趙廉, and earned his living by doing business. He lived there for four years; but he was killed however by Japanese gendarmes shortly after the Victory in August of 1945.

The collected works of Yü Ta-fu were published between 1928 and 1931 by the Pei Hsin Book Co., under the title of *Ta Fu Ch'üan Chi* 達夫全集. It contains seven volumes altogether. They are: 寒灰集*, 鷄肋集*, 過去集*, 奇零集*, 敝帚集*, 蕨薇集* and 斷殘集*. Besides these, he wrote 閑書* (1936, 良友); 達夫日記*, etc.

Translations: 拜金藝術 (*Money Writes* by U. Sinclair, 北新); 小家之伍 (Selected European and American Short Stories, 北新), etc.

The essays on Yü Ta-fu were collected by 素雅 in his 郁達夫評傳 (1932, 現代) and by 賀玉波 in his 郁達夫論 (光華). Chao Ching-shên 趙景深 also wrote a book on Yü Ta-fu, entitled 郁達夫論 (1933, 北新).

197. Yü Yang-ling 余揚靈

Also named 余致力. Pen-names: 徐懋庸, 高平, 揚, etc.

Essayist, and literary critic. He received only junior middle school education. He acquired from self-study all the necessary knowledge about literature and foreign languages. At the age of 20, he went to Shanghai, where he studied in the Lao Tung Middle School 勞動中學, and began to contribute to *Tzŭ Yu T'an* 自由談 (Free Talk), a literary supplement of the newspaper *Shên Pao* 申報, edited by Li Lieh-wên 黎烈文 His works were highly appreciated by the latter. His writings were published also in the magazines *Shên Pao Yüeh K'an* 申報月刊, *Chung Hsüeh Shêng* 中學生 (The Juvenile Student), *T'ao Shêng* 濤聲, and *Wên Hsüeh* 文學 (Literature).

His first collection of essays, entitled *Ta Tsa Chi* 打雜集, published in 1935, with a preface written by Lu Hsün 魯迅, was enthusiastically received by the Chinese youth. And in 1936, he published one volume of popular articles on literature, entitled *Chieh T'ou Wên T'an* 街頭文談* (Street-Side Literary Opinions 光明).

During the Sino-Japanese War, he went to Yenan, the former capital of the Red Régime, where he taught in the Lu Hsün Institute of Arts 魯迅藝術學院,

Besides the works mentioned above, he also wrote *Tsên Yang Ts'ung Shih Wên I Hsiu Yang* 怎樣從事文藝修養 (1936, 三江); *Wên I Ssŭ Ch'ao Hsiao Shih* 文藝思潮小史 (1947, 生活); *You Ch'ü Ti Jih Chi* 有趣的日記* (1935, 新中國); etc.

198. Yuan Ch'ang-ying 袁昌英.

(1894 —   )

T. 蘭紫. Playwright, and essayist. Born in Liling, Hunan. Wife of Yang

Tuan-liu 楊端六, a professor of economics at Wuhan University. She studied literature first at Edinburgh University, where she received her M.A. degree, and then at the Université de Paris. Upon returning to China, she was appointed professor at the National University of Law and Political Science of Peiping 國立北京法政大學, and then at the China Institute 中國公學 at Woosung, the National Central University 中央大學, and the National Wuhan University 武漢大學. During the Sino-Japanese War, she lived in Loshan, Szechwan, to which place the Wuhan University moved. After the Victory over Japan, she returned to Wuchang, still holds the position at Wuhan University.

Works: *K'ung Ch'iao Tung Nan Fei Chi Ch'i T'a* 孔雀東南飛及其他 (containing six pieces of plays); *Yin Ma Ch'ang Ch'êng K'u* 飲馬長城窟 (a five-act play); *Fa Lan Hsi Wên Hsüeh* 法蘭西文學 (French Literature, 1933, 商務); *Fa Kuo Wên Hsüeh* 法國文學 (French Literature, 1944, Chungking, 商務); *Shan Chü San Mo* 山居散墨* (collection of essays, 1937, 商務); *Hsing Nien Ssŭ Shih* 行年四十 (1945, 商務); etc.

199. Yuan Hsi 袁　犀.

(1919 —　　　)

Novelist, and short-story writer. Born in Mukden. After the Mukden Incident of 1931, he went to Peiping, where he attended the I Wên Middle School 藝文中學, and was then transferred to the Northeast Middle School 東北中學. With the outbreak of the Sino-Japanese War, he returned to the Northeast to do underground work, and was arrested by Japanese gendarmes in 1938. Regaining freedom in 1940, he began to write a novel *Ni Chao* 泥沼 (1940, 文選刊行會), to describe the emotion of the Chinese people under the Japanese rule. His later novels are: *Pei Ch'iao* 貝殼* (1943, 新民印書舘); and *Mien Sha* 面紗 (1944, 新民印書舘). His collection of short stories is called *Sên Lin Ti Chi Mo* 森林的寂寞 (1943, 華北文化書局). From 1941 on, he lived in Peiping. After the Victory over Japan, he edited a literary magazine *Liang* 糧, which ceased publication after issusing its first number. Later he went to Changchun.

200. Yuan Mu-chih 袁牧之.

Pen-name: 袁梅. Playwright. Born in Ninghsien, Chekiang. Before the Sino-Japanese War, he was a member of the Fuhtan Dramatic Group 復旦劇社, and a film star. During the War he joined the Communist Régime at Yenan. In the autumn of 1946, he married Miss Ch'ên P'o-êrh 陳波兒, a famous Communist actress, at Harbin.

Works: *Ai Shên Ti Chien* 愛神的箭 (a play, 1930, 光華); *Yen Chü Man T'an* 演劇漫談 (1933, 現代); *Shêng Ssŭ T'ung Hsin* 死生同心 (1936); *Hsi Chü Hua Chuang Shu* 戲劇化裝術 (世界); *San Ko Ta Hsüeh Shêng* 三個大學生 (新時代); Ling Ling 玲玲 (a play); *Liang Ko Chio Sê Yen Ti Hsi* 兩個角色演的戲 (新月); *Chung Lou Kuai Jên* 鐘樓怪人* (a play, 世界), etc.

1500 MODERN CHINESE NOVELS & PLAYS

by

Jos. Schyns （善秉仁）

& others

NOTE

The reviewed books are classified under the names of the authors. The authors are classified in alphabetic order according their English transliteration. Because of insurmountable difficulties, it has been impossible for us to classify the different books of each author in a strict chronological order.

1500 MODERN CHINESE NOVELS & PLAYS

PRESENT DAY FICTION

1. 好年頭　*GOOD YEAR*[1]　　　1 vol. 106 p. by **艾霞遺**
　　　　　　　　　　　　　　　　　1935　春光書店

The author — a woman — presents a vivid picture of village life in China, and of the hardships of the Chinese peasants. She describes how they toil from morning to night without enough food to live; and when they have a good harvest, instead of their conditions being improved, they become poor as the prices fall and their money has to go to pay their debts.

Here and there it presents some scenes taken from the daily life of a peasant. It can be read by those who want to become acquainted with peasant's life in China. *A very good book.*

2. 愛與恨　*LOVE OF HATRED*　　　1 vol. 149 p. by **艾王龍**
　　　　　　　　　　　　　　　2nd. edit. 1946　百新書店

P'ing is a young professor who has loved Shu-fang since his earliest years, and their love is reciprocal. Shu-fang's father, however, forces her to marry another man, whereupon P'ing marries one of his students.

They are still united, however, by the great love between them.

The love of P'ing's wife for her husband is also described. She admits the indignity of her situation but knows her own worth.

In the end, the first love triumphs over conjugal love. *For adults.*

3. 南行記　*SOUTHWARD BOUND*　　　1 vol. 170 p. by **艾　蕪**
　　　　　　　　　　1933　文化生活出版社　*See Biogr.* 1

A Chinese goes to live in Kunming but is not able to find any work there. He travels through Burma and there he recites stories on the public highway. Afterwards he becomes a "boy" and then a school teacher.

Interesting descriptions of the countries visited. *For mature people.*

4. 夜景　*NIGHT SCENE*　　　　1 vol. 245 p. by **艾　蕪**
　　　　　　　　　　　　　　　1936　文化生活

Two stories describing scenes of daily life. The author tells us, above all, of poor people who are suffering and unhappy. *For everyone.*

---

1. Mr. Wu Ping-chung (吳炳鍾) took the lion's share in the translation of the titles of the reviewed books. The others were excerpted from Mrs. Su Hsiue-lin's Introduction, which was translated by Miss Shuping Kuai (蒯淑平). We acknowledge here our gratitude for this difficult work. (J.S.)

5. 芭 蕉 谷 *PLANTAIN VALLEY*

1 vol. 223 p. by 艾　燕
1937 商務印書館

Three novels.

The first describes the conjugal life of a woman, engaged in trade, who has had four husbands. The second tells of the agitated existence of a school in disorder. The third presents us with some aspects of ordinary life.

For mature people only because the author is too realistic and sows his pages with shallow villifications. *Not for everyone.*

6. 春 天 *SPRING*

1 vol 69 p. by 艾　燕
1940 良友復興圖書公司

It is Spring. Some poor peasants are voluntarily cleaning the irrigation canal of the village, but the one who is profiting from it the most, Yi Lao-hsi 易老喜 , a rich peasant, not only refuses to help, but has in addition, spoilt the canal. He wishes moreover, to appropriate the only piece of land of a poor widow.

On the day that the canal is being cleaned the old Yi Lao-hsi threatens her while she is catching a few fish, and on the evening of the same day, his son goes to her house to intimidate her. There he breaks everything and seriously injures a poor peasant whom he finds in the widow's house. She herself escapes bodily injury only through defending herself with a knife, and her clothes are torn to shreds and her fish, the only food she has got, are taken from her.

The poor peasants are furious but do not dare to accuse Yi Lao-hsi or to punish him. He is too powerful. Moreover, he is connected with an opium smoker who is a man with many irons in the fire, whom everyone fears.

The story ends with the departure of the wounded peasant with only two dogs keeping him company.

The language used is sometimes vulgar, with plenty of curses and encouragements to hate and vengeance.

To be kept back because too violent and full of hate. *Not for everyone.*

7. 海 上 閒 話 *VOYAGE CHATS*

1 vol. 96 p. by 安 世
1930 北新書局

A collection of anecdotes and short stories, witty but shallow and disconnected. The style is lively and pleasant. *For informed readers.*

8. 傳 奇 *TALES*

1 vol. 257 p. by 張 愛 玲
6th. edit. 1945 建東印刷公司

Stories happening in the Chinese, Eurasian, and European world of Shanghai and Hongkong. Written in a very free and modern style.

Well written and often absorbingly interesting to read, most of these love stories end unhappily.

They should *not be recommended to anyone,* however, because of the free life described in them and because of a number of risky and low expressions that occur in them.

9. 流 言 *SO IT IS SAID*

1 vol. 163 p. by 張 愛 玲
2nd. edit. 1945 五洲書社

p. 1 Youthful memories.
p. 11 The author herself.
p. 17 Life in a city.

p. 24 On names.
p. 29 Struggles and troubles in Hongkong.

p. 41 Shanghai.
p. 43 Views.
p. 49 On the subject of clothes.
p. 57 One always returns to one's first loves.
p. 58 On women.
p. 68 Films.
p. 71 On the theatre.
p. 73 More films.
p. 77 Attitude of Chinese and of Europeans toward the theatre.
p. 86 Friendly talk.

p. 89 Secrets of a writer.
p. 98 To write is not easy.
p. 100 Education.
p. 120 An urchin beaten by a policeman.
p. 103 On poetry.
p. 108 Conversation in a train.
p. 109 The author in the family home.
p. 122 Painting.
p. 131 On dancing.
p. 143 More on painting.
p. 144 The writing profession.
p. 155 On music.

For everyone.

10. 紅玫瑰 *A RED, RED ROSE*   1 vol. 122 p. by 張愛玲
1945 北京沙漠書店

1. Love adventures of a man before his marriage. He first falls in love with a half-breed. Then he abandons her for a Chinese who obtains a divorce for his sake. And in the end he marries the girl chosen by his mother.

2. A young employee in Shanghai becomes enamoured with a young man, but after she learns of his scandalous life, she breaks with him.

3. An european bachelor of Shanghai has several mistresses whom he receives in his house.

4. An old schoolfellow of the author makes confidences. She loves her professor who is already married.

Not to be recommended to anyone.

11. 匪窟生活 *IN THE DEN OF BANDITS*   1 vol. 136 p. by 張健庵
1924 晨報社

A story about brigands. Very interesty and written in a easy language. *For everyone.*

12. 京西集 *WEST OF THE OLD CAPITAL*   1 vol. 91 p. by 張金壽
1943 華北文化書局

Of workmen, labourers, and the poorer people in the country around Peking. Of life in workshops. *For everyone.*

13. 春明外史 *ROMANCE OF THE IMPERIAL CITY*
3 vol. 392, 532, & 593 pp. by 張恨水
3rd edition; 1929 北京書局 *See Biogr. 3*

Book not to be recommended to anyone; the author gives too much descriptions of the houses of prostitution etc.

N. B. — During an interview accorded to one of our collaborators, the author made known to us that the books examined under the numbers: 28, 29, 31, 32 33, 34, 35, 36, 38, 41, 42, 43, 46, 48, 51, 52, 53, 54, 56, 57, 58, 61 and 62 all published under his name, were not written by him.

14. 啼笑因緣 *FUNNY AFFAIR*   1 vol. 340 p. by 張恨水
2nd edition 1939 玲玲書社

Fan Chia-shu, a young rich man from Hang-chow, went to Peiping to study. There he lived with one of his cousins, who, together with his wife, formerly a singer, brought him into society. He enjoyed himself and was introduced to a modern girl who was very rich. Her name was Hao Li-na. The author represents her with a good heart and generous character. Chia-shu refused to enter into intimacy with her, as he preferred quiet fun to dancing halls. He got acquainted with a singer, Feng-hsi, with whom he fell in love and lived on intimate terms. In the meantime Chia-shu, who had a noble heart, made an acquaintance with an old man Kuan Chou-feng, a fencing master. The latter was the father of a girl Hsiu-ku. The latter is a real pearl: good character and golden heart. She loved Chia-shu but kept her feelings to herself as she wanted to draw him out of certain difficulties, and this she did with the help of her father who owed gratitude to the man. One day, Chia-shu was called back to Hang-chow to his sick mother. Meanwhile Feng-hsi was forced by her family to marry a general. On his return to Peiping, the young man suffered cruelly from this infidelity. Meanwhile Feng-hsi lost her mind as the general illtreated her.

The book ends by the noble act of Hsiu-ku who left Chia-shu in "tête à tête" with Hao Li-na.

This book is very interesting and popular.

This volume *can be read by grown up people* without any offence.

15. 續啼笑因緣 FUNNY AFFAIR (suite)   1 vol. 318 p. by 張恨水

The author presents the marriage of Fan Chia-shu with Hao Li-na. Splendid marriage, but of short duration, for they divorced after several months. In the meantime Kuan Chou-feng and Hsiu-Ku trapped Feng-hsi's husband and killed him. Feng-hsi thereupon left the general's house and was put in an insane asylum. Little by little she recovered herself but became very poor, and became a prostitute in Tsinanfu. Here once more she was saved from danger by Hsiu-Ku in the company of her father. Chia-shu married her. Hao Li-na, after a disorderly life, entered a buddhist convent, and Hsiu-Ku disappeared. This sequel is not so good as the first volume. Hao Li-na is represented with a new character. The interest flags and the moral standard is lower. More daring descriptions. *Can be read only by informed readers.*

16. 金粉世家   6 vol. by 張恨水
1944   東方書店

The author took up a task which was above his capacity. The result of it is a stream of gossip while his intention was to draw the picture of a "great family."

Mr. Chin, a high official, lived together with his wife, concubines, four sons and several daughters. His aim in life was to collect money. He treated his children with severity and little intelligence. Their mother managed the house affairs. The three eldest sons were corrupt fellows. They had good positions at the ministry. They spent their free time outside their home, and on their return they quarrelled with their wives. The author describes such scenes with every detail. The fourth son was a very careless young man; he amused himself with servants and girlfriends. One day he met a student Leng, who was of modest family. He fell in love with her. He rented a court in the Leng's neighbourhood and got acquainted with the family.

Yen Szu, the fourth son, gradually won the love of his ideal Ch'in Ch'iu (Miss Leng). The latter feared to become a daughter-in-law in Chin's family, but at last love conquered her fear, and she accepted Yen Szu as her husband. At the beginning all went well, but soon one of the daughters-in-law picked a quarrel with the married couple, for she was mad at Yen Szu's refusal to marry her cousin. She succeeded in bringing the latter in to contact with Yen Szu. Yen Szu also patronized prostitutes. After Mr. Chin's death the family began to fall apart. Their relations became unpleasant, and their mother decided to leave; thus the family bonds were broken. Ch'in Ch'iu, who became a mother, realized that her husband neglected her, and she resolved to have no relations with him in future. She escaped with her child during a disorder caused by fire. Yen Szu spent his time with girls and finally departed to Europe, to study. . .

The author does not tell us any more about Ch'in Ch'iu, after her flight. Yen Szu, after his arrival to Europe, joined a theatrical group.

The book is swallowed by the youngsters, especially by students. The author introduces us to the lives of rich families. The book *should not be recommended to anybody* because it approves of divorce, and concubinage.

The book however contains no immoral scenes.

17. 滿江紅   1 vol. 341 p. by 張恨水

1943 啓智書店

An artist, who was an ex-professor of Tientsin, sailed from Chinan to Nanking. During the trip he met a girl who seemed to be a student. In reality she was a cabaret girl. The artist fell in love with her. The rest of the novel is a maze of complications. In spite of the girl's profession, the author wants us to sympatize with the girl. He describes her struggles while she tried to emerge from her surroundings; he also shows her aim to set up a good family of her own.

May be read *only by grown up people,* owing to some risky descriptions.

18. 北雁南飛 *THE BIRDS FLY SOUTH*   1 vol. by 張恨水

京津書店

In the last days of the Empire, a small provincial clerk sent his son — a boy of fifteen — to a private school in the neighbourhood. The principal of the school was a severe tutor of the old type. Altogether, there were twenty students, one of them a girl, the tutor's daughter. This one was only fourteen and was engaged to an ugly fellow whom she hated. She fell in love with our hero. The author tells us about all the means by which the young people sought to communicate with each other. Finally, an interview, which was rather sentimental, took place. In order to continue their relations they employed some school-servants. In the end they caused a quarrel between two poor families, and through their fault one student was dismissed. On this our hero left the school. *Not to be recommended to young people.*

19. 北雁南飛 *THE WILD GOOSE FLYING SOUTH*   4 vol. 485 p. by 張恨水

1946 北京書店

The precedent book consisted of only 14 chapters, while this volume has 38. In the added chapters we are told of the adventures of the same characters as in the other book and in such a boring way that the reader is made to fall asleep standing. The hero and heroine try to accomplish a happy marriage but do not succeed. *For adults.*

20. 胭脂淚 *THE LADY CANNOT BE HAPPY*   1 vol. 298 p. by 張恨水

1946 萬象書屋

In order to avoid marrying a merchant's son whom she does not love, a young lady leaves her family and lives alone. In spite of the cautions of her friends, she accepts an appointment as the secretary of a departmental director of a ministry. This latter has intentions on her and wants to take her as his concubine. The heroine, however, insists on his obtaining a divorce from his wife. The director refuses, and the young lady turns over a new leaf and again leads an honest life.

There are no immoral descriptions in this book and the illigitimate situations are not pushed too far. The author even has good intentions for he wishes to show the unhappiness of those who defy the old traditions. He is to be congratulated on his good will in this instance for up to now he has not spoilt us in this respect. The subject itself seems, however, rather dangerous, and because of it we do not recommend the book, although there is no great reason why it should be kept back. *Not for everyone.*

21. 香妃怨 *THE FRAGRANT PRINCESS*   2 vol. 271 p. by 張恨水
1946 百新書店

In these two volumes the author tells us of the amourous adventures of several young people. Two of them end in committing suicide, two others finally obtain the paternal consent to their marriage, and as for the heroine, Hsiang Fei, her story just tails off.

The book in question is badly constructed, containing only low class anecdotes with scenes over which it is better to draw a veil. And furthermore, the author writes with calculated effect, for on page 195, he himself tells us of the evil wrought by bad books. He cannot, therefore, deny his own responsibility.

Apart from the moral point of view, his work has not the slightest literary value.

We wish to warn all directors of consciences, both Christian and non-Christian, of the great dangers brought on by the reading of such frivolous books. *Proscribed.*

22. 丹鳳街 *STREET OF RED PHOENIX*   1 vol. 264 p. by 張恨水
3rd. edit. 1946 山城出版社

This novel first appeared under the title of 負販列傳. The author tells us of the inhabitants of a certain quarter of a large city. His characters are all poor people or small tradesmen. Their story is not interesting.

A girl is given as a concubine to a wealthy man. She consents to this course hoping to alleviate the poverty of her mother. She is loved by a poor young man, who is driven away by the maternal uncle of the heroine. Her friends try to save her from the unhappy conditions in which she finds herself, but fail.

The author provides for a sequel. *For everyone.*

23. 熱血之花 *FLOWERS OF PURE EMOTION*   1 vol. 116 p. by 張恨水
2nd. edit. 1946 百新書店

Identical book with that by 馮玉奇 under the title of 血淚花.

It is a mystery how the same book can be claimed by two different authors. *For everyone.*

24. 大江東去 *AS FLOWING WATER RETURNS NOT*   1 vol. 260 p. by 張恨水
1946 教育書店

The author is to be congratulated that for once he has produced a proper and even a well written book.

An officer who has been ordered to the front entrusts his wife to a brother officer, to conduct her to Hankow. The friend remains at a proper distance from the lady but nevertheless, renders her considerable services, so that she becomes attached to him, under the pretext that the silence of her husband proves that he has died on the field of honour. The friend, however, is faithful to his mission and does not respond to the advances of Ping-ju (冰如). They learn soon after, that the husband is not dead and is coming to Hankow. He is received coldly by his wife who insists on a divorce. The husband consents and with the formal document of divorce in her pocket, Ping-ju goes to importune her friend who, however, gives her an excellent lesson by turning his back on her.

The husband, who has consented to the divorce only because he has been forced by circumstances, would like to take back his wife, but she is afraid of losing face and sends him away. Upon this, both, the husband and the friend, volunteer for a perilous mission and leave together for the front.

It is to be hoped that the author will give us more books of this nature. *For everyone.*

25. 落霞孤鶩 *SUNSET CORMORANT DANCE*   4 vol. 637 p. by   張恨水
                                                       1931   世界書局

The author narrates the life of Lo Wu, who was sold, after her mother's death, to the family Chao and was treated as a slave. One day she warned Professor Chiang against a great danger threatening him; he escaped in time. Next Lo Wu was put into an orphanage in the same room with Yü Ju. Both girls had a good character: the former was more simple, the latter more intelligent. Mr. Chiang, on his return to Peiping, saw Yü Ju's photo displayed at the orphanage and asked her to marry him. Though Yü Ju was in love with him, she refused, and asked him to marry Lo Wu, to whom she owed a debt of gratitude. She herself was obliged by her superior to marry Wang, a poor tailor, and their marriage was very unhappy while her friend's was a happy one. Yü Ju's parents-in-law, in order to increase their business, sent her to pay a visit to Liu's powerful family, whose son, a rake, wanted to seduce her. She turned him down and never again visited the family. Yü Ju continued to be in love with Mr. Chiang and after having a few dates with him in a park their love increased. When Lo Wu heard about it she pointed out to her husband, without jealousy, the danger of their rendezvous. Yü Ju, being warned, also promised never to meet Mr. Chiang again. Wang, being held in contempt by Yü Ju, began to pay frequent visits to prostitutes and was compelled to leave his home, but being penniless he stole some money from his wife. Lord Liu had him arrested; in order to save Wang his parents forced Yü Ju to sell herself to Liu. She obeyed out of fear, but once her husband was set free, she disappeared, leaving her friend, Lo Wu, in despair.

A good novel with fine characters, though some of the passages are frivolous. *For experienced persons.*

26. 夜深沉 *THE NIGHT IS WELL IN HER COURSE*   2 vol. 564 p. by   張恨水
                                                       1941   百新書局

The Ting family adopts a little girl. She has talent and studies actively. She is seduced by a student who afterwards abandons her to sell her to a general. The heroine, however, manages to escape and goes back to the stage. A manager of a factory seduces her in turn. Then the young Ting goes in search of his so-called "sister" but is not able to find her. He then marries a girl who is also seduced by the manager and who dies in childbirth. It is then expected that Ting will finally marry his "sister" but once again the manager prevents him.

There is nothing particularly upsetting in this book but it has an unhealthy atmosphere. *For adults.*

27. 滿城風雨 *THE TOWN IS SCANDALIZED*   3 vol. 651 p. by   張恨水
                                                       1935   上海大衆書局

A student from a province fell in love with a remote cousin. Some soldiers, on their way, captured him and made him their general's secretary. He managed to escape and tried to reach his home with the aid of a Catholic missionary. On his way back, he passed a town, where he made acquaintance with Choufeng, who was also his cousin. In her company the student passed through many war-time adventures. He treated his companion as his fiancée. Returning to his native city, he found the latter occupied by the Japanese. These put him into prison. To save his fiancée from starvation, he was forced to accept the post of Hsien-chang. The "Yi Yung Kiun" with his brother at the head, recaptured the city. To wash away his disgrace, he took the command of "Kan Szu Tui", and died at the head of his men. On learning about his death, Chou feng threw herself into the river and was drowned.

In this book there is one daring scene; for this reason, the book *may be given to the grown up people only.*

28. 春去花殘 *THE FLOWERS ARE WITHERING* 1 vol. 64 p. by 張恨水
1936

A story of little literary value. A married man had illicit relations with a married woman. The adultery was discovered by his legal wife, and the two were divorced. The divorce was followed by the marriage of the guilty ones. But on the wedding day the new wife left her lover. . . The shock drove him mad. His first wife died of sorrow. *Not to be recommended to anyone.*

29. 摩登小姐 *THE MODERN MISS* 1 vol. 134 p. by 張恨水
1937 奉天三友書局

In this book of little interest, the author wanted to present to us a "modern girl". The said girl had a number of flirtations; in the author's opinion these numerous flirtations classify a young girl as a "modern".

Besides several curses and a daring scene — this is hinted at rather than described — there is nothing offensive in this book.

This "modern" girl clearly cannot be set as an example. *For informed readers.*

30. 鐵血情絲 *OF BRAVERY & LOVE* 2 vol. 454 p. by 張恨水
1938 廣藝書局

The story of warriors (former T'ai-P'ing soldiers) and their followers. It narrates their attempts to rescue people who had been kidnaped by brigands. The main characters are true artists in their profession, and the brigands have no choice but to behave well.

An innocent novel although tiresome. *No reservation* from the moral point of view.

31. 離恨天 *FOREVER SORROW* 1 vol. 101 p. by 張恨水
1940 世界書局

A student Li·Chi fell in love with Yün Hsien. The young couple promised to make an excellent marriage; in the family, moreover, everybody agreed, with the exception of Yün Hsien's stepmother. The latter succeeded in setting her husband against the young couple. The girl, who saw that the marriage had failed, fled from her parents' home and entered a buddhist convent as a postulant. Li Chi set out at once to look for his bride. For this reason he disguised himself as a novice bonze. He travelled over a year and finally succeeded in finding his bride. He returned home and informed Yün Hsien's father. The latter departed at once to bring his daughter back. In the meantime she had to leave the convent as it was plundered by brigands. She escaped to Shanghai where she found a job. Her master, after having seen her, desired to have her as his concubine. Yün Hsien refused, but the boss made some bold attempts. Our heroine resisted by striking him and escaped in the night only to land in a hospital. Here her father found her; after some days she died. Li Chi who witnessed her death, attended the funeral. After this he entered a convent.

In this book there is one unbecoming scene, but *the atmosphere in not offensive.*

32. 春江淚痕　*TRAGEDY BY THE RIVER*　　1 vol. 85 p. by 張恨水
　　　　　　　　　　　　　　　　　　　　　　　　　　　　　奉天東方書局

A young man from the North was a newspaper man in Shanghai. His friends introduced him to a girl, whom he married. The newly married couple were happy and departed for their honey-moon trip to Hangchow Lake. The husband's mother fell sick and the couple departed for Jehol. After one year of married life the young woman died in childbirth. Her husband set off on a voyage, in order to forget his grief. *For everyone.*

33. 襤衣鴛鴦　*LOVERS IN RAGS*　　1 vol. 155 p. by 張恨水
　　　　　　　　　　　　　　　　　　　　　　　1940　積記書社

Lewd descriptions. *To be proscribed.*

34. 水不解花　　　　　　　　2 vol. 160 & 136 p. by 張恨水
　　　　　　　　　　　　　　　　　　　　　　　1942　文藝書局

This book presents a love affair in a real Chang Hen-shui style. A man makes love to four women. The author merely relates his ordinary theme. The hero left his legal wife and was followed by her rivals.

Various unhealthy situations are presented in such a way as to make them seen quite natural.

The book ends in a Chang Hen-shui vein : by a divorce, new marriage and suicide.

In this book there are no obscene passages. But it is *not recommended to anyone* owing to its unhealthy atmosphere.

35. 少年繪形記　　　　　　　　　　　1 vol. 233 p. by 張恨水
　　　　　　　　　　　　　　　　　　　　　　　勵進出版社

Chou Chi-ch'un was the first of his class at middle school. His old father was very happy about it. He related to his friends the hardships and sacrifices he had endured in order to pay his son's school fees. The old parent was well rewarded, for all his troubles. His son was well educated, diligent and helpful at home.

The young hero soon fell in love with a fine girl. These young people engaged themselves to be married. During Chi-ch'un's illness his bride revealed what noble feelings she had for him.

After some time Chi-ch'un came to live in Peiping. As could be expected in a novel of Chang Hen-shui, our hero found himself connected with a modern girl, who by her tricks and presents made him forget the country girl. He also forgot his kind father and the sacrifices that the old man had endured. At first he wanted to resist his new feelings, but finally the Peiping girl won.

Chi-ch'un's professor came to know this and wanted to force the girl to break her relations with the hero, but in vain. This young modern girl persuaded Chi-ch'un to marry her. (Thus the first volume ends.) *For grown up people.*

36. 情天恨海　　　　　　　　　　　1 vol. 169 p. by 張恨水
　　　　　　　　　　　　　　　　　　　　　1939　大東書局

A young man fell in love with a comedian, but his father would not give his consent to their marriage unless his son passed four years at a foreign university. Soon, however, the son was taken as a hostage by brigands; he was then rescued by an American missionary and his adopted daughter, who was Chinese. The latter fell in love with him. Owing to the fact that he was told that his former bride was dead, he got engaged with the adopted daughter. Finally he met the comedian in a factory, where she worked. She had been kicked out by her mother, who wanted to give her as a concubine to a rich man. She refused as she wanted to remain faithful to her fiancé. The young man, meeting her under such conditions, loved her all the more and resolved to marry her. He took her to his father. The latter, in a dramatic scene, told them that they were brother and sister. After this the young man returned to the missionary's daughter and married her. On their return they found that his father and daughter had departed to do penance for their sins.

A very nice novel. Its characters are very beautiful, which is an unusual thing for Mr. Chang Hen-shui.

Although it contains a number of immodest expressions, *that should not keep grown up people from reading it.*

37. 秘密谷 THE SECRET VALLEY   2 vol. 328 p. by 張恨水
1941 百新書店

Mr. K'ang Pei-ch'uan found himself forsaken by his girl-friend. He met at the club three men who were talking about an expedition to an unknown land, which was said to be inhabited (they called it "Mi-Mi-Ku"). As this region was not from K'ang Pei-ch'uan's native village, he joined the expedition. When they reached their destination they found the region inhabited by people, who had been separated from the world since the time of the Ming. Our two heroes wanted to flee but could not. The expedition returned to Nanking with the "king" and his wife. The "king" died as a rickshaw-coolie. Mr. K'ang volunteered to bring back the king's wife to the mountains. *This book may be read by everyone.*

38. 冷月孤魂   1 vol. 160 p. by 張恨水
1942 奉天大東書局

Subject: A student from a well to do family lived in Shanghai in modern university surroundings. Around him fluttered three damsels. One was very rich and worldly; she left him. The second one was of a once influential family with whom he fell passionately in love; this romance ended as she died of consumption, faithful to him in spite of many temptations. The third girl was his own cousin, a gay and modern girl who finally won him.

Form: Easy to read, the book has no literary value whatever.

Meaning: The work is rather farciful, for in this book money flows like water, luxury is scattered, the exams are passed without any preparation....All this takes place in an imaginary world.

Morals: No description is immodest.

Several equivocal situations, and much sloppy sentiment. From a moral point of view the worst thing is flirtation with several girls without any intention of marriage, which is described as the natural thing to do.

The reading of this book will not bring any profit to the reader. It should *be proscribed* from college libraries, schools, and other educational institutions.

39. 如此江山 SIC TRANSIT GLORIA MUNDI   2 vol. by 張恨水
1941 百新書店

A story of a young man and a girl who were engaged. During a voyage, this young man met a girl who won his interest; thus arousing the jealousy of his fiancée. To put an end to all this, the young man resolved to sail to Europe, but the two girls attemped to prevent him.

Quite innocent. Lack of action. *For everyone.*

40. 現代青年 *MODERN YOUTH* 3 vol. by 張恨水
1941 三友書店

A father of a poor family made superhuman efforts in order to give his son a chance to study. The latter was an intelligent and clever fellow and it seemed that he was to have an excellent future. He engaged himself with a poor young girl, who was faithful to him. In the meantime he departed to Peiping to continue his studies. Here he fell in love with a rich girl; he was ignorant of the fact that she was a "half-sister" of his betrothed. He began to lead a bad life and his father, who came to correct his errors, could not find him and died of despair, in the poor girl's home. The latter, who learned about her fiancé's infidelity, was in despair and committed suicide. When our hero learned about these two deaths he repented and came to mourn and ask forgiveness at his father's tomb.

A realistic novel; the author does not condemn the lack of conscience and filial devotion. He describes with sympathy the seductions and careless living. *Not to be recommended to anyone.*

41. 桃李花開 1 vol. 190 p. by 張恨水
1942 廣藝書局

The heroes of this book all carry the odour of brothels. We are presented with some immoral stories about illegal amusements, union with concubines etc.

The atmosphere is certainly unhealthy. Although there are no obscene descriptions, it seems to us that *this book should be proscribed* owing to its unhealthy atmosphere.

42. 月暗花殘 1 vol. by 張恨水

A student fell in love with a girl and his love was reciprocated. He continued his studies; in the meantime his friend's father died and she was taken as a concubine by her landowner. The legal wife of the landowner received her well, but when she saw that the concubine was pregnant she became jealous. In order to get rid of her she provoked a seduction scene between her nephew and the concubine. The scandal was known and the concubine was sent away. She found her former friend; they lived together for six years as a "brother and sister"!! After this period her innocence was proved and she became the legal wife of the Landlord. His former wife deprived of her rank committed suicide.

This book approves of concubinage and the cohabitation of girls and boys. This can lead astray the young readers. The seduction is described in a raw way. For these reasons the book is *to be proscribed.*

43. 海月情花 1 vol. 167 p. by 張恨水
1947 上海遠東出版社

Mr. Chang Hen-shui would have done a great favour to his readers if he had not written this novel. It is the love story of a certain Ho Hsien-sheng, so obscene that the author of these lines had to throw the book aside, after having read only a score of pages. *To be proscribed.*

44. 平滬通車 *PEIPING SHANGHAI EXPRESS* 1 vol. 200 p. by 張恨水
1941 百新書店

A certain Mr. Hu, a banker, took the Peiping-Shanghai express. He travelled first class. His cabin contained two berths. He was the only occupant. A young lady entered the train; she had a first class ticket, but she had not reserved a berth. She was therefore obliged to install herself in the dining-car, while the employee looked for one. This lady started a conversation with Mr. Hu who came to take a cup of coffee in the restaurant.

He consoled the lady and wanted to give her his cabin, but after some civilities Mr. Hu was tempted to seduce the lady. They passed a night in the cabin. The lady surprised the banker by declaring that she was his niece. The next day our couple talk love. . . . . Mr. Hu proposed to dismiss his wife and to marry his niece, who was a divorced woman. During the next night, the lady gave a narcotic to Mr. Hu and stole 120,000 dollars, which he had to take to Shanghai, and left the train. Our hero awoke and discovered the theft. He had had to do with a professional thief.

Mr. Hu regretted his error; having been rich he now fell into utmost poverty; meanwhile the lady continued her profession.

A very absorbing book. The lesson which the author draws out is excellent. But nevertheless *it can not be given to everyone.*

45. 美人恩 *HER GRACIOUSNESS*   1 vol. 249 p. by 張恨水
                                        2nd edition 1941   上海世界書局

An interesting book to read. A young man Hung Shih-yi, poor as Job but with a good heart, fell in love with a girl of low birth; the latter's name was Hsiao Nan. He spent all the little money he earned and sold his things, in order to lighten the girl's situation and to save her parents. Hsiao Nan's mother had a low and vile character and was ready to sell her conscience for a little sum of money. Her blind father was a devoted Buddhist, with a noble character. The young girl soon forgot her benefactor and joined a dancing troupe. A young man from this troupe was interested in her and they promised to marry each other. At this time a rich young man appeared on the scene. At first this man got a good job for Hung Shih-yi and asked him to obtain our heroine for him as his concubine. Hsiao Nan agreed to this and went to live with the drunkard. Her mother, who was bribed with a big sum of money, also consented to this union. Only her father who was disgusted with the whole affair, left the house and entered a buddhist convent. Hung Shih-yi, who was disgusted with the services which Hsiao Nan demanded from him, left the city and became a soldier. The dancer, whom our heroine promised to marry, likewise left the city and became a school teacher in a village. One day these two rejected suitors met together. They realized that Hsiao Nan, by her way of rewarding them, had given them a chance to form their characters: hence the title. *Not to be recommended to anybody.*

46. 孤鴻泛史   1 vol. 137 p. by 張恨水
                                              1941   文華書局

A novel of a modern girl who separated herself from a "good friend" in order to love another.

The author presents some theories about marriage which are contrary to good morals. This book contains no obscene passages. *It may be read by informed readers.*

47. 蜀道難 *TORTUROUS ROAD*   1 vol. 119 p. by 張恨水
                                           1941   上海百新書店

Description of the difficulties met by a lonely lady on a long voyage. The author relates to us the numerous accidents which happened during the voyage between Hankow and Szechwan, in a boat. All these difficulties vanished with the appearance of a man who took an interest in the lonely travelling lady. . .But not every lady wants to become intimate with the man who helps her. Our lonely lady had the same opinion. The young man, about whom the book relates, finds this out after they land. *This book can be read by everyone.*

48. 愛人的謊話 *HER LIES* 1 vol. 137 p. by 張恨水
1942 文華書局

A young Peiping girl, Miss Chao, was the daughter of a concubine. She was promised in marriage to a certain Mr. Fang. She hated the latter very much. Miss Chao had some relations with Mr. Chou, whom she renounced for the idealistic patriot Mr. Mao. In the meantime her family interfered, and forced her to marry Mr. Fang. But our heroine refused and sought refuge at Mao's place. The latter soon forgot all his ideals and was occupied only with his friend.

In this book there is one frivolous description and an equivocal insinuation. *Some reserve.*

49. 天上人間 1 vol. 126 p. by 張恨水
3rd edition 1943 奉天文藝書局

A young girl of a good family refused to marry the man who was selected for her by her parents. She fled from her home and published her refusal in a newspaper. The other party accepted the refusal and our heroine sailed to Shanghai. Here she married the one she loved. Before the marriage ceremony took place they lived together for several days. By this they showed that they cared neither for morals nor for conventions. After a year the husband became unfaithful and lived with a singer. He was accused by the so-called brother of the singer and cast into prison. In the prison he learned about his wife's illness and wrote her a letter. She forgave him but after his release he nevertheless did not dare to return home.

This book is *not to be recommended to anyone*. The author talks lightly about marriage bonds.

It contains also two immoral scenes.

50. 燕歸來 3 vol. 173 & 179 & 197 p. by 張恨水
1943 啓智書店

A Nanking student, at the death of her father, related her hardships to her four friends. A terrible famine caused the dispersion of her family in Kansu. She was sold as a slave in order to save her parents from death. Her adopted father treated her as his own daughter and made her study. Now she wanted to return to Kansu in order to try and find her family and also to work on the social improvement of her native country. The four friends, who were in love with her, proposed to accompany her to her native place. At the moment of her departure one already renounced his proposal and remained behind. The description of the voyage, with remarkable geographical and historical features, is accompanied with philosophical reflections, which are at times trivial. In the course of the trip the three friends returned one by one to Nanking, each giving an excuse, but in reality they returned because their hope to marry her had vanished. She however soon made acquaintance with an engineer. *This book may be read by everyone.*

51. 雨梨濺花 1 vol. 128 p. by 張恨水
1942 同光書局

Obscene descriptions. *To be proscribed.*

52. 大地回春 2 vol. 175 p. by 張恨水
1943 遠東出版社

Two friends adopted a girl as their "sister". One of them had to travel, during which period the other took the girl with him. Their constant jealousy made life intolerable to her and she soon was sent back. Her friend, who could not find peace, departed to Shanghai to study. Here he found his former girl-friend in a brothel. He saved her from this dangerous place. The novel ends up by a double-marriage, as another figure has appeared on the horizon.

Some daring passages. *For informed people only.*

53. 落英繽紛   1 vol. 121 p. by   張恨水
                                        1943   勵志書店

A story of a rich Tientsin man who took a concubine; the latter was an actress. The actress succeeded in dissipating his fortune.

The author uses all his imagination for describing a rich man's dwelling. He describes such things as: decoration, furniture etc., very skillfully and in full detail.

A dull book. *The book may be read by everyone.*

54. 艷陽天   2 vol. 261 p. by   張恨水
                                        1943   上海遠東出版社

The author wants to describe a platonic love between a married man (Mr. Huang) and a young girl (Miss Ni). Mr. Huang was unhappy with his wife, as the latter had a passion for gambling, and seemed not to realize the necessity of love between the spouses. Anyhow, she was "broadminded" enough not to reproach her husband after she discovered his love for Miss Ni. She embezzled some money from her rival. Miss Ni was a "modern girl", but according to the author she did not pass the limits of "platonic love" with the married man. She was a "women of character" and would not submit to the will of her father, who wanted to marry her to a certain Mr. Li. The latter saved her family from ruin. Mr. Li thought that money could do everything, but this girl despised his wealth. Finally however she was compelled to submit to het father's will: so she pretended to give her consent but on one condition, namely: that Mr. Li's financial aid would be put off until the wedding day. On the fixed day she escaped to Peiping (after taking a lot of money from Mr. Li). On her arrival in Peiping, she fell sick and was found in this condition by her father and her fiancé. The two men, after they had found her, fought between themselves; and a lawsuit ensued. Miss Ni died, overcome with emotion.

This book must *not be read by everyone.* The readers must be warned against the dangers of platonic love.

55. 京塵影事   6 vol. by   張恨水
                                        1943   新新書店

Stories about the frivolous life lead by ten cabaret girls.

During entertainments, tea-parties and walks, each of the ten singers tried to extort money from their friends. Some succeeded, others failed. *May be read by informed people.*

56. 香閨淚   2 vol. 169 & 166 pp. by   張恨水
                                        1943   百新書店

Wang, a student, was loved by two girls, Hsi Lien and Li Ying. He had been their tutor. These two girls left their homes in order to find him. Hsi-Lien, out of love, sacrificed herself, thus uniting Wang with Li Ying. These two fled from Tientsin to Shanghai. Here they continued their studies. They also celebrated their marriage at Wang's place, after his father had given his consent.

This book should *not be recommended to anybody* owing to its big number of immodest descriptions and its pessimistic atmosphere.

57. 落花流水   2 vol. 194 p. by   張恨水
1943   遠東書局

A young doctor, Chen Hsi-wen, fell in love with Ma Shu-min who was already engaged. She promised the doctor to break her engagement but, forced by her parents, she married her former fiancé. Chen Hsi-wen, on learning of this marriage, committed suicide; Ma Shu-min did not know about it. She was very unhappy with her husband, who was an epileptic and had illicit relations with a divorced woman. On discovering their correspondence, Ma Shu-min made a scene to her husband; the latter wanted to kill her, but she escaped back home, where she learned of Dr. Chen's death.

This book can be read *only by informed people,* not because of daring descriptions, but owing to its pessimism and very realistic atmosphere.

58. 錦城春秋   2 vol. 223 p. by   張恨水
1943   遠東出版社

Hsü Ch'iu-min, a student and the son of a commander, after having parted with his girl-friend Pei Lu-yin, had arrested a revolutionist who attempted to assassinate General Liu. The latter in reward, promised him his daughter, Ts'an Chu; — this was not very pleasing to the young hero. The arrested revolutionist was found to be Pei Lu-yin's father; our hero rescued him as his girl-friend had insisted on it, but he himself disappeared with Ts'an Chu. The son of a General fell in love with Lu-yin, not knowing who she was. Her father was again arrested and executed, and she herself took flight. Meanwhile commander Hsü joined the fight against the revolutionary troops with whom was his son, Ch'iu-min, and his fiancée Ts'an Chu, who was a hospital nurse. During the fight commander Hsü was wounded; he died under the care of Ts'an Chu, who later on took care of Ch'iu-min, and the couple got married. The revolutionists won; general Liu fled abroad. His son met Pei Lu-yin, and they got married. One day our four young heroes met each other in a park.

In this book there are two unbecoming scenes: General Liu's concubine wanted to get hold of Ch'iu-min and her husband's son. *To be read by informed people only.*

59. 似水流年   *TIME FLOWS LIKE THE RIVER*   2 vol by   張恨水
2-nd edition. 1944   羲生印刷局

Adventures of an Anhwei student in Peiping. Realistic descriptions of the life led by girl and boy students. The moral lesson of this book is good: virtue is rewarded and vice is punished.

Nevertheless the book can be given *only to grown up people,* owing to its extremely daring realism.

60. 綠珠小姐   *MISS LU CHU*   2 vol. 246 p. by   張恨水
1943   文明書店

A young student, Lu Ch'ing-ch'ao, lost his parents and all he had in a flood at Hankow. He went to Shanghai to ask help and advice from his uncle, who received him very coldly. Our young hero seeing this left his uncle and managed to live relying only upon himself, though this parting was painful to him, as he was in love with his cousin. After many struggles he made good with the help of another young girl. Soon after the young people fell in love with each other, but Lu Ch'ing-ch'ao still continued to dream of his cousin. After a long interval his cousin gained the upperhand, and the other girl sacrificed herself by going abroad.

Many good characters are found in this book, though some indecent scenes are also described. *For informed people.*

61. 熱血冰心   1 vol. 122 p. by 張恨水
                                              1944 惠迪吉書局

Three young girls fell in love with *one* rich young man, who in his turn liked all three of them. As the time went by he fell in love with one of them, and had illicit relations with her. His mother, seeing him very often absent from home, offered him a fourth girl as a bride. The young man accepted, and they got married. In the mean time one of those three girls committed suicide, because she could not bear the young man's infidelity, persuading the girl who had lived with him to do the same. The young man, recently married, was so shocked that, in order to make up for his sins, he entered a Buddhist convent and did not return to his wife any more. The third girl went to the temple in search of the young man; she failed to find him and threw herself into the lake. Immoral theories. *For informed people.*

62. 春之花 *FLOWERS OF SPRING*   1 vol. 115 p. by 張恨水
                                                        1943 上海遠東出版社

A story of a young student who fell in love with a girl at first sight. The two got along very quickly and promised to marry each other after a few meetings.

In this book there are no immodest passages, but it is so sentimental that it must only be read *by well informed readers.*

63. 秦淮世家 *SCIONS OF A NANKING FAMILY*   1 vol. 224 p. by 張恨水
                                                    2nd edition 1940 新新書局

Chang Hen-shui describes in this novel a circle "sui generis" in Nanking.

The heroes of this novel are a family consisting of mother and two daughters, one of whom was a singer, and several friends. This time the author is to be congratulated for presenting to us people with fine characters and dignity (even the two girls).

The story ends dramatically: a rake offended the two girls; one of these avenged herself by killing the offender's girl-friend; the fellow killed her and in turn was killed by the victim's friend.

The atmosphere of this book is too full of vengeance; many expressions are too crude. *For informed readers.*

64. 斯人記 *IT HAPPENED TO SUCH A MAN*   2 vol. 502 p. by 張恨水
                                                        1940 百新書店

Here is a veritable monument, but alas, a monument of stupidities! We cannot, however, refrain from admiring the fecundity of imagination of the author to be able to produce such a mass of insanities!

To make a resumé of this book is as difficult as to resolve the quadrature of a circle. Everything is mentioned and in addition, a thousand other things.

The action is, however, concentrated chiefly on the singsong girls. And this subject gives a fetid atmosphere to this book even though it has been well edited before reaching our hands. After its perusal one gasps for a breath of fresh air. *Not to be recommended to anyone.*

65. 風流艷史 *AN AMOROUS BIOGRAPHY*   1 vol. 161 p. by 張恨水
                                                        1942 志同書店

A mandarin has carnal relations with his adopted daughter. His wife becomes jealous and gives her in marriage to a young man with no money. After she has been married only a few months, the young woman falls into the hands of an official, who has no conscience, who insists on her obtaining a divorce, and installs her in a separate house.

An immoral book full of crude details. *Proscribed.*

66. 傲霜花 *UNDAMAGED BY FROST*   1 vol. 366 p. by 張恨水
                                                              1946 百新書店

Life of the school teachers and professors during the war in Chungking.
Lively written and interesting. *For everyone.*

67. 虎賁萬歲 *LONG LIVE THE ARMY*   1 vol. 344 p. by 張恨水
                                                              1946 百新書店

Ch'ang-tê during the war. Epopée of a Chinese regiment who killed some 20 000 Japanese. *For everyone.*

68. 在大龍河畔 *BY THE BIG DRAGON RIVER*   1 vol. by 張秀亞
                                          1936   上海風社 *See Biogr. 4*

Very fine sketches made by the author at the time when she was still a pagan. Very fine and poetical descriptions of nature. The author goes into the smallest details. *For everyone.*

69. 幸福的泉源 *THE SOURCE OF HAPPINESS*   1 vol. 73 p. by 張秀亞
                                                                      1941

A young student from "Fu-Jen" university, diligent, pious and serious. At the same university a cousin of the young man; she is kindness itself though a bit jealous of a third person, pagan, by the name of Wen Ch'ing, who appeared on the scene and was noticed by the student. Wen Ch'ing, studious and diligent but proud, likewise fell in love with him. And here was the irony of fate: Wen-Ch'ing had been introduced to the young man through the cousin. The later was jealous and vexed when she saw the sudden change in his feelings. Loosing all hope she departed to Shanghai wishing Wen Ch'ing and her cousin "good luck". The young student saw the danger of allying himself with the pagan; but Wen Ch'ing was converted to the Catholic faith after her illness and an accident which happened to the student. Thus the obstacle to their marriage was overcome.

The book is *recommended to young people* before their marriage. It was written by the author just after her baptism.

70. 皈依 *CONVERSION*   1 vol. 46 p. by 張秀亞
                                                              1941

The friendship of a little boy Hua and a little girl Chih remained the same after they grew up. All of a sudden sorrows came. Hua departed to another city to study in a college. As the time passed by, his letters to Chih became rare, and one day he stopped his correspondence. After a number of years the young man came back as a seminarian and explained to Chih why he had stopped his correspondence: he was converted and wanted to become a priest in order to do good in the future.

During a flood Chih's father was saved by an unknown person, who was accidentally found to be Mr. Hua. His self-sacrifice became an example to Chih and led her to the Catholic faith and the three vows.

71. 銀蛇 *SILVER SNAKE* 1 vol. 323 p. by 章克標
1929 金屋書店 *See Biogr.* 6

Some college professors and their wives are trying to find a suitable girl for a bachelor colleague to marry. A pearl is soon marked out but quick work is needed as another suitor has appeared upon the scene.

The story begins well but what follows is of no interest. The successive adventures of the bachelor are recounted to us, and they are quite improper, proving that he is not an honest gentleman. The war overtakes the lovers in Hangchow. The heroine flees to Shanghai, and the second hero goes to join her there. Thus ends the first volume, after regaling us with a sufficient number of improper details. *Not to be recommended to anyone.*

72. 我們的故鄉 *OUR HOMETOWN* 1 vol. 269 p. by 章 浪
1937 一般書店 *See Biogr.* 7

1. 死亡線上 p. 1-41. Of a poor family with whom live two relatives. Not having anything left to eat, because of the exactions of the Japanese, the son decides to enrole in the volunteer army. The police take away their last dollars with which they had wanted to save the head of the family.

2. 村中之友 p. 43-80. Miseries during a flood.

3. 兒歸 p. 81-102. A father, driven to desperation by hunger, sends his son to steal from a neighbour. The son is brought back dying, having been beaten into this condition by the propertied man.

4. 雪夜小景 p. 103-109. A poor mother and her baby.

5. 賠錢貨 p. 111-185. Of a very poor family where all the girl babies are killed upon birth.

6. 我們的故鄉 p. 186-269. Three acts. A patriotic play.

A Manchu family is presented. The father, who has lost his wife under the Japanese, is a very good patriot. The eldest son is a lazy fellow. The second becomes a volunteer (Yi-yung Chun). When they refuse to sell their factory to the Japanese, they are threatened by a spy. The father resists and is killed. The eldest meets the same fate. The daughter-in-law, who has a weakness for the spy, dies bravely. The younger son revenges these deaths.

In these stories the author shows his sympathy for the oppressed, and is not exempt from revolutionary spirit. *For everyone.*

73. 空谷蘭 *ORCHID OF THE VALLEY* 1 vol. 172 p. by 張六合
1939 誠文信書店

A young English viscount, having finished his military services at India, came back to England to live with his mother and cousin, both of whom wished that he would marry his cousin. The viscount nevertheless fell in love with a poor girl, whom he finally married. Quarrels arose, because the cousin made up her mind to revenge herself. She publicly humiliated the new viscountess, who did not know much about the etiquette of the noble families. The viscount shared the humiliations of his wife, and life in the castle became impossible, as the managing of the household had passed into the cousin's hands. Not being able to bear it any longer, the viscountess left the castle and was believed to have perrished in a railway accident. He then married his cousin. After seven years the first wife of the viscount reappeared. She was not recognized by her husband. In the meantime the viscount's second wife died in an accident and our hero found again the first wife and, with her, his happiness.

Interesting novel; easy and fluent style. *For everyone.*

74. 孤兒苦鬥記 *AN ORPHAN'S STRIVING* 1 vol. 210 p. by 張勉寅
1941 東方書店

The story of a child who is found and adopted by a juggler, who makes his way in the world. Of his virile education. *For everyone.*

75. 風流歌女 *A FLIRTING CHORUS GIRL* 1 vol. 121 p. by 張 蓬
1946 上海大明書局

A dancer of good family marries the director of a factory in spite of the fact that she is already engaged to someone else. Her former fiancé attends her wedding and she learns that he is an intimate friend of her husband. As the latter is ignorant of their relations, he often leaves them together, until one fine day he finds them abusing his confidence. Surprising them in the act, the director behaves in an unforeseen fashion, for he commits suicide, leaving his fortune to the two who have been so unfaithful to him.

The book contains some very crude details. *Proscribed.*

76. 鬼影 *SHADOW OF THE GHOST* 1 vol. 241 p. by 張少崆
1930 北平震東印書館

A series of nine stories inspired by the decadent school in the style of Yü Ta-fu, and at the same time full of Zola's realism. In the first story the author describes "how an immodest woman deceived men in a sarcastic manner such as to provoke laughter". At the same time he describes the "grief of a lost love" (Introduction to the book). The rest of the volume is written in the same vein. In addition the author relates "the story of his love affairs, over which his friends are asked to shed their tears". (Introduction). By this the author "wants to prevent his friends from falling into the plight, in which he found himself." (Introduction)

This book is *not to be recommended to any reader.*

77. 江南女兒 *A SOUTHERN GIRL* 1 vol. 141 p. by 張十方
1946 百新書店

Several young girls wish to devote themselves to the country during the Japanese invasion. Their subsequent life is told us by the author.

A dull book. *For everyone.*

78. 一年 *A YEAR* 1 vol. 418 p. by 張天翼
上海良友圖書印刷公司 *See Biogr. 10*

A commonplace story about magistrates' employees. It shows their greed for money and fame, their lack of shame, and their insecurity. The author reveals us the means by which they extort money from people. He shows their low and cheap life.

The book ends by showing how the hero commits suicide. *For everyone.*

79. 蜜蜂 *BEES* 1 vol. 288 p. by 張天翼
2nd edition 1933 現代書局

A collection of short stories. These novels describe military life, the soldiers' relations with their officers and superiors. A description of a Chinese in foreign service. In the last story he describes the children's feelings towards bees.

This book contains a number of shocking details in the second novel. *For informed readers.*

80. 移行 *REMOVAL*   1 vol. 310 p. by 張天翼
1934 上海良友圖書印刷公司

Nine short stories.
1. A servant's anxiety about his son.
3. A wife from a rich family tried hard to have patience with her husband, who lost his job.
4 How a rich family became poor.
5. Story of two little friends.
6. False promises of a rich man to a poor woman whom he dishonoured.
7. The breach between the young man and his girl-friend, as the latter prevented him from doing his duty.
8 The marriage of a girl, who was a Communist, to a rich manufacturer.
9. An important individual, whose visit was very unsuccessful. *For informed readers.*

81. 洋涇浜奇俠 *AN UNLIKELY CHIVALROUS MAN*   1 vol. 247 p. by 張天翼
1936 新鐘書局

As the author remarks in the preface, the book is written for grown up people. His narratives are interwoven with love scenes under the pretext of country love, and he has no fear of coarse expressions. His story: A young man, aged 15, went to a fencing school where the atmosphere was imbued with superstition. He hoped to leave the school after one year, and then the enemies of his country had better be careful!! In the first fight in which he took part, he was unsuccessful and did not fulfil his hopes, for he was wounded in spite of his so-called invulnerability. In a dream, brought on by the fever, he continued to fight. *Everyone is to be warned against this book.*

82. 在城市裏 *IN THE CITY*   1 vol. 524 p. by 張天翼
1937 良友公司

A man named Ting goes to the city to visit his rich relatives. Through 500 pages there is a description of the families he is connected with. Everything he sees and everything he hears is put down, all without any real observation or depth.

The author aims at irony, but it hardly seems to us that he will interest the reader as much as a Lao She or a Lin Yü-t'ang. *For everyone.*

83. 清明時節 *ARBOR DAY*   1 vol. 164 p. by 張天翼

清明時節 p. 1-107. The embarrassment of a landlord who owns a property upon which is the graveyard of another family.
搶案 p. 108-126. A dull account of an attack by bandits. The village defends itself.
友誼 p. 127-164. A worthy soul intrigues for a position, but his efforts and suppers lead to no result. *For everyone.*

84. 同鄉們 *PEOPLE FROM MY TOWN*   1 vol. 179 p. by 張天翼
2nd. edit. 1939 文化生活

Four stories.
1. 夏夜夢 Dream of an unhappy young singer.
2. 侶 伴 About a husband without a will of his own. His wife works in his place.
3. 同鄉們 Working companions.
4 陸寶田 Story of a yamen employee. Misfortunes congregate on his head due to the ridicule of his comrades. *For everyone.*

85. 追 *THE PURSUIT*

1 vol. 213 p. by 張天翼
2nd. edit. 1939 開明書店

This book contains a few fairly well told stories, but also a number of risky allusions, **and** a great number of platitudes. *Not to be recommended to anyone.*

86. 奇怪的地方 *A STRANGE PLACE*

1 vol. 125 p. by 張天翼
6th. edit. 1940 文化生活出版社

A useful book for children.

The rich child: he is spoilt, changeable, hard on his equals and on poor children.

The workman's child: he is honest and straight, and has pity for poor children.

This book will be read with fruitful results by rich children, but the author shows **too** much partiality, and does not give a real picture of rich children. "Ab uno etc."

In the preface the author denies the existence of demons because noone has ever seen **them**. In addition to this questionable position, the book gives the impression that **the** differences between the classes is entirely the fault of the rich. *For everyone.*

87. 好兄弟 *GOOD BRETHREN*

1 vol. 190 p. by 張天翼
文化生活

Fairy stories. *For everyone.*

88. 張天翼選集 *AN ANTHOLOGY OF CHANG T'IEN YI*

1 vol. 306 p.
1927 上海萬象書店

Eight stories criticizing wildly modern society from every point of view.

Modern teachers are criticised in "Ch'un Feng"; in "Pao Ming Fu Tzu" it is poor parents who wished to give an education to their childern (the latter turned out to be scamps).

In the story "Ch'eng Yü Hen" the pro and anti Communist movements are criticised; and free love in "Wen Ju Chih Tsao Chih.

In the fifth story the patriarcal system is described.

The criticism of patriotism and national defence are dealt with in the sixth and seventh.

The style is very simple and easy to read; it contains almost no descriptions but is chiefly dialogues. The author is rather poor in psychological analysis; at times he appears to be rather frivolous and raw in his expressions.

The book is *not to be recommended* owing to the author's scepticism on the problems of modern life. The author advises his readers to take no part in the movements of ideas.. which is the very point for which Chinese critics condemn the author. (Cfr. Introduction of the book).

89. 跳躍着的人們

1 vol. 234 p. by 張資平
1930 文藝書局 *See Biogr. 13*

This book is *not to be read by anyone* as it attacks religion (pp. 7, 61, 69), has immodest tendencies, and reveals the revolutionary and communistic ideas of the author.

90. 群星亂飛 *STARS FLY*

1 vol. 255 p. by 張資平
1931 上海花華書局

The heroine, Mei-Ling, a student at a music and dancing school, was in love with Kuo Hsiung, a fine lad but of a weak character. Her mother wanted them to get married but her father, who was in America, was against it. He returned to Shanghai unexpectedly, with great ambitions, wanting his daughter to become as rich as American movie stars, and marry a rich fellow. Mei Ling, being watched almost as a prisoner, deceived his vigilance and went to live with her boy-friend, from whom she had a child. But, threatened by Mei Ling's obstinate father, the young couple was frightened and Mei Ling returned to her parents, leaving her child at Kuo Hsiung's family. In China, the life of an actress is more difficult than in America, and our heroine had no success in it. This greatly disappointed her father, especially when she refused proposals of two young men from a rich family, which she had done to revenge her father. Finally her father left his family and mother-land, and sailed for America never to return again. After he left, Mei Ling returned to her boy-friend. — This book is directed against the arbitrary authority of parents who thwart their children in their reasonable inclinations and prevent their happiness.

The father is an obstinate and hard man, with exceptionally queer character, which makes the story strange and incredible. Apart from one or two reflections hostile to religion, there is nothing offensive in this work. *Can be read by grown up people.*

91. 上帝的兒女們 *GOD'S CHILDREN*   1 vol. 344 p. by 張資平
1932 新文藝書局

The author gives us his personal ideas on several families of protestant pastors, as well as on their religion in general, and this in the form of a novel. Evidently the real meaning of Christian life is overlooked by this superficial and erotic author. Also, in this big volume, he only succeeds in giving us "table-talk"! He presents the protestant people, and the Chinese who hold to this religion, as hypocrites at the service of Mammon. All individuals described in this book misbehave themselves; their private lives are shocking, and they justify themselves by passages from the Bible! It is useless to give a summary of all the love stories which are scattered through this book. *This novel is to be proscribed,* owing to many daring passages, and to the author's tendency purpose of presenting the Christians as hateful characters who call themselves "the children of God". *He also ridicules Christian dogmas.*

92. 明珠與黑炭 *PEARL & CHARCOAL*   1 vol. 332 p. by 張資平
5th edition 1934 光明書局

A former university student was unemployed, and supported his wife and little daughter by borrowing little sums of money from his friends. The characters described might be material for a good novel. But we must not forget that this book is written by Chang Tzu-p'ing, and therefore must contain "triangular love"!

Indeed our hero met with some of these adventures, and the author tells of two, with plenty of details. The novel ends with the baby's death, and we are sure the mother is going to die of grief having lost her child.

Not to be recommended to anyone, owing to its theories on free love and immoral passages.

93. 冲積期化石 *ALLUVIAL FOSSILS*   1 vol. 204 p. by 張資平
8th edition 1935 上海大新書店

Descriptions of school life led be the Chinese pupils in the primary and middle schools, during the first year of the Republic, and also in Japan.

The book is full of considerations on the organisation of public institutions, on school work, on teachers, on the life and psychology of the pupils and on many other similar questions.

The author does not spare his blames and criticism, but scatters them without discrimination. His stay in a Protestant school does not seem to have left a good impression on him, quite the opposite. He ridicules his teachers, and describes blameworthy adventures of a minister's daughter.

The book contains all sorts of opinions and reflections, which, are at times justified. It can be read *by informed people.*

94. 約伯之淚 *THE TEARS OF JOB*   1 vol. p. 165-238 by 張資平
上海藝光出版社

1. 梅嶺之春 pp. 165-186. The heroine, a young girl student, stayed in the house of her distant relative, who was a teacher in a middle school. Although the girl was engaged, they fell in love with each other and a child was born.
For grown up people.
2. 約伯之淚 pp. 186-215. Last confidences of a student, dying of consumption, to a girl-student, with whom he was deeply in love, and of whose future marriage he has just been told.
For grown up people.
3. 懺悔 pp. 215-237. A very interesting story, in which the hero regretted his egoism and hardness towards his family and describing the joy he felt in helping them and showing his affection and devotion towards them.
For everyone.
This book is for grown up people.

95. 姊夫 *BROTHER IN LAW*   1 vol. 146 p. by 張資平
1939 藝譯書店

A student from Tientsin came to Peiping to continue his studies, and stayed with his relatives. In this family there were two young sisters; one serious, the other less so. Both of them fell in love with the young man, who prefered the elder, but their parents gave him the younger as a bride. Finally all was settled by the death of our hero's fiancée, who, on her death-bed, wished the young man to be happy with her rival. *For everyone.*

96. 戀愛錯綜 *COMPLICATION IN LOVE*   1 vol. 240 p. by 張資平
1939 中華書局

An orphan, Che San, was brought up in an inordinately rich family of Shanghai. He first studied at home, then went to a Protestant school and finished by becoming a Christian. He wanted to become somebody, was full of good-will, but had a weak character. He was in love with Mrs. Liang Tze-yun, and at the same time with her daughter and a servant by the name of Li Hsien. This last, the offspring of Mr. Liang's liaison before his marriage, was courted by the gardener Kung-er and by the son of the family, Jui Hsiang; moreover she was coveted by Mr. Liang himself. Hence arouse jealousy between Che San, Kung-er and Jui Hsiang on one side, and between Jui Hsiang and his father on the other.

Jui Hsiang, born eight months after Mr. Liang's marriage with Liang Tze-yun, was the offspring of the latter's intimacy with her sister's husband, an artist.

The story of all these relations in told in full detail.

During a trip to Hongkong, Jui Hsiang declared his love and proposed to Li Hsien. Love was mutual, but as for marriage, there were obstacles: difference of situation, father's jealousy, and at least Li-Hsien suspected it. . .consanguinity. In order to reach his aim, Jui-Hsiang devised a ruse. He described the animosity of the workmen in his father's factory against his father, frightened his mother and sister and advised them to leave their house at Kiulung, and go as soon as possible to the Queen's Hotel at Hongkong. He wrote to his father not to come at all, the workmen being unwilling to negotiate except with his son or his representative.....Miss Li Hsien. A few days later the family was back in Shanghai. Jui Hsiang and Li Hsien remained to settle disputes in the factory..... and they were married, Li Hsien's fear of consanguinity having vanished after disclosures made by Jui Hsiang's sister. Che-san was dismissed. In Shanghai he became a teacher..... maintained his connexions with Mrs. Liang, his former mistress, and still dreamt of Li Hsien to whom he was writing numerous letters which remained unanswered. The subject and atmosphere of this book are *objectionable for all readers.*

97. 母愛 *MATERNAL LOVE*　　　　1 vol. 188 p. by 張資平
　　　　　　　　　　　　　　　　　　　　1942　大連啓東書社

Hsi Chün, daughter of a professor of chemistry, was destined to marry the best pupil of her father. She did not consent to this marriage, and ran away with Li Mei-ling, who also had illicit relations with an actress. But he was disappointed with the latter and attached his attention to his wife.

Meanwhile Hsi Chün took interest in Keng Tzu-chung, with whom she went to Japan, leaving her childern with her first husband. Soon Hsi Chün got a disease from her lover, and the later left for Shanghai while she was in hospital. During her stay in hospital she made acquaintance with a medical student, and after having recovered, went with him to Shanghai. Here she left him and joined her former lover Tzu-chung who helped her to become an actress. In the meantime her first husband married again, but lived in poverty. His eldest son died and the husband killed his second wife and tried to commit suicide. Hsi Chün, when she learned about it, tried to save her two childern, but failed to do so and commited suicide.

This book is *not to be recommended to anyone.* It relates only divorces and illicit love affairs, besides some frivolous scenes.

98. 苔莉 *T'AI LI*　　　　　　　　1 vol. 175 p. by 張資平
　　　　　　　　　　　　　　　　　　　　1942　啓文印書館

This book describes a young family where T'ai Li was believed to be "the wife" but in fact she was only a third concubine. Meanwhile her husband left her and returned to his legal wife, while a young student, K'o Ou, fell in love with T'ai Li. His love was returned, and they lived together. Soon after a young girl was given in marriage to K'o Ou, which promised him a brilliant future, but being in love with T'ai Li he was unable to leave her. After graduating K'o Ou was called home. He and T'ai Li travelled together and promised each other not to part. At home K'o Ou was introduced to his fiancée, Liu, but in spite of her beauty he did not want to leave T'ai Li. During a storm, they threw themselves into the sea. *To be banned;* owing to some daring scenes.

99. 飛絮 *CATKINS*　　　　　　　1 vol. 144 p. by 張資平
　　　　　　　　　　　　　　　　　　　　1943

The novel relates how two young people were in love with each other; the young man was not accepted by his girl-friend's parents, who wanted their daughter to marry Mr. Lu. The girl kept on rejecting Mr. Lu's advances, and used to express her love to Mr. Mei sometimes very openly. At last, under the threats of her father, she had to accept Mr. Lu. Before their marriage took place, she was seduced by Mr. Mei who was drunk at that moment, having taken to drinking owing to the fact that he was deprived of the girl he dreamed of. Mr. Lu learned about it only after the marriage; when a child was born to him he acknowledged it as his own, but our heroine's aunt interfered, and in the presence of Mr. Lu advised the young woman to return to Mr. Mei. She had been for a whole year, the secret wife to Mr. Lu, from whom she had a child; she died the same day, *To be banned,* owing to its immoral scenes and unhealthy descriptions of love.

100. 張資平小說選 *AN ANTHOLOGY OF CHANG TZE P'ING* 1 vol. 304 p.
1928 上海新興書店

A series of thirteen stories which mainly describe the life of Chinese students in Japan. They also describe the economic difficulties of a teacher, who was paid very little to support his wife and children, etc.

Not recommended to anybody, owing to certain immodest passages, dishonest love intrigues, and immoral insinuations.

101. 張資平選集 *AN ANTHOLOGY OF CHANG TZE-P'ING* 1 vol. 181 p.
1935 萬象書屋

p. 11 The family of a poor teacher whose wife was expecting a second child.
p. 24 The same family after the child was born.
p. 51 A farewell letter of a young man, who was sick, to his girl-friend who had married another fellow.
p. 82 Two young people were in love with each other, but the girl preferred to marry a rich man. Her boy-friend also got married but his wife died. After ten years our two heroes met again.
p. 111 A young girl, poor and bethroted in her childhood, began to work for a protestant pastor, who treated her so badly that she was compelled to return to her fiancé.
p. 135 Unsuccesful love.
p. 155 A poor Japanese family whose daughter is a mother of a child "without father". One day the child disappeared and was never seen again.
p. 173 Another unsuccessful love. *For informed people.*

102. 不同集 *DIFFERENT* 1 vol. 223 p. by 章英
1934 樂華圖書公司

The author gives us an outline of the situation of China in 1934, after the Japanese invasion. Very revolutionary spirit. *For enlightened people only.*

103. 孤鴻淚史 *ALONE* 1 vol. 178 p. by 張有斐
1946 春明書店

A young man of good family whose parents are both dead, accepts a post as a tutor. He is soon asked to leave, not because of any fault on his part, but because several ladies in the family have fallen in love with him.

He then goes to his own tutor where he is badly received. His tutor does not want to give him his daughter in marriage, but gives her, instead, to another who is a good-for-nothing. Upon this the hero of the book leaves for Shanghai to earn his living there.

The daughter of the tutor manages to make her father believe that she has died and also goes to Shanghai where she becomes a teacher. After her father has died of chagrin and disappointment, she returns home to live with her mother.

The young man also becomes ill from chagrin and disappointment, and he ends up by dying in spite of the care lavished upon him by the heroine who hastens to his bedside.

The mother of the girl also dies, and she herself enters a convent. *May be read by anyone.*

104. 書獃子 *THE BOOKWORM*   1 vol. 309 p. by 章玉清
                                                              文光書局

A collection of little tales for pupils of primary schools. There are farces and adventures among them. All very interesting and told in an attractive manner. *For everyone.*

105. 名號的安慰 *CONSOLATION FROM THE TITLE* 1 vol. 177 p. by 常 工
                                                              1930 景山書社

1) A newly married couple; the wife was in love with another young man. After three months of marriage she tried to attach herself to her husband, but after the first child was born, she parted with her husband for good.

2) An engaged girl was waiting for her fiancé's return. He returned but, alas, married. After the interference of the girl's father, the wife of the young man committed suicide. The girl took to flight.

3) The mayor of a city, unable to get money for the soldiers, as demanded by the government, hanged himself.

4) A rash judgment of a husband who suspected his wife.

5) A married man had illicit relations with a widow, who was his wife's friend. When the child was born the father adopted him, and the widow disappeared.

6) Tribulations of a good fellow.

7) A father went to buy "Hsi-kua" accompanied by his son, who died of thirst; the father refused to give his "Hsi-kua" in order to save his son.

8) Illegal meeting of two lovers.

9) An imprudent, but innocent girl, was expelled from a school.

10) A father, who lost two children, killed the third one.

11) Marriage of a married man with a young girl.

In this book there are many daring details and immoral theories. *Not to be recommended to anyone.*

106. 愛的新教育 *NEW EDUCATION OF LOVE*   1 vol. 223 p. by 趙錦華
                                                              1941 國光書店

The life of a young man from his attendance in a primary school until he enters society.

He cannot serve as a model for our youth because he is lacking in religion and a true ideal. *For everyone.*

107. 春江風月   1 vol. 224 p. by 趙學榮
                                                              1944 義生書局

A description of a Ch'ien family, who, after being very rich, fell into poverty. The author wanted to write a "realistic" novel. He succeeded only too well. . .as the content of his book is nothing but a juxtaposition of scandalous events.

As for composition and style, this novel has no value.

Properly speaking there are no obscene descriptions, but the book constantly verge on immorality. *To be proscribed.*

108. 春夢遺痕 *MARKS*   1 vol. 98 p. by 趙學榮
                                                              1940 義生書局

Amorous adventures of a rascal who is spending to much time in brothels. *Not for everyone.*

109. 故鄉之春 *SPRING IN MY HOMELAND* 2 vol. 188 p. and 199 p. by 趙恂九
大連實業洋行出版

A story of which the plot is laid in a Manchurian village.

Ch'en Wěi-tou, the son of poor peasants, is a good worker, sober, and has an excellent character. Sui Yu-ying, a girl who lives near by, is of the same condition. She is of a natural goodness, has an agreeable exterior, and is very industrious in everything pertaining to the house. As their parents are on very good. terms, the two young people have many chances of seeing each other, and it is not long before their hearts are seized by love. The author gives us in detail the intimate conversations of the heroes.

The father of Yu-ying is looking for a suitable party for his daughter and promises her to a good-for-nothing in the neighbouring village. From this great grief descends upon the young people. Their meetings become even more frequent. Their love becomes greater and their grief increases in proportion.

A few days before the intended marriage, Wei-tou becomes seriously ill of his grief. In the meantime, news has come that Yu-ying's bethrothed has died which produces an amelioration in the state of the hero.

The love that unites the two young people has been noticed for some time by a friend of the family, who now comes forth as match-maker and arranges the bethrothal of the pair who are thus rendered happy.

The plot of this story is simple. The author's chief aim is to describe Manchurian usages and customs. His ambition (expressed in the preface to the book) is to surpass "The Good Earth" of P.S. Buck. He has not, however, succeeded, as his talent is far inferior to that of the celebrated novelist. But in spite of this, his book is very interesting and makes us understand the life of a Chinese village.

Certain passages may be considered risky, and we do not believe that the intimate conversations between the young villagers correspond with reality. And let it be added that the author finds that P. Buck has only blackened the character of the Chinese in her celebrated novel. *For grown-up people.*

110. 春夢 *SPRING REVERIE*   2 vol. 140, 150 p. by 趙恂九
1939 誠文信書局

Still another popular romance of no value, written in an elementary style and with very little action, and no serious basis whatever. It is about the sentimental history of a professor. The author admits all the most advanced ideas, free love, divorce, suicide, etc. This book cannot have other than disastrous effects on the young. *Not to be recommended to anyone.*

111. 他的懺悔 *HIS REPENTANCE*   1 vol. 136 p. by 趙恂九
1941 實業洋行印刷部

Wei Chi-cheng, a young professor, returned from the university in Japan, and found himself compelled to marry an old-fashioned woman. He married, but soon after took a divorce and married a modern girl. This one was so modern that she deceived Chi-cheng. Chi-cheng bitterly regretted his divorce; he was happy to live the rest of his life with his first wife.

As long as the author describes all the evils of divorce and of extremely modern girls the book is good. But his discourses are too long, and he discusses too much on love. *The book is only for informed people.*

112. 鸞飄鳳泊 *THE SCATTERED TWO*   1 vol. 123 p. by 趙恂九
1941 實業洋行出版部

Three novels.

1. Two students, cousins, fell in love with each other...The parents, suspecting it, called back the young girl in order to arrange her marriage with the one her heart had chosen. The young girl, being ignorant of their intentions, was alarmed, and eloped with her sweetheart. The latter, seeing his resources had come to an end, sold his cousin to a house of prostitutes. —

2. Again two students who were in love with each other; the parents arranged a marriage between the girl student and another young man...our two sweethearts took to flight.

3. A professor fell in love with one of his students. She left the school, and the professor found her a place in the city where she stayed. One day the object of his love shammed illness, went to hospital and called her lover, where the two young people declared themselves married. —

This book cannot be read but by grown up people on account of theories which it contains.

113. 苦鄉綺夢錄 *ROMANTIC ADVENTURE IN A MELANCHOLUS MOOD*
1 vol. 120 p. by 趙亦新
1941 天津書局

This book is composed of short anecdotes, travelling notes, having invariably for its theme maidservants, pretty girls, with whom the people flirt just for amusing themselves. Hence the theme is of little interest, at times coarse, but always vulgar. *Not to be recommended to anyone.*

114. 癡情錄 *TENACIOUS DEVOTION*   3 vol. 162, 188 and 219 pp. by 趙亦新
1946 勵力出版社

This is the same book as the one reviewed under the title 畫帶青絲 *Proscribed.*

115. 畸人 *THE HERMIT*   1 vol. 110 p. by 趙伯顏
1928 上海新宇宙書局

A romance of a Chinese student in Berlin. He fell in love with a young girl, whom he met in a train, and got introduced with her through the mediation of his friend. The young girl seemed to return his love. At this our hero was called back to China by his dying mother. During this absence his friend took away his beloved one, and on his return to Germany, he found them married...Disgusted, the Chinese student left for Heidelberg. The following year he received news, that a child was born to the young couple.

Nothing dangerous, but the author attaches little importance to the fact that the hero was already married in China. *For enlightened readers.*

116. 在草原上 *ON THE PRAIRIE*   1 vol. 174 p. by 趙宗濂
1940 輔仁文苑社 *See Biogr. 18*

Short stories taken from life. many of them about the family. Most of them can be read by everyone, but it would be unwise to put them in the hands of our catholic students.

The less edifying are: "The wet-nurse Yü" p. 93 "Li Hun" p. 133 and "Lung Ta-ko" p. 159. *Only for grown up people.*

117. 父與子 *FATHER & SON*　　　　　1 vol. 166 p. by 趙蔭棠
　　　　　　　　　　　　　　　　　　　　　1944　新民印書館

A series of twenty short stories of which seventeen can be read by everyone. A reservation, however, must be made on No. 14, No. 16, and No. 18, owing to certain offensive or unhealthy descriptions contained therein. *Not to be recommended to anyone.*

118. 影 *IN THE SHADE*　　　　　　　　1 vol. 228 p. by 趙蔭棠
　　　　　　　　　　　　　　　　　　　　　1945　華北作家協會

Still another of those books that spread a nauseous atmosphere. And to think that it has been written under he auspices of a literary society of North China. All that the author has been able to imagine is to describe a man of some forty years, of good heart, but feeble character, running from one courtisan to another. In the beginning chapters he does this in company with some friends. Through the rest of the book he dwells in concubinage with one of the above persons.

One has to make an effort to find the qualities of this author that are lauded by the newspaper reviews, for it is impossible to discover a single serious sentence in this book. It has an unhealthy atmosphere. *Everyone to be dissuaded from it.*

119. 難為情 *GAUCHE*　　　　　　　　1 vol. 277 p. by 陳秋圃
　　　　　　　　　　　　　　　　　　　　　1944　東亞書店

Li Han-ch'in, from the North of Shensi, a student of Peiping University in the College of Arts, was a serious young man, hard-working, good-looking and seemed to be a good boy. . .but with financial difficulties. Moreover he led a modest life. Two girl-students, besides other young girls, sought his friendship. At first he became intimate with Li Shu-yin, who was in an other department in the same university. Soon a student from his department, Pei Li-fang, intervened; she was richer and modern. The two girls helped him through his increasing difficulties. He tried to find a source of income to continue his studies. At first he became temporary lecturer, but did not succeed. Thrown into prison through false accusations, he was able to come out thanks to steps taken by the girls. The friendship with Shu-yin had increased; only quarrels with her brother compelled him to renounce the young girl. Then he returned to Li-fang. Other young girls, one more audacious, also tried to trap him. But in vain. His friendship with Li-fang for a time was very strong. But soon she left him for a cousin who returned from Paris. A novel, which Li Han-ch'in had written in the meantime, was not accepted by the press. Disgusted, he tried to commit suicide. Luckily he was saved in time; and was brought to a hospital. Shu-yin, who had learned about it from the newspaper, went to visit him; the first and true love was resumed. *For informed readers.*

120. 革命的前一幕 *PRELUDE TO REVOLUTION*　1 vol. 226 p. by 陳銓
　　　　　　　　　　　　　　　　　1934　上海良友圖書公司　*See Biogr. 19*

Ch'en Ling-hua fell in love with a nice girl Hsü Meng-p'in, and they promised to marry each other. Ling-hua had to complete his studies in America. His friend Hsü Heng-shan advised him to renounce his love, in order to concentrate fully on his studies. He also advised him to consecrate his life to the well being of China. But Ch'en Ling-hua desired to remain faithful to his bride. Meanwhile Heng-shan was introduced to Hsü Meng-p'in, and fell in love. He was ignorant of the fact that she was the betrothed of his friend, who was in America. After trying to conquer his feelings he finally gave up and resolved to make Hsü Meng-p'in his companion in life. On his return from America Ling-hua learned about his friend's love for his bride and believed that the latter shared his love. He lost all his hope and aim in life and was in despair. But he could not but admire the good qualities of his friend. All this time Hsü Heng-shan was ignorant of the ties between Ch'en Ling-hua and Hsü Meng-p'in, declared his love to the latter, and asked her to become his wife. He was surprised with the refusal and even distressed until he discovered the cause. He then acted very generously. He wrote to both of his friends a letter, in which he wished them good luck. He then departed from them and became a simple soldier in the revolutionary army. He sacrificed his life to the revolution which was to save China.

This novel is well written, though based on false ideas. The story is related in a healthy atmosphere. Its heroes have fine characters. No daring situations are presented in this book. Life's problems, its goal and significance are shown in a fine and realistic way. But somehow all the solutions appear insufficient to the heroes, even the Christian solution. *For everyone.*

121. 死灰 *DEAD ASHES*   1 vol. 197 p. by 陳　銓
                                             1935 大公報承印部

A Chinese student passed his vacations in the company of a young girl in Berlin. They loved one another but the girl refused to marry him as she did not want to follow him to China. The author describes the daily events and the relations of the two lovers. The book ends with the departure of our hero to another city where he was to receive his degree. On the last page of the book the author tells us how the young man was dying in a hospital, while his girl-friend was marrying another man.

There are no obscene passages or descriptions, but nevertheless this book should *not be recommended to the readers* as it gives too many details of the intimacy between the two lovers.

122. 彷徨中的冷靜 *HESITANT YET UNCONFUSED*   2 vol. 663 p. by 陳　銓
                                             1935 Com. Press 商務印書館

This romance is laid at the beginning of the revolution. The principal hero is a young man of good character who is affable in his relations with his family and his friends. The heroines are also of good character, and the author shows a great reserve in describing the frequent relations between the chief characters. The girl that the principal hero choses dies a victim of the revolution. Nevertheless the story ends with his marriage to one of the other central personages of this romance.

What the author may be reproached for are interminable passages, stories that never seem to end, and useless descriptions of events without importance. The book, however, contains some beautiful passages and above all, beautiful characters.

Although there are a few passages that are a little too expressive, we believe that this book may be read by anybody. *For everyone.*

123. 藍天 *THE BLUE SKIES*   1 vol. 110 p. by 陳恩風
                                             新京書局

Miss Wei Chou, a respectable young girl loved Ching Hua, an excellent student from a good family. Hsiao Lan, a friend of the latter, was equally in love with this young girl, but he sacrificed himself because he saw that Wei Chou had a good influence on his friend. He exhorted the latter to try to mould Ching Hua's character, as he often sinned through his weakness. Ching Hua was addicted to drinking and Wei-Chou saw herself unable to correct him. She sacrificed her love and became a nurse in a hospital. There, she was present at the death of her childhood friend, Hsiao Lan, who in his last farewell wished her to do a lot of good in the future.

This book *can be read by all.* The heroes are all under the strong influence of

Protestantism. For them God exists and religion is a conviction. They pray, celebrate Christmas in the family. . . but drinking for them is a sin without remedy.

124. 迷戀的情婦 *THE MISTRESS*   1 vol. 248 p. by **陳福熙**
                                                          1936 上海大光書局

A collection of stories written in a very simple style. The author presents us with a cross section of society, and gives us a number of character studies of unhappy or original people.

Certain reservations should be made on the stories entitled 四封情書, 老來紅 and especially on the first in the book, 迷戀的情婦, in which there is an analysis of the morbid sentiments of a young man who ends up by committing suicide. *Not to be recommended to anyone.*

125. 浮雲集 *YOU CAN'T TAKE IT WITH YOU*   1 vol. 112 p. by **陳福熙**
                                                          1936 北新書局

A collection of brief accounts written in an easy style. Among other subjects, the author tells of fishing, of life in a village, of the hard life of labourers, of the New Year, of young married people between whom love is dead, etc. etc.

One of the tales is told in rather too light a tone. *May be read by anyone.*

126. 不安定的靈魂 *UNSETTLED SOUL*   1 vol. 314 p. by **陳翔鶴**
                                                  1927 北新書局 *See Biogr. 20*

1. Some perverse advice.
2. Complaints of a widower on account of his deceased wife.
3. A mother advised her son to marry a girl he did not love.
4. Action and conduct of a little girl; her influence on her surroundings.
5. A young man owed his aunt a big debt of gratitude. On completing his studies he returned to her house, but found her dead. . .
6. A sad story of a man who did not find peace.
7. A man was congratulated for his good fortune. .but, in reality, he was very unfortunate. *Not to be recommended.*

127. 獨身者 *THE BACHELOR*   1 vol. 236 p. by **陳翔鶴**
                                                               中華書局

Four short stories written in a rather difficult style. *For everyone.*

128. 窗帘 *WINDOW CURTAIN*   1 vol. 184 p. by **陳果夫**
                                  ...   1931 黎明書局 *See Biogr. 21*

A number of humourous short stories based on folklore, and afterwards, a succession of little scenes.

Well conceived and characteristic. *For everyone.*

129. 茶葉棒子 *SHORT STORIES*   1 vol. 232 p. by **陳白塵**
                                                  1937 開明書店 *See Biogr. 23*

馬棚灣 A quarrel between passengers and a boatman in which the passengers win.
夜 Of two families of pitiful people. A married couple who are blind earn a living by singing. A small trader works from morning until night to keep his wife, who, together with the blind husband, die, while the other two remain "united".

茶葉棒子 Fights and quarrels between boys in the street and students over a girl who works in a tea shop.

起早 About young ladies travelling, their arrogance in ordinary times and their cowardice in face of danger.

李大扣子上學 An evening school for adults.

蠢動 Story of workmen and their chiefs.

The author has talent and writes well, but all these tales contain very coarse language. The author seems to have poured out his whole repertory to such an extent that the reader is nauseated. Also some improper details are included. *For grown-up people.*

130. 小魏的江山 *WEI'S SPHERE OF INFLUENCE*   1 vol.201 p. by 陳白塵
1937   文化生活

1. Adventures and misfortunes of Hsiao Wei who is put into prison. Of the organisation of the prison where the hero is the recipient of blows and curses, and disputes occur between different sections. The author possesses a large vocabulary of strong words!
2. About a hospital in which there is a great number of sick people and of coffins. The prescriptions of European doctors are not known, and only Chinese medecine is taken. Disputes occur frequently.
3. The diary of a political prisoner and of his companions. They are tortured when they are cross-examined to hasten their confessions. A high official visits the prison, the prisoners are set free, and they sup together. *For everyone.*

131. 海外繽紛錄   2 vol. 267 & 225 pp. by 陳辟邪
上海春明書店

In these two volumes, the author presents the life of Chinese students abroad, mainly in Paris. The author does not mention their studies, and it appears that these students know but two things: to spend their free time in cafés, and to amuse themselves with women.

A big number of obscene passages. *To be proscribed.*

132. 像樣的人 *THE ELITE*   1 vol. 241 p. by 陳涉
1937 良友圖書公司

The book tells how the moneyed class exploits the poor in China. The well-to-do people stop at nothing.

The description of an abortion obliges us to make serious reservations. *Everyone to be warned against the above.*

133. 情海斷魂 *LOVELORN*   2 vol. 343 & 444 p. by 陳慎言
1939 天津書局   *See Biogr. 24*

A newly-married couple, in love with each other, were separated and compelled to divorce by their mother-in-law, an arbitrary and extremely mean woman. The divorced woman had placed herself under the protection of a professor, who came back from America. The latter fell in love with her, but remained always dignified and did many services to the lady. He kept an old love at the bottom of his heart: the object of his love had left him, in order to marry a very rich man...this marriage was imposed by her parents. Because the woman herself was deeply in love with her first lover, she went to importune this last one, who stayed with his favorite in Paitaho, There she beseeched him to marry her, as her first husband was dead. The professor was still in love with her, but he sent her back, believing himself to be honourably pledged to his favorite. His first love, grieved by this repulse, commited suicide. The husband of his favorite was love-sick, and was continually calling his wife, who also...kept in her heart the memory of her husband; but her mother-in-law was on the watch and the obedient son did not dare to resist this tyranny.

One day, the professor was taking a walk with the young divorced woman; haunted by the memory of his first love, he moved away from his companion for a moment, fell into a pool by the side of the road and was drowned.

Despair of the favorite. . ! But in spite of all, being in love with her former husband, and knowing that he was sick because of her ,she went to see him in the hospital outside the city of Peiping. A cousin of this man, who was destined to become his wife, made a scene and told the husband that his mother died of anger after she had learned about the reconciliation of the two spouses. The obedient son considered himself to be the murderer of his mother and died in grief; his wife also died near his bed.

The book is exciting; unexpected situations, many tragic scenes! Sad endings. Much prolixity. No objectionable descriptions. The author describes well the misfortunes of a family caused by an arbitrary mother-in-law, and also the fatal consequences of divorce. *May be read by informed people.*

134. 海上情葩　　　　　　　　　　　　　1 vol. 194 p. by **陳慎言**
　　　　　　　　　　　　　　　　　　　　　1940　義文書局

The novel took place at navy quarters in Foochow. A young and brave marine lieutenant and a nurse from the methodist hospital loved each other tenderly, and thought of getting married in the near future. In the meantime the lieutenant's friends wanted to dissuade him from marrying this nurse, and advised him to choose the admiral's daughter. This one indeed, though worldly and extravagant, had a big influence. The lieutenant refused, but in the mean time had to join a naval expedition. The admiral's son availed himself of the hero's absence and tried to seduce the nurse; his sister, who detested the young girl, helped him in his plan. Our heroine resisted. The admiral's son decided then to resort to force; but the nurse threw herself into the water. She was saved by fishermen and her enemy made a new attempt, but the victim was saved this time by her fiancé, the lieutenant, who came back from the expedition, covered with glory. Upon this, our two heroes got married.

For grown up people owing to one scene which is rather wild.

135. 名士與美人　*NOTARIES & LADIES*　　1 vol. 186 p. by **陳慎言**
　　　　　　　　　　　　　　　　　　　　　1940　義文書局

Two friends from the South came to Peiping. The first came accompanied by a prostitute whom he later forsakes for a singer. The second succeeded in finding a good position, thanks to the concubine of his senior clerk; in a hospital he found another good match... *Everyone to be dissuaded from reading it.*

136. 花生大王　*PEANUT KING*　　　　　　1 vol. 190 p. by **陳慎言**
　　　　　　　　　　　　　　　　　　　　　1940　華龍印書館

A poor student, very intelligent, married a young and very rich girl from Shanghai, during their studies in America. Back in Shanghai, he lived for some time at the expenses of his wife's family, but this life of a parasite was hateful to him. He left for Peiping and Tientsin to make his career. He succeeded. In the mean time his wife and his sister-in-law came to join him in Tientsin. He became intimate with his sister-in-law, who became his concubine; his wife, after some scenes, finished by getting used to this state of things. Finally the heroes of this book finished in bankruptcy on account of risky speculations. Thus vice was punished. *For everyone.*

137. 恨海難塡   1 vol. 276 p. by 陳慎言
                                                      1941 北京華龍印書舘

A loving couple was accidentally separated by the young man's father. This father, a mean person, ignored the affection his son had for the young girl. One day he met the latter accidentally and made advances to her. The girl detested him, but did not dare to show her antipathy because this man had business with her father. She did not know that he was the father of her exiled friend. It the end, in order to save the honour of her family, which had been compromised in a big opium affair, she agreed with reluctance to live with this person. The night which followed their marriage, she wounded him and herself in order to defend her chastity. They were taken to a hospital and the son, who was far away, was called back. Dying, the father enjoined his son to take care of a certain girl, who, he said, "is your mother-in-law!" The young man on learning this, and on discovering that his mother-in-law was his old love, was in despair and gave up his plan of marrying her. The young girl saw him again and learned that he was the son of her so-called "husband". . .Hence, more despair.! She thereupon made a resolution to enter a Buddhist convent.

This book is interesting for its descriptions of the ways of living and "doing business" of rich men.

With the exception of one scene, there is nothing objectionable in this book. *Can be read by grown up people.*

138. 幕中人語 *CONFIDENTIAL*   1 vol. 174 p. by 陳慎言
                                                      2nd edition. 1941 華龍印書舘

A young girl by the name of Chin tzu was given as a concubine to a voluptuous official. By mutual consent with the acknowledged wife, she succeeded in preserving her chastity. But after a few months, when the wife was ill, the "K'o Chang" violated Chin tzu. The latter did not want to live dishonoured. Having arranged for her mother's future she drowned herself together with a young man whom she loved.

The author gives us a very fine character in the person of Chin tzu. . .Some scenes are carried a little too far, but the book *can be read by grown up people.*

139. 貴族女兒 *AN ARISTOCRATIC GIRL*   1 vol. 132 p. by 陳慎言
                                                      北京華龍印書舘

A young lady, having divorced her husband a few months after their marriage, because of his misconduct, lead a very dissolute life. . .She became a prostitute, then a general's concubine, and finally a dancing-girl. After a few years, she was converted under the influence of her doctor and became a fervent Buddhist.

Some frivolous scenes. *For informed readers.*

140. 薄命女兒 *THE POOR GIRL*   2 vol. 149 p. 147 p. by 陳慎言
                                                      北京義文書局

A young man brought shame on several young girls by his frivolity. Deceived in their hopes, they became Buddhist nuns.

The book describes the frivolous life of unemployed girls; it gives us also some fine characters. The interest is not always maintained. Some frivolous scenes. *To be read only by grown up people.*

141. 心盟 *THE SPIRITUAL ALLIANCE*   2 vol. 192 & 190 p. by **陳東哲**
1941　勵力出版社

This book presents the life of several young men and girls, their deeds and ideas. A number of happy weddings are described in the course of the story. The modern ideas and relations between the sexes remain dignified; but owing to the description of an act of vengeance in which one heroine, in order to avenge her father's death, murders the poor victim in cold blood, this book can be read *only by experienced persons.*

142. 爐邊 *FIRESIDE*   1 vol. 168 p. by **陳煒謨**
See Biogr 25

A collection consisting of an essay and seven stories. We are told with full detail of the life in certain academic circles in Peking of which the author has been a member. Then follows a rather crude incident in which the author took part during an academic session. The book ends with a few descriptions of domestic life.

The above is written in a careless style and the subject matter is without elevation. *For mature people only* due to certain crude details.

143. 一個女作家 *AN AUTHORESS*   1 vol. 118 p. by **沉櫻（陳鍈）**
1935　北新書局 *See Biogr.* 26

Four stories.
All four deal chiefly with the problems of life which confront the newly married. They contain no immodest descriptions. The first story dwells unduly on the particulars of child birth, and is *thus unsuitable for single persons.*

144. 女性 *THE FAIRER SEX*   1 vol. 266 p. by **沉　櫻**
1934　生活書店

A collection of stories.
1. 女性　A happy married couple, but the wife is afraid of having a child and goes to the hospital to obtain an abortion. *Not for everyone.*
2. 主僕　Story of a servant. *For everyone.*
3. 時間與空間　A beautiful love affair ends unhappily because of the inconstancy of the girl. *For everyone.*
4. 我們的塾師　An old-fashioned master. *For everyone.*
5. 舊雨　Marriage makes the man unhappy. On the necessity for emancipation. *Not for everyone.*
6. 生涯　Shattered love between two students. *Not for everyone.*
7. 張順的犯罪　Tribulations of a poor soldier. *For everyone.*
Simple stories and well written, but the author seems to approve of free love. *For adults.*

145. 倦旅 *TIRED SOJOURN*   1 vol. 122 p. by **陳月昭女士**
1925　梁溪圖書館

This book is of the small incidents of daily life. The characters described are mostly women teachers. The point of view is protestant. *For everyone.*

146. 風塵三傑 *THE THREE SWORDSMEN*   2 vol. 112 & 114 p. by **鄭證因**

These two volumes are taken from a series of books about popular Chinese heroes. The author describes exploits of the heroes, ordinary and extraordinary. *This book may be read by everyone.*

147. 武林俠踪 *THE SWORDSMEN'S HATRED* 4 vol. 170, 144, 115, 174 p. by 鄭證因
藝林書店

Swashbuckler romance.

A cavalier is slain in an encounter. His son revenges him and wounds his adversary, whose son, in turn revenges his father, and so forth. *For everyone.*

148. 家庭的故事 *STORY OF A FAMILY* 1 vol. 258 p. by 鄭振鐸

2nd edition 1931 開明書店 *See Biogr.* 27

This book deserves its title indeed. It is composed of sixteen stories. All of these deal with home life or intimate things attached to it.

On the whole this book is well written. We think that these tales should please the Chinese for they narrate chiefly daily events. The author seems to be well acquainted with the life he describes.

There is little left to comment upon. In the fourth tale, divorce is described by the author as a usual and natural act. The marriage which followed this divorce turned out to be an unlucky one. The author leaves us the impression that his heroes would be far happier if they had refrained from this divorce. There are a number of coarse details, but the author does not draw attention to them. This book *may be read by all.*

149. 海燕 *SEAGULL* 1 vol. 212 p. by 鄭振鐸
1932 新中國書局

Literary criticisms, accounts and souvenirs of journeys. Special attention should be paid to the severe criticism of sentimental romances and swashbuckler romances, and to the criticism of the use of illustrations in Chinese books. The author reveals the value of illustrations in the old romances and the bad taste of the illustrations in modern books for the young. He also criticises journalistic morals in Shanghai. *For everyone.*

150. 三年 *THREE YEARS* 1 vol. from p. 264 to 329 coll. by 鄭振鐸
上海藝光出版社

Scenes from ordinary life. A young woman given to gambling, a faithful servitor, a husband ill and abandoned, a happy family fallen into misfortune, etc. *For everyone.*

151. 鄭振鐸選集 *AN ANTHOLOGY OF CHENG CHEN-TUO* 1 vol. 256 p.
1936 萬象書局

p.	11	Expelling a communistic professor. An effort is made to uproot his influence.	p. 221	Sea-swallow.
p.	38	On the T'ai-p'ings.	p. 224	Religion.
p.	85	A mediator goes to the enemy who keep him, but he escapes.	p. 228	Arabs.
			p. 232	A beautiful road in Suchow.
p.	144, 170	Mythology.	p. 237	On insects.
p.	190, 195	On the novel.	p. 240	Description of Nature.
p.	202	Aspects of literature.	p. 243	The cat.
			p. 248	Students.
p.	215	Farewell to the fatherland.	p. 251	The impassive people. *For everyone.*

152. 鄭振鐸選集 *AN ANTHOLOGY OF CHENG CHEN-TUO*

256 p. **現代創作文庫**

1936 萬象書店

In addition to a number of poems and extracts, this anthology consists chiefly of historical accounts that the author has slightly revised. Some of them are useful from an educative or patriotic point of view, but they are too serious for the very young. *For everyone.*

153. 結算 *ACCOUNTS SETTLED*   1 vol. 309 p. by **征 農**

1935 生活書店

Twelve stories:

1. A mother was working hard, spoiled her children and suffered for it later on.
2. Exploitations by the owners and their emissaries.
3. Cruelties of landowners.
4. A starving woman wanted to buy some corn; the rich men refused to sell, because the prices were too low.
5. A young man returned home after two years in prison. . .His mother had died of grief.
6. Peasants were summoned by force and were made to work "voluntarily" for the soldiery!
7. The hard life of peasants.
8. Some grain was carted to the market but there were no buyers.
9. Efforts to unite a peasant village with the civilized world. . .Disputes, murders.
10. Village scenes.
11. Advantages and disadvantages of being deaf-and-dumb.
12. Marriage and remarriage and. . .their consequences. *For all.*

154. 打火機 *LIGHTER*   1 vol. 241 p. by **鄭伯奇**

1940 良友公司 *See Biogr. 28*

1. 打火機 Story of a fire-lighter found again. *For everyone.*
2. 普利安先生 Portrait of a foreign employee. *For everyone.*
3. 偉特博士的來歷 If you do me in the eye, I'll do you worse in the eye. *For everyone.*
4. 不景氣的插話 The unhappiness of a domestic. Out of work, he drowns himself. *For everyone.*
5. 白沙枇杷 Events in a cafe. *Not for everyone.*
6. 港香的一夜 A night in a hotel in Hongkong. *Not for everyone.*
7. 重逢 A young man gives an account of a visit to a courtisan. *Not for everyone.*
8. 幸運兒 A financial crash. *For everyone.*
9. 懇親會 Cordial relations in a tea house. *Not for everyone.*
10. 聖處女的出路 Stupid lucubrations against the Catholic religion. The author shows a complete lack of understanding of the Catholic religion and demonstrates a paucity of wit in his calumnies against it. *Not to be recommended to anyone.*

　　Throughout the book the author lacks seriousness, and is constantly introducing the reader into the private chambers of courtisans. *Not to be recommended to anyone.*

155. 上海的秘密 *SECRETS OF SHANGHAI*   1 vol. 130 p. by **鄭 燕**

3rd. edit. 1946 中國出版公司

Of the deplorable side of life in Shanghai. *Proscribed.*

156. 嫁後光陰   *WHERE LIFE BEGINS*   1 vol. 187 p. by 程瞻廬
1939   文藝書局

In this novel we are introduced to two couples who got married. One family was happy, the other unhappy! A third person intervened; she took the happy wife to the house of an artist and thus succeeded in provoking the jealousy of the husband. After this, divorces and many intricacies! This finished by the marriage of the former happy wife and the artist. . .But. . .the unhappy wife and another person were equally in love with the artist. . . .Vexed, these two entered the establishment of Zikawei in order to do penance.

In this book it is too much spoken of divorce. . .*all young people must be dissuaded from reading it.*

157. 滑頭國   *A COUNTRY OF SHREWELS*   1 vol. 78 p. by 程瞻廬
1940   上海大衆書局

A comic story telling of the adventures of three brothers in the kingdom of sharpers. The author makes a number of puns and brings in inscriptions that, read from right to left, mean exactly the opposite of what they say when they are read from left to right. *For everyone.*

158. 白紗巾   *THE CASE OF THE WHITE SCARF*   1 vol. 145 p. by 程小青
上海大衆書局

Detective story.

Mr. Chia is killed, after which two detectives pursue a man who had been seen after the murder in the room that was the scene of the crime.

In the end, through overhearing a conversation, the detectives discover that a female employee of the customs is the guilty one. She believed that she acted in self-defence. *For everyone.*

159. 浮浪者   *THE ROAMER*   1 vol. 134 p. by 程碧冰
3rd. edit. 1933   上海文藝書局

A young man of advanced ideas solicits a position in a school but without success. His father is very dissatisfied with him and turns him out of the house. His mother, however, intervenes and obtains permission for the son to go and continue his studies in Shanghai. The young man goes there but finds himself disillusioned in no time, whereupon he returns, quite content, to the paternal roof.

The book describes at length the revolutionary ideas of the son and also shows the wrong that parents commit in treating their children too severely.

The author also shows that the advanced ideas of youth are not of a nature to save society. *For everyone.*

160. 丁香花悲痛小史   *THE PITIABLE LIFE OF LITTLE LILAC*
1 vol. 434 p. by 李博多
1941   北平北堂印書館

This book relates how the Wu family, robbed by brigands, fled to Cho-chow where they settled down. Here they lived in the house of a school mistress. Their daughter helped the school mistress in her work and desired to be baptized; her mother was also eager to receive the new faith and was finally baptized before her death; the girl met with many oppositions from her father, who did not want to see his daughter baptized. Their change of residence did not deflect her from her worship of God. After some time she returned to Cho-chow, where she died a saintly death.

This book presents a very good story and teaches a good lesson. *For all.*

161. 睢鳩 *CUCKOO SONG*　　　　　1 vol. 164 p. by 季　時
　　　　　　　　　　　　　　　　　　　1930　中華印書局

In this novel the marriage question is put forward. The author studies the problem of marriage and chooses the middle road. He first tells of parents who refrain from drawing up a contract until the children have known each other for some time. Then the author shows how a marriage, arranged by parents, turned out to be an unlucky one. He ends up by describing the honeymoon of a third couple; he thinks that a honeymoon is the most desirable event for modern youths.

All should be advised against reading it, as it contains a number of obscene passages.

162. 孟麗君 *MISS MENG*　　　　　　1 vol. 372 p. by 戚綠荷
　　　　　　　　　　　　　　　　　　　1936　大達圖書局

Two young men fall in love with a young lady. In order to decide who will have her affections they compete at archery. The loser, however, refusing to submit to this verdict, and through his family relations, brings about the ruin of the winner. The young heroine, dressed in men's clothes, escapes in company with two other young ladies, and her fiancé also goes away. Each one, separately, strives to save the ruined family. Owing to their spirit of sacrifice, their virtues, and their heroic acts, they are successful and the hero marries all three young ladies.

Apart from this polygamous marriage, there is not a reprehensible word in this book. Sin is punished and virtue rewarded. *For everyone.*

163. 隋煬帝艷史 *ROMANTIC LIFE OF AN EMPEROR-YANG OF SUI*
　　　　　　　　　　　　　　　　1 vol. 202 p. by 齊東野人
　　　　　　　　　　　　　　　　2nd. edit. 1946　中央書店

Indecent stories without any head or tail about the harem of an imperial court. *Proscribed.*

164. 飛紅 *PINK PETALS*　　　　　　1 vol. 193 p. by 蔣江秋
　　　　　　　　　　　　　　　　　　　1928　群衆圖書公司

A man who is already married takes a second wife and lives with her. It is not long before both regret their act but for different reasons. The husband detaches himself from the wife, while she seeks consolation elsewhere.

This book should be proscribed because of the theories it vaunts, and also because of certain very crude details that are repeated a number of times. *Proscribed.*

165. 綠箋 *GREEN STATIONERY*　　　　1 vol. 114 p. by 蔣逸霄
　　　　　　　　　　　　　　　　　　　1928　古城書社

This novel, in the form of letters, strongly denounces the authority of parents in affairs of marriage. A rich girl from Tientsin and a poor professor sincerely love each other. They meet regularly but still keep up a moving, passionate correspondence besides. Their love is thwarted by the girl's father who has promised her to another man, without the girl's consent.

The subject and the pagan outlook *call for reserve.*

166. 衝出雲圍的月亮 *MOON'S OUT*   1 vol. 283 p. by 蔣光慈
1930 北新書局 *See Biogr.* 29

The author describes the enthusiasm of the Communists of the 3rd International that will give the world a new freedom. Faced with the failures of 1928 they cool down and get disillusioned. If they cannot rebuild, they will at least tear down.

The book then continues with a series of obscene descriptions in which a young Communist woman aims at upsetting everything by giving free play to evil passions. She justifies her own immorality by alleging that she "thus revenges herself on this rotten capitalist society".

This *book must not be found in any, even university, libraries.*

167. 三對愛人兒 *THREE PAIRS*   1 vol. by 蔣光慈
1932 上海月明書店

A collection of naturalistic, erotic and immoral stories.

This book *must be condemned* on the grounds of the immorality of the descriptions and the Communism of the author who gives the impression of being satiated with voluptuousness.

168. 蔣光慈小說全集第一集 *COLLECTED STORIES BY CHIANG KUANG-TS'E*
(Vol. I) 442 p. 3rd. edit. 1932 新文藝書店

1. 李孟漢與雲姑 p. 1-37. A young Korean tells, in a school of Moscow, of the death of his parents, the fidelity of his fiancee, and her death. Revolutionary spirit. *Not for everyone.*

2. 一封未寄的信 p. 37-49. A letter in which there is question of an illicit love. *Not for everyone.*

3. 革命戰線歸來的王曼英 p. 49-155. A revolutionary girl leaves her parents for the army. She does not attain her ideal there. She then leads a licentious life in order to injure the rich. A child that has been picked up reminds her of her duty. Lascivious descriptions. Revolutionary spirit. *Proscribed.*

4. 徐州旅館之一夜 p. 155-175. A young husband, called home by his wife who is ill stays in a hotel with a prostitute. The latter has only just started on her profession. She recounts her unhappy history, and he pities her. Revolutionary spirit. *Not for everyone.*

5. 橄欖 p. 157-199. The vengeance of a concubine who kills her husband. *Not to be recommended to anyone.*

6 長信一封 p. 199-309. Misfortunes of a young man whose parents died victims of a cruel man of wealth. Revolutionary ideas and full of vengeance. *Not to be recommended to anyone.*

7. 求耦 p. 309-329. A poet in search of a friend. *Not for everyone.*

8. 東京之旅 p. 329-421. Diary of the author written in Japan. *Not to be recommended to anyone.*

9. 歸家 p. 421-442. A murderer whose family has been killed by soldiers. *Proscribed.*

This book is written in clear and easy language that ought to please people. Communist and revolutionary ideas are expressed in it from beginning to end. It contains also a great number of obscene descriptions. Morals do not exist for the author. His watchword is vengeance and revolution. *Proscribed.*

169. 蔣光慈小說全集第二集 *COLLECTED STORIES BY CHIANG KUANG-TS'E*
(Vol. II) 1 vol. 460 p. 3rd. edit. 1932 新文藝書店

1. 兄弟夜談 p. 1-33. A revolutionary son opposes the marriage arranged by his parents. *Not for everyone.*
2. 一切都永別了 p. 34-181. A young wife, daughter of a Russian nobleman, has to flee her country during the revolution. She arrives in China where she is forced to prostitute herself in order to gain a living for her husband. She becomes ill and prepares to commit suicide. *Not to be recommended to anyone.*
3. 汪海平與吳月芬 p. 182-217. A protestant nurse falls in love with a wounded revolutionary. The latter dies in a subsequent scuffle, whereupon she renounces God and drowns herself. *Not to be recommended to anyone.*
4. 毅然走革命正軌的王曼英 p. 218-357. (Sequel of a story in the first volume). A girl pays no attention to her remorse but continues her licentious life to the harm of society. She ends in falling in love with an old acquaintance. Together they gives themselves up to the real revolution. Lewd atmosphere. *Proscribed.*
5. 哭淑君 p. 359-460. A revolutionary professor lives with a girl who is also devoted to the revolution. He does not love her, but fancies a coquette. Regrets overtake him. *Not for everyone.*

The whole book is written in a clear and simple style. Its aim is to propagate revolution and communism. *To be proscribed.*

170. 蔣光慈小說全集第三集 *COLLECTED STORIES BY CHIANG KUANG-TS'E*
(Vol. III) 1 vol. 404 p. 1932 新文藝書店

1. 最後的微笑 p. 1-191. Various pictures of a revolutionary. Subject: a young workman becomes an assassin for the good cause, and eventually kills himself.
All this is presented to us as a matter of course! *Not to be recommended to anyone.*
2. 老太婆與阿三 p. 193-207. Two portraits. *Not for everyone.*
3. 紀念若瑜 p. 208-404. Loveletters between the author and the one who became his wife. *Not to be recommended to anyone.*

171. 蔣光慈小說全集第四集 *COLLECTED STORIES BY CHIANG KUANG-TS'E*
(Vol. IV) 2nd. edit. 1932 新文藝書店

The whole book is a picture of the communist revolution. *Proscribed.*

172. 夾竹桃 1 vol. 163 p. by 江 流
1945 馬德增書店

Four stories.
1. An account dealt with in a realistic-romantic way of adventures in a Peking courtyard.
2. and 3. without interest.
4. A young girl devotes herself to the support of her father and small brothers. For them she sacrifices both love and marriage. A very pathetic story. *For everyone.*

173. 夜工 *NIGHT SHIFT* 1 vol. 211 p. by 蔣牧良
1937 文化生活出版社 *See Biogr. 30*

A collection of stories nearly all of which aim at social reform.

1. 夜工 p. 1-24. In spite of instinctive repugnance, a woman worker in a factory ends in giving in to the solicitations of her employer. *Not for everyone.*

2. 生死朋友 p. 24-47. An employee in an office, Mr. Hung (洪) dies in misery. Under the pretext of helping the widow and children, his friend manages to obtain an allocation from the administration after energetic representations. It happens, however, that Mr. Hung once borrowed money from this "friend", who therefore keeps most of the money that he has raised. *For everyone.*

3. 肉 p. 47-53. A captain, under pretext of enforcing discipline, shoots a corporal who had dared to allude to his sodomitical habits. *Not for everyone.*

4. 三七租 p. 55-94. A farmer is forced by his poor condition to pay the excessive rent demanded by a hard landlord who is, moreover, a gambler. *For everyone.*

5. 分泉 p. 95-113. In order to force his brother to give him his share of the patrimonial inheritance, Lao Chiu resorts to a kind of extortion by cutting off his finger. *For everyone.*

6. 印刷間的一夜 p. 113-126. In order to repay a debt that his mother has contracted, under necessity, Hsiao Ti-tzu has to work at night in a printer's. There he discovers proof that his employer is working for the Japanese. He reproaches his employer with this rather insolently, which results in a fight that lands Hsiao Ti-tzu in prison. *For everyone.*

7. 雷 p. 129-147. Mr. Ch'ueh has squeezed the cereals destined for the victims of a flood. A violent storm overtakes him on the way. He thinks he is menaced by the God of Thunder and hopes to move him by his repentence and promises. *For everyone.*

8. 吃壽酒 p. 149-159. A grandmother does not mind showing her grandson that she prefers her granddaughter. *For everyone.*

9. 懶捐 p. 161-185. Wu Ta-t'ou-tzu (吳大頭子) has not cultivated opium. He cannot pay, because of his poverty, the $45 of "special" tax that the tax collector insists on levying, and is thrown into prison. *For everyone.*

10. 拂曉的攻擊 p. 185-211. An account of a violent combat between soldiers and bandits, seasoned with barrack-room language and coarse expressions. *Not for everyone.* Can be recommended with caution. *Not for everyone.*

174. 旱 *BAKNIGLY DRY*

1 vol. 74 p. by 蔣牧良
1940 良友復興圖書公司

During a time of great drought a procession is organised in honour of Lung Wang to pray for rain. The old Ch'en considers that the persons responsible for this misfortune are Mr. Chao Kuan-tsung, a hard and rapacious man of means who has caused several people to be put into prison, and who has pocketed the money destined for public works (in this case, an irrigation canal), and a bad woman who is a procuress of girls for the neighbouring city.

Now Chin A-ko has a wife and children. His father has died and is awaiting burial. But there is no money in the house, not even any provisions. He hopes, therefore, to be able to borrow enough for his immediate necessities, and to save his harvest that is perishing.

He goes to his sister first but she is not able to help him having herself been the victim of a robbery.

A friend then undertakes to introduce him to a rich man. He does not dare to go but he goes eventually, not being able to do anything else. He is received harshly and coldly. Overcome, he returns home and makes a scene with his wife and children. His mother, however, succeeds in calming him.

He is desperate. A friend surprises him in this sad state, who eventually advises him that Ch'uan Sheng-man could lend him the necessary sum. She happens to be the procuress.

The poor man decides to sell his daughter who is fourteen years old. He tells his wife and extorts a consent from her through violence. But after having delivered his daughter, he is again seized with despair.

On the way home he learns that the old Ch'en has robbed him of the water he had provided for his own fields, and a fine battle ensues.

Apart from a few expressions that are rather low or too realstic, it is a beautiful book. *Can be read by everyone.*

175. 月上柳梢頭 *MOON'S OVER THE WILLOW TREE* 1 vol. 122 p. by 蔣山青
1927 上海出版合作社

A collection of sloppy love stories. Nothing risky, but a sultry atmosphere full of sighs and easy tears. Gives exaggerated descriptions of the state of mind of lovers. Altogether unwholesome.
Unsuitable for younger people.

176. 秋蟬 *DAYS ARE NUMBERED* 1 vol. 206 p. by 蔣山青
1926

1) A young girl is ill. She is afforded every care to save her life. The mother is anxious because her son died of the same disease. The heroine dies.
2) Anxieties caused by a sick person.
3) An orphan is refused all commerce with women which renders him extremely unhappy. Finally he is allowed to become engaged and he is as though reborn. His happiness, however, is not of long duration.
4) A wedding is being celebrated. The bride, however, has someone else in her heart and they fear for her happiness.
5) Various psychologies before marriage.
6) A young man upon whom a betrothal is being imposed thinks of an old man of his native village who was faithful to his fiancée who had died young.
7) Diary of a sentimental girl.
8) Memories brought on by seeing a funeral in the street.
9) Memories of an old lady.
10) Letter to a dead friend.
Not for the young.

177. 燕都小霽 *IN PEKING* 1 vol. 124 p. by 姜華
1927 北京書店

A book without any serious idea, and containing nothing but love-sick fancies.
Not for the young.

178. 酒家 *THE BAR* 1 vol. 220 p. by 羼先艾
1934 新中國書局 *See Biogr. 32*

A collection of ten stories.
1. 詩人朗佛羅，到鑛西去，四川紳士和湖南女伶，酒家 These are tales of gallantry and love.
2. 血泡粑的典禮 Three merchants are staying in an inn. They are served 泡粑 of an unusual size. The oldest of the three tells his two companions the history of this phenomenon. In order to construct a road across the territory of the Miao, the mandarin in charge had to destroy a tomb that was in the way, and thus he stirred up an insurrection. He died a victim to it, but his wife very courageously made good her escape, defending herself bravely. She was made a prisoner later and died with her breast bared to receive the blade. To

commemorate her courage, the Miao dip their 泡粑 in blood during their feasts of victory.

3. 美麗的夢 A merchant dreams of making a fortune. He makes straw sandels such as are worn by soldiers. The city is then pillaged by soldiers. He escapes the pillage but with the departure of the soldiers, his dream dissolves.

4. 遷居 Difficulties encountered by a young couple in search of a peaceful and convenient residence.

5. 鹽巴客 The author has to stop at an inn during a journey. He is lodged in a poor room with a porter. The story of this good working man makes him change his opinions and sentiments towards those who are less fortunate than himself.

6. 僕人之書 A student who has already graduated at last manages to get employment as the gate-keeper of a school. He is satisfied with his condition. He writes a long letter to his old teacher in which he gives an account of his mortifications and the misfortunes that have occurred to him since he left school, the history of his family, of his sister who died through devotion to her people and her country, and of his father who has died from consumption.

7. 被遺忘的人的故事 The finding of an old romance, left behind by a relative who was a childhood friend suggests the telling of the story of this friend and of this book.
Not for everyone.

---

179. 鹽的故事 *THE STORY OF SALT*   1 vol. 155 p. by 蹇先艾
    1937   文化生活

1. There is a scarcity of salt. Only one powerful family has some in their shop. Instead of helping others they keep it by force.

2. . . . .

3. The revolutionary spirit is blowing among the young, but as for their parents. . .

4. How an official enriched himself and acted.

5. The misery of an employé.

    The second story has been torn from the book that we have in hand. The other four are for all readers.
For everyone.

---

180. 避難日記 *DIARY OF A REFUGEE*   1 vol. 95 p. by 簡易從
    1940   國民書店

1) 揚州十日記 The story of the siege of Yangchow.

2) 再生紀略 Another war story.

3) 虎口餘生記 An uninteresting story.

4) 再生紀選錄 About a battle.
For everyone.

---

181. 淪落青衫 *DOWN AND OUT*   3 vol. by 倩倩
    1941   志新書店

    A very complicated love story. A young man is loved by at least four girls. He chooses the poorest. Although put off, a general's daughter continues to protect him. Follows a series of complications: a rascal who deceives the hero's wife, some murders, etc. Finally the author unites the hero and the general's daughter.

    No risky descriptions. The author's flippancy calls for reserve as does his account of the exaggerated freedom in the relations between persons of both sexes.
Very objectionable.

182. 圍城 *BESIEGED* 1 vol. 479 p. by 錢鍾書
1947 晨光出版公司 *See Biogr. 33*

A novel about a young man's travels to the interior and abroad, his romance and daily life.

In general, the author's skill in describing is manifest and the selection of characters reveals a promising pen. When necessary, he displays a fine sense of humour, and can be successfully sacarstic.

However, his technique is altogether a failure. The story he tries to relate in this book, does not warrant such a long narrative, nor the time he allegedly took. (2 years, as is written in the preface.)

The book is prolix and the plot thin. It does not seem worthy of the time and energy the author spent on it.

The author cannot refrain from being pedantic i.e. giving unnecessary and irrelevant foreign slogans and maxims (German, Spanish, French, Italian, etc.), a fact which repels most readers. Anybody could have done that by referring to a dictionary.

There is one passage highly suggestive of carnal desire, so *the book is better proscribed and kept away from the young people,* who can spend their time in reading more worthwhile books.

183. 兩只毒藥杯 *TWO CUPS OF POISON* 1 vol. 69 p. by 倩兮
1931 震東印書館

A young man is loved by two girls, and hesitates in his choice. To his own despair and the girls' disappointment he has to part with both of them.
For all.

184. 多情恨 *REGRETTED* 1 vol. 238 p. by 錢一燕
1946 上海大明書局

Many pages that say nothing. This book is composed entirely of love affairs between people of easy means, who have no great regard for morals. *Not to be recommended.*

185. 桃色慘案 *THE ROSY MURDER* 1 vol. 174 p. by 茜蒂
1940 大連實業印書館

Detective stories. The detective's adventures do not show much ingenuity.
The last story contains a few objectionable passages. *For informed readers.*

186. 血淚想思 *INDELLIBLY ENGRAVED* 1 vol. 119 p. by 茜蒂
2nd. edit. 1946 上海百新書店

This book is of the agitated and sentimental life of several young people who give themselves up to revolutionary aetivities.
The morals are too free. *Not to be recommended to anyone.*

187. 青的花 ·*BLUE FLOWERS* 1 vol. 318 p. by: 靳以（章方叙）
1934 生活書店 *See Biogr. 2*

A collection of short stories:
1) A widow muses about the love she felt for her first sweetheart.
2) This sweetheart well advanced in age now, comes to her home; she does not see him but makes her children wait on him. She talks to herself about her love and disillusions.
3) A rich man adopts a good looking young man in order to deceive women. He starts the realization of his plan but the young man flees.

4) A man, cheated by his wife, courts any woman he runs into.

5) A sick boy falls in love with a nurse while in hospital. A doctor wins the girl.

6) A Russian singer leaves her husband to lead a free life. She loves him all the time, though, even when he becomes poor. One day she is found murdered.

7) A teacher looks after his ailing wife; both Christians; the wife dies and the husband finds solace in a sermon preached by the parsons.
For all.

188. 蟲蝕 *WORMEATEN*   1 vol. 228 p. by 靳 以
1934 良友圖書公司

A number of short stories which contain nothing immoral. The last stories present the government in Manchuria; as this government is foreign, it is opposed by the author.
For everyone.

189. 羣鴉 *CROWS*   1 vol. 205 p. by 靳 以
1934 新中國書局

父親 : of the love for and the great severity towards his children of the father of the author.
黑影 : a letter of complaint written by a young man to his friend on the subject of his unfaithful fiancée.
困與疚 : economic difficulties of a young man who has recently married.
女閡君 : impressions and disillusions of the first love of a young girl.
姊姊 : family memories.
結束 : a young man breaks off with his unfaithful fiancée.
羣鴉 : imprudent gossips are punished for their ridiculous talk.
旋: story of an unfaithful girl who repents.
This book might be useful to students in big cities. *For everyone.*

190. 珠落集 *GLISTENING*   1 vol. 204 p. by 靳 以
1935 文化生活出版社

Literary essays telling of two happy girls, a young widow finding her happiness in her child, a quarrel between husband and wife, a wandering minstrel etc. etc. *For grown-up people.*

191. 秋花 *AUTUMN BLOSSOMS*   1 vol. 175 p. by 靳 以
1936 文化生活

Story of a man who has contracted tuberculosis when in prison. He goes to be looked after in a hospital, which, however, reminds him of prison because the rules are so severe and the staff so unobliging. He then goes to a sanitarium and there he dreams constantly of two women he knew formerly. One comes to nurse him in reparation for the wrongs she has done him, but our hero is in nowise grateful. The other woman whom he still loves, is married, but she consents to a last meeting against her better judgment. The sick man succumbs.

There is nothing actually unhealthy in this book, but plenty of tears! *For everyone.*

192. 血與火花 *BLOOD & FIRE*   1 vol. 84 p. by 靳 以
1946 萬葉書店

Descriptions of atrocities committed by the Japanese and the misery caused by eight years of war. The book is full of patriotic spirit, and calls for action in the re-construction of China. *For everyone.*

193. 黃沙 *YELLOW SAND*   1 vol. 230 p. by 靳　以
                                                    1936　文化生活

去路　A husband who has been driven from his home by the enemy, has lost his mother, his wife and a child far from his native province. He has another child remaining to him. Reduced to misery, he is taken in by a friend, but urged by the memory of those who belonged to him, he goes alone into the night to the tomb of the dead.

殘葉　About an individual who makes a vow and believes in Buddha because after liberating a courtisan, he abandoned her to another person who has no conscience!

雪朝　An old employee is replaced, under orders from the new director, by a modern young lady.

亡鄉人　Tragic history of a family of fugitives.

雨季　Of a wife who is seriously ill.

Under sentence, she still remains full of hope. Contains a word against religion that refutes itself.

過載的心　Story of a little defeatist employee.

黎晨　Tragic story of a poor family.

黃沙　Story of one who has escaped.

About the author is a past master in the description of the misfortunes from which society suffers. His book leaves a sad and melancholy impression which the author explains himself in a postcript.
For everyone.

194. 渡家　*THE FERRYMAN*   1 vol. 203 p. by 靳　以
                                                    1937　商務印書館

A collection of short stories written in a fine style. *For everyone.*

195. 貓與短簡　*CAT & OTHER ESSAYS*   1 vol. 131 p. by 靳　以
                                                    1937　開明書店

First a series of *tuan-chien.* Then the letters of a man who is disillusioned by the departure of his mistress and the death of his mother, whose death by the way, is told in a touching and elegiac fashion. The book ends with a number of short essays. *For everyone.*

196. 殘陽　*THE SETTING SUN*   1 vol. 244 p. by 靳　以
                                                    2nd. edit. 1939　開明書店

A dozen or so well written short stories. The author tells chiefly of the miseries of daily life.

A slight reserve should be maintained over the seventh story in which the adventures of a young Chinese with a Russian woman are described. *For grown-up people.*

197. 遠天的冰雪　*ICE-BOUND*   1 vol. 170 p. by 靳　以
                                                    1937　文化生活出版社

Here is a very beautiful book. The author dwells in a very touching manner on maternel love.

1st. sketch. A small child longs for his absent mother.

2nd. sketch. A severe father and a loving mother.

3rd. sketch. Two frolicsome children.

4th. & 5th. sketch. Maternel love that touches the sublime.

6th. sketch. The death of a mother.

A book *to be recommended to everyone,* especially to the young.

198. 蕲以短篇小說一集 *SHORT STORIES BY CHIN-YI (BOOK I)* 1 vol. 467 p.
1937 開明書店

The majority of these short stories are laid in big centres, chiefly in Shanghai and Harbin. Some tell of Russian emigrés in China, but most of them have love for the subject. The author shows us mainly the unhappy side of this passion indicating that there is no rose without a thorn. *For everyone.*

199. 遭遇 *ENCOUNTERS* 1 vol. 148 p. by 金 魁
1940 文化生活

Story of a young man that education has made into a misfit.

The son of a peasant goes to study in the town. His father enables him to do so at the price of great sacrifices, believing that he is assuring the future of the young man in this way.

When, however, the son returns home, his studies accomplished, he cannot adapt himself to the life in the country. Neither can he be happy with his wife. Thoroughly disgusted with everything, he obtains money by an abuse of confidence, and is thus enabled to escape back to the town, where, after a number of denouments, he sinks lower and lower, ending in suicide.

This book gives a good picture of life in the country, and moreover, presents a real problem. The tone throughout is perhaps, too consistently somber, coming from the fact that the author is too keen to work out his thesis. *For everyone.*

200. 花柳病春 *SPRING FEVER* 1 vol. 165 p. by 金滿城
1937 各省大書局 *See Biogr. 35*

An essay and two comedies.
1) A humourous essay on modern customs. A young man of twenty five asks his father to find him a fiancée. The father grants his wish and finds one. She is one year old. In his rage the young man goes out, meets a beautiful girl student, a prostitute by profession, and falls in love. She plays up to him and swears undying love. He takes her to the pictures; they exchange presents. He promises her to go against his father and to marry her the next day. At two in the morning he arouses his father and makes a scene witnessed by the neighbours. After some arguments the father gives his consent. The next day the two get married; the third day, they separate, the boy having found out what kind of woman he has married.

Strictest caution on account of improprieties and blasphemies directed against God, Jesus Christ and the Blessed Virgin.
2) A ghost, carrying his own body, enters a surgeon's study. He wants his body examined in order to find out why he never had any success with women. After the operation he has no money to pay the surgeon with, so he enters his service as gatekeeper to pay his debt.

Another ghost enters, a woman, and old friend of the first ghost. She comes to tempt the surgeon. The first ghost discovers them and starts a fight. She escapes declaring that she loves neither of them.

Very objectionable.
3) A girl comes to Peking in search of her fiancé who has not been heard of for several years. He tells her that he is in love with another woman. In despair the girl drowns herself. *Not to be recommended to anyone.*

201. 少女的懺悔錄　*HER CONFESSION*　　　1 vol. 221 p. by　敬樂然
　　　　　　　　　　　　　　　　　　　　　　　　1941　益智書店

A diary of a young woman who was married to a rich man in spite of her unwilling-ness, as she loved a poor youth. Misfortune followed her even in her married life; her husband, who was a gambler, died. Her parents-in-law blamed her for it, and drove her out of the house. She had to sell her belongings in order to pay the debts of the deceased one. Thus she found herself penniless with a small baby. The latter fell sick, and she had to become a prostitute in order to pay the doctor's bill. She died in despair with the name of her boy-friend on her lips.

A fine book with good and easy style; some passages are full of poesy. It contains no frivolous passages, but owing to its atmosphere it *can be read by instructed people only.*

202. 海落　*THE FALL*　　　　　　　　　　1 vol. 127 p. by　敬樂然
　　　　　　　　　　　　　　　　　　　　　　　　1941　益智書店

A book on the "eternal triangle"; it contains rather a long discussions about the problem: which of the two women should one choose? Generally one makes an unlucky choice. *For instructed persons only.*

203. 秋海棠　*HE IS CALLED BEGONIA*　　　1 vol. 396 p. by　秦瘦鷗
　　　　　　　　　　　　　　　　　　　　　　　　1944　東方書店

Description of the unhappy life of Ch'iu Hai-t'ang, a popular actor.

Being in love with the concubine of a good liver of Peking, he sees his love answered. A daughter is born from this union. When the good liver is informed of the affair, he kills the woman servant of his concubine and mutilates the countenance of the hero, who flees with his daughter and renouncing his profession, works with his hands to obtain a living for himself and his cherished daughter.

The latter, being very intelligent, educates herself and takes music lessons in secret. Ch'iu Hai-T'ang is forced to flee to Shanghai to avoid his enemies. There he lives in misery. In order to save the life of his daughter, he is forced to resume his old oc-cupation, and engages in musical entertainments, thus being enabled to live in slight ease.

One day the concubine arrives in Shanghai and recognises her daughter in a per-formance. They plan to go together and surprise Ch'iu Hai-t'ang, who has never given his address to his wife, not wishing her to share his unhappy life. The love between them however, has remained very much alive.

When they arrive in the room of the hero they find him dead!

A beautiful story containing several very lovely characters. The sentiments of the father towards his daughter and vice versa are magnificent.

A few passages are too realistic. *For grown-up people.*

204. 軟玉溫香　*VOLUPTUOUS LIFE*　　　1 vol. 220 p. by　秦瘦鷗
　　　　　　　　　　　　　　　　　　　　　　　　1947　大中華書局

An extremely boring romance, in which the author jumps from one subject to an-other. It fails to rouse the slightest flicker of interest and is moreover, an ammoral book, *not to be recommended to anyone.*

205. 埋劍集 *MY SABRE Y HAVE BURIED*   1 vol. 61 p. by   秦佩珩
1943 天津書局

Tales written by an author well-versed in the Catholic religion.

The first story is a mixture of the Christian religion with superstitions. A girl who is the victim of sorcery, cannot get back the heart of her lover. Suffering from this check in her affections, she drowns herself, at the same time demanding pardon of God. *For everyone.*

206. 相思草 *LOVE-SICK*   1 vol. 180 p. by   青   鸞
1941 上海中央書店

A man's adventures with taxi-girls. The author shows how the hero plays up to them and is each time deceived. *Very objectionable.*

207. 夢裏的微笑 *A SMILE IN A DREAM*   1 vol. 241 p. by   周全平
1925 光華書局 *See Biogr. 36*

Three stories about love thwarted by the inflexible rules of tradition. The only consolation of the ill-stared lovers is their faithfulness to each other.

The book is very much in the "Blood and Tears" line of literature of which Yü Ta-fu is the chief representative, but it presents a higher moral standard.

Unsuitable for younger people because of its sentimentality and utopian idealism.

208. 他的懺悔 *HIS REPENTANCE*   1 vol. 149 p. by   周全平
1935 大新書局

A collection of short narratives. *For everyone.*

209. 周全平創作選 *AN ANTHOLOGY OF CHOU CH'UAN-P'ING*   1 vol. 162 p.
1936 上海仿古書店

Some works of the author describing the economical and social difficulties of young people.

A pessimistic atmosphere but sain morality and social ideas. *For everyone.*

210. 江北人 *A NORTHERNER*   1 vol. 196 p. by   周信華
1942. Yen-chow-fu. *See Biogr. 37*

An employee of Peiping (native of the South) was discharged by his senior clerk. Soon his family (there were two ugly children) was brought to most dismal poverty. They sold all they had, and to their confusion had to borrow money. Their Christian neighbour helped them with great charity. Forced by poverty, the father became a rickshaw man. A third child was born, this one very beautiful!

They could not nourish him, and the mother gave him to a Christian family. The former employee Chiang Pei-jen was earning his daily bread; the wife undertook a little commerce, and their son had followed his father's example by becoming a rickshaw man to a nabob, in whose house his sister was living as a servant.

They were happy, but regretted the abandoned child. The adopted child was studying in middle school, and sometimes it was his father who pulled his rickshaw... .The child learned from the others that he was an adopted one. From that moment he went in search of his parents, but all his efforts were fruitless. Finally, a Father from "Fu-Jen" University advised him not to go on with his quest, but to pray for the conversion of his parents. Hope of seeing them again in heaven restored peace to the child. *For all.*

211. 挽救 *SAVED* Zikawei 1 vol. 68 p. by 周信華

The author wants to provide young Catholics with interesting and edifying reading, capable of increasing the apostolic spirit.

A zealous priest was utilizing sports to attract young people, and in that way to renew the Christian life of his parish. That is the outline of the book. *For our young people.*
(Cf. Bulletin Catholique de Pékin, 1942, p. 46).

212. 西諾亞人 *CHINOIS* Zikawei 1 vol. 182 p. by 周信華

A poor family: the father was a fish dealer, and the mother was dead. Poverty forced them to place their daughter in the family of her fiancé, where she was treated as a slave. She fell ill and became a Christian in a hospital directed by nuns. Her father died also as a Christian, and relied on the charity of the missionary for the education of his children.

The family of a missionary adopted them; they went to France where they were well received, and proved themselves to be good and clever children. *For all.*
(Cf. M.v.W. Bulletin Catholique de Pékin, July 42)

213. 雲凛菊流 *THE DISPERSED* Yenchowfu. 1 vol. 213 p. by 周信華

(Cfr. Bulletin Catholique de Pékin, April 1944, p. 187.). *For all.*

214. 天津一美兵 *AN AMERICAN SERVICEMAN IN TIENTSIN*

1 vol. 48 p. by 周信華
1946 中國天主教文化協進會

Under the agreeable and popular form of a recital of the adventures of an American soldier in China, the author attempts a comparative study of China and America, of their customs, character, mentality, defects and respective qualities. The hero is a very sympathetic person who goes under the name of *"Ta-hao jen"* (the excellent man). He is a Catholic, and in telling of him, the author is able, without emphasising the fact, to bring to the reader some points of the doctrine of the Church.

A book to be recommended to all categories of readers. *For everyone.*

215. 泡影 1 vol. 140 p. by 周信華
1947 上智編譯舘

A shepherd, 謝南壽, who has been an orphan since his childhood, had married at the age of 28. On this occasion, his master had presented him with a few mow of land, to recompense him for having once saved his life. The couple, however, are envious of the good fortune of their master whose son is an officer, and their most ardent wish is to have an equally brilliant son. To this end, they indulge in all kinds of superstitions; but when their craving for a child is finally fulfilled, the wife gives birth to a girl! Though being convinced that there is nothing to gain from a girl, they nevertheless let her live, but they give her the name of 招弟, hoping that this will lead to their having a male child.

A second child arrives, but it is again only a girl. She lives only a few days, saving thus her parents from becoming murderers, as they had planned to do away with her.

At last, however, the long expected son is born. But his arrival is accompanied by a great deal of bad luck, and under stress of poverty, the parents sell their daughter to a Catholic orphanage where she is baptized. Not very long after, a good husband is provided for her, who makes his fortune, becoming rich. This circumstance, however, remains unknown to the girl's parents.

Meanwhile, the latter, being still haunted by their dream of future grandeur, send their son to school. He, however, conducts himself badly, so that his parents are forced to sell their last bit of land to pay his debts.

When he takes more and more to bad courses, his father dies of grief. 招弟, whose place of residence has in the meantime been discovered, pays for his funeral from which 元貴 is altogether absent, and takes her mother with her.

A few years after, 元貴 is found dead on the public road.

In this novel, the author wants to expose the sad consequences of a bad education. *For everyone.*

216. 旱災 *DROUGHT*   1 vol. 130 p. by 周楞伽
                                             1935 中華書局

旱災   There is a drought. The peasants try to save the harvest by carrying water over their land. The authorities bring a hydraulic machine to replace hand labour. Urged by curiosity, the peasants attend the first demonstration in great numbers. They see that the results are marvellous, but consider that the machine would be too expensive to run. One of them, however, profits of the occasion, and some of the peasants would like to bargain for the machine. Another is jealous, and excites them against it, wishing to create trouble. Disputes arise, bad language is thrown about, and a free-for-all ensues. The machine is taken away.

A delegation from the village then goes to the neighbouring city to ask for help from the authorities. An accident occurs before the offices of the subprefecture when two men from the village are killed by the guards.

In 村居日記 the author goes on a visit to his brother in their native province. There is a drought. The people in their native place are extremely poor. He gives some money to his brother to defray the expenses of his stay, and to regale him, buys some delicacies. Others learn of this. Their jealousy is excited and they believe that the visitor is a rich man. Some bad characters plan to do him injury. They wish to relieve him of his goods and pillage his brother's house. His brother is alarmed and grieved. In order to restore peace, he returns to Shanghai.

In 小貓 the author tells us of a difference that occurred between him and his wife on the subject of cats. His wife loved the white one, while the black one, which she maltreated and hated, was his favourite. Eventually they come to terms.

永久的感傷 During some troubles in the city, a mother takes her child into the country to her farmers. The child makes friends with the son of a farmer. Five years later he finds his friend sad and in poor health. The trouble is due to his not having obtained permission to marry the girl whom he loved and who now has died in another family. He is encouraged by the other who persuades him to sacrifice himself for the good of society. *For everyone.*

217. 煉獄 *PURGATORY*   1 vol. 610 p. by 周楞伽
                                             1936 上海微波出版社

Social novel. The action begins in Shanghai during the war of 1932-34, and ends in the North when the fighting has moved there. The author describes life in modern Shanghai: capitalists, educators, boy and girl students; strikes and students' riots; he further deals with gambling houses, prostitutes, seductions; village life, the misery of the peasants and exactions by the landowners. He also tells of the war against the Japanese, the patriotism of Chinese youth and the corruption of the higher classes. These descriptions are intended to give us an idea of China's "purgatory". *Very objectionable.*

218. 失業 *UNEMPLOYED*   1 vol. 256 p. by   周楞伽
北新書局

A collecion of short stories. The first is for enlightened people only; everyone is advised against reading the second; the rest are for everyone. *Not to be recommended to anyone.*

219. 田園集 *PASTORAL*   1 vol. 314 p. by   周楞伽
新鐘書局

A collection of seven stories.

旱災 p. 1-126. cf. no. 216. *For everyone.*

源泰米行 p. 127-164. An opulent rice merchant thinks of nothing but how to increase his wealth. During a famine, people are angry with him and his daughter, whom he has neglected and elopes with a young man, taking papa's cash box with her. *For everyone.*

夜渡 p. 166-192. Bandits rob travellers. What follows. *Not for everyone.*

私鹽船 p. 193-218. A young boatwoman has a dream. She has to be content with less which, however, proves to be her happiness. *Not for everyone.*

木匠 p. 219-250. A husband boasts of having killed his inconstant wife. He is taken at his word. *Not for everyone.*

招兵 p. 251-286. A poor peasant, father of a family, joins the militia. Regrets are not slow in coming. A tragic sequel. *For everyone.*

村居日記 p. 287-314. cf. no. 216. *For everyone.*

There are some details in three of the above stories that are not for young readers.

220. 月球旅行記 *TRIP TO THE MOON*   1 vol. 196 p. by   周楞伽
1940   山城書店

A journey to the moon etc. in the style of Jules Verne. *For everyone.*

221. 小泥人歷險記 *ADVENTURE OF A DOLL*   1 vol. 170 p. by   周楞伽
3rd. edit. 1941   山城書店

Stories for children. *For everyone.*

222. 吳鈎集 *THE INVALUABLE*   1 vol. 226 p. by   周黎庵
1930   宇宙風社

Critics on literature and three short stories without interest. *For everyone.*

223. 瘋狂世界 *THE WORLD IS MAD*   1 vol. 117 p. by   周嫩春
1946   象萬書店

Love story of two young people. Very risky descriptions. *Not to be recommended to anyone.*

224. 輕煙 *NEBULOUS*   1 vol. 207 p. by   周楞伽
1941 Shanghai, 群立出版社

A young teacher leaves his school to go to Shanghai to work for "social progress". He thus abandons his sickly young wife for whom he has nothing but pity.

After he has arrived in the big city, and in spite of the warnings of enlightened friends he falls in love from the very first day with a "beautiful" lady teacher. He becomes a willing dupe and sacrifices for her his affections, his friends, and his ideals.

In time his eyes are opened but only when it is too late.

This book may serve as a lesson to young people open to advice. *Not for everybody.*

225. 可愛的學校   *A WELL LIKED SCHOOL*   1 vol. 305 p. by   **周天籟**
1930   春江書局

Description of life in a school. *For everyone.*

226. 小老虎   *TIGER CUB (Story of a boy)*   1 vol. 396 p. by   **周天籟**
1936   三民圖書公司

Story of a young man, his infancy, his life as a student. his adolescence, his adventures, and his misfortunes. *For everyone.*

227. 甜甜日記   *THE DIARY OF DULCIDA*   1 vol. by   **周天籟**
1941   三民圖書公司

The diary of the adventures of a little boy; of his life at home, at school, and his relations with his little girl friend. Fresh and entertaining. *For everyone.*

228. 風流千金   *THE FLIRTING DAMSEL*   2 vol. 324 p. by   **周天籟**
1946   文光書局

Still another book fit only to throw upon a dirt cart. Here is described the scandalous life of a girl in Shanghai. *Proscribed.*

229. 梅花姑娘   *MISS PLUM*   2 vol. 328 p. by   **周天籟**
1946   文光書局

Below average. Conversations and letters between two young people. In the end they get married against the will of the girl's mother. The girl is not, for that matter, a model of filial devotion.

Very objectionable from the moral point of view.

230. 春之戀   *SPRING LOVE*   1 vol. 156 p. by   **周天籟**
1946   勵力出版社

A student who is already married succeeds in seducing a young divorcee after giving her a promise of marriage.

The author approves of divorce, free love, and misconduct. There are no obscene descriptions in this book but the atmosphere is immoral. *Proscribed.*

231. 亭子間嫂嫂 *THE LADY TENANT IN THE ATTIC*   2 vol. 719 p. by   **周天籟**

In over seven hundred pages of small print we are given the story of a girl forced by circumstances into secret prostitution. The story is told by a neighbour who is a novelist by profession and has to write all day long to earn his living. The author tries visibly to present an apology for the girl. He has certainly read and is influenced by "La Dame aux Camélias", to which he alludes more than once.

According to the author, the heroine of his story is reduced to the circumstances he describes entirely because of the fault of society and the inequality of social conditions.

Although the woman concerned has certain good points to her character, and the book does not contain many crude details, it is easy to understand that it can be put into the hands of *only those who are aware of its dangers.*

232. 風流寡婦 *THE MERRY WIDOW* 1 vol. 250 p. by 周天籟
1947

The detailed recital of the excesses of a young widow in Shanghai. Although the details are not too precise or too exciting to the imagination, nevertheless the nature of the story is enough to place it in the proscribed class. *Proscribed.*

233. 花月良宵 *NIGHT OF TRANQUILLITY* 1 vol. 140 p. by 周天籟
1946 春明書店

The sentimental experiences of a rascal aged sixteen years who passes off as a pupil of an art school.
Here the author gives us another proof that his moral level is very low. *Proscribed.*

234. 多產集 *FERTILE* 1 vol. 233 p. by 周文（何穀天）
1936 文化生活 *See Biogr. 61*

A collection of narratives describing the life of soldiers and the small happenings of daily life. *For everyone.*

235. 烟苗季 *WHEN THE OPIUM PLANTS ARE BUDDING* 1 vol. 380 p. by 周 文
文化生活

In this book the author describes military life, and especially what happens in a certain headquarters. He deals with life, hate, dissensions and jealousies, and the revenge taken by high officers.
The book ends without satisfying the reader who wonders how the story should end. Nevertheless it is an interesting volume and agreeable to read, although it contains some crude expressions. *For everyone.*

236. 烟苗季,後部 *SEQUEL TO THE PRECEDENT* 1 vol. by 周 文
2nd. edit. 1938 文化生活

The author has decided to narrate in this volume the development of the events given us in the preceding book. And he does so by giving us an extremely dramatic solution.
The sequel, however, is not as interesting as the first book. And again he has no tendency to avoid crude words and expressions. *For everyone.*

237. 在白森鎮 *AT THE WHITE FOREST VILLAGE* 1 vol. 109 p. by 周 文
1940 戾友復興圖書公司

A mandarin puts down his rival, who in turn, puts down the man who has taken his place. *For everyone.*

238. 東京小品 *MEMOIRS OF TOKIO* 1 vol. 297 p. by 周簷剝

Part. I. The author describes the Japanese at home and does it sympathetically.
Part II. The life of Chinese students in Japan of the hardness of their lot, and also of their sentimental adventures. A journey to West Lake in Hangchow.
Part. III. Subjects from actual life.
For everyone.

239. 鄉村 *VILLAGE*　　　　　　　　1 vol. 173 p. by 周毓英
1934 民族書局 *See Biogr.* 41

A village revolution. A rich landowner exploits his tenants. They get together and state their terms, which the landowner refuses to meet. They strike. He tries to force them into submission but they force their conditions upon him.

For the benefit of all, the rich man's possessions are taken charge of by a committee of family heads.

Objectionable because of the description of an attempted rape.

240. 秋心集 *MELANCHOLY AS IN AUTUMN*　　　1 vol. 198 p. by 朱企霞
1937 北新書局

A collection of poems, narratives and philosophical discussions.
1) Lyricism and poetry with the figure of the well-beloved in the background.
2) Memories of the mountains of the West.
3) Story of the saw.
Considerations follow on a variety of subjects. *For everyone.*

241. 孱兒集　　　　　　　　　　　　1 vol. 424 p. by 朱企霞
1929 北新書局

A collection of tales.
1) The author pretends that he is Maupassant and makes the characters of that wellknown writer pass before us with their particular characteristics.
2) A certain gentleman makes new friends in Peking. He expects them to visit him but as he has to wait a long time he gets impatient and goes to the barber. In the meantime, his friends arrive, but finding that he is not in, they go away again. He runs after them but in vain. Disappointed, he goes away.
3) A married couple review their married life. They have regrets and make good resolutions.
4) A disfigured man falls into the hands successively of two wives who are very devoted to him. He is rather soured but in the end, he learns how to smile again.
5) During a flood. Tittle tattle and extortion of the women.
6) A student is forced into marriage. He learns to love his wife and is loved in return. In the long run, however, he has enough of it, and goes away.

Other tales are included, all without much value. The author allows himself too many liberties from the moral point of view.
For mature people.

242. 愛侶恩愁 *MIXED WITH LOVE & HATRED*　　1 vol. 178 p. by 朱鴻儒
1946 正氣書局

The book opens with an ill-assorted household, where the husband is out of work, while the wife, who has come from a large and wealthy family, loves luxury and leaves her husband for anyone who can give her some of the comforts of life.

The hero eventually finds a job in Shanghai. He goes, leaving his wife behind. She passes her time with loose companions who help her to spend the money painfully earned by her husband. After a while, she separates from him completely and marries a friend who happens to come along.

Many years after, the first husband who has become very rich and powerful, comes to visit his former wife in the miserable hotel that she lives in with the children of her second marriage. There he gives her a magnificent present, for he has always been conscious of his responsibilities. And he takes away her eldest child who is his own son.

The book ends with the marriage of the hero. His first wife attends the wedding in the role of a discreet and jealous spectator.

As the book contains many crude passages *it is not to be recommended to anyone.*

243. 晦明 *DUSK*   1 vol. 214 p. by 朱炳蓀
1939   和平印書局   *See Biogr. 45*

A newly-married couple: the husband is a peaceful, industrious man, very much in love with his wife. She is rather childish; she was in love with her husband while they were at school, but now she feels more like a sister towards him.

A returned student makes a pass at the young woman; she falls for him without, however, being unfaithful to her husband. Gradually she realizes that this young man is just a mean self-indulgent fellow. She then throws him over and confesses her fault to her husband, who shows kind understanding. They start on a trip to revive their first love.

A beautiful book that shows clearly the danger of unrestrained love. A few passages are slightly *objectionable.*

244. 一個苦兒努力記 *HE WAS AN ABANDONED CHILD*   1 vol. 448 p. by 朱平君
1940   國光書店

A book written with the aim of edifying young readers. It is the story of an abandoned infant who makes his way in life. In the end, he has the happiness of finding his mother and of obtaining a good position. *For everyone.*

245. 金銀花 *GOLDEN & SILVER FLOWERS*   1 vol. 101 p. by 朱瘦菊
2nd. edit. 1946   正氣書局

A novel which has for theme how the rich exploit the poor.

A family where the daughter has been extremely imprudent, select a poor relative as her husband with the object of saving their face. The young man is cajoled into the marriage with magnificent promises.

After the baby is born, however, he is no longer needed, and divorce is proposed. Tormented by the caprices of his wife and the intolerance of his father-in-law, the young husband goes out of his mind. *For adults.*

246. 背影 *MY FATHER*   1 vol. 129 p. by 朱自清
9th. edit. 1940   開明書店   *See Biogr. 46*

Of the family of the author, of his journeys by land and by sea, and of his surroundings.
For everyone.

247. 逾越節 *THE PASSOVER*   1 vol. 87 p. by 朱雯
1939   文化生活出版社   *See Biogr. 47*

1/Description of the agony of Jesus-Christ.
2/A faithfull servant.
3/The story of Oedipus.
For everyone.

248. 月夜 *MOONLIT NIGHT*   1 vol. 86 p. by 川島（章廷謙）
1928 2-nd edition   北大新潮社   *See Biogr. 11*

Amorous dreams and aspirations; dangerous for young people and unprofitable for all.

249. 怨鳳啼凰 *THE SORROWFUL PAIR*   4 vol. 166, 172, 178, 172 pp. by   鍾吉宇
1931   上海鄉雲圖書公司

The action takes place in Shanghai. The author presents a young "bourgeois" family: a virtuous wife, the only nice character in the book, and a thoughtless husband. After a few weeks of marriage he carries on a flirtation with an old girl friend. This results in divorce. The book ends with the reconciliation of the married couple. In the meantime the author describes the life of young men in Shanghai, of a few emancipated girls and some debauchees.

The book is unsuitable for all classes of readers.

250. 離巢燕 *AWAY FROM HOME*   1 vol. 200 p. by   鍾超塵
1936   北京小實報版

The story of a young girl, unwanted by her parents and adopted by a Buddhist nun. She is initiated in magic art which will enable her to help the oppressed and avenge injustice. *For all.*

251. 幽僻的陳莊 *THE ISOLATED TOWN*   1 vol. 403 p. by   儁 聞
1935   北平文心書業社

An interesting book for those who want to know village life in China. The author describes a big family: Ch'en. They are rich, influential and exploit their fellow villagers to enrich themselves. He then introduces us to another family: T'ien, reduced to poverty in a short time because of the son's negligence. A true rascal, he, together with a friend, defies the Ch'en family. He puts fire to their crops and goes unpunished.

The book deals with everything that interests a farmer: the crops, the ways of getting a good price for them, floods, taxation by the military, etc. Village life is well described: virtuous and other women, clashes and enmity between old Ch'en and young T'ien who court the same woman. The book ends with the threats of T'ien against Ch'en.

The author also describes sympathetically the wretched life of Mrs. T'ien, forsaken by her husband; also Mrs. Hsiao-pei, at first a virtuous woman, who yields to temptation.

The book is well written. Three passage (pp. 26, 27, 28; 299; 395) call for some reserve. *For informed readers.*

252. 三月天 *THE THIRD MOON*   1 vol. 70 p. by   屈曲夫
1940   文化生活

逼   A father of a poor family disembarrasses himself of a girl baby who is born and whom he cannot afford to keep. His young son has seen him and disinters the infant!
霧   Adventure of two urchins.
碰   A quarrel between two jolly dogs which comes to an arrangement. The one in the wrong, who is a very conceited fellow, is glad not to have to kowtow in apology to the other.
三月天   Some portraits and ordinary incidents.

The author is not afraid of round words. *For everyone.*

253. 花蕊夫人 *A LADY AT COURT*   1 vol. 51 p. by   范烟橋
1946   日新出版社

1) A concubine is taken away. She commits suicide in preference to forfeiting her honour. The title is the name of the concubine.
2) A poet in hot water with two fiancées.
3) A girl (Huang) is captured by Manchu soldiers. She becomes the wife of the King of Nanking and presents him with a daughter.

4) A celebrated damsel of the end of the Ming.

5) A pirate chief is driven out of Taiwan. He seeks refuge in Siam where he saves the dynasty but perishes miserably himself.

A few tales follow of the Manchu conquest. *For everyone.*

254. 風塵集 *TURMOIL OF THE WORLD*   1 vol. 151 p. by **方　敬**
1937　晨友圖書公司　*See Biogr. 49*

A collection of short narratives, containing the story of a manufacturer, family memories, story of a poor family, of an original person, childhood memories, story of a rich family, meeting a friend, rivalries between officers, of religion, etc.

Written in easy language. *For everyone.*

255. 枕上集 *BEDSIDE VOLUME*   1 vol. 246 p. by **方　西**
1938　商務印書館

1. A rich man in search of a second concubine. *Not for everyone.*
2. An obedient son is ridiculed. *Not for everyone.*
3. Injustice of the rich to the poor. *For everyone.*
4. A wife sacrifices herself in her own way to procure opium for her husband. *For everyone.*
5. Tribulations of a poor farmer. *For everyone.*
6. Concerning a poor man who is expropriated from land. *For everyone.*

For mature people.

256. 春風楊柳 *THE SPRING TIME WILLOW*   1 vol. by **方奈何**
1938　昌明印刷所　*See Biogr. 51*

This book relates how one young man was loved by five girls but, being very generous, they decided to move away in order to let him choose for himself. The result of this was that none of the five was chosen.

It contains a number of immoral scenes. *To be strictly reserved.*

257. 管他呢 *LET HIM BE*   1 vol. 224 p. by **芳艸（彭家煌）**
1928　北新書局　*See Biogr. 127*

A student haunted by the memory of women loses his mind.

This book is a mass of ridiculous stuff that *everyone should be dissuaded from reading.*

258. 桃園 *THE PEACH ORCHARD*   1 vol. 147 p. by **廢名（馮文炳）**
3rd edition 1930　開明書店　*See Biogr. 57*

A dozen short stories. They are written in lively and good style. The descriptions are harmless. *This book can be read by everyone.*

259. 橋 *BRIDGE*   1 vol. 384 p. by **廢　名**
1932　開明書店

A large volume without much meaning or action. The author describes the life of a little boy and of two little girls. Their lives are quite ordinary.

The book is written in fastidious style, but the question occurs during its perusal, whether the multiple relations between the three heros are normal, and whether they are an example to place before Chinese children? *For everyone.*

260. 伍子胥 *WU TZU HSU* 1 vol. 111 p. by 馮　至
1946 文化生活出版社 *See Biogr.* 53

An episode of ancient history told in easy modern language. The author transports us to the time of Confucius and relates to us the history of the King of Ch'u and how his faithful servitor, Wu Tzu-hsu, had been treated. The story gives in detail the legend of the second son of the above hero. *For everyone.*

261. 春華露濃 *SPRING DEW* 1 vol. 193 p. by 馮　蕎
1941 上海萬象書屋

The life of prostitutes in Shanghai. *A bad book which should be banned.*

262. 糕檲西施 *THE LOVELY WAITRESS* 1 vol. 155 p. by 馮若梅
1942 二酉出版社

The author relates how a country girl accidentally met with a number of dangerous situations. Although bad luck followed her, she resisted the temptations and protected her chastity.

This book is very interesting but the rather vivid description of the situations with which the girl met, *makes it unsuitable for younger people.*

263. 八年 *EIGHT YEARS* 1 vol. 175 p. by 鳳　子
1945 萬葉書店 *See Biogr.* 52

This book is composed of two parts. The first contains a number of sketches on various subjects, and the second has several character portrayals among which are a few rather worldly figures. *May be read by anyone.*

264. 綠綠堂隨筆 *SKETCHES BY FENG TZE-K'AI* 1 vol. 97 p. by 豐子愷
10th. edit. 1946 開明書店 *See Biogr.* 56

A series of short articles. The author tells of his family, and his children; of painting, education, and art. He also gives a child's diary. This book has plenty of humour but its philosophy is supercial. *For everyone.*

265. 車箱社會 *IN THE THIRD CLASS COACH* 1 vol. 255 p. by 豐子愷
1935 瓦友圖書公司

1. Reminiscences of a journey in a train.
2. On a theme dear to true Chinese.
3. Boring ceremonies.
4. Misfortunes caused by friends.
5. Rich children and poor children.
6. The misery of the poor.
7. Anxiety over examinations.
8. Views of cities.
9. A rustic hairdresser on a boat.
10-15. Scenes on a boat and anecdotes.
16. Long live the snows of yesteryear!
17. Fishing.
18. For and against vegetarians.
19-21. Notes on painting.
22. Everything is relative.
23. Various pastimes.
24. Memories.
25. Thoughts suggested by the season of great heat.
26. Rumours of the town.
27. Art and books.
28. Journey in a bus.

For everyone.

266. 率眞集 *UNSOPHISTICATED* 1 vol. 189 p. by 豐子愷
1946 萬葉書店

1st. Part. Description in three chapters of the beautiful house of the chief character and of Japanese atrocities.

弘一法師 Story of a monk who is a musician and a painter.

掉丐師 Describing the life of this monk who is the master of the author.

沙坪小屋的鵝 A goose who guards the house like a dog.

逃難 Flight before the Japanese.

2nd. Part. On art and especially on painting.

3rd. Part. Short tales of ordinary life.

For everyone.

267. 竹林的故事 *TALE OF A BAMBOO GROVE* 1 vol. 206 p. by **馮文炳**
1925 *See Biogr. 57*

A great number of stories, mostly about family events. *For all.*

268. 熱情的女人 *AN EMOTIONAL WOMAN* 1 vol. 110 p. by **馮又奇**
1946 上海明星書店

This book is written by a certain Dr. Chang Ching-sheng (張兢生) whose books are banned by the police. That is the reason why his subsequent work is issued under another name. *Proscribed.*

269. 春在人間 *SPRING IS HERE* 1 vol. 202 p. by **馮又奇**
1946 大中華書局

About a young man who loves two girls and is loved in return. After a year, this false situation is discovered by the two young ladies who both break with him.

The book is full of sentimentalities. *Not for young readers.*

270. 寫郎憔悴 *ON ACCOUNT OF HIM* 1 vol. 204 p. by **馮又奇**
1946 中華書局

A great deal of ink has been wasted on very little matter. We are told in this book of an unhappy love, but it proves a very dull affair. *May be read by anyone.*

271. 落花夢 *MIDST FALLING PETALS* 2 vols. 158 p. and 176 p. by **馮又奇**

A Chinese student in Japan becomes engaged to a Japanese girl. Recalled home, his dying mother forces him to marry a Chinese girl. The young man obeys but declares to his wife that he does not consider her as such. After which, his fiancée arrives, but when she learns of his marriage, she returns home. Whereupon our hero turns to his Chinese wife. *For everyone.*

272. 海棠紅 *THE TREES ARE BLOOMING* 2 vol. 219 p. by **馮又奇**
春明書店

The book presents a sory of a young girl who lived with a widow as a companion. One day she saw a young handsome youth on the street and fell in love with him. After some time she told about her love to her companion who offered to act as a "go-between". Afterwards, the widow mentioned all this to her friend who, pretending to be "the handsome youth", visited the girl by night and received a charm as a token, but lost it. Another man, finding the charm, resolved to visit the girl but he lost his way and entered the room of the land-lord, who was killed during the quarrel. The girl thought that the handsome youth was the murderer and swore revenge. The trial took place in Shanghai and the heroine was married to the "handsome youth" without knowing it, but finding out his identity she planned to kill him. At the end the guilty ones were found and thus the life of the handsome youth was saved.

As this book has a number of daring and vulgar descriptions, *everyone should be advised against reading it.*

273. 香海恨 *REGRET OF ROMANCING*   2 vol. 246 p. by 馮玉奇
                                                                    1939 上海智識出版社

This book narrates how Kan Yü-hai was introduced to Mei Hsiang-lien with whom he fell in love. After he had brought her to Shanghai — where a friend asked him to cooperate in editing a newspaper — they lived together for more than one year as brother and sister, since lack of funds prevented them from getting married. In spite of the temptations they remained true to each other. After a short illness Hsiang-lien died and Yü-hai joined the Chinese Red Cross.

This novel contains a number of realistic passages but ignores the realities of life. *With caution even for informed readers.*
(The same novel is published under the title: 孤島淚)

274. 紙醉金迷 *THE SURRENDER TO TEMPTATION*
                          2 vol. 170 & 148 pp. by 馮玉奇 and 余碧珺女士
                                                                    1940 春明書店

Story of a very rich family. The father who was a wild youth lived with a woman twenty years ago, and had a son, but soon left her and married someone else. From her he had a daughter. The illegal son saved the daughter from death and the latter asked her father to help the rescuer who was very poor. When the father came to help his daughter's rescuer he discovered that he was his son.

After some time misfortunes fell on the family and they became very poor. The father killed himself. His eldest daughter ran away, while the eldest son killed his mistress and her new lover, who happened to be his own brother. Their mother was sent to an insane asylum. *Everybody should be advised against reading his book.*

275. 燕翦春愁 *SWALLOWS ARE HERE*   2 vol. 226 p. by 馮玉奇
                                                                    1941 中央書店

Love story about two young revolutionists and three girls. This novel is very interesting and is full of tragic-comical situations.

The book describes the marriage of one of the young men with one of the girls, thus breaking off with the other who was his fiancée. At the end the young wife died thus straightening out the situation. The other youth married the third girl.

As this book holds a number of risky details it may be read *only by informed readers.*

276. 舞宮春艷 *ROMANCE IN THE DANCING HALL* 2 vol. 172, 192 p. by 馮玉奇
                                                          3rd. edit. 1941 大文書局

Exactly the same book as 香妃怨 by 張恨水. It is difficult to understand how the same book can be attributed to two different authors, and such books often run into several editions!!! *Proscribed.*

277. 陌頭柳色 *WHEN THE WILLOWS BUD*   1 vol. 238 p. by 馮玉奇
                                                                    1941 新華印書館

This book presents the story of a Huang Hai-ming, a young student from Hang-chow. During his stay in Shanghai he got acquainted with Chin Ling — who happened to be also a native of Hang-chow. He fell in love with her and, though one of his cousins was deeply in love with him, he preferred Chin Ling and finally married her. His cousin lost all hope and disappeared.

Although this book presents a number of rather sentimental love passages and in spite of its many scenes of disaster and tragedy, *it may be read by anyone.*

278. 春花秋月 *CHANGING ON THE SEASONS*   1 vol. 118 p. by **馮玉奇**
                                                                  1942 義生印書舘

This story narrates a life of a tailor's daughter, who was so poor that she could not even pay her school fees. She allowed a friend to help her but when he was accused by another friend she left him and lived with the latter. After some time he left her. This act enraged the girl for she was pregnant and swore to avenge herself. Later she met her seducer without being recognized. They took to each other and, as his former wife had given him his divorce, he married her. She remained true to her resolve and killed him on their wedding-night. *For informed readers.*

279. 婚變 *THE CLEAVAGE*   2 vol. 130 & 157 pp. by **馮玉奇**
                                                                  1942 上海智識書店

The author describes a big rich family which lived in Shanghai. It consisted of five sons, three of whom were married while the fourth refused to marry. His fiancée was given to his youngest brother, but owing to her tuberculosis she died before the marriage took place. After some time the sister of the deceased was given him as a wife but he could not forget his first wife. After a long period he came to love his wife but she died in child-birth.

This book contains a number of interesting details about the life of big families. As this novel contains a number of daring passages it *calls for strict reserve.*

280. 泣殘紅 *THERE IS BLOOD IN HER EYES*   1 vol. 254 p. by **馮玉奇**
                                                                  1943 廣藝書局

A young man falls in love with a girl and at the same time with her cousin. The girl leaves for Peking and falls into bad company into which she marries. Soon after she dies for the country.

Some immoral passages are given. In by far the greater majority of his books, this author does not trouble himself the slightest about morals, and his heros are not activated by any moral law. *Proscribed.*

281. 百花洲 *THE ISLE OF FLOWERS*   1 vol. 188 p. by **馮玉奇**
                                                                  1943 廣益書局

A young boatwoman is betrothed to a young professor who abandons her, suspecting her of misconduct. She is, however, innocent.

After a number of casual love affairs, he discovers her in the company of an intimate friend. In the meantime he has learnt that she was innocent, but he has fallen in love with another. The book ends with two happy couples.

Without indulging in actual obscenity, the author grases the edge of the abyss. *Proscribed.*

282. 金屋淚痕 *THE LADY HAS TEARS*   1 vol. 246 p. by **馮玉奇**
                                                                  1943 華英書局

We are told of the misfortunes of a poor girl of good character, whose fiance is imprisoned, and who is seduced by the manager of a factory who is an accomplished rake. In the end, the latter is killed by the prisoner, who has been set free, and the hero and heroine meet again. The heroine, however, loses her husband after only a few months of marriage.

This book contains several immoral passages. *To be condemned.*

283. 江上烟波 *RIVER MIST*   1 vol. 280 p. by **慈水馮玉奇**
          2nd. edit. 1945 春明書店

A hotchpotch of love affairs between young people who, mutually sacrificing them-selves, are forced to change the object of their affections, but continue to revolve in the same circle.

A well sustained story containing several admirable characters. *For everyone.*

284. 一代紅顏 *BEAUTY DOES'NT LAST*   2 vol. 136, 183 pp., by **馮玉奇**
          2nd edition 1946 正華書局

愛紅 a young girl, falls in love with a young man who is also coveted by a rich young widow. Driven by jealousy, she adopts the young girl and thus gets hold of the young man.

愛紅 then turns her attention to the son of a general and marries him soon afterwards. A few days after the marriage, she kills her father-in-law and her husband, who were responsible for her father's death. She then poisons herself, advising her former fiancé to work for the good of the country.

There are some troubling passages, and the vengeance scene is objectionable. *Not to be recommended to anyone.*

285. 明珠淚 *THE DEBUTANTE'S SORROW*   1 vol. 120 p. by **馮玉奇**
          1946 廣藝書局

A very wealthy man in the decline of life, decides to divide his possessions between his three daughters. The two elder ones are bad wives, but the youngest is a good girl, who is secretly engaged to a poor young man.

On the day of the partition, the elder sisters succeed in deceiving their father by flattery, whereas the younger one is cursed by him on account of her straightforwardness. The result is that the former receive all the wealth, and the younger sister nothing at all. She leaves in the company of her fiancé, with poverty as her part.

There are some rather troubling passages. *For grown-up people.*

286. 夜鶯啼月 *THE NIGHTINGALE*   2 vol. 174 p. by **馮玉奇**
          1946 春明書店

A young girl falls the victim of a Shanghai dandy. She leaves her son with a friend and returns to her native village where she marries.

Ten years afterward, her husband dies and she returns to Shanghai. She takes with her the daughter born in the country. In the big city, her two children meet, and as they do not know they are brother and sister, they fall in love. The illigitimate son abuses his sister, but when he learns the real identity of his friend, he commits suicide.

After these events, the mother returns to the country with her daughter.

The author is well-intentioned as he wishes to show the dangers of such a place as Shanghai, but his manner of doing it is not to be admired. Also certain details of the book, together with the suicide, are to be deplored. *Not to be recommended to anyone.*

287. 啼笑皆非 *STUNNED*   1 vol. 165 p. by **馮玉奇**
          1946 春明書店

The story of the misfortunes encountered by a very courageous girl when engulfed by the Japanese invasion. After being deceived by a good for nothing, she is sold into a house of prostitution. She then finds herself a concubine, and again she changes her condition in becoming a dancing girl. In the end, she marries a man much older than herself. This man has a son whose wife is much older than himself, and it transpires that she is no other than the mother of the heroine. Thus the mother has become the daughter-in-law of her own daughter!

Such a situation causes readers to moralize, and it would be better if the author was satisfied with such an effect instead of exhausting his cerebral muscles to entertain people with far-fetched predicaments. With him, marriage is a very unstable institution, and this book does not fail to contain a number of crude descriptions. *Not to be recommended to anyone.*

288. 歧途 *ASTRAY* 　　　　　　1 vol. 139 p. by 馮玉奇
　　　　　　　　　　　　　　　　　　　　　1946 正氣書局

The aim of the author in this book is not reprehensible as he wishes to put youth on guard against the dangers of loose relations.

The fall of a girl who is already affianced is described, and also the means employed by a man of no morals to pervert women.

The book, however, *is not to be recommended* because it contains too many crude passages, besides which, it exploits the desire for vengeance.

289. 燈紅酒綠 *HERE'S TO THE LADIES* 　1 vol. 209 p. by 馮玉奇
　　　　　　　　　　　　　　　　　　　　　1946 大中華書局

A young man falls in love with a girl. He is of open and affable character, and he is accapared by the heroine and her family.

A denoument occurs when the hero confesses that he is a spy of low extraction, but in spite of this, the marriage is consummated, because the girl love him for what he is, and does not care about his past.

This book lacks action and contains too many sentimentalities for young readers. *Not for everyone.*

290. 霓裳曲 *LIEBESLIED* 　　　　　　1 vol. 79 p. by 馮玉奇
　　　　　　　　　　　　　　　　　　　　　1946 晨鐘書局

A young girl revenges herelf on two suitors who have killed her fiance. Contains several immoral scenes. *To be condemned.*

291. 香花春濃 *THE FLOWERS GIVE SCENT* 　1 vol. 145 p. by 馮玉奇
　　　　　　　　　　　　　　　　　　　　　　1946

A young student falls in love with a girl who is poor but of a good family. After many denouements they end in being united in marriage.

This romance is pure nonsense and of no value.

One page is very crude. *Not to be recommended to anyone.*

292. 浮雲遮月 *THE MOON IS VEILED* 　　1 vol. 142 p. by 馮玉奇
　　　　　　　　　　　　　　　　　　　　　　1946

A young man, handsome, moneyed, and of good conduct, is the centre of attraction of three girls. They are, his cousin who is a serious girl of good character, the daughter of a general — she is poor but also of good character — and a coquette. The second is eliminated because of a seeming inconstancy, and the third whom the young man loves very much, dies of chagrin after a misunderstanding, so in the end only the cousin remains.

The hero is full of admirable sentiments throughout the story, and shows weakness for only a moment, when his house is burnt and his mother perishes in the flames.

This romance should have been a very beautiful one, but unfortunately it is marred by a number of descriptions that, although they are not pushed too far, are nevertheless obscene. *Proscribed.*

293. 鵑 *CUCKOO*   1 vol. 155 p. by **馮玉奇**
                                    1946   上海永康書店

A romanticised account of war. We are told of the resistance of the inhabitants of a certain village, and in particular of several young people. This book might be instructive should a new war break out.

Here and there it is a little crude. *For everyone.*

294. 遺產恨 *CURSE ON THE INHERITANCE*   1 vol. 138 p. by **馮玉奇**
                                    1946   廣藝書局

A brother and a sister try to obtain from a maternal uncle the property that he has appropriated from them.

A good many pages on a dull story.

Contains some light-minded touches. *Not for everyone.*

295. 秋水長天 *THE RIVER REFLECTING THE AUTUMN SKY*
                          1 vol. 163 p. by **馮玉奇**
                                    1946   春明書店

An episode of the resistence under the Japanese occupation. Unfortunately the sensual and sentimental element dominates. It is a pity that the author is not able to remain on a more elevated level and mixes patriotic sentiments with too intimate scenes of love-making. *Not to be recommended to anyone.*

296. 春閨怨 *HER COMPLAINT*   1 vol. 196 p. by **馮玉奇**
                                    1946   春明書店

A girl of good character is given in marriage to the son of a "collaborator", whose family suspect her of infidelity and therefore treat her harshly. Her husband is a good-for-nothing. He smokes opium and frequents the society of dancing girls.

At the end of the war, the head of the family and his son are arrested by the police, and the family is reduced to misery, besides being covered with shame.

The heroine engages on a patriotic course.

For adults only due to certain crude details. *Not for everyone.*

297. 燕語鶯啼 *THE BIRDS ARE SINGING*   1 vol. 164 p. by **馮玉奇**
                                    1946   春明書店

A romanticised story in which we are told of the acts of collaborators, and the exploits of the resistence to the Japanese invasion.

Contains certain details to be reprouved. *Not for everyone.*

298. 春殘夢斷 *GONE WITH SPRING*   1 vol. 162 p. by **馮玉奇 邵鈞軒**
                                    1946   武林書店

In order to save his ailing mother, a son becomes a thief. His gesture is, moreover, of no use because his mother dies. He is thrown into prison and his sister, Hsiao Yü (小玉), sells herself as a slave in order to buy a coffin for the mother.

The son of the house where Hsiao Yü is a slave treats her well, and even falls in love with her. His mother, however, throws her out upon learning that her brother is a thief. The son takes her back into the house but Hsiao Yü dies under the maltreatment of his mother. The son, Chung-ming, (仲明) then takes her corpse to give it decent burial, and curses his mother and a jealous cousin.

This book makes interesting reading, but is not to be recommended to young people because of the too great intimacy between Chung-ming and Hsiao Yü and the curses against the mother. *Not for everyone.*

299. 民族魂 *ESPRIT DE CORPS*   1 vol. 157 p. by **馮玉奇**
                                                 1946 廣藝書局

Another book in which this author takes patriotism as his theme, and illustrates this sentiment in describing the resistance in a village under Japanese occupation.

Heaven grant that he writes more books of this kind, and gives up the sentimental romances with loose morals that he usually indulges in. *For everyone.*

300. 妾無罪 *THE LADY IS INNOCENT*   2 vol. 145. 150 p. by **馮玉奇**
                                                 2nd. edit. 1946 春明書店

Decidedly Mr. Feng Yü-ch'i has very little imagination or rather, his imagination is always haunted by the same impure images, unbelievable encounters, ambiguous rendez-vous, beastliness and filth, incests, young people of different sexes sleeping in the same bed, and so forth.

He does not go quite so far as pornography in this volume, but he touches the limit in his scenes of love-making. *Proscribed.*

301. 我一生之情史 *MY ROMANCE*   1 vol. 62 p. by **馮玉奇**
                                                 1946 上海宇宙書店

A man who is married to a woman whom he does not love, tells of his experiences and sentimental life with a girl. *Not to be recommended to anyone.*

302. 比翼鴛鴦 *CLOSE AS TURTLE-DOVES*   1 vol. 159 p. by **馮玉奇**

雪箏 loves 琴仙 and she is loved in return, but her father gives her in marriage to another. On her wedding night, she is abducted from the bridal chamber and made a prisoner. The instigator of this event was no other than 枝 , an old school mate, who became desperate when Hsueh-cheng was prefered by the man she loved.

After one year, the frustrated husband marries Ying-chih, believing Hsueh-cheng is dead. Hsueh-cheng marries Ch'in Hsien.

This book is found on all the stalls and must be read by a great number of people. The plot is well sustained but owing to a rather risky scene on p. 79, *it cannot be recommended.*

303. 雁南歸 *SOUTH BOUND FLIGHT*   1 vol. 101 p. by **馮玉奇**
                                                 1946 晨鐘書局

A book without much unity of action.

The following are described: young girls looking for employment in Shanghai, another girl attached to a young man, a good liver flirting with a dancer, a rich old man who wants to found a hospital, etc.

Contains a rather crude scene. *For adults.*

304. 綠窗艷影   *THE BEAUTY IN THE WINDOW*   1 vol. 104 p. by 馮玉奇
1946   晨鐘書局

Sequel of the preceding volume.

The two sisters fall in love, one with the good liver, and the other with the young man. The former is treated so badly, that she commits suicide. The latter sacrifices her love in favour of the girl friend of her lover, and kills the seducer of her sister. *For adults.*

305. 百合花開   *LILACS*   1 vol. 250 p. by 馮玉奇
1946   春明書店

Two young men fall in love with two girls, who are coverted at the same time by two men of ripe age. In the end the young men have the advantage.

Contains some troubling descriptions. *Not to be recommended to anyone.*

306. 鏡月花   *IMAGES*   1 vol. 148 p. by 馮玉奇
1946   廣藝書局

About a family quarrel. The only son is engaged. His sister wishes to obtain her share of the family fortune, on the insistence of a bad companion, who abuses her confidence and promises her marriage.

After the division has been made, the heroine discovers that her companion is already married, and he is nothing but a swindler. Upon this, she commits suicide after writing a letter to her brother, in which she expresses her regrets at the way she has treated him and their mother.

Contains some crude details. *Not for everyone.*

307. 血淚花   *BITTER TEARS*   1 vol. 114 p. by 馮玉奇
1946   春明書店

It is to the credit of this author that he seems to have made an effort to free himself for once from the dirt that he usually deals in.

In this story he gives us the history, alas fictitious, of a young heroine who sacrifices her love for her country. *For everyone.*

308. 罪   *IT IS A CRIME*   1 vol. 178, 180 p. by 馮玉奇
1946   上海武林書店

The author tells us of the inconstancies of Ssu-ma Ch'ao (司馬超) and his companions. They spent their time in gambling, in visits, and in amusing themselves with women of light reputations. One of these last, surnamed Chang, leads the hero onto a less dangerous path.

The environment described and certain offensive details *oblige us to dissuade everyone from reading this book.*

309. 孽   *RETRIBUTION*   1 vol. 370 p. by 馮玉奇
1946   武林書局

This book is the sequel of 罪. The author tells in detail a series of events that occur in the family Ssu-ma Ch'ao (司馬超), and those of his relatives.

The hero is imprisoned for misconduct, several members of his family die, and thirty-six other events occur, all without the slightest interest.

For adults only because of the amoral atmosphere.

310. 霄 *NOCTURNE* 1 vol. 299 p. by 馮玉奇
1946 武林書店

Mr. Feng Yu-ch'i is afraid that the readers of 罪 and 孽 are anxious about the fate of the heros described in those books, but we can assure him that no serious reader will be worried in the slightest regarding them. Such mediocre characters are not worth thinking about.

This volume is the sequel of the above mentioned novels and here is described part-cularly the sentimental life of 司馬光, and the moral resurrection of his eldest brother.

The developments and dialogues are drawn out to such an extent, that the reader is relieved to arrive at the last page. It is regretable that the author has stretched his material to fill a trilogy, and it would have been better if he had remained within the limits set by his talents. *Not for young readers.*

311. 花落春歸 *WHEN SPRING IS LEAVING* 1 vol. 150 p. by 馮玉奇
1946 春明書店

春明 a young student, is forced to accept as his bride a girl whom his parents had chosen for him. She soon reveals her true nature, and 春明, convinced that he will never be happy with her, leaves her, giving her her freedom.

He then falls in love with a poor girl whose name is 花枝. She suits him better than a rich girl, as she has a very good character. He marries her without the consent of his parents, and they live happily together.

When 春明 falls ill, his wife is compelled to exercise an improper profession in order to give him the necessary care. She, however, resists all temptations.

When her husband is restored to health, one of those who tried to seduce her, invents calumnies about her to her husband, so that he repudiates her. She avenges herself by killing the slanderer and dies in hospital in the presence of 春明 who has come to implore, her pardon.

Not to be recommended, on account of certain too realistic details.

312. 解語花 *SHE DOES UNDERSTAND* 1 vol. 139 p. by 馮玉奇
1946 春明書店

Two young people who are poor, but educated, marry after some developments that have threatened their happiness.

After their marriage, they live in decent circumstances and are happy. There is a friend, however, who has a weakness for the young wife, and because of him their happiness is in danger for a time. Things resume their proper course after his departure.

This book is for mature people only, because of the too pronounced feelings of vengeance in the characters, and because the relations depicted between the opposite sexes are too free. *Not for everyone.*

313. 花石因緣 *PREDESTINED LOVE* 1 vol. 102 p. by 馮玉奇
1946 春明書店

Sequel to the preceding book.

The tempter becomes a buddhist monk. After a time, he returns home but continues to observe his vows and refuses intimate relations with his wife. He cannot be persuaded to change his mind. *For adults.*

314. 黃金禍 *THE CURSE OF GOLD* 1 vol. 131 p. by 馮玉奇
1946 廣藝書局

We are given a picture of a disunited family at the mercy of an unfaithful compradore, who intrigues for the hand of the daughter of the house. *For adults.*

315. 藝海雙珠 *TWIN PEARLS*   1 vol. 122 p. by 馮玉奇
1946 廣藝書局

The action of this story occurs behind the scenes of a theatre. We are presented with two comedians who end up unhappily. The heroine, who is nevertheless a good girl, is abandoned by her fiance on the pretext that her theatrical life has changed her. She has, however, remained faithful to him.

There is nothing immoral in this book, but the general atmosphere *may be dangerous for the young.*

316. 千紫萬紅 *ADORNED WITH FLOWERS*   1 vol. 135 p. by 馮玉奇
1947 廣藝書局

Exactly the same book as that which has been reviewed under the title 藝海雙珠 *For adults.*

317. 鸞鳳鳴春 *CHANT DU PRINTEMPS*   1 vol. 178 p. by 馮玉奇
1943 華英書局

The author wishes to show how illicit love always ends badly but he does it by giving the most obscene descriptions, stopping at nothing. *Proscribed.*

318. 滄桑痕 *THE WAKE OF CHANGES*   1 vol. 136 p. by 馮玉奇
1946 上海滙文書局

The father of a family drives out one of his daughters and breaks with a friend who intercedes on her behalf. His daughter sets up housekeeping in the town with a friend and they consider themselves as married. In the meantime, the father has divided his goods between the two elder daughters who show him the door once they have laid a firm hold on the money. He then goes in search of his youngest daughter and is very kindly received. The two bad daughters are punished eventually by their fate.

Contains some very crude descriptions. *Not to be recommended to anyone.*

319. 海上風雲 *STORM ON THE SEA*   1 vol. 104 p. by 馮玉奇
1946 三益書店

The story of an unhappy marriage. The husband seeks his pleasure outside and neglects his wife. He is looking for a suitable party for his sister in order to derive some profit for himself. The book ends by an attempt at suicide by his wife.
Not to be recommended to anyone.

320. 歇浦春夢 *IS IT TRUE*   1 vol. 116 p. by 馮玉奇
1946 三益書店

The sequel to the preceding book. The wife in question recovers and gives some perverse advice to her own daughter. And the story ends with the flight of the heroine taking her daughter with her.
Not to be recommended to anyone because of the crude descriptions it contains.

321. 生之哀歌 *THE ELEGY OF LIFE*   1 vol. 149 p. by 馮玉奇
1946 上海滙文書局

Four friends who have graduated from university find themselves without money. No. 1 attempts suicide but is prevented by No. 2. No. 1 then decides to return to his native village. Nos. 2 and 3 find jobs. A girl installs herself with No. 2. The relations of the friends become complicated. In the end they all leave for the front. *For everyone.*

322. 蝶戀花 *ATTRACTED* 1 vol. 155 p. by 馮玉奇
1947 上海復新書局出版

The exploits of a lost sheep. A bad book that should be *proscribed*.

323. 花月爭艷 *REVELLING IN CHARM* 1 vol. 138 p. by 馮玉奇
上海廣益書局出版

Of a bad household. Madame misconducts herself. Her husband has seduced a wellgrown girl. A young man is engaged as tutor to the son of the house. He falls in love with the adopted daughter. Madame falls in love with the tutor, and in order to arrive at her ends, she engages the adopted daughter to a doddering rich man. The daughter, however, runs away with the tutor. *Not to be recommended to anyone.*

324. 傾國傾城 *FOR HER THE NATION CRUMBLES* 1 vol. 187 p. by 馮玉奇
1947 中央書店

A young doctor makes the acquaintance of two sisters. Soon after, he goes to Europe to finish his studies. When he returns, he finds the elder of the sisters married and the other a nurse in his own hospital. He marries the younger sister.

The elder becomes a widow after which she devotes herself to patriotic work. *For mature people.*

325. 慾海回瀾 *THE FINAL TEMPTATION* 1 vol. 157 p. by 馮玉奇
1947 春明書店

The story of a young woman who, after the reported death of her husband at the front, makes advances to a friend of the latter. The end is tragic. For the two heros of the story become buddhist monks while the heroine loses her mind. There are also some indecent details. *Not to be recommended to anyone.*

326. 人間地獄 *INFERNO ON EARTH* 1 vol. 143 p. by 馮玉奇
1947 上海廣大書局

Domestic stories that are hardly decent and that are somewhat "high" in odour. *Proscribed.*

327. 殘羽 *THE WINGS ARE INJURED* 1 vol. 113 p. by 島公 (潘晃公)
1933 天津書局 *See Biogr. 126*

Collection of stories and short novels. Several of them are well written and the author shows some psychological insight. He writes chiefly about love and pity. A small number of scenes are taken from the daily life of Chinese people.

From a moral point of view the book is acceptable, but a realistic scene in the story "Ping-yeh" *makes it unsuitable for young people.*

328. 情海生波, 隱刑 *AN INVISIBLE TORTURE* 2 vol. 118 & 189 pl. by 島公
1942 京津出版社

A young man returns from the city to his native village, meets a poor girl and seauces her. He loves her and promises to marry her later on. Back in the city he courts a rich girl whom he does not love, and marries. At the same time he carries on with a public woman. When his wife gets wind of this she asks for a divorce. At this juncture the young man meets the country girl he seduced. He still loves her and she has remained true to him — but he asks her to sacrifice their love lest his wife should hear of it. The girl, who has a noble disposition, consents and, secretly, commits suicide. His wife, having collected proofs of his infidelity, insists on and obtains a divorce. This does not move the young man very much as he feels sure of the country-girl's affection. He goes back to his village in search of her, fails, and dies in utter wretchedness.

Many objectionable descriptions, especially in the first volume. *To be banned.*

329. 生還   *THE RETURN*   1 vol. 318 p. by 毘　工
                                                              1937   天津大公報舘

A story of a young couple who met in a streetcar. They fell in love with one another, but the young woman was married. This obsacle, however, was pushed aside by the young man and they both escaped to Singapore where the young woman felt happy as she preferred the ardent love of her lover to the quiet and respectful love of her husband. The latter sought after the couple and found them but they escaped again by going to China. The young woman died on board ship and her body was buried in the sea. Her seducer felt no remorse for his crime as his principle was "one must not resist love". But nevertheless in his old age he admitted that there were laws which had to be obeyed by every individual.

The book professes pantheism and advocates free love. *To be proscribed.*

330. 山胡桃   *WALNUT TREE*   1 vol. 370 p. by 傅東華
                                                        1935   生活書店   *See Biogr. 58*

This volume is composed of 1) various subjects, 2) literary criticism, 3) dissertations on literary subjects. *For everyone.*

331. 淚花   *TEARS*   ·   1 vol. 143 p. by 霍佩眞
                                                        1930   北京工大消費社出版

Short stories, mostly of unhappy love affairs. Some of them contain scenes that are rather shocking. *Everyone should be dissuaded from them.*

332. 紅顏女兒   *THE DAMSEL*   1 vol. 225 p. by 韓　護
                                                              1941   關東出版社

A story of two girls who in a period of a few months live a gay and disorderly life; they even lived as prostitutes but were soon disgusted with it and came back to normal and good life.

Although the book does not contain any obscene descriptions, the atmosphere is unhealthy. *For informed readers.*

333. 默愛   *UNTOLD LOVE*   1 vol. 397 p. by 郝東哲
                                                              1946   百新書店

Several young people who are friends prepare for weddings and act the role of intermediaries.

One young man falls in love with a lady who although rather touched by him, refuses his offers because she has a vengeance to wreck. The hero then selects another victim. After she has achieved her act of vengeance, his first conquest leaves for France in the company of a lady friend.

The spirit of vengeance of which the book is full is to be deplored. *For everyone.*

334. 逸如   *YI-JU*   1 vol. 288 p. by 郝蔭潭
                                                              1929   沉鐘社

A young man and a girl have loved each other for two years. One day, during a walk in the pei-hai, the young man asks for the hand of the girl who wishes to consent, but does not answer in so many words. The hero, believing that her silence indicated a refusal, leaves the city and becomes ill from disappointment. His life from henceforth is miserable. He ends by joining the revolutionary movement, and dies a victim of his act.

The girl is equally faithful, and continues to be sad, constantly thinking of her friend. When she hears of his death, she becomes grievously ill on the very same day, is moved to the hospital, and there she allows herself to die, not wishing to survive her friend.

All this could have been avoided by a word of explanation from the heroine, or a little more confidence on the part of the hero.

The book is interesting to read although too long for such a simple plot. We believe that it would be better *not to recommend it to young people,* because of the pessimistic and defeatist spirit of the characters.

335. 雪 *SNOW* 1 vol. by **黑嬰 (張又吾)**
1937 千秋出版社

The love affairs of a young man with a cinema star. Insipid, with no intrigue. *For mature people.*

336. 刻意集 *DELIBERATELY ENGRAVED* 1 vol. 138 p. by **何其芳**
2nd. edit. 1939 文化生活 *See Biogr. 59*

1. An account and description of a nocturnal outing in a boat after a heavy snowfall.
2. A sentimental interview between two women teachers who are friends and about to separate.
3. The author tells how he became a writer.
4. ditto.
5. Poems.

For everyone.

337. 曖昧 *NONE TOO HONORABLE* 1 vol. 214 p. by **何家槐**
1933 上海良友圖書公司 *See Biogr. 60*

Eight novelettes, well written, present us with a true picture of life led be married couples in modern times, it also show the lives and customs of the new middleclass. The most successful is the one under the title "Li". The two last ones contain some daring passages. *For informed readers.*

338. 寒夜集 *COLD NIGHT* 1 vol. 252 p. by **何家槐**
1937 北新書局

A collection of 14 stories. In the first one a wild young man lives a gay life in Shanghai. Nothing else interests him; even the death of his only son does not affect him; but old age brings him remorse. The third story describes the young couple who fell in love with each other during the boat-cruise. "Han Yeh" describes the struggles of a poor mother and her five children, and the birth of the sixth one which caused a struggle between the maternal love and the temptation to kill her new-born baby; she yielded, and afterwards remorse tormented her. "Yü T'ien" showes to what lengths some people can be bored on a rainy day at home. The other tales are worthless. This book *can be read by all, save the second story* which presents a young man seducing a woman.

339. 春色惱人 *SPRING TROUBLES ME* 1 vol. 206 p. by **何海鳳**
1947 大中華書局

The aim of the author in this romance is to demonstrate that a young man ought to give all his love to a single girl. He bases his assertion on reason and tradition. Whoever shares his heart deceives and is deceived. *Not for the young.*

340. 分 *DIVIDE*   1 vol. 221 p. by 何穀天
                                          2nd. edit. 1933 文化生活 *See Biogr. 61*

A collection of five stories.

The author seems to be a great pessimist, for that is the characteristic note of these tales. In addition, he has the air of being a defeatist. His heros are all failures, and do not have the courage to swim against the courant.

The book is sown with the most vulgar expressions in the Chinese vocabulary. *For mature people.*

341. 懺悔 *REPENTANCE*   1 vol. 157 p. by 奚如 (吳奚如)
                                          1936 良友公司 *See Biogr. 176*

A quite ordinary novel with rather unbelievable developments.

The two sons of a farmer of Hupeh remain attached to the family property even after the death of the father. The elder has two children while the younger has none. The wife of the younger refuses the offer of the elder to allow her to adopt one of the children. The child in question one day complains to his mother when he has been scolded by his aunt. The two women quarrel and the brothers separate after dividing the farm.

The younger brother wants to adopt a maternal nephew which would mean that his land would pass to a member of a family of another name. A family gathering commands him to give up the plan, upon which his wife seeks a quarrel with the elder brother, who during the dispute, first kills his sister-in-law with an axe, and then his brother. The murderer runs away but is overcome with remorse. The representatives of the family wish to hush up the affair with money, but the guilty man is eventually condemned to death. *For everyone.*

342. 四朵花 *FOUR FLOWERS*   1 vol. by 奚識之
                                          2nd edition 1941 智識書店

A protestant book translated from English but with names and places changed. As the customs and way of living are different the book presents a strange and even ridiculous atmosphere for Chinese readers.

The story of a good family. We first assist at the marriage of the eldest daughter. The second daughter then accompanied her aunt to Europe on a study tour. The third daughter refused to marry a young man because she found his character unsuitable for her taste. The youngest daughter was in love with him but her love was not returned. This book is a good one and *can be read by everyone.*

343. 散花天使 *THE FLOWER SCATTERING ANGEL* 1 vol. 125 p. by 夏風
                                          2nd edition 1941 上海武林書店

A story of a youth who promised to marry a girl but as he was urged by his parents to marry another he broke his promise. Nevertheless he loved both of them; the disappointed girl was taken ill and died. The book contains a number of indecent scenes and the atmosphere is unhealthy. *Strict reserve.*

344. 假鳳虛凰 *AFFECTED LOVE*   1 vol. 125 p. by 夏風
                                          2nd. edit. 1946 上海武林書店

A young man falls in love with a dancer who is already kept by a rich man. His parents, however, force him to marry the girl chosen by themselves. The hero of the tale loves his wife but his love for the dancer also remains quite lively.

A solution to the problem is found in the death of the dancer; and henceforth the young married couple, now rendered happy, think with emotion of the one who has gone.

The book does not contain any descriptions that are too provoking; nevertheless *it should be proscribed.*

345. 檸檬糖　*LEMON DROPS*　　　　　1 vol. 199 p. by 夏孟剛
　　　　　　　　　　　　　　　　　　　　　　　　　　　　1933

The author is a journalist publishing a collection of short stories which, on the whole, gives a characteristic note to the work.

菊姑娘　A young girl loves her cousin　who has married another. Her secret is discovered at her death.

新聞記者夫人　A journalist is apt to neglect his wife. On the anniversary of their wedding, she changes the text of an interview written by her husband for his paper. This particular article is greatly praised by the readers of the paper. The journalist eventually decides to let his wife share in his work. *For everyone.*

346. 當爐豔乘　*ROMANCE IN THE BAR*　　　1 vol. 297 p. by 夏　冰
　　　　　　　　　　　　　　　　　　　　　　　　　1939　天津書局

A worthless book and a dangerous one from a moral point of view. The author deals with frivolous and silly subjects. He features surroundings which should be better left unknown to all decent people. This book contains no obscene descriptions but the atmosphere is so objectionable that the book is *unsuitable for all classes of readers.*

347. 我離開十字徜頭　*THERE I LEFT THE CROWD*　1 vol. 42 p. by 向培戾
　　　　　　　　　　　　　　　　　　　　　1927　光華書局　*See Biogr. 64*

A travelling diary of a youth who fled from Peiping during Tuan Ch'i-jui's dictatorship to South China to join the revolution. *For all.*

348. 萍絮集　*ACCIDENTAL MEETINGS*　　　　1 vol. 206 p. by 蕭　艾
　　　　　　　　　　　　　　　　　　　　　　　　1943　新民印書舘

A collection of short stories.
Tao Hsi : Life of boon companions.
Lin : Gossip between neighbours.
Lao Chow : The troubles of a servant in a civil court.
An Fen : Chin Eur-yi was very skilful with the brush; he obliged hundreds of people with his services. He was arrested on the eve of his daughter's wedding; his people visited the persons he helped before, hoping they would intervene in his favour. . .but they turned a deaf ear.
Ts'an Yue : A story of a young couple and their struggle for life.
Mu : The hard life of a "daughter-in-law".
Loa Ya : The sorrows of a teacher in a boarding school.
Ti Yi chang : Love story; rather dull.

In this book we have a good description of Peiping life. *This book can be read by grown up people.*

349. 鬼　*AN APPARITION*　　　　　　　　1 vol. 185 p. by 蕭　艾
　　　　　　　　　　　　　　　　　　　　　　　1945　華北作家協會

1. 烟雲 : miseries of an artist.
2. 一條心 : blackmail for a raise in salary.
3. 婦道 : complaints of a country woman on modern life.
4. 鬼 : miseries of literary men.
Some of the expressions used are too strong. *Not to be recommended to anyone.*

350. 籬下集 *FLOWERS ON THE FENCE*   1 vol. 208 p. by 蕭 乾
2nd. edit. 1936   商務印書館 *See Biogr 65*

A series of short stories. Slight reservations to be made on them. *For mature people.*

351. 夢之谷 *THE VALLEY OF DREAM*   1 vol. 312 p. by 蕭 乾
1937 文化生活出版社

A young man goes south and obtains a teaching position. He falls in love with a girl. After some time, he returns to Peking to continue his studies.

In the meantime, his friend, who has remained in the South, becomes the concubine of a rich man.

When the hero learns of it, he goes to save her, but his friend does not want to be saved. *For everyone.*

352. 江上 *ON THE RIVER*   1 vol. 318 p. by 蕭 軍
1936 文化生活出版社 *See Biogr. 151*

Three stories which describe life in Manchuria.

In the first the author describes life in a big village, where the rich illtreated the poor and offended "Lao Chin", the protector of the forest.

In the second, we have, a description of the hard life among river workers, and their love for their children.

In the last the author presents the love story of a traveller.

This book presents a number of beautiful Chinese expressions and fine descriptions. The author possesses one fault and that is : he swears freely and likes coarse expressions. However, in spite of these faults, the *book may be read by everyone.*

353. 十月十五日 *THE FIFTEENTH OF OCTOBER*   1 vol. 204 p. by 蕭 軍
1937 文化生活出版社

A modern writer who despises the old conventional rites (p. 172) and contents himself with simple co-habitation which, according to him, can also be just temporary. In addition he holds all religion in horror, especially the Catholic religion (pp. 48 and the following). He despises priests and the Church. *Not to be recommended to anyone.*

354. 牛車上 *ON A BULL WAGEN*   1 vol. 106 p. by 蕭紅 (張廼瑩)
1936 文化生活出版社 *See Biogr. 8*

The life and reminiscences of the childhood of the authoress. She describes especially her sister-in-law, her idle uncle who is also a thief, and a faithful servitor. *For everyone.*

355. 曠野的吶喊 *CRIES FROM THE WILD*   1 vol. 154 p. by 蕭 紅
1946 上海雜誌公司

Short narratives on incidents that occurred during the Japanese occupation. They are well-written and the author appears to be a good psychologist. His tales are well sustained. *For everyone.*

356. 紅粉知己 *A FEMININE ALTER EGO*   1 vol. 94 p. by 蕭 玲
1946 藝文書店

This is a story with a school background, but do not expect anything serious. The intellectual level of the author does not rise to that. All that he has been able to produce is a relation of insanities and immoralities. He tells of the love affairs and dirty conversations of young people, of their relations with each other, and occasionally a few obscene details are thrown in. *Proscribed.*

357. 新生 *NEW LIFE*   1 vol. 99 p. by 蕭 吳
1946   新世紀出版社

1) Japanese atrocities during the war.
2) An artist leaves occupied China and goes to the other side, but one would say that
that had not benefited his country.
3) A courageous woman is going to rejoin her husband. On the way she learns of his
death through an accident. She decides to devote herself to the education of her child.
4) Financial difficulties of professors.
5) How the people understand nothing of the general interest.
For everyone.

358. 葡萄園 *VINEYARD*   1 vol. 176 p. by 謝人堡
1942   唯一書店 *See Biogr. 66*

A collection of short stories. Exception is taken to the first one only as it contains
an unhealthy atmosphere. It describes how a prostitute is forced to drink wine in order
to amuse her partner. She hates wine and became sick. The remainder of the book can
be read by everyone.

Stories beginning with page 34, 76, 84, 111, and 137 are worthy of mention, and
they are *recommended to everyone.*

359. 春滿園 *THE GARDEN IN FULL BLOOM*   1 vol. 114 p. by 謝人堡
1944   北京馬德增書店

A cinema novel.

A young rake was so rakish that he could not find a girl-friend. At the age of fifty
he met with one of his former friends, who was at one time his fiancée. Although she had
been left by him, she remained faithful to him.

A frivolous book. *Only for enlightened people.*

360. 寒山夜雨 *THE COLD NIGHT'S RAIN*   1 vol. 145 p. by 謝人堡
1944   勵力出版社

Ma Ming-yüan married Huang Mei without his father's consent; the latter disinherited
him after the news was broken to him. Owing to this, a discord arose in the young family
and Huang Mei left Ma Ming-yüan. The latter became a director of a new school, and
finally married the daughter of the founder of the school. When Huang Mei came to know
it she drowned herself. *For enlightened people.*

361. 月夜三重奏 *TRIO IN MOONLIGHT*   1 vol. 138 p. by 謝人堡
1944   馬德增書店

Huang Li-chün, a Shanghai actress, came to Peiping; there she met three young
men who liked her very much. Two of them fought for her and Chow Feng-chih was
the winner. After a journey to Shanghai for family affairs (a rapacious bonze claimed paternal
rights over her) the girl came back to Peiping and her friend. They agreed to live together
and for this purpose they rented a bungalow in the Western Hills. No formal marriage
took place; a child was born. The husband soon began to spend his wife's money and
resumed his licentious habits. In a very short time he wasted all his wife's wealth and
money, and left her. She was obliged to become a servant, while he took up a law career.

One day he was confronted with a prisoner accused of theft. It was his own son
Chow Yü. He had no way but to condemn him to prison for five months. When Chow
Yü's term was over, his father offered him employment. Chow Yü consented, provided his

mother would not be separated from him. When they began to look for her they could not find any trace, and thus the son worked and lived with his father. But at the end he suddenly disappeared and left no trace behind him. *For informed people.*

362. 模範作文 *MODELS IN COMPOSITION* 1 vol. 646 p. put together by 謝元逸
1933 黎明書店 *See Biogr. 67*

Selections from the works of well known modern authors as: Lu Hsün, Mao Tun, Yeh Shao-chün, Ping Hsin, and Yü Ta-fu. All these are *recommended for middle-school students.* Reserves are made for other readers owing to the unhealthy mentality of Yü Ta-fu, the social tendancies of Mao-Tun, and the import of Lu Hsün's stories.

363. 幻醉及其他 *ENCHANTED* 1 vol. 216 p. by 謝冰季
1929 中華書局

The author presents to us a collection of well written stories. Everyone can read them. The story 幻醉 is worthy of special attention. The author analyzes the sentiment of a newly married couple anticipating their honeymoon. The husband's death (he was a naval officer) put an end to all these beautiful dreams. His wife became insane. *For everyone.*

364. 溫柔 *TENDER LOVE* 1 vol. 109 p. by 謝冰季
1946 上海華中出版社

Five tales in which the authoress tries to show the influence that women have on men.
This is her theme and also the love of a bored woman of the world. She does not seem, however, to understand the meaning of real love. *Not for the young.*

365. 一個女兵的自傳 *AUTOBIOGRAPHY OF A WOMAN SOLDIER*
1 vol. by 謝冰瑩
1941 近代出版社印行 *See Biogr. 68*

This autobiography was written at the request of Lin Yü-t'ang who placed Hsieh Ping-ying among the best writers of China.
The story of a girl who rebelled against the old Chinese traditions, customs and society. She chose unlimited freedom, communism and free love. She divorced her husband after five months of married life. She studied in a modern school and became a soldier. Her parents wanted her to marry a young man whom they selected; at first the girl refused and fled from home but her parents compelled her to return. She had to marry the man in order to escape again. The second time she fled to Shanghai where she became a reporter, and gave herself to the revolution.
This book should *not be given to everyone,* owing to its revolutionary feelings.
It contains a good description of the struggle for equality among men. But the desire for freedom is too strongly expressed in this volume. (The authoress is too partial to Zola, Maupassant, Dostoyevsky etc.).

366. 鐵苗 *"THE INVINCIBLE MR. MIAO".* 1 vol. 289 p. by 熊佛西
1946 *See Biogr. 70*

The story of a teacher of strong will and model conduct who flees to free China during the Japanese occupation. His students go with him. Some of them do good work; others weaken. In the end the hero is assassinated, but his work continues.
The story is banal. Under cover of patriotism, the author sometimes forgets reality and follows the bent of his own imagination too much. *For everyone.*

367. 情絲淚痕 *TEAR STAIN* 1 vol. 157 p. by **徐哲身（鄔應坤）**
1938 上海春明書店

It is very hard to make a good synopsis of this book. Nothing but love and flirtation. *Everyone is advised against reading it.*

368. 雙妹淚 *THE SORROWED SISTERS* 2 vol. 476 p. by **徐哲身**
2nd edition 1936 大眾書局

A story of two sisters who were drawn into the revolutionary turmoil after the death of their parents. During their flight one was caught by bandits, the other by soldiers. Raping, adultery and murder ensued. After many adventures the sisters met again and resolved to avenge themselves. Finally they murdered their seducers.

For this deed they were sentenced to death.

The book is a mere series of seductions. *To be banned.*

369. 白話玉梨魂 *THE "YU-LI-HUN" IN VERNACULAR* 1 vol. 207 p. by **徐忱亞**
1944 益智書局

A novel of a professor who fell in love with a widow who lived in the same courtyard. They wrote letters for a time and when the professor proposed to her she refused. After this the widow arranged a meeting with her sister-in-law, who was married by force to the professor. The widow blamed her sister-in-law for this marriage, and died of sorrow thinking of the sacrifice of her unbold love for the professor. A good novel, *can be read by everyone.*

370. 女人的魔鬼 *DEVIL TO THE LADIES* 1 vol. 118 p. by **許躋青**
1929 中國書局

Seven short stories: of a betrayed woman, of a faithful young wife, a diary, the story of a rickshaw coolie, a story of the war, of the hold of foreigners on China.

Some of the details in this book are *not for young readers.*

371. 暮春 *LATE SPRING* 1 vol. 140 p. by **許 傑**
2nd edition 1925 光華書局 *See Biogr. 71*

This book contains two novels. The first one describes the meeting of two persons who were in love with one another 20 years ago, but whom fate had separated. As he was going to the funeral of his wife, she was going in the same direction in the company of her sick husband. The meeting revived lots of memories. Back home he wept over his wife and his lack of love for her. A few days later he paid a visit to his lady-friend, whose husband had recently died. Thus the two lovers were finally united to each other.

The second novel presents a picture of a married couple. The wife loves her husband, while the latter refuses to live with her. The parents interfere; in the end the husband tires of it all and goes away. *Everybody is advised against reading it.*

372. 慘霧 *DARK FOG* 1 vol. 299 p. by **許 傑**
2nd edit. 1928 Commercial Press

A collection of narratives giving a cross-section of family life, village life, and society in China. *For everyone.*

373. 剿匪 *ROUTING THE BRIGANDS* 1 vol. 134 p. by **許 傑**
1929 明日書店

錫鑛塲 Of workmen in a factory who are treated like slaves. Eleven people are killed in an accident, and the employees fire at the women who have come to mourn the dead.

Several of them are killed. And all this is happening while the director of the factory is resting in the arms of his concubine.

剿匪   Soldiers give chase to bandits. A few risky allusions.

七十六歲的祥福   Details of sons who have devoted themselves to the revolution.

In this book the author shows his discontent with modern society and his great sympathy for the communist revolution. *For adults.*

374. 闊太監   *THE RICH EUNUCH*   1 vol. 133 p. by 徐劍膽
1936 實報叢書之十七

Li Wang, chief eunuch (Tai Chien) lived happily with his wife and a servant. He was very rich and enjoyed life; his wife was a young and charming lady, but was avaricious as she was of poor origin. Wang Wen-t'ai, an ugly and brutal man, was formerly one of the Li Wang servants, but after the fall of the Empire he had no means to support himself. As Li Wang was a good man he often helped his former servant, but his wife disapproved of these deeds, and there were quarrels in the family. Wen-t'ai, who saw that Li Wang avoided him, and that he was urged to do so by his wife, began to hate both women, the wife of Li Wang and the servant. One night as Li Wang was sleeping he had a terrible dream and heard the moaning of the two women. In his anxiety he returned home very early and found them both killed.

The police interfered and suspected T'ien Yu cheng — a student 一, who fled. The latter had illicit relations with the servant's wife and was advised by Liu Pa to flee in order to avoid complications. His mistress had confided to him that her husband was the murderer, and Liu Pa, when questioned, revealed the whole story. Wang Wen-t'ai was arrested and finally confessed his guilt.

The atmosphere is immoral, and some descriptions are rather immodest. *Everyone is to be advised against reading the book.*

375. 青 年   *YOUTH*   2 vol. 131 & 140 pp. by 徐劍膽
1940 大華書局

The hero of this book was a good and very intelligent boy, but of low birth. With the help of his friends he became a bankclerk and after some time was promoted to a well paid position. After his promotion he broke his friendship with his friends, misbehaved and got married. But owing to his misconduct he could not stay any longer in Peiping and after stealing the bank's money he fled to Shanghai. The police traced him and brought him back to Peiping where he was found guilty and sentenced to death. *For everyone.*

376. 巴黎的鱗爪   *HERE & THERE IN PARIS*   1 vol. 182 p. by 徐志摩
2nd. edit. 1928 新月書店 *See Biogr. 72*

巴黎的鱗爪   Obviously the author has retained from his visit to Paris some love stories and a visit to an artist. A narrative that is apt to agitate the reader.

The rest of the book is composed of reflections on different problems and aspects of life.

The whole book is well written, and the late poet, whose loss we all regret, often gives expression to beautiful sentiments. *Not to be recommended to anyone.*

377. 自剖   *HARA-KIRI*   1 vol. 210 p. by 徐志摩
2nd. edit. 1928 新月書店

Poetical descriptions, elegiac memories, and impressions of journeys, all in a very high flown style. *For everyone.*

378. 愛眉小札 *LOVE LETTERS*   1 vol. 209 p. by **徐志摩**
                                          1936 良友文學叢書

The author's diary. In this book the author confesses his feelings towards his future wife Lu Hsiao-man. The second part of this book is Hsiao-man's diary. The whole book appeared in 1936 to commemorate the fifth anniversary of the author's death.

There is question only of love between the two. *It is not recommended for young people,* although there is nothing coarse or vulgar; the author shows himself to be a courtly gentleman.

379. 落葉文集 *FALLEN LEAVES*   1 vol. 168 p. by **徐志摩**
                                          5th edition 1937 北新書局

A collection of philosophical as well as economic discussions. Beautiful style, but the theories are far from being orthodox. *For informed readers.*

380. 徐志摩遺著精選 *MASTERPIECES OF HSU CHIH-MUO*   1 vol. 168 p.
                                                           更新出版社

1. A critical study of literary works. *For everyone.*
2. Various poems. *Not for everyone.*
3. Story of a betrayed woman.
4. Visit to the studio of a painter.
   Agitating descriptions. *Not to be recommended to anyone.*
5. Various memories of the author. *For everyone.*
Not to be recommended to anyone.

381. 回家 *GO HOME*   1 vol. 134 p. by **許欽文**
                                          1926 北新書局 *See Biogr. 73*

A young man from the South desired to make his fortune in Manchuria. On his way he was already desilusioned; and still more so as soon as he reached his destination. Many other people had made the same plans had also failed. The material and moral conditions did not live up to his expectations. With empty pockets he heturned to the South, where life was easier.

The intention of the author is not bad, but certain descriptions might be *dangerous for young people.*

382. 趙先生的煩惱 *TROUBLES OF MR. CHAO*   1 vol. 160 p. by **許欽文**
                                              2nd. edit. 1927 北新書局

The heroine has a feeble character but is a good sort. She loves her husband but that does not prevent her from flirting in her spare time. The hero loves his wife in spite of everything, but is wrong in being too weak with her. The "admirer" is an unenterprising man.

Moral: triangular love does not make for happiness but complicates life terribly. *Not for young readers.*

383. 鼻涕阿二 *THE DIRTY AH-ERH*   1 vol. 129 p. by **許欽文**
                                          1927 北新書局

This book presents the fate of women in China. The heroine of this book, who was the second child in a family, was neglected at home, but did not rebel against this as it was the custom. At school she was better treated and found some sympathy from a youth who tried to kiss her; according to the custom, she struck him. When this incident was related to her father, his contempt increased, and he married her to a stupid fellow. After the latter's death she was given as a concubine to a rich man. Here she took advantage of her position and ill-treated her maid, thus avenging her fate. She also constantly quarrelled with the wife of the rich man. The death of the rich man brought her harder struggles for a living; in the end she fell into poverty and died. According to holy custom a number of superstitious rites were performed over her. *For all.*

384. 幻象的殘象 *BROKEN PIECES OF AN ILLUSION* 1 vol. 197 p. by 許欽文
1928 北新書局

A collection of short stories.

1) Friends meet to plan the delivery of their comrade out of prison; after heavy drinking and eating they decide to call another meeting.
2) An invitation to a play was refused by a guest, but when he was told that his girl-friend was also invited, he accepted it.
3) The meeting between an officer and his girl-friend.
4) Three friends talk about "love".
5) A youth saw his girl-friend with another man while he was waiting for her.
6) A story of a school-master who fell in love with one of his pupils, but his love was not answered. After some time he came to know that she was sought after by the police, as she was a criminal.
7) The quarrel between two friends on account of a girl.
8) A story of an unsuccessful wooing of a warried woman by a married man, who finally returned to his wife.
9) A story of a youth who was refused by his girl-friend; it relates how he used force in order to possess her.
10) Disillusion of a lover.
11) Confession of a deceived lover.
12) Comedy played by two children.
For experienced people only.

385. 蝴蝶 *BUTTERFLIES* 1 vol. 104 p. by 許欽文
2nd edition 1929 北新書局

An allegory, the object of which is to promote free love. The way in which the author-poet presents the theme gives him the opportunity to defend his thesis in a very suggestive manner. *All are warned against this book.*

386. 一罐酒 *A JUG OF WINE* 1 vol. 222 p. by 許欽文
北新書局

A collection of thirteen stories, among them a number extracted from newspapers. Some of these stories are harmless, but the majority are unprofitable reading. The author favours divorce, free love and suicide. *Everyone is warned against this book.*

387. 彷彿如此 *SEEMINGLY THUS* 1 vol. 177 p. by 許欽文
1928 北新書局

Little love tales without interest. In spite of the beautiful language employed by the author, this book is *not to be recommended to the young.*

388. 線襪及其他 *SOCKS AND OTHER STORIES* 1 vol. 272 p. by 許欽文
2nd edition 1938 北新書局

A collection of twenty-four short sketches; little description; a very easy style. Poor plots. *This book is for everybody.*

389. 潘金蓮愛的反動 *UNCONVENTIONAL LOVE*   1 vol. 340 p. by 許嘯天
美美書屋

In a long preface the author poses as a champion of feminine emancipation, especially in matters of love. The trouble with Chinese women is that they lack personality, character and idealism and that they are not in a position to provide their own needs. This occasions coquetry, artifice and insincerity. This is even more the case with girl students. — They take advantage of entering school to dress elegantly and to take liberties with the sole purpose of securing an obliging companion who will provide them with money and jewels. They do not possess the sincere, true love which is imperative in married life to ensure permanent harmony and happiness. This mercenary love is against woman's dignity and makes her a plaything in man's hands. The author wonders what is the difference between them and prostitutes. Then he poses P'an Chin-lien, heroine of the novel Chin P'ing Mei, as an example. She shows strength of character and a true, constant and ardent love. She refuses to be at the beck and call of the rich Shan Ta, and to be married against her will to Wu Ta. On the other hand, how sincere her first love for Meng Tai; how ardent her passion for Wu Song! It is true that she poisoned Wu Ta and misbehaved with Hsi-men Ch'ing. But this happened because social conditions and time-honored custom did not permit her to provide for herself independently of men, to be really herself and to materialize her ideal of love.

A considerable part of the book is nothing but the repetition of the adventures of Wu Song as related in the "Shui Hu Chuan"; the rest is a reproduction of the novel "Chin P'ing Mei". *To be banned.*

390. 荒謬的英法海峽 *THE ABSURD DOVER CHANNEL*   1 vol. 117 p. by 徐訏
1939 *See Biogr.* 74

A novel.

While the author was crossing the English Channel he was captured and carried off by pirates to a country where conditions were ideal.

The ruler of the island fell in love with a Chinese girl and asked our hero to plead for him. In the meantime Mr. Hsu was sought after by two girls who wanted to marry him; he refused to marry any of them as he wanted to go back to China and was afraid his wife would not be happy there. At last he had to marry the one he loved less. . . At this moment he awoke on the deck of a ship which was about to reach England. The whole was merely a dream. In this utopia-land girls and boys were fine but rather free in their relations. But nothing immodest can be found in this book. *For all.*

391. 鬼戀 *AN UNCANNY LOVE*   1 vol. 110 p. by 徐訏
1941 夜窗書店

A young man meets a woman at night. After several encounters at the same hour, she confesses that she is a spirit. Having followed her one night, he passes the night in her house without approaching her. The next day he surprises her dressed like a buddhist nun. She explains to him that it is thus she expiates certain crimes. All this causes the hero to fall ill. His nurse falls in love with a handsome young man who visits him frequently and who is no other than the heroine disguised as a man. After a certain number of denouements, the young man and his attendant are forced to admit that they have loved the same person and have both been deceived by her. *For grown-up people.*

392. 一家 *ONE FAMILY*   1 vol. 140 p. by 徐訏
1940 夜窗書店

A history of the Lin family and its decay. The second daughter-in-law, wishing to

be separated from her husband, advised her parents-in-law to sell their property and depart for Shanghai. The family took her advice and, with little money, sailed off to Shanghai
and lived in great style. Misfortune followed them. First their father died, then the third
son took to flight, and finally the mother died. The first daughter-in-law, whose husband
had been dead for some time, left the family. The second daughter-in-law was sucessful
in her action against her husband, — a good but weak character and lived independently in
the future. *For everyone.*

393. 海外的情調 *FOREIGN ATMOSPHERE*   1 vol. 121 p. by 徐　訏
　　　　　　　　　　　　　　　　　　　　　　　　　　　　　　　　1940 夜窗書店

In this book a man tells of his amorous adventures in Europe. *Not to be recommended to anyone.*

394. 吉布賽的誘惑 *GYPSY'S ENTICEMENT*   1 vol. 121 p. by 徐　訏
　　　　　　　　　　　　　　　　　　　　　　　　　　　　　　　　1940 夜窗書店

An obscene story of experiences told in the first person. *Very objectionable.*

395. 費宮人 *THE LOYAL FEI—(Story of a heroic Lady at court)*
　　　　　　　　　　　　　　　　　　　　　　1 vol. 250 p. by 徐　訏
　　　　　　　　　　　　　　　　　　　　　　2nd. edit. 1940 宇宙風社

A collection of tales and short stories.
　　The author tells how a maid servant takes the place of a princess to save her, about
a woman who believes that she has been betrayed by her husband, and there is a tale of vengeance. Later we are told of a lover who wishes to commit suicide, and of an employé
who is injured in a disturbance. *For everyone.*

396. 春韭錄 *THE FIRST GREEN*   1 vol. by 徐　訏

　　Satirical essays mixed with a good dose of humour.
1)　Difficulties of finding a lodging.
2)　A girl who is ill owing to the loss of a key comes to sit on the cushion on my sofa.
She jumps up and I discover that she has been sitting on the very key she lost. Instant
recovery of her health.
3)　A fantasy on portraits.
4)　The wife annoys her husband with her constant praise of permanent waves. When
he is tired out he allows her to go to the hairdresser in spite of the poverty of the family.
The wife returns with her "permanent" — but without her charms.
5)　Where to spend the holidays is the great question. He wants to go to the sea, while she
prefers the country. For a thorough agreement, they should go to both, but as it is necessary
to be economical, one takes a bath, while the other refreshes herself on the terrace.
6)　My sister is dying of consumption. As I wish to be like her, I want to have consumption too!
7)　All the ladies of the lodging visit an exhibition. They are pretty well bored.
8)　My sister who is as beautiful as an angel goes to Paris where she grows so fat that
she loses all her beauty. After she returns home, her beauty also comes back, but her friend
becomes ugly due to change of climate. *For everyone.*

397. 精神病患者的悲歌 *ELEGIE OF AN INSANE*   1 vol. 198 p. by 徐　訏
　　　　　　　　　　　　　　　　　　　　　　　　　　1943 3rd edition 光明書局

　　A story of a young Chinese who nursed a neurotic European girl. . . in Paris.
　　He followed the sick girl to the dance-halls where he fell in love with one of her

companions.

A lewd book, full of stupidities and big talk. *To be proscribed.*

398. 風蕭蕭 *THE WIND IS GROANING* 2 vol. by 徐 訏
1947

In this book there is much talk about love; yet it would be wrong to call it a love story; it is a spy story.

The action is well sustained without too much side tracking.

The principal characters of this book, Pai-p'in and Mei Ying-tzu, are spies, the former for the Chinese, the latter for the American government. Both have a strong love for their country and are ready to sacrifice everything to their cause. All their activities — social life, dancing, friendships and relations with the Japanese-are guided by their ideal. Even personality, according to Mei, is subject to the common good. The problem of the individual's relation with society is hinted at in many passages.

Hsü, who tells the story, is also an interesting character. He is an inveterate bachelor so engrossed in his work that he goes unmoved through many complications where others would have sought the gratification of their possessions. His love for his country makes him join the intelligence organization. The end of the book shows a possible union of Hsü with Hai luen.

This book is not a realistic picture of life nor is it a social novel. The imaginary in the characters does not make them unreal, although it might be misleading. The platonic love of Hsü, the innocence of the two women who move in the midst of corruption, yet are not in the least affected by it, are, to put it mildly, strangely unusual.

The book touches on a lot of problems but does not resolve any. There is in the book a vague mysticism, slightly disquieting, yet capable, in the case of Mei and Pai, of inspiring far-reaching self-sacrifice.

The book may impress the reader at first as a love story; it would be a mistake to look upon it as such. It is a spy story; not, may be, a real one, but with a "mystery" twist.

The story moves on undisturbed and without being sidetracked by secondary interest. *For informed readers.*

399. 衘頭文談 *OVERHEARD IN THE STREET* 1 vol. 189 p. by 徐懋庸(余揚靈)
1936 光明書局 *See Biogr. 197*

Short articles on literary subjects. Without great value. *For everyone.*

400. 有趣的日記 *AN INTERESTING DIARY* 1 vol. 86 p. by 徐懋庸
1935 新中國書局

The diary of a Belgian doll in Brussells telling other dolls the story of the war, ol her mother and her family, of the vexations committed by the Germans and of the final deliverance. *For everyone.*

401. 四代女性 *FOUR GENERATIONS OF WOMEN* 1 vol. 72 p. by 徐碧波
1946 日新出版社

Short tales seasoned with wit and humour.
1) The generations follow each other but do not resemble each other. Four generations of girls.
2) A father and two sons. Good people but pursued by misfortune.

A few very short stories follow. *For everyone.*

402. 粉紅蓮 *PINK LOTUS*   1 vol. 74 p. by **徐碧波**
                                               1946   日新出版社

1) A marriage that turns out badly, and a forced marriage.
2) The frivolous occupations of the employees of a firm.
3) A poor girl deceived and persecuted by rich people.
4) Why were they divorced? A tragic misunderstanding.
5) Ghosts? No, they were bandits. A happy ending.
6) Scenes in a hospital.
7) My bag reminds me of tender memories.
8) The dreams dissolve and change into maternal love. *For everyone.*

403. 紅顏啼血記 (二集) *BLOOD IN HER TEARS*   1 vol. 104 p. by **徐剌兒**
                                               1934   蔚文書局

A very ordinary novel of a disobedient son, who left his home after robbing it of all
its precious objects. He spent them all on prostitutes and then returned home, but later
again revolted against the authority of his parents.

The book is rather dull and uninteresting; *it can be read by informed people.*

404. 乍浦遊簡 *TRAVEL TO THE PORT OF CHAPU*   1 vol. 113 p. by **徐蔚南**
                                  2nd. edit. 1937   開明書店 *See Biogr. 76*

For those who like beautiful descriptions. The author possesses a power of observation
that is out of the ordinary and is able to transfer well all that he sees. The whole book
is a succession of little pictures under the form of letters. *For everyone.*

405. 鶯燕分飛 *THE SEPARATED*   2 vols. 118 & 130 p. by **許亞農**

                                               1946   北京書店

A romance with no head or tail. We are told of the amorous exploits of a boring
gentleman, and of his relations with women. As the author seems to be a specialist in such
matters and obsessed with them, other characters of the same calibre as the main hero are
added, and the story is seasoned with their galantries.

This is a book that *everyone should be dissuaded from reading* because of the in-
direct apology for brothels that it contains, and also because of certain crude passages fit only
to entertain a guardroom.

406. 虹 *RAINBOW*   1 vol. 240 p. by **胡山源**
                                  3rd. edit. 1940   中華書局 *See Biogr. 77*

虹 p. 1-26. A student is deceived through a pair of gloves and the donor.
手套 p. 27-48. A lady who has a marriageable daughter wishes to attract young men to her.
珂蓮 p. 71-90. A friendship that is badly responded to.
盧光斗 p. 91-110. Meeting with an old acquaintance.
秋雨 p. 111-132. Talk among students.
蕫嫣的傷心 p. 133-148. A servant who is faithful and very attached to her employers
黃大利 p. 149-188. Description of an original character.
五里湖之雨 p. 189-219. Little incidents of ordinary life.
幾個忘記不了的面孔 p. 221-240. Sketches of some personages.
    A well written book in simple style and with good psychology. *For everyone.*

407. 胡適新選 *A NEW ANTHOLOGY OF HU-SHIH*   1 vol. 184 p. by **胡 適**
1945 大文書店 *See Biogr. 78*

A series of stories about love affairs. They contain descriptions of unfaithful women, rapes and adulteries, stories of mothers-in-law, etc. All written in a very light and risky fashion. *Everyone to be deterred from above.*

N.B. Is this book written by this famous author? We doubt about it. (J.S.)

408. 聖徒 *THE HOLY DISCIPLE*   1 vol. 154 p. by **胡也頻**
1927 新月書局 *See Biogr. 79*

A number of stories easy to read for their lively and humorous style. Nevertheless they show the pessimistic and fatalistic disposition of the author, and the majority of the stories have sad and bad ending. As the book contains nothing immodest it *can be read by all.*

409. 西冷橋畔 *BY THE SHELON BRIDGE*   1 vol. 146 p. by **胡雲翼**
1933 北新書局 *See Biogr. 80*

Several short stories dealing with the advent of the Kuomingtang and the set back it suffered after the May 30 affair. *For everyone.*

410. 蜀山劍俠傳 *WONDER-WORKS FROM SZECHWAN — (A Phantasy)*
1 vol. 200 p. by **還珠樓主**
2nd. edit. 1937, Tientsin 文嵐移印書局

First of a series of books of adventure approaching the character of the old romances. It consists of a succession of battles and revenges between different sorts of warriors, men, women, beasts etc. All are of a really superhuman ability. The book is at the same time a mass of superstitions.

Certain pages are hardly decent: pp. 44, 77, 121 and the following. *For grown-up people.*

411. 輪蹄 *TRAMPED*   1 vol. 124 p. by **還珠樓主**
1943 勵力出版社

A very dull book about a juxtaposition of events around a central character. Contains some unorthodox theories. *Not for everyone.*

412. 陳迹 *RELICS*   1 vol. 236 p. by **黃仲蘇**
1940 中華書局 *See Biogr. 81*

Short stories, letters, personal impressions, translations, and literary studies.

To be recommended to mature readers. The judgements on Zola, Maupassant, and Flaubert should be read with reserve. *Not for everyone.*

413. 音樂之淚 *THE TEARS OF MUSIC*   1 vol. 204 p. by **黃仲蘇**
商務印書舘

Three stories.

1) A young man who is studying in Europe falls in love and marries without considering the fact that he is already engaged and has a girl waiting for him in his native country. Upon his return to China, he teaches in Peking. His fiancée follows him secretly, and one day when he is telling of his marriage to his pupils, she faints. She is taken to a hospital and dies there after a last adieu with her ex-fiancé.

2) A Chinese student is studying in America. His fiancée is studying in Paris. The hero falls in love with Mary, the daughter of his landlady. Another lodger is also in love with

her, who comes to blows with the student and eventually reveals the fact that he is her father. Mary then gives up the student and sends him the letters from his fiancée that she had intercepted.

3) Still another story of a Chinese Joseph and a European Putifar, that is to say, how a Chinese student is pursued by the advances of his landlady. *Not for the young.*

414. 罪惡 *CRIME*   1 vol. 199 p. by 黃心眞
                                                          1928   上海新宇宙書店

The servant of a brothel describes the attractions of the prostitutes. He is showing the life of the clients, and as he becomes jealous of them he tries to imitate them. Then a series of obscene stories. *Ta be banned.*

415. 姊夫 *BROTHER-IN-LAW*   1 vol. 146 p. by 黃歸雲
                                                          1928   眞美善出版社

Exactly the same book as that reviewed under the title 姊夫 by 張資平. The authorship of this book was erroneously attributed to Chang Tzu-p'ing during the Japanese occupation. *For everyone.*

416. 曼麗 *MARY*   1 vol. by 廬隱 (黃廬隱)
                                                          北平文化學社 *See Biogr. 82*

A series of stories describing the excesses of the movement for the new culture. *For everyone.*

417. 廬隱自傳 *AN AUTHOBIOGRAPHY BY LU-YIN*
                                                          1 vol. 132 p. by 黃廬隱

The autobiography of the authoress.

She describes her infancy and adolescence. Although maltreated by her parents, the young women succeeds in making her way.

Religion has no attraction for the writer. As a pupil in a protestant school, she was forced, according to her own account, to embrace the religion. Later she becomes an apostate and in her book, she justifies this act, obviously putting the blame on religion. To be read *only by enlightened readers.*

418. 雲鷗情書集 *LOVE LETTERS*   1 vol. 161 p. by 黃廬隱 and 李唯健
                                                          1931   上海神州國光社

Love-letters which were written by a youth and his girl-friend. From the beginning to the end these letters give evidence of an exalted and morbid love. The love sentiments are accompanied with the most insane figures of speech. It takes a lot of courage to read this book to the end.

The book certainly has real literary value; but it must have disturbing effects on anybody's imagination. *For informed readers.*

419. 憂鬱的歌 *A DIRGE*   1 vol. 226 p. by 荒煤
                                                          1936 文化生活出版社

Short stories in which the author describes in a realistic fashion the smallness of men living together in society. The author knows Catholic principles but is incapable of applying them to ameliorate the situations described. He considers them rather as a hindrance on the "free life".

Told in easy language. *For grown-up people.*

420. 失戀之後 *AFTER I WAS REFUSED* 1 vol. 366 p. by 黃素陶
5th edition 1933 大中書局

A married man being separated from his wife, whom he never loved, sought an "ideal woman". Soon he was introduced to one with whom he fell deeply in love. When their love was at its full bloom the girl was informed about his marriage; on hearing this she left him; neither his great passion, nor his divorce could bring the girl's love back to him. Our hero suffered greatly because the girl began to appear with another young man, but even this act of hers did not kill his love for her, and he remained faitful to her forever.

There is nothing obscene in this novel; however, *everyone should be advised against reading it* because it despises the marriage bonds and exalts love too much.

421. 艷夢 *DULCID DREAMS* 1 vol. 168 p. by 紅綃
3rd. edit. 1946 武林書店

Ming tells in a joking, and often cynical fashion, of his life with his wife and two of her friends who live with them.

From the moral point of view, the book should be proscribed, because from beginning to end, it is scattered with extemely risky and suggesstive details. *Proscribed.*

422. 夜鶯曲 *SONG OF THE NIGHTINGALE* 1 vol. 168 p. by 紅綃
4th. edit. 1947 上海武林書局

The same book as the precedent, only under another title. *Proscribed.*

423. 鳳凰嶺 *MOUNT PHOENIX* 1 vol. 94 p. by 紅雪
1942 和平印書局

A few stories of no value, chiefly on family life. *For everyone.*

424. 流亡 *EXILE* 1 vol. 250 p. by 洪靈菲
1928 上海現代書局 *See Biogr. 85*

A worthless revolutionary book. The hero lived with a revolutionist girl, Man Man, while he was away from his own wife and home. The couple were persecuted by the police and roaming all the time. After two years Chih Fei returned home, but stayed only for a short period, and neither his wife's nor his parents' prayers could hold him at home. When he came to Singapore he lost all his money and decided to return home. Here he did not know what to do; a letter from his mistress, who went to study in Peiping after his departure to Singapore, made him decide to continue his revolutionary career, and he came to Peiping.

A very poisonous and bad book as it defends free love and divorce; it also contains many immoral scenes. *This book should be proscribed.*

425. 五奎橋 *WU KUEI CH'IAO* 1 vol. 129 p. by 洪深
2nd. edit. 1946 鐵流書店 *See Biogr. 87*

The title is the name of a bridge belonging to the Chou family, the chief land-owners of the village. Some of the fields cannot be watered because of the bridge. The inhabitants of the village wish to destroy it but the Chou family oppose the project. In the end the villagers revolt and destroy the bridge.

Anti-superstitious spirit, and a little revolutionary. *May be read by anyone.*

426. 爲法小品集 *PROSE* 1 vol. 238 p. by 洪爲法
1936 北新書局 *See Biogr. 88*

A series of short stories about the manners and customs of Shantung, written with a vigorous and humorous pen. *For everyone.*

427. 長跪 *KNELT ON THE GROUND*   1 vol. 128 p. by 洪爲法
                                             3rd. edit. 1937 大光書局

A series of stories describing chiefly the sad side of life. *For everyone.*

428. 情書一束 *A BUNDLE OF LOVE LETTERS*   1 vol. by 衣萍 (章衣萍)
                                             7th. edit. 1929 北新書局 *See Biogr. 5*

The book has been prohibited since its appearance and the author himself calls it
a bad book. The tendency of this volume is to give instruction in free love to young people.
In this the author is completely successful, for he gives evidence of being a past master
in the art of teaching evil.

The book consists of sensual letters between young people of the opposite sexes,
and the narrations of love experiences that they contain are extremely sordid. *To be condemned.*

429. 少女日記 *DIARY OF A MAID*   translated by 衣萍 and 鐵民
                                             2 vol. 254, 195 p. 1927 北新書局

The translation of a foreign book of which neither the title nor the author are
given. It consists of the diary of a girl of fourteen and a half who describes her daily
life. The entries are scattered with physiological details that she learns of in conversations
with her friends.

A bad book. *To be condemned.*

430. 櫻花集 *CHERRY BLOSSOMS*   1 vol. 226 p. by 衣萍
                                             3rd. edit. 1929 北新書局

This book is composed of small talk, criticisms and souvenirs, of a play, allusions
to the other works of the author, and sketches, etc.

The author also presents us with his ideas on morals, but they are quite different
from ours. He makes a great deal of propaganda for one of his bad books.

The present volume contains many passages offensive to good morality. *Proscribed.*

431. 枕上隨筆 *BEDSIDE BOOK*   1 vol. 82 p. by 衣萍
                                             1929 北新書局

Banal sketches and reminiscences that are sometimes stupid and cynical. *For adults.*

432. 友情 *FRIENDLINESS*   1 vol. 220 p. by 衣萍
                                             2nd edition 1931 北新書局

In this book the author describes to us certain people who were overcome by the
difficulties caused by the economic and political situation of China at the period described.
Some found escape by throwing themselves into the Revolution, others could not find in
that a solution to the difficulties of their lives.

The author is realistic; his realism is of a low class which compels us *to class his
book among those prohibited.* Moreover his theories are absolutely corrupt.

433. 窗下隨筆 *BENEATH THE WINDOW*   1 vol. 94 p. by 衣萍
                                             4th. edit. 1932 北新書局

Anecdotes about a number of well-known people, some without any particular point,
some very amusing (such as the one about Wang erh-feng-tzu), but all interesting.

The book includes a rather crude description of a rape. *For grown-up people.*

434. 桃色的衣裳 *PEACH-COLOURED RAIMENT* 1 vol. 255 p. by 衣 萍
北新書局

According to the author there are no morals among writers. This premise is well illustrated in the present volume composed of love letters, a diary, and souvenirs. Marriage, ceremonies, and laws are vain words to this writer. The only realities for him are free love and love without restraint. The fact that the author shows no self-respect is his own affair, but it is a pity that he does not respect the public by refraining from such rubbish. The only thing his books are fit for is to throw on the fire! *Proscribed.*

435. 情書二束 *TWO BUNDLES OF LOVE LETTERS* 1 vol. 185 p. by 衣 萍
1934 上海樂華圖書公司

This book is composed of a series of love letters and a diary. In it the author exposes his immorality and preaches free love. For him there is nothing serious in life. The only thing that counts is carnal satisfaction. *Proscribed.*

436. 黃繡球 2 vol. 208 p. & 208 p. by 頤 絹
新民社生活部

A novel written between two periods: that of the old novels and that of the modern literature. This book has an easy style and is written in the "pei hua" language, but is a little bit tiresome. The story describes how a working woman raised herself above the condition in which women lived in those days, and became a "Mdme Roland" (the author's expression). She performed great service for the emancipation of woman. *For instructed persons.*

437. 小江平遊滬記 *AN EXCURSION IN SHANGHAI*
2 vol. 288 & 138 p. by 一舸女士(褚雪松)
1932 新明書店 *See Biogr. 48*

This book relates how Chiang P'ing, hearing about the allurements of Shanghai, went there to enjoy the "air of freedom". He succeeded only too well, and became a frequent visitor of Shanghai dives. This book contains nothing but the description of foolish, vulgar, and often obscene "experiments". *This book is to be banned.*

438. 日記文學叢選 *SELECTED DIARIES* 1 vol. 334 p. collected by 阮无名
1933 南強書局

A collection of extracts from intimate journals. Extracts from the best authors are included, among others, memories of the period of civil wars by Kuo Mo-jo, 郭沫若 passages in more lofty language by Yu P'ing-po. Hu Shih in his notes on the songs, popular with the sing-song girls of Hangchow, gives some examples that *call for a slight reserve.*

439. 希望 *HOPE* 1 vol. 260 p. by 柔石(趙平復)
1930 商務印書舘 *See Biogr. 17*

A collection of twenty eight stories. The author describes the social conditions of different classes. The majority are harmless; some call for strict reserve because of vulgar and immoral descriptions.
The 17th, 21st and 23rd are *very objectionable.*

440. 二月 *THE SECOND MOON* 1 vol. 257 p. by 柔 石
1929 春潮書局

A university student named Hsiao, after several years of study in various universities, is invited by an old friend, T'ao, to teach in the middle school run by the latter.

There is a young widow living in the same locality, who is the mother of two children, and whose husband has died in the war. T'ao, on his side, has a sister, T'ao Feng, who is free in her manners and coveted by several young admirers.

Hsiao, a sympathetic person, is presented to us in a rather vague fashion. What is most remarkable about him is his generosity and impressionability.

As the widow is without means of existence, Hsiao gives her half his salary and arranges for her daughter to enter the school where he is working. The mother is of very good character, and is extremely touched by the generosity of the young man towards her. T'ao Feng, however, falls in love with him, and gives up her other admirers for him. Their relations are cordial and dignified.

The widow now is stricken with another misfortune. Her little son of two years dies. She is so overcome that she decides on suicide. Hsiao tries to prevent her, and with that end in mind, proposes marrying her although such a course is repugnant to him. Nevertheless, in a paroxysm of despair, the widow hangs herself. Her daughter is taken to the T'ao family to be later taken by Hsiao, who after the death of the widow, is undecided what to do.

He loves T'ao Feng and is loved in return, but he cannot decide on marriage. Under the pretext of an excursion into the hills, he goes for ever. Then T'ao Feng, urged by her great love, leaves to search for him in company with her brother.

It is a beautiful book, well written and interesting. The author certainly has considerable talent. Nevertheless the platonic relations of the hero with the widow and with T'ao Feng run the danger of not remaining indefinitely in the spiritual sphere.

There is, however, nothing shocking in this work. *May be read by anyone.*

441. 卷葹 *CHIUAN-SHEH*　　　　1 vol. 62 p. by 淦女士 (馮淑蘭)
　　　　　　　　　　　　　　　　1927 北新書局 *See Biogr. 55*

A romantic novel of a girl who was promised to a youth of the same neighbourhood. She departed to Peiping to study; here she met a lover and loved him after the new fashion i.e. "with a holy and free love alone worthy of the name". Soon she was obliged to return home, and in spite of all family traditions, she held to the newly established rights — to choose as she pleased —. Hence she found no other way out but to commit suicide.

For informed readers only, owing to the theories put forward.

442. 黍差 *THE DARKER CORNERS*　　　　1 vol. 200 p. by 高　深
　　　　　　　　　　　　　　　　　　1945 新民印書館

The author wishes to show in half a dozen stories certain abuses of contemporary society, such as war, opium, prostitution, plurality of employments with the official class, their bad example, etc.

Certain descriptions are too sensual, viz. p. 34 and the following, and p. 194 and the following. *Not to be recommended to anyone.*

443. 男與女 *MAN & WOMAN*　　　　　　1 vol. by 高雲池

A collection of short stories which show the relations between men and women.

1) A romance that ended with a happy marriage.
2) A story of a youth who resolved to give up his fiancée, as he thought that she would be happier with one of his friends; he wrote her a letter saying that he had died. After some time she married another boy friend, but when the truth was revealed the shock killed her.
3) A story of "spiritual" infidelity in marriage. A married woman who constantly thought

and dreamed about her first boy-friend.

4) A man, who possessed no courage to kill himself, resolved to enjoy life first. He won money in a lottery, and began to spend money like a fool; finally he found himself in a brothel where he committed suicide.

5) A story of a girl who was afraid to return home, as she was to be married to a man she did not love. The matter was settled favourably.

6) A girl student who poisoned herself, as she did not want to marry without love; her fiancé did the same thing.

7) A married couple found consolation where they should not.

8) A concubine, who was very indignant at the sufferings inflicted on women by men who do not love. She died in childbirth but her husband was not affected.
For instructed persons only.

444. 少 女 的 苦 悶 *MAIDEN SORROW*　　　　　1 vol. 179 p. by **高雲池**
　　　　　　　　　　　　　　　　　　　　　　2nd edition 1937　上海南星書店

A story of Miss B., a modern girl who had many disappointments in her loves; all her boy-friends turned out to be unfaithful; finally she married the man whom she liked best. For a time perfect love reigned in their house, but disappointments began as she found out that her busband had no livelihood and ran after other girls. However, everything was settled in the end.

This book *should be strictly reserved* as the author describes immodest scenes and presents very strange ideas about love and marriage.

445. 隨 糧 代 徵 *COLLECTED WITH TAX IN KIND*　　1 vol. 472 p. by **高　詠**
　　　　　　　　　　　　　　　　　　　　　　　　　　1940　文化生活

Of oppressors and the oppressed. In giving us a picture of the latter, the author paints with a masterly hand two peasant families. He gives life to the story by weaving in the sentimental relations of the children of these two families. Everything described in very correct term as the love between them is an honest and true one.

As for the oppressors — they are concentrated in the Chao family. The injustices they commit and their shady sides are given to us by the author in occasionally trivial and risky fashion.

In the course of the story, a new sub-prefect full of good intentions, wishes to agitate in favour of the families that have been driven to misery. The Chaos are alarmed, and through machiavellian means, succeed in obtaining a change of officials. A new functionary, who is a member of their clique, is appointed, and the scramble for spoils begins again. Murders are committed and the "haves" triumph over the "have nots". The poor, and especially the peasant families mentioned in the beginning, are deprived of everything. They even have to sell their land to satisfy the rapaciousness of the Chaos.

The book ends with the departure of the two poor heros who leave in the night to revenge themselves upon their oppressors.

A finely conceived book, although it is a little too leftist. The author knows his subject and the attention of the reader is held to the end.
For adults only, because of the spirit of the book and certain trivial descriptions.

446. 半 夜 潮 *MIDNIGHT LAKE*　　　　　　　1 vol. 98 p. by **耿小的(耿郁溪)**
　　　　　　　　　　　　　　　　　　　　1939　新北京報社 *See Biogr. 89*

A story of a Tientsin girl, already engaged to a young man; she fell in love with a professor while she was studying in Peiping University. The professor was also in love with her and they planned to get married, but the first fiancé interfered and won the love of his fiancée again.

Nothing blameworthy, from a moral point of view, is related in this book, but *girls should be warned against reading it.*

447. 紅葉譜 *RED LEAVES*   1 vol. 72 p. by 耿曉堤
北京書店

Two professors fall in love with the same student. One obtains her hand but it does not take long for him to become indifferent to her. Ten years after, the other professor meets his old friend and their love revives stronger than ever. The husband discovers his wife's correspondance with the other professor, and they agree to a divorce. The heroine believes herself abandoned by her friend, and therefore seeks him out and shoots him with a revolver. At the very moment of her crime, she learns that she has been labouring under a misunderstanding, and her friend was still in love with her. In despair, she kills herself.

This book is *not to be recommended* because of this extra-conjugal love, and the approbation of divorce that it contains, not to mention the killings.

448. 六君子 *THE SIX GENTLEMEN*   1 vol. 271 p. by 耿小的
1937 新華書局

Several teachers found a new school that flourishes for a time.

Then misfortunes occur. Things are stolen, including four girls! The principal loses his health because of it, and the control of the school comes under a buddhist priest. The school sinks gradually.

The book is amusing to read because it describes very well the weaknesses of modern teachers and students. *For everyone.*

449. 太液秋波 *AUTUMN IN PEKING*   1 vol. 123 p. by 耿小的

A dull and rather empty book, which describes the life in an official's residence. It shows how their time is spent, on such things as stirring up quarrels between other officials, wrecking homes and causing divorces.

Although there are no raw scenes, this book can be read *by instructed people only.*

450. 天花亂墜 *PETALS FROM ABOVE*   1 vol. 179 p. by 耿小的
1939 糸葉書店

The first part of the book features the life of present day students. The only important item of the curriculum seems to be making love and being courted. In one exceptional case the affection is sincere and enduring.

The second part features the same students after their marriage. The marriage of the two who knew real friendship turns out to be a success. The others behave in marriage as they did in their flirtations. They keep busy separating and getting divorced.

The author does not object to such goings-on. Although there are no immodest descriptions, the book is still *very objectionable.*

451. 烟雨芙蓉   2 vol. 214 p. by 耿小的
1939 義成書局

This book describes the life of Peiping citizens, with poor attempts at humour. A Peiping family became poor, owing to the fact that they scatterred money in a foolish way.

At the end they became rich by winning the lottery prize.

This volume has no literary value, but provides an hour of rest while reading it. From the moral point of view, it contains a number of passages which contain double meanings, and a number of shocking scenes. There is *no danger for instructed persons to read it*.

452. 時代群英 *BEST OF THE ERA*　　　　1 vol. 271 p. by **耿小的**
　　　　　　　　　　　　　　　　　　　　　　1940 天津勵力出版社

A novel relates how a number of friends established a school for girls which, judged by the program, might be considered as a free university. The discipline of the university was so low, that its students were everywhere but in shool. The directors planned to organize a number of festivals, in which girls had to take part, but the lack of discipline forced them to close their school.

This book contains some unbecoming allusions; hence it *should be reserved for instructed persons.*
(This book appeared in 1946 under the title 花燭之夜).

453. 磊落 *MANLY*　　　　　　　　　1 vol. 114 p. by **耿小的**
　　　　　　　　　　　　　　　　　　　　　　1940 大華書局

The scene of this story took place at the Men Tou Kow mines. The hero of the story, Lao Hao, was adopted by a miner, who lost his legs in an accident while he worked in the mine. When Lao-Hao grew up he married, but in the very near future quarrelled with his parents-in-law. He refused to work and forced them to sell their land; with that money he bought a mine which he himself managed. Bandits, who came to know about his act, paid him a visit — while Lao Hao was away — and carried off his wife and a friend. On his return, Lao Hao was obliged to pay a heavy ransom, after which he was so poor that he was obliged to search for manual labour.

No risky passages. The book itself is very interesting, as it contains vivid descriptions of a miner's life. *For everyone.*

454. 愛的驚濤 *SUDDEN STORM*　　　　1 vol. 159 p. by **耿小的**
　　　　　　　　　　　　　　　　　　　　　　1942 光記書局

In these modern times teachers of girls' middle schools have to go through quite an ordeal! The one presented in this book loves a girl who lives in the same compound as he. Several pupils of his as well as a goodly number of their friends are also in love with him. Intrigues and inextricable entanglements never end.

Life in modern schools, as described by the author, bustles with activity so that no time is left for study.

The book abounds in false theories and frivolities. *Very objectionable.*

455. 馬牛風 *IRRELEVANT*　　　　　　1 vol. 134 p. by **耿小的**
　　　　　　　　　　　　　　　　　　　　　　1943 新華書局

The author describes with a certain amount of wit and humour the life in a given school. It is not edifying — far from it! The book is composed of wanton conversations among students, a dangerous pastime! Schools of this standard may exist, but that does not alter the fact that the perusal of this book cannot lead to any good whatsoever. *Only for mature people.*

456. 鸞飛鳳舞 *TURTLE DOVES* 1 vol. 104 p. by 耿小的
1943 世界鉛字公司

A story of an actress whose bills were paid by several lovers. It contains a big number of obscene passages. *To be banned.*

457. 女姓公敵 *COMMON ENEMY OF THE LADIES* 2 vol. 123 & 116 p. by 耿小的
1943 華萩書局

Here the author describes the love escapades of a young journalist — reporter by the name of Liu. The book contains little interest for readers, as it has no original ideas and is written without any effort. Mr. Liu, in spite of his bad reputation, was pretty successful among women, but nevertheless was a poor specimen. The frivolity of the book *calls for strict reserve.*

458. 青平斷 *FULL HOUSE* 1 vol. 131 p. by 耿小的 (曉堤)
1943 新華書局

In this novel we go through a maze of burlesque situations.

A girl who is going to be married, has had intercourse with her cousin and is afraid this will be known after her marriage. So she provides a substitute on her wedding day. After many tragicomic events, the author manages a happy end: three married couples.

There is not one serious idea in the whole book. It will be widely read because the plot is as fascinating as that of a good detective story. *For informed readers.*

459. 隄邊月 *MOON BY THE RIVER BANK* 1 vol. 119 p. by 耿郁溪
1943 藝林書局

The story relates how Mr. Chang fell in love with Wang Mei, but the latter had a rival by the name Chiang, who decided to separate them. In order to carry out her plot she introduced Miss Li who was to separate the loving couple; the effect of her scheme was disastrous as Mr. Chang fell in love with Miss Li. After some time Li leaves Chang and marries one of her former boy-friends. Mr. Chang tries to forget his sorrow in hard work.

As the atmosphere in rather unhealthy, this book *can be read by instructed people only.*

460. 菩薩蠻 *SERENADE* 2 vol. 235 p. by 耿曉堤 (小的)
1943 新華書局

This book describes the condition of the common people in Peking under the political and social conditions of 1943. It is a satire against a certain nation, not mentioned by name. The setting is a big compound in which many families live: a married bonze, an employee, a rickshaw coolie, etc. They all have the same trouble: how to make both ends meet under pressure of social conditions. The daughters, although brought up well, soon learn how to earn some money. The desire for luxuries achieves their moral ruin. They are at first seduced by rakes and afterwards sold to houses of ill fame. Another of the girls described marries a man who is in the opium racket; she brings comparative wealth to the rest of her family. The other families become constantly poorer and end in utter dejection.

Nothing risky. The author aims at defending the poor and therefore attackes the well to do. In one passage he accuses "Lao T'ien Yeh" of injustice against the poor. *For informed readers.*

461. 鸎唱鵑啼 *THE CANARIES SING*   1 vol. 142 p. by **耿郁溪**
                                                   1943 藝華書局

Li Yü-seng is presented in this book; he fell in love with two girls and finally had to make a choice, as both of them loved him. He chose Miss Yang, a beautiful and rich girl. The two lovers remained engaged for a long time. After Miss Yang left the university she was seduced by Professor Ma, and had to leave her fiancé in order to marry Ma; the latter was often absent and Yang found out that he was already married to a country girl. After this she wanted to go back to Li, but on the way felt sorry for her sins and drowned herself. Li had always been faithful to her; but when he met his former second girl-friend he found out that he still loved her, and married her. *For informed readers.*

462. 輕雲蔽月 *THE MOON IS VEILED*   1 vol. 146 p. by **耿小的**
                                                   1943 藝林書局

A story of a school professor who was married to a country girl by his parents; he had three sons. After some time he left his family and came to live in Peiping. During his stay in Peiping his friend gave him a girl of fifteen, on condition that he helped her through school. The girl lived with him. After she finished her studies, she obtained a position in an office. After living with the professor for ten years, she left him. The professor was seized with despair.

Although this book contains nothing indecent, the atmosphere is too sentimental. *For instructed persons only.*

463. 梁先生 *MR. LIANG*   1 vol. 76 p. by **耿小的**
                                                   1944 新華書局

A collection of short stories, one as meaningless as the other; it might make some people of doubtful education laugh . . . but it should not be put into the hands of serious people. These stories are full of obscene allusions. *Strict reserve.*

464. 微塵 *SLIGHT DUST*   1 vol. 70 p. by **耿郁溪(小的)**
                                                   1944 銀麗書屋

This book is a satire on a certain administration. The author denounces the chaotic situation of the modern schools. He pretends to be a witness of what he is relating.

The events took place in a normal school outside of Peiping wall. The pupils were a collection of poor individuals. These young students never opened their text-books for they followed the example set for them by the professors who never mounted their rostrum. The government paid for all expenses; the money was divided and put out at interest. The superfluous money paid for the picnics and outings during the holidays under the professor's supervision. During one of the outings the director of the school paid a visit to the wife of a professor while he was away. At the same time the bursar paid a visit to director's wife. When the pupils came to know the fact they were shocked. The professor made an accusation against the director and obtained his well-paid post.

In the preface, the author remarks that we cannot expect much from those students when they will be the instructors of the coming generation. *For grown up people only.*

465. 疎雲秋夢 *AN AUTUMN DREAM*   1 vol. 97 p. by **耿曉堤**
                                                   1944 銀麗書屋

A story of a poor youth who fell in love with a rich girl. He was a good son and a hard working fellow. His fiancée, owing to her riches, was vain. They planned to get married and sought after the necessary funds for the marriage. The girl tried to obtain a position, thus coming in contact with a number of frivolous people, who took advantage of her simplicity and led her along the road to ruin. The youth, who thought that she was lost to him, married another girl; when this was made known to his former fiancée, she fell so low that after a short time, during which she was a waitress, she committed suicide. *For instructed persons only.*

466. 喜遷鶯 *THUS THE CANARIES FLY*   1 vol. 99 p. by **耿小的**
1946 北京書店

The father of a family frequents the company of a singsong girl and breaks with his wife. His life becomes impossible, he is so torn in both directions. In the end the singsong girl goes away.

The subject of the book is *not for young readers.*

467. 落花時 *WHEN THE FLOWERS FALL*   1 vol. 163. 169 p. by **耿小的**
1946 正氣書局

In this book the author describes what happens in a Peking household. It is an account of Chinese folklore that is not lacking in interest.

The people are depicted in a picturesque and witty fashion.

The morals of the characters are, however rather crude. They are convincing, but sometimes it is better to draw a veil over the truth! *For adults.*

468. 幽情蜜意 *DELICATE LOVE*   2 vols. 158 & 185 p. by **耿郁溪**
1946 天津勵力出版社

Love in the university, love that is not love yet is all the same! One of the couples is sincere — they often quarrel, once with a good result — and everything is arranged in the end. A proper betrothal takes place. Another couple comes to bad end and lands in prison.

Contains some rather risky passages. *For mature people.*

469. 情漂愛燄 *THE FLAME OF CONSUMING LOVE*
3 vols. 92, 132, & 114 p. by **耿曉堤**
1946 北京書店

It has to be admitted that the author has a certain narrative talent and he is not completely denuded of wit. But his stories are too frivolous to entertain the leisure hours of a serious person.

The present volumes prove this. Actually they are about the amorous affairs of some students in Peking who live together and whose principal occupation is flirting.

All this reads easily, and it is even possible that the author has good intentions, but it is impossible to call this kind of stuff literature. *For mature people.*

470. 意可香 *LOVELY*   1 vol. 158 & 185 p. by **耿郁溪**
1947 勵力出版社

A social novel describing life in the universities of Peking. The author shows how people can be changed by love affairs that are an obstacle to serious study and lead the students to ruin. The cause of these commotions is, according to him, the coquetry of the girls who are nothing but gold diggers.

This book might prove instructive to some people, but it runs the danger of harming the young. *Not for everyone.*

471. 離鄉集 *AWAY FROM HOME*   1 vol. 182 p. by **戈　壁**
                                                   1944　新民印書館

1) Two men from the country, pushed by misery, allow themselves to be hired in the service of the state. Their salary is the very smallest possible and not enough to support their families. One of them is further overcome by misfortune for he falls off a ladder which incapicitates him from work for a very long time. His friend looks after him and has recourse to all sorts of expedients to keep body and soul together. Needless to say, they are thoroughly miserable.

2) The author is recalled to his old home by his father falling seriously ill. He arrives too late to see his father and finds that the latter has already been buried. The family is very numerous and divided among themselves. The village is old fashioned and nothing goes smoothly. Thoroughly discouraged, the author returns to where he ·came from.

3) A bird is caught in the hall. Being in captivity, it refuses to eat even though the greatest trouble is taken to discover its tastes. The bird dies.

4) The touching story of a neighbour.

5) Two friends are delivered from embarrassment. One of them is a drunkard.

6) An expedition against bandits.

    Some other tales are contained, none of which have much interest. *For everyone.*

472. 昨夜 *LAST NIGHT*   1 vol. 70 p. by **顧仲雍**
                                              2nd edition 1927　北新書局

    Four novels are presented in this book written in a flowing style which can be easily read by everyone. It describes life as it is, daily scenes and events. The second novel is unbecoming. *For instructed persons.*

473. 在北極底下 *UNDER THE NORTH POLE*   1 vol. 126 p. by **顧均正**
                                                            1940　文化生活 *See Biogr.* 92

    Three stories, fantastic and scientific.

1. Hypnosis exercised by the Japanese on America.
2. Epidemics in Germany.
3. A curious Nobel Prize.

For everyone.

474. 電子姑娘 *MISS ELECTRON*   1 vol. 166 p. by **顧均正**
                                                   開明書店

    Vulgarisation of certain physical phenomena. *For everyone.*

475. 落花夢 *A ROSY DREAM*   1 vol. 215 p. by **顧明道**
                                                 See Biogr. 93

    A student falls in love with a girl student. Their relations are extremely courteous.
    The girl, however, is recalled by her stepmother and given in marriage to a good-for-nothing.
    The heroine does not wish to consent and commits suicide, whereupon her friend hangs himself not far from her tomb.
For cautioned readers, on account of these suicides.

476. 紅妝俠影 *A CHIVALROUS DAME*   1 vol. 119 p. by **顧明道**
                                                       春明書店

    Romantic and adventuresome deeds of Miss Kao Fei-ch'iang and her father and of his adopted son, Nieh Kang.

Of a noble character but impulsive, independent, proud and somewhat fierce, Kao Fei-ch'iang refuses at first to submit to the desire of her father that she marry Nieh Kang. Kao Fu, a follower who bears a grudge and who is of a jealous temperament, flatters her in everything, and regards coldly her relations with her adopted brother. During a journey to Shansi, her father is slain in a dastardly manner by his sworn ennemy, Hsieh Ta-wu. And soon after, Nieh Kang, having disagreed with our heroine, leaves to look for the murderer of his master.

Kao Fei-ch'iang is at the head of a caravan conducting a rich literatus to his domicile when they encounter brigands. She overcomes them and learns from one of them the refuge of her father's murderer.

On her way to take her revenge, she meets an unhappy literatus on the point of committing suicide because his wife has been raped by a military chief. Our heroine consoles him and promises to bring him his wife on the following day; whereupon she goes to the ravisher's yamen and succeeds in escaping with the victim.

Soon after, urged by a thirst for vengeance, she goes to her father's murdered and provokes him. She fights him and is victorious, but falls into an ambush. On the point of dying, she is saved by Nieh Kang. The murderers of her father and the tyrant fall under their blows.

The people are full of gratitude towards them and shower presents on them. Returning to Tientsin the two heroes married. *Not for everyone.*

477. 紅顏薄命 *THE BEAUTIFUL HAS NO LUCK* 1 vol. 190 p. by **顧明道**
2nd edition 1936 奉天三友書局

The story takes place during the Sung dynasty. A beautiful girl suffered ill-treatment from her step-mother. After the death of her father, our heroine was led away by an officer, in order to marry her to one of his cousins. But her beauty was noticed by the son of a high official, who resolved to seduce her. Therefore the girl was allured to a convent where the abbess persuaded her to remain a virgin; she gave her consent, but in the near future had to fight against the proposals of the official's son. Her friends killed the latter as well as the abbess and our heroine was set free. Then she became sick and died.

The idea in this book is good but due to some obscene passages *everyone should be warned against reading it.*

478. 歌女淚痕 *THE CHORUS GIRL HAS TEARS* 1 vol. 139 p. by **顧明道**
1939 三友書局

The author narrates the life of an actress, Hung Mu Tan, a beautiful character and comparatively virtuous. Hung Mu Tan loved a youth, but being an obedient daughter, she married a low character, as the latter was her mother's choice. She was very unhappy in her married life, for her husband led a bad life and spent all they earned. In the end he was thrown into prison. In the second volume the story will narrate how she was saved by her former friend.

Strictly reserved, as there are a few passages which describe the husband's misconduct.

479. 紅蠶織恨記 *WOVEN WITH MISERY* 2 vol. 139 & 161 pp. by **顧明道**
1941 國元書店

A novel.

The scene took place in a girls' school in Kiangsu. The chief characters are school mistresses and their lovers. Love stories, scenes of jealousy and some sincere friendships are presented in this book. It is rather pessimistic and contains two suicides of school teachers.

Everyone is advised against reading this book, owing to some obscene descriptions and immoral adventures.

480. 惜分飛 *THE PARTING* 3 vol. 244 200 & 210 ppp. by 顧明道
1941 上海春明書店

Episodes from students' life are described in this book. Some couples married after completing their studies. Two of these marriages were unsuccessful (the principle heroine is the unlucky one). The book also depicts the opposition between the ancient and modern worlds. The author ascribes to the female characters more energy than to his male characters.

The style is easy but the novel is rather complicated. There is plenty of detail but the main plot is poor. The end of this book is rather sad. *For enlightened people.*

481. 奈何天 *YE GODS, YE GODS!* 2 vol. 226 & 221 p. by 顧明道
1941 啓智書店

The Li family was ruined by bandits, and only one son remained alive; his name was Teh Wo. In order to provide a living for himself Teh Wo became a tutor in the Ch'en family where his pupil was a modern girl Ch'en Yü-hsüeh. He also was a tutor in a poor family where the mother tried hard to marry her daughter A-Mei — his pupil — to him, but he refused as he loved Ch'en Yü-hsüeh, though his love was without response. The latter fell in love with a vain fellow who was a married man. Teh Wo departed to Shanghai where he found a job, and at the same time helped to edit a revolutionary magazine. After some time he fell ill. In the meantime A-Mei became a concubine to a rich man. She found Teh Wo and took tender care of him; thus he recovered from his illness, and found a job with a good salary. During this time Yü-hsüeh and Yeh Pu-fan fled, having robbed their folks. At the end of the novel Teh Wo met Yü-hsüeh who was sick and died, cursing the man who ruined her.

There are no obscene passages, but the author approves of suicide, concubinage and free modern life. *For enlightened people only.*

482. 吳門碧玉 *THE DAMSEL FROM SOUTH* 2 vol. 136 & 144 p. by 顧明道
2nd edition 1943 東方書店

Ch'ing P'ing and Chu Cheng have long been in love with each other. Ch'ing P'ing becomes a teacher in a girls' school where he gets acquainted with Yun Yin, also a teacher; she is a rich girl and has a good character. The principle of the school acts a go between, but Ch'ing P'ing wants to be true to Chu Cheng. In the mean time Chu Cheng has taken a job in a factory. The manager courts her and she does not succeed in escaping his attentions. In her determination to be faithful to her young man, she thinks of suicide but, as her family depends on her earnings, she finally accepts the manager's advances. At that juncture Ch'ing P'ing proposes to her but she feels that she cannot accept him. Ch'ing P'ing marries Yun Yin. Chu Cheng is broken-hearted.

Fine characters. The misfortunes of the poor, especially of the girls, are caused, according to the author, by the passions of the rich who abuse their power to satisfy their every whim. The author gives unduly detailed descriptions of how this is done. On that ground *the book calls for some reserve.*

In vol. I chapter IX, the author confuses Catholic priests with Protestant ministers; he speaks of the priest's wife.

483. 野草閒花 *RANDOM LOVE*   1 vol. 232 p. by **古燕居士**
                                        1933 環球書局

Story of two young men who frequent bad houses. During the recital, one carries off the concubine of the other, from which event disputes arise, but an arrangement is come to. Nevertheless the girl continues to meet her lover and ends by being taken by him for good.

A licentious atmosphere. *Not to be recommended to anyone.*

484. 海底撈月 *NEEDLE IN THE HAYSTACK*   1 vol. 171 p. by **關菁英**
                                        1941 實業洋行出版部

A story of a girl who left home in order to study in another city, where she met a former acquaintance. Little by little they fell in love with one another, but as he was married the girl was in despair. After some time the girl was called home, where she was married to a man who was a bandit. One day her husband fired at a group in which he thought is his wife, her boy friend and another person. Actually he wounded his own sister and the wife of a friend. After this accident he fled, and our heroine renewed her friendship with her friend, who was then a widower.

As this book contains a number of love scenes and presents a romantic atmosphere, it can be read *only by instructed people.*

485. 風網船 *SAIL BOAT*   1 vol. 212 p. by **關永吉**
                                        1945 華北作家協會

This book contains five stories. The first is a good description of poor people forced to leave their village because of famine. They are on their way to the unknown. The second tells of yamen employees and their occupations.

In the third the author shows his keen observation in his admirable descriptions of the hard life of peasants.

In the fourth he depicts a litle hamlet isolated by water. And in the last he gives us a picture of love that is full of humour.

The last two are only for informed readers.

486. 牛 *CATTLE*   1 vol. 154 p. by **關永吉**
                                        1935 大楚報社

Some old families of peasants are forced to leave the country to establish themselves in the town because of the exactions of certain tyrants. One family that has sought refuge in Tientsin is divided when it is time to return to the country. Eventually one of the sons decides to return to cultivate the soil.

On the way he falls in with thieves who take away the little money that he has. Therefore, when he arrives in the village, he has to struggle against a number of obstacles. The difficulties of the peasants are great, especially as they are exploited by those in power.

Our hero finds that he is not able to conduct a successful struggle with all his enemies, and therefore returns to Tientsin to avoid being utterly undone by them. He retains his courage, however, and reckons on returning to the village later to clean it of all these vampires.

The intention of the author is to show the love the peasant has for the land and the fascination that it exercises on those who have loved it.

For mature people only because of certain crude passages.

487. 童年彩色版 *BOYHOOD IN TECHNICOLOUR* 1 vol. 152 p. by 狂 夢
1942 大華印刷局

A collection of literary essays. The author touches on all sorts of subjects, constantly reverting to the main theme of the book — friendship. The book is well written and the author demonstrates his poetic quality and sensitiveness in everything he describes. Sometimes, however, his main theme is expressed in such a way as to lead the reader into reverie, but in spite of this we believe that the book *may be read by anyone.*

488. 落葉 *LEAVES FALL* 1 vol. 154 p. by 郭沫若（開貞）
1928 上海創造社出版部 *See Biogr. 96*

A collection of forty one letters which are supposed to be written by a Japanese girl, who fell in love with a young Chinese studying in Japan. The latter married, according to the old custom, by his parents, was dissatisfied as he loved the Japanese girl. Owing to his veneral disease he could not accept her love. The girl was protestant and she saw her faults; she often expresses christian feelings.

Owing to the very sentimental atmosphere, as well as the passionate love for a married man this book is fit to be read by *informed readers only.*

489. 水平線下 *BELOW THE HORIZON* 1 vol. 200 and 90 p. by 郭沫若
1929 上海創造社出版部

Dissertations of Kuo Mo-jo on different subjects which moreover, are of little interest.

The book is made up of notes of travels, thoughts on soldiers, disputes between husband and wife, etc.

What strikes one more than anything is the socialist ideas of the author. Several dissertations treat avowedly of Socialism and Communism. *For grown-up people.*

490. 郭沫若選集 *SELECTED WORKS OF KUO MO-JO* 1 vol. 233 p.
萬象書屋

This book presents a collection of short novels.
1) The last days of the emperor whose conscience was not at ease.
2) The separation of Mencius and his wife.
3) Confucius' hunger. He suspects one of his followers, and finally sees his error.
4) The life of a weak man, and his Japanese wife, who left him because of his character.
5) Some details about the hero of the preceding story.
6) A story how a thief brought back stolen books.
7) The meeting of two friends.
8) A story of a wise man.
9) A story of a hero who killed the king and minister of the neighbouring country, and finally killed himself. His sister and a friend set out to find his body, but at the end they fled.
10) A plot in the imperial court.
11) A story of two school girls — their professor, and a wonderful tree.
12) A story about every day events.
13) A life of a military officer who gave his life in a rescue.
14) A story about hens.
15) Author's thoughts about his mother.

As this book contains a number of risky descriptions, and also the fact that the author seems to approve of suicide, it is to be read *only by informed readers,* especially as the author denies the existence of God.

491. 黑貓與塔 *BLACK CAT*   1 vol. 172 p. by 郭沫若
                                                    1930 仙島書店

1. 黑貓 Marriage of the author and political events in Szechwan.
2. Löbernicht 的塔 Events in the life of Kant.
3. and 4. already reviewed (No. 490).
5. 葉羅堤的墓 A love-affair between a brother-in-law and a sister-in-law.
6 and 7. already reviewed (No. 490).
8. 喀爾美蘿姑娘 A father of a family loves another woman. He is ready to commit suicide if he cannot have her.
For grown-up people.

492. 歸去來兮 *RETURNING*   1 vol. 256 p. by 郭沫若
                                                    1936 北新書局

Excerpts from the author's diary. Like his other writings, a great love of his country animates them.

The writer says he is indifferent towards the various sects, but praises the Zikawei mission for its patriotic spirit during the Japanese occupation. It appears to us that he has never investigated the religious question, seeing that he dared to say that the Catholic Church does not permit bathing!!! *For everyone.*

493. 黑貓 *BLACK CAT*   1 vol. 69 p. by 郭沫若
                                                    3rd edition 1942 現代書局

Autobiographic story. At 14 the author's fiancée dies. He resolves never to get married, and declines an offer by a certain Cheng. Although his people seems to approve of his resolve, his mother, later on, insists on his getting married. The author describes his feelings when he learns that a fiancée has been found for him. She is said to be good looking, well educated and her family is of the same social standing as his.

Going back to his native village, he finds it in revolutionary excitement. He tells us of his opinion about the revolution and the New Republic; he describes the nationalism of the young, the unrest caused by the military, the sack of Chiating and the consequent banditry. The civilian population buys rifles and organizes its own defense.

In the auhor's village two such organizations are set up: one headed by his uncle calls itself "pao-wei-t'uan"; the rival group, headed by a certain Yang lang calls itself "pao-an-t'uan". The feud between the two groups brings about the murder of Yang lang.

During this period of unrest his fiancée's people keep urging him to get married. The author's parents ask for his consent. He describes his inward struggle and emotions; he gets tired of being bothered like that and finally consents.

Then he describes the marriage ritual and attempts an explanation of its origin and meanings, the feeling he had when he first saw his bride, her painted face, her bound feet. He visits her family and tells us of his impressions.

The murder of Yang-lang is brought before the tribunal. The author follows the accused to Chiating. He travels to Ch'eng-tu with his sister-in-law.

In the end he tells how his brother took a second wife, and describes the chaotic condition in Szechwan. *For all.*

494. 蘇聯紀行 *TRIP IN THE U.S.S.R.*   by 郭沫若
                                                              1946

This book's title is enough to indicate its character, when we known from other sources the author's ideas; it is a plea in favour of the Russian Soviet regime.

Invited by the Russian government to travel in U.S.S.R. at their expense, Kuo Mo-jo paid his debt of gratitude in this book, which is lively and interesting. It shows industrial regions of Russia, where he sejourned from the 25th June to 16th August 1946.

Let us quote a short paragraph that is, so to speak, a digest of the book: "In Russia I was extremely well entertained. After leaving Moscow by airplain I visited Leningrad, Stalingrad, Tashkent, Samarcande and Toltoi's grave in Yasnaia Poliana. I visited many research institutions, museums, factories, kolkozes, universities, colleges, children's parks. I was present at all sorts of plays, operas, concerts, dancefestivals. I interviewed many workers, peasants, intellectuals, writers, artists and engineers. I was 50 days in U.S.S.R. Although my visit was not a long one, I believe I saw more than some of those who have lived there for 50 years." (Introduction). *For enlightened people.*

495. 郭沫若代表作 *AN ANTHOLOGY OF KUO MO-JO* 1 vol. 295 p.
三通書局

This book presents a number of different narratives.
P 1. The life of the author after he left Szechwan and his stay in Japan.
p. 62. Past events.
p. 117. Events during the author's campaign against the Northern armies.
p 222. A short family drama.
p 274. Punch and Judy scenes.
For all.

496. 塔 *THE TOWER* 1 vol. 325 p. by 郭鼎堂
4th. edit. 1930 商務印書館

A collection of essays on Kant and his fancies, then about a young man who loves his sister-in-law, and then several plays in which one suicide succeeds another. *Everyone to be deterred from it.*

497. 口供 *THE AFFIDAVIT* 1 vol. 98 p. by 郭子雄
1930 中華書局

A number of essays, speeches, and sentimental memories, as well as other narratives, all of which are written in a declamatory style.
It also contains a number of patriotic events from students' life. *For all.*

498. 桂公塘 *KUEI-KUNG POND* 1 vol. 220 p. by 郭源新(鄭振鐸)
1937 商務印書館 *See Biogr.* 27

Patriotic recitals grouped around the invasion of the Mongols and the T'ai P'ing Rebellion. *For everyone.*

499. 取火者的逮捕 *THE CATCHING OF THE FIRE-SNATCHER*
1 vol. 230 p. by 郭源新
1934 生活書局

The book presents several episodes of Grecian mythology such as the theft of the fire and Jupiter's misconduct. The young people of the earth rebelled against the selfishness of the gods, and in the struggle they used the strength of the fire. The gods took shelter on the summit of Mount Olympus, but the mountain disappeared in a terrific cataclysm. Thus men were the conquerors. *For all.*

500. 天堂北獄 *HEAVEN & HELL*   1 vol.85 p. by **藍天使**
上海文新書局

This book features life as either a heaven or a hell. It describes conditions among the lower classes in Shanghai. *To be proscribed.*

501. 老張的哲學 *LAO CHANG'S PHILOSOPHY*   1 vol. 268 p. by **老舍（舒慶春）**
1932, 商務 *See Biogr. 137*

A realistic novel which describes the struggle between the old spirit of the deformed *li-chiao* and the new free and intellectual culture. The story shows how a young couple wanted to get married for love but the "Old man" Chang opposed them, as he wanted his girl for financial reasons to marry a politician. The young man interfered and owing to his courage he won the situation.

Although the book contains a number of passages in which Christians are slightly ridiculed, it *can be read by all.*

502. 離婚 *DIVORCE*   1 vol. 264 p. by **老舍**
1933 良友

This book describes the life of an official in a magistrate's office, showing the daily occupation of the officials. The said official was persuaded by his friend to bring his wife and children to town; on the arrival of his wife he realized that she was clumsy and old; so he began to dream about a young woman who lived in the same yard, whose husband was away and lived with another woman. Our hero remarked the sad results of divorce, and in spite of his passion for the young woman he gave up hope of divorcing his wife, and finally gave up his job and retired, with his wife and children, into the country.

Although the disadvantages of divorce are well stressed, some descriptions are bold and vulgar. The book may be read *by adults only.*

503. 趙子曰 *THUS SAYS CHAO*   1 vol. 348 p. by **老舍**
1933 商務

This book narrates the doings of Chao Tzu-yüeh and other youths, students of Peiping University. The action takes place first in Peiping and then in Tientsin. The book is of small interest to readers save for the successful satire which shows the life of modern students and their interest in all but study.

As there are no obscene passages, and though one immoral allusion is found at the end of the story, the book can be read *by all.*

504. 趕集 *COUNTRY FAIR*   1 vol. by **老舍**
1st edition 1934

Collection of 15 short stories:
1. 五九 A story of a Chinese who spent his time in disparaging everything in his own country.
2. 熱包子 A beaten woman disappeared from her conjugal home, then reappeared six months later, to the joy of her husband.
3. 愛的小鬼 A young married lady received a letter from her so-called cousin, which aroused the jealousy of her husband.
4. 同盟 A story of a man, a theorist on love, who wanted to study female psychology.
5. 大悲寺外 A story of a teacher, very devoted to his pupils, who died the victim of an intrigue; at a meeting he was hit with a brick. His murderer, a senior pupil of his, would have a sad life.

6. 馬褲先生 A passenger in the train between Tientsin and Peiping was constantly calling the boy, as if he were at his exclusive service.

7. 微神 A story of a young man, forced to leave his country in order to subsist; when he returned to China, he heard that his fiancée was a prostitute, and wanted to get her out of this vile profession by marrying her; he came back and found that she had died in childbirth.

8. 開市大吉 Singular proceedings of two partners starting a hospital; extremely ingenious as well as humoristic logrolling.

9. 歪毛兒 A misanthrope related his life to a friend, describing mankind as extremely hateful; a little bit abnormal.

10. 柳家大院 A family believed to be "civilized", modern, because it was reading the newspaper, presented a scene of perpetual dissensions; at the end the daughter-in-law of the house hanged herself and her parents demanded a big sum from her tormentor.

11. 抱孫 Against the will of her mother-in-law who is horrified by modern medical methods, a young woman goes to a hospital for a difficult delivery. The old lady is much pleased with the result but, against the doctor's advice, takes mother and baby home immediately. Both die.

12. 黑白李 A story of two brothers, of whom the elder constantly sacrifices himself for the younger, finally he even offered his life in order to save his brother, and was shot in his stead.

13. 眼鏡 A story of stolen spectacles which ended on the nose of a smart rickshaw-man; but when in danger he threw them on the ground in order to see more clearly, as they inconvenienced his sight.

14. 鐵牛和病鴨 The diverse fortunes of two former students of agriculture who both had little success at the university; the more fortunate stood in the way of his former schoolfellow, who had refused him a place in his house.

15. 也是三角 Two former soldiers associated themselves in order to live more easily; they were satisfied even with a "common" wife. . .Painful situation and a sad life for the three partners.

For enlightened people.

505. 櫻海集 *FORREST OF CHERRIES*   1 vol. 292 p. by 老 舍
                                          1935 人間書屋

上任 The tribulations of a military leader who cannot make two ends meet. *For everyone.*

犧牲 A returned student from America does not like the life in China. He marries, but his wife runs away after a few months. *For everyone.*

柳屯的 Story of a concubine who rules over the legitimate wife, and all the family, and even the village. *For everyone.*

未一塊錢 Speculations on what one can do and not do with a dollar. *For everyone.*

善人 A satire against women who preside over committees devoted to charitable works. They neglect their own families. *For everyone.*

鄰居們 Quarrels between neighbours. *For everyone.*

月牙兒 Confessions of a prostitute. Being forced to adopt this kind of life, she describes to us her clients. As her trade is an illegal one, she finishes in prison. But there her condition seems still more enviable than her former life. *Not for everyone.*

陽光 A girl of a wealthy family wishes to live her own life. She dreams of nothing but love, liberty, and divorce. *Not to be recommended to anyone.*

506. 小坡的生日 *THE BIRTHDAY OF LITTLE PO*   1 vol. 156 p. by 老 舍
                                                      1935 生活

A simple tale of the adventures of a Chinese boy in Singapore.

The first part is interesting and reminds us of Lichtenberger. The second part narrates the dream of our little hero and is rather prolix. In this book the author gives us his opinion about the various races living together in the port city, describing each race with its characteristic qualities and shortcomings. Very original outlook. This book can be read *by all.*

507. 蛤藻集   *CLAMP & WEED*   1 vol. 100 p. by 老 舍
1st edition 1936 4th edition 1946

6 short stories and one of average length:

1) 老字號 A store became bankrupt and was swallowed up by its rivals because it remained true to the old trading methods.

2) 斷魂槍 A story of a general and his rifles.

3) 聽來的故事 A student, who was endowed with no talents, reached the highest position, owing to protection and introduction.

4) 新時代的舊悲劇 A novel of average length about common graft and revenge. It is the hidden struggle between the police commissioner and his underlings. They used almost identical methods of graft, but the chief succeeded in causing the death of the rival who was plotting for his job.

5) 且說屋裡 A crafty, ill-famed politician got himself elected president of an association, but owing to his behaviour he roused the feelings of the pupils of the school where his favourite daughter was studying. He telephoned to the school demanding his daughter's return home; but in vain. This girl was the daughter of his 11th concubine, and was "determined to preserve all the virtue of the house". She however, happened to be the one who appeared at the head of the crowd of demonstrators, carrying the flag.

6) 新韓穆烈德 A student, full of fine dreams about social justice, during the holidays left for home and determined to increase the wages of his father's employees. But when he reached home he learned that his family had been ruined by the economic crisis.

7) 哀啓 A terrible story of a rickshaw coolie's daughter who was kidnapped for ransom. The man received no help from the police nor from any benefactor to pay the money. He took revenge by killing the kidnappers, while his daughter died in tortures.
For everyone.

508. 老牛破車   1 vol. by 老 舍
1937

In this book the author relates his literary experience and theories. It is enough to give a list of the chapters to know the contents of the book.

1) How I wrote "Lao Chang's philosophy" 老張的哲學.
2)   ,,   ,,   ,,   "Chao Tzu says" 趙子曰.
3)   ,,   ,,   ,,   "The two Ma" 二馬.
4)   ,,   ,,   ,,   "Little Po's birthday" 小坡的生日.
5)   ,,   ,,   ,,   "Ta Ming Lake" 大明湖.
6)   ,,   ,,   ,,   "Memories of the Cat's city" 貓城記.
7)   ,,   ,,   ,,   "Divorce" 離婚.
8)   ,,   ,,   ,,   "My collections of novelettes"
9)   ,,   ,,   ,,   "Niu T'ien Tz'u's biography" 牛天賜傳.
10) On Wit.
11) On description of the setting.
12) On description of the characters.
13) Profitable employment of facts and events.
14) Language and style.
For everyone.

509. 駱駝祥子 *RICKSHAW BOY* 1 vol. 238 p. by 老 舍
1937 文化生活出版社

A penetrating but pessimistic social and psychological study.

A country fellow comes to Peking and becomes a rickshaw-coolie. He is a fine man, physically, not afraid of work and determined to make good. He has confidence in himself, is honest and has a keen sense of dignity. His hard work and frugal life enable him to realize his boldest dream: he buys his own rickshaw and becomes a free man.

Hard times soon arrive. Soldiers rob him of his savings and of his rickshaw. Then he is tricked into marrying his employer's daughter. At first he resists, and after his weakness he feels degraded. Although he is supposed to inherit his employer's comparative wealth he tried to avoid the marriage. From then on he sinks gradually lower; his health is impaired and his prospects are thereby ruined. After the death of his wife he has a chance to marry an honest woman, but he lets the opportunity go by.

Then he becomes irregular in habit, neglects his work; takes to drink, abandons all self-discipline until he ends discouraged and wretched. The author finds the reason for all this in the social conditions and the individualism of our time.

The book is well written; the character of the hero, his emotions, his hope and despair are skilfully analyzed. The outlook is rather pessimistic.

A few unbecoming passages. *For informed readers.*

510. 二馬 *THE TWO MA'S* 1 vol. 448 p. by 老 舍
1939 開明書店

Erh Ma goes to England to live with his father. They have a curio-shop. Their life is described, their relations with their landlady and with the family of the minister who converted Erh Ma's father to Protestantism.

They live an uneventful life but the author finds ample opportunity for sarcastic remarks — often to the point — about foreigners in general and Englishmen in particular, who detest the Chinese. He does not forget the shortcomings of his countrymen either. China, according to the author, is not appreciated because she is a weak country and foreigners only bow to the strong.

The book makes interesting reading but it will not further the mutual understanding between East and West. It will rather strengthen the Chinese displeasure with those arrogant, haughty Europeans whose prejudice he occasionally exaggerates. It might be useful to foreigners as it shows the susceptibility of the Chinese to criticism directed against their country and their indignation at the ostracism inflicted on them.

The author seems to approve of free love. *For informed readers.*

511. 文博士 *DOCTOR WEN* 1 vol. by 老 舍
1941 振光排印局

The story relates how a young Chinese finished his studies in U.S.A., and returned to China. He could not use his knowledge in his motherland, and was very disappointed. In the end he married a rich girl from Chinan, whose family found him a position — but not in line with his education —. As the time passed he forgot all his ideas and studies, and came to the conclusion that it was better to get a good position, for which it was not necessary to go and study in U.S.A.

This book can be read *by all.*

512. 小快船 *BATEAU* 1 vol. 198 p. collected by 老 舍
1941 作者書社

A collection of stories edited by Lao Shê but written by other people.

p. 1 小快船 by 陳瘦竹

The daughter of a ferryman is betrayed by a young man of wealthy family who promises that he will marry her. After she is abandoned she commits suicide. Her fiancé kills the seductor. A well-handled story.

p. 65   夏夜夢 by 張天翼

A girl who has been sold into a brothel very young believes that memories of her tender childhood have returned to her. She allows herself to be recked by dreams of freedom and a worthy life.

p. 108   麗麗 by 汪錫鵬

A succession of unhappy circumstances make a worthy girl sink in the world. She is in danger of ending up as a prostitute.

p. 157   鼻子 by 萬迪鶴

Tribulations of a writer afflicted with a red nose, who does not know whether he should be cured of this infirmity.

For grown-up people.

513. 老舍幽默集   *HUMOROUS STORIES BY LAO-SHE*   1 vol. 72 p.
1942   大連滿大書局

Little tableaux and descriptions in which Lao Shê traces, with his mordant and ironic pen, the mean aspects of his environment. *For everyone.*

514. 黑白李   *CONTRASTING BROTHERS*   1 vol. 128 p. by 老 舍
1943   滿大書局

The author paints for us with his customary animation some pictures of daily life: a childhood friend, a very busy lady, a bankruptcy, and stories of family life. *For everyone.*

515. 牛天賜傳   *THE LIFE OF NIU T'IEN-TZ'U*   1 vol. by 老 舍

A story of a childless merchant who found, one day, a baby on his door-steps, and adopted it. When the child grew up he hired teachers for him: the first one was too serious, the other too careless and easy. The latter, after borrowing some money from the merchant, disappeared; hence our hero was sent to school, from which he was expelled in a very short time. His foster mother could not bear the grief and died. Now the young man again continued his studies at home, but after some time he fell in love with a girl whom he met at a scholar's home. The merchant died also of grief and sorrow, and left the young man with no money; his fiancée also left him. At the end the young man was saved by his second, careless teacher, who became rich and wealthy through the borrowed money. This teacher, after he had settled all the orphan's affairs, brought him to Peiping. This book can be read *by all.*

516. 老舍短篇集   *SHORT STORIES BY LAO-SHE*   1 vol. 215 p. 1944

A collection of selected pieces identical, except for two tales, with the collection, 趕集 of the same author. A good anthology that gives us characteristic examples of the author's humour. *For everyone.*

517. 老字號   *OF LONG STANDING*   1 vol. 199 p. by 老 舍
1945   盛京書店

A collection of short stories.

In the preface, the author tells us that he describes the things and people of Peiping as they really are; sometimes ridiculous, sometimes sad.

A number of realistic stories require *some reserve.*

518. 東海巴山集 *SEA & MOUNTAIN* 1946 1 vol. 196 p. by 老 舍

A collection of stories written during the war.

1) 火車 Railway passengers were awakened by a fire on the train in which many were burned.

2) 兔子 A youth with the nickname "rabbit" became a singer but was a failure owing to his weak voice; finally he died of T.B.

3) 殺狗 Patriots who were arrested by the Japanese during a secret meeting.

4) 東西 An ex-student regretted that he studied in England and not in Japan, for it would have enabled him to cooperate more easily with the Japanese. At the end he helped a Jap to steal some precious objects from a tomb.

5) 浴奴 Two young men established a bath-house; the clients were Japanese. These two also arranged to provide two prostitutes. Realistic incidents of low class milieus, where the Japanese were the principal characters.

6) 一塊豬肝 A conversation between a hospital nurse — who showed her joy when she was useful to the wounded — and a young spy — who understood nothing about patriotic feeling.

7) 人同此心 Three men handed together and planned to drive the Japanese out of the city which they were occupying. They carried out their plan with the help of bombs and bullets.

8) 一封家信 A man who worked hard was far from his home, and resolved to send his savings to his wife. He received a letter from the latter which was full of reproach for his avarice.

9) 戀 A collector of curios and precious objects consented to cooperate with the Japanese against his own will, provided that his collection would be intact.

10) 小木頭人 A fable of little "wooden-head" who bravely went to fight the Japanese. He returned home safe and sound because the bullets had no effect upon him. . .while his brother became a "literate" man.

11) 不成問題的問題 A rivalry between two bosses in an agricultural farm; one, who was serious and studied agriculture, had a good harvest, the other who was lazy and incompetent and had not completed his studies, succeeded in ousting the former.

12) 一筒炮台烟 The admirable unselfishness of a young husband who discovered a big sum of money hidden by accident in a present. He returned the money against the will of his wife. "In that way our son will be born clean": the husband concluded.

For enlightened people.

519. 惶惑 *FRIGHTENED & PUZZLED* 2 vol. 621 p. by 老 舍

1st edition 1946 晨光出版公司

A long novel in three parts, each of which contains two volumes of 300 pages. The intention of this book is to give an accurate description of war-time conditions in Peiping. For this reason the daily events of a Pekinese family are placed before the readers. This family, by the name Chi, consisted of four generations, namely: the great-grandfather of 80 years, his son, three grandsons — who were the main characters in the story, their wives and finally the eldest grandson's child. It was the eldest grandson's duty to look after the house, but he was uncertain whether to go away and join the army in the interior in order to fight for his country, or remain at home. At the end he resolved to stay in Peiping, but with regret. The second grandson, Shuei Feng, on the contrary, had no scruples and began to help the Japanese. He obtained a well paid position and an influence gratifying to his self-esteem. He was a frequent visitor in circles of cooperators, and associated with traitors. The third, Shuei Chin, without completing his studies at the university, left to join the army in the interior; he was the hero of the family, but his name was seldom

mentioned. These three brothers present a different attitude towards the invaders. Their neighbours were patriots save one Kuan family which was despised as its members had become servants and hangers-on of the Japanese. They were ready for any well paid job offered by the Japanese. Mrs. Kuan was happy because she obtained the position of principal in a school for Japanese soldiers. Kuan's friends were also corrupt. In the course of the novel the author describes various ceremonies by which the Japanese celebrated their victories in Shanghai, Nanking etc. He also describes the low sentiments of the traitors.
For enlightened people.

520. 偷生 *LIVING SURREPTITIOUSLY*   2 vol. 692 p. by 老 舍
1st edition 1946 晨光出版公司

This is the continuation of the preceding book, and the second of the three parts. While we witness the advance and retreat of the armies and the psychological effect produced on the Chinese, we observe chiefly the intrigues of the traitors. The Chi family is now in the background and the Kuan family are the main characters. Mr. and Mrs. Kuan present themselves as undesirable people from whom all good patriots flee as from disease. Although they felt the growth of the ditch between themselves and their neighbours, they nevertheless seemed to prefer their position to the "opinion of the neighbours". The other cooperators, with whom they kept acquaintance, were also bad. Pretending to be united in one association of cooperators, in their hearts they remained rivals and hated one another. They were jealous of each other for they all strived to obtain the same positions. There were no open quarrels but each person tried to oust his friends, which only increased their hatred against the victims. Shuei Feng was in this way deprived of his position through the avenging act of a conspirator. In patriotic circles the Chi family was never mentioned. The father of the three brothers — Shuei Chuen, Shuei Feng and Shuei Ching — was arrested and beaten by the Japanese for disobeying certain orders. He killed himself through shame. He had led a quiet life in the background and his disappearance did not affect the scene. Shuei Chuen hesitated all the time between his duty and his family. He reproached himself for his lack of courage in remaining at home. Some subordinate characters met with a violent death in the course of the story, either at the hands of Japanese, or in unsuccessful attacks on the city.
For enlightened people.

521. 貓城記 *PEOPLE OF MARS (A Phantasy)*   1 vol. 272 p. by 老 舍
1946 復興書局

A Chinese aviator landed on Mars. His machine broken to pieces, prevented his return to the earth. He relates his experience in the first person. He found himself in the kingdom of cats, the most ancient and the most civilized of nations inhabiting this planet. The Cats are represented as being indolent, cruel, corrupt, gluttonous, without organization, cowardly, and ready to contend with each other. Their national food was made up chiefly of "enchanted leaves" which appeased the temper, but sapped all energy, and promoted indolence and inactivity. Money in circulation was called "kuo-hun", the national spirit. After a stay in the country, the hero of the novel went to the city in order to observe morals and education. All the indications of decadence were visible to his eyes. In primary school, degrees were granted to pupils on the first day of school. Discussions between intellectuals were endless. Museums were empty, as all the objects of art had been sold to foreign nations for millions of "kuo-hun". The statesmen were amusing themselves with big dinners, while the enemy was invading the territory. The enemy came from the East, from the kingdom of Dogs; they were smaller in height than dwarfs, did not look to be very intelligent, but thirsted with rapacity and cruelty. In the army of Cats, disloyalty broke out and generals deserted and allowed themselves to be bribed; resistance was rapidly falling down. The aviator-explorer was the witness of a complete destruction of the nation of Cats. He stayed six more months on Mars planet; then, taking the advantage of a French aeroplane, he returned, safe and sound, to his "great, glorious, and free China."

According to Chinese critics, this witty fiction is a pungent, social satire on the nation, scarcely disguised behind the frame of this feline kingdom; a satire, they add, which assumes the appearance of a caricature, of a very provoking joke, but sometimes very enjoyable. The author, moreover, says himself that the first motive which incited him to write this book was a feeling of discouragement due to military and diplomatic failures.

For all.

522. 火葬 *CREMATION*   1 vol. 125 p. by 老舍
1946, 1st and 2nd edition

A war-time novel on a patriotic subject, the author having devoted his pen to propaganda. Two young men, Ting and Liu, were pretenders to the hand of a young lady Wang, daughter of a "chü-jen" who was esteemed in his town. When the war broke out, Wang (the chü-jen) and Liu, in order to protect their property, found it quite natural to go over to the side of the Japanese, who entrusted them with important posts in the city. During this time, young Ting, a lieutenant in the national army was given a mission to penetrate into the city in which his sweetheart live. He had 32 men with him, and their orders were to massacre the Japanese garrison and the traitors. Liu, knowing of his rival's appearance, made arrangements to kill him. Miss Wang was ashamed of her father, detested Liu and loved no-one but Ting; thus it was with deep affliction that she learned of the death of her fiancé. But the unexpected attack was successful, as the population joined forces with the 32 heroes who were ordered to infiltrate into the city: the Japanese were massacred in big numbers, and the houses of the traitors were set on fire, Wang and Liu perished in the skirmish. Miss Wang joined the Chinese army in order to find employment in the service of her country.

For all.

523. 微神集 *WEI SHEN*   1 vol. by 老舍
1st edition 1947

This collection contains 17 tales, of which 11 had already appeared in the above collection (cf. 趕集 from No. 5 to No. 15 included).

The following are the details of those not yet published.

1) 上任 Dismissal of an official who had been promoted little by little.
2) 犧牲 Description of a student who, on his return from U.S.A., spent his time in boasting about that country and running down his own. He seemed to speak of "sacrifice" all the time but his selfishness had no limits.
3) 柳屯的 A family which had become Protestant, was guilty of lax conduct, especially after the arrival of a concubine who was a zealous propagandist of the religion. The intention to criticize and ridicule Protestantism is clear.
4) 毛毛的 A family drama. A husband with a university degree and his two wives form the main characters.
5) 善人 The classical example of a woman who had nothing to do and who was very selfish; she spent her time in trivial matters but she tought that she was saving the world. A hypocritical social worker.
6) 鄰居們 Disputes between two neighbouring families, interwoven with martial incidents, where a bad boy was a recent convert to the Protestant faith.

For enlightened people.

524. 老舍幽默傑作集　*BEST HUMOROUS WORKS OF LAO-SHE*

1 vol. 117 p. by 老　舍

1946　上海毅力書局

A book that is full of humour. It contains nothing contrary to good morals, but sometimes ambiguous expressions are used and the ideas expressed are not orthodox. *Not for the young.*

525. 庶務日記 *DIARY OF A PURCHASING CLERK*　1 vol. 116 p. by 老向（王向辰）

1945　時代圖書公司　*See Biogr. 165*

A satire on the life of government officials. The descriptions are vivid and lively, written in a good style, showing the occupations of high officials in the form of a diary, where it appears that most of their time is spent in courting the wives and daughters of their bosses, neglecting their duty and the welfare of people. He also states that owing to their preoccupation with their personal welfare, they plot against each other, each trying to succeed in winning the master's favour. The accounts are often the source of worry; so much money is spent to please the ladies! But after a good dinner and some drinks the boss usually loses his adamantine air.

A few risky insinuations. *For informed readers.*

526. 黃土泥　*YELLOW EARTH*

1 vol. 170 p. by 老　向

1936　人間書屋

About thirty short tales. The subject of nearly all of them is life in the country. The author knows his background perfectly well and describes with zest the usages and customs in the country. Many of these tales are very interesting.

The last twenty pages of the book in our hands were missing so they have not been examined. *For everyone.*

527. 全家村　*ŢUAN CHIA TS'AI*

1 vol. 182 p. by 老　向

上海宇宙風社

We are introduced to a national hero, who lost his right arm and four fingers on the left hand. The government wanted to look after him but he refused. A hospital supplied him with a wooden arm. The hero imagined all the time that he had lost his heart too, and after his arm was restored he went in search of the former. When he arrived home he found that everything was changed, and was much displeased. His kinsfolk celebrated his return, during which our hero fell asleep. In his dream he was presented with different hearts; one of straw, one of wood, and the third one of iron. When he awaked he demanded for the iron heart.

This book is like a fairy tale, very innocent and simple. It can be read *by all.*

528. 良田　*GOOD LAND*

1 vol. 135 p. by 雷妍（劉植蓮）

1943　大華印書局　*See Biogr. 108*

This is a Chinese version of "The Good Earth" by Pearl Buck.

Asked to treat the same theme as the American author Miss Lei produced this book.

She has not the power of observation and analysis found in Pearl Buck, but equals her in expressing feelings and emotions.

The book gives a faithful description of life on the land and of the affection between married people.

Hao Ta, farm hand of Mrs. Lin's, loves a poor girl. Mrs. Lin arranges for their marriage which takes place on the same day as his younger brother's. Hao Ta is happy and is soon better off. Hao Erh is not so sound as his elder brother.

The book describes Mrs. Lin, generously helping those around her. She is persecuted by her brother-in-law, a mean character. The book describes weddings, funerals, famine and banditry.

The characters in the book often show passionate love, but always between the right persons. *For all.*

529. 阿鳳 *FENG, THE GIRL*   1 vol. 124 p. by   冷　西
 1931   中華書局

This book contains seven short stories which deal chiefly with love: free love, divorce, etc. None of these stories is commendable. The first three novels will upset any serious person; they should be banned. The others can be read by grown up folks; the atmosphere is unhealthy for the young generation. *To be proscribed.*

530. 羅帳秋風 *THE BREEZE IS CHILLING*   1 vol. 176 p. by   冷香樓
 1946   百新書局

The story begins with an engaged couple. The girl's step-mother wishes to separate them and to give the girl as a concubine to a rich old man. The heroine escapes and goes to Tientsin in search of her fiance. The latter, in the meantime, has got involved with an actress. Everything ends happily, however, and the principals are married. *Not for everyone.*

531. 斷腸風月 *LOVE IS SAD*   1 vol. by   冷　氷
 1946   三益書局

The romantic tale of a young man of good family which, however, is devoid of interest. He abandons the girl chosen by his parents. The old people intervene but the young ones pay no attention to them. The favoured girl dies, and there is a suicide to round out the affair. *For everyone.*

532. 唐小姐 *MISS T'ANG*   1 vol. 216 p. by   李阿毛
 1942   大連實業印書館

The author tells us of the life of two sisters. The elder, Yu Wei, is typist to a manufacturer. She has a serious character and falls in love with an employee of the same firm, who named Hsiao Ch'en who seems to return her sentiments.

The younger sister, Ch'in-p'ing, is impulsive and has no reserve. Directly Hsiao Ch'en makes her acquaintance, he falls in love with her and marries her.

Yu Wei suffers a great deal from this marriage, but, in spite of it, rests attached to her brother-in-law.

The director of the factory falls in love with her and asks her hand in marriage. Yu Wei, however, has no great regard for his character, and refuses him after she has discovered that he has been flirting with her sister.

This is an uninteresting novel as it is lacking in plot. *For everyone.*

533. 雨後殘蕾 *FLOWERS THAT SURVIVED THE STORM*   黎正甫
 1935   傳信印書局

Five students are staying together in Peking and are well-served by an amah no longer in her first youth. Their conversations are very animated and always charitable. One day they go for a walk, and find a girl lying unconscious in the road. They take her home, and ask the amah to look after her. The latter develops an affection for the child who recounts her adventures. As the result of a notice in the newspaper, the father of the child comes and wishes to take her home.

This is an edifying book. Several of the characters are Catholic, and in it, the author shows the force of Christian charity. *For everyone.*

534. 暴風雨前 *THE CALM BEFORE THE STORM*   1 vol. 328 p. by **李劼人**
2nd. edit. 1940 中華書局 *See Biogr.* 97

A novel of which the scene is laid during and immediately after the Boxer Rebellion, and treating of the cultural and social revolution of China. It is mostly about students.

In contains too vivid descriptions of their amorous relations and multi-angular love affairs. *Not for the young.*

535. 西山之雲 *CLOUDS OVER THE WESTERN HILLS* 1 vol. 145 p. by **李健吾**
1928 上海北新書局 *See Biogr.* 98

A book of selected short stories: the first three are only an outline while the fourth is well developed. It describes the life of a melancholy youth who fled to Western Hills in order to cure his sorrow. There he fell in love with a Manchu woman. The latter was poor, as her husband was a soldier and she had also to support her old mother and adopted son. Her husband tried to persuade her to accept the wooing of the student but she, being honest, resolved to die.

Sentimental and fatalistic. *Some reserve.*

536. 壜子 *THE JAR*   1 vol. 206 p. by **李健吾**
1931 開明書店

A collection of nine stories which partly deal with love, and partly with military life. 又一身 describes the life of a soldier who died from wounds. Thus he followed the fate of his grandfather and father, who were both military men. It describes the sorrow and grief of his grandmother and mother.

末一個女人 describes the mother's revenge on a soldier, who killed her only son; it presents a scene of horror.

These stories are not without a certain tragic beauty. In the first two, there is too much love-making between unmarried persons and also a number of objectionable descriptions (p. 129 and 84). *For informed readers.*

537. 希伯先生 *MISTER HIPPO*   1 vol. 90 p. by **李健吾**
2nd. edit. 1940 文化生活

A collection of tales, memories, and sketches.

Of a worker who becomes a hero, a portrait, a strong woman, another portrait, a memory, a literary anecdote, the love of women, the theatre, and reflections on many things and people. *For adults.*

538. 大街的角落 *THE STREET CORNER*   1 vol. 151 p. by **黎錦明**
1936 北新書局 *See Biogr.* 99

Six stories.

All of these are rather dull and present no interest to the reader. The third contains an objectionable passage. *For informed readers.*

539. 春粧豔影 *IN GRAND ATTIRE*   1 vol. 95 p. by **李涵秋**
1939 東方書店

This book presents us with a festival period during which the guests acted and recited poems. The young men all had their girl friends. There was a young man who fell in love with a poor girl with a bad reputation. He went and lived with her; but as he was very lazy, the girl had to earn the living for both of them. At the end the girl died. *Everyone should be warned against reading it.*

540. 鳳女多情記 *THE DAMSEL IS LOVELORN*   2 vol. 128 p. by 李醒非
1943 京津小小書店

The sentimental experiences of a young person, first as a girl, then as a young wife, and eventually as a public woman. *To be proscribed.*

541. 佳人淚史 *DAMSEL IN SORROW*   3 vol. by 李醒非
1946 平津國民書店

Although the title is different, this is the same book as that reviewed under the name of 鳳女多情記

A sequel has been added here in the form of the third volume. This volume, however, should also be proscribed, as it contains nothing but vulgarities seasoned with dirt. *Proscribed.*

542. 白衣天使 *AN ANGEL IN WHITE*   2 vol. 223 p. by 李薰風
See Biogr. 101

A story of Mr. Hu who was seriously ill; his concubine, Wang Ai-li, wished to kill him in order to possess his money, but as she was unable to do so herself she tried to win Dr. Feng to her plan. The latter was seized with remorse and took poison. All this affected Wang Ai-li so much that she was brought to the hospital. Here she saw how a nurse was seduced. The latter, being good, resolved to die; she took poison, but as it was not strong, she was cured; in the meantime the concubine stole the nurse's poison and mixed it with her husband's food. Somehow she was caught while doing so. After being informed, Mr. Hu threw her off and she had to earn her living in a dancing hall. *This book can be read by adults.*

543. 北京明星 *A STAR OF PEKING*   2 vol. 164 & 164 p. by 李薰風
1940 華新書局

The story narrates how Liu Cheng-ai wanted to meet Miss Chien; for this reason he went to a brothel, where he sought his friend Ch'en Ta-shao who arranged the meeting. But Miss Chien was not attracted by Liu and asked for jewels from Ch'en. The latter had no money so Liu Cheng-ai promised to get some. After his return his wife quarrelled with him, but at the end she gave him a sum to pay for his debts and found him a good job. Later Liu Cheng-ai succeeded in making his wife unfaithful and stole her jewels. Now that he possessed jewels and a good position, he booked a room in a hotel and invited Miss Chien. The latter was not satisfied with the jewels as they were common. Further romantic adventures between the hero and other women are then described.

The book was first printed as a serial in the "Shih Pao". *Very objectionable.*

544. 雨下殘荷 *PERSECUTED BY RAIN*   2 vol. 202 & 214 p. by 李薰風
1940 北京義文書局

This book contains two parts: the first is an essay about drama. The second describes the life of a girl who was an opium-addict. She married; later on she was sold to a brothel. After some time she was sent to a reformatory. *For experienced people only.*

545. 北國春秋 *THE NORTHERN COUNTRY*   2 vol. 143, 166 p. by 李薰風
1941 鴻文書局

A girl of very good character hesitates between two suitors. One is a cousin of licentious habits, the other a serious student. She does not love the former but her mother desires the match.

The cousin abuses her to such an extent that she plunges into a disorderly life. The other, however, looks after her in spite of her degradation and helps her to die decently. *For everyone.*

546. 北京花　*PEKING FLOWER*　　　1 vol. 160 p. by 李薰風
1941　同化印書館

A novel in which three girls are described; the first two were the daughters of rich parents; the last was a poor girl of low origin, but was bestowed with even more beauty and a finer character than the two other girls. She keeps her serenity in every misfortune and her example encourages the two rich girls. There is hardly any sequence in the various scenes. Although one passage deals with a boy who tried to seduce a servant there is nothing shocking in it. *For all.*

547. 桃李門牆　*BLOSSOMS OVER THE WALL*　　2 vol. 191 & 185 p. by 李薰風
1942　勵力出版社

A novel that is rather poorly written. The story is very disconnected.

It describes the life of boy and girl students, their flirtation and indifference towards their studies; even the coming tests do not bring them back to their work. One of the characters, Mr. Chao, the director of the school, had a fiancée — a rich American girl — during his stay in U.S.A. After his studies he returned to China, and married a Chinese girl. His former fiancée — the American girl — came to China and tried hard to win back his love, but she did not succeed as Mr. Chao remained faithful to his Chinese wife. He even regretted his frivolous time in U.S.A.

Many objectionable descriptions, equivocal allusions and off-colour insinuations. *Unprofitable reading for anyone.*

548. 野薔薇　*WILD ROSES*　　　2 vol. 112 & 162 p. by 李薰風
1942　百新書店

A stupid book. It is impossible to make head or tail of the adventures of the young men and girls involved.

As the story holds some lewd passages, *everyone should be advised against reading it.*

549. 春城歌女　*A SING-SONG GIRL*　　2 vol. 191 & 218 pp. by 李薰風
1943　奉天大東書局

A novel which presents Mr. T'ien, a professor, who fell in love with a girl he saved and supported. His wish was to make her an actress. He also paid and supported her folks. Among his descriptions, the author, scatters love-scenes which are very unbecoming Although she promised to marry, the girl was trapped by a mandarin who succeeded by getting a good position for her father. Finally she became his concubine . Mr. T'ien, who was greatly shocked by this news, could not help in any way. Owing to the illtreatment in her new house the girl began to feel remorse for her ingratitude towards her benefactor; she soon fell sick and was taken to a hospital. Before her death she asked to see her benefactor, but he arrived too late. *All are advised against this book.*

550. 學府風光　*COLLEGE SCENE*　　　1 vol. 166. p. by 李薰風
1946　文興書局

The author tries to describe modern student life. He does not, however, touch on anything serious. The whole book consists of nothing but conversations between students of their amorous experiences.

There are no immoral passages, *but people should be dissuaded from reading this book,* as it runs the danger of distracting the imaginations of students.

551. 路柳牆花　*UNFORESEEN*　　　　　　by 李薰風
1947　勵力出版社

The same book as that reviewed as No. 548. *Not to be recommended to anyone.*

552. 再生集 *REBIRTH*   1 vol. 314 p. by **李輝英**
                                              1936 新鐘書局 *See Biogr. 102*

A collection of a large number of essays written in clear and easy language. The author touches upon many subjects, but has a marked preference for the various evils that society suffers from. He likes to describe the sufferings of the poor, and different essays describe certain sections of society. From the moral point of view there is nothing to take exception to, but some of the subjects dealt with, are not suitable to readers who are too young. Nevertheless, as the author does not give any improper details, we consider that the book may be read by anyone. *For everyone.*

553. 人間集 *MAN AMONG MEN*   1 vol. 237 p. by **李輝英**
                                              2nd edition 1937 北新書局

A collection of seven stories which are all written in a good style. This book may, with the necessary caution, be read *by informed readers.*

554. 津門艷跡 *AN AMOROUS EVENT IN TIENTSIN* 2 vol. 175 p. & 165 p. by **李然犀**
                                              1941 大陸廣告公司印刷部

A collection of stories.

These stories show how powerful men from Tientsin intervened in disputes in order to restore peace.

On page 181 there is a vulgar conversation about a frivolous woman; owing to this the book is *only for enlightened people.*

555. 畫廊集 *GALLERY OF PICTURES*   1 vol. 181 p. by **李廣田**
                                              1936 商務印書館 *See Biogr. 103*

1. A gallery of pictures.
2. Captain of the civic guard.
3. Impressions on the manuscript of a diary.
4. Memory of a friend.
5. A madman who drowns himself.
6. Meeting of two brothers.
7. A melancholy recital.
8. Impressions of Autumn.

Very good style. *For everyone.*

556. 灌木集 *BUSHES*   1 vol. 228 p. by **李廣田**
                                              2nd edition 1946 開明書店

A fine collection of essays that *everyone may read.* The author likes to describe characters and psychology. Nature too comes to life under his pen.

557. 現代小說精選 *A TREASURY OF MODERN SHORT STORIES*
                                              1 vol. 254 p. coll. by **李公耳**
                                              1936 春明書店

A collection of short stories by different authors, who write chiefly on love; as the atmosphere is unhealthy, *everyone is advised against reading it.*

Some novels as "Kung Yüan chung," "Shu Tai tzu" "Tsao Wu ti" clearly show the outlook of the book.

558. 崇高的母性 *LOFTY MOTHERHOOD*   1 vol. 114 p. by **黎烈文**
                                              1946 文化生活出版社 *See Biogr. 104*

First the narrator confides in the reader regarding his wife whom he met in France while he was a student there. Then we are given the story of a man who planted a tomb with white roses. A few reminiscences end the book. *For everyone.*

559. 蛇蝎美人 *BEAUTIFUL BUT DANGEROUS*   1 vol. 100 p. by 李 明
1946   業餘出版社

We are told how a young man originally of good character is ruined through bad company when he goes to town.

The moral of the book is good but it contains descriptions that are not for the young. *Not for everyone.*

560. 白夜 *NIGHT THAT IS NOT DARK*   1 vol. 181 p. by 麗尼（郭安仁）
1937   文化生活 *See Biogr.* 95

Vivid descriptions of the misery of China. *For everyone.*

561. 津沽春夢 *A ROMANCE IN TIENTSIN*   2 vol. 115 & 110 pp. by 李山野
天津河北出版社

1. A story of an honest "defender of right" who killed a number of soldiers and officers, because they seduced members of the weaker sex.
2. Story of a rich man who got his money in an illegal way: he spent his life in the company of prostitutes.

As this book contains a number of immoral descriptions *it should be banned.*

562. 紅粉小牛   1 vol. 162 p. by 李山野
1941   昌明書店

The book relates how Hung Yen, who was the adopted daughter of a rich family, lived illicitly with her "brother" T'ien Lin, who built a hotel where they lived; after some time his lawful wife found out and also came to live in the hotel. Hung Yen's real mother urged her to ensnare another rich man; in order to succeed she pretended to be a virtuous girl. *Everyone should be advised against reading it.*

563. 香閨夢 *DREAM IN A FRAGRANT CHAMBER*   1 vol. 235 p. by 李山野
1946   正氣書店

Account of a good peasant family who are forced to leave their village because of consecutive famines. They make a painful journey to Tientsin in the hope of finding work. The misfortunes of the daughter are also given. Some rakes try to seduce her. This last aspect gives a particular atmosphere to the book, which makes it unsuitable for young readers. *Not for everyone.*

564. 雙鳳伴凰 *TWO AFTER THE SAME LASS*   194 p. by 李鐵民
奉天東方書店

A student from a middle school fell in love with two girls who also admired him. One of the two girls had an admirer, who was her cousin. The latter, out of jealousy, attempted to kill his rival. The first attempt caused a serious but not fatal injury, while the second one completely failed. Meanwhile the student's school-mates resolved to arrange the ceremony for the "double-marriage". His rival was very glad when he found out that the father of his ideal refused to give his consent to the double-marriage, as he considered it to be "bigamy". The girl became sick, but this did not change her father who, in spite of his wife's scoldings and even blows, refused to give his consent. The same students resolved to outwit the old man; for this purpose they placed a doll in the place of the sick girl and again asked her father whether he would give his consent now his daughter was dead. Not knowing that it was simply a doll, the father, thinking that his daughter was dead, gave his consent. Thus, the student married the two girls and everyone was happy. This book contains no lewd scenes but its theories are evidently false. *To be reserved.*

565. 青青河畔草 *MEADOWS ARE GREEN* 1 vol. 95 p. by 李紫尼
1946 江城出版社

A young man, having finished his studies, joins the air force. He conducts him-self heroically, is wounded and taken to a hospital where a young nurse falls in love with him. But the pilot wants to remain faithful to a girl from his native village, who for him represents the ideal woman. Having, however, been separated from his ideal during all the years of the war, he finishes by marrying the nurse. On the day of his marriage, he receives the order to start out on a new mission.

Shortly afterwards, his young wife is wounded and dies. His "ideal" then returns to the scene. She becomes blind from the effect of poison gas used by the enemy. When the war ends, the pilot tries again to marry her, but the heroine prefers continuing to work for her country, in spite of her blindness.

A beautiful war novel. *For everyone.*

566. 爬山虎 *THE IVY* 1 vol. 147 p. by 李韻如
1937 協光印刷公司

A number of short stories. *For everyone.*

567. 錦秀集 *WORDS OF PEARL Essays by* 林語堂 *put together with notes* by 梁廼治
朔風書店印行

The author condemns the bustle and yearning for success which was brought to China by the Americans. He praises the Chinese "dolce farniente". In "Chinese humanism" the author deals with the meaning of life. Unlike the solutions of Christianity and Buddhism, the Chinese answer is remarkable for its absence of hope in a next life. The lesson is "all happiness is to be taken from life itself." Next the author tries to prove his point of view by giving some examples. In T'ao Yüan-ming, he discovers an ideal epicurian. Chang Ch'ao belonged to the same school and furthermore he approved of concubinage and nudism.

This is enough to pass a judgement on the book and to warn the reader about the materialistic and hedonistic outlook of the author. *Everyone should be advised against reading it.*

568. 天津小姐 *MISS TIENTSIN* 2 vol. (I & II) 108 & 100 pp. by 梁丙周
3rd edition 大通書局

A novel of Chia Tzu-yü, who was sixteen years old when he fell into poverty. He had such a fine character and good education, that four Tientsin girls fell in love with him. Three of the said girls were rich.

In this book there is nothing serious apart from the description of the character of the poor girl. The book contains no risky scenes but it will disturb the reader's imagination. *For grown up people.*

569. 天津小姐 *MISS TIENTSIN* vol. III by 梁丙周
3rd edition 1938 大通書局

More adventures of Chia Tzu-Yü and the four Tientsin girls. In these scenes our hero remains all the time in the back-ground.

The author describes some scenes between the Tientsin girls, showing their jealousy. Then he describes the flight of Chia Tzu-yü who joined general Chao's army.

This book contains a number of frivolous scenes. *Only for grown up people.*

570. 摩登花　*A VERY SOCIAL GIRL*　　　2 vol. 78 & 109 p. by 　梁丙周
　　　　　　　　　　　　　　　　　　　　　　　　　　1938　大通書局

Two volumes of a series that is still incomplete. This is a stupid book considered and criticized from every point of view. It chiefly contains descriptions of the flirtations of a rake. No passage can be called obscene, *but all border on the immoral.*

571. 鳥語花香　*BIRDS SING & FLOWERS BLOSSOM*　2 vol. 143 & 153 pp. by 梁丙周
　　　　　　　　　　　　　　　　　　　2nd edition 1943　聚勝堂立記書局

Liang Ping-chou is a very dangerous author from the moral point of view. We have another proof of it in this book.

This book is of no interest and has no main theme. In spite of this, it is in the second edition. The reason is that the author has the trick of bringing his young people together. He does not pass the limits of decency but, somehow, by very frivolous descriptions, he troubles the imagination. This book is *to be proscribed.*

572. 桃源　*PEACH FOREST (A Phantasy)*　　1 vol. 106 p. by 梁世熙
　　　　　　　　　　　　　　　　　　　　　　　1940　義文書局

An account of a journey to and from T'ao-yuan, and of excursions in its environs. It contains descriptions of places and of Nature in different seasons.

During the course of the recital the author tells us of the love affairs between girl and boy students, and especially of the sentiments of the principal personage, Mr. Mu, towards two young ladies, Hsiao Ling and Chu Ju, and a little girl, Wen Hsien.

These relations, formed with a view to walks, celebrations, etc. occur too frequently and above all, are too sentimental.

For this reason it seems that *this book should be classified among those held back from young readers.*

573. 阿弓　*AH KUNG*　　　　　　　1 vol. 71 p. by 列躬射
　　　　　　　　　　　　　　　　　　1936　東方文藝社

A rather commonplace story of a certain Ah-Kung. *For everyone.*

574. 黑屋　*THE DARK ROOM*　　　　1 vol. 204 p. by 漣清
　　　　　　　　　　　　　　　　　　1937　商務印書館

Nine stories. Descriptions of ordinary life in the town and in the country. Usages and customs. Also abnormal situations in China. *For everyone.*

575. 鞭苔下　*SCOURGED*　　　　　　1 vol. 120 p. by 林珏
　　　　　　　　　　　　　　　　　　1946　萬葉書店

We are here given a number of incidents that happened during the Japanese occupation. As such incidents have been too familiar and we are still too near them, they do not have any great interest for us.

This book, moreover, contains some crude details. *Not for very young people.*

576. 嫂夫人　*SO MADAME IS CONTEMPLATING SEPARATION?*
　　　　　　　　　　　　　　　　　1 vol. 180 p. by 林鳳
　　　　　　　　　　　　　　　　　　1945　北京沙漠書店

An intellectual has married a country woman who cannot adapt herself to the ways of the town and remains a peasant. A divorce naturally follows.

Our hero then marries an ultra-modern woman and his life changes entirely. It becomes, in fact, a continual succession of fetes, dances, excursions, etc. to such an extent that he cannot do any serious work. Life becomes a hell for him. He wishes to have a child, but his wife prefers abortion. When he is ill, she does not want to nurse him from fear of being infected. Summoned to his bedside when he is dying, his wife is bored and before going, first smokes a cigarette. And she does not go until after she has fed her little dog.

An excellent book for modern youth thinking of marriage. *For everyone.*

577. 神怪諷刺 *SATIRE*   2 vol. 93 & 91 p. by 林修千
                                                    1946 經緯書局

1) Forty-two ghost stories. Gruesome tales without literary merit.
2) The heroic acts of brigands, mandarins, demons. Magical rites.

Not for those who are too young as their imaginations would be stimulated in an undesirable way. *Not for everyone.*

578. 金田鷄 *A GOLDEN FROG*   1 vol. 118 p. by 林蘭編
                                                    1933 開明書店

A collection of popular little stories to tell to children. *For everyone.*

579. 明朝 *TOMORROW*   1 vol. 188 p. by 林曼青
                                                    1929 亞東圖書館

A story of a poetic and enthusiastic young student who fell in love with several women. At first he resisted the temptations of a prostitute; this is described in undue detail; he also resisted the love of a woman who was about to get a divorce. The author also describes this minutely. Finally he let himself go finding a thousand excuses for his lust and his sin. *This book should be proscribed.*

580. 濃烟 *THICK SMOKE*   1 vol. 488 p. by 林參天
                                                    1936 生活書店

The aim of the author is to inform us of the state of education in Malaya, but although his book is voluminous, he has not attained this end. Instead of telling us about education, he tells us of uses and customs in the Malayan islands.

The book lacks interest, and the author congratulates himself a little too much, taking for granted that his own country is as modern as the city of Paris, and as if the Malayans were in comparison, extremely backward.

He also claims that religions have become out-of-date in the scientific age. And in addition, there are some crude details delineated in his pages. To be recommended *with caution* to people warned of the dangers.

581. 京華烟雲 *MOMENT IN PEKING* 3 vol. 333, 269 & 251 pp. in Engl. by 林語堂
                                                    See Biogr. 106

Lin Yü-t'ang introduces us to two big Chinese families: one of a rich merchant Yao, and the other of a high official Tseng. The period involved comprises two regimes — Imperial and Republican. The principal character is Mu Lan, the eldest daughter of Mr. Yao. She is pretty, intelligent, with a happy-go-lucky character. Her sister, Mu Ch'ou, has a more solid character. Mu Lan, in her childhood, was lost during a journey and was found by a female Boxer, from whom she was ransomed by Mr. Tseng. She came to like Tseng's family and was married to one of their sons, a lazy but kind fellow. Before her marriage she got introduced to K'ung Li-fu, a young intellectual of great promise, whom she came to like, though she always remained dignified and true to her fiancé. K'ung Li-fu married her sister, Mu Ch'ou, who succeeded in calming down his advanced ideas. When the revolution broke out in Peiping Mu Lan's daughter was killed. This loss and the sad plight of Yao's family, brought about by the bad conduct of her brother, Ti Jen, made her leave for Hangchow and thence for the interior in order to escape foreign occupation. In this book the author describes the life of these two families under two different regimes, namely:

the conservative Empire and the revolutionary Republic. All this upheaval does not break the constancy of old people, but makes the young lose their balance. To complete the picture, Lin Yü t'ang introduces us to Mr. Niu, the minister of finance, and his family. This set-up allows the author to describe: firstly Mr. Yao, a sedate man, who seeks his happiness in Taoism and does not reject modern ideas; secondly Mr. Tseng, a resolute official of the old regime who admits no compromise; and lastly Mr. Niu, a merchant and profiteer of the old regime. Next he describes the young generation: Mu Lan, a modern woman, though restrained in her modernism; her brother, Ti Jen, an erring fellow; Mr. Tseng's sons, swimming between two currents; and his daughter-in-law (née Niu), who divorced her husband, being dissatisfied with the old regime of Tseng's family; Li Fu, a young intellectual, who wants to destroy everything. Lastly goes the youngest generation who openly ally themselves to the new ideas. Lin Yü-t'ang introduces us to all these undercurrents of society without passion and violent shocks which is one of the good qualities of his book, and distinguishes him from Pa Chin and young modern authors. *This book* however, *can be read by experienced persons only,* as the author approves of divorce and concubinage and describes, though with reserve, a few bedroom scenes. This great work was greatly expurged: in the first edition we have a description of the grip the foreign countries had on China; there is also a description of "agreements" with regard to frontiers and foreign concessions, and scenes of invasion. A powerful work that will be in vogue for many years to come, as the revolutionary spirit of China is described calmly, and its set-up is on firm grounds. It is longwinded at times, but nevertheles interesting for non-Chinese readers. It gives us a detailed picture of family and social life in China.

582. 瞬息京華 *MOMENT IN PEKING*   1 vol. 314 p. by 林語堂

A resume of "Moment in Peking" reviewed under No. 581. The Chinese title of this present volume may be translated as "A Moment of Repose in Peking". The present volume is a compressed and expurgated version that may be placed in anyone's hands, but it has less flavour than the original. *For everyone.*

583. 雛 *CHICKS*   1 vol. 200 p. by 楳魂女士 & 文濤先生
                                                               1932

The authors (a man and a woman) present their letters; each letter is accompanied by their latest literary product. The letters deal almost exclusively with impressions and emotions. The book is written in a difficult language and a would-be poetical style.

Many passages are obscure and long-winded, the authors getting lost in an attempt at psychological analysis. They want to bring home to the reader the influence of social conditions on the minds of the people. The main theme is the disastrious effect of the "old style" marriage.

Several essays are depressing. One, the diary of a grandmother, gives a clear idea of the position of women in big Chinese families. *For all.*

584. 花之寺 *THE MONASTERY OF FLOWERS*   1 vol. 182 p. by 凌淑華
                                                          1928 新月 *See Biogr. 107*

In this collection, of a dozen short stories, the authoress describes some intimate dramas in which she proves a good psychologist.

1. A strange desire.
2. A melancholy memory.
3. A deception caused by love.
4. Meeting of a man with his girl friend.
5. Conversation between two sisters.

7. Rendezvous between a couple.
8. A septegenarian and his family.
9. An egoistic mother.
10. Friendship between girls.
11. Waiting that ends in a drama.

6. An unhappy marriage.   12. A memory.

A reserve to be made on the tenth story that describes a sensual, friendship.

585. 女人   *WOMEN*   i vol. 191 p. by **凌淑華**
                                                      1930 商務印書館

A book which contains a number of descriptions of women taken from real life.

1. A life of a school-girl; her life later when she has children to support.
2. Description of a widow servant who sacrificed her life for her soldier son.
3 Description of a devoted wife who gave her life for her ailing husband.
4. Busy women.
5 A young married couple in love.
6. A girl who was in love with her fiancé, but left him because she felt that she would harm his future by her marriage.

All the descriptions are well drawn; some however are too realistic, as in No. 1, and *should not be read by young students.*

586. 小哥兒倆   *ALLEGIANCE*   1 vol. 262 p. by **凌淑華**
                                                      1939 良友復興圖書公司

A dozen stories well told and full of life and freshness, especially the first. Some risky passages but the book may be read by anyone. *For everyone.*

587. 柳惠英   *MISS LIU*   1 vol. 137 p. by **凌淑華**
                                                      1943 盛京書局

1. A girl loves a young man to distraction.
2. Moving house.
3. Dress-making.
4. Love of a maid for her son.
5. Regrets of a girl student for having gone abroad.
6. A woman meets her old flame.
7. A very proud girl student and her idyll with a young man.

For everyone.

588. 痴情鴛侶   *THE STEADFAST LOVERS*   1 vol. 119 p. by **劉志剛**
                                                           1944 東亞書局

A story of a young woman who was disappointed with her marriage. She lived for a number of years with her husband. The latter died and she was given into a marriage to another man whom she also hated. The only comfort she had was her child and the memory of her first boy-friend. After the death of her second husband she became a prostitute. One day she met her former boy-friend but he was very poor and could not buy her freedom, so they committed suicide together. *To be proscribed.*

589. 支那女兒   *CHINESE DAUGHTER*   1 vol. 221 p. by **劉大杰**
                                3rd. edit. 1932 北新書局 *See Biogr. 111*

姐姐的兒子 During a time of great cold, a woman who has brought her sister's child with her, to arouse pity in charitable people's breasts while she begs, sees it die before her eyes. *For everyone.*

支那女兒 Sorrows and death of a Chinese child whose father has married a Japanese after the death of his first wife. *For everyone.*

妹妹! 你瞎了 A bride of one day sacrifices her happiness and her life for the revolution. Her husband follows her to death. *For everyone.*

殘花 Of extra-marital love affairs; melancholy; and suicides. *Not for everyone.*

妻 A young married couple have been happy for five years, but as they have no child, the husband takes a concubine. *Not for everyone.*

夜 Psychology of the poor. *For everyone.*
櫻花時節 Departure for Japan. *For everyone.*

590. 昨日之花   *YESTERDAY'S FLOWERS*   1 vol. 256 p. by   劉大杰
1933

A collection of short stories.

The majority of these stories deal with love. In several of them we find some frivolous passages that are not very harmful. A description in the last story (p. 228-9) is objectionable. But nevertheless the book can *be tolerated.*

591. 渺茫的西南風   *BLOWING GENTLY FROM THE SEA*   168 p. by   劉大杰
1928 北新書局

Eight short stories, sentimental and monotonous; all of them rather vaguely imply that love must be different from what it was in "old style" marriage.
1) A young man's regret; a misunderstanding causes him to break with his girl.
2) A young man, engaged to be married, finds another girl, more worthy of his affection. He marries neither.
3) Following a conversation with his girl friend, a young man recalls sentimental and sad memories.
4) Remorse of a soldier on his death bed.
5) Letter breaking off an engagement.
6) Faithful wife; an unfaithful husband.
7) A young man drops flowers into a river in remembrance of a girl-friend.
8) Four symbolic descriptions of love.

This book contains *nothing objectionable,* but it lacks all originality.

592. 三兒苦學記 *STRIVING OF A POOR BOY*   1 vol. 253 p. by   劉大杰
5th. edit. 1939 北新書局

The tribulations of a little boy who lives with his mother in her family, and who is passing through his apprenticeship to life. *For everyone.*

593. 故事的罈子 *RECEPTACLE FOR STORIES*   1 vol. 228 p. by   劉大白
1934 黎明書局 *See Biogr. 112*

This book consists of forty-five stories. The first thirty stories deal with the old literary examinations. The rest are stories having daily life as their main theme. Some are mythological stories. *For everyone.*

594. 西星集 *STAR ON THE WEST*   1 vol. 152 p. by   柳存仁
1940 宇宙風社

1. Three essays on education with a great deal of advice based on experience.
2. An analysis and criticism of Shadick's book on Lao Ts'an Yu-chi.
3. A criticism of Feng Sheng Yen-i.
4. A detective story.
For everyone.

595. 角落裏 *IN THE CORNER*   1 vol. 121 p. by   劉鈍安
2nd. edit. 1940 文化生活

A banal story of some students who, with their teacher, find themselves forced to leave their school and to work with their hands. *For everyone.*

596. 春鴻遺恨 *AN UNFORGOTTEN REGRET*   2 vol. 226 & 212 pp. by   劉渥水
The story relates the loves of Chin Ch'iu-hen, a rich young Peiping merchant. He

was employed as a manager of a firm in Manchuria. He was a frequent visitor to the brothels and soon took an interest to Miss Hu. They planned to get married but the girl died. Chin gave her a splendid funeral. Our hero tried to forget his first love but failed. Out of charity he was interested in Miss Li and procured for her a job as a teacher. When love was about to bloom he was called to Peiping where his parents urged him to marry Miss Chu. However he intended to remain faithful to Miss Li; she gave up her rights, thus obliging Chin to marry Miss Chu.

Everyone is advised against reading this novel as the atmosphere is unhealthy.

597. 夜都會 *METROPOLITAN NIGHT*   1 vol. 139 p. by 柳 因
                                                2nd. edit. 1946   百新書店

An intimate diary in which we are given a description, day by day, of the relations of the supposed writer with the girls he keeps. There are no particularly crude details in the book, but people should be prevented from reading it because of the complete lack of moral sense in all the characters. *To be condemned.*

598. 春夢留痕 *SLIGHTLY ENGRAVED IN MEMORY*   1 vol. 162 p. by 劉雲行
                                                            1946

Four narratives and a novel. The author understands city inhabitants well, and his first piece is a fine study of the people in a city. Each family is well characterised. Occasionally a few rather broad details creep in.

The novel is well constructed and very interesting. It contains, however one page that is rather risky. *For adults.*

599. 春水紅霞 *SUNSET ON THE SPRING LAKE*   2 vol. 188 & 286 pp. by 劉雲若
                                                中北書店 *See Biogr. 113*

This novel centers around actors, players, and prostitutes. The author has no knowledge of moral law and his book is full of lewd scenes and also immoral theories. *To be proscribed.*

600. 湖海香盟 *THE OATH OF FIDELITY*   3 vol. 131, 141 & 144 pp. by 劉雲若
                                                            五洲書局

This story relates how an engagement was broken between Jen Yi-sa and Chu Hsü-hu, as the former became an actress. However the young man was enchanted once more when he saw her on the stage. In the meantime his parents procured a new fiancée for their son. As soon as our hero saw his new fiancée he fell in love and asked her to marry him, but the damsel refused. After this our hero wrote a love-letter to his former fiancée; he gave up her stage career and married him.

A daring description is found in the first volume on page 81.
For informed readers.

601. 歌舞江山 *THE WORLD DANCES*   1 vol. 246 p. by 劉雲若
                                                1929   新華書局

The story of General Lu who condemned an official to death. Soon after the execution this general was saved by Tsu Yung, who happened to be the son of the executed official; but coming to know about his father's fate, the young man planned to escape in order to return and avenge his father's death and promised to marry a girl who would help him. On the evening that was set for his departure along with the girl he had promised to marry, he was seized and brought to the sister of the general's concubine. The general recognized the young fellow and wanted to reward him by giving him the girl as his wife. At first the hero refused but at the end, mislead by a letter of his former fiancée, he married the concubine's sister.

Very objectionable on account of numerous immodest passages.

602. 花市春柔記   1 vol. 194 p. by 劉雲若 & 戴愚盦
     1940 新華書局

The story of a young married man, who was very rich. One day he fell in love with a prostitute's daughter. Another prostitute was jealous of the girl. The book relates how each woman tried hard to hurt and annoy the other.

This book is *to be proscribed* owing to its lewd descriptions.

603. 小楊州志   *OF THE SECOND YANG-CHOU*   2 vol. 227 p. by 劉雲若
     1941 天津書局

The story of Mr. Hsieh who was married to Yen Min. The latter was not satisfied with one husband and Ying-Ssu — a man who lived in the same yard — filled the lady's want. A young woman fell into the hands of these three scamps, who forced her into sin in order to pay her debts. Mr. Hu visited her and wanted to save her by marrying her. Chapters seven and eight deal with different people: a certain lady was accused of crime and the magistrate intended to punish her, but she succeeded in seducing him.

An immoral book. *To be proscribed.*

604. 燕子人家   *THE SCION*   2 vol. by 劉雲若
     1941 新聯合社

A story of a young intelligent man, who was very poor. He married a rich girl, who was unfaithful to him; hence a divorce. After the divorce he met a girl who was persecuted by her step-mother.

A number of unbecoming scenes. *For grown up people.*

605. 情海歸帆   *RETREAT FROM LOVE*   11 vol. by 劉雲若
     1941 京津出版社

Immoral story of a prostitute. The book presents a number of immoral ideas and descriptions. The author openly attacks Christian (monogamous) marriage. *Proscribed.*

606. 迴風舞柳記   *THE WILLOWS DANCE TO THE BREEZE*
     1 vol. 135 p. by 劉雲若
     1942 天津唯一書店

Another of the endless novels by Liu Yün-jo. Love stories, the characters of which constantly change. The scene of this novel is the frivolous world of Tientsin.

Everyone is advised against reading it, as it contains some risky passages, as well as revolutionary theories about marriage and divorce. The atmosphere is unhealthy.

607. 紅杏出牆   *RED FLOWERS OVER THE FENCE*   6 vol. by 劉雲若
     1943 藝光書店

The story of a young married couple; the husband found his wife guilty of infidelity with his friend, and left her. Soon he fell in love with a pock-marked girl and later with one of his wife's friends. Meanwhile his wife sought for him unsuccessfully and finally married his friend. More adventures follow. The wife first returned to her rightful husband, then back to her lover, and again to her husband. The book ends by describing the parting of the wife with her lover in the hospital. After this scene she committed suicide and her husband followed her example. A bad book which offends morals. *To be proscribed.*

608. 粉黛江湖   *THE WORLD OF DAMSELS*   4 vol. by 劉雲若
     1943 天津流雲出版社

A story of an actress who was a star in a little travelling group. She had two hard problems in her life, the first being to marry a divorced man she had saved from committing suicide. The second problem was even harder. She wanted to find her mother and if necessary to avenge her. The latter had been abducted by a military leader.

This novel is rather loosely knit. Although the style is easy, it contains some unhealthy theories, as well as some lewd situations, though these are not unduly detailed. *To be proscribed for young people.*

609. 姽嫿畫英雄 *PORTRAIT* 3 vol. 130, 124, 138 p. by 劉雲若
1945 北京書店

A young man employed in a bank is obliged to marry to keep his place. He is thus faced with a big problem: to marry for love or for a practical reason? The book ends without a solution.

The young man described has a good character and irreproachable principles, but the theories of the author on the subject of marriage and free love are quite contrary to Christian laws of conduct. For this reason the book is *not to be recommended to anyone.*

610. 雪艷春姑 *A REFINED DAMSEL* 1 vol. 126 p. by 劉雲若
2nd. edit. 1946 北京崇文書店

Two girls love the same young man. One is good and serious while the other has a bad character and is inclined to employ every means to attain to her end.

The hero prefers the former. The rest of the book consists of nothing but the vain machinations of the unsuccessful rival.

Not to be recommended because of certain crude details.

611. 香閨夢 *ILLUSIONED* 1 vol. 235 p. by 劉雲若
1936 唯一書局

Exactly the same book as that written by Li Shan-Yeh under the same title. Who the author is, is difficult to say. *For mature people.*

612. 白河月 *MOON OVER THE WHITE RIVER* 1 vol. 325 p. by 劉雲若
1947 正新出版社

This novel tells us of the Japanese occupation. Obviously we are given a dose of atrocities, and the role of collaborators is described. Neither are the members of the resistence left out. Some of them are ruined because of the fatal attraction that gold and women have for them. The victory was a recompense for good patriots while it brought punishment for traitors.

Historical details are mixed with love affairs. *Not for those who are too young.*

613. 換巢鸞鳳 *SHUFFLED* 2 vols. 151 & 153 p. by 劉雲若
1947 勵力出版社

Morbidly amorous descriptions. A rich man, due to his wealth, endulges himself, going from one woman to another. *Proscribed.*

614. 醉裏 *INTOXICATION* 1 vol. 218 p. by 劉黑芷
2nd edition 1928 商務印書館 *See Biogr. 114*

A collection of short stories.
1. Hu P'ang-tzu, after becoming rich, gave a dinner with music and actresses.
2. Ken Shen, having a number of adventures, made up his mind to become a bonze, but he did not persevere.
3. Life of a doctor who married in his middle age and was deeply loved by his wife.
4 A story about an unhappy young wife.
5. What there is to see at a Japanese hotel.
6 A woman, returning from a festival, conversed with her lady-friend, but thought all

the time about a male-friend.

7. A visit to a sick aunt where the visitor met a girl of whom he was afraid.

8. Scene between lovers in a boat .... and then twenty years later.

9. The life of a peasant.

10. Accident on a river.

11. The sad death of a sick man.

12. The arrival of a concubine.

13. Celebration after the birth of the fourth child.

14. A professor, himself desperately ill, conforts his family.

15. Farewell letters to a mistress.

16. The thoughts of a rich man while he rests in an inn, during his journey. He ponders over the social difference between himself and the poor folks he sees around.

17. Misfortunes of a pedlar who was hanged during the revolution.

For everyone.

615. 愛之奔流 *THE WAVE OF LOVE*   1 vol. 282 p. by **羅西（楊儀）**
                                    1943 戞友圖書公司 *See Biogr. 182*

Yü Tzu seduced a young girl. They went to live as man and wife, in opposition to the will of the latter's parents. Her sister Yü Chin, was noticed by Man Tzu, a rich young man. The parents were equally opposed to this marriage. Nevertheless the two sweethearts mutually resolved never to give in and to love each other till death. Man Tzu, on his return from a trip, was compelled by his father to marry his cousin in order to refloat the family economy. The married people did not love each other. Meanwhile, Yü Chin revealed to Man Tzu that she would soon be a mother. . . .Alarmed, he sent her to Shanghai for her confinement. On her return, Yü Chin went to importune Man Tzu in order to make him fulfil his duties as a father. Man Tzu came to love his wife and she him, so that he wanted to dismiss Yü Chin; the latter enticed Man Tzu's wife to an appointment, killed her and then committed suicide.

This book is *to be proscribed;* it contains some daring passages, and moreover it vindicates triangular love. On page 212, it contains an odious comparison referring to the Catholics.

616. 你去吧 *YOU MAY PROCEED*   1 vol. by **羅　西**
                                            1928 大光書局

Lascivious and pornographic scenes. *To be proscribed.*

617. 空山靈雨 *SLIGHT DRIZZLE*   1 vol. 120 p. by **落華生（許地山）**
                                    1935 文學研究會 *See Biogr: 75*

A great number of small anecdotes and essays in simple and cultivated language. *May be read.*

618. 解放者 *THE EMANCIPATOR*   217 p. by **落華生**
                                            1933 星雲堂書店

Eight short stories and a play; well written; lively and slightly satirical.

1) Salon of Fei Tsung-li. A picture of how profiteers exploit the ignorant public under pretence of charity.

2) Three "doctors" return from America. They show off their cheaply acquired titles.

3) Story of a wretched blind man. Nobody pities him.

4) A Chinese prison.

5) A woman of a well-to-do family has to become an amah. She gradually be-

comes a thief and ends up by committing suicide.

6) Tells of a girl's romantic adventures complicated by political activities in the rising Republic party.

7) Influence by "foreign" ideas, a frivolous woman becomes disgusted with her husband.

8) A schoolteacher's wife studies in France where she has a lover. Determined to get a divorce she returns to her country with her lover. She falls in love with her husband. A happy ending.

9) A play about false ghosts.

For all.

---

619. 春桃 *PEACH IN SPRING* 1 vol. 391 p. by 落華生等著
1935 生活書店

Selection of short stories by well known writers. Well written and full of action. They centre around the hardships of the common people. *For all.*

---

620. 春王正月 *THE FIRST MOON OF A LUNAR YEAR* 1 vol. 233 p. by 羅洪女士
1936 上海良友圖書公司 *See Biogr. 115*

A silk dealer went bankrupt and was harassed by his creditors, especially around the New Year. Rather dull; no conclusion.

---

621. 活路 *THE WAY OUT* 1 vol. 147 p. by 羅 洪
1945 萬葉書店

A collection of ten tales. The author particularly describes the miseries of peasants, soldiers, etc.

Also included are several sketches of children, and a very sympathetic description of maternal love. *For everyone.*

---

622. 苦果 *BITTER FRUITS* 1 vol. 450 p. by 羅皚嵐
1935 大公報社 *See Biogr. 116*

A young man, having finished his studies in France, is about to marry a cousin of his.

Just at that time he makes the acquaintance of the daughter of a compatriot who had saved his life when he was abroad. He marries her shortly after. On the day of his wedding, however, he is arrested on the accusation of a political enemy who covets his wife. She finally yields to the enemy in order to save her husband's life.

The latter's party emerges victorious from the political struggle. His adversary takes to flight, taking his victim with him, only to abandon her half-dead on the road.

Subsequently, our hero marries his first betrothed, but he is not happy, as he is haunted by the memory of his first wife.

He leaves his mother and his wife to take vengeance on his enemy. . . . the two abandoned women die of grief.

Well constructed novel. *For everyone.*

---

623. 創 *WOUNDED* 1 vol. 208 p. by 羅皚嵐
1939 東亞印書局

The story of a yamen employee which contains chiefly an account of the waggish tricks of his son told in a pretty realistic style. Curses abound. The employee referred to is discontented with his mediocre position, sells all that he possesses, and engages in speculations. He loses his money, becomes ill, and dies. His wife, who is an opium smoker, sells her furniture, and her clothes, and ends in misery. *For everyone.*

624. 生人妻 *THE STRANGER'S WIFE*   1 vol. 115 p. by 羅　淑
1938 文化生活 *See Biogr. 117*

1. 生人妻 A poor woman is sold to a wealthy old man. On the day of her going to her new husband, she takes to flight, is injured on the way, and follows her first husband.
2. 橘子 Quarrels and tears over a sale of oranges.
3. 劉嫂 Story of a maid thrown out because she took to drink. Whatever happened she had to live. A rather vulgar story.
4. 井工 A coarse story of a young workman.
The book ends with a story by Pa Chin and Chin Yi. *For everyone.*

625. 米夫子   1 vol. 149 p. by 陸　堅
1941 大地圖書雜誌公司

A number of short stories fairly well written but without great interest. *For everyone.*

626. 里門拾記 *COUNTRY LANE*   1 vol. 211 p. by 蘆焚（王長簡）
1935 文化生活出版社 *See Biogr. 163*

A dozen sketches of the native village of the author, containing descriptions of character types and recounting adventures.
The style is rather jerky, not flowing, with a tendency detrimental to morals. *For grown-up people.*

627. 黃花苔 *YELLOW PETALS*   1 vol. 155 p. by 蘆　焚
1937 良友圖書公司

1. Family memories.
2. A description. A family scene.
3. Memories of a dead friend.
4. Story of a mother.
5. A modern woman. Reminiscences.
6. A childhood friend.
7. The story and hopes of a shepherd.
For everyone.

8. Joys of childhood.
9 Nocturnal dreams.
10. The croaking of frogs.
11. Lanterns for the dead.
12. Poetic memories of Peking.
13. A child's game.
14. On a journey.
Etc. etc.

628. 江湖記 *PERAMBULATION*   1 vol. 170 p. by 蘆　焚
1938 開明書店

Memories of the country with descriptions. *For everyone.*

629. 看人集 *SIGHT SEEING*   1 vol. 103 p. by 蘆　焚
1939 開明書店

Student life.
1 A student in France. 2. Stories of former students. 3. A fable.
For everyone.

630. 新女性的日記 *DIARY OF A MODERN LADY*   1 vol. 251 p. by 陸笑梅
1938 上海希望出版社

The diary of a young married woman. Her marriage was not of her own choice but made under the pressure of her parents. She is unhappy, for her character and her husband's are not congenial. Her "literary" relations with another man are also the cause of continual disputes between them.
Her husband is jealous. Moreover he has other faults. He is a gambler and often stays out all night.
The heroine is faithful to him, but insists too much on the right of an independent

life for women, on their right to form their own relations, etc.

She considers marriage as a source of vexations and as an obstacle to being of service to society (p. 163). According to her, free love would be a better solution to the social development of women. The children could be educated in a state institution (p. 107).

The heroine has not the slightest idea of the serious side of marriage, nor of its obligations. Here and there in the book there are raw passages and hard words concerning parents.

Nevertheless the heroine has one admirable quality, and that is her love for her child. *Not to be recommended to anyone.*

631. 吶喊 *CRIES*   1 vol. 272 p. by 魯迅（周樹人）
2nd edition 1923 文藝叢書 *See Biogr. 39*

1) *Diary of a simpleton;* attacks against society.
2) *K'ung Yi Chi* (cf. No. 638).
3) *Yao:* (cf. No. 637).
4) *Ming T'ien:* A poor widow who brought her child to a quack.
5) *Yi Tien Hsiao Shih:* a rickshaw-coolie, in a minor accident, presents himself to the police.
6) About the times when the pig-tails began to fall.
7) *Storm in a glass of water:* A fervent revolutionist cuts his pig-tails .... The pig-tail may again be introduced!?. . .It is only a rumour.
8) *Ku Hsiang:* (cf. No. 638).
9) *Ah-Q:* (cf. No. 635).
10) An official's life, his difficulties in receiving a decent salary.
11) After the student failed in his exams he departed from home in order to look for a hidden treasure, first in town then in the country, inspired to do so by some mysterious sign. After one day his body was found.
12) The author's dislike for cats, because they are enemies of white rabbits.
13) A Russian professor who reared frogs; hungry ducks ate them.
14) The author dislikes the city theatre; he relates his impression of a popular comedy he saw in his youth.
15) The author's fight against the enemies of the revolution.

All these stories are written between April 1918 and October 1922. Lu Hsün is at the height of his talent 吶喊 is his master-piece. Anyone who is interested in knowing his principal ideas on the society of 1911 as well as the revolution should read this book. It is written with ease and beauty. For serious readers there is no reserve to make. Two short pieces against Providence refute themselves. The famous "Ah Q" is the longest as well as the best piece written by Lu Hsün. It expresses his deep disillusion regarding the revolution and the establishing of the republic. This novel shows how the ardent revolutionists were the first victims of the revolution while the scamps and swindlers filled their pockets with gold and richess. The story of the simpleton presents a lovely theme; he who dreamed of ideal life and human sympathy found a wretched end. It is a master work of psychology and bitter irony. The true sentiments of Lu Hsün and his opinion of the new regime and its leaders show on every page. *For everyone.*

632. 彷徨 *HESITATION*   1 vol. (incomplete) by 魯 迅
A collection of novels.

1 *Tsu Fu:* The author revolts against "numerous abuses and ritual practices".
2 A novel which presents the mentality of the ordinary man.
3. Typical example of an "old style" divorce suit.
For everyone.

633. 故事新編 *OLD STORIES RETOLD*   1 vol. 177 p. by 魯 迅
3rd edition 1936 文化生活出版社

A novel in which Lu Hsün relates, in his own way, certain incidents taken from history and legend. Too realistic. *For informed readers.*

634. 歸家 *GOING HOME*   1 vol. 222 p. by 魯 迅
1926 生活社

Nine short stories.
1) Punch and Judy scenes; old tales which are applied by the author to the officials to ridicule them.
2) The value of gold; economically China is not able to compete with foreign countries. He advises us to fight imperialism and the foreign concessions.
3) Fashions: The author ridicules fashion.
4) Dull; a young man freed from prison resolved to help his folks but on his return he found them all dispersed. Thus his dreams were destroyed. Socialistic tendencies.
5) Triumph of Realism over Romanticism.
6) The lamentations of a widow who lost her only child; the author made acquaintance with the child just before his death.
7) Humorous story of a good fellow who was looking for a book.
8) Kuei Chia: After a long absence, Pai Lu-su returned home; he was received coldly but in the end everything was settled.
    For everyone.

635. 阿 Q 正傳 *THE TRUE STORY OF AH-Q*   1 vol. 56 p. by 魯 迅
國學書店

Ah-Q is very pleased with himself. Even after the most crushing humiliations he invariably manages to find a quiet corner in which to nurse his hurt pride. Thus his self-conceit grows with every blow. A crawling coward in the presence of the strong, he is haughty and cruel towards the weak.

Having made his own life impossible in his village, he goes to the city in search of a living. He soon returns after having associated for some time with a gang of highway robbers.

When the revolution spreads to the nearest town he contemplates joining the movement and thus securing a means to get even with his enemies and satisfy his ambitions.

Accused of burglary of which he is innocent, he talks so wildly as to give the magistrate — who needs a scape-goat — enough ground to pin the crime on him. He is executed without ever clearly realizing what was really happening.

This story has become very popular in China. It has been translated into many languages. "Ah-Q," a recent article says, "is the only character out of contemporary Chinese fiction that actually lives in the minds of the people."

In the person of Ah-Q the author brought together all the inbred defects against which the Revolution was directed.

Profitable reading for informed readers, *permissible to everyone.*

636. 唐宋傳奇集   2 vol. by 魯 迅
1929 北新書局

The style of this novel is classical; its language difficult.
It presents the goings on in the imperial harem. *For well informed readers.*

637. 藥   *MEDICINE*   1 vol. 35 p. by 魯 迅
1940

     A lugubrious story of two young people, of whom one is consumptive, who died after taking medicine containing the blood of an executed man. They are buried and both the mothers come to visit their graves in the public cemetary. *For everyone.*

638. 魯迅創作選集   *SELECTED WORKS OF LU-SHUN*   1 vol. 127 p. 1921
Four essays.

1   *K'ung Yi Chi*: Description of a scamp who completed his studies, but instead of using them to provide a living he lived by theft. He spent his days in the restaurant but at the end died in poverty.

2   *Yao*: Hsiao Hsuan, a consumptive youngman who died after he took some medicine that should have cured him. The medecine was made of the blood of an executed man. Lu Hsün declared war on quacks and superstitions.

3.   *Ah-Q*: cf. No. 635.

4   *Ku Hsiang*: After a long residence in the city Lu Hsün returned to his native town. In his native town he left like a stranger. Life is a mystery, there are no beaten paths, each must find his own way.

     For everyone.

639. 古奇觀   *CURIOUS TALES OF OLD*   1 vol. 491 p. by 陸高誼
3rd edition 1937   世界書局

     This book contains a series of quaint stories about olden times. Some of them hold a number of risky passages. *All are to be advised against reading it.*

640. 小小的心   *A TINY HEART*   1 vol. 132 p. by 魯 彥
2nd edit. 1934   天馬書店 *See Biogr. 168*

1.   A newspaper man interests himself in a boy; the boy is after all very much like a slave bought by his master and abused at will.

2   A love passage between two youngsters.

3.   A petty scandal in a school.

4   A young fellow loses weight, puts on weight, and wants to lose it again.

5.   Discovery of a tree called "Lung yun".

6   English exercise in school:

             — She :   Good morning.
             — He :   Will you marry me?
             — She :   Come back in three years.
             — He :   Good bye.

7.   Humorous story.

     For all.

641. 河邊   *THE RIVERSIDE*   1 vol. 223 p. by 魯 彥
1936   上海良友圖書公司

     Six stories.

1.   During three years an ailing mother waits for the return of her son.

2   A peasant goes to Shanghai.

3.   An opium racketeer dreams of piling up money. He is robbed. He is accused and the legal proceedings cost so much that he despairs of ever getting rich.

4   A widow, mother of two children, returns to her native country. Although she is poor she is thought to be well off. All kinds of complications arise from this false supposition.

5   A man risks some money in a lottery hoping to win. While the lottery is drawing he has a nervous breakdown.

6.   An aged schoolmaster has already lost his two sons in the prime of their life. His third son is among his pupils and dies of the same disease as his brothers.

For all.

642. 屋頂下 *UNDER THE ROOF*   1 vol. 220 p. by 魯   彥
2nd edit. 1936 復光書局

Seven stories, each of them is a psychological study of a different class of people:
Ch'a-lu enmity between two villages, stronger than cholera and death.
Wu ting hsia quarrels between a mother-in-law and her daughter-in-law. They separate.
Pao lü two kids, always quarrelling, yet inseparable.
An shih an unhappy widow adopts a son; he leaves her and she feels again lonely.
Ping a gibe at quacks.
Li mu story of a maid. From all her misfortunes she learns one lesson: in order to succeed one must deceive people.
Hu-hsü a poor poem on moustaches.

Some reserve.

643. 野火 *CAMP FIRE*   1 vol. 446 p. by 魯   彥
The story unrolls in a village which the author uses to describe to us the tyranny of the authorities and the sufferings of the poor people. The events unfold before our eyes just as in a play.

There are some well-intentioned young people who wish to bring about a reign of justice in the country but they find themselves baulked all the time by those in power. A love affair between one of these young people and a daughter of the enemy ends in nothing. And the book ends with the failure of the young people who are put into prison under the accusation of collaborating with the communists. *For everyone.*

644. 靈海潮汐 *MENTAL TIDES*   1 vol. 204 p. by 盧隱（黃盧隱）
1937 開明書店 *See Biogr.* 82

A short story with a thesis demanding the emancipation of Chinese women, especially in marriage. The author — a woman — denounces the sad situation of women in China. *For everyone.*

645. 海濱故人 *FRIEND BY THE SEA*   1 vol. 259 p. by 盧   隱
2nd edition 1935 商務印書館

A collection of short novels and stories. A very easy and beautiful style with plenty of freshness. The author likes to describe married women. *May be read by everyone.*

646. 象牙戒指 *AN IVORY RING*   1 vol. 238 p. by 盧   隱
This book presents a true history of the poetess Shih 石評梅 (+ 1928).

At the age of eighteen she fell in love with a married man (he was a man of letters). She refrained from pursuing him but nevertheless she remained true to him. At the same time a married man fell in love with her and proposed to her, promising to divorce his wife.   She refused him and he committed suicide. The poetess felt guilty of his death and tried to forget her sorrows in drink and other modern pleasures of life. She died three years later.

A sad and rather pessimistic book. *For informed readers.*

647. 愛園 *THE GARDEN OF LOVE*   1 vol. 126 p. by 盧隱女士

A girl student who is already betrothed falls in love with her teacher, and follows him to Shanghai where she gives herself to him. But the recipient of her love is not faithful and falls in love with another girl, who, however, dies, after which he marries the heroine.

Here is the common theme of the stories in this collection. *The young should be strongly dissuaded from reading this book,* for only love and pleasure count with this author. Neither chastity nor fidelity pose any problems for her.

648. 玫瑰的刺 *NO ROSE WITHOUT THORNS*   1 vol. 254 p. by 盧隱女士
                                          2nd. edit. 1935   中國書局

It is true that "roses have thorns" and that the damage wrought by the thorns is greater than the pleasure given by the perfume of the rose! In ten stories of which the second contains seven shorter ones, this thesis is proved by the authoress in a masterly fashion.

In clear style exposing melancholy sentiments, Lu Yin gives us in the first story an allegory in which she gives human sentiments to birds. The second convinces us with a wealth of proof that perfect happiness is not of this world. The third tells of the love affair of a student in Japan. The fourth is the story of a fugitive. The fifth and the sixth are love stories, while the bitterness of love is especially dealt with in the seventh and the eighth.

The ninth describes to us how a girl endoctrined by a free-thinker can fall low. And the last gives an account of a sentimental conversation.

This book is certainly a reflection of the soul of the authoress. In her other works, she has preached of divorce, free love, and other advanced ideas. These theories, it is obvious, engender only resentment, chagrin, and disillusion, of which the present publication is a proof.

From the moral point of view, this volume should be reserved for adults as it does not divide clearly enough sane ideas from dangerous ones. Moreover, these love stories are too vivaciously and too pessimistically told. *Not for everyone.*

649. 棘心 *A HEART IN THORNS*   1 vol. 338 p. by 綠漪女士（蘇梅）
                                 8th edition 1937 北新書局 *See Biogr. 141*

Authobiography of the authoress. Su Mei was born in the province of Anhwei. After she had completed her studies in the Normal School in Peiping, she received a scholarship in 1921 to the Sino-French University of Lyons. She did not tell her parents about it until the day of her departure, as she was afraid of a refusal. During her stay in France, a fellow-student fell in love with her and proposed to her. She refused him, as she wanted to remain loyal to her fiancé, who was studying to become an engineer in U.S.A. This fiancé was selected by her mother and our heroine did not know him. As she had a great love for her mother, she did not object to this choice. The same love inspired her to resist all temptations.

During an illness she made the acquaintance of Catholic Sisters. Their self-sacrifice and the fine sentiments of Miss Pei Lang, her bosom friend, induced her to study the Catholic doctrine. Nevertheless she had no intention of being converted, and her objections to the Faith remained. But in spite of all these, she was attracted by the beautiful Catholic ceremonies, as she was herself an artist. When she learned that her mother was very ill, and was cured due to the fervent prayers of her friends, she made a vow to become a Catholic.

The news from China and from her folks was very alarming, and she returned to her home, after an absence of more than two years in Europe. During her stay in France, she had visited Montmartre Basilica and this visit left a beautiful impression on her.

In China, authors of great talent are the only ones who can hope to see many editions of their works. This book has had eight editions in a few years. This alone proves its value. This celebrated authoress has become popular among young readers, not by providing them with raw stories-as is often the method adopted by authors-but by giving them a true and realistic narrative of her youth.

In her narratives, she gives a delicate analysis of her affection towards her mother and her girl-friend Pei Lang, and also shows her loyalty for an unknown fiancé chosen by her mother. Furthermore she describes the various crises of her "troubled heart" and the difficulties on her road to the Catholic Faith. While we read this book, we are struck with the great sincerity of the writer and the loftiness of her sentiments. Her sincerity wins our sympathy. We heartily congratulate the authoress for having given us a master-piece, and express the hope that the teachers will put this novel into the hands of modern youth. They will find in it lofty and generous sentiments, and they will learn to write, for the style of the book is clear, fluent and simple.

(Cfr. R.F.O.Brière in his article on Su Mei in "Bulletin de l'Aurore" 1943, pp. 920-933 and Tientsin "I-che-pao" March, 28th, 1948).

For everyone.

650. 綠天 *THE GREEN SKIES*   1 vol. 124 p. by **綠漪女士**
                                        7th edition 1928   北新書局

"The author describes little incidents of home life, often in symbols, and celebrates married love. Seemingly insignificant things are often endowed with poetical greatness. She shows real sympathy with all animate and inanimate beings, living the life of the plants and insects and stirred by their emotions; she shows interest in all they do; talks to them; her fingers conjure beauty on all she touches. She compares herself to Mr. Seguin's goat, for she is likewise fascinated by freedom, feels one with nature and is attracted by summits. The most strikingly characteristic piece is the "Story of the gold-winged Butterfly"; it describes in symbolical terms her life in France. The butterfly, the bee, the dragonfly, the cricket and the worm, represent the people with whom she lived in France. This fable unmistakably shows her love of the supernatural, the symbolic, of imagery. She may seem to lack creative imagination for she always features personal experiences or actual events, but she possesses in a high degree a poetical imagination that transplants the most prosaic events into a world of beauty. In the preface to a volume of fables by another author she says "I love fables and mythological legends. As a child I always had the "Hsi Yu Chi" at hand, and now the tales of Anderson and Oscar Wilde never leave me. I have a deep admiration for Greek mythology."

(O. Brière S.J. Renseignements du bureau sinologique No. 369 p. 3).

For all.

651. 閒話上海 *SHANGHAI*   2 vol. 204, 192 p. by **馬健行**
                                     1940 國光書店

A mass of stupid information on what is going on under the surface in Shanghai.
Not to be recommended to anyone.

652. 太平愿 *CARNIVAL*   1 vol. 195 p. by **馬 驪**
                                   1943 新民印書館

The title of this book is taken from one of its stories. It presents a good description of the general hope of the people. They ask all the time for peace but they never get it as calamities succeed each other, such as drought, famine and brigandage.

1) 生死路 The story reveals the hardship of a pagan family; drought, famine, quarrels, and brigandage pursue it. The old parents had to leave their home; they begged that

their daughter may be spared, but she was abducted and her father died while trying to save her. Her mother returned home but found the people so unfriendly towards her that she resolved to kill herself on the doorsteps of her enemy. This book gives a good description of the peasants' hardships. There are a number of obscene popular songs.

2) 太平願 A description of a big Chinese village. Eur Hu, who lived like a lord at the expense of the villagers, was a lazy man. But the folk feared him and obeyed him as their master. One day he asked them to have a troupe of comedians but they could not afford it; while they were discussing their problem bandits came to loot the village. The villagers were sure that Eur Hu had a hand in it and one bold man went and told him so, but he paid for this act with his life.

3) 生髮油 Brilliantine. Wang Ho one day discovered that his wife had illicit relations with old Liu, and Chao San was their accomplice; quarrels ensued in which everyone took part. During this time soldiers arrived and arrested Wang Ho. No immoral passages, but a number of bad songs and risky descriptions.

For informed readers.

653. 驅驊集 *STEEDS*   1 vol. 104 p. by **馬 驪**
                                                 1945 中國公論社

pp. 1 and 28 : the author describes in two short stories the painful existence of certain poor writers. Trivial expressions.

p. 51 : The gentleman will soon be conferred a doctor's degree.

p 57 : waiting for her fiancé.

p. 71 : tribulations of a small merchant.

p. 88 : a village school.

The above book is well written and very interesting. *For everyone.*

654. 筆伐集 *MIGHTIER THAN THE SWORD*   1 vol. 232 p. by **馬子華**
                                                 1937 北新書局

A collection of eight stories.

The tone of this book is rather anti-imperialistic, opposed to a certain power and at the same time anti-European. *For everyone.*

655. 春之罪 *THE FAULT OF SPRING*   1 vol. 153 p. by **茅以思**
                                                 1930 中華書局

Five well written stories. The first two describe the experiences of actors. The third is the story of a cat; the last two present a number of letters to a girl-friend.

There is nothing shocking; the book may be read *by everyone.*

656. 幻滅 *DISILLUSION*   1 vol. 90 p. by **茅盾（沈雁氷）**
                              10th edition 1946 開明 *See Biogr. 133*

This novel shows us the spirit of "Young China", especially of girl-students. Miss Chang, the principal character of the book, knows only failure and disillusion in the pursuit of her revolutionary and sentimental ideal.

In the circles described ideals are very often mixed with gross egoism. The life of the heroines is clouded with passion; in their sentimental life they know no bonds and the idea of marriage doesn't even enter their heads. A couple of dangerous descriptions. *Unsuitable for all classes of readers.*

657. 動搖 *UNCERTAINTY*   1 vol. 165 p. by 茅　盾
                                              14th edition 1946　開明書店

This novel describes the activity of a local Republic Party bureau and of the various organizations attached to it: unions and youth groups.

Their reforms do not lack thoroughness: buddhist nuns, widows, concubines and slavegirls are "freed". They gather some twenty women, and train them in view of a subsequent marriage.

In another village five women are "freed" — two of them nuns — and distributed to the bachelors of the village.

The office workers' union state their terms and after long negotiations, they are accepted by the employers. But occasionally similar solutions are only arrived at after riots and murders.

The hero of the book, a local dictator, succeeds in being accepted by the revolutionists and in bossing the local party bureau. This enables him to realize his own unsavoury plans. The women's training centre becomes a brothel under his direction.

The characters in the book have no morals but the author does not unduly feature immorality. *For informed readers.*

658. 追求 *SEARCH*   1 vol. 175 p. by 茅　盾
                                              4th edition 1946　開明書店

This book describes the mentality of university students.

One of them, Si Hsun, was a pessimistic man, and tried to commit suicide but failed. Another student Man Ch'ing who was disgusted with the political life as he could not practice his ideas from a social and revolutionary point of view returned to his professor's career, but met again with disillusions. He met the same disillusions in his married life. Miss Chang Ch'iu-liu on the contrary did not believe in social and patriotic ideals. She resolved to lead a free and independent life, and spent her youth looking for strong emotions. At the end of the book a doctor found out that she had venereal disease. Wang Chao-chung another student, was a very optimistic fellow and succeeded in life rather well. On the eve of his marriage his optimism was shaken by the sudden death of his fiancée.

The conclusion to be drawn from this book is that life is a bitter farce which breaks all hopes and frustrates men from attaining their aim in life. The author proves that he possesses in a high degree the "psychological sense," but unfortunately no moral sense. One of his principal characters, Miss Chang, strongly approved of a girl, who, in order to procure her living, became a prostitute.

A number of raw descriptions. *Cannot be recommended to anybody.*

659. 虹 *THE RAINBOW*   1 vol. 273 p. by 茅　盾
                                              10th edition 1940　開明書店

A novel about a girl, Mei, who was a revolutionist as well as an anarchist. The scene of the novel began at Chengtu where Mei fell in love with her cousin; the latter, a disciple of Tolstoy, refused to marry her, for he was afraid that he could not make her happy. Her father married her to a merchant with a bad reputation. She fled to Chungking after some months. Here she turned down several proposals and departed to Shanghai. The author describes the deeds of Trotsky's partisans in that city. Here Mei fell in love with a communist; she has no objections against triangular love. The story ends rather abruptly and without conclusion.

The book is considered to be a masterpiece but it exhales nothing but revolution, pessimism, defeatism and fatalism (e.g. p. 49). There is not a single noble character among the thirty under review. Mao Tun is imbued with the ideas of Tolstoy, Nietsche, Schoppenhauer, Maupassant. . .The novel is rather prolix; the author mixes a lot of unsound doctrines with the narrative. The atmosphere of the book is dangerous.

Mei is a double-faced woman; sometimes she acts as a revolutionist; sometimes she appears to be attracting men by her beauty, but throws them off later on with cold indifference. Sometimes she becomes sentimental in order to find a new consoler.

This book can be considered as one of those propaganda writings of which Lu Hsün says in his "Eur Hsin Chi" "revolution literature resembles a man — who is the author — standing in two boats at the same time: one boat is literature, the other revolution; he shifts his balance according to circumstances." *Everyone should be advised against reading it.*

660. 野薔薇 *WILD ROSES* 　　　　1 vol. by 茅　盾
　　　　　　　　　　　　　　　　　　　　　　　1931 大江書舖

"Wild Roses".

Five stories containing the same psychology as found in "Eclipse".

Here five girls disclosed the same confusion in the presence of contemporary conditions. They were moved to pity by their lot and wept over it; some even committed suicide. To use the language of a critic, if "Eclipse" gives a general picture of modern society, "Wild Roses" emphisizes every element composing the picture.

These girls failed everywhere. They were not prepared to play the new social roles they desired. Their characters were not equal to their good intentions. The tragedy of their despair so impressed the author, that it decided his literary career. "Mao Tun, Un peintre de son temps" by: Rev. F. O. Brière S.J. (Bulletin de l'Aurore 1943 T. III 4, No. 1). *Very objectionable.*

661. 宿莽 *JUNGLE LAW* 　　　　1 vol. 154 p. by 茅　盾
　　　　　　　　　　　　　　　　　　　　　　　1932 大江書舖

A collection of short stories.

1) 色盲 A youth who loved two girls was advised by a friend to practise free love, but the young man refused and chose one of the girls; but the latter was already engaged so he had to propose to the other. Having made up his mind, he happily awaits the answer.
2) 泥濘 Plea in favour of the Chinese Communists.
3) 蛇蝶 A girl who made a plea against marriage was flattered by a letter from one of her suitors.

The other stories are of a revolutionary feeling. *Young people are advised to avoid reading it,* as it presents a communistic atmosphere.

662. 三人行 *THREE MEN ON THE ROAD* 　　　　1 vol. by 茅　盾
　　　　　　　　　　　　　　　　　　　　　　　開明書店

In this novel, Mao Tun describes how three rural notables, after much struggle, joined the revolutionary party. For the first time we find in Mao Tun's works a convinced, cool revolutionary leader who is convinced of his vocation; the kind Pa Chin likes to present.

"Mao Tun, Un peintre de son temps" by Rev. O. Brière S.J. (Bulletin de l'Aurore 1943 T. III 4 no. 1). *For informed readers.*

663. 路 *THE ROAD* 　　　　1 vol. 166 p. by 茅　盾
　　　　　　　　　　　　　　　4th edition 1936 文化生活出版社

The book centres around discontent and strikes in a certain university. The students fail in their attempted reforms because the authorities depend on the assistance of the police.

Hsing, the hero of the book, is portrayed in the centre of this reform. He knows the actual order of things must be upset but is very undecided as to everything else.

At the same time Mao Tun describes the evolution of Hsing's feeling towards Tu Jo, a girl student.

One of his friends is in jail, and there he finds more talent than among the professors of the university. This adds to the rage of Hsing, who gets wounded in a riot and lands in hospital. After his final interview with Tu Jo, he writes to his parents, saying farewell to his family in order to throw himself unreservedly into the social struggle.

The revolutionary spirit of the book calls for *some reserve.*

664. 子夜 *MIDNIGHT*   2 vol. 279 & 296 p. by 茅　盾
1942　關東出版社

The author describes in this book the social life of economic and industrial circles in Shanghai. He recounts the philanthropic intentions of one particular man, which after initial success, met with so much opposition that he was finally compelled to give them up. This book contains a great number of characters and it is difficult to distinguish one from another.

This book has a socialistic outlook on life. It calls for *strict reserve* because of immodest descriptions.

665. 子夜 *MIDNIGHT*   1 vol. 577 p. by 茅　盾
1932　開明書店

Cfr. criticism of 子夜 in No. 664. In this edition, Chapter IV is left out. Nevertheless this edition still contains a number of obscene descriptions. *Everyone should be warned against reading it.*

666. 春蠶 *SILKWORMS*   1 vol. 257 p. by 茅　盾
2nd edition 1933　開明書店

A collection of novels which describe the conditions of peasants and merchants. Reveals strong anti-foreign feelings; opposes superstition.

The *first* and the *fourth* are *for informed people* while the *second one* should be *proscribed,* as it contains a very immodest scene.

667. 話匣子 *CHATTER BOX*   1 vol. 250 p. by 茅　盾
1934　良友文學叢書

This book is divided into two parts. In the first, we are presented with a number of descriptions, memories, and sketches. The second part deals with literature, authors, incidents, literary translations, etc. *For everyone.*

668. 多角關係 *A MULTIANGULAR AFFAIR*   1 vol. by 茅　盾
1936　生活書店

A new description of Shanghai's industrial life. The author considers this book as the continuation of "Midnight". He paints the bad life of a young man whose habit it was to deceive girls; hence the title. He also relates how the young man's father was besieged in his factory by workers. Both of them, father and son, have the same vices: vanity and love for easy life. Mao Tun tried his best to show the ridiculous side of their lives.

The book is a repetition of the author's pet ideas in a much inferior form.

"Mao Tun, Un peintre de son temps" by Rev. F. O. Brière S.J. (Bulletin de l'Aurore, 1943 Tome III 4 No. 1). *For instructed people.*

669. 泡沫 *FOAM*   1 vol. 236 p. by 茅　盾
1936　上海文學社

A collection of short stories containing scenes of social life. *For everyone.*

670. 烟雲集 *SCUD*

1 vol. 307 p. by 茅盾
1940 良友文學叢書

烟雲 Some risky details. *Not for everyone.*
擬浪花 Good. *For everyone.*
搬的喜劇 Small officials living in the fear of having to move. Of their narrowness. *For everyone.*
大鼻子的故事 A little beggar taking part in an anti-Japanese demonstration. *For everyone.*
一個眞正的中國人 An upstart enriching himself under the cover of pretending to work for the good of the people. *For everyone.*
水藻行 Two poor workers vexed by the injustice of officials. *For everyone.*
手的故事 Of the preparation for the war against Japan and a portrait of the mentality of officials in provincial towns. *For everyone.*

671. 第一階段的故事 *THE FIRST STAGE*

1 vol. 365 p. by 茅盾
1946 百新書店

A sketchy account of the events in Shanghai at the beginning of the 1937 "incident". These pages are full of strategical discussions between boys and girls, so-called students who are full of patriotic fancies. There is, however, a complete lack of positive patriotic action.

The book is sown with humour; a little too much for the tragic situation described.

This is not a consecutive narrative, but an account of the opinions of different classes of society. *For everyone.*

672. 霜葉紅似二月花 *RED AUTUMN LEAVES*

1 vol. 251 p. by 茅盾
1946 上海華華書店

Youth is full of good sentiments and ready for all sacrifices; roused to enthusiasm by generous ideas, it wishes to ameliorate the sad state of humanity. The world, however, is egotistic and interprets everything badly, even the ideals of youth. Thus things drift. *Not for the young.*

673. 有志者 *MAN OF RESOLUTION*

1 vol. 134 p. by 茅盾

A number of stories that are quite interesting. *For everyone.*

674. 他 *HE*

1 vol. 244 p. by 茅盾
1936 上海雜誌公司

In this book the author presents us with a selection from his short stories. Unfortunately, his choice is not to be recommended to the youth in our schools as he gives us, in fact, only a number of sensual love affairs. *Not to be recommended to anyone.*

675. 茅盾代表作 *AN ANTHOLOGY OF MAOTUN*

1 vol. 290 p.
三通書局

A number of selected novels and stories taken from Mao Tun's works. The author describes the life of modern peasants who are ready to join the revolution; he also presents some sketches of married life. One of his stories describes the state of mind of young women at the time of emancipation.

In the last novel the author presents us with a vivid description of a girl's suicide due to disappointment in her love affair. Everyone should be warned against reading this book, as it presents unhealthy atmosphere and ideas. "詩與散文" is very objectionable.

676. 茅盾代表作選 *AN ANTHOLOGY OF MAO TUN*

1 vol. 352 p.
1941 上海全球書店

A collection of short stories which, *with the exception of* 烟雲 and 創作, stories of the

married life of the young generation, can be read *by everyone.*
Mao Tun here describes the life of the middle classes.

677. 茅盾選集　*AN ANTHOLOGY OF MAOTUN*　　　1 vol. 265 p.
　　　　　　　　　　　　　　　　　　　　　　　　　　　　　　　1940

　　　Selections from Mao Tun's works. The author deals with the revolution, its crisis, and the hardships that people had to endure. He narrates an episode of the Chapei incident. In some of his essays the author upholds the literary and social revolution and poses as a patriotic propagandist for the present war.

　　　Everyone should be advised against reading this book, especially against some pieces in the novels: 騷動 and 詩與散文; some present a number of risky descriptions.

678. 魚　*FISH*　　　　　　　　　　　　1 vol. 212 p. by　梅娘（孫嘉瑞）
　　　　　　　　　　　　　　　　　　　　　1943　　　　*See Biogr. 142*

　　　A collection of short stories which describe feminine psychology in matters of love. These stories all contain a bitter and fatalistic notion of life, hence they should be read only by enlightened people. These novels contain passages offensive to morals.

侏儒 p. 1. An idiot child who found a protector, and gave his life for her.

魚 p. 24. A dramatic description in the form of a monologue of an unhappy love. The first part possesses literary beauty.

旅 p. 75. A usual travel episode.

黃昏之獻 Huang Hun chih hsien p. 83. A story of a writer who was unhappy in marriage, and sought sentimental adventure through a newspaper's advertisement. However it was only a joke.

雨夜 p. 103. A young woman who went to a dance in order to find some consolation ─ was cought in a storm on a beach. She was a victim of an assault but was lucky enough to escape in time.

一個蚌 p. 125. A novel of a girl who fell in love; a tragic misunderstanding end the happiness.

　　　All these novels should be read by *informed readers only.*

679. 蟹　*THE CRAB*　　　　　　　　　1 vol. 227 p. by　梅　娘
　　　　　　　　　　　　　　　　　　　　　1944　華北文化書店

　　　A collection of six stories.

1. A meeting in the night.
2. Confidences of a deceived woman.
3. Love story through an advertisement.
4. Barber's dream which never came true.
5. Invitation to some girls by their friends.
6. Hsieh. A novel describing the Sun family, which was ruined through lack of steady management.

　　　The style is easy and good in this book. *It can be read by enlightened people.*

680. 熱情的書　*A VOLUME OF WARM FEELING*　1 vol. 191 p. by　孟　朗
　　　　　　　　　　　　　　　　　　　　　　　　1946　上海復旦出版公司

　　　Letter from a girl to her fiancé, in which she tells him in ever so many different ways all the things that are told by people in love with each other, that is, nothing of importance. *Only for grown-up people.*

681. 石獅　*STONE LION*　　　　　　　1 vol. 232 p. by　米星如
　　　　　　　　　　　　　　　　　　　　　1932　開明書店

　　　Fairy stories. About the demon of war, symbol of the oppression of the humble. Who is the most powerful: the warrior or the magician, the demon or the king? Compassion for mice. A fairy story. Happiness in works of mercy etc. *For everyone.*

682. 如夢令 *WAS IT LIKE DREAM?* 1 vol. 313 p. by 穆儒丏
開明書店

A girl who has been sold into a house of ill fame finds herself liberated and married to a very rich man. After his death, she gets into touch again with her father and brothers who profit of the occasion by extorting as much money as they can out of her. In spite of her generosity, she is forced to throw them out of the house. Before letting them depart, however, she gives them each a present, and then leaves herself for a foreign country.

The heroine is an admirable character. *For everyone.*

683. 南北極 *NORTH POLE AND SOUTH POLE* 1 vol. 275 p. by 穆時英
1934　現代書局　*See Biogr. 119*

A collection of novels. A few of these are harmless from the moral point of view, while the others should be proscribed, especially "Nan Pei Chi" which describes the misconduct of a young man. *To be proscribed.*

684. 黑牡丹 *BLACK PEONY* 1 vol. 206 p. by 穆時英等
1934　上海良友圖書印刷公司印行

This book contains ten novels written by well known authors, several of them are harmless from the moral point of view. The one named "P'eng-Yu Liang" points a good moral. But the story by Pa Chin as well as the last two (pp. 165 & 189) contain objectionable descriptions. The second novel presents an unhealthy atmosphere. This book can be read *by informed readers.*

685. 現實的故事 *A STORY OF REALITY* 1 vol. 98 p. by 乃麟
1946　建業出版社

Some little tales about the great city, but all very dull indeed. A book that falls below the average standard.
Not suitable reading for children.

686. 百合集 *THE LILY* 1 vol. 108 p. by 倪貽德
1929　新北書局　*See Biogr. 120*

A collection of short stories.
1. A school master, who married one of his pupils, could hardly support her; after some time she became unfaithful to him and asked for a divorce.
2. A story of a girl who became poor owing to her infidelity to her friends.
3. Same theme as the second story.
4. A country girl became a restaurant waitress in Shanghai; a serious youth fell in love with her.

This book contains a number of risky descriptions, together with false theories about divorce and abortion. *To be reserved for informed readers.*

687. 殘 *BROKEN* 1 vol. 198 p. by 倪貽德
1930　北新書局

We are given an account of a group of musicians in the country. Among them is a girl who is already engaged but, in spite of this, she has two other suitors, a cousin and another young man. The cousin has no luck but his rival is successful to such a degree that he takes advantage of the heroine. The latter, seized with panic, proposes that they escape to Europe, to which her lover consents.

The cousin who has been refused drowns himself when he learns of their departure.
For adults.

688. 飢寒人　*THE STARVED*　　　　　1 vol. 110 p. by 歐陽山（楊儀）
1937　北新書局　*See Biogr. 182*

A collection of four poor stories; unhealthy atmosphere, especially in the first story. *Not to be recommended to the young people.*

689. 七年忌 *THE SEVENTH ANNIVERSARY MEMORIAL*　1 vol. 282 p. by 歐陽山
1935　生活書店

A collection of poorly written stories. The author shows an utter lack of taste. The big number of quarrels, vulgar expressions and immodest allusions oblige us to reserve this book *for informed readers.*

690. 潘金蓮　*P'AN CHINLIEN*　　　　　1 vol. No. 4 by 歐陽予倩
1928　新月

A story of a young slave girl who refused to become a concubine to her master. After the refusal the master gave her in marriage to a person whom the girl disliked. The slave girl loved the brother of her husband, who also returned her love. When her husband heard about this love he poisoned the woman.

This book contains a few immodest expressions, and, as the theme of the story is bad, this book is to be reserved *for enlightened people.*

691. 滅亡　*DESTRUCTION or DEATH*　　　1 vol. 226 p. by 巴金（李芾甘）
20th edition 1946　開明書店　*See Biogr. 100*

"Death" is the story of a young man who resolved to devote his life to the revolution to better the people's conditions. This man was in love with a girl, but he deemed this contrary to his ideal. His partner was arrested and shot for distributing Tu Ta-chin's — hero's name — magazine. Tu thought that he was responsible for the death of his partner who left a widow and a child. In spite of the prayers of his fiancée, he commits suicide.

The tone of this story is bitter, often violent, marked with melancholy and sadness. A passionate and extremist book that was welcomed by the critics who called the author a "romantic and anarchist revolutionist."
(Renseign. du Bureau Sinol. No. 382 p. 2. 0.　Brière S.J.). *Everyone should be warned against reading this story.*

692. 光明　*GLORY*　　　　　　　　1 vol. 181 p. by 巴　金
4th. edit. 1935　新中國書局

This is the second collection published by the author, the first being entitled 復仇 Most of the contents of this book are extremely pessimistic and sentimental.
The chief ones are as following:
愛的十字架　A story of a family that struggles against misery through natural pride. It costs the life of the wife.
奴隸的心　Two school-mates, one rich, in whose family are several female slaves, and the other poor whose mother misconducts herself to pay for his studies. It is the latter who lives a life that is useful to society although he ends up by being shot by the government for his political activities.
狗　Bitter sarcasm on the excesses of the fashion of having bare legs. Sensual.
生與死　The story of the shattered love of a young man who in spite of exhortations to live a more laborious life, indulges in pessimism and eventually dies of it. The inanity of all effort and of all work.
未寄的信　Tells of a love affair between a Chinese student in France and an Austrian. The young man is inconstant and ends up in breaking off the affair. *Not to be recommended to anyone.*

693. 海底夢 *SEA DREAM* 1 vol. 131 p. by 巴 金
8th. edit. 1941 開明書店

This novel was written in 1935. It can be considered as the counterpart of 滅亡 Whereas the hero of the latter is a young man who is devoted, body and soul, to the revolution, the present volume is about a girl who is animated by the same sentiments.

Being the daughter of a rich family, she begins her life in passing her days pleasantly. Then one evening, after having passed the day with the gilded youth of her circle, she meets with an accident. On her way home, her car runs over a poor widow. In reparation for this accident, she is forced to undertake the living expenses of the son of the widow. Thus she comes to know the world of the downtrodden.

Soon she begins to love her protege, and prefers to leave her home to share the fate of the pariahs of society. Together they devote themselves to the revolution that they hope will liberate the oppressed classes from the tutelage of moneyed capitalists. The revolution that they have dreamed and planned for is, however, snuffed through the intervention of soldiers, and the young man meets his death in it. Before dying, however, he is comforted by the vow made by the heroine to continue the struggle.

The heroine fulfils her vow, and soon she is found in prison. Her father, who has influential friends, wishes to save her. He visits her in prison, and asks his daughter to sign a declaration regretting her revolutionary activities, and he promises that it will secure her release. He also tells her of her mother's death from chagrin and anxiety over herself. He prays her to reform her thinking and to return home with him to afford him some comfort in his old age.

The prayers and tears of her father fail to persuade the heroine to give up her revolutionary career. Weeping herself, she tells him that she cannot commit perjury and go against her own oath. She must continue to struggle for the deliverance of the oppressed, the "slaves".

The whole book is an allegory where China is the "slave" and Japan is symbolized by the ruling class. *For mature people.*

694. 春天裡的秋天 *AUTUMN IN SPRING* 1 vol. 129 p. by 巴 金
1932 開明書店

Still another book by Pa Chin reflecting the mentality of "Young China" and accusing contemporary society and the family system. The story begins with the suicide of the brother of the hero, for which, according to him, the parents are responsible. Then follows a love affair between the hero and his sweetheart, Jung, who sometimes consoles him and sometimes treats him coldly. A friend advises him to work, as the sole purpose of life is not making love. Jung is called home to her sickly mother and wishes to break off the affair. This means new sorrows for the hero. The book ends with the death of Jung who leaves a letter in which she swears fidelity to the hero and takes exception to the fiancée that has been chosen for him by his parents.

After this there is no more "Springtime" for our hero!
Only for mature people as the book is too sad and melancholy.

695. 砂丁 *THE ANTIMONY MINE* 1 vol. 125 p. by 巴 金
4th. edit. 1940 文學叢書

Of the hard life of miners exploited by industrialists who care for nothing except money.

The author dwells too much on the tyranny of employers and urges too strongly revolt against the social system that permits such injustices.

The book has a very pessimistic flavour. *For grown-up people.*

696. 新生 *NEW LIFE*   1 vol. 239 p. by 巴 金
16th edition 1946 開明書店

Li Ch'ing-shu, (fiancée of Tu Ta-chin, hero of "Death") became a revolutionist after the death of Tu Ta-chin. Li Ch'ing-shu tried hard to convert her brother; finally she succeeded through the help of a girl and three other friends, directors of a revolutionary magazine. Li Ch'ing-shu's brother, Li Leng, left Shanghai in order to help the revolutionary movement in another city. In this city he started a general strike; he was arrested and sentenced to death.

In this second novel, in places written like a diary, the hero is more human and natural than in the first story. The author's philosophy shows that a suicide is a worthless act for the revolution, while the execution of Li Leng's is a glorious and fruitful one as his blood will inspire thousands of revolutionists to continue his struggles. (Renseign. du Bureau Sinol. No. 382 p. 2. 0. Brière S. J.). *Everyone to be warned against the above story.*

697. 霧 *MIST*   1 vol. 102 p. by 巴 金
New edition 1947 開明書店

This is the first part of the trilogy "Love". Chou Jou-shui, a young but successful author, falls in love with Chang Jo-lan. He knows that she loves him but he does not declare his love.

Before he went to Japan to study, his parents had married him to a girl whom he did not love; he has two children. For many years, he lived separated from his wife and the idea of going back filled him with horror. His parents insisted on his returning home. The voice of his conscience was imperative. He could not decide to give up Chang Jo-lan, nor his literary career. His friends advised him to divorce; but still he hesitated.

In the end he decided to break with Jo-lan, and returned home to find that his wife had been dead for over a year. Thus he realizes how his irresoluteness stood in the way of his happiness.

The author advocates divorce and considers the system of concubinage as contrary to the good of the family.

For informed readers.

698. 雨 *RAIN*   1 vol. 195 p. by 巴 金
New Edition 1947 開明書店

The story presents Mr. Wu, who after his wife's death found consolation in the company of his former girl-friend Hsiung Chih-chün. At her place he met Cheng Yü-le, his former admirer; she, however, killed herself as Mr. Wu refused to remember their love. Mr. Wu was reproached by his friends for taking no interest in revolution owing to the fact that he spent all his free time with Miss Hsiung. She, in order to save Wu from being charged with the death of Yü-le, married Cheng Yü-le's husband. She informed Mr. Wu of the fact, asking him not to be down-hearted, because she was ill and would not live long. *For informed readers.*

699. 電 *LIGHTNING*   1 vol. 124 p. by 巴 金
New Edition 1947 開明書店

A novel of young revolutionists who were pursued by police during their night meetings. They took to flight; five were hit by bullets; two were killed; the rest of the group managed to escape to the country.

One of the group had to occupy an important position in the city; Wu Jen-min volunteered but in the end his admirer took his place.

Pa Chin prefers this novel owing to the spirit of the revolutionists who are ready to sacrifice their lives in order to reach their goal. *For informed readers.*

700. 人生 *LIFE ON EARTH*

1 vol. 166 p. by 巴　金
1942　文化社

Of the life of a child from his earliest years to adolescence. *For everyone.*

701. 海外雜集 *NOTES FROM A VOYAGE*

1 vol. 102 p. by 巴　金
4th. edit. 1940　開明書店

In 1927 the celebrated author went to France to pursue his studies. This book is the description of his journey there.

In contains nothing original, being an early work. Some of the expressions used are trivial, and there is a lack of understanding of Christianity. *For everyone.*

702. 雪 *SNOW*

1 vol. 124 p. by 巴　金
1st edition 1932 5th edition 1940

A production of his younger days in the author's early style; hence passionate, morbid and over-romantic. A young man told his fiancée that to set her free from her masters and to give her freedom, it was necessary to get married; so he would go and work in a mine where he was sure to earn money quickly in order to set up a house. Attracted by the wonderful promises of the mine directors he went to work, but was soon disillusioned: working conditions were the worst imaginable, causing much illness and many deaths; those that tried to escape were shot down by the police. One day, the mine was flooded; all the miners were drowned including our hero. The directors suffered no loss and hired another squad of workmen. The young fiancée, unaware of her lover's death, died after one year of solitary life and hard work, but she died with her lover's name on her lips. *Not to be recommended to anyone* owing to its revolutionary spirit.

703. 髮的故事 *ABOUT HAIR*

1 vol. by 巴　金
1st edition 1936 6th edition 1940

A collection of four novelettes.

1. *A story of hair:* A white hair found in a book recalled to mind how one of the author's revolutionary friends had been cornered by the police, and discovered that his hair had suddenly turned white in presence of the danger that threatened to overwhelm him; this had saved him, for the police did not recognize him.

2. *Rain:* Two friends talked about a girl's disappearance due to the revolutionary upheaval. How hard it seemed to inform the girl's mother about this disaster. It contains the last confidential letter of the prisoner before her death.

3. *Under the window:* A lover came to talk with his fiancée — a servant — during the night. His grief when he found out that she had left with her masters for the interior owing to rumours of war, instead of following him as he had suggested to her.

4. *The star:* A writer came to visit a former mistress whom he still loved, but found out that she was living with one of his friends; in spite of this he had a long conversation with her, but their lives were in danger, for a band of brigands having being once driven off returned to threaten and attack the town. Cannonade, Lewis guns, runnings to and fro, various meetings of friends deciding what steps to take. It was necessary to separate. The young man wept, but a star arose amidst his tears; he realized that he must imitate the secret work and self-sacrifice of his friends in the cause of society and the revolution.

Not to be recommended owing to its revolutionary spirit.

704. 憶 *MEMORIES*

1 vol. 136 p. by 巴　金
1st edition 1937 10th edition 1947　藝光出版社

As the title shows, the book contains the author's personal memories.

1/*Memories:* His suffering when his parents died.

2/*First memories:* His first impressions as a child about his parents; a narrative in rhytmic prose or free verse; very touching.

3/*His Home:* His life in Chengtu during his childhood; he witnessed the death of his father and mother, several brothers and cousins. He saw the spread of the new ideas in Szechwan, the social evolution and revolutionary upheaval. At the end he left for France.

4/*Belief and action:* His first contact with an anarchist and his social humanitarianism; he read the influential magazines in vogue and, collaborating with his brothers, produced pamphlets.

5/*Youthful experience:* How he cooperated or directed several magazines that would each be suppressed one after the other; the first because the author took up a position in favour of "short hair".

6/*My eldest brother:* How he admired his eldest brother, a partisan of the new ideas; opposition between the young party who were modern, and the uncles who were tyrannical and out of fashion, was the cause of his many sufferings. This too was responsible for the publication of his great trilogy. In the end his eldest brother committed suicide owing to monetary difficulties. Sorrow of the younger brother.

7/*On the threshold:* Narrative of the fortunes of his first translations or of his first stories, especially the biography of a Russian or Polish revolutionary.

8/*I am leaving Peiping:* Impressions in the form of a letter about a residence of three weeks in the old Capital in 1935.

9/*Various memories:* Inner struggle between his liking for the pen and the disgust he sometimes feels. His intimate contradictions and weaknesses. Let us quote a revealing phrase: "I realize the greatness of Dante, Shakespeare and Goethe, but I prefer Tolstoi, Dostoieski and Artsybashev."

For everyone.

705. 短簡 *SHORT LETTERS*　　　　　　1 vol. 172 p. by 巴　金
　　　　　　　　　　　　　　　　　　　　1937　上海良友復興圖書印刷公司

In this book Pa Chin answers his friends who asked him to explain his ideas and characters in "Chia", "Ch'un" and others of his writings. In some cases Pa Chin advised revolt against the old family system; sometimes he recommended patience, but chiefly he encourages his readers to believe in life and future. *For everyone.*

706. 點滴 *TINY BITS*　　　　　　　　1 vol. 88 p. by 巴　金
　　　　　　　　　　　　　　　　　　4th edition 1940　開明書店

A collection of short stories and essays in literary criticism, very simple but rather romantic and whimpering. Anticipating this kind of criticism, Pa Chin answers that his emotions matched his revolutionary spirit, as "his tears are tears of freedom" *For everyone.*

707. 家 *HOME*　　　　　　　　　　1 vol. 497 p. by 巴　金
　　　　　　　　　　　　　　　　　21st edition 1941　開明書店

Description of an old style Chinese family and its modern problems. Four generations live under the same roof; the youngsters grow restive under the rigid rule of the old family head.

The main character, Chüeh Hui, is the most violent rebel against the time-honored privilege by which the parents can make and unmake the life of their children, and even get them married against their inclination.

The oldest son, Chüeh Hsin, loved his cousin and was loved by her but had to give her up in order to marry the woman chosen for him by his father. He represents the young people who are too weak to stand up against the old despotism and prefer to sacrifice their convictions.

Chüeh ming has more vigour but still needs the backing of his brother Chüeh hui's fierce determination in order to keep his resolve never to marry the girl his father chose for him.

The maid with whom Chüeh hui was in love was intended to become a concubine to an old man. She killed herself on the eve of her wedding. The family provided the old man with another maid who had to be forced into marrying.

Disgusted with these goings-on, Chüeh hui leaves his home. Freed of the hidden hatred which his uncles and his grandfather's concubine foster against him, he feels all restraint hindering the pursuit of his aspirations lifted from him; he is overcome with emotion when he contemplates — endlessly — the hardships caused to him and all modern young people. He wants to consecrate himself to emancipation and the new ideal. This ideal, which remains vague and undefined, is inspired by his hatred and love.

The book is rather depressing and bitter. It will unsettle young minds; may be tolerated *for informed readers.*

708. 春 *SPRING* 1 vol. 547 p. by 巴 金
11th editiion 1941 開明書店

春 is a sequel to 家 The theme is the same. The heroine of this story, Kao Shu-yin, was engaged by her father to a dandy of a Ch'ih family, and refused to marry him, hence arose some family quarrels, well described by Pa Chin. At the end Kao Shu-yin yielded to her parent's decision and considered the matter as her "unhappy lot"; later on she learned that she had to "thwart" her parent's decision. This was told to her by her cousins Chüeh Hui, Chüeh Ming and the latter's fiancée. They related to her how their cousin died of chagrin as she was given in marriage to a person whom she did not love. This narration caused Kao Shu-yin to rebel openly; she fled to Shanghai where Chüeh Hui awaited her.

Chüeh Hsin's character has not changed: "he would like, but he dares not"! He saw clearly the defects of the old regime, but had not enough courage to resist. A poor specimen.

In this book they laugh at their uncles who, secretly, keep concubines and abuse the servant girls. The eldest son is well aware of the corruption, but has not got the guts to do anything about it . . thus preparing the end of the clan.

The book contains a number of coarse expressions, frivolous scenes between the uncles and the servants and the quarrels which follow.

The revolutionary spirit in the book is at times too violent. Although the theme is "freedom to choose one's wife" the author also advocates disobedience. *For informed readers.*

709. 秋 *AUTUMN* 1 vol. 705 p. by 巴 金
4th edition 1942 開明書店

This third part of the celebrated "trilogy" contains no principal character, as the author describes secondary scenes such as the unexpected episode "Mei". A lazy young man, worse than Chüeh Hsin, got married; his faults were due to his lack of education for which his father was guilty; the latter fixed the marriage and everyone expected it to be an unhappy one, but it turned out to be the contrary. This volume describes a number of quarrels between Shu Hua — a sympathetic, energetic person — and his uncles, as they were the cause of the household's ruin. The story shows Chüeh Hsin as a lazy and unlucky man; it presents his failure due to the weakness of his character (During the scenes that are described Chüeh-Hsin wept fifteen times.)

This book contains neither immorality nor exaggeration in the revolutionary spirit. *For everyone.*

710. 憇園 *GARDEN OF LEISURE*　　　　　　1 vol. 248 p. by 巴　金
　　　　　　　　　　1st edition 1944 3rd edition 1946. 文化生活出版社

In this novel, two tragedies are interwoven, though without close connection. The connection is made by the narrator, who is telling two stories that took place under his eyes at almost the same time, and partly at the same place.

The first story is about the wretched life of the head of a family, who was obliged to sell his house, and, as he could not live in peace with his wife and eldest son, preferred to sacrifice himself for the domestic good. From then on he lived in the street like a beggar. His youngest son found him and wanted him to return home; although he visited his home from time to time, the eldest son treated him with such brutality that at the end he died alone in the street from illness. The book describes the sorrow of the youngest son when he learned about his father's death.

In the house sold by the wretched hero of the above tragedy — ironically named "house of quiet", — another tragic story was about to happen. The new master of the house married a second time; his new wife tried to tame her step-child. The child, encouraged by his uncles, resisted his step-mother's efforts. At the end the father realized the goodness of his wife's advice and planned to withdraw the child from the influence of his uncles and aunts by sending him to school. One day, without his parents knowledge, he was invited to a swimming party and was drowned. *For everyone.*

711. 小人小事 *INSIGNIFICANT EVENTS*　　　　1 vol. 85 p. by 巴　金
　　　　　　　　　　　　　　　　　1945 文化生活出版社

This small book contains a collection of five stories written during the war.
1. 猪與雞 Dispute between a tenant and the owner of a house arising from the fact that herds of pigs and hens were loose in the property and were leaving marks of their passage; this caused the owner to evict the tenant.
2. 兄與弟 Relations between two brothers; after a fire in which several people were burned to death, the elder brother buried the younger.
3. 夫與妻 A cursing scene between husband and wife which ended when the police threatened to put them under arrest.
4. 女孩與貓 A little girl reared a cat that was sometimes absent from home for a considerable time; after one of these absences, the cat returned one day and died on the girl's doorstep. She buried the cat carefully.
5. 生與死 A dying wife who requested her husband to wait a year at least before marrying again.
For everyone.

712. 火 *FIRE*　　　　　　　3 vol. 249, 292, 314 p. by 巴　金
　　　　　　　　　　　　　　　　7th edition 1946 開明書店

Although these three volumes have the same title they compose a rather loose trilogy: looser still than some others by the same author. Hence, we must make a separate digest of each volume.

Volume I

In the first volume the author completely attains his object, which is to describe the war in China. The novel begins with the battle of Shanghai (August — November 1937). We see the actions of a group of young men and women who were animated with patriotic ideas contrary to those of their parents, who were a prey to defeatism and possessed no thought save of their personal welfare. Some of them published and edited magazines preaching a war of resistance, others of the young group were working in the hospitals and caring for the wounded. But the chief centre of action was a patriotic Club which the foreign police regarded with suspicion for they were afraid of trouble with the Japanese. As the battle progressed, sadness laid a heavy hand on the hearts of all, for Chapei, west of Shanghai, and Nantao fell into the hands of the Japanese. To avoid police interference the Club decided to depart for the interior and devote itself to war propaganda in the front lines. In the meantime, a love intrigue between two of our heroes sprang up which will be continued in the next two volumes.

No objection can be made from a moral point of view. *For everyone.*

Volume II

In the course of the second part, we follow the wanderings of the same group of friends in the interior devoting themselves to holding up the courage of the people; they spent their time in staging patriotic plays and inciting the people to join the guerilla ranks; and in that way they had good success. As the Japanese advanced they withdrew farther into the interior towards Hankow in order to reform their ranks, for the war had indirectly thinned them out. Two actors joined the guerillas; a third who allowed himself to seek sentimental adventures was killed by a Japanese bomb; a fourth, suffering from shock in a bombardment was forced to rest in a hospital. During this retreat, the friends endured a very long exhausting journey on foot. This time the book has no intrigues.
For everyone.

Volume III

The third and last volume of the trilogy has very little connection with the foregoing. In the background, however, the love affair begun in the first volume appeared to end in marriage. In fact one of the young men was killed by Japanese bullets; the other was thrown into prison. But this intrigue was a mere — the — way, a "deus ex-machina" that helped to link up the third volume with the two others. As a matter of fact, this novel deals with the psychological description of an exemplary Protestant family of which the head, who was an assiduous reader of the Holy Scripture and son of a minister, made an effort to conform his life with his ideal. In this man's home, union was perfect without a shadow according to the teaching of the Gospel.
For everyone.

---

713. 第四病室 *WARD NUMBER FOUR*   1 vol. 364 p. by 巴 金
1946 晨光出版社

Describes the sufferings, the pleasures, the visits and conversations of the sick in a hospital, undisturbed by any romantic affairs. Jokes, complaints and various reflections go hand with the monotony of the long days in hospital. There are the dying that arouse pity, the dissatisfied, who run away, and others who await the cure impatiently. In spite of all, the interest lags, so that the reader has no easy task to reach the last of these 364 pages. The novel proceeds in diary form, and hence in the first person singular, from Thursday, June 1st, to Sunday 18th, thus including the day when the allied troops set foot in Normandy, to which event there is a passing allusion. The sick man, who was the narrator, made friends with a nurse, but the friendship remained a wholesome one, since the latter advised the young man on their parting: "Be good, pure, and useful to your neighbour". The sick were all civilians, and there is scarcely any allusion to the war. *For everyone.*

---

714. 寒夜 *COLD NIGHT*   1 vol. by 巴 金
1st edition 1947

The story of a husband who saw that his wife was drifting farther from him and tried hard to hold her back. The latter, after fourteen years of married life and in spite of having a child aged thirteen, had no scruples at leaving her home. Furthermore she formed an illicit friendship outside, rather a platonic one on her part, as she never showed great interest in her new friend. What forced her to leave home was the continual disagreements with her mother-in-law; at times she had qualms of conscience and returned for a short period to her home. Her husband was failing in health owing to T.B. and was from time to time driven by sufferings to drink, but he soon took hold of himself again. At the end, the wife left home for good and departed with her new partner into the interior. Soon afterwards, the abandoned husband died. Let us note that he had asked himself the question "After death is there not a soul that continues to live? Can we ever see again the dear ones of former days?" A question without an answer, this was his conclusion. After his death, his mother and his son left for a new residence. The former wife one day returned to visit her family, but as she found no one, she was seized with remorse and asked herself: "Ought I to return to my son or return to Lanchow my new country"? *For enlightened people.*

715. 短篇小説選 *SHORT STORIES*   1 vol. 32 p. by 巴　金
4th edition 上海中央出版社印行

A collection of three stories.
1. 復仇 A medical doctor when asked about the nature of "happiness" replied that it is found in revenge. To give proof of his saying he presented an example of a Russian murderer who committed his crime to avenge his wife who had been raped by two officers. The author does not approve of this assertion.
2. 初戀 Mr. T'ang relates that his marriage was not for love but for convention, as he loved only once, in France. He also tells of the life he led in France and his first love.
3. 狗 A story of an orphan who thought that he was of the lowest class and placed himself on the level with dogs.
　　　The third is said to be one of the finest pieces in Chinese literature. *Objectionable.*

716. 巴金選集 *AN ANTHOLOGY OF PACHIN*
1936 上海萬象書屋

　　　A collection of novels by Pa Chin. All of these can be read by anyone except the last one, where the author approves of a mother who sells her body in order to give a good education to her son. In the preface Pa Chin denies the existence of God. *For informed readers.*

717. 巴金代表作 *AN ANTHOLOGY OF PACHIN*
1940

Pa Chin presents some biographical material in the first part of this book; the second part contains eight stories and four essays.
He describes a modern woman, her spirit of sacrifice and the lack of freedom in choosing a husband. He also gives us a vivid description how hard it is to find a lost child etc. The last story is "Kou". (see 715).
His essays deal chiefly with psychological training, social spirit, the influence of a mother, of servants, and of an elder brother on a child. He attacks the opinion that life is not worth living, and speaks of his own "weight of memories". *For everyone.*

718. 青龍滾 *THE BLACK DRAGON FALL*   1 vol. 70 p. by 白　峯
天津書局

　　　Several narratives written with a Catholic atmosphere.
　　　In one of these stories, the author touches on the question of abandoned infants, and he gives two reasons for this evil — the existence of natural children, and superstitions. *For everyone.*

719. 老處女 *AN OLD MAID*　　　　1 vol. 184 p. by 白序之
　　　　　　　　　　　　　　　　　　1934　上海大東書局

The author has talent and proves in these tales that he also has humour. Most of these tales deal with the oddities of old maids who, late in life, take a fancy to handsome young men. Other examples of feminine eccentricity are also given. The last few pieces in this collection consist of memories spicily recounted.

Although they are presented with irony, young people should, however, avoid acquaintance with some of the specimens included in this book. *Not for everyone.*

720. 蘇青與張愛玲 *ON SU-CH'ING & CHANG AI-LING — TWO MODERN WOMEN WRITERS*　　1 vol. 107 p. by 白鷗編
　　　　　　　　　　　　　　　　　　1945　北京沙漠書店

Interviews with and ideas of the above two lady writers who are in great vogue at the present moment and much read by young people.

Many subjects are dealt with, but chiefly marriage and the employment of women. Subsequently an appreciation of the two authoresses is given and the book ends with a few passages written by them.

Their ideas are the modern ones in fashion, which cannot serve as a guide to our young people. *For grown-up people.*

721. 山徑 *MOUNTAIN PATH*　　　　1 vol. 173 p. by 白文
　　　　　　　　　　　　　　　　　　1938　文化生活

Of excursions in the mountains, coming across the miseries of the poor, fear of robbers. *For everyone.*

722. 大澤龍蛇傳 *UNCOMMON*　　3 vol. 155 p. 116 p. 126 p. by 白羽
　　　　　　　　　　　　　　　　　　1943　唯一書店

Story of bandits and heros.

Hsiao Pei-lung, having escaped from soldiers, is saved by a certain person whose daughter he marries. The book also recounts the subsequent adventures of Pei-lung. *For everyone.*

723. 戀家鬼 *THE HOME HAUNTER*　　1 vol. 105 p. by 白羽
　　　　　　　　　　　　　　　　　　1944　福成合印刷局

A book full of humorous stories; some of them contain a number of coarse expressions. *For everyone.*

724. 離婚 *DIVORCE*　　　　1 vol. 120 p. by 潘漢年
　　　　　　　　　　1928　上海光華書局 *See Biogr. 123*

A collection of interesting and lively short stories.
The style is vivid and simple. The scenes are well described and can be read with great ease. The story "他和他" (T'a Ho T'a) is down-right obscene. *To be banned.*

725. 馮小青 *FENG HSIAO-CH'ING*　　1 vol. 144 p. by 潘光旦
　　　　　　　　　2nd. edit. 1929　新月書店 *See Biogr. 125*

We are first presented with a biography of the famous Ming poetess of the title (Feng Hsiao-ch'ing). Then the author tries to explain her life and work according to Freudian theory. Finally we are given a few of the writings of the poetess herself.

This book is suitable for mature people only because of the approach of the author. *Not for everyone.*

726. 想飛的紙   *PAPER THAT YEARNS TO FLY*   1 vol. 155 p. by 鮑維湘
2nd. edit. 1934   北新書局

Stories for children. *For everyone.*

727. 霧裏重慶 *CHUNGKING IN THE MIST*   1 vol. 59 p. by 北 鷗
1946   作者出版社

Life is hard during the war in Chungking, with difficulties piling up that cannot be overcome. But clouds disappear when victory comes, and the sky becomes clear again.

In this book, the author juggles too easily with threats of divorce. *For grown-up people.*

728. 前線戀 *LOVE ON THE FRONT LINE*   1 vol. 172 p. by 北 鷗
1946   作者出版社

This novel is enacted at the front during the Sino-Japanese war. Although the author had a good chance to produce a creditable novel within the frame of the war, he has given us only a romance conceived by a haunter of boulevards. What he tells us of the war is very elementary, and we are given the impression that the high command are more concerned in amusing themselves than in prosecuting the war.

As for the plot, it is the ordinary one of novelists with no inspiration, containing ignoble love stories.

The heroine, Miss Hsu, who is the only creditable person of the book, remains in the background. The author prefers to narrate the adventures of people of lighter behavior.

From the moral point of view, this book is *not to be recommended to anyone,* not because it indulges actually in immoral descriptions, but because it is apt to lead the imagination to such subjects.

729. 喜訊 *GOOD TIDINGS*   1 vol. 180 p. by 彭家煌
2nd edition 1936   復光書局 *See Biogr. 127*

A collection of short stories, a few are interesting, others are very ordinary. The book should be reserved for grown up people, as it contains some descriptions as in "Tso Yeh" — of an aged man who spends most of his time among prostitutes —., and in "Ch'ao Shen Miao" where the atmosphere is *very unhealthy for young readers.*

730. 剪影集 *SILHOUETTES*   1 vol. 251 p. by 蓬子 (姚蓬子)
1933   上海良友圖書印刷公司 *See Biogr. 189*

Seven short stories.
1. The story of two brothers, one rich and arrogant, the other poor but good.
2. A story of revolt against the rich.
3. Floods — famine. It presents a heartless rich man, who was killed by workers.
4. A drunkard's story.
5. A story of a poor merchant, his troubles, struggles and his ruin.
6. A novel of a young man who met a prostitute, and his fall.
7. The meeting of two former lovers, and their parting.
   The first five are for everyone, but the two last are *only for informed people.*

731. 盔甲山 *THE ARMOUR HILLS*   1 vol. 103 p. by 畢基初
藝術與生活社

Stories of braves and brigands and the sufferings of the poor. *For mature people.*

732. 迷朔鴛鴦 *THE CONFUSED TURTLE DOVES*   1 vol. 304 p. by 必　周
1936 京報印刷部

A story of a family which lived in Paoting-fu. It consisted of parents, a son, a daughter and a cousin. The son had a student friend with whom his sister was violently in love. The parents wanted their son to marry his cousin, but the youth refused. He was in love with a girl who was seduced by a scamp. As this girl ran away, our hero was in despair and went to see his friend, who had become a girl (having concealed her sex on the death of her father). Our hero fell in love with her and at the same time his sister got engaged to a young man who saved her from bandits. The cousin, who still loved our hero was, of course, very unhappy but the author found a way out by marrying two girls to our hero. After the wedding these "children" return to school. *For informed readers.*

733. 掘金記 *GOLD RUSH*   1 vol. 72 p. by 畢奐午
1936 文化生活 *See Biogr. 128*

Verses and a few tales.

Certain of the expressions used do not correspond too much with reality. *May be read by all.*

734. 姑姑 *MY AUNT*   1 vol. 72 p. by 冰心（謝婉瑩）
4th edition 1937 上海北新書局 *See Biogr. 69*

Four stories.

1) A novel of a young man who worried because his ideal married one of his gambling friends.
2) The author sees the success of her first dinner, and sadly thinks of her mother all the time.
3) An invitation sent by a young married woman to her former friend; the latter had enough sense to decline.
4) The story of two babies who were born on the same day in a hospital. . . One was the son of a rich family the other of a poor.

This book presents fresh and good pictures. *For everyone.*

735. 超人 *SUPERMAN*   1 vol. 149 p. by 冰心女士
2nd edition 1933 上海商務印書館

A collection of literary essays and letters of a sick girl. She is not afraid of death as the world never attracted her. She considers death as only an apparent separation.

Beautiful style and great ideas. This book is considered to be one of the masterpieces of the author. *Profitable reading.*

736. 去國 *SAILING ABROAD*   1 vol. 152 p. by 冰　心
1933 北新書局

A collection of short stories.

In this collection there is a novel with a title "Ch'ü Kuo" where the author describes a student's impressions after his return from U.S.A. The style is very fine, fresh, poetical and natural. It presents beautiful feelings. *For everyone.*

737. 冬兒姑娘 *MISS TUNG-ERH*   1 vol. 161 p. by 冰　心
1935 上海北新書局

This book presents three interesting stories.
1 A story of a Peiping girl of the working class .
2. A novel of a girl who was adopted by an American woman — the latter was very

happy with her child. The child slowly realized that she was Chinese. . . . The story tells of her growing up and becoming a woman.

3.   A description of the salon of a modern lady.

This book can be read by everyone.

738.   往事   *REMINISCENCE*   1 vol. 124 p. by   冰　心
                                                      13th edition 1940   開明書店

Ping Hsin is one of the most refined of the woman authors in modern China. She is a Protestant.

In this book she shows her delicate sentiments and reveals herself as a true poet.

It is a collection of memories in which she sings of man (her mother, her friends, and her children), and nature (the snow, a storm at sea, moonlight, the stars, the flowers, etc). She gives proof of a great gift of observation and noble feelings. The influence of Protestantism is also seen. *For everyone.*

739.   冰心小說集   *STORIES BY PING-HSIN*   1 vol. 341 p.
                                                   5th edition 1936   上海北新書局

A collection of the best novels and works of Ping Hsin are presented in this book. The preface contains her autobiography; she then presents a number of short stories. These show us that Ping Hsin is really a poet and a great author. She has the gift to express the most noble sentiments: her love of nature, of her mother, of her children. She touches on everything that can lift up people. Although she is a protestant and is strongly influenced by her religion, this should not prevent Catholics from reading her books.

For everyone.

740.   冰心女士小說集   *ANTHOLOGY OF PING-HSIN'S STORIES*
                                          1 vol. 119 p. by   冰心女士
                                          Collection :   近代文學名著
                                          2nd. edit. 1930   上海新文學社

1. 悟   A student receives a letter from a friend explaining his conception of life and of the world. Being an orphan without support or a friend, he finds men egoistic, society hard, and life full of suffering and tears. His ideal cannot be any other than to satisfy his hunger and assuage his thirst. He does not believe at all in love. He becomes ill, however, while taking a walk, and has to enter a hospital. When he is convalescent, the student refutes the arguments of his friend. For the whole universe bears the mark of love, the love of the Creator towards His creatures, the love of a mother for her children, the love of Nature, and of friends.

In another letter addressed to his sister, his friend explains how it is he is accused of lack of virility. He exposes his psychological state, and explains the difficulty he has in expressing adequately his thoughts and feelings.

2. 去國   A graduated engineer wishes to serve his country, the young Republic of China. Because of his ideals, he refuses magnificent offers made to him in America. After returning home and furnished with a letter of recommendation from his father to a friend, he goes to Peking to look for a job. He becomes a member of a useless bureau. There is no work to do. All they do is to indulge in gossip. After several months he returns to America, disgusted and distressed.

3. 一個軍官的筆記   The diary of an officer. He leaves his parent to join the war. He meets his men at the station. He is so moved that he cannot speak to them. Why do we have fratricidal, inhuman war that cannot really accomplish anything? He is then wounded. He has a friend and relative in the opposite camp who comes to visit him. They remember the vow they made as children never to fight each other again.

4 一篇小說的結局 A girl student describes a novel. It is about a mother who reads and re-reads the last letter written by her son just before he goes into battle. She is waiting for him this evening. Someone enters the room. . . but it is not her son.

5 六一姊；莊鴻的姊姊；最後的安息；一個兵丁；姑姑. These are five narratives full of interest. The author reveals herself a fine psychologist. She excells in penetrating the most intimate sentiments of children and in describing their souls, their joy, their pain, their sensibility, their friendship, and their sympathy. *For everyone.*

---

741. 寒夜集 *COLD NIGHT*   1 vol. 102 p. by 冰 瑩
1947 *See Biogr. 68*

1. 傑作 A writer in needy circumstances. He was asked to write an article, but had to wait for his payment. In the meantime he was offered a positiion; as he did not receive the money for his article, he accepted the job.
2. 骨頭 Also about a writer in needy circumstances.
3. 名片 A story of a student who had just completed his studies.
4. 玫君低頭笑了 What a girl was thinking during the time when her fiancé paid her a visit and wished her a Happy New Year.
5. 陳嫂子想了半夜 A scene from village life.
6. 因為老師不在的原故 A dispute in a school.
    For everyone.

---

742. 濤語 *THE WHISPERING BILLOWS*   1 vol. 235 p. by 許梅女士 (石評梅)
1931 神州國光社 *See Biogr. 135*

    Languishing effusions. Friendships too sweet for words. *May be read.*

---

743. 三山奇俠   1 vol. 230 p. by 不肖生
1932 藝光書店 *See Biogr. 63*

    "The Marvellous Heros of the Three Mountains" is an epic whose subject is common enough in Chinese literature. Such books exalt the chevaliers or knights who go around redressing wrongs, revenging innocent people, and slaying bandits. They are always endowed with extraordinary powers, in this case differentiated by the three schools of Chinese boxing and fencing that they follow. *For everyone.*
Note: A synopsis of this kind of romance is impossible because it would be too complicated. They contain too many characters and the events are too difficult to trace. It might be added that although such romances may be read by anyone and they do not contain anything contrary to good morals, nevertheless they are not to be recommended. Many parents and educators have discovered that they excite young imaginations too much. (Jos. Schyns).

---

744. 土 *DIRT*   1 vol. 178 p. by 沙 里
1945 新民印書館

    After an introduction that makes us think of the famous saying, "After us the deluge", the author ends by arriving where he should have begun.
    Description of peasant life with the underlying idea that civilization only kills it. *For everyone.*

---

745. 苦難 *DIFFICULTIES*   1 vol. by 沙汀 (楊同芳)
1937 文化生活出版社 *See Biogr. 186*

    A collection of short stories which contain criticism of the life led by present-day officials. *For all.*

746. 土餅 *MUD CAKE*   1 vol. 203 p. by 沙 汀
                                                      1932 文化生活

A series of stories describing the miseries occasioned by bad administration and other calamities such as famine, war, the soldiery.

A slight reserve should be made on the fourth story in which abortion is mentioned, and on the tenth because of a number of crude words employed. *For grown-up people.*

747. 獻給年青女友 *WRITTEN TO YOUNG LADIES* 1 vol. 155 p. by 沙駝 (王志聖)
                                                      1942 大興書籍文具店

A book of lay morals containing practical advice for young girls in middle schools and for young women.

After giving an account of the various stages by which women have become emancipated during the past few years, the author gives advice on adolescence, preparation for marriage, and for the young mother. The author's psychology is rudimentary and often false. The work seems to have been inspired by certain American manuals of psychology of second order. It does not contain a single word on some real problems such as conjugal relations and the psychological and social difficulties that they may lead to.

The book should *not be recommended* because of its mediocrity.

748. 豐年 *A PROSPEROUS YEAR*   1 vol. 190 p. by 山 丁
                                                      2nd edit. 1945 新民印書館

A series of tales, of players, story tellers, scenes in a train, and in the country. *For mature people.*

749. 夢 *A DREAM*   1 vol. 190 p. by 邵鈞軒
                                                      1946 上海大明書局

A young woman has been married for seven years and is the mother of two children, when she meets her former fiance whom she has always loved and who loves her. As she is maltreated by her husband, she listens to the perverse advice of her friend, and runs away with him. She takes her daughter with her, leaving her son behind. Her new found happiness, however, is of short duration as her new husband dies after only a few months, the victim of a bombardment.

In the second part, we are told of the subsequent existence of the heroine and that of her daughter. The latter falls in love with a young man who proves to be no other than her own brother.

The book ends with the death of the daughter and the suicide of the mother.

It makes very interesting reading, although the extra-conjual love and the suicide at the end are to be deplored. *For adults.*

750. 殘碑 *THE RUINED MONUMENT*   1 vol. 336 p. by 沈起予
                                                      1941 辰友復興圖書公司 *See Biogr. 129*

This book brings us back to the period of the beginning of the Kuo min tang party.

A young man, who found that his purse was empty and hence was unable to continue his studies, begged board and lodging from his uncle, who finally employed him as a servant. His girl-cousin was living under the same roof with him, but after a short stay he left the house and entered a school of the new Republican Party.

Later on the said party entrusted him with a position in the city of Hankow where the young man restored order, as he was ordered to do. Here he met a number of his old boy-friends as well as his girl-cousin. When the political situation was at its climax one of his enemies took advantage of the moment and accused him before his elders. The young man was afraid and ran away accompanied by his cousin who later became his wife. *For informed readers.*

751. 慈母 *LOVE OF A MOTHER* 1 vol. 143 p. by 沈嬹銓
5th. edit. 1946 三益書局

A young man of light character returns from the town where he has lost at gambling the whole fortune of his family. His mother, however, receives him affectionately and puts him on the right road again.

The hero manages to obtain the sympathy of the local doctor and is received as his partner. He even manages to obtain the hand and the affections of the daughter of his patron. The young people are very happy together. And when the doctor dies, the hero inherits his practice which is worth a considerable amount.

One day, however, he is called to a consultation in Shanghai where he finds his old comrades. There he gambles again, and again loses everything, this time, the fortune of his new family. He is seized by the police and is condemned to a year in prison. After his release, he goes home where he learns of the death of his mother and of his wife, both of whom have died of chagrin. An old woman servant receives him and repeats the same words that his mother used upon his former return from indulging his favourite vice.

A good book with a moral point of view. A few love affairs that are described are not too suggestive. *May be read by anyone.*

752. 夢裏家園 *DREAMING OF HOME* 1 vol. 128 p. by 沈心池
1946 正氣書局

The story of an impoverished family that is without the slightest interest. *May be read by anyone.*

753. 刧後桑田 *IN THE WAKE OF DISASTER* 1 vol. 128 p. by 沈心池
1947 正氣書局

The sequel of the family history begun in the preceding volume. *May be read by anyone.*

754. 孽海情侶 *PURE LOVE IN A WORLD OF LUST* 1 vol. 127 p. by 沈心池
1947 上海正氣書局

The odyssey of a damsel who becomes a dancer. Her environment is not interesting. *Not for the young.*

755. 塵海浮沉 *TOSSED BY THE TIDE* 1 vol. 120 p. by 沈心池
1947 上海正氣書局

Sequel to the above, consisting of a mass of nonsense. *Not for the young.*

756. 懺悔女郎 *PENITENT DAMSEL* 1 vol. 134 p. by 沈鴻麗
1946 上海前進書店

A girl student, of versatile character, has many suitors but she does not like any of them. She shies at her admirers and retires within herself.

A very dull book. *Not for the very young.*

757. 死灰 *ASHES* 1 vol. 113 p. by 沈松泉
1927 光華書店 *See Biogr. 130*

This book presents a diary and letters, which contain an exaggerated account of the love of a romantic whimperer. In this book it is the men who are always ready to weep. The love-affairs here described have a very sad ending. *For informed readers.*

758. 少女與婦人　*MAID AND WOMAN*　　1 vol. 177 p. by 沈松泉
　　　　　　　　　　　　　　　　　　　　　　　　　1928　光華書局

Unhealthy reflections on girls and married women. The author seems to be a man whose chief aim in life is carnal pleasure, which is the criterion of his acts and thoughts. *Proscribed.*

759. 醉吻　*AN INTOXICATING KISS*　　1 vol. 107 p. by 沈松泉
　　　　　　　　　　　　　　　　　　　　　　　　1929　光明書店

Four short stories.
The first tells us of the love affair of a young married man with a friend of his childhood. The second is a rather broad farce that takes place on the wedding night of a former friend. In the third, a married man gives excellent advice to a girl who is infatuated with him. The fourth describes a love that dies. *For grown-up people. Not for students.*

760. 鴨子　*DUCKS*　　　　　　　　1 vol. 285 p. by 沈從文
　　　　　　　　　　　　　　　　　1926　北新書局　*See Biogr. 131*

Amusing comedies and tales for children. Without always being of great literary value, they are nevertheless pleasingly written. *For everyone.*

761. 阿麗思中國遊記　*ALICE IN CHINA*　　1 vol. 280 p. by 沈從文
　　　　　　　　　　　　　　　　　　　　　　　　1928　新月書店

Little Alice and her companion ran away to China, a country full of animals which spoke and acted like human beings. — This book relates the events which took place in a dream. *For children.*

762. 石子船　*BOAT CARRYING MARBLE*　. B 1 vol. 143 p. by 沈從文
　　　　　　　　　　　　　　　　　　　　　　　　1930　中華書局

Several stories that are easy reading, without intrigue nor depth, but well written and interesting. A slight reservation to be made on them. *For mature people.*

763. 旅店及其他　*THE INN*　　　　　1 vol. 148 p. by 沈從文
　　　　　　　　　　　　　　　　　　　　　　　　1930　中華書局

A collection of six stories.
PP. 1—19: A story describing the events that took place before the marriage of an engaged couple. *Proscribed.*
PP. 19—33: A young widow with a stainless past ran a boarding house, but was unable to resist the temptations of a traveller who lodged for the night. *Strict reserve.*
PP. 33—41: Aking planned to marry but met with some objections from his friend, who finally succeeded in preventing the marriage. *Not for everyone.*
PP. 41—59: Seven huntsmen who prefer a free life rebel against the civil authorities, who are represented here as modern tyrants. The huntsmen are finally beheaded. *Not for everyone.*
PP. 59—89: A satire on the oddities of a poet who, being infatuated with himself, sought popularity by admiring all that was foreign and despising all that was Chinese. This story shows the modern outlook of the young generation. *Not for everyone.*
PP. 89—148: An author in a melancholy mood, met a girl-singer. After resisting temptation, he was finally led along the road to danger. *Not for everyone.*
This book presents an unealthy atmosphere. *To be banned.*

764. 如蕤集 *THE JU JUI COLLECTION*   1 vol. 351 p. by **沈從文**
                                                         1934 生活書店

    This book presents a collection of 11 short stories.
1) cf. resume No. 771.
2) Three girls, would-be poets, discuss a thousand things, and talk about a friend of theirs: that night they are told that she has died.
3) Vexations caused by soldiers.
4) Street scenes.
5) A number of people in the fighting lines.
6) Life in a slum.
7) The ill-treatment of prisoners.
8) The daily occupations of a young girl.
9) Episodes from prisoners' life in the neighbouring cells.
10) Night adventures in trenches, spies in the front lines.
11) The romance of a couple who get married.
For informed readers.

765. 八駿圖   *THE EIGHT CHARGERS*   1 vol. 167 p. by **沈從文**
                                                         1935 文化生活

    Stories written by the author for his wife. Several of the adventures with courtisans contain lascivious descriptions. *Not to be recommended to anyone.*

766. 從文小說習作選 *STORIES BY SHEN TS'UNG-WEN*   736 p. by **沈從文**
                                                         1936 上海良友圖書公司

    Collection of short stories and tales; in 4 parts.
1) 短篇 14 short stories, widely different in nature, often interesting for their descriptions of people's habits (peasants, fishermen etc.).
2) 月下小景 Ten legendary stories: No. 5, 扇陀, presents folkloristic interest: hunters tell their yarns; one of them relates how a monster, half man half deer, prevents rain from falling; a girl 扇陀 decides to seduce him in order to save the country from starvation; several girls go with her and swim, all naked, in a lake; the ruse works and prosperity comes to the country together with the rain.
3) 神巫之愛 Story in six parts: a magician visits a village temple, he is besieged by the girls who are all in love with him; he turns them all down except two sisters.
4) 從文自傳 18 episodes from the life of the author. He tells how he joined the army and started writing.
    Lively and realistic writings. No description is obscene or unduly detailed, but the general tone is amoral, and several stories are, after all, rather frivolous.
For informed readers.

767. 月下小景   *IN THE MOONLIGHT*   1 vol. 249 p. by **沈從文**
                                                         1936 上海復興書局

Collection of superstitions and fairy stories.
p. 1 A hopeless passion; suicide of the two lovers.
p. 26 How certain ladies succeed in persuading a hermit to quit his solitude.
p. 64 A very generous son of a king.
p. 122 A physician who protects animals.
p. 124 A robbery at the imperial court. The robber is almost caught but he escapes.
p. 150 Speculations on the heavenly regions. Conclusion: be content with what you have.

p. 199   On the infidelity of women.
p. 211   Love stories.
For grown up people.

768. 一個女劇員的生活   *LIFE OF AN ACTRESS*   1 vol. by 沈從文
1939   上海大東書局

A young "star" belonging to a dramatic troupe in Shanghai had three admirers and, though her pride was flattered, she refused all of them with some mocking. She was a selfish girl until she met the fourth lover whom she married.

This novel has an easy as well as elegant style, and contains no indecent passages. *For everyone.*

769. 主婦集   *HOUSEWIVES*   1 vol. 122 p. by 沈從文
2nd. edit. 1940   商務印書館

1   First anniversary of a wedding. Passion is calmed by now, but affection remains.
2.   Tragic adventure of a workman.
3.   Portrait of an uncle and a nephew.
4.   Vulgar story of a good liver.
5   Unhappiness of a student separated from his family.
For everyone.

770. 新與舊   *THE NEW & THE OLD*   1 vol. 237 p. by 沈從文
1940   上海良友復興圖書公司

A collection of novels which describe modern China. Very lively and realistic descriptions, but, from a moral point of view, it calls for *some reserve.*

771. 如蕤   *JU JUI*   1 vol. 100 p. by 沈從文
1941   上海大陸書報社

This book presents three stories that stress the power of love.

1) Narrates the adventures of a beautiful girl courted in vain by a number of young men. After some time, when her life was in danger, she was saved by a young man with whom she fell in love. The young man was indifferent for a considerable time but in the end he fell in love with her. She left him in order to keep fresh the memory of this love which had cost her so much to attain.

2) Describes how a woman succeeded in winning the love of a genius by guile. It shows how she dominated him after winning his love. This book should be reserved only for adult persons, owing to coarse expressions.

3) Narrates how the king's son of a Miao tribe was endowed with such beauty and perfect character that everyone considered him as an ideal man whom no woman dared to seek in marriage. One day he was carried away by the song of a girl and swore that he would marry her. He sought for her and finally succeeded in his search.

This book can be read *by everybody.*

772. 沈從文選集   *SELECTED WORKS OF SHEN TS'UNG-WEN*   .   1 vol. 266 p.
1936   上海萬象書屋

A selection of short stories which present a number of love-scenes, as well as events from army life. The author describes military life as a dull and mechanical one though nevertheless very realistic. He describes love as an inborn attraction of man towards woman, which fails at the end. Woman is represented as an enchanting and unattainable creature whose psychology differs greatly from man's. *To be strictly reserved.*

773. 上元鐙 *LANTERN FESTIVAL* 1 vol. 174 p. by 施蟄存
2nd. edit. 1933 新中國書局 *See Biogr. 134*

Memories of childhood. *For everyone.*

774. 小珍集 *SMALL BUT PRECIOUS* 1 vol. 194 p. by 施蟄存
1936 良友公司

A collection of eight stories, very well written and interesting to read, containing a description of an employee who has a false claim — namely, the superiority of the milk of the diary over the milk of the cow — of automobile accidents, etc. etc.

To end up two married people without children go to the Nai-nai Miao and return each with a child. This last tale calls for a certain reserve. *Not for everyone.*

775. 善女人的行品 *A KIND LADY* 1 vol. 222 p. by 施蟄存
2nd edit. 1940' 良友復興圖書公司

Discussions on the question of marriage and the rights and duties of women.
The author here presents us with a series of examples in which carelessness and lack of consideration brought disaster and in some cases wrecked the happiness of married life. *For everyone.*

776. 捕蝗者 *LOCUST EXTERMINATOR* 1 vol. 72 p. by 石 靈
1935 中華書局 *See Biogr. 145*

The burning sun dries up everything in the fields. Add to this catastrophe, a plague of locusts & vexations from soldiers, and you will have an idea of the misery of the peasants.

Rain comes at last. The locusts disappear. The local official puts up a notice. That all this cannot revive the dead harvest! *For everyone.*

777. 蠶蛻集 *CAST OFF* 1 vol. 166 p. by 史 岩
1929 上海廣益書局 *See Biogr. 136*

This book contains some short stories with modern drawings which are perhaps too modern for the unexperienced.

The author also gives a series of very melancholy love letters. *For informed readers.*

778. 京俗集 *CUSTOMARY IN PEKING* 1 vol. 209 p. by 司 徒
1941 朔風書店

病後 p. 1-21. Humorous remarks on doctors and hospitals. *For everyone.*
熱風 p. 22-41. Sport between officials. Some of the words have a double meaning. *Not for everyone.*
不明白 p. 42-70. A poor family. Child psychology. *For everyone.*
溪邊 p. 71-87. Quarrels and idle talk, that are not very edifying. *Not for everyone.*
人物 p. 88-102. In an office. Rather dull. *For everyone.*
妹妹 p. 103-131. A humorous sketch of the advantages of having an elder sister, and the disadvantages of having to look after a younger sister. *For everyone.*
三人行 p. 132-144. The story of a false ghost that ends in the death of the one who thinks he has seen it. *For everyone.*
心與物 p. 145-160. Coldness between a married couple. The clouds disperse. *For everyone.*
隱創 p. 161-189. A young woman, who has died, finds on her tomb the one she longed to meet for many years. *For everyone.*

婚前 p. 190-209. A vanished dream. *For everyone.*

The author likes to indulge in humour and succeeds very well.

779. 浣錦集 *CLEAR STREAM*   1 vol. 226 p. by 蘇青(馮和儀)
1944, 10th. edit. 天地出版社 *See Biogr. 54*

A very popular book. Considering the subjects treated and the realism of the authoress, one is not surprised at the success of this book.

Is this success deserved? We believe not. We do not deny the great talents of the authoress, but her success is derived chiefly from the fact that she is a woman and she dares to say everything. From that she obtains her great hold over modern youth. Certain of her compositions are little master-pieces, but her principles are not ours. *Not to be recommended to the young.*

780. 結婚十年 *TEN YEARS OF MARRIAGE*   1 vol. 189 p. by 蘇 青
10th edition 1944 天地出版社

This book is, as the author terms it "a romantic story". A young woman describes her unhappy married life. First she describes her wedding with its ceremonies: later on, she describes her new home. As her husband had to go to Shanghai in order to continue his studies, she also left for Nanking to study, as she could not live in peace with her parents-in-law. Her studies were soon to be interrupted, as the time of her confinement approached. During her studies she had some platonic relations with an artist, whom she could not forget all her life.

She gave birth to a girl, and the family was very angry with her for they wanted a boy. Then follows a detailed description of her convalescence. After she had recovered she left for Shanghai, as she felt lost in the family. After she joined her husband she realized that the latter had ceased to love her. She went to the country and gave birth to a child, again a girl, who soon died of hunger. When peace was restored, her husband began a law practice; during this period a third girl was born. The husband's family was in despair and despised her completely. Her husband was a very weak character and soon lost his situation; at the same time he fell in love with his wife's friend. Misfortune fell on the family; during this time the fourth baby was born and, although this time it was a boy, she did not win her husband back. She complained about it to her family, her husband refused to support her; her father-in-law died of anger at his son's misconduct. She was then divorced, after ten years of married life.

This book was composed in 1944 and it went through twelve editions in one year. The author possesses a real talent, so everyone is eager to read it as the theme interests the young generation.

From the moral point of view we must make some objection. In several chapters the writer does not hesitate in using coarse words and in describing realistic scenes. But she wrote down what she felt and experienced without unduly insisting.

The authoress does not approve of divorce (cf. the appendix to the book); nevertheless the book *is not to be recommended.* She forgot that married life is only possible when both sides make mutual concessions, and with a little good will on both sides the marriage would have been a happy one.

781. 濤 *SWELLING WAVE*   1 vol. 122 p. by 蘇 青
1945 天地出版社

This book contains a number of dissertations, narratives, descriptions and mainly personal memories. The authoress gives her impressions about men, love, summer heat etc. She remembers her childhood, her student days, and her life as a newspaper-editor. At the end she presents her opinion on her own published books.

It must be admitted that this new authoress has a real talent; her style is very lively, fresh and easy to read. She deals in an original way with her theme which is usually very interesting. But nevertheless we have to make *some objection* to her book from the moral point of view; she advocates birth control and some of her opinions are rather advanced. However the majority of the pieces are good.

782. 屠龍集 *THE DRAGON IS SLAIN* 1 vol. 170 p. by 蘇雪林 (蘇梅)
2nd edition, 1945, Commercial Press. *See Biogr. 141*

The first part of this book gives us some short stories written by the author during the Sino-Japanese war. As in other compositions Mrs. Su shows herself as a master in describing human feelings.

The second part is a collection of lectures given by her at different occasions. The most interesting part is without doubt her dissertation about the religious thoughts at the end of the Ch'ing dynasty. For the outsider it may become a real revelation how near educated Chinese were at this time to western religion represented by Protestantism and Catholicism. Speeches to students show the high patriotic spirit of the author and her ability to catch the feelings of her audience. *For everyone.*

783. 蟬蛻集 *THE CICADA'S SHELL* 1 vol. 116 p. by 蘇雪林
1945, Commercial Press

A volume of historical sketches, full of human interest and faith in the destiny of China without, however, ignoring the shortcomings of the national character.

The first six have an identical setting: the resistence of the Ming scholars against the onrushing Manchu hordes.

They feature the whole list of possible attitudes towards the invader, from sublime heroism down to the most debased toadyism. They emphasize the love of freedom, deeply rooted in the hearts of the literati and their undaunted spirit in the face of the enemy.

Was it an excessive love of individual freedom or an inbred distrust of each other, even when threatened by a common danger? Or was it the deep-seated contempt of physical force and the certainty that the spirit can never be put in bonds? A civilization — over-refined — miscalculating the power of vigorous primitives?

As a matter of fact, such riches of national pride and spirit of sacrifice as might have made the country impregnable, was, helas, wasted. That often gives tragic beauty to most of the stories. The deeds inspired by a courage and faith second to none in the world, were doomed to failure in as much as they were not parts of a concerted action. Very much like a delicate flower lost in a welter of towering rocks. It takes a writer as sensitive to real beauty as Miss Su, to be able, in the midst of dry historical research, to pause and pay tribute in spite of the surrounding desolation.

The seventh story takes place earlier in the Ming period when the Japanese raiders infested the China coasts. It again illustrates individual courage and the versatility of the masses.

The stories are so true to life that they might have been written about the events of the last twenty years, if the author had not insisted on historical accuracy.

Well built and extremely well written, they make profitable reading for everyone and have a real educational value.

Miss Su suggests in her preface that these stories — and many, not yet written, found at the same source-are suitable for the stage. In skilful hands they certainly would enrich the national theatre; they contain everything a dramatist may look for. *For everyone.*

784. 蘇綠漪創作選 *AN ANTHOLOGY, OF LU-YI*   1 vol. 146 p.
1936   上海新光書店

A collection of seven stories and four essays. These stories are full of poetry; they show that the authoress possesses the most beautiful feelings. The book may be read by everyone, and ought to be *recommended to young people*.

785. 反倭袍 *RAIDERS FROM THE EAST*   6 vol. 1430 p. by 敖六山
1934   大衆書局

The tunic mentioned in the title was a mark of distinction conferred upon officials, who had distinguished themselves in the campaigns against Japan during the Yuan and Ming Dynasties. In this work we are told about the family of a high functionary named T'ang, living under the Emperor Cheng Te (1506-21), who has inherited a tunic of this kind. His rival, Chang P'iao, who has not been allowed to look at the tunic, tries to injure him before the Emperor, who is good-hearted but sensual, and allows himself to be circumvented.

T'ang has seven sons and a daughter. The eldest son is fighting on the frontiers, the sixth has married the younger sister of the Emperor, and the seventh is sworn brother to one named Tiao. The latter has a wife, Liu, whose extra-marital adventures with a neighbour, Wang Wen, have been the subject of a romance. The present work is actually a refutation of the earlier romance, the argument of the author being that Wang Wen who was put into prison for murder, inspired the former romance which, therefore, was an act of vengeance.

Most of the book is devoted to the adventures of the T'ang family. Condemned to death on a false report, the whole family seeks refuge in flight. The son finally saves the Emperor from the hands of rebels and his family receives the imperial pardon.

The book is full of digressions and adventures that are more or less connected with the principle theme. It also contains a number of descriptions that are *dangerous from the moral point of view*. Moreover, it has no literary value.

786. 脫韁的馬 *FLED FROM REINS*   1 vol. 122 p. by 穆 青
1946   自強出版社

A young man from the country who has been in the army for two years asks for a few days leave to go to his native village. He discovers that during his absence neither his family nor his village have changed in the slightest. He decides to stay there to ameliorate the material conditions of his family. The mayor, however, talks of hunting out "deserters" with the hope of making a little "squeeze". Our hero engages in a struggle with him. During the night he has a magnificent dream in which his native village appears as a model village. He wakes up, however, and confronted with the sad reality, he decides to return to his regiment.

A good book and well written. *For everyone*.

787. 鳳還巢 *THE RETURN*   1 vol. 147 p. by 孫長虹
1943   啓智書店

A young man and a girl lived together as husband and wife, the girl's mother being against their marriage. Only after a son was born could they urge her mother to give her consent.

Everyone is warned against reading this book, as it contains some free theories on "free love" and divorce, as well as a number of very raw expressions.

788. 山野掇拾　*STEPPES*　　　　　　　1 vol. 296 p. by　孫福熙
1923 北新書局 *See Biogr. 143*

A description in 82 chapters of a summer vacation passed in a village of Savoie by a Chinese student studying in Lyon. He tells of his journey and his stay in the country. He found it very agreeable as the people that he stayed with were kind and hospitable. As it was during the war, he helped with the work in the fields. After six weeks he returned to Lyon. *For everyone.*

789. 愛神的玩偶　*DOLLS OF CUPID*　　　1 vol. 150 p. by　孫孟濤
1930 中華書局

This book presents five short stories.
1. A quarrel during a cinema show.
2. A novel of a young man whose love was not returned, as his girl loved another man. But her love was not returned either, as the man loved another girl.
3. A teacher fell in love with one of his pupils; the latter had no courage to say she did not love him but one day the teacher met her with her lover.
4. Two former admirers of the bride relate during the wedding dinner what a worthless woman the bride was.
5. A married man found himself in the snares of a married woman; the latter made a new coat for him. He was put into prison and after his release fifteen years later, he saw the same coat on another man . . . his son!
　Everyone is advised against the book.

790. 玄武門之變　*MUTINY ON THE HSUAN-WU GATE*　1 vol. 202 p. by　宋雲彬
2nd. edit. 1939 開明書店

1. Successors of Yao.
2. Ta Nan fails to deliver his brother.
3. Compromising documents are burnt. General joy.

4. Advent of the Ch'in.
5. An embassy.
A dozen or so other historical events follow.

For everyone.

791. 罪巷　*RED LIGHT DISTRICT*　　　　2 vol. 228 p. by　大梁酒徒
1940 兄弟印刷局

Should anyone want proof that an author is able to write two volumes without saying anything let him read this book.

The first volume contains more than one hundred pages. It describes how a very young woman was given as a concubine to an old but rich man.

A boring book, it nevertheless makes us acquainted with Chinese folklore and many Chinese proverbs.

The atmosphere is unhealthy and *only permissible to informed readers.*

792. 秋雨銷魂錄　*AN AMOROUS AUTUMN NIGHT*　2 vol. 204 & 182 pp. by　戴愚盦
1941 文利書局

This book is obscene. *It has to be banned.*

793. 地之子　*THE SON OF THE EARTH*　　　1 vol. 256 p. by　台靜農
1928 未名社出版 *See Biogr. 149*

A collection of short stories which contain a lot of criticism on modern society, its vices and ill manners. The book contains some fatalistic and subversive ideas. *For informed readers.*

794. 最後的掙扎 *LAST STRUGGLE*   1 vol. by **唐次顏**
1936   上海南星書店

Three short stories.

1. Hsin Chin, a very sentimental young man, saw how his girl-friend was given as a concubine to an opium-seller; in spite of this fact they continued their correspondance through a friend. The concubine asked him to save her. The young man visited her friend, with whom he fell in love. At the same time he also loved an actress, but in spite of all this, he left the three girls, and sailed off to Europe to study.

2. A mother's grief after the death of her child and her envy for another mother, who had a child.

3. A young married woman parted with her former lover; the parting took place in an alcove.

The second is for everyone, but the other two are very objectionable.

795. 妻子的妹妹 *MY WIFE'S YOUNGER SISTER*   1 vol. 210 p. by **唐次顏**
3rd edition 1939   上海南星書店

A collection of five stories. These stories present love scenes in a very romantic and exciting manner: the atmosphere is rather unhealthy and *unsuitable for all classes of readers.*

796. 摩登老夫子 *GRANDPA'S INDIAN SUMMER*   1 vol. 223 p. by **悼 萍**
北平平凡社

This book presents the family of an old general; he has four concubines and fifteen children. All the members of the household, especially the women, lacked the most elementary modesty.

Though the book has no indecent descriptions, nevertheless its atmosphere is so immoral that it ought *to be banned.*

797. 白荷花 *WHITE LOTUS*   1 vol. 136 p. by **田 父**
1946   日新出版社

A rather disconnected novel about the late war. Several love affairs are dealt with. In one, the heroine, Ting, ends in a proper marriage. Her brother, however, is not so fortunate, as he is abandoned by his wife. There are other characters with more or less important roles. Although they play at being in love, they fight very well when faced with the enemy.

Some of the love scenes are rather crude. *For informed readers.*

798. 春宵集 *NOCTURNE*   1 .vol. 133 p. coll. by **天廬編**
1933   光華書局

Six tales written during an agitated period and showing the excitement of the authors against Japan.

The most remarkable of them is that of Pa Chin that relates a very curious story.

This one and the sixth in the book might very well trouble the imagination of the young. Apart from these, the others may be read by everyone. *Not for everyone.*

799. 三姑娘 *MADEMOISELLE SAN*   1 vol. 99 p. by **田舍郎**
1946   百新書店

An immoral book. The author forgets that he should better do his laundering at home. The book features criminal and incestuous relations. *To be banned.*

800. 三姑娘 *MADEMOISELLE SAN* 2 vols. by 田舍郎
1946 百新書店

See review No. 799. The present book is a sequel. *Not to be recommended to anyone.*

801. 小裁縫 *APPRENTICE TO THE TAILOR* 1 vol. 128 p. by 田舍郎
1946 上海

The story of a tailor and his relations with some low down women. A mass of ridiculous stuff without the least seasoning of wit. *Proscribed.*

802. 荒 *BARREN* 1 vol. 155 p. by 田 濤
1940 文化生活 *See Biogr. 153*

A collection of nine stories written in beautiful style.

1. A nocturnal journey in the snow. A story is told that ends dramatically.
2. A poor mother who is ill sells her little daughter before dying.
3. Children's quarrels.
4. Bird of prey. A tragic description.

5. In the fields. The father works. The son is a lazybody.
6. Miseries of the poor.
7. A crude idyll.
8. Misery of the poor.
9. ditto.

For everyone.

803. 希望 *HOPE* 1 vol. 108 p. by 田 濤
1946 萬葉書店

Five stories with the aim of rousing patriotic sentiment. The heros and heroines of the first four of these tales devote themselves to the good of the country. Their families and the people around them oppose their plans in general, from which fact, conflicts arise.

The fourth tale ends tragically — the eldest brother is killed by his own sister. There is also a scene in which a revolt against God is described.

Immature readers should be warned of the dangers. *May be read by anyone.*

804. 燄 *FLAME* 1 vol. 208 p. by 田 濤
1946 大道出版社

A story about imagined guerillas. The country people, whose houses have been burnt, flee into inaccessible places from where they attack the Japanese. The story is rendered piquant by the presence of an unfaithful young wife.

Some of the love scenes are too crude. *Not for everyone.*

805. 夢裏人生 *LIFE IN DREAM* 1 vol. 68 p. by 田蘊瑾

Stupidities and vulgarities, of no value, either literary or from the point of view of the composition. *Not to be recommended to anyone.*

806. 舊京新潮 *NEW WAVES IN THE OLD CAPITAL* 1 vol. 88 p. by 田蘊瑾
1944 北平錦社

The author's intentions are commendable He exposes the excessive freedom that characterizes present-day relations between boys and girls in Peiping. One long description is very provocative. We consider that the book *must be prohibited* on that ground.

807. 陳素芳的日記 *DIARY OF A DAMSEL*   1 vol. 112 p. by **丁琴女士**
1933 上海大申書社

The tragedy of a poor girl. After being sold into a house of courtisans at the age of twelve, she is later given in marriage to a merchant who, however, abandons her after the birth of her first child. The heroine falls in love with an employee who is not indifferent to her either, although he is already married. He wishes her to finish her studies although her age — twenty-six — is an obstacle. She subsequently suffers from a nervous malady, and receives letters from her friend full of good advice. He ends by praying her to marry someone else. This advices aggrevates her malady and she has no other way of resolving the question but suicide. *For mature people.*

808. 在黑暗中 *IN THE DARK*   1 vol. 270 p. by **丁玲 (蔣冰之)**
1930 *See Biogr. 31*

Four short stories. The title of the book expresses the conclusion that follows all four : Life deceives our hopes and aspirations.
夢珂 : The story of a girl student. Shocked by the voluptousness of men, she is on her guard against temptation. Soon, feeling in spite of herself the attraction of the senses, and pressed by want of money, she becomes an actress.
莎菲女士的日記   In the form of a diary we follow the psychological effects of the physical awakening of a girl dying of tuberculosis.
暑假中 : Pictures the life of some teaching girls. Devoted to their work, they nevertheless experience a certain psychological discomfort. One finds a remedy in marriage, the others in greater devotion to their work.
阿毛姑娘 : The story of a young wife, poor but happy and well liked by her in-laws. Allured by the pleasures of life, she begins to dream of luxury and contemplates leaving her home to live a more worldly life. Unable to realize her dream she becomes gloomy and uncommunicative, is taken ill and, losing all hope, commits suicide.
Dangerous for girls because of a morbid outlook. Unsuitable for boys because of sensual and unduly detailed description of feminine emotional life.

809. 韋護 *WEI-HU*   1 vol. 156 p. by **丁 玲**

The hero of the book, Wei Hu, is a queer character, hard to fathom. He loves literature, art, progress. He is fascinated by some social ideas, a plan, a conviction the author never clearly defines. Passionatelly in love with Li Chia, he is at first afraid to turn traitor to his ideal.

Li Chia is a student tired of going to school. Like Wei Hu, she is a puzzling character, strongly convinced of her superiority. After a few months of living together and transports of love, Wei Hu is reclaimed by his ideal and walks out on her.

The book describes an emancipated environment with much freedom in the relationship between both sexes. Marriage is not mentioned; free love is the normal thing. That, together with the vagueness of the hero's ideal, the air of dissatisfaction and pessimism emanating from the book, and a few unbecoming descriptions make the book *dangerous reading*.

810. 一個女人 *A WOMAN*   1 vol. 107 p. by **丁 玲**
1930 中華書局

Six love stories with the aim of elucidating the form and the reason of love in a woman.

The author writes as an egoist in her relations with the other sex. According to her, man is drawn by an irresistible force to woman, even when the latter is indifferent to his advances. In spite of everything, he continues to hope for her favours.

Woman loves to be sought after by man, even when she is cold to him. She considers man always egoistically. And man would be unhappy if he knew the real sentiments that animate woman. *Not to be recommended to anyone.*

811. 意外集 *UNEXPECTED* 1 vol. 240 p. by 丁 玲
1936 良友公司

1. 松子 cfr. No. 814. *For everyone.*
2. 一月二十三日 Winter for the rich and Winter for the poor *For everyone.*
3. 陳伯祥 An original. *For everyone.*
4. 八月生活 Picture of life in a factory. *For everyone.*
5. 團聚 An impoverished family reunited in misery. *For everyone.*
6. 莎菲日記第二部 Some notes that have little interest. *For everyone.*
7. 不算情書 Love letters in spite of the title. *Not for everyone.*
8. 楊媽的日記 A few very ordinary facts. *For everyone.*

Ting Ling shows herself a good psychologist in these tales. The fifth one especially, indicates the depth of her sentiment. Written in beautiful style.

812. 母親 *THE MOTHER* 1 vol. 236 p. by 丁 玲
1940 良友文學叢書

Man Cheng, a young widow and mother of two children, struggles valiantly to make a living out of her little farm. Having overcome most difficulties she becomes attached to the land. Invited to the city, she first resists the appeal, but, gradually weakened by old memories and family associations, she yields. There she learns of a world of novelties: schools etc., until finally, in spite of her thirty years of age, she starts going to school herself. Completely absorbed by the city, she sells her farm. The only remainder of her old love of the land is a desire to spend her vacations in the country.

Then comes the invasion. Everybody gets panicstricken and thinks of fleeing before the approaching enemy. *For all.*

813. 我在霞村的時候 *WHEN I WAS IN THE VILLAGE OF GLOW*
1 vol. 169 p. by 丁 玲

新的信念: pp. 1-36. An old woman who has been persecuted by the Japanese, devotes herself to patriotic propaganda, and this in a very energetic and stimulating way. Somewhat too realistic.

縣長家庭: pp. 37-60. A child of eight, daughter of a "hsien-chang" is enrolled in Ting Ling's militia and refuses to return to her parents.

入伍: pp. 61-94. Exploits and sentiments of a soldier accompanying journalists to the front.

我在霞村的時候: pp. 98-128. The author tells of her influence on a young girl who has followed the Japanese army to the front.

秋收的一天: pp. 129-144. Harvest day with the Communists.

壓碎的心 pp. 145-156. Ideal soldiers — obviously Red soldiers!

夜: pp. 157-169. History of a family — showing the good influence of Communism!

The book is written in very simple language, revealing nevertheless great mastership. It is throughout Communist propaganda, in an unostentatious way that makes it even more dangerous.

Those who have lived under the Communist regime, are under no illusion and cannot but regret that an author of quality such as Ting Ling should stoop to vile propaganda of this kind. Not for everyone; *only for mature people.*

814. 丁玲代表作 *AN ANTHOLOGY OF TING LING'S WORKS*

三通書局

莎菲女士的日記： Diary of a girl of eighteen. Describes the awakening of passions： unsuitable for young people.

年前的一天： Awakening of disorderly love.

閻集： *For all.*

一月廿三日： Describes the hopelessness of the poor during winter, and the false charity of rich officials.

水： Magnificent description of a flood; bearings on the class-struggle.

奔： Peasants, oppressed by heartless officials, look for a living in Shanghai factories; life there is worse.

松子： Story of an urchin. *For all.*

給孩子們： Story for children.

他走後： Purposeless dreaming of a lovesick girl.

　　　　Strict reserve.

815. 豐年 *GOOD HARVEST*　　　　　　　1 vol. 189 p. by 丁　山

Ten stories. Description of the life of the poor and of their feelings. Too much realism. *Objectionable.*

816. 小事件 *A MINOR EVENT*　　　　　1 vol. 139 p. by 丁　丁
　　　　　　　　　　　　　　　　　　　　　　　　1942　建國書店

A small volume of tales with no serious basis. The author seems to like to tell tales and the book is full of dialogues.

The book has very little worth.

From the moral point of view, some objections could be made to the last story, but the author seems to be ridiculing the abnormal situations that he describes. *May be read by anyone.*

817. 黃昏 *DUSK*　　　　　　　　　　1 vol. 288 p. by 丁　文
　　　　　　　　　　　　　　　　　　　　　　　　1932　人文書店

Short stories, descriptions, miscellaneous, taken mainly from every day life. Nothing much happens. *For everyone.*

818. 少女懺悔錄外集 *HER REPENTANCE*　　1 vol. 345 p. by 拓　荒
　　　　　　　　　　　　　　　　　　　　　　　　1941　新地書店

This book has for theme the unhappy love life of the heroine, Lin. Married into a rich family, it is not long before she sees her husband take to opium and other women. She protests, struggling against the old-fashioned attitude of the family, and reprimands her parents-in-law. Soon after, she succeeds in separating from her husband, and goes to live with an old friend, Shih-ch'ing.

They are poor and without support, but nevertheless they are happy in spite of their poverty. But at the end of his resources, and in order to seek means of subsistence for his wife, Shih-ch'ing is forced to leave her temporarily to go to Singapore where he has a post.

During his absence, a friend of the family permits himself certain liberties with Lin. But as she wishes to remain faithful to her husband, she invites a lady friend to live with her. This ruse, however, is not very successful, for when Shih-ch'ing returns unexpectedly, he surprises his wife in the company of his friend. Lin protests her innocence, but her husband does not believe her, and leaves her.

Mad with love and in despair, Lin searches through the whole of Shanghai for him, and in the end finds him in prison into which he has been cast, a victim of his opinions. Lin continues to love him madly and waits for his release from prison.

This book is the counterpart of the one reviewed under the name of the author Ching Lo-jan. It holds the readers interest and the heroine is a very courageous and sympathetic person, but it is not to be recommended because of the easy recourse to divorce contained in the book. *Not to be recommended.*

819. 黑幕的故事　*THE ACTUAL BACKSTAGE*　　　1 vol. 88 p. by 蒼　丁
1946　建業出版社

A lot of ridiculous stuff with which the author wishes to tell us what goes on under the surface in Shanghai. *Not suitable reading for young people.*

820. 快樂生活之秘訣　*SECRETS OF A HAPPY LIFE*　　1 vol. 117 p. by 蒼德玉
1943

The way to live happily! In this book, the relations between married people are discussed, and we are told what is necessary to live happily. We are given a lot of advice of which some is excellent. The whole book exhales the Christian faith, and although it is written by a protestant, *may be read* by Catholics.

821. 詩人的情書　*LOVE LETTERS OF A POET*　　1 vol. 209 p. by 曹雪松
1931　上海現代書局

A young poet leaves his wife whom he does not love, and goes away with a friend who abandons him in her turn, leaving their child with the father. She dies soon after.

The young man then falls in love with a cousin (who is his correspondant) who comes to live near him in Shanghai. He becomes famous through a play, in which he describes his adventure with the woman who abandoned him, but new misfortunes are in store for him. His mother dies, his cousin is recalled home to be married to another, and he himself is killed by the new friend of the heroine of his play. His last letter is an appeal to his cousin to revenge him.

This book which is composed of letters, should be proscribed. The author admits of divorce, free love, vengeance, etc. It also contains some obscene pages. *To be proscribed.*

822. 心的慘泣　*BEMOANING*　　　1 vol. 130 p. by 曹雪松
4th edition 1932　大東書局

A very good boy, fond of his mother and of a tender disposition, left home to study. Soon he fell in love with a girl, though his mother had selected for him another fiancée. Hence arose one of those family quarrels, which, at the present time, cause so much grief to many young Chinese people.

The author narrates in detail the psychological situations through which our hero passed. This description does not prove anything and in no way excuses divorce, free love and suicide, which the author proclaims.

Young people are advised against reading this book.

823. 絕地 *CORNERED*   1 vol. 136 p. by 草 明

A woman who has been abandoned by her husband for several years keeps an inn where her small child cooks for the patrons. She is on the most intimate terms with the latter who are the workmen of the locality. Misery arrives with the war and it is only due to one of her clients that she does not die of starvation.

One day she notices that the land upon which her shanty is built is being measured. Assuming that the landlord has ordered this to be done, she profits of the occasion to exercise her charms upon him. She soon learns, however, that the authorities have building plans which necessitate the pulling down of her shanty. She resumes flirting with the masons.

While her hut is being demolished, she suffers as though her heart was being torn from her breast. In the end, she says goodbye to the workmen and goes off to a far destination.

An unedifying tale, and *not to be recommended to anyone.*

824. 試郎心 *TO TEST HIS FIDELITY*   1 vol. 118 p. by 曹乃文
                                              1935 文光書店

A commonplace story about the flirtation of students of a certain university with the belle of the campus. Four young men sue for her hand. As each of them possesses certain qualities, the girl hesitates to pick her choice.

One day, during a walk, she is bitten by a dog and brought to a hospital. Her wounds are negligible but she has herself bandaged all over and sends alarming notes to her four beaux. Three of them jump to the conclusion that her looks must be irreparably ruined and do not turn up. The remaining faithful admirer gets the prize. *For all.*

825. 恨相逢 *SHOUDN'T HAVE MET*   1 vol. 112 p. by 曹乃文
                                              1941 上海文化報社

Love letters. Hsia meets Mrs. Yen and falls in love with her. Both are married and this makes marriage impossible. Hence an inward struggle between love and reason.

Hsia becomes more and more passionate in his utterances. Mrs. Yen tries to reason; but her armour shows weak spots.

They are determined not to touch the forbidden fruit and to love each other with a pure, spiritual love.

Their mutual affection grows; their imaginations are fired; they desire the impossible; but their reason still disapproves; their desire is unfulfilled.

They begin to curse their destiny, even the "li-chiao" still their reason wins; regretfully they decide to break the ties that hold them.

Hsia expected new energy and happiness in love; it makes him wretched and tired of living. He finally regrets ever having met her.

One page is *objectionable;* several unbecoming insinuations; on p. 12 suicide is advocated.

826. 恨相逢 *I WISH WE HAVE NEVER MET*   1 vol. 112 p. by 曹乃文
                                              文化服務社

Both he and she are married to other people but nevertheless they love each other. The book in question is composed of forty-nine letters that they have written to each other. In addition to corresponding, they have rendezvous which are not innocent. She has more courage and sense of duty than he, for she refuses to take the last step. The correspondence ceases and they end in hating the moment that they first met.

The letters are well written and it is a pity that they are addressed to the wrong people. *For informed readers.* (Same book as the precedent).

827. 碧玉簪 *JADE HEADWEAR*　　　1 vol. 87 p. by 曹鐵苻
　　　　　　　　　　　　　　　　　　　　　　1943 廣藝書局

The scenario of a film with the same title.

During the Ming Dynasty, the academician Wang disciple and co-provincial of the minister, Li, has a son to whom the latter wishes to give the hand of his daughter. This last who has received a careful education, has another suitor, a cousin whose disorderly life is a scandal. The rejected suitor makes a go-between write a letter supposedly signed by the girl, and this letter together with a hairpin, is discovered by the academician's son after his marriage. He does not want to make a scandal, but he moves to an apartment separated from the rest of the house. The fraud is discovered when the husband, who has come out first in the official examinations, is presented by the Emperor with the hand of an imperial princess. He is reconciled with his wife.

An inoffensive romance but not worth much. *For everyone.*

828. 線上　　　　　　　　　　　　　　1 vol. 170 p. by 曹　原
　　　　　　　　　　　　　　　　　　　　　　1943 大華印書局

A poor family tries to mount a little on the social ladder, but their efforts are in vain. The result of all their striving is a worse condition than before.

A rather pessimistic book. *For everyone.*

829. 秋雨殘花 *SCATTERED*　　　　　1 vol. 165 p. by 鄒雅明
　　　　　　　　　　　　　　　　　　　　　　1947 上海大明書局

Friendships between girl and boy students and the results of these friendships. *Not to be recommended to anyone.*

830. 烽火情侶 *LOVE AMIDST WAR*　　1 vol. 97 p. by 鄒雅明
　　　　　　　　　　　　　　　　　　　　　　1947 大明書局

The story of a love that brings a whole village into the ranks of the guerillas. They offer a strong resistance to the Japanese upon whom they inflict heavy losses. The hero dies during the war while his wife, who is the heroine of the romance and of the resistance, marries another guerilla chef.

The book contains one rather crude description. *For mature people.*

831. 一個商人與賊 *A MERCHANT & A THIEF*　1 vol. 98 p. by 曾今可
　　　　　　　　　　　　　1933 上海新時代書店 *See Biogr. 158*

Features two men: a businessman and a thief. The author does not see any difference between them. The business man has everything to make him happy: money and a good wife. As he only desires to make more money and seek amusement with more women, he is unhappy. He dies alone, wretched. The other is poor; his wife and child are starving; at his wits' end he takes to stealing. Caught red-handed, he is punished. Such is the injustice of social conditions.

The author writes an easy and clear style. A few passages call for a certain reserve. *For informed readers.*

832. 魯男子 *LU NAN TZU*   1 vol. 377 + 11 + 39 pp. by   曾　樸
眞美善書店 *See Biogr. 159*

The heroes of the book are champions of the freedom to choose one's partner for life; they oppose the old marriage custom.

One, Hsiao Hsiung, carries his principles through to the bitter end, and commits suicide because he is not given the right to marry whom he chooses. His girl follows his example.

The other, Lu Nan tzu, being weaker, yields and accepts the bride chosen for him. *Very objectionable.*

833. 大俠馬長江 *MAH THE HERO*   1 vol. 166 p. by   毒　蟲
1943 勵力出版社

Describes the fight of a colonel against bandits near Harbin. *For informed readers.*

834. 懷鄉集 *HOMESICK*   1 vol. 250 p. by   杜衡（戴克崇）
1936 復興書局

A number of stories. The one called "Jen yü nü-jen" is rather cynical and vulgar. The author sets little store by the virtue of women. With the exception of this story the book may be read *by all.*

835. 漩渦裏外 *WHIRLPOOL*   1 vol. 334 p. by   杜　衡
1941 良友文學叢書

A private school; the school-board has appointed Mr. Wang principal; pupils and teachers are displeased with the nomination.

Hsü Tzu-hsiu has taught English for twenty years; he has a strong character and devotes all his energy to the welfare of the school. His wife and son have died. He has a daughter, Shou-mei. He is interested in a young man Fan Cheng-min and helps him to a teaching job in the school.

The school-board meets to appoint a new principal. One party wants a certain Ch'eng in the hope of furthering their own little interests. The other wants Mr. Hsü who will further the interests of the school. Fan Cheng-min agitates for the latter party. The first party does not let matters rest: they write to the papers, slinging mud at Shou-mei, and, on the day of the vote, they have Cheng-min imprisoned. Ch'en is appointed.

Mr. Hsü, who is ill, ignores these events. But when a dinner is given in honour of the new principal, he gets up and delivers a speech that leads to a general strike. *For all*

836. 徒然小說集 *STORIES BY T'U-JAN*   1 vol. 168 p. by   徒　然
1933 生活書店

A collection of short stories, well written, taken from every-day life. Psychological studies depicting working people, students and country people in their own environment.

There are some rather crude details, but the book may nevertheless be read *by everyone.*

837. 冥寥子游 *MING LIAO TZE'S TRAVEL*   1 vol. 67 p. by   屠緯眞
1940 西風社

An official retires and goes on a journey. He is a Taoist and aspires at perfection as taught in his religion. The book deals with his experiences. *For all.*

838. 杜鵑花 *AZALEA*   1 vol. 233 p. by 段可情
1934 現代書店 *See Biogr. 160*

Six short stories.

These stories deal with a great variety of subjects; a young girl sold to a brothel, rescued and going back; an unhappy dancing girl, kept by three men; an unhappily married woman, beaten by her husband and dying in hospital. The last story is about a young man who leaves his home to join the revolutionists. Ten years later he returns to see the peasants against the landowners. He is arrested and executed. *For informed readers.*

839. 憎恨 *RESENTMENT*   1 vol. 299 p. by 端木蕻良
1946 文化生活出版社 *See Biogr. 156*

1) Two young people guard the fields at night.
2) A family reunion on the anniversary of an unhappy event.
3) A military expedition that is lost at first but afterwards found.
4) A miserly monk.
5) Death of a miser.
6) Tribulations of a young beggar.
7) A considerable number of fox-skins are demanded. The people cannot suffer such exactions and revolt.
8) A little sick boy who is dying wants to go home.
9) An unedifying couple demand a roof over their heads for the night. The house burns down and the couple perishes.
10) A prison scene.

The author's language is too crude. *For mature people.*

840. 科爾沁旗草原 *STEPPES OF THE KHORCHIN BANNER*
1 vol. 518 p. by 端木蕻良(曹之林)
1939 開明書店

This new-realist novel describes a group of people emigrating to East Mongolia. The conclusion of the book is that one must sacrifice oneself in order to live a new life. There is no Communist tendency, but the author intends to prove that the family and society must be reformed. The realization of this reform presents knotty problems. Philosophically the book beats about the bush, and fails to suggest a real solution.

The heroes of the book give up their native country for "a new life" that is never clearly defined. They prove to be so many weaklings. The principal character is a coward, lacking courage to keep his promises or to stand up for his convictions.

In spite of its shortcomings the book may be called a masterpiece. It contains powerful descriptions, especially that of the immigrants in the first chapter. Social conditions in Mongolia are magnificently described.

Some immodest passages, especially in Chapter 9. Much unbecoming language. *Very objectionable.*

841. 將軍的故事 *THE STORY OF A GENERAL*   1 vol. 111 p. by 東平
1937 北新書局

A collection of short narratives mostly about soldiers.
An uninteresting book. *For everyone.*

842. 年輕人 *YOUNG FOLKS*   1 vol. 314 p. by 慈 燈
                                    1943 新京開明圖書公司

A married man, father of two children, leaves his family and goes to Peiping. There he gets acquainted with a girl with a reputation. On the eve of his second marriage his wife and children arrive in Peiping and put an end to his adventure.

This story fills 200 of the 314 pages. Follow meaningless stories, revealing the pen of a not very promising novice. *For informed readers.*

843. 三根紅線 *THREE PIECES OF RED STRING*   1 vol. 298 p. by 萬國安
                                    1943 四社初版部

A book that will please Chinese readers. It describes minutely the experiences of some people fighting a certain foreign power. A few light scenes. *For informed readers.*

844. 火葬 *CREMATED*   1 vol. 223 p. by 萬迪鶴
                 1935 上海良友圖書印刷公司 , *See Biogr. 162*

A collection of short stories. That on page 93 entitled 王家 happens in an atmosphere of debauch. *Not to be recommended to anyone.*

845. 七世奇緣 *SEVENTH REINCARNATION*   1 vol. 168 p. by 王繼廷
                                    昌明印刷所

Tells of the metempsychosis of two taoist fairies. They misbehave in heaven and are driven out. Back on earth as a man and a woman, they are explicitly forbidden to marry. A deity interferes each time they are about to get married. Only after their seventh rebirth are they allowed to marry. *For well informed readers.*

846. 小姐生活 *A LADY'S LIFE*   1 vol. 48 62 18 p. by 王奇新
                                    1946

Description of the fickle life of what the author calls "modern women." The descriptions are mostly immoral. *Proscribed.*

847. 滿園春色 *THE AMOROUS GARDEN*   1 vol. 58, 60 p. by 王奇新
                                    1946

This author would do better to sweep the streets than to be a pest to the young in offering them such filth. *Proscribed.*

848. 無襠褲子   1 vol. 64 p. by 王企梅
                                    中興書局

A book like this makes one wonder how it is possible to produce such stupid stuff. *Condemned.*

849. 成名以後 *AFTER FAME IS HERE*   1 vol. 202 p. by 王家械
                                    1936 中華書局

Collection of tales and short stories, several of them very interesting. The author shows psychological insight. *For all.*

850. 七山王 *KING OF THE SEVEN HILLS*   157 p. by 汪劍鳴
                                    2nd edit. 1939 廣益書局

Story of the fight against a secret society. They aim at overthrowing the Manchu house. Several seductions. *For well informed readers.*

851. 虎窟擒王記 *CORNERING THE TIGER IN ITS DEN* 1 vol. 138 p. by 汪劍鳴
1942 春明書店

Ch. 1. A gang of bandits commit burglary in Hongkong.

Ch. 2. After first making good their escape, they are spotted on a ship.

Ch. 3. They blow up the ship, save their own lives and that of a young woman. The chief's lieutenant pretends she is his niece.

Ch. 4. They sail on a freighter.

Ch. 5. Revelry in which the young woman takes part. Drunk, she is carried to bed by the lieutenant.

Ch. 6. The other members of the gang wonder if she really is his niece.

Ch. 7. She is not. Obscene passage.

Ch. 8. According to the papers the chief of the gang has been murdered. His lieutenant is suspected of the crime.

Ch. 9. While they split the proceeds, the lieutenant poisons five of the gangsters and makes off with the booty.

Ch. 10. The young lady goes to the villa of a rich Chinese; she is not admitted.

Ch. 11. The chief of he gang, who is still alive, thinks that his lieutenant owns that villa.

Ch. 12. The chief plans to kill his lieutenant and goes to the villa. The man who lives there is not a member of the gang, but a detective who prepared a trap for them to walk into. When the lieutenant enters the house the chief kills him. The young lady walks in and kills the chief. She was a friend of the detective!

Very objectionable because of obscenities in chapters 5 and 7.

852. 魔窟 *THE DEMON'S DEN* 1 vol. 205 p. by 汪劍鳴
昌明印刷所

Rambling miscellanea rather than detective stories. The detectives are very commonplace and their efforts so disconnected as to produce no effect. *For all.*

853. 血淚英雄 *WITH BLOOD AND TEARS* 1 vol. 223 p. by 王誌之
1926 東方書店

Some literary pieces in which a great deal is made of the revolutionary cause, the sacrifices that have been made for it and those that have yet to be made, and of the conflicts brought on in its train, etc. Mention is also made of love. *For everyone.*

854. 河流的底層 *BED OF THE RIVER* 1 vol. 222 p. by 王秋螢
1942 大連實業洋行

The author describes the life of young men and women; they pass their time in pleasure and laziness. Under pretence of studying, they live an easy life, far away from their parents' control. The hero of the book is an exception; he takes life seriously, studies hard and is engaged to be married to a solid girl. They have every chance of making good. Gradually the young man is carried away with the gay life around him and is heading for a complete disaster. After a few years he recognizes his error; but it is too late. His fiancée, who was poor, could not wait for him for five long years and is lost to him. Nothing but vain regrets remain with him.

The author gets lost in superfluous detail but shows keen wit. Although the argument is commendable, the book calls for some reserve because of some risky details. *For informed readers.*

855. 竹葉集 *BAMBOO LEAVES*   1 vol. 171 p. by 王春翠
1936 天馬書店

The authoress touches on the feminine problem in these pages. But it is question-able whether she has a happy touch. Certain pages, because of their very peculiar character, are not suitable reading matter for young people. *For mature people.*

856. 惱人春色 *SPRING BOTHERS*   2 vol. 441 p. by 汪仲賢
上海萬象書屋 *See Biogr. 164*

A young man rejects the fiancée chosen for him by his father to follow the dictate of his heart. After some time he marries without the consent of his father who disinherits him. It is not a happy marriage and the wife is unfaithful. He leaves her and learns that she had been married to another man all the time.

Many prolixities. Unbecoming passages make it *unsuitable for younger people.*

857. 胭脂紅淚 *UNFORTUNATE WOMAN*   4 vol. 101, 92, 103, 98 p. by 王新民
1946 北京書店

Young people from the country go to live in the city. Two sisters are soon involved in the feverish life there, and they end in marrying a general who maltreats them.

The book finishes dramatically. The general kills his wife. She however, has a friend who kills the general, and who is taken to prison for it.

The book contains interminable boring passages. *For adults only.*

858. 俠義英雄譜 *THEY ARE CHIVALROUS*   4 vol. by 王醒愚
1941 北京書店

Extraordinary achievements of ancient heroes. Much fighting; a few scenes call for strict reserve. *For well informed readers.*

859. 尋親奇遇記 *IN SEARCH OF HIS PARENTS*   1 vol. 199 p. by 王修和
3rd. edit. 1941 山城書店

Adventures, accidents, and incidents that are occasionally very interesting. *For everyone.*

860. 楊花別傳 *HISTORY OF YANG-HUA*   2 vol. 162, 170 pp. by 王雪佳
1940 大華書局

A series of love intrigues, rather loosely construed, of three girls trying to rope in a young man who has money. Another story is about a young man who is after a woman's money and tries to marry her.

An immoral book with an utterly offensive atmosphere. *Very objectionable.*

861. 孤雁 *A BIRD LOST FROM THE FLOCK*   1 vol. 178 p. by 王以仁
1933 *See Biogr. 166*

1. The author presents himself to his readers.
2. Condition of soul of a poor teacher.
3. The hard life of the same teacher.
4. His misfortunes only increase.
5. Going home. His love for his mother.
6. He falls lower and lower, (he becomes a gambler).
7. The end of the unhappy hero.
   Much too pessimistic. *For adults.*

862. 殉 *SACRIFICE*   1 vol. 232 p. by 王任叔
2nd edit. 1929 上海泰東圖書局 *See Biogr. 167*

Eight short stories. The first tells of a woman who refuses to accept a girl as her daughter-in-law because she is too much emancipated. The second describes a family in distress; the third is about an ill-fated man. Several stories are about robbers. Another presents a match-maker in action. The last story is about a young man who goes mad and nails his own father to a scaffolding. A gruesome tale.

    Rather depressing reading. *For all.*

863. 捉鬼篇 *AFTER THE DEMONS*   1 vol. 207 p. by 王任叔
上海新城書局

1) Agitated elections. The candidates are mistaken for ghosts. Consequences of popular superstitions.
2) Consultation with a lawyer when he takes fright.
3) Financial difficulties of professors upon whom subscriptions for patriotic works are levied.
4) A corpse on the railway line.

    Two uninteresting tales follow.
For everyone.

864. 嬌喘 *SHE IS TIRED*   1 vol. 73 p. by 王平陵
1946 百新書店 *See Biogr. 169*

    The theme of this story is that people without conscience always succeed, while honest peole, in spite of their abilities, fail.

    For adults on account of some crude details.

865. 柚子 *THE GRAPEFRUIT*   1 vol. 186 p. by 王魯彥
1926 北新書局 *See Biogr. 168*

    Widely different compositions, all inoffensive. The story 小雀兒 tells us what the Chinese sparrows think of their country. It is an exquisite satire of the rivalry between Kuomintang and Kungch'antang youth groups and of their hollow phrases. *For all.*

866. 黃金 *YELLOW GOLD*   1 vol. 186 p. by 王魯彥
1928 人間書店

    A number of stories. The fourth is about a slightly insane individual and a thief who discovers that his wife is unfaithful. He has his revenge. A few immodest passages. *For informed readers.*

867. 西風殘照 *AUTUMN SETTING SUN*   1 vol. 246 p. by 王似雲
1946 百新書店

    So many pages, just to tell stories without head or tail! The principal personages are servants or low class people. *Not to be recommended to anyone.*

868. 王獨清選集 *AN ANTHOLOGY OF WANG TU-CH'ING*   1 vol. 237 p.
1936 萬象書店 *See Biogr. 170*

p. 72   Last preparations for the great revolution. It fails.
p. 124 Chinese students in France.
p. 148 Confucius.
p. 165 Life of the author. (Communistic tendency).
p. 187 Several writers. (Communistic tendency).

p. 194, 202 Short addresses with a communistic tendency.

p. 205 Nosce te ipsum. (Communistic tendency).

p. 209 Letter to a French friend.

p 214 Visit to Suchow.

Everyone to be warned against the above.

869. 王獨清選集 *AN ANTHOLOGY OF WANG TU-CH'ING*

238 p. **現代創作文庫**
1936 萬象書屋

The author is a modern poet who has studied in Italy and travelled in France. A third of the work is composed of poems in modern style about his travels. There are also two plays and two novels included. The rest of the work consists of various extracts, the most interesting of which is about the literary society, 創造社 in whose activities the author has taken part almost since its early beginnings. *For everyone.*

870. 春雨之夜 *NIGHT OF SPRING RAIN* 1 vol. 256 p. by **王統照**
1933 商務印書舘 *See Biogr. 171*

Selections. Many are well written but the ideas are not always commendable; some are objectionable, for instance the second story. *Unsuitable for younger people.*

871. 山雨 *MOUNTAIN RAIN* 1 vol. 370 p. by **王統照**
3rd. edit. 1938 開明書店

Evolution of the peasants. Under the influence of foreigners, the soldiery, brigands and other afflictions, the peasant is leaving for the industrial centres. *For everyone.*

872. 去來今 *RETURN* 1 vol. 152 p. by **王統照**
1940 文化生活

A series of stories written in the old style. *For everyone.*

873. 春花 *SPRING FLOWERS* 1 vol. 300 p. by **王統照**
1941 良友文學叢書

An interesting picture of the state of mind of the students during the Revolution. The hero of the book is a staunch revolutionist but the hardships in bringing about his ideas wear him out. Discouraged, he enters a monastery, but leaves it after six months. Back in the movement he gains new confidence in his mission and throws himself into the struggle. *For all.*

874. 一葉 *A LEAF* 1 vol. 150 & 89 p. by **王統照**
1923 商務印書舘

The diary of a young man who lives in Peking and studies at one of the universities, consisting of a chronological record of unimportant events : his childhood in the paternal mansion, his relations with an adopted sister, at school, his relations with a professor, an illness, etc. *For everyone.*

875. 王統照選集 *AN ANTHOLOGY OF WANG T'UNG-CHAO* 1 vol. 258 p.
1936 萬象書屋

p. 9. A young man falls in love with a Russian girl and marries her. They are arrested (the man committed a murder some time before). The hero swears vengeance on those who imposed upon his wife during his absence.

p. 35. Drought and distress; prayers for rain; fights against bandits.

p. 60. The story of a monk.

p. 81. Portrait of a girl student.

p. 94. On leaving the hospital a patient thinks of a girl friend who nursed him.

p. 107. Meditation on life and death.

p. 117. Two friends; one has a screw loose and probably committed a crime.

p. 132. Conversation with a little boy.

p. 142. Childhood memories.

p. 154. An opium den.

p. 161. Thoughts about Japan.

p. 165. Conversation with an old man.

p. 172. A boy whose qualities are not appreciated.

p. 181. A new town.

p. 189. Conversation between old friends.

p. 198. Meditation in a grave-yard.

p. 202. A busy street in Harbin.

p. 205. On the beach.

p. 214. A strange fellow traveller.

p. 222. Excelsior!

p. 225. Sunshine after rain.

For all.

876. 長相思 *FOREVER REMEMBERED* 2 vols. 152 & 212 p. by 公磊王研石
1933 誠文信書局

A young man from Peking goes to Harbin to finish his studies and to perfect himself in the Russian language. Soon he finds himself in close relations with three girls, one of whom is especially taken up with him. He is recalled to Peking and complications in his love affairs are caused by a rich man of not very strict morals. Nevertheless everything ends happily, and the young man achieves a good marriage. *For everyone.*

877. 浮沉 *FLOATING* 1 vol. 338 p. by 王余杞
1938 星雲堂書店 *See Biogr. 173*

A poor orphan, forsaken by her friends, marries a student who also forsakes her. Falling from bad to worse, the heroine gets in touch with two soldiers. One of them wants to save her and gives her money to that end. She spends the money looking for her husband whom she finally finds. He gets rid of her by recommending her to the protection of one of his friends. The other soldier still tries to get hold of her but she finds refuge with her husband's friend. Immodest details. Wrong outlook on life. *Very objectionable.*

878. 粉牡丹 *PINK PEONY* 2 vol. 205, 104 pp. by 王曰叟
1940 北大書局

Romance of chivalry for the greater part inoffensive. At least one chapter is downright obscene.

A mean attack on the idols of Tantrism; records of the morals of Buddhist nuns; descriptions of adultery; a number of obscene insinuations. *To be banned.*

879. 七封書信的自傳 *AUTOBIOGRAPHY IN SEVEN LETTERS*
1 vol. 116 p. by 魏金枝
1928 人間書屋 *See Biogr. 174*

Seven letters and a few essays by a man who was once headmaster in a school. Dissertations on politics, morals, education, and a thousand and one other subjects. *For informed readers.*

880. 白旗手 *WHITE SIGNALER* 1 vol. 237 p. by 魏金枝
1933 現代書局

Four short stories. The first — the longest of the four — describes how soldiers settle on a village during a crimping expedition. It relates disputes and conversations among soldiers and some less edifying episodes. It is interesting because it describes rather faithfully one of the sore spots of China.

The second is taken from life at barracks. The last two are love stories. One is rather inoffensive. The other abounds in immodest details. As a matter of fact, throughout the book the author never minces his words. *Very objectionable.*

881. 流外集 *EXILING*　　　　1 vol. 222 p. by 味 徹
　　　　　　　　　　　　　　　　　　　1936 中華書局

Twenty or so pieces in which the author gives us his descriptions and ideas on a good many things. He tells us of actual conditions in China and makes a number of comparisons with foreign countries.

The author does not lack wit and sometimes his remarks are to the point. Nevertheless, his ideas are not ours. For example the piece entitled 男女之間 should be read with discretion, even though the ideas expressed in it are excellent. *May be read by anyone.*

882. 她竟變心了嗎 *WAS SHE CHANGED?*　　1 vol. 155 p. by 韋月侶
　　　　　　　　　　　　　　　　　　3rd edition, 1937. 萬象書局

A student falls in love with a young girl. When she is forced to return home, the young man goes to the Southern islands.

On his return later on, he finds his sweetheart as his brother's concubine, but with her virtue intact. He escapes with her to the South. *For grown-up people.*

883. 夢裏的情人 *THE LOVER OF MY DREAMS*　1 vol. 214 p. by 韋雨蘋
　　　　　　　　　　　　　　　　　　　　1937 萬象書屋

Psychological study of love. Three characters: a young man and two women. He is a quiet but impressionable boy. He meets one of the women when travelling. The other woman is a young widow, a protestant, set on ensnaring the young fellow. When his infatuation with the first woman cools down, the widow succeeds in her plans. He then learns from his brother that he is not her first victim; that finishes all between them.

The spirit of the book is wholly objectionable; several descriptions are immodest. *Strict reserve.*

884. 新婦女書信 *LETTERS OF A WOMAN*　　1 vol. 178 p. by 韋月侶女士
　　　　　　　　　　　　　　　　　　　　1933 廣益書局

Letters treating of love, marriage, and divorce — all without the slightest regard for morality. The author establishes herself on a single principle, "liberty in everything." *Not to be recommended to anyone.*

885. 春蠶 *SILKWORM*　　　　　　1 vol. 309 p. by 韋月侶女士
　　　　　　　　　　　　　　　　　　　1937 希望出版社

A young girl student reads a great number of romances and she wishes to experience in herself the sentiments of the characters she reads about. With this end in view, she meets a poor young musician, and love is soon born between them. On the point of returning on holiday to her parents, she wishes to give proof of her great love. In the following pages and at great length, the author describes a scene in an alcove in which the heroine gives this proof. But after she has returned home, her parents oppose this union.

The young couple refuse to admit defeat, and the hero succeeds in eloping with the girl. They go to Shanghai where they live together. However, the heroine has a haemorrhage and dies after five days, while her lover is taken by the police for having seduced a minor.

This book is *to be proscribed* because of the really obscene description that it contains. It is astonishing that a woman is not ashamed to write in this fashion!

886. 蓉蓉 *FLOWER* 1 vol. 192 p. by 聞國新

華北作家協會 *See Biogr. 175*

Yung-yung, a peasant girl, has ambition; much more than her fellow-villagers. This is due to the fact that she is friends with the village teacher. Her parents approve of the companionship, although there never was a promise of marriage. She herself only thinks of marriage as of a means to bring her wealth. In his admiration her lover is ready to ignore her less idealistic view on marriage. During the vacation the girl's parents die; left alone, she wants to go to her lover. A far relation of hers pretends to bring her to him but sells her to a woman of easy virtue. Yung-yung succumbs to her way of life. The village teacher finds her in this deplorable position and wants to save her, but he has not got the money to buy her freedom. Yung yung dies in that condition, a victim of social conditions.

This last part is brushed in even more realistic colours than the rest of the book. *Very objectionable.*

887. 落花時節 *WHEN THE FLOWERS WITHER* 1 vol. 190 p. by 聞國新

1944 新民印書館

Fourteen short stories. The author describes in them miseries of all sorts, those of an oppressed child, of a teacher, of a student, of a young girl who is persecuted, etc. *For everyone.*

888. 革命外史 *ANECDOTAL HISTORY OF THE REVOLUTION*

1 vol. 112 p. by 翁 仲

1928 吳越書店

This book records a few events from the time when the Revolutionary Army took power; true to life descriptions of scenes familiar to those who lived in China at that time.

Several episodes and speeches call for strict reserve, although the author himself disapproves of them. A few pages are obscene (89, 90, 91). *Must not be found in any library.*

889. 兩度生死 *TWICE THROUGH THE GATES OF DEATH*

1 vol. 118 p. by 武承揚選

1946 美華書局

Detective stories.
1) A detective discovers a criminal through a special cigar.
2) A double murder. The detective discovers the murderer to be a so-called friend.
3) A mysterious robbery is solved.
4) A husband who disencumbers himself of four wives from whom he is divorced. He is locked up.
5) A detective who has been threatened himself arrests a band of malefactors.
For everyone.

890. 實言棒 *LIAR'S STAFF* 1 vol. 45 p. 吳翰雲編輯

1933 中華書局

A small volume of a collection of stories for children.

After reading some volumes of this series, it seems to us that the whole series can be given to children. *For everyone.*

891. 陷阱與誘惑　*TRAP & TEMPTATION*　　1 vol. 82 p. by 吳逸明
　　　　　　　　　　　　　　　　　　　1946　建業出版社

Eighty-two pages of ridiculous stuff! The author wishes to put us wise regarding the tricks played by the fraudulent society in Shanghai, but it would have been better if he had refrained. *Not to be recommended to anyone.*

892. 北極風情畫　*LANDSCAPE OF THE NORTH POLE* 、1 vol. 219 p. by 無名氏
　　　　　　　　　　　　　　　　　　6th. edit. 1946　無名書屋

A Chinese officer refugeeing in Siberia, tells of his romance with a Polish girl, also seeking refuge in those regions.

After the departure of the officer for China, the heroine commits suicide, and the former seeks oblivion on an isolated mountain.

The book contains the description of a great love, but the author makes out no case for marriage and morals. It does not, however, contain any passages that are carried too far. *Not to be recommended to anyone.*

893. 野獸,野獸,野獸　*BEASTS, BEASTS, BEASTS.*　1 vol. 530 p. by 無名氏
　　　　　　　　　　　　　　　　　　1946　時代生活出版社

A young man who for years had taken an active part in the revolution and had been in prison, changes his mind and comes back to healthier ideas and to true freedom, which he had sought in vain in his former struggles.

Some disputable theories. *Not for everyone.*

894. 塔裡的女人　*WOMEN IN THE TOWER*　　1 vol. 152 p. by 無名氏
　　　　　　　　　　　　　　　　　　1947　時代生活出版社

A bonze related his adventures. When he was still young he met a young and good girl. Three years afterwards they fell in love but he could not marry her as he was already married and had children. After three years he advised her to marry another man. But the latter was a rake. The girl left him and departed to live in solitude. Ten years afterwards the bonze met her again. She had changed very much . . . her mind had lost its clarity! It was then that he left her and became a bonze. Their love remained platonic. *For instructed persons.*

895. 西柳集　*WESTERN WILLOWS*　　1 vol. 397 p. by 吳組湘
　　　　　　　　　　　　　1934　上海生活書店 *See Biogr. 179*

A collection of ten stories. The first is about a young married woman, who, in order to continue her frivolous life, refused to feed her child, but finally maternal love won. The second is a story of a nurse's affection for a little child whom she nourished. The third is a story of a prodigical son. Next come two love stories. The next one is a story of a big boy who was fed by a woman's milk, a very vulgar story. The four last stories contain psychological description of modern life.

The author has a pleasant style; his descriptions are vivid and realistic; his expressions are sometimes coarse and vulgar, especially in the fourth and fifth stories. *For enlightened people.*

896. 飯餘集 *WITH PLATES SERVED*   1 vol. 158 p. by 吳組湘
2nd. edit. 1936 文化生活

1. Calamity in an entire country, and tribulations in a family.
2. Domestic portraits.
3. A series of dreams.
4. A woodcutter.

5. Two women in disaccord with their husbands.
6. A father repents of not having loved his dead child enough.
7. Things seen at Taishan.

For everyone.

897. 林沖夜奔 *THE EXILE OF A MAN*   1 vol. 156 p. by 吳永剛
1940 國民書店

Episodes from Shui Hu Chuan with Lin-chung as principal character, arranged for the stage.

We readily agree with the author when he contends that those in power must be just and give a good example. We must disagree with the methods he advocates to realize this ideal. *For informed readers.*

898. 玉君 *YU CHUN*   1 vol. 167 p. by 楊振聲
5th edit. 1933 北京書局 *See Biogr. 181*

Story of a young man who looks after a girl during several years. They are devoted to each other with a noble, pure and exclusively spiritual love. *For informed readers.*

899. 去國的悲哀 *SORROW OF NOSTALGIA*   1 vol. 242 p. by 楊鐘健
1929 北平平社

Description of a student's travels. He resides in Europe for several years. Comparison between European and Chinese ways of living.

For informed readers because of the anti-religious opinions of the author.

900. 桓秀外傳 *THE STORY OF HUAN-HSIU*   1 vol. 149 p. by 楊剛
1941 文化生活 *See Biogr. 183*

Two novels.
1. A good girl conceives a beautiful dream, but her life actually is a hell.
2. About a very unhappy family. The hero has two wives, who are always quarrelling with each other.

An interesting book to read but too realistic. The author is not afraid of calling a spade a spade. *For mature people, not for young students.*

901. 公孫鞅 *KONGSUN YANG: A Statesman*   1 vol. 69 p. by 楊剛
2nd. edit. 1941 文化生活出版社

A historical narrative of the time of the Seven Kingdoms (4th. century B.C.) 公孫鞅 is known in history as the Count of 商鞅. Descended from an impoverished but noble family, he succeeded, pushed by his egoism, in elevating himself on the social scale. Under the 魏 he already had a certain influence. And under the 秦, he was promoted to a count of lesser degree. Later he became chancellor, and henceforth the "law" was the inspiration and standard of all his acts. Everyone had to submit to the law. No exception was allowed, not a single noble nor even the Crown Prince.

Due to his integrity, the country was put into order and knew peace. He was created a count of the highest degree, and restored to this dignity, he made the state of 秦 a vassal of 魏.

The nobles, however, resented his too great rigidity, and in the end, he succumbed to their attacks. *For everyone except children.*

902. 燕子李三 *SEE THE SWALLOW* (*An Extraordinary Burglar*)
1 vol. 105 p. by 楊六郎
1947 萬國書店

A collection of stupidities that have no value whatever. *Not to be recommended to anyone.*

903. 他的天使 *HIS ANGEL*
1 vol. 196 p. by 楊騷
1928 北新書局 *See Biogr. 184*

1 His "angel" is the girl who flirts with everyone. *Not for everyone.*
2 The "host" is an old lover on his way to the red paradise. *Not to be recommended to anyone.*
3. A young communist, pursued by the police, runs away, leaving his girl friend. Communist tendency. *Not to be recommended to anyone.*
4. Exploitation of the blacks by the whites. *Not to be recommended to anyone.*
5. A symbolic dream. (Communistic tendency). *Not to be recommended to anyone.*

904. 記憶之都 *A CITY OF REMEMBRANCE*
1 vol. 315 p. by 楊騷
1937 商務印書館

1. 記憶之都 p. 1-42. Two sister stars fall in love with a man on this terrestrial globe. The elder descends to the earth to make the human rise towards her younger sister who meanwhile picks some fruit for her dearly beloved. A god punishes her for three years, and the elder sister stays on the earth. *For everyone.*
2 心曲 p. 43-189. A colloquy between a young man and a nymph which is full of poetry, and in which the author's imagination is very fecund.
It contains, however, too much sentiment for the young. *Not for everyone.*
3. 迷離 p. 190-315. Conversations full of poetry. Sentiments exchanged between young people. Here again the author shows much imagination. Many words used are pure poetic juggling, with no basis on reality. *This piece is not to be recommended to the young.*

905. 神州亞森蘿蘋 *A CHINESE ARSENE LUPIN*
1 vol. 147 p. by 楊時中
1941 大業書局

About detectives tricked by robbers. Sherlock Holmes and Watson arrive in Shanghai, but they are not able to get the better of Chinese robbers. The Chinese detectives also meet with nothing but mortification. *For everyone.*

906. 夢斷香魂
2 vol. 124, 123 pp. by 葉光華

何泰來 is a very talented painter; he is proud and independent. Being handsome, he is a sure success with women. Having a tender heart, he succumbs simultaneously to the charms of two young women, who both love him passionately. In consequence of some misunderstanding, one enters a Buddhist nunnery, the other commits suicide. Utterly disheartened he drowns himself.

A very mediocre book. A few scenes are well written, many are long-winded and superfluous.

One or two unbecoming descriptions. *Objectionable.*

907. 處女的夢 *DREAM OF A GIRL*   1 vol. 123 p. by 葉靈鳳
4th edition, 1931   上海現代書局   *See Biogr. 190*

Five short stories:

妻的恩惠 A writer without talent profits from his gifted wife. *For everyone.*

摩伽的試探 The story of a young girl. Rather crude details. *Not for everyone.*

處女的夢 A young girl meets the writer of her dreams. *Not for everyone.*

國仇 A Chinese student in Japan wants to abuse a woman-servant. *Not to be recommended to anyone.*

秋的黃昏 A woman is unfaithful to her husband. *Not to be recommended to anyone.*

落雁 A man falls into a trap, but escapes danger. *Not to be recommended to anyone.*

908. 鳩綠媚   1 vol. 289 p. by 葉靈鳳
光華書局

Collection of short stories, well written but obscene.
To be banned, especially because of the second story 浴 in which youth is taught evil.

909. 稻草人 *THE SCARECROW*   1 vol. 213 p. by 葉紹鈞
4th edit. 1927   商務印書館   *See Biogr. 191*

A book for the young. Stories in which nature, the birds, the plants talk to men. They are illustrated with simple but suggestive drawings.

It is a *profitable book* for *youngsters.* It will teach them to love nature and to know the better side of man.

910. 城中 *IN THE CITY*   1 vol. 157 p. by 葉紹鈞
2nd. edit. 1927   開明書店

A collection of nine stories, very well written in easy, clear style, and repanding a pure atmosphere. *For everyone.*

911. 火災 *FIRE*   1 vol. 197 p. by 葉紹鈞
1930   商務印書館

A work of which the theme is love, but elevating love, e.g. love between married people, towards children, for Nature etc. According to the author, it is the lack of such love that is the cause of all disorder. *For everyone.*

912. 未厭居習作 *WITHOUT SATIETY*   1 vol. 211 p. by 葉紹鈞
1935   開明書店

Little events of ordinary life — usages and customs. Written in beautiful language and with quite a lot of humour. *For everyone.*

913. 線下 *UNDER THE LINE*   1 vol. 235 p. by 葉紹鈞
1935   商務印書館

A collection of short stories well-written and *to be recommended* to all readers.

914. 四三集 *ODDS & ENDS*   1 vol. 348 p. by 葉聖陶
1936   良友文學叢書

A collection of stories, interesting and easy reading. Of the life of students and professors; of schools; of life in the country and in Shanghai. *For everyone.*

915. 隔膜 *COLDNESS*   1 vol. 160 p. by 葉紹鈞
                                                              1938   商務印書舘

Selected writings of Yeh Shao-chün. They deal with all kinds of subjects: life at home, in the country, at school etc. Some selections are excellent in their freshness and simplicity. Slight objections might be raised here and there, but not important enough to make the book unsuitable, even for youngsters. *For all.*

916. 未厭居習作 *MY ELEMENTARY WORKS*   1 vol. 211 p. by 葉紹鈞
                                                    3rd. edit. 1939   開明書店

An excellent book about excursions, plants, Spring, and ordinary events. *For everyone.*

917. 古代英雄的石像 *STATUE OF AN ANCIENT HERO* 1 vol. 139 p. by 葉紹鈞
                                                    2nd. edit. 1941   開明書店

A collection of allegorical tales and fables. *For children.*

918. 葉紹鈞代表作 *AN ANTHOLOGY OF YEH SHAO-CHUN*   1 vol. 304 p.
                                                              1941   三通書局

pp. 1, 12, 22 Scenes in a school	p. 136 Reception of an American.
p. 28 Waiting for the postman.	p. 142 Pessimistic thoughts.
p. 34 Enthusiasm extinguished.	p. 147 A mother and her child.
p. 43 Children's speech.	p. 151 Miscellaneous.
p. 46 Story of an earthquake.	p. 155 Newly weds.
p. 52 Situation of the schools.	p. 160 Expectation.
p. 57 Against superstitions.	p. 173 About a garden.
p. 64 Conversation with an unhappy wife.	p. 182 The wife is ill.
p. 86 The parents are shot. The grandmother survives with a small child.	p. 186 A fresh and musical morning.
	p. 188 The spectre of phthisis.
p. 99 A girl cruelly treated.	p. 194 A young widow loves the child of a neighbour.
p. 104 The boredom of making visits.	
p. 133 A little boy goes for the first time to school.	p. 206 Ships.
	p. 217 Ships.
p. 122 A young mother.	p. 220 On flowers.
p. 127 A woman badly treated.	p. 222 Visit to buddhist monks.
p. 131 Promenade of a young couple.	p. 231 Memory of a dead friend.
p. 133 Two love letters.	

Also some stories for children. *For everyone.*

919. 葉紹鈞代表作 *AN ANTHOLOGY OF YEH SHAO-CHUN*   340 p.
                                                              1940   三通書局

A book worth recommending to students both for its stylistic qualities and for its contents. *For all.*

920. 星 *STARS*   1 vol. 105 p. by 葉　紫
                                              1935   上海文化生活出版社 *See Biogr. 192*

An excellent person is given in marriage to a cruel man who maltreats her. In spite of this she remains faithful to him. During a revolution, she escapes and marries a teacher who is very considerate towards her. Together they work for the good of society, and thus our heroine knows some months of happiness.

After the revolution has been put down, her husband takes her back together with the child of the teacher, to which she has given birth in the meantime. He continues to maltreat her. And her son dies at the age of six years. Faced with this new sorrow, the heroine loses patience and escapes towards the unknown.

The book has a slight communist tint. *For everyone.*

921. 浮生集 *ROAMING LIFE*   1 vol. 387 p. by   **葉永蓁**
1934   生活書店

Various pieces. Considerations more or less profound on different subjects, among others, dreams. No cash. No tears. *For everyone.*

922. 山寺暮 *DUSK AT THE MOUNTAIN MONASTERY*   1 vol. 172 p. by   **嚴文井**
1937   良友公司

A collection of ten essays and narratives. In a careful and vigorous style, the author describes walks, Nature, and the details of ordinary life, mixed, however, at times with rather free comments. *For everyone.*

923. 錢 *MONEY*   1 vol. 289 p. by   **言　永**
大連啓東書社

The author wants to prove that money often causes disorderliness and unhappiness. He introduces us to a rich merchant who thinks his wealth is given solely to enjoy life. We are told about his family life, the two concubines he takes to satisfy his whims. Both of them only think of his money and compete to make him spend it on them. When, in the end, they succeed in ruining him, he sees his error and starts an orderly life.

The author can tell a good story. The first part of the book is well built and full of action. The second part is full of vulgar realism. Some of his characters reveal a repelling cynicism. *Very objectionable.*

924. 嚇美國嗎 *IS THAT THE U.S.?*   1 vol. 87 p. by   **尹　庚**
2nd. edit. 1937   文化生活

Reminiscences of one who has lived in America for a long time. About a girl who disappeared during a meeting, various incidents, at a curio dealer's etc.

All these tales are laid abroad. *For everyone.*

925. 枕上集 *BEDSIDE*   1 vol. 246 p. by   **友　西**
3rd. edit. 1940   商務印書舘

Local descriptions of opium smokers, the oppression exercised by village potentates, etc.

Without much psychological value. *For everyone.*

926. 離絕 *DENOUNCED*   1 vol. 171 p. by   **雨　嵐**
1927   光華書局

Letters making up a complete novel. The love described is sound. One *objectionable passage.*

927. 遙遠的愛 *LOVE FROM AFAR*   1 vol. 164 p. by   **郁　茹**
1946   自强出版社

A girl of revolutionary stock has married a good bourgeois. After several years of happiness, the wife finds her life empty, and joins the "party". Henceforth she devotes herself to the poor — the ideal woman. Her husband, however, leaves her. She has no grudge against him and does not think of re-marrying. She devotes herself to good works and retains her optimism.

In the end the ex-husband joins his lot with a young man who has made advances to the wife but has been refused.

Apart from the separation of the husband and wife, there is nothing questionable from a moral point of view in the book. *For everyone.*

928. 雞冠集 *COCK'S COMB*　　　1 vol. 92 p. by **予且（潘序祖）**
1934　四社出版部　*See Biogr. 124*

A pamphlet without any value whatever. It deals with questions connected with marriage. The author adds a number of witticism and sayings of famous men. Several of his opinions about divorce and free love are condemnable and the witticisms are often off-colour. *For informed readers.*

929. 兩間房 *TWO ROOMS*　　　1 vol. 166 p. by **予　且**
1937　中華書局

Collection of rather frivolous short stories. 秋 and 案壁之間 are *very objectionable.*

930. 迷羊 *LOST SHEEP*　　　　1 vol. 164 p. by **郁達夫**
1928　上海北新書局　*See Biogr. 196*

Autobiographic story of the love of a young man and an actress. He met her in a small town when she was on a tour; soon they became very intimate, ran away and lived together during two months. He is completely carried away by his great passion; the woman soon loses interest and again thinks of the stage. One morning she takes advantage of his prolonged sleep to walk out on him. All his efforts to find her foil.

The book is well written; the style is fluent and clear. No descriptions are too unbecomingly minute. The immoral atmosphere, and the analysis of the hero's feelings and impressions caused by his passion make it *very objectionable* reading.

931. 春潮 *SURF IN SPRING*　　　1 vol. p. 239-287 by **郁達夫**
上海藝光出版社

Three stories recounting the unhappy adventures of students.

The first tells of two students who are candidates for the official examinations under Ch'ien Lung. The second is an idyll about two children, and the third is about the intimate life of two students at the Normal University. *For grown-up people.*

932. 郁達夫文集 *WRITINGS OF YU TA-FU*　　　1 vol. 140 p.
國風書店

A good number of these stories may be read by all. Two call for the strictest reserve; one on p. 7 that is equivocal, one on p. 73 where the author describes his relations with a prostitute.

The book is written in a brilliant style. *Very objectionable.*

933. 達夫全集第一卷寒灰集 *COLD ASHES*
7th edit. 1931　北新書局

This first volume contains several short, inoffensive literary essays, and a number of short stories. They are melancholic in tone, sarcastic and morbid. In a letter to a student, who will shortly take his degree, Yü Ta-fu vents his spleen upon the military, declares that all certificates are worthless and that stealing is the only way to success. He advises the young man to do so.

In the stories 茫茫夜 and 秋柳 there are indecent details; the author shows how poorly he estimates chastity. *Very objectionable.*

934. 達夫全集第二卷雞肋集 *CHICKEN'S RIBS*

2nd edition 1928 上海創造社

Second volume of writings by Yü Ta-fu. The first story is about a student in Japan. He is given to melancholy, takes to self-abuse, repents but falls again. The young man later witnesses a shocking scene in a room adjoining his; in the end he seduces a servant. *Very objectionable.*

935. 達夫全集第三卷過去集 *THE PAST*   377 p.

3rd edit. 1928 上海開明書店

In this volume the author tells us of love affairs (some are his own), temptations and filthy thoughts; all this is coated with melancholy and miscontent. Here again, we realize how morbid and abnormal Yü Ta-fu's tendency is.

As the author's talent is unmistakable, *only well informed readers,* who are engaged in literary study, may be permitted to read the book.

936. 達夫全集第四卷奇零集 *TRIVIA*   273 p.

2nd edit. 1928 上海開明書店

Fourth volume of selections from Yü Ta-fu, dealing chiefly with literary subjects. In his political and social considerations he shows Marxist tendencies. Some essays are inoffensive. *Very objectionable.*

937. 達夫全集第五卷敝帚集 *OLD BROOM*   250 p.

1928 現代書局

Biographies, studies on literature, poetry, culture, etc. The author seems to be a staunch follower of J.J. Rousseau. *Objectionable* because of false theories.

938. 達夫全集第六卷薇蕨集 *UNIMPRESSIVE FLOWERS*   1 vol. 183 p.

2nd edit. 1931 北新書局

This book contains nine stories. The author as always is showing here a melancholic and morbid streak. *Not to be recommended to anyone.*

939. 達夫全集第七卷斷殘集 *SCATTERED PIECES*   1 vol. 323 p.

1933 北新書局

This book contains essays on novels and literature and prefaces to some of his own books; this part is followed by narratives and descriptions, the last four of which are mainly translations of Nietsche & Rousseau. *Not to be recommended to anyone.*

940. 郁達夫代表作 *AN ANTHOLOGY OF YU TA-FU*

三通書局

Yü Ta-fu is a sentimental, effeminate, morbid writer.

Unsuitable for younger people, his books must be read with the greatest caution even *by well informed readers.*

941. 達夫代表作 *AN ANTHOLOGY OF YU TA-FU*

1928 上海春野書店

A number of short stories by Yü Ta-fu. One describes how a man, having lost his wife, takes to drink. Another portrays a dreaming, unsociable poet. The third deals with the behavior of a young man and a prostitute.

The stories are full of immodest details which make them *dangerous for younger people.*

942. 達夫短篇小說集上冊 *SHORT STORIES OF YU TA-FU* 1 vol. 307 p.

1935 上海北新書局

A number of short stories in which the author shows himself a sentimentalist and often a cynic. Several may be safely read by everybody. Others must be reserved to well informed readers. Some are unsuitable reading for students, viz. pp. 83, 84 & 112 and the whole of 秋河. *Very objectionable.*

943. 達夫短篇小說集下冊 *SHORT STORIES OF YU TA-FU*

1935 北新書局

Another selection of stories by Yü Ta-fu. Some may be read by everybody; but the volume as a whole is unsuitable for younger people, for most stories contain morbid ideas and many passages are unbecoming. *Very objectionable.*

944. 繡囊記 *THROUGH AN EMBROIDERNED PURSE* 1 vol. 156 p. by 俞天憤

1936 中原書局

A good book and to be recommended. It tells how riches allied to indulgence lead to ruin, and how virtue, industry and charity lead to happiness. *For everyone.*

945. 怒海鴛鴦錄 *TOSSED BY FATE* 162 p. by 于次溪

1940 大華書局

Na-na, formerly a student, becomes a dancer. Two young men fall in love with her. She prefers the poorer of the two but puts off marriage awaiting better days. In the meantime she gets married to an old nabob who, obligingly, dies in a short time, leaving her a big fortune. With her newly acquired wealth she sets out for Shanghai, finds her lover and goes abroad with him.

The book makes interesting reading, but the language and the ideas make it unsuitable for all classes of readers. *Very objectionable.*

946. 劫灰 RUINS 1 vol. 115 p. by 沅君 (馮淑蘭)

1929 北新書局 *See Biogr.* 55

1. Robbers ransack a village.
2. An unhappy woman.
3. A recently widowed woman finds solace for her deep sorrow in a second marriage.
4. A teacher is accused of being in love with one of his pupils. To prove the fact a compromising letter is stolen.
5. A teacher loves one of his pupils. She leaves the school.
6. A husband, unjustly suspected by his wife, proves his innocence.
7. A love affair.
8. An unintelligible lucubration.
   For all.

947. 時間 *TIME*   1 vol. 202 p. by 袁 犀
                                        1945 文昌書店 *See Biogr. 199*

In the present work the author gives us six short stories. A resumé of two of them will give a sufficient idea of the class to which they belong.

1. 手杖 The narrator is a neurasthenic whose doctor has advised a rest in Tsingtao. He knows nobody there and goes to a hotel where he makes the acquaintance of a servant. The love affairs of the latter are described, and form the chief theme of the story. One of her lovers is a painter who has held an unsuccessful exhibition in Tsingtao; another is a musician who has come to convalescence from consumption, who, however, does not dare to avow his love. The servant marries the artist and the musician has a haemorrhage. The narrator meets the servant in his turn, and she is abandoned subsequently for a concubine.

2. 絕色 The author meets a beautiful young man in a dancing hall in Tientsin. This Adonis is pursued by a number of females. He eventually seduces a girl whose family once maltreated his aunt. He does not rest until she dies and he himself commits suicide.

This collection also contains several sarcastic discussions aimed at Providence.

The triangular love affairs are described without too much crudity, but the general tone of the book makes reading that cannot be recommended.

From the literary point of view, this book has no value at all. *Not to be recommended to anyone.*

948. 貝殼 *SEA SHELL*   1 vol. 196 p. by 袁 犀
                                        2nd edit. 1942 新民書局

A young woman has been seduced by another man two months before her marriage. The author describes coarsely the woman's fears before her confinement. She travels, in company of her sister, so that her husband may not know of the thing. More adventures follow.

The book is offensively realistic. *Very objectionable.*

949. 愛河情波 *DISTURBED LOVE*   1 vol. 140 p. by 浣 梅
                                        1946 正文書店

A sentimental romance and an adventure story at the same time. The hero is a very good character, and at the same time he is a good detective. He ends by marrying the chosen of his heart after surmounting many obstacles.

The style of this book is ordinary, but the plot is interesting. *For everyone.*

950. 西湖三光 *WEST LAKE*   1 vol. 176 p. by 員子沙
                                        1928 泰東圖書公司

Little tales written in carefully chosen language but without much value except for the last.

The subject of the last is a boy who has been brought up in a temple. He comes into contact with the world and being attracted by the opposite sex, he runs away. During a certain time, he lives with a prostitute who ends up, however, in driving him out. Having no resources, he becomes a miserable beggar. Finally he returns to the temple where he is re-admitted after receiving pardon for his transgressions. And later, he becomes abbot of the very same temple. *For mature people.*

THE FOLLOWING FICTION ARE WRITTEN
BY VARIOUS AUTHORS.

951. 十 年 *A DECADE*　　　　　　　1 vol. 376 p. col. by 夏丏尊 etc.
　　　　　　　　　　　　　　　　　　　　　　1936 開明書店

　　A number of literary essays by well known authors. This book contains *nothing that can affect one's morals.*

952. 玉蘭花下　　　　　　　　　　　1 vol. 147 p. coll. by 壬　秋
　　　　　　　　　　　　　　　　　　　　　　盛京書局

玉蘭花下 by 壬秋 p. 1-19. A girl has a beautiful dream a few hours before her wedding. Her sister shatters her dream with one word.
　　The dream is a little too suggestive for young people. *Not for everyone.*
在醫院裡 by 柳月女士 p. 20-60. A child is ill in the hospital. His father, who loves him very much, cannot take care of him properly, because the grandmother holds the reins and she detests the child. She even refuses to pay the hospital expenses. The child takes poison.
　　This ending obliges us to place a reservation on this story. *Not for everyone.*
安壽的死 by 倪宛仙女士 p. 61-69. Death of an infant. The mother tells of his birth, how she nursed him, and of his death. Certain details are not for readers who are too young. *Not for everyone.*
離家的前夜 by 緗緗女士 p. 70-80. A young mother renounces her studies from love of her baby. *For everyone.*
春痕 by 馮沅君女士 p 81-126. Love letters. Without interest. *For everyone.*
給 S 妹的信 by 謝冰瑩女士 p. 127-147. Letter to an old friend. Very forcefully written but also very violent and at times, cynical. *For everyone.*

953. 名家創作小說選 *SELECTED FAMOUS WORKS* 1 vol. 238 p. coll. by 任倉厂
　　　　　　　　　　　　　　　　　　　　　　　　　1936 上海經緯書局

1) 春風沉醉的晚上 by 郁達夫. The author meets a girl who wishes to raise him a little. *For everyone.*
2) 一個男人和一個女人 by 丁玲. The relations of a young man with two different women. *Not for everyone.*
3) 密約 by 張資平. The platonic relations between a married man and a woman in the same condition. *Not for everyone.*
4) 一侍女 by 蓬子. A young girl is invited by an old friend who departs without paying the bill. *For everyone.*
5) 一個村子 by 胡也頻. A beautiful village is pillaged and put into a state of confusion. *For everyone.*
6) 他們戀愛了 by 魯彥. A childhood friendship. *For everyone.*
7) 黑白李 by 老舍. Two brothers love the same girl. The elder retires in favour of the younger. *For everyone.*
8) 姑姑 Cfr. No. 247. *For everyone.*
9) 理智的勝利 by 謝冰瑩 A friendship without hope. *For everyone.*
10) 新同學 by 許欽文. Two students talk of a new arrival. *For everyone.*

11) 夫婦 by 沈從文 An amorous couple discovered in the act. *For everyone.*
12) 幽靈 by 巴金 A curious visit. *For everyone.*
13) 新生 by 腓兆 Consequence of a revolutionary act. *For everyone.*
14) 奇遇 by 張天翼 Impressions of a baby. *For everyone.*

954. 遙遠的風沙 *SANDSTORMS FAR AWAY*   1 vol. 242 p. by **老舍 等**
              1947 三聯出版社

A collection of eleven stories.
1) 遙遠的風沙 by 端木蕻良 p. 1-22. "Sandstorm Afar". A military convoy in Mongolia, the life of the desert, brigands. Certain passages are vulgar and crude. *Not for everyone.*
2) 且說屋裡 by 老舍 p. 23-42. "Scenery in the House". Of two Chinese officials in accord with the Japanese before the war. An excellent description of the mentality of old officials. *For everyone.*
3) 小魏的江山 by 白塵 p. 43-80. "Wei's Access to Power". Of prison life and how Wei managed to climb up in the world. *For everyone.*
4) 回家 by 劉祖春 p. 81-90. "Back Home". A man who has been with the resistance returns home after an absence of six years. His mother had a great love for him and his sister a very lively affection. But life is sad in a deserted house and the neighbour despises people without a job. *For everyone.*
5) 風雨 by 嚴文井 p. 91-117. "Rain and Wind". *For everyone.*
6) 紫 by 青子 p. 118-142. "The Violet". A sentimental story in which the poetical and psychological point of view is emphasized. *For everyone.*
7) 逼 by 屈曲夫 p. 145-161. "Oppression". A very touching story of an infant who is made to disappear but is found by his brother, aged ten. Contains tragic description full of beautiful sentiments. *For everyone.*
8) 冰天 by 劉白羽 *See Biogr. 110* p. 162-188. "The Frozen Territory." Of a military expedition in the north. A sergeant has joined it to revenge his mother. He dies frozen to death. *For everyone.*
9) 長江上 by 荒煤 p. 189-204. "On the Yangtze". Of travellers on the river. Contains vulgar language. *Not for everyone.*
10) 包身上 by 夏衍 p. 205-222. "Sold to the Contractor". The conditions of slave women working in the factories of Shanghai. *For everyone.*
11) 矮簷 by 蕭乾 p. 223-242. "Low Graves". Of a widow and her only son, and of his life at school. Well written. *For everyone.*
     The stories numbered 1,2,3,4,6,7, and 11 have a certain literary value.

955. 秋雁集 *AUTUMN FLIGHTS*   1 vol. 164 p. by **劉大杰 等**
              1942 一流書店

     Several stories. Of the regrets of a girl hesitating too much in choosing a husband, of an abandoned soul, of girl and boy students, of a theft committed by a poor man, and memories of childhood. *For everyone.*

956. 迷茫 *UNCERTAIN*   1 vol. 242 p. by **盧焚等作**
              1947 三聯出版社

     A collection of twelve stories by different authors.
1) 迷茫 by 盧焚 p. 1-11. "Uncertainty". Description of a girl of rather ripe age, her brother, and his friend of the female sex. In a student demonstration in Peking against the Japanese, the hero is assumed to heave disappeared, and his friend is wounded.
2) 團聚 by 丁玲 p. 12-36. "A family re-union." The story of a family, formerly in easy circumstances, that has fallen into misery.

3) 手 by 蕭紅 p. 37-56. "The hand". A country boy in the university.

4) 特別勳章 by 罪烽 p. 57-73. "A special decoration." An officer serving with the Japanese kills his own son who is with the guerillas.

5) 查災 by 沙丁 "Inspection of a place where famine reigns." Here is described the tragic murder committed by a refugee.

6) 糠粢 by 香菲 "Paddy-husk Stew". Of a starved family.

7) 出關 by 楳西 p. 85-95. "Destination Northeast". Of Chinese peasants deceived and sold as labour slaves in Manchuria.

8) 三個 by 周文 p. 96-110. "Three of them". Of the life of three young apprentices.

9) 初步 by 奚如 *See Biogr. 83* p. 111-116. "The first step". The beginning of socialisation in a Russian village.

10) 酒船 by 紺弩 *See Biogr. 121* p. 117-126. "The Floating Bar". Opium smokers in Szechuan.

11) 犯 by 葛琴 *See Biogr. 90* p. 127-183. "The guilty one". A young apprentice is unjustly accused. The end is tragic.

12) 一月二十三日 by 丁玲 p. 184-219. "The 23rd. January". A camp of refugees and some rich people.

With the exception of story number 11 this book is without interest. *For everyone.*

957. 中學文學讀本散文乙選 *READING FOR HIGH SCHOOL*
1 vol. 304 p. coll. by 曹聚仁
1931 群衆圖書公司

This collection is composed of two parts.

1. Of critical and historical essays on literature and literary styles from Liang Ch'i-Ch'ao to Hsu Chih-mu. Various tendencies are represented that have had a great deal of popularity, especially the pragmatism of Dewey.

2 Of narrations and memories of journeys.

The choice in this selection is suitable for middle school students. Certain themes, however have a rather dangerous tendency. *Not for everyone.*

958. 遲暮 *LATE IN THE EVENING*
1 vol. 356 p. by 郁達夫
2nd. edit. 1935 生活書店

A collection of tales by various authors, containing nothing against religious faith or good morals. Some strong language is used, especially in the tales by 罍沙 and 張天翼. *For mature people.*

959. 遲暮 *LATE IN THE EVENING*
1 vol. 346 p. by 郁達夫等
2nd. edit. 1935 生活書店

1) A meeting of old friends on the lake at Hangchow. How we have aged! Where is the good time when we had no worries?

2) Haunted by her memory, I propose marriage to a girl I have met casually, by accident, and who has left a great impression upon me. Then I learn of her sad death. When I see her corpse, it makes me see all her life in vision. She loved me but could not accept my proposition because she was forced to sell her body to all comers to support her old father.

3) A strained situation between mother-in-law and daughter-in-law. The former does not want to give up any of her authority, from which fact quarrels are born. In the end the two persons concerned resort to separation.

4) Of poor farmers. Their poverty forces them to get rid of a new-born infant. They resort to all sorts of expedients but nevertheless cannot succeed in making two ends meet.

5) There is a ship that cannot continue her voyage. The passengers are obliged to descend. They claim damages and obtain justice.

6) Portrait of an exploiter. Contains very strong language.

7) An old friend begins to lose his reason. Because of this he avoids his old acquaintances and thinks that everyone despises him. These suspicions and doubts deprive him completely of his reason.

8) A prisoner returns home after eighteen years in prison. He is received with open arms by his wife, but he does not have the courage to begin life all over again.

9) There is a gathering to pray for rain. As the country is not peaceful, the people go armed, and, in actual fact, they are attacked by bandits. Victims fall on both sides. *Not for everyone.*

960. 現代書信文作選 *AN ANTHOLOGY OF EPISTOLARY STYLE*
1 vol. 218 p. 1932　上海青年書店
by famous authors.

In this volume we are given a series of model letters written by famous authors. There are three kinds of letters included: letters concerning contemporary affairs, lyrical and poetical letters, and descriptive letters. *For everyone.*

961. 現代說明文作選 *AN ANTHOLOGY OF DISSERTATIONS*
1 vol. 216 p. 1932　上海青年書店
by famous authors.

1) 經的大意 by 章太炎 Dissertation on the classics.

2) 教育與政治 by 梁啓超 In order to have a solid government, it is necessary to begin by taking care of education.

3) 美術的起源 by 蔡元培　The origin of art.

4) 介紹我自己的思想 by 胡適 The personal ideas of Hu Shih. He first learnt to doubt and then to think. Science stands in the place of religion for him. He prefers material civilization to spiritual civilization. His literary revolution was founded on history. His ideas on the ancient literature.

5) 猥褻的歌謠 by 周作人 Broad expressions and such like subjects in literature.

6) 小說的藝術 by 黃仲蘇 The art of the novel.

7) 從牯嶺到東京 by 茅盾 Dissertations on novels.

The four following dissertations are literary discussions.

12) 性愛的痛苦 by 謝六逸 Dissertation on erotic marifestations. Not to be recommended. *Not to be recommended* because of the last dissertation.

962. 現代記叙文作選 *AN ANTHOLOGY OF DIARIES, DESCRIPTIONS OF JOUR-*
　　　NEYS ETC.
1 vol. 226 p. 1932 上海青年書店
by famous authors.

1) 九年的家鄉教育 by 胡適　The story of his childhood. His relations with his parents, the difficulties of numerous families, his studies, and his relations with other children.

2) 旅行印象記 by 李石岑 A man who has travelled in the countries of Europe and who has noticed certain advantages of foreigners over Chinese.

3) 我的旅行 by 胡愈之　Return to China from Paris via Germany. Esperanto.

4) 旅行雜記 by 朱自清　Various remarks.

5) 從北京到北京 by 孫伏園　Impressions and things seen.

6) 今津記遊 by 郭沫若 Holidays in Japan.

7) 感傷的行旅 by 郁達夫 A journey in China.

8) 槳聲燈影裡的秦淮河 by 俞平伯 In a boat in the moonlight.
9) 在波蘭 by 郭子雄 Journey and stop-over in Poland.
10) 我的祖母的死 by 徐志摩 Ideas of children on death. His own ideas when adolescent on the death of his grandmother. He is an atheist.
11) 兩法師 by 葉紹鈞 Visit to buddhists.
12) 我的讀書的經驗 by 章衣萍 Youthful studies.
For mature people.

963. 現代論難文傑作選 *AN ANTHOLOGY OF QUESTIONS OF THE MOMENT*
1 vol. 214 p. 1932 上海青年書店
by famous authors.

Questions of the moment.
1) Comparison between Chinese and American students. What is lacking in our students. By Ts'ai Yuan-p'ei.
2) The literary revolution. By Hu Shih.
3) Modern literature. By Lo Chia-lun.
4) The new literature. By T'ang Fu.
5) The end of the old literature. By Lu Hsün.
6) The new historical method. By T'ao Wen-ho.
7) The old literature. By Tai Hsing-chao.
8) The power of the new literature. By Liang Shih-ch'iu.
9) Literary liberty in the universities. By Tung Jo-chien.
10) The art of lecturing. By Lin Yu-t'ang.
11) Right way of thinking. By Chu Tzu-ch'in.
12) Analysis of love. By Yu P'ing-po.
For everyone.

964. 現代小品文傑作選 *AN ANTHOLOGY OF BEST CONTEMPORARY TALES*
1 vol. 218 p. 1932 上海青年書店
by famous authors.

A choice of short tales by well-known writers. They are different in character, critical, lyrical, descriptive, of memories, etc., mostly ironic and imaginative.
For everyone.

965. 現代日記文傑作選 *AN ANTHOLOGY OF BEST CONTEMPORARY DIARIES AND ACCOUNTS OF JOURNEYS*   1 vol. 218 p. 1932 上海青年書店
by famous authors.

1) 馬上日記 by 魯迅 His occupations, visits, and correspondence.
2) 勞生日記 by 郁達夫 The author in Canton. Visits, schools, relations, letters. His writings.
3) 寄小讀者通訊十八 by 謝冰心 Her journey to America.
4) 苦雨齋之一週 by 周作人 Facts and acts.
5) 書生的一週間 by 趙景深 His works.
6) 廣州大火下的日記 by 楊振聲 A fire in Canton.
7) 倚枕日記 by 章衣萍 The author being ill is nursed by his wife.
8) 伏中日記 by 許欽文 Dog days.
9) 戰時日記 by 王禮錫 The battle of Chapei. What the author did.
10) 首途記 by 周全平 A ship near Nanking after the battle in Shanghai.
For everyone.

966. 現代詩傑作選 *AN ANTHOLOGY OF BEST CONTEMPORARY POEMS*

1 vol. 160 p. 1932 上海青年書店

by famous authors.

A collection of modern poems. Difficult to judge from the literary point of view, they are inoffensive from the moral point of view. *For everyone.*

967. 現代小說傑作選 *AN ANTHOLOGY OF BEST CONTEMPORARY STORIES*

1 vol. 348 p. 1932 上海青年書店

by famous authors.

阿 Q 正傳 by 魯迅 Cfr. No 635.

創造 by 茅盾 Cfr. Works of Mao Tun.

蘇堤 by 巴金 Three friends are on the lake at Hangchow. One of them wishes to visit a famous spot but the boatman refuses to take them there for fear of not being paid. Everything, however, is arranged amicably.

葉羅提之墓 by 郭沫若 An idyll between brother and sister-in-law.

春風沉醉的晚上 by 郁達夫 A returned student from Europe. He lives miserably but remains honest.

病夫 by 葉紹鈞 Sentiments of a writer who believes that he has T.B.

中年 by 沈從文 An author of mature age leaves Shanghai to go to Peking. The love affairs of the young, however, do not find him indifferent.

失散 by 趙景深 Quarrels of married people.

元蔭嫂的墓前 by 鄭振鐸 A husband who remains faithful to a wife who has died, even though her conduct was not irreproachable when she was alive.

分 by 謝冰心 The story of a new-born infant.

幽弦 by 黃廬隱 A curious story.

花之寺 by 凌叔華 A celebrated husband falls into a trap.

年前的一天 by 丁玲 Two writers who are married live in misery.

歸途 by 落華生 A gloomy tale.

扇子 by 施蟄存 Idyll between two students.

手指 by 穆時英 The martyrdom of women and girls engaged in winding silk from cocoons.

阿河 by 朱自清 The author takes an interest in a servant.

青松之下 by 王統照 The story of an unhappy girl student.

These stories are all written by famous authors and together they constitute some of the best work in contemporary literature. *May be read by mature people.*

968. 彩虹 *THE COLORFUL RAINBOW* 1 vol. 154 p. by various authors.

1928 上海泰東圖書局

First series of a collection of speeches, talks, short stories and poems by different authors. The exquisite stylistic quality of the collected material makes the book most enjoyable. *For all.*

969. 半日遊程 *HALF DAY'S TRIPS* 1 vol. 165 p. by various authors.

1934 上海良友圖書公司

A collection of short stories by different authors. Very superficial. Widely different style. *For informed readers.*

970. 貪官污吏傳   *CORRUPT OFFICIALS*   1 vol. 95 p. by various authors.
1936 宇宙風社

A collection of stories by different authors dealing with the multiple corrupt practices in the public service since the beginning of the Republic. *For all.*

971. 屠蘇 *NEW YEAR'S BEVERAGE*   1 vol. 199 p. by various auhors.
1926 光華書店

A collection of poems, essays and sketches by various authors.
Pagan outlook. *For informed readers.*

972. 星海 *CONSTELLATION*   1 vol. 266 p. by various authors.
1924 Commercial Press.

Selected passages chosen by well-known authors. *For everyone.*

973. 八年 *EIGHT YEARS*   1 vol. 126 p. by various authors.
1946 上海大華出版社

A young girl refugee amuses herself with a cat. Souvenirs of Chungking and Kunming. Street scenes. A young woman ceded to a third person. Patriotism drowned in a bottle of brandy. A city dweller returned to the country makes some reflections. The son of T'ien Han risks his life for the country. Particularities of Chungking. A few short stories follow. *For everyone.*

974. 三種船 *THREE TYPES OF BOAT*   1 vol. 340 y. by various authors.
1935 生海書店

A collection of stories in simple but pleasant style. Mostly descriptions of every day events. *For all.*

975. 中國近代短篇小說選 *AN ANTHOLOGY OF MODERN CHINESE SHORT STORIES*   by various authors.
1941 上海中英出版社

Short stories by Lu Yen, Pa Chin, Lu Hsün, Kuo Mo-jo, Yü Ta-fu, Chang T'ien-yi, Yeh Shao-chün, and Hsieh Ping-hsin, with English translation. *For all.*

976. 現代小說選 *AN ANTHOLOGY OF MODERN NOVELS*
1st. vol. by various authors.

A series of novels by well known authors. Some of these stories are harmless, from the moral point of view, as for instance the first and the second; the majority however can be read by·adults and *experienced people only.* As grounds for this decision, cf: pp. 43,. 58., 59., 73 among many others.

977. 現代小說選 *AN ANTHOLOGY OF MODERN NOVELS*
2nd vol. by various authors.

Another collection of stories taken from works of a number of great authors. They can be read *by all.* The following are worth reading: "Ku Hsiang" by Lu-Hsün and "Shui" by Ting Ling.

978. 灰色的鳥 *GREY BIRD*   1 vol. by various authors.
1928 創造社出版部

A collection of stories by seven authors. Mostly love stories, often morbid, occasionally verging on the immoral, especially those by Yü Ta-fu and Kuo Mo-jo. *Strict reserve.*

979. 闊 *RICHES*   1 vol. 163 p. by various authors.
                                           1941   奔流文藝叢刊社

1) A critical study on Pa Chin's trilogy, "Home", "Spring", and "Autumn".
2) What is happening in the next room.
3) Translation from the Russian. On the courage of a woman.
4) Village scenes. Contributions are demanded.
5) A parasite.
6) A play translated from the Russian.
            A man is cited as a witness in a law case. It is thought that he will not return.
They sell his goods and even dispose of his wife, when he suddenly comes back! *For
mature people.*

980. 淵 *ABYSS*   1 vol. 162 p. by various authors.
                                           1941   奔流文藝叢刊社

1) Reproaches against an old student who is conducting himself badly at the university.
2) A Japanese professor is invited.
3) Fleeing before the enemy. The story of an adopted brother.
4) A peddler reduced to misery.
5) An indomitable woman devotes herself to her country.
6) A one act play. About a loose and hysterical journalist. *For everyone.*

981. 汎 *THE FLOOD*   1 vol. 174 p. by various authors.
                                           1941   奔流文藝叢刊社

1) An unfaithful military telegraphist.
2) The soldiers in the military hospital are abandoned by the army and surrounded by
the enemy on three sides.
3) A professor who cannot maintain his family asks for a raise. Unacceptable propositions
are made to him. He is replaced, and falls into despair.
4) A police official under the Japanese. He is shown where his duty lies. He listens to
the counsel of his friend and quits his job.
5) A gentleman goes to Shanghai to engage in trade. His vexations.
6) A man who is considered a coward enlists as a volunteer.
7) A soldier who has lost his way is arrested.
8) Idyll on a boat.
For everyone.

982. 決 *FAREWELL*   1 vol. 197 p. by various authors.
                                           1941   奔流文藝叢刊社

            A collection of articles and stories.
1) An unhappy child.
2) A story laid in the Caucasus, by Tolstoy.
3) A student, who is the son of a traitor, enlists with the nationalist army.
4) Speculations on rice.
5) The election of Roosevelt.
For everyone.

983. 現代小說文庫第十六輯 *AN ANTHOLOGY OF MODERN NOVELS*
        (BOOK I)   1 vol. 218 p.
                                           上海更新出版社印行

p. 1 故鄉 by 魯迅 After a long absence the author returns to his native province.

Farewell to the paternal home.

p. 14   藥 by the above. A young tubercular takes medicine soaked in blood. He dies.

p. 42   人力以上 by 郭沫若 After a long period of study abroad, it is very difficult to get used to home again.

p. 70   人妖 by 郁達夫 A young convalescent goes for a walk against the advice of his mother. He follows a girl until he loses sight of her.

p. 107 銀 by 張資平 Chinese students in Japan.

p. 112 自殺 by 茅盾 A woman who has been betrayed commits suicide.

p. 140 病 by 許欽文 During an illness. . .

p. 157 蜜柑 by 沈從文 Meeting of male and female students.

p. 164 夫婦 by the above. A young couple give themselves up to demonstrations that are not for the public eye!

p. 178 離家的一年 by 冰心 A boy thirteen years old begins his studies. Successes and reverses.

p. 196 一對度蜜月去的人 by 胡也頻 A young married couple go on honeymoon to Hsi-hu. Unhappily they die in Shanghai.

For grown-up people.

984. 現代小說選二集 *AN ANTHOLOGY OF MODERN NOVELS (BOOK II)*
1 vol. 209 p.

芒夜 by 郁達夫 The hero leaves for a new post in the interior. His moral and amorous propensities.

故事 by the above. Very strange story.

by 魯迅 Chinese mythology.

鳳波 by the above. A story of the time of the beginning of the Republic.

愛的十字架 by 巴金 Farewell letter of a man who intends to commit suicide.

啞了的三弦琴 by 巴金 Visit to a prison in Siberia.

煩悶 by 冰心 A pessimistic student.

去國 by the above. Disillusion of a student returned from abroad. He goes away a second time.

牛 by 葉楚傖 Fable of a buffalo and agricultural instruments that fail in a rebellion.

鄉愁 by 滕固 A telegram saying that her lover has died in Japan. She marries another. The telegram was false, but what can be done about it? *For grown-up people.*

985. 現代中國散文選 *MODERN CHINESE ESSAYS* 2 vols. 511 p. by various authors.
1930 上海江南文藝社

Part. I. Articles of Hu Shih. The eminent Philosopher develops in them the ideas that are so dear to him. He shows himself under his true colours, positivist, materialist, and atheist. His ideas are dangerous, and moreover, out of date. *Not to be recommended to anyone.*

Part II. Descriptions by authors of literary distinction, and some letters of Yü Ta-fu. One description is of a deplorable crudity.

Proscribed.

986. 日記與遊記 *DIARIES & TRAVEL STORIES* 1 vol. 197 p. by various authors.
1937 啓明書局

A collection of souvenirs of journeys, and extracts from the individual diaries of several well-known contemporary writers.

魯迅 His diary has the characteristics of all his work. The style is flowing, cold and sarcastic. The reader does not know whether to laugh or to cry. He is always animated with the desire to reform society.

周作人 Works of the first period of the author in a very imaginative style.

胡適, 俞平伯, 朱自清 Journeys to Tsing-hui Ho.

郭沫若 Extracts from the life of the author in Japan.

郁達夫 Romanticism and pessimism. This writer has published a good many personal journal.

田漢 The life of the author in Japan and his love for his fiancee.

徐志摩 Notes on a journey in Siberia. Etc. Etc.

For everyone.

987. 模範遊記文選 *COLLECTED TRAVEL STORIES* 1 vol. 226 p. by various authors.

2nd. edit. 1937   光明書局

A selection, signed by the chief authors of China, of descriptions of model journeys. Their names alone are enough to guarantee the value of the book.

Nevertheless, if it is wished to use this collection as a textbook in our colleges or seminaries, some pages should be eliminated, not because they are too risky, but because they contain some rather wanton comparisons and images.

May be read by everyone.

988. 學生遊記文選 *SOME TRAVELLING SKETCHES WRITTEN BY STUDENTS*

1 vol. 102 p. 1943   北京書店

Descriptions and travel impressions culled from the works of the best writers. Modern style.

Its chief failing is that it does not quote the names of the authors.

Some of the expressions used are slightly shocking. *For everyone.*

989. 雪潮 *AVALANCHE BLAST*   1 vol. 157 p. by various authors.

Anthology of poems by well-known modern writers.

The poems date from the beginning of poetry written in the modern style. Their literary value, and especially their rhythm, are not remarkable, although often the ideas retrieve somewhat the defective form.

Some of the poems are rather crude. *For mature readers.*

990. 現代十六家小品 *SHORT PIECES BY SIXTEEN CONTEMPORARY AUTHORS*

1 vol. 490 p. 1934

Most of the articles collected here are occasional essays written for literary reviews. They are short, without much significance, and only in rare instances representative of the author.

周作人 Three prefaces and several nice compositions that are rather banal in character.

俞平伯 Two prefaces and some descriptions. About the moon that reminds him of a dead friend. A melancholy essay on shattered love.

朱自清 A discussion on modern literary movements. Recollections of a voyage with Yui P'ing-po on the river near Nanking.

白種人 A sarcastic essay on the pretentions of Europeans. Difficulties of too early marriage.

鍾敬文 Literary essays on Nature and her poets.

蘇美 Descriptions of Nature of which the first is full of melancholy.

茅盾 Literary essays and impressions of the theatre — nothing characteristic.

落華生 Short tales, one on the origin of his name.

郭沫若 Some liberties in the last article.

郁達夫　Essays full of melancholy, especially the one about the death of his son.

魯迅　The only author whose personality is reflected in the slightest and who is always seeking to instruct or influence the reader. In the essays included here the humour and sarcasm are directed against his compatriots.

The rest is banal.

For everyone except the story by Kuo Mo-jo.

991. 月光下　*IN THE MOONLIGHT*　　　　1 vol. by various authors.
1946　建國書局

1) Vexations and despair of a friend. Help is given him and his wife gives him good advice.

2) Women of the resistance during the Japanese occupation.

3) A guerilla leader in Mongolia who became a national hero during the Sino-Japanese war.

4) A member of the Korean resistance. He leaves his mother to revenge himself upon the Japanese. Ten years later, he returns to see his mother and the day after, she dies.

5) Patriotism of a young man of Dairen.

For everyone.

992. 小花　*SMALL BLOSSOMS*　　　　1 vol. 137 p. 中學生社編
2nd. edit. 1940　開明書店

A collection of popular narratives. Those of Chin-yi and Pa-Ching are especially remarkable. *For everyone.*

993. 沒有光的星　*STARS THAT SHINE NOT*　　1 vol. from p. 553 to 738
by various authors.
1945　新民印書館

1. Fickle moods of a melancholy young man. *For all.*

2. A passionate love story. *For all.*

3. Another love story. *Not for everyone.*

4. The free life of cinema stars. *Not for everyone.*

994. 新進作家小說選　*AN ANTHOLOGY OF NEW NOVELISTS*　　1 vol. 213 p.
by various authors.
中華書局

A series of stories of which the common theme is the sufferings of the people. Different authors describe to us in tragic fashion the miseries occasioned by a flood and the unscrupulousness of a compradore. Other stories tell of family rivalries and jealousies between step-mothers and step-daughters. Still others show us the sufferings of the unemployed, the vexations caused by landlords, and the extremes to which the best people are sometimes driven.

Although the book contains enough bitterness, we believe, nevertheless, that it may be read by everyone. *For everyone.*

995. 中篇小說集　*A COLLECTION OF MIDDLE-LENGTH SHORT STORIES*
1 vol. 198 p. by various authors.
Coll. 1941　華龍印書館

1. A good girl, forced by her mother, is seduced by a rich man. In despair she commits suicide. Her fiancé remains faithful to her.

2. Dream of an unhappy girl.

3. The agitated life of a woman who is deceived.

4. Story of a drunkard.

These stories are well written and interesting but the subject matter is sometimes of a nature liable to trouble young imaginations. *For mature people.*

996. 學生時代 *SCHOOL DAYS* 1 vol. 168 p. by various authors.
1942 益文印刷局

The accounts of various celebrities of their student years. By Lu Hsün, Mao Tun, Hu Shih, etc. *For everyone.*

997. 十三作家短篇名作集 *SHORT MASTERPIECES OF THIRTEEN AUTHORS*
1942 新民印書館

A collection of thirteen short stories by young writers of whom only the first shows any talent. The book was published under the Japanese occupation and is necessarily deprived of any serious subject. It contains nothing but sentimental stories without moral elevation. It reflects the temporary conditions in which it appeared. *Not to be recommended to anyone.*

998. 中華童話 Booklets for children edited by 中華書局

This list is incomplete.

1) 沙淑敵 A recital of battles. *For everyone.*
5) 滎陽城 A war episode at the beginning of the Han Dynasty. *For everyone.*
7) 血書衣 A law case under the Impress Wu of the Tang Dynasty. *For everyone.*
9) 無頭箭 A strategy of war. *For everyone.*
10) 函谷關 A minister is rewarded for his charity towards the unfortunate. *For everyone.*
12) 炭煮飯 A buddhist monk gives a lesson to a rich glutton. *For everyone.*
14) 狐中毒 A child succeeds in killing two wolf-ghosts that haunted his home. *For everyone.*
20) 癡人福 A little idiot keeps on talking so foolishly to a girl who has been dumb since birth that he makes her laugh. (We are given the details of her birth). In the end the foolish boy's tricks draw speech from the girl, so that she learns how to talk, and he receives a thousand dollars as a reward. *For everyone.*
23) 移山力 Heaven helps an obstinate man to move a mountain. *For everyone.*
24) 神道碑 The story of two ministers who are jealous of each other. *For everyone.*
26) 紅燭淚 A prince, who is travelling with his concubines and servants, is robbed. The robbers are found due to a ruse on the part of a maid servant. *Not for everyone.*
27) 千金恨 Of a mandarin who loves nothing but money. *For everyone.*
28) 江東橋 An episode in the wars that put the Mings on the throne. *For everyone.*
30) 玉面貓 The fidelity between the master and his cat. The master is given a beautiful girl in exchange for his cat. *Not for everyone.*

999. 世界童話 Booklets edited by 中華書局

This list is incomplete.

1) 二王子 How a Russian prince found a princess to marry. Marvels without any head or tail. *For everyone.*
3) 法螺君 The marvellous adventures of the Baron Crack told by himself. *For everyone.*
4) 驢公主 The princess runs away to escape marrying her foster father. She finds a prince charming. A fairy story. *For everyone.*
5) 鐵王子 The adventures through which an urchin delivers his brothers and sisters from dragons. *For everyone.*

6) 夢三郎　A boy delivers a princess and marries her. *Not for everyone.*

7) 指環魔　How a poor boy succeeds in marrying a princess due to his charitable acts and a magic ring. *For everyone.*

8) 卜人子　The animals help their benefactor who ends in becoming king and marrying a princess. *For everyone.*

9) 驚人談　Charlemagne and Roland go to fight the Saracens out of pride. They pass by 愛爾柴輪 which is a 寺院 of the 基督教 where 上帝 is adored. The superior, 僧正 gives the king as gifts the handkerchief of Christ, the hat that He wore before His death, a nail from His feet, the knife and plate which Christ used in eating, and a hair from St. Peter's beard. There is an image that represents the pope with a tiara on his head anointing Charlemagne. Due to these holy emblems, the army walks through a lake dryshod and Charles cures a blind man and a dumb man. Then they arrive in Constantinople where the king of the Turks entertains them to a dinner of surprises, after which the warriors forget to sleep telling of their exploits, and exaggerating them to an incredible degree. Roland says: "I can blow so hard that my breath will uproot trees" etc. After the Turkish king has heard everything he forces the boasters to make a demonstration of their power. The warriors, however, come off with flying colours, for they do everything as they have said. Having observed their magic power, the Turkish king submits to them and Charlemagne builds a big church in Paris for the veneration of his relics. This mass of nonsense should not be given to children to read. *Not for everyone.*

10) 大洪水　In order to avoid giving his daughter to the pagoda, a father slays the guardian of the mountain. *For everyone.*

11) 幸禍花　A poor young man delivers three princesses through magic means and marries one of them. *For everyone.*

13) 黃金船　A young man steals a flying boat and goes for a joy ride with a young lady who steals it in her turn. The young man punishes her, then changes his mind and marries her instead. *For everyone.*

14) 黎伯爵　The story of "puss-in-boots". A fox helps a poor fool to marry the daughter of a rich man . *For everyone.*

15) 黑足童　A young man marries a princess because he understands the language of beasts. *For everyone.*

16) 大食童　The hero calls for meat directly he is born. In order to obtain food, he steals, lies and kills, and plays practical jokes, but in the end, he reforms. *For everyone.*

17) 三孃題　Three brothers quarrel over one girl. One gets her, and another has adventures that make him forget his two brothers. *For everyone.*

18) 雪中牙　A bear gets hold of a talkative girl whom he keeps secretly for a year. *For everyone.*

19) 龍宮使　An admirable little tale that consoles one for the nonsense in the others. *For everyone.*

20) 林中女　A pretty tale, although it contains images that are rather indecently exposed. *For everyone.*

22) 小人鼻　A boy is tranformed into a monster by a wizard. He gains his original shape and saves a princess from the same predicament. *For everyone.*

23) 夜光劍　A gambler wins a princess at gambling. She cures him of his bad habit. *For everyone.*

24) 小獵師　The adventures of a young hunter. He delivers a princess from bad dragons, who becomes the ruler. *For everyone.*

26) 搖動笛　A boy makes a princess laugh through his magic power, and is rewarded for it. *For everyone.*

27) 金色鳥　A young man with a magic horse delivers a princess and marries her. *For everyone.*

30) 惡戲術　The jokes of a poker. *For everyone.*

31) 木馬談　Story of the Trojan horse. Princesses and concubines are taken away into captivity. *For everyone.*

44) 薔薇姬　A nobleman wishes to marry a princess who rejects him. He transforms himself into a petal and is eaten by the young lady who thereby conceives a girl, etc. Incomprehensible to children. *Not for everyone.*

45) 九傀儡　The ninth statue that a young man has to find is a beautiful girl for him to marry. *For everyone.*

46) 金髮姬　Three animals that have been saved by a young man help him in his matrimonial projects. *For everyone.*

1000.　文學, 一週紀念號, 第三卷, 第一號

1934　生活書店

A collection of tales and romances that cannot be recommended to young people because of indecent passages that it contains, and because of dangerous ideas. *Not to be recommended to anyone.*

SOME FICTION WITH NAME OF AUTHORS LACKING.

1001.　父子之間　*BEFORE FATHER AND SON.*

1 vol. 304 p.
1935　良友圖書公司

1) The younger son is a good for nothing in open disagreement with his father. One day, he departs for the front where he is killed.

2) The son follows the example of his father, an inveterate gambler and an opium smoker. He steals from his parents from which family quarrels arise.

3) Flirting between two young emancipated people. A quarrel and a reconciliation.

4) A farce with soldiers.

For everyone.

1002.　雨夜槍聲　*REPORT OF GUNS*

1 vol. 230 p.
1946

An absolutely Chinese detective story. A very successful attempt at this kind of writing. A synopsis is not given as it would detract from the pleasure of reading the book itself. *For everyone.*

1003.　稚瑩　*CHIH YING*

1 vol. 386 p.

The heroine who is an only daughter and rich has a weakness for her cousin. The father of the latter opposes their betrothal and seeks out another party for his son. In the meantime the girl has become attached to another young man. Nevertheless she is engaged to her cousin whom she no longer loves. When, however, she learns that her cousin wishes to marry another person, she takes advantage of this situation to separate from him. Thus the happiness of the four persons concerned is secured. *For everyone.*

1004. 姊妹花 *SISTERS*   1 vol. 84 p.
                                                    3rd edit. 東方書店

Relates the sufferings of a family driven out of their home by bandits. The interest of the story lies in the fact that it features real life. *For informed readers.*

1005. 迷惘 *CONFUSED*   1 vol. 155 p.
                                                           益智書局

Describes the love of a student; a pure and steady love bearing the promise of a happy marriage. Unfortunately the girl marries a friend of the hero. At the end this friend acknowledges that he wronged his friend. But that does not quite satisfy our hero.

Although no objection can be raised against anything written in the book, it must be reserved *to informed readers* because its atmosphere will upset younger imaginations.

1006. 愛的代價 *THE PRICE FOR LOVE*   1 vol. 261 p.
                                                            Moukden

After having had an affair with a film-star, Huang Leng-chiu marries and makes a living writing. His wife is inconstant and stops loving him. He leaves his home that she may be free.

Soon two girls, one rich, one poor, show interest in him. They travel with him, stay in Chinan and Shanghai. There he runs into the film star who manages to embezzle a lot of his money.

The author has endowed the hero and the two girls with a very pleasant disposition and keeps the reader in constant suspense as to which of the two girls will be preferred. Towards the end of the book the group returns to Peiping where Leng-chiu divorces his wife. The rich girl steps aside so that his love for the poor girl may have its course.

A very interesting book, the only objection being that the author seems to approve of divorce. *For informed readers.*

1007. 鴛鴦夢 *DREAM OF THE TURTLE DOVES*   1 vol. 114 p.
                                                        上海新文化書社

A young litterati who is very handsome, and his two friends make the acquaintance of some beautiful women. The hero then meets some more ladies who are educated and beautiful.

The book contains some obscene passages and therefore should be forbidden to young people. *Proscribed.*

1008. 紅燈籠 *RED LANTERN*   1 vol. 238 p.
                                                              1937

1) An unhappy poor man sees a passenger go past in the night carrying a red lantern. Pushed by his poverty, he kills the man and robbs him. In the morning he perceives that he has killed his son who had come to save him from his misery.

2) Some boatmen are surprised by three soldiers who rob them and abuse the wife of the chief boatman. In despair, he lets the boat crash on a rock and the whole family perishes.

3) Women will always be a mystery. The hero waits for a lady friend who does not come. The one he calls in to fill the gap absorbs the refreshments that have been prepared, then furnished with a good sum, abandons him to look for her own friend.

4) The painful separation of two Chinese friends in New York.

5) A Chinese who has returned from America receives a visit from an old American friend. He confesses that his life at the present moment is like being in a prison with gold bars.

6) A little girl who is maltreated by her stepmother runs away. She passes her nights in the moonlight, until discovered by the police, she is placed in a good home.

7) The memories of a professor. He sees again two old students of his who had been friends. One was locked up by the police as a communist, and the other did not leap into the breach for his friend.

8) A lover's quarrel, about Chinese in America. They quarrel, then they sulk, but in the end they make it up.

9) A famous man retires but he is not serious about it and does not persevere.

10) A quarrel between children that finishes badly.

11) Maternal love akin to madness.

12) A writer divorces his old fashioned wife and marries something more modern, but he lives to regret it when it is too late.

13) A grandmother gives advice to her grandson who is taking things to his father in prison.

14) Breaking into a shop with a tragic end.

For everyone.

1009. 毀滅 *DESTRUCTION*   1 vol. 176 p.

益智書局

A very ordinary love story mixed up with unedifying details. *For adults.*

1010. 紅粉飄零 *TOSSED BY FATE*   1 vol. 126 p.

上海北方書局

A doctor falls in love with a girl student named Shu-min who loves him in return, but on his avowal tells him that she has been betrothed since a tender age.

The girl student is recalled by her parents to be married and is very unhappy over the affair. Her husband, it so happens, also cherishes the lively memory of another love. After a scene in which Shu-min guesses this secret, she runs away and they separate.

The heroine, who has regained her freedom, then learns that the rejected doctor has committed suicide in despair, jumping into the sea during a voyage to Japan.

Overcome with unhappiness, Shu-min becomes a buddhist nun.

As the author does not approve of either the divorce or the suicide in his story, we see no reason to place reservations on this book. *May be read by anyone.*

1011. 春夢 *DREAM IN SPRING*   1946, 1 vol. 83 p.

The unhealthy and lovesick lucubrations of a poor married man who remembers a girl who has forsaken him.

The author approves of free-love and divorce. The book is full of nonsense. *Not to be recommended to anyone.*

1012. 恐怖 *TERROR*   1 vol. 151 p.

1928

踐踏: Luxuries of the rich and hardships of the poor. Strikes.

恐怖: Labourers revolt against capitalistic oppression. The army is called upon to disperse the rioters.

我在懺悔： Letters in which bolshevism is preached.
夜話： On being fired a factory-hand is approached by socialists, fomenting strikes.
從上海到蘇州： A batch of workmen arrested for striking.
    A revolutionary book; improper language.

1013. 收穫 *THE HARVEST*   1 vol. 155 p.
                                        1937   生活書店

    Two novels. In one the hero is a workman who flies the red flag over his chimney. In the other, the Japanese occupation is the subject.
    Nine letters of Lu Hsün written during his last illness.
    Poems.
    Six articles on politics and literary usages.
    A few souvenirs and anecdotes.
    Dissertation on the campaign of 1924-26.
    Analysis of a book by Ai Ssu-ch'i.
For everyone.

Miscellaneous

ESSAYS, POEMS, DIARIES, TRAVELS,
BIOGRAPHIES, LETTERS, ETC.

1014. 靈飛集　*LING FEI*　　　　　1 vol. 140 p. by 張次溪
　　　　　　　　　　　　　1939　北京印刷廠　*See Biogr. 14*

A collection of documents relating the story of a famous prostitute of the Boxer period, when Peiping was occupied by the allied troops.
　　The book in itself is not bad, but being a story of a prostitute-heroine, it is better not to put it into the hands of those who do not know the story. *The book gives the impression of glorifying debauchery.*

1015. 關於丁玲　*ABOUT TING LING*　　　　　by 張惟夫
　　　　　　　　　　　　　　　　　　　　　　1933

Review and criticism of the life and work of Ting Ling: incomplete, superficial, and biassed. *For everyone.*

1016. 新傳統　*THE NEW TRADITION*　　　1 vol. 334 p. by 趙家璧
　　　　　　　　　　　　　1936　良友圖書公司　*See Biogr. 15*

History of the novel in the U.S.A. from the civil war until 1914. *For everyone.*

1017. 小妹　*YOUNG GIRL*　　　　　1 vol. 125 p. by 趙景深
　　　　　　　　　　　　　1933　北新書局　*See Biogr. 16*

A little sketch. Then lengthy prattle about the author himself, his studies, his books, his biography, his marriages, his relations, his preference in literature. To end up, a study of the caricaturist, Max Beerbohm. *For everyone.*

1018. 青年日記　*DIARY OF A YOUTH*　　1 vol. 238 p. by 趙景深
　　　　　　　　　　　　　1937　上海北新書局

Selected essays gathered from a competition organized in 1934 by the review "Ch'ing Nien Chieh". The theme was a "Vacation Diary". The first essay is especially remarkable. *For everyone.*

1019. 文人翦影　*PROFILES OF LITERARY MEN*　　1 vol. 122 p. by 趙景深
　　　　　　　　　　　　　　　　　　　　　　北新書局

The author of this book had many connections with other authors of Young China. This little book contains recollections of their friendship, little souvenirs and anecdotes;

physical, moral and literary characteristics of forty-four authors. For example : Mao Tun is of small stature and is a good translator, : Yeh Shao-chün, an ardent worker and a serious man, was a good host, etc. *For everyone.*

1020. 歐行日記 *TRIP TO EUROPE*   1 vol. 124 p. by **鄭振鐸**
1924   上海良友圖書公司   *See Biogr. 27*

Travelling diary. The author describes for his wife, his impressions during his voyage to and his stay in France. *For everyone.*

1021. 兩棲集 *AMPHIBIOUS*   1 vol. 248 p. by **鄭伯奇**
1937   良友   *See Biogr. 28*

Criticisms on literature & authors; nine letters on novels, translations, etc. Criticisms on movie pictures & filmstars. *For everyone.*

1022. 自己描寫 *SELF DESCRIPTION*   1 vol. 226 p. by **徵文當**
1935   開明書店

A collection of extracts from papers managed by students. Interesting because they expose the mentality of young people of a few years ago. The interest of these extracts, however, is not even throughout. *For everyone.*

1023. 爾都集   1 vol. 261 by **紀果庵**
1944   太平書局

29 articles on the society, family, food, etc. etc. *For everyone.*

1024. 華髮集 *BEAUTIFUL HAIRDRESS*   1 vol. 166 p. by **周黎庵**
1940   蔚溪書屋

Articles from journals giving appraisals of authors, personalities, and events. *For everyone.*

1025. 夜讀抄 *FROM NIGHT READINGS*   1 vol. 313 p. by **周作人**
1934   北新書局   *See Biogr. 40*

Review of a whole series of books, Chinese, European, and Japanese.
Themes very diverse : customs and myths, cries of little hawkers, Greek mythology, etc. . . .
   Two themes are quite improper: a case of the alternation of sex of a Danish woman and the psychology of passion; quotations in which bestiality is called inoffensive. Nevertheless none of the descriptions is immoral. Finally all kinds of essays : about a clock, about eunuchs, etc. . The style is good but difficult.

1026. 藝術與生活 *OF ART AND LIFE*   1 vol. 468 p. by **周作人**
3rd. edit. 1940   中華書局

Dissertations on Chinese literature. The author recommends to his readers a number of Chinese, Russian, and Japanese stories. And at the end of the book, he is found in ecstasies before a village built upon communist ideals.
   The author understands nothing about biblical inspiration and puts the Bible on the same footing as mythology. *Not for everyone.*

1027. 過去的生命   *LIFE THAT IS PAST*   128 p. by   周作人
                                                        1933   北新書局

Forty poems and short essays, mostly occasional pieces and sketches. The collected material reveals great poetical charm and literary value. *For all.*

1028. 苦茶隨筆   *OF THE SAVOUR OF TEA*   1 vol. 345 p. by   周作人
                                                        1935   北新書局

   A collection of literary criticisms, prefaces and postscripts to various works. Also included are the memories of the last moments of two of the author's friends, 劉復 and 馬隅鄉. *For everyone.*

1029. 風雨談   *MIDST WIND & RAIN*   1 vol. 265 p. by   周作人
                                                        1936   北新書局

   Essays on various subjects and dissertations on authors and literary works. *For everyone.*

1030. 苦竹雜記   *SIMPLENESS IN TASTE*   1 vol. 313 p. by   周作人
                                                        1936   良友圖書公司

   Various essays mainly on literary subjects, written in agreeable style and containing interesting literary criticisms. *For everyone.*

1031. 瓜豆集   *SILENT BEAUTIES*   1 vol. 302 p. by   周作人
                                                        1937   宇宙風社

   Chou Tso-jen presents us here with about thirty sketches. The subjects dealt with have been furnished by his personel reading. Sometimes it is a word, sometimes an idea that attracts his attention. His reflections are not profound. What pleases the Chinese reader the most is his play on words or on the tones of the characters in question.
   Here are some of the subjects dealt with : devils, virginity, green peas. He also mentions his brother, Lu Hsün.
   The syle of the book is stiff, and official in tone. While Lu Hsün, and the "Young China" has adopted "pei-hua", Chou Tso-jen has clung to a style that is rather difficult to understand. *For everyone.*

1032. 藥味集   *WITH BITTER TASTE*   1 vol. 254 p. by   周作人
                                                        1942   新民印書館

   Twenty-two essays in good style, but rather difficult.
   Short articles on several Chinese and Japanese authors. Sketches on the custom of throwing little peas (a Japanese superstition), also some sketches on Japanese customs, habits etc, which please the author. *For all readers.*

1033. 秉燭後談   *TALKS UNDER CANDLELIGHT*   1 vol. 173 p. by   周作人
                                                        1944   新民印書館

   Of events of the moment and souvenirs. Surveys of reviews and magazines. *For mature people.*

1034. 周作人代表作   *AN ANTHOLOGY OF CHOU TSO-JEN*

258 p.   **現代作家選集**

Peking 1941   三通書局

Also essays on literary subjects written in good style. *For everyone.*

1035. 石門集 *STONE GATE*   1 vol. 196 p. by   **朱　湘**

2nd. edit. 1935 Commercial Press.   商務印書館   *See Biogr. 43*

This collection contains a short play presenting a case of metempsychosis, a poem in free verse, and poems in modern style telling of the intimate sentiments of the author towards Nature and Men. He excells in psychological analysis and is able in a few touches, of sketching the various stages of a sentiment. A great number of the poems reflect the severe judgement of the author on himself and on others.

He believes in God and invokes Him with respect. He describes occasionally the struggle of the soul to dominate the animal nature of man. His poems are full of rhythm.

The high literary value of several of the poems and the nature of the sentiments described, such as deception, love, melancholy, oblige us to reserve this book for adults. *Not for everyone.*

1036. 海外奇霓君 *WRITTEN FROM FOREIGN LAND*   1 vol. 156 p. by   **朱　湘**

1934   北新書局

This book consists of the letters written by the author to his wife, while he was working for his doctor's degree in America. In them he shows a great attachment to his wife and two little children. Full of solicitude for his family, he sends money regularly, is interested in their health and in all the details of their daily life.

We are also given many details of life in America, and the remarks made about the Americans are also interesting to foreigners. *For everyone.*

1037. 孟實文鈔   *WORKS OF MENG-SHIH*   1 vol. 208 p. by   **朱光晉**

1936   良友文學叢書   *See Biogr. 44*

Literary studies, mostly on poetry. *For everyone.*

1038. 你我 *JUST YOU & I*   1 vol. 244 p. by   **朱自清**

1936   商務印書館   *See Biogr. 46*

A number of selected pieces followed by very interesting criticisms and comments.
Useful for gaining an acquaintance with some of the good writers of the   文學研究會
For everyone.

1039. 西太后列紀   *ANECDOTES ABOUT THE EMPRESS DOWAGER*

1 vol. 107 p. by   **菊　華**

1940   國民書店

The history of the Empress Ts'i Hsi. It is presented by the author in the manner of foreign writers. *For everyone.*

1040. 水邊 *WATERSIDE*   1 vol. 105 p. by   **廢名 (馮文炳)**

1944   新民印書館   *See Biogr. 57*

Impressionistic poetry. Embellishments on Nature. Natural and simple but not very lyric. *For everyone.*

1041. 浪花 *SURF*   1 vol. 217 p. by G. F. 女士
1927 北新書局

A collection of poems of which one part was written while she was still a student. These poems date from the first attempts at poetry in pei-hua. They are almost without rhythm, and they are of very mediocre value. The other part consists of translations of short poems from various foreign poets, Carlyle, Coleridge, Blake, Tennyson, and many others. These translations do not reveal the poetry of the original. *For everyone.*

1042. 還鄉日記 *GOING BACK TO MY HOME TOWN*   1 vol. 94 p. by 何其芳
1939 上海良友復興圖書公司 *See Biogr.* 59

A small collection of literary essays in which we are presented with the deductions of the author on literature, a journey, a road, a sub-prefecture, life in the country, etc. *For everyone.*

1043. 模範散文選註 *AN ANTHOLOGY OF BEST ESSAYS*   coll. by 何光霽
1 vol. 318 p. 光明書店

Essays by classic authors for use in schools.
Part. I. Dissertations on modern ideas, literature etc.
Part. II. Discussions on education, youth etc.
Part. III. Narratives, descriptions, travels etc.
For everyone.

1044. 平屋雜文 *PROSE*   1 vol. 184 p. by 夏丏尊
1935 開明書店 *See Biogr.* 62

This work is a collection of narratives, sometimes humorous, but very often based on irony. It also contains personal memories, account of actual happenings, reflections on actualities, and some prefaces originally written for other works. Most of the pieces in this collection are derived from the review 中學生 and therefore are suitable for students of middle schools. The author is an example of a writer who finished his studies at the end of the old regime, but who is entirely modern in both style and ideas. *For everyone.*

1045. 文心 *INSTRUCTIONS ON WRITING COMPOSITIONS*
1 vol. 272 p. by 夏丏尊 & 葉聖陶
1934 開明書店

Studies of style under the form of little narratives. The object of the authors is to draw the attention of students to everything that is useful in the study of language. *To be recommended to everyone,* especially to professors.

1046. 現代遊記文選 *SELECTION OF TRAVEL STORIES*   put together by: 笑我

1. An excursion to the mountains.
2. Another excursion to the mountains.
3. A few days in Hsuchow.
4. A trip in the snow-covered mountains.
5. The Hsi-Hu and its neighbourhood.
6. A train journey.
7. After reading this one feels glad not to live in Nanking.
8. Shanghai forever!
9. Trip to Hsuchow; the meeting of good soldiers and patriots.
10. Return home. . . dinners in the magistrate's office.
11. Market day.
12. Impressions of the Hsi-Hu. Social problems.

13. A trip to the mountains and lakes. Meeting Europeans in all places.	fakirs.
14. Pa Chin's ecstasies on Nature.	22. Colombo, Venice, Florence, and Rome.
15. Beauty here and there.	23. Through Siberia.
16. Rivers, mountains and lakes.	24. A fine article on Japan.
17. Descriptions of Nature.	25. Excursion to Japan.
18. Historical mountains.	26. A trip to the mountains of Japan.
19. Views of Ceylon.	27. Again about Japan
20. Westminster Abbey.	28. Journey in France.
21. Harbin, U.S.A. and its automobiles; *For everyone.*	29. Berlin.
	30. New York.

1047. 冰心詩集 *POEMS BY PING-HSIN*　　1 vol. 315 p. by **謝冰心 (謝婉瑩)**
1933　北新書局　*See Biogr. 69*

This collection of poems is characteristic of the manner of the author. The subjects dealt with, the descriptions of Nature that it contains, and the sentiments expressed are full of charm although sometimes rather affected. It is poetry of the elite that rarely reflects the struggles and problems of the actual world. *For everyone.*

1048. 志摩日記 *CHIH-MO'S DIARY*　　　　　　1 vol. 236 p.
1947　晨光出版公司印行　*See Biogr. 72*

愛眉小札 and 小曼日記 cf. works by Hsiü Chih-mo.
一本沒有顏色的書 Drawings and texts presented to the author and his wife.
西湖記 The author's diary from September 7th 18 to October 28th of the same year. He tells us about his vacation on the well-known lake. His diary is well written. Students from middle-schools, and universities will gain great advantage from reading these pages.
眉軒瑣語 The author's diary written during the first months of his marriage. *For adults.*

1049. 現代中國女作家 *CONTEMPORARY WOMEN WRITERS IN CHINA*
by **黃 英**
1931　北新書局　*See Biogr. 82*

A literary and critical study of the most prominent authoresses that have appeared recently. An interesting book for students of literature, but to be read *with reserve* because of the point of view of the author.

1050. 中國小說的起源及其演變　　　　1 vol. 132 p. by **胡 適**
1934　上海正中書局

On Chinese Fiction. *For everyone.*

1051. 參差集　　　　　　　　1 vol. 266 p. by **侍桁 (韓侍桁)**
1936　良友

Literary criticism. *For everyone.*

1052. 民眾戲劇概論 *ON POPULAR PLAYS*　　1 vol. 254 p. **谷劍塵編**
1933　民智書局

A historical manual on both the Chinese and the foreign theatre. *For everyone.*

1053. 創造十年 *A DECADE OF WRITING*　　1 vol. 272 p. by 郭沫若
1933　現代書局 *See Biogr. 96*

Autobiography and activities of the author during the years 1918-24.
Interesting in connection with the study of contemporary Chinese literature. *For everyone.*

1054. 我的幼年 *MY CHILDHOOD*　　1930 by 郭沫若

This is the first volume of Kuo Mo-jo's autobiographical writings. He recalls memories of his childhood until the age of 16 (1893-1909). He already appears to be a rebel, opposed to authority. Turned away from school in Chiating, his native town in Szechwan, he departed thence to Chengtu. *Not to be recommended to young people.*

1055. 反正前後 *ANYWAY*　　1 vol. 213 p. by 郭沫若
1931　現代書局

Kuo Mo-jo traces the history of the revolution in Szechwan with which he was intimately connected. He tells us of several interesting episodes. *For everyone.*

1056. 沫若詩集 *POEMS*　　1 vol. 360 p. by 郭沫若
1936　上海復光書店

This book presents rather sentimental and sensual poetry. The author shows himself capable of poetic fervor. This book can be read, under the guidance of a serious teacher, by the students of "Kao-chung".
It would be very useful if some passages were excised before the book is used by students. *Very objectionable.*

1057. 北伐途次 *NORTHERN EXPEDITION*　　1 vol. 170 p. by 郭沫若
1937　潮鋒出版社

The author gives us a historical account in this book of the siege of Wuchang in 1926. *For everyone.*

1058. 怎樣解決你的婚姻 *YOUR MARRIAGE PROBLEM* 1 vol. 247 p. by 李　復
1944　大陸書店

Miss Li has a correspondence column in a magazine. The young who have marriage troubles or other difficulties present their cases to her and she gives her answer. This book is a real study of morals in contemporary China.
All sorts of cases are dealt with, ill assorted marriages, love affairs, abandoned mothers, triangular complications, cases of ill-treatment by the husband, etc. etc.
The answers indicate the legal measures that may be taken to solve the various cases. The consultant tends towards modern solutions, love above all, and easy divorce.
The book evidently cannot serve as a guide for Catholics. Nevertheless it is interesting to those who speculate on morals. *All should be dissuaded from it.*

1059. 偏見集　　1 vol. 304 p. by 梁實秋
1934　正中書局 *See Biogr. 105*

The whole book is about literature. According to the author, there is no revolutionary literature. Class struggle has no place in literature. According to him, poetry should serve to express the aspirations and sentiments of the people.
He also deals with some particular literary problems.
A thoughtful and serious study. *For everyone.*

1060. 遠人集 *BONNIE FAR AWAY*   1 vol. 187 p. by 林 榕
                                                                  1943 新民印書館

Essays on various subjects, Nature, flowers, trees, etc. Also poetic descriptions. *For everyone.*

1061. 孔子之學 *WISDOM OF CONFUCIUS*
                              1 vol. 67 p. Chinese & English text by 林語堂
                                     上海一流書店社 *See Biogr. 106*

This book is recommended to foreigners who want to study Confucianism, or at least to acquire some notion of Confucius' career, doctrine and influence. The author is criticised by many for his interpretation of the texts. He shows us in this book his stand with regard to Confucianism. He respects it as a human culture and as the foundation of social life, and considers it powerful enough to withstand Communism, or rather to change it if it takes root in China. As a political system, advocating the restoration of a feudal regime, he thinks that Confucianism is antiquated. According to his point of view, the greatest rival of Confucianism in China is not Christianity but western thought and activity. *For informed readers.*

1062. 吾國與吾民 *MY COUNTRY AND MY PEOPLE*   2 vol. 464 p. by 林語堂
                                                                  1939 光明書局

This book contains some fine pages in simple and pleasant style. It is also an instructive book which gives a better knowledge of China and the Chinese, makes us respect their qualities, and be indulgent to their shortcomings. These pages also introduce us to the intellect of modern pagans, official classes and new students. The author appears to be a spectator with a materialistic point of view, who is satisfied with the present moment, likes his leisure, and finds pleasure in little joys which life provides for us. He avoids thinking about the big problems of life and takes nothing seriously. Lin Yü-t'ang is persuaded that "In the Chinese Christians" (p. 129) there do not exist the necessary qualities to make good, which shows that, though he was capable of composing a good-sized book, he knows nothing or almost nothing of the history of Catholicism in China and that he judges his fellow countrymen after his own sensual outlook. Mr. Wu Ching-hsiung, a doctor of Law and a man of judicious character, a personal friend of Lin Yü-t'ang as well as codirector of the "T'ien-Hsia Monthly" says in his commentary on this book: "After pointing out as the dominant quality of the Chinese character "the supremacy of the human mind" (p. 77), Dr. Lin throws out near the close of the book a bold challenge: "Whoever said that the Chinese civilization is a spiritual civilization is a liar" (p. 344). T'ien-Hsia Monthly Vol. 1 1935 p. 471.
This book should be read with great prudence:
1) Owing to the materialistic atmosphere.
2) Owing to Lin Yü-t'ang's attitude towards religion.
3) Owing to his theories on marriage.
It is not to be recommended to anybody.

1063. 生活的藝術 *"THE IMPORTANCE OF LIVING"*   by 林語堂

This book intends to show that man must return to nature. Man's image has been deformed by scholars, scientists, theologians, sociologists, etc. The author arrives at the conclusion that man is a puzzle. According to Lin Yü-t'ang, men took the wrong road to happiness, for they were blinded by power, wealth and glory. These only complicate life. Man's restlessness is the source of all misfortune. The author advises us to go back to nature and its simplicity. "Dolce farniente" is our true religion. Dr. Lin then describes his ideal of human life : — it is a mixture of "Taoism, Confucianism and modern materialism." In one place he says "Life is a joke". Let's take advantage of the little pleasure that it gives us. "The importance of living" is a bad book. The materialistic ideas are put forward as a thesis and then developed throughout the book. The author laughs at "Dogma" and tries to make the whole structure of Catholic theology look ridiculous. He takes his stand in front of religion like a judge in front of a prisoner.

There is nothing settled or systematical in the book. The author merely puts forward his "opinions", that is : a lot of ideas on various topics. He is superficial and avoids the difficulties he dares not confront. His literature is cheap wit and he knows that he is successful only in the eyes of surfeited American materialists. He makes an impression of one who is composing an Encyclopedia of the "objections against religion". Let us not be too hard on his swelled head. According to Catholic belief, unbelievers and even the persecutors of religion can obtain grace. "God loves me so much that he will not condemn me to hell", he says; this shows that he did not loose all his faith. This book is *to be proscribed.*

1064. 中國聖人 *CHINESE SAGE* 1 vol. 151 p. by **林語堂**
1941 朔風書店

Reflections on China, on Confucius, on the humiliations imposed on the Chinese by foreigners, on force, on the qualities and defects of the Chinese. *For everyone.*

1065. 翦拂集 *SALUTING YOU* 1 vol. 184 p. by **林語堂**
1928 北新書局

The author tells us of Peking and Shanghai. The subjects that he deals with are miscellaneous, brigands, education, the administration, etc. Everything passes through his sieve. Noticeable in this work is the American bias which has struck the author and which he develops even more conspicuously in his later books. *For everyone.*

1066. 林語堂代表作 *AN ANTHOLOGY OF LIN YU-T'ANG* 1 vol. 336 p.
1941 三通書局發行

A selection of Lin Yü-t'ang's essays.
1. A caricature of a modern rich man during vacation period.
2. Author's opinion on concubinage and divorce. He does not give any solution for the three problems but prefers concubinage to divorce.
3. Criticism on nudism in a jocular vein.
4. 記性靈 a psychological essay expressing the author's sympathy for materialism.
5. Some extracts from "Moments in Peking".
All are advised against reading this book.

1067. 語堂作選 *SELECTED WORKS*
國風書店刊行

This book contains twenty essays and sketches on different subjects.
1. 迷人的北平 very good.
2. 裸體運動 less edifying; although the author ridicules nudists, he indulges in frivolous descriptions.
3. 天月山的和尙 is capable of disturbing delicate consciences.
4. 有不爲 on page 40 the author says "I can never remember to have committed a sin. I think that my morality is like that of other men and if God's love for me is half that

of my mother's, he will never condemn me to hell. If I do not go to Heaven, then "the earth is doomed".

Not to be recommended to anyone.

1068. 語堂幽默文選　SELECTED HUMOROUS SKETCHES　1 vol. 152 p.

上海萬象書屋印行

A selection of humorous sketches, literary and social criticisms are presented in this book. Excepting its humorous and literary value the choice is rather poor, and it contributes in no way to the reader's education.

This book is dangerous as the author's ideas about marriage are wrong.

1069. 幽默小品集　SELECTED HUMOROUS ESSAYS　1 vol. 83 p. by 林語堂

朔風書店印行

Good humorous essays. The most interesting are: "How I spent the Chinese New Year", and "I have bought birds".

This book is the best of Lin Yü-t'ang's works which can be given to an ordinary reader. *For everyone.*

1070. 秋窗集　LOOKING AT AUTUMN　1 vol. 209 p. by 另　境

泰山出版社　*See Biogr. 94*

Discussions of literary subjects. Souvenirs of Lu Hsün. *For everyone.*

1071. 航海的故事　SEAFARER'S TALES　1 vol. 94 p. by 劉虎如

3rd. edit. 1939　開明書店

Adaptation of an English book on maritime discoveries since Marco Polo. *For everyone.*

1072. 青年禮儀常識　ETIQUETTE FOR YOUTH　1 vol. 137 p. by 盧　經

1944　農業進步社印刷部

A handbook of politness, showing Protestant influence. It can be consulted by everyone, but must not be used as a text-book in a Catholic milieu.

1073. 墳　TOMB　1 vol. 264 p. by 魯　迅

1941　魯迅全集出版社　*See Biogr. 39*

Little essays published between 1907 and 1925 by Lu Hsün. The first pieces are in the old style: those after 1907 in pei-hua.

Some pieces of scientific aspect are of darwinistic inspiration in which, however, the author's knowledge seems rather scanty.

In these essays the author touches on very important problems such as the equality of the sexes, the duty of parents, & married life. He gives no clear-cut solution but he serves us some apposite ideas in his incisive and pregnant style.

A savory note is not lacking, as for instance, in "Concerning moustaches" and "the National Curse".

The ideas are not presented in a very subversive manner. Slight reservations, however, should be made for the young. *No reservation is necessary for grown-up readers.*

1074. 野草 *WILD GRASSES* 1 vol. 80 p. by 魯 迅
1941 魯迅全集出版社

The "Wild Grasses" of the title drink in the dew of Heaven and rainwater just as the flesh and blood of dead bodies, says the author.

This little book presents us with 23 short pieces, in 80 pages: descriptions, tales, observations, and dreams. One finds in them Lu Hsün's habitual qualities of observation and style, but in spite of this, one is obliged to admit that the subject matter is nevertheless rather slight.

No danger is incurred by the grown-up reader. Certain diatribes against Providence are without violence even if they cannot be said to be without malice. There is a final summing up of Jesus which is baffling: to whit, "Those who slew the Son of Man were more vile than those who slew the Son of God!"

The general note sounded by this series is pessimistic: "the young make me feel that I still am moving among the living." This is the conclusion arrived at by the author. *Not to be recommended to everyone.*

1075. 集外集 *EXTRA* 1 vol. 166 p. by 魯 迅
1935 群衆圖書公司

Reflections on Sparta and patriotism. About the adventures of the author with Yang Shu-ta etc. *For everyone.*

1076. 夜生清 *THE NIGHT IS ON HER COURSE* 1 vol. 110 p. by 魯 莽
1946 日新出版社

Adventures of the journalist Lu. Not a love story, but what he has seen and heard during his career. *For everyone.*

1077. 雀鼠集 *SMALL CREATURES* 1 vol. 160 p. by 魯彦 (王魯彦)
1939 文化生活出版社 *See Biogr. 168*

Essays on education and duty, the fidelity of a dog, scenes in a tram, struggle between merchants, thieves, mice, etc. etc. *For everyone.*

1078. 驢子和騾子 *THE DONKEY & THE MULE* 1 vol. 230 p. by 魯 彦
1935 生活書店

A collection of tales.

The author has real talent. He knows how to describe Nature, and to analyse sentiments, and reveals himself a true poet. *For everyone.*

1079. 偷閒小品 *LEISURELY PIECES* 1 vol. 236 p. by 馬國亮
1935 良友圖書公司

A collection of sketches in a jocular vein on the following subjects: a thief, too much hair and baldness, illnesses and insomnia, modern girls, etc. *For everyone.*

1080. 印象,感想,回憶 *IMPRESSIONS, FEELINGS, MEMORIES* 1 vol. 105 p. by 茅 盾
5th. edit. 1940 文化 *See Biogr. 133*

Anecdotes describing Chinese life in general and student life in particular. *For everyone.*

1081. 速寫與隨筆 *PROFILES* & *SKETCHES*   1 vol. 219 p. by **茅 盾**
6th. edit. 1946 開明書店

A series of articles divided into three parts.
I. Memories of Tokyo. The noise of the streets, cherry trees in blossom, the parks, the public cemeteries, etc.
II. Considerations on Shanghai. Comparison between the new and the old Shanghai.
III. Stories. Descriptions of Nature. Harvest time. The miserable life of Shanghai etc.
For everyone.

1082. 茅盾散文 *PROSE OF MAOTUN*   1 vol. 270 p.
1933 上海天馬書店

A collection of Mao Tun's essays. The author deals with many subjects with rather a skilful hand. Several of these essays are interesting and are worth reading. The style is elegant and simple.
There are no daring passages, but his ideas are not always orthodox. *For informed readers.*

1083. 晞露集 *DEW AT DAWN*   1 vol. 116 p. by **繆崇群**
1933 星雲堂書店 *See Biogr. 118*

A number of well written essays in a simple style. The author presents his childhood memories before and after he entered school; he also recalls his friendships as a boy and a youth. Unbecoming details. *For informed readers.*

1084. 近五十年中國思想史   1 vol. 432 p. by **郭湛波**
1936 北京人文書店

Biographies and details on the principal leaders of China before 1930. *For everyone.*

1085. 讀和寫 *ON READING* & *WRITING*   1 vol. 182 p. by **沐紹良**
2nd. edit. 1939 開明書店

Literary compositions for students. *For everyone.*

1086. 畫人行脚 *NOMADISM OF AN ARTIST*   1 vol. 181 p. by **倪貽德**
1934 良友圖書印刷公司 *See Biogr. 120*

Souvenirs, recollections, and sentimental reflections of an artist. His aim is to talk about painting, but he often forgets his avowed subject. *For mature people.*

1087. 話柄 *MY STORY*   1 vol. 126 p. by **白 羽**
1939

The autobiography of the author. During the perusal and until the last page of the book, one looks in vain for the reason why this man has thought it necessary to write all this stuff.
Insipid, without interest. *For everyone.*

1088. 冰心遊記 *"TRAVELS" BY PING-HSIN*   1 vol. 105 p. by **冰心（謝婉瑩）**
1935 北新書局 *See Biogr. 69*

Notes of a journey from Peking to Suiyuan. Excursions made during the course of the journey.
Many descriptions of old houses, cities, and of Nature. *For everyone.*

1089. 寄 小 讀 者 *LETTERS TO MY YOUNG READERS* 1 vol. 242 p. by 冰心女士
4th edition 1927 北新書局

This book contains twenty nine letters written for the "Children's page" of a literary magazine. The author describes her trip to and residence in U.S.A. The style is elaborate; subject matter and expressions are chosen to please children. At the end of the book a dozen little incidents that happened to the author during her stay in U.S.A. are related.

1090. 閒 情 *LEISURELY* 1 vol. 101 p. by 冰心女士
3rd. edit. 1935 北新書局

A number of essays and poems by Ping Hsin. In the second essay one has the impression that the author is somewhat under the influence of pantheism. *For everyone.*

1091. 南 居 印 象 記 *DOWN SOUTH* 1 vol. 84 p. by 沈美鎮
1929 開明書店

Descriptions of Malaya, of the trees, fruits, and agriculture there. A few curious myths are included. *For everyone.*

1092. 廢 郵 存 底 *OLD LETTERS* 1 vol. 164 p. by 沈從文
1936 文化生活出版社 *See Biogr. 131*

A collection of letters dealing with literary criticism and containing a number of philosophical comments. *For all.*

1093. 記 丁 玲 *ABOUT TING LING, THE AUTHORESS* by 沈從文
1934 良友文學叢書

A biography of Ting Ling until 1932. It gives a good idea of the person dealt with and her work, but from the historical opint of view leaves something to be desired. *For everyone.*

1094. 記 胡 也 頻 *ABOUT HU YEH-P'IN* by 沈從文
1932 光華書局

A collection of personal memoires concerning Hu Yeh-p'in, valuable for those who wish to know him. *For everyone.*

1095. 湘 行 散 記 *SOJOURNING ON THE HSIANG RIVER* 1 vol. 144 p. by 沈從文
1936 商務印局館

In these pages the author describes a journey by boat on the river. He gives evidence of a talent for observation far above the ordinary. Nothing escapes him in Nature, Man or things. He has carefully observed and described everything that has occurred to his imagination. Another merit of the book is that it is written in simple and flowing style. Unfortunately it is regrettable that in his descriptions the author never omits mentioning questionable stories of ladies and rather spicy details. There is nothing to criticise seriously in this book, but the nature of the tales and the meaning implied in some oblige us to reserve it *for adult* reading only.

1096. 燈 下 集 *UNDER THE LANTERN* 1 vol. 192 p. by 施蟄存
1937 開明書店 *See Biogr. 134*

A collection of notes, impressions, and literary criticisms. *For everyone.*

1097. 龍套集 *AN INSIGNIFICANT ROLE*　　　1 vol. 104 p. by 索　非
1946 萬葉書店 *See Biogr. 139*

Brief views of various social and ethical questions. *For everyone.*

1098. 現代中國散文選 *A COLLECTION OF MODERN CHINESE PROSE*
1 vol. 351 p. by 孫席珍編
1935 人文書店 *See Biogr. 144*

A collection of modern prose of the best contemporary writers, Chou Tso-jen, Lu Hsün, Yü P'ing-po, Chu Tzu-Ch'ing, Yeh Shao-chün, etc. The pieces selected consist mostly of short accounts, extracts from diaries of journeys, reminiscences, preface from various works, etc. *For everyone.*

1099. 海天集 *HORIZON ON THE SEA*　　　1 vol. 213 p. by 唐　弢
1936 新鐘書局 *See Biogr. 150*

Dissertations on literary forms. Criticisms of well-known writers. Shows much erudition. *For everyone.*

1100. 天廬談報 *MEMOIRS OF A JOURNALIST*　　1 vol. 77 p. by 天廬主人
1930 光華書局

A dissertation on the press, on the exterior form, its aim, its influence, etc. Also about the co-operation of women in the contemporary press. *For everyone.*

1101. 新鏡花緣 *STRANG CRUISE*　　　3 vols. 910 p. by 天涯淪落人
1936 京報

Three friends visit nineteen countries and the following is a description of those regions, country by country.
1) The land of dissolute morals. Equality of the sexes reigns there.
2) A kingdom resembling ancient China.
3) A region with no fixed calendar and the inconveniences brought on by this.
4) A puppet state. Satire against Korea under the Japanese.
5) Here reigns a dictatorship and militarism.
6) In this country enormous rats are tamed.
7) A country where no work is done and where people walk in couples.
8) A country where they live like children according to the dictates of nature.
9) A place where everything is made of glass and transparent.
10) Here domiciles are regulated. All families consist of three persons.
11) In this country everything is strictly regulated according to law.
12) Here beauty reigns.
13) Land of superstitions.
14) A simple people.
15) In this place suicide is epidemic.
16) Here riches rule.
17) Long live the theatre and long live the "Stars".
18) A people given to opium.
19) A kingdom of women victorious over the opium fiends.
For everyone.

1102. 蹉跎集 *HESITATING*   1 vol. 174 p. by **丁　丁**
                                                        1942 建國書店

Chiefly about the author himself and his literary life. He also discusses Chinese and foreign poetry. *For everyone.*

1103. 寶貝兒 *PUPIL OF MY EYE*   1 vol. 55 p. by **臧克家**
                                          1946 萬葉書店 *See Biogr. 155*

A collection of verse in simple style describing a cross section of the modern world. *For everyone.*

1104. 徬徨歧途 *ON THE CROSSWAY*   1 vol. by **王志聖**
                                          1942 edited at Dairen.

The correspondence box of the Hsi Feng Review.
Questions and answers. The answers are given according to what is most natural in a given case (human, natural point of view). The following questions are dealt with: society, the family, sexual initiation, anomalies of sentiment, relations, marriage, morals, illnesses.
There is good advice in the book, but reserves should be made concerning what it says on birth-control and divorce. *For informed readers.*

1105. 柱宇談話集 *WANG CHU-YU'S COLUMN*   1 vol. 246 p. by **王柱宇**
                                                        1941 天津書局

Articles that have appeared in the papers. Of customs, accidents, ideas, reflections. *For everyone.*

110⌐. 當代女作家書信 *LETTERS OF MODERN WOMEN WRITERS*
                              1 vol. 193 p. collected by **汪定九編**
                                          4th. edit. 1937 中央書局

Letters of the best known women authors. Subjects: their daily life, their intimate life, the political and social situation. *For everyone.*

1107. 歐遊散記 *EUROPEAN WANDERINGS*   1 vol. 211 p. by **王統照**
                                          1930 開明書店 *See Biogr. 171*

Notes of a journey to Europe. The author describes chiefly England and Holland. Of things seen and observed. *For everyone.*

1108. 片雲集 *A SINGLE PIECE OF CLOUD*   1 vol. 173 p. by **王統照**
                                                        1934 生活書店

Literary essays.
Speculation on poetry and philosophy. Pagan outlook. *For informed readers.*

1109. 青紗帳 *VEGETATION*   1 vol. 148 p. by **王統照**
                                                        1936 上海生活書店

Literary essays. In "Tu-shu-chi-kan" the author comments on a page of Spinoza and professes Atheism. In the eleventh he ridicules the streetcorner predication of the protestants. *For informed readers.*

1110. 夜行集 *NOCTURNAL WALK*   1 vol. 162 p. by **王統照**
                                                 1936   生活書店

The majority of these selected pieces are poems in modern style, mostly evoking impressions of travels abroad. *For everyone.*

1111. 茶墅小品 *PROSE*   1 vol. 140 p. by **吳秋山**
                                          1937   北新書局

A collection of essays that often have a very learned air, but we do not believe that they will succeed in stirring the readers.
    The last essay is missing in the copy of the book that we have read. It therefore, has not been checked. *For everyone.*

1112. 床上隨筆 *WRITTEN IN BED*   1 vol. 65 p. by **楊集生**
                                           1931   開明書店

Reflections and witticisms. Without any value whatsoever. *Not for everyone.*

1113. 給姊妹們 *TO MY FELLOW LADIES*   1 vol. 314 p. by **葉 舟**
                                              1941   光明書店

Letters from young girls and the corresponding answers, in which the subjects of the day are dealt with.
    The solutions given are not always orthodox and cannot be considered the standards to follow by our young people. *For mature people.*

1114. 雜拌儿 *POT-POURRI*   1 vol. 222 p. by **俞平伯**
              3rd. edit. 1930   開明書店 *See Biogr. 194*

A collection of historical studies and literary criticisms. Interesting for contacting the prose and mentality of the author.

1115. 燕郊集 *BY PEKING*   1 vol. 268 p. by **俞平伯**
                                        1936   厪友圖書公司

A collection of literary essays on various subjects, written in a limpid style, half pei-hua and half wen-yen, in the manner of Chou Tso-jen. The book contains prefaces originally written for different works, and also notes on poems. At the end there is a translation of a piece of writing by Edgar Allan Poe.
    A work with literary value. *For everyone.*

1116. 屐痕處處 *THE WAKE OF MY TRAMPING*   1 vol. 249 p. by **郁達夫**
                                      上海復興書局 *See Biogr. 196*

A collection of travelling notes. *For everyone.*

1117. 達夫日記集 *DIARY OF YU TA-FU*   1 vol. 373 p. by **郁達夫**
                                            1935   北新書局

Personal souvenirs that depict the epicurean life of the author. He does not take conjugal fidelity seriously. His book is of a morally low order, and contains realistic and provoking details. *Not to be recommended to anyone.*

1118. 閑書 *WRITTEN WITH NO PURPOSE* 1 vol. 281 p. by 郁達夫
1937 瓦友圖書公司

A collection of literary essays, of extracts from the diary of the author, of accounts of journeys, all unedited up to the appearance of this book. It contains very few traces of the known pessimism of the author. *For adults.*

1119. 山居散墨 1 vol. 245 p. .by 袁昌英
1937 Commercial Press *See Biogr. 197*

Essays and critics in a very good style. *For everyone.*

1120. 勞者自歌 *THE LABOURER'S SONG* 1 vol. 227 p.
1934 生活書店

Twenty four essays in easy style. Psychological, folkloristic and with a certain amount of humour. *For all.*

1121. 懸想 *DEEPLY CONCERNED* 1 vol. 365 p. published by 生活書店編
生活書店

The second volume of the correspondence box of the Sheng Huo Publishing Co.
1) Questions and answers concerning education. Education has become a commercial affair, and the heads of schools are not free in the choice of students.
2) Employments. The difficulty of graduates in procuring employment.
3) Propaganda in favour of small families, against clans.
4) Diverse questions concerning marriage. Liberty of the young. Studies should be finished before indulging in amorous adventures. Widows have the right to re-arrange their lives, etc. etc.
5) Political and social questions.
6) The position of China in the world.

No harm can be done in reading this book as long as the advice is not blindly followed. *May be read by anyone.*

1122. 某夫人信箱第一輯 *LETTERS TO MRS. X* XVI + 352 p.
1939-1940

A selection of letters written by the readers of the "Shih Pao" Peiping, to Mr. Chang T'e-sheng. Under the pen name 某夫人, the latter published the original letters and his answers.

The writers of the letters, boys and girls of Peiping, are harassed by the conflict between the traditional Chinese moral code and social prejudice on one hand, and the modern idea of emancipation of the individual and scientific progress on the other.

Writing these letters they hope to find the balance of values for their emotional and family life.

The answers are sometimes very wise and prudent and show the author markedly influenced by (American) Protestant teachings. He is at his best when he deals with the problem of filial piety and its adaptation to modern principles. As a whole his advice is based on personal discipline, tolerance and courtesy; he also emphasises social and individual responsibility. He is often very vague in his application of Christian doctrines as his readers are supposed to know only a natural moral code.

Some points are subject to reserve; although he condemns divorce, mainly on natural grounds, he recommends it in some difficult cases. He follows for that matter the Chinese law which approves of a remarriage following a divorce with the consent of both parties. Touching on the question of birth control, he advocates continence but describes, without condemning them, contraceptive methods and devices, and gives the address of the bureau of "Birth-control" opened by Protestant missionaries in Peiping.

The author adds the summary of a book by Rev. Weatherhead, dealing with sexual life. In this book self-abuse is looked upon as an indifferent action, about which the old prejudice should be discarded.

The book may *only be read by priests and by laymen who have had a solid philosophical and religious formation.* It may help them in their work among the youth of the cities.

1123. 某夫人的信箱 *LETTERS TO MRS. X*   1 vol. IV + 365 p.
1940-1941　沙漠畫報社

The appreciation of vol. I goes for vol. II. The letters are written by the same set of people and the answers by the same author. They were published partly in the 實報 partly in the 沙漠畫報 We, therefore, only refer the reader to the preceding book.

Teachers of ethics and moral theology ought to read the book in order to keep pace with modern Chinese ideas, especially on matters of sex, and to illustrate their classes with living examples.

1124. 未名合本   1st and 2nd vol.
1928-1929　北平未名社版

This periodical strongly opposes Kuomintang principles in government. It advocates rioting, propagates menshivist ideas and preaches anarchy. Judged from Christian and moral points of view it must be condemned.

University students or priests who make a serious study of modern Chinese literature, may find this magazine useful as it expresses fairly accurately the mood of a very influential group of scholars in China. It shows clearly why so many authors are alleged to have Communist sympathies. It also helps to understand why Chinese youth is said to show the same tendencies, an intimation which should not be too readily given credit to.

1125. 天才夢 *ILLUSION OF GENIUS*   154 p.
1940　西風社選編

A collection of the best compositions written on subjects suggested by the Shanghai monthly Hsi-feng. The greater part treats of family affairs such as the death of a young wife; the death of a younger sister, married too young and against her will; belated remorse for the sorrow caused to a deceased relation. Some deal with divorce, occupations (especially professional dancing), the difficulties in finishing school and the hardships of starting on a career. Finally T'ien ts'ai meng, that gives the title to the book; a girl explains how she intends to develop her talents and the difficulties of this task.

The book contains lively descriptions; it shows youth's characteristic but often utopian yearnings for happiness. The story of the dancer is objectionable. *For informed readers.*

1126. 供狀 *THE CONFESSION*   1 vol. 214 p. by different authors.
1941　西風社徵文集

A collection of articles by different authors. In the first five one of them voices his dissatisfaction with his own life. Another discusses the distress of illegitimate children; others deal with abnormal persons : mentally diseased and illtreated children. In chapter 6 two conceptions of life are given : one materialistic, one somewhat spiritualistic but scarcely uplifting.

From a moral point of view, no objection can be raised against the book. *With due caution* it may be given to younger people.

1127. 樊籠 *AN INVISIBLE CAGE*

1 vol. 200 p.

1940 上海西風社

Brief compositions collected in a competition.

Most of the pieces treat of marriage and the family, on such subjects as lack of liberty, concubinage, and precocious marriage. They deal with sad, oppressed life without hope.

The book points to the absence of ideals in the heathen family and shows the attitude of the young towards marriage. *For grown-up people.*

1128. 大腿戲 *BURLESQUE*

1 vol. 270 p. 西風社編

西風社

1) A cross section of society. Worldly dancers, worldly guides, courtisans, beggary, fraud, orphanages, theatres.
2) Problems. Abortions, very early marriages, prostitution, suicide, birth control, cremation, crimes.
"Boystown" of R. Fr. Flanaghan.

A great many risky and false theories. *Not to be recommended to anyone.*

1129. 木偶戲 *PUPPET-SHOW*   Articles from the Review 西風信箱第四集

1 vol. 320 p. 1941   上海西風社發行

Questions and answers chosen from the correspondence section of the review, "Hsi-feng". These questions and their corresponding answers concern very different subjects, but they are chiefly on the difficulties encountered by modern youth, their opposition to tradition etc. Often the answers are full of humour and in general they are to the point.

Nevertheless these answers cannot serve as directives to Christian youth. *Not to be recommended to anyone.*

1130. 青年婚姻問題 *MATRIMONIAL PROBLEMS*

Cath. Miss. Press. Wu-hu; An-hwei.

Love does not stop at sacrifice, even of one's life. Has not love produced many martyrs? Why is it that married love, love of the purest kind, so often makes martyrs in a different sense? The author finds three reasons:
1. The old style marriage ought to be excluded from Christian communities.
2. Influence of surroundings: this is traced back to lack of education; parents must form the characters of their children.
3. Incompatibility: might be avoided by making a more careful choice guided by love. One must be prepared to help the other even if some self sacrifice is involved.

The author does not stress sufficiently the necessity of self-improvement in order to prepare for a virtuous conjugal life.

(Cfr. M.v.W. Bull. Cath. de Pékin, June 1941)

Read the book before recommending it to anybody.

Fiction Translated

1131. 四姊妹 *"THE FOUR SISTERS"* 　1 vol. 326 p. by *Louisa Alcott*
5th edit. 1941 Christ. Lit. Soc. Sh'hai

On the cover of the book is printed: "It is doubtful whether any American writer has given more pleasure to young readers than Louisa M. Alcott in her picture of four sisters living together, growing up, and finally marrying happily." *For all.*

1132. 小婦人 *"LITTLE WOMEN"* 　1 vol. 219 p. by *L. M. Alcott*
3rd edit. 1937　啓明書局

See nr. 1131. This is another translation of the same book.

1133. 一個舊式的姑娘 *"AN OLD-FASHIONED GIRL"*
1 vol. 440 p. by *L. M. Alcott.*
translated by 李葆貞
商務印書館

A very fine story telling of the beneficent influence of a serious young girl on a family that is no so good. All of it framed in a love story.

An educative book that *should be recommended.* Occasionally it is somewhat monotonous.

1134. 藍窗 *"THE WINDOW"* 　1 vol. 327 p. by *Temple Bailey.*
3rd. edit. 1941. Christian Lit. Society, Shanghai.

On the cover of the book is inscribed: "Character sketches, contrasting the simple, truthful, natural girl with the shallow, sophisticated society girl; the strong, up-right, high-principled student with the lax, easy-going, ease-loving type of man. Also a delightful love story." *For everyone.*

1135. 美娥出走 *"THE LITTLE GIRL LOST"* 　343 p. by *Temple Bailey.*
2nd. edit. 1940 Shanghai, edit. by *"Christian Literature Society".*
On the cover of the book is inscribed: "The book is a delightful and wholesome novel. It deals with one of the chief problems of life — marriage. Although one would not call it great literature, it is extremely interesting and pleasant to read".

This story obviously is not for children, but may be read *by everyone of a certain age.* Our Christians should be informed that it is edited by protestants and terminology such as "shang-ti", "mu-shih" etc. should be explained to them before this book is given to them.

1136. 天曉得 *"HEAVEN KNOWS"* 　1 vol. 155 p. by *Margaret Brown.*
1939　上海廣學會

Story of a peasant who left his home to seek his fortunes in Shanghai. There a number of mishaps awaited him. During the war in Shanghai, he was wounded and attended to at a first aid station where he was converted to protestantism. Disappointed in his hopes of making a fortune, he returns to his native province.

Book for everyone. It contains protestant propaganda, but is not too pointed.

1137. 大地 *"THE GOOD EARTH"* 1 vol. 352 p. by *Pearl S. Buck.*
translated by **胡仲持** 1940 開明書店

Wang Lung, a poor farmer, marries a servant of the rich Huang family. The couple live on their little plot and become more and more attached to the land. Also their desire to possess more land grows steadily. Famine drives them South. Military disturbance in the city enables Wang Lung to enter a rich mansion with the populace and to lay hands on a big amount of gold. Back at his native village he buys the fields of the rich Huang family. He can afford to send his sons to school and also to indulge in a few vices. He visits tea-houses and marries a concubine. Later his eldest son makes him buy the big Huang residence. The second son, a model of avarice, markets the products; the third runs away and joins the army. In his old age Wang Lung takes one more concubine and returns to the house of his first married days to die.

The book exhalts the love of the land. In every misfortune this love keeps Wang Lung's courage up. It is too realistic and therefore only suitable *for informed readers.*

1138. 元配夫人 *"THE FIRST WIFE"* 1 vol. 144 p. by *Pearl Buck.*
4th. edit. 1940 啓明書局

Part I. 1) An old-fashioned woman has to give place to a modern woman.
2) A peasant is scolded by his daughter-in-law.
3) The way a foreign woman behaves.
4) The seduction of a modern girl.
5) A badly assorted marriage.
6) Disillusion of a student.
Part II. 1) The revolution does not bring the happiness dreamt of.
2) Deplorable results of the revolution.
3) Idem. 4) Idem.
Part III. Disasters caused by the Blue River.
For everyone.

1139. 秘密花園 *"THE SECRET GARDEN"* by *Francis H. Burnett.*
1 vol. 252 p. 1940 Commercial Press.

The book tells of how two children, ill in both body and soul, find health in a free life with Nature and in relations with other children. *For everyone.*

1140. 人猿泰山 1 vol. 355 p. by *E. R. Burroughs.*
1938 大文書店

An English family perishes on a ship that is adrift. The son, one year old, is taken away and brought up by a monkey. T'ai Shan, the boy, lives among monkeys but feels himself superior to them. Gradually he awakes to his higher qualities that make him a human being. One day white people land on the island and he realizes that he is of their kind. A little later, he finds occasion to show off his strength, by saving the life of a girl. As he cares for her, he accompanies her to America, but his love is not requited. The book may be read *by all.*

1141. 寶窟生還記 1 vol. 262 p. by *E. R. Burroughs.*
1931 商務印書館

Ninth volume of a series dealing with the adventures of Tarzan, the man-ape, presented as a knight-errant who protects the weak against strangers, adventurers and Arabian merchants. *For all.*

1142. 處世奇術 *"HOW TO WIN FRIENDS"* by *Dale Carnegie.*
3rd. edit. 1939, Tientsin 正中印刷局

Translation of Dale Carnegie's "How to win friends and influence people" The author, president of the "Institute of effective speaking and human relations", campaigns in lectures and conferences for more intelligent human relationships based on the laws of psychology. In two hundred pages he condenses his long experience.

A typical American book, it gives little space to speculation; directly workable formulas are illustrated with striking, living examples.

The subdivisions of the book will suffice to give an accurate idea of its contents:
1. Fundamental techniques in handling people.
2 Six ways to make people like you.
3. Twelve ways to win people to your way of thinking.
4. Nine ways to change people without giving offense or arousing resentment.
5. Letters that produced miraculous results.
6. Seven rules for making your home life happier.

Everybody's desire for a feeling of importance and for the esteem of others lies at the base of all the author's techniques. Therefore they can be boiled down to two main principles: one positive — praise judiciously; one negative — do not criticise wildly.

Everybody may profit by reading this book.

The author places Christ on one line with Buddha and Confucius but always respectfully.

The part in which he touches on sex in marriage is inoffensive. *For all.*

1143. 雨後斜陽 *"THE MASTER REVENGE"* 1 vol. 312 p. by *H. E. Cody.*
3rd. edit. 1941. Christ. Lit. Soc.

On the cover of the book is inscribed: "This is the story of a good young man who was trapped. After twelve years of bitterness he was able to regain his reputation. He then treated his enemies with the spirit of Christ and thus took "Master Revenge". The whole story is very moving." *For everyone.*

1144. 天上舵工 *"THE SKY PILOT"* 1 vol. 195 p. by *Ralph Connor.*
3rd. edit. 1939 廣學會

On the cover of the book is inscribed: "An exciting adventure story of pioneer days in Western Canada. A spiritual light is kindled in the hearts of rough men by God working through the life of the Sky Pilot". *Can be read by everyone.*

1145. 戰地行 *A VISIT TO THE FRONT* 1 vol. 90 p. by 居里小姐
1945 中外出版社

Eve Curie, the daughter of the famous chemist, Mme. Curie, gives a very interesting account of her visit to different theatres of war in 1941-42.

Starting from America, she visited the front in North Africa in company with the son of Winston Churchill. Later she took part in the retreat of the Germans in Russia. From there she went to Burma, and on to India where she had a long interview with Gandhi. Her sympathies are leftist, with revolution and for the liberty of the oppressed classes. A visit to a Russian church gives us an idea of the so-called "religious liberty" of the U.S.S.R., where youth has no conception of religion any more. The authoress herself is a free thinker.

If as a preliminary, the reader is forewarned, the book may be read *by anyone.*

1146. 神曲:地獄 *"LA DIVINA COMMEDIA - INFERNO"* by *Dante Alighieri.*

1 vol. 210 p. 1939 商務印書館

A translation in prose of the first part of the "Divine Comedy".

This translation is poorly done, and at times incorrect, and cannot be understood by those who are not familiar with the history of the Middle Ages. *For everyone.*

1147. 波納爾之罪 *"THE CRIME OF SYLVESTER BONNARD"* by Anat. France.

現代書局

The book is made up of two distinct parts. In the first, called "La Buche" (a block of firewood) an old book-lover, Sylvester Bonnard, discovers a valuable manuscript that he has long been looking for. After a lot of vicissitudes the manuscript is given him as a present by an Italian countess in return for the block of firewood he sent her some years before. At that time the countess, then a widow, lived in extreme poverty.

The second part is called "Jeanne Alexandre". In a boarding school Sylvester Bonnard finds the grand daughter of Clementine de Lessay, towards whom he once fostered an ardent but timid love. He takes the girl's interest to heart. When he learns that she is harshly treated by the head mistress and that her guardian covets and tries to seduce her, he helps her escape, unaware of the legal consequences. Matters arrange themselves favourably. Sylvester Bonnard gives her a substantial dowry so she can marry as her heart dictates.

No objection can be raised against the moral or ideological contents *of the book.* In many places it becomes sententious.

It is one of the rare books of Anat. France that are not on the ecclesiastical Index, where his "opera omnia" are mentioned.

N.B.: According to abbe Bethléem, Anat. France is one of the most impious and immoral contemporary writers. Well informed readers can be permitted "Le crime de Sylvestre Bonnard", "Pages choisies", "Albums pour la jeunesse", edited by Hachette, and, with some reserve, "Abeille", "Nos enfants", "Le livre de mon ami".

There exist the following Chinese translations:

1. Le livre de mon ami 友人之書, 金滿成譯, 北新書局.
2. Abeille 蜜蜂, 穆木天譯, 泰東書局.
3. Le lys rouge (A mixture of licentiousness and piety) 紅百合, 金滿成譯, 現代書局.
4. Jocaste 喬加斯突, 顧維雄等譯, 商務印書館.
5. Thais (Argument: lust, incontinence, impurity of the flesh and the spirit constitute the raw material of all sanctity). 女優泰綺思 徐蔚南譯, 世界書局.
6. Le chat maigre 藝林外史, 李青崖譯, 商務印書館.
7. Sur la pierre blanche (Ex professo contra fidem). 白石上. 陳聘之譯, 商務印書館.

1148. 少年伴侶

1 vol. 146 p. by *R. Frayerman.*

translated by 俞荻 1940 山城書店

Contradictory sentiments in the breast of a girl are presented. She first falls in love with a boy student in the school they both attend, and then with the adopted son of her father, who is brought into the family through his second marriage. After detesting him in the beginning, because he has robbed her of her father's love, she falls in love with him, but in vain.

This is a Russian book that discusses co-education, and shows a great liberty in regard to divorce. *For grown-up people.*

1149. 煉 獄 *"PURGATORY"* from the *"COUNT OF MONTE CHRISTO"*
by *Alex. Dumas.*
1 vol. 195 p. translated by 翟伊文 中華書局

The captain of a ship dies. The second-in-command, a young man twenty years old, replaces him. But before dying, the captain had given him two letters. One was addressed to the Isle of Elbe where Napoleon was exiled, and the other was addressed to someone in Paris. As he considers that the fulfillment of the last wishes of a friend is a sacred trust, the young man prepares to acquit himself.

He finds his fiancée at Marseilles when he returns there, and their marriage is decided upon. But he has a rival, who, with two jealous and spiteful comrades, swear to undo him. An anonymous letter is addressed to the police, with the consequence that a few hours before his wedding, he is arrested. The second letter is discovered, and as there is a conspiracy afoot to liberate Napoleon, he is put into prison as a dangerous character.

After a period of seclusion in a subterranean cell, he makes the acquaintance of his neighbour. His new friend teaches him history, English and other practical and useful subjects. He also tells him his own past history and reveals the secret of a treasure hidden in an island. His old companion then dies. He substitutes himself for the dead body and is thrown into the sea. He escapes through swimming and is picked up by smugglers. He goes to the island where the treasure is and gathers it. Then he returns to Marseilles where he finds his old father receiving assistance from his fiancée.

This book is a translation of a part of the romance of Dumas père entitled, "Le Comte de Monte Christo."
This part of the novel may be read *by everyone.*

1150. 女 性 的 禁 城 *"CRANFORD"*   1 vol. 163 p. by *E. C. Gaskell.*
1937 啓明書局

Conversations between ladies on the subject of certain small points of honour. Harmless tales of what has happened in various families etc. *All very innocent.*

1151. 愛 羅 先 珂 童 話 集 *STORIES FOR CHILDREN*   1 vol. 227 p. by *V. Eroshenko.*
translated by 魯 迅
2nd. edit. 1935 商務印書館

Essays and short stories translated by Lu Shün. *For everyone.*

1152. 幸 福 的 夢   1 vol. 119 p. by 高爾恰克等
1946 萬象書店

The first tale 家 by Poljanov describes a difficult birth. It is told, however, in a decent manner.

The second, 遺產 by Baghy is an exhortation to generosity, to gratitude, and other good sentiments.

The three following are the best, being three of Grimm's Fairy Tales For Children. *The last ones* are not so good and are *not for children.*

1153. 四 騎 士 *"LOS CUOTRO JINETES DEL APOCALIPSIS"* by *Vincente Blasco Ibanez.*
1 vol. 399 p. 1936 商務印書館

The action takes place during the first world war. The novel involves two families, one French, one German, but related. The author contrasts the first and her "liberal" education with the second, moulded on reglemented lines.

When the war breaks out, Germany is mechanically on the march, while France moves "democratically" but with her heart in it.

Jules, the hero of the book, has a love affair with a woman who lives separated from her husband. She gives him up when duty calls and lovingly nurses her husband who is heavily wounded in the war. Although he is an Argentinian by nationality, Jules thinks that he must do something for France, his father's country, and enrolls. His father goes through the occupation and the retreat of the Germans and meets one of his nephews who is an officer of the German army. The hero is killed in action; his family visits his grave. The marriage of his sister to an invalid veteran opens a vista of what the next generation will be.

Some descriptions are too realistic. *For informed readers.*

1154. 鮑志遠 *PAO CHIH-YUAN: HIS ADVENTURES* 1 vol. 137 p. by *H. Ibsen.*
translated by 石靈 1939 萬葉書局

A drama on a sociological theme in four acts.

A banker has married for money, in spite of which he becomes bankrupt and is pursued for his debts.

The hopes of the parents are centred in the son, for they look to him to save them from their financial condition. He, however, deceives them, and marries the girl of his heart, leaving the paternal roof. *For adults.*

1155. 劊子手 1 vol. 282 p. by *G. Q. Johnson.*
1941 上海西風社

Dissertations on social life abroad, especially in America. They touch on criminals, detectives and judicial institutions abroad. *For all.*

1156. 妻 *THE WIFE* 1 vol. 122 p. by *Valentin Petrovich Katayev.*
translated by 朱葆光 Chungking 1945 中外出版社

A Russian officer is returning to his post on the Orel front. On the way he meets a girl, Petrovna Nina. She is also going to the front to visit the tomb of her aviator husband who was killed the year before. The cemetery happens to be recovered the following day during a fresh offensive.

Most of the story is taken up with the account, told by Petrovna, of how she met Andrew at Sebastopol, of their love, their marriage, and his death. The love that she describes is a pure one without agitated sentimentality.

The book does not contain a single displaced word of exaggerated apology for communism. The moral to be learnt from it is that work gives meaning to a life that seems to have been broken.

From the literary point of view and because of the description of life in the U.S.S.R. that it contains, this book is an excellent example of contemporary Soviet literature. *For everyone.*

1157. 狂人與死女 *"THE TALE OF A MANOR"* 1 vol. 176 p. by *S. Lagerlöf.*
1935

A student neglects his studies and family for his music. He has to start in business in order to remake his fortune, but has bad luck, and goes mad.

A gipsy girl has been adopted by a clergyman; being dangerously ill, she is believed to be dead and is buried. The madman saves her from her ghastly predicament. With much patience and love she succeeds in curing his illness. *For all.*

1158. 冬天的樂園及其他 *"THE LEGEND OF THE CHRISTMAS ROSE AND
OTHER STORIES"*
4th ed. 1941 Christ. Lit. Soc.

Six Christmas stories by Selma Lagerlof, Nodier, etc.

In one of the stories the monks of oriental religions are given the same qualifications as Catholic monks. *For informed readers.*

1159. 吾家 *"OUR FAMILY",*   1 vol. 288 p. by 林阿苦, 亞娜
translated by 黃景華 1940

In eighty or so chapters the two daughters of Lin Yü-t'ang, aged 13 and 16, give us their family impressions, and tell us of their journeys abroad and of their return to China, their native country to which they have always remained attached. The influence of their father can be seen on each page, and under his direction, they have learnt the art of living. We need not however, congratulate Lin Yü-t'ang too much upon the way he has educated his daughters, as we observe no trace of religious education — in fact, the contrary! (Cfr. chap. 69).

Apart from this chapter of which the contents refute themselves, the perusal of this book should be a good recreation for the readers, and will help them to understand Chinese psychology better. *For everyone.*

1160. 我是希脫拉的囚徒   1 vol. 468 p. by *Stephan Lorant.*
上海棠樣社

Stephen Lorant is a Hungarian publicist. He was arrested in Munich during the Hitler putch and, never knowing why, was in prison for six months. *For all.*

1161. 青鳥 *"THE BLUE BIRD"*   by *Maeterlink.*
1932 文學研究會

In the "Index", "Omnia opera" of this author are condemned.

1162. 如此人生 *"THOSE FITZENBERGERS"* 2 vols. 108 p. and 110 p. by *Helen Martin.*
translated by 王敏. 天津德泰印字舘

An industrialist, father of a family, has associated with him as his secretary, an educated and pretty girl to whom he becomes attached, neglecting his duties as a husband and a father. His wife feels herself abandoned and sends the daughter, whom the father loves, to a relative, and soon afterwards drowns herself with her other two children. The industrialist then marries his secretary, and after the death of the aunt to whom she was sent, the daughter returns to the paternal roof. Such is the situation related to the daughter by her dying father, which until now has been a secret from her. Her father has become moody and there is a coldness between them. Her step-mother detests her and makes her feel it. The villagers avoid her and do not even allow their children to be friendly with her. The poor girl finds herself alone without a single friendly soul to confide in or to whom she could open her heart.

Nevertheless there is a boy who, without the knowledge of his violent and obstinate father, has become her friend. They scheme together to evade the paternal vigilance, and meet secretly at night. But the boy leaves soon after to enter university. They write to each other, however.

The family of a pastor now comes to the village and installs itself there. The girl becomes a friend of the new arrivals and is treated as a member of the family. She is held in high esteem by them, and is able to pursue her literary studies under the guidance of the clergyman and his wife.

Now the boy who has gone to the university is a model and intelligent student, very highly regarded by his superiors. He is admitted into the family of the President of the university, where he becomes friends with his son and makes the acquaintance of his daughter, Aida, an intelligent but rather melancholy girl.

A book appears entitled "A Village Tragedy". The book is a great success but the author is unknown. Aida's brother, however, is completely charmed with it.

During the holidays, the two young people originally referred to, see each other again. The boy, who has become conceited, breaks his relations with the girl whom he now considers inferior to himself. She, however, maintains her affection for him and proves it.

There happens to be a jealous young woman, of bad character, who is pursuing him assiduously although repulsed and snubbed all the time. She trumps up a charge against him and he is put into prison. His old friend then intervenes and when the truth is known, he is set free and his honour reestablished.

The girl's father dies and she goes to New York to continue her studies. Recommended by the clergyman and his wife, the author of "A Village Tragedy" is warmly received into the family of the President of the university.

Some time after, when her girlhood friend finds her, she is already married to the son of the President. And her old friend is dismissed by Aida who loves her like a sister.

This book takes up the emancipation of women and presents us with scenes of American love-making. The local circumstances, time, and persons involved have to be taken into consideration in permitting this book to be read by any particular reader or category of readers. *Not for everyone.*

1163. 人心 *"NOTRE COEUR"*　　　　1 vol. 294 p. by *Guy de Maupassant.*
　　　　　　　　　　　　　　　　　　　　　　1935　中華書局

According to Emile Faguet, Guy de Maupassant is "the greatest realistic story-writer of the century". According to Jules Lemaitre, "he loves and searches after the most violent manifestations of physical love, egotism, and naive ferocity... He is extraordinarily sensual and he is so complaisantly, with fever and passion". (From "Les Contemporains", 1st. series, p. 300).

A bad book. *Proscribed.*

1164. 生活的藝術 *"THE ART OF LIVING".*　　　1 vol. 150 p. by *A. Maurois.*
　　　　　　　　　　　　　　　　　　　　　　1944　李木書屋

Considerations on love, marriage, the family, friendship, philosophy, work, pleasure, and old age. *For grown-up people.*

1165. 最佳短篇小說 *"THE BEST SHORT STORIES"*　　　by *Edward J. O'brien.*
　　　　　　　　　　　　　　　　　1 vol. 138 p. 1940　大地圖書公司

A series of war stories. Life in the trenches. *For everyone.*

1166. 西部前線平靜無事 *ALL QUIET ON THE WESTERN FRONT*
　　　　　　　　　　　　　　　　　　　　　　by *E. M. Remarque.*
　　　　　　　　　　　　　　　　　1 vol. 365 p. 1930　水沫書店

In writing this book the author obviously has the aim of inspiring his readers with the horror of war. In order to arrive at this end he describes his own experiences and those of some of his comrades in the war. During the course of the book he tells, in an extremely realistic fashion, of life at the front, behind the lines, in barracks and on leave.

According to him, the soldier loses completely his personality and becomes a sort of machine without a will of his own, and at the mercy of his officers. He fights because he cannot do otherwise, and his only ambitions are for material pleasures such as to eat and drink and to have women. He has no fixed aim.

After the horrors that we have known twice within a quarter of a century, noone will approve of slaughter; nevertheless we believe that most of the combattants who have fought are worth more than the heros of Mr. Remarque. Moreover, it seems to us that this book is an insult to the majority of the soldiers who served in the first world war.

From the point of view of morality, we consider this vulgar portrait of the soldier reprehensible, as also the shocking realism of the author. Besides which, serious reservations must be made over certain pages that are of an extreme crudity. *Not to be recommended to anyone.*

1167. 苦戀   1 vol. 322 p. by *Schnitzler.*
Translated by 劉大杰 1932 中華書局

After two years of widowhood, Berthe Garlan, a famous pianist, sees the portrait of an old friend in an illustrated review. She writes to him, hoping for results.

She wants to go with her friend, but he will not allow her, preferring her acquaintance at a distance. The widow is so indignant that she wishes to commit suicide. She finds the world very unjust where a woman is unclassed when she misconducts herself while a man is free to do whatever he likes. *Proscribed.*

1168. 飢餓 *"FAMINE"*   by *Simenov.*
Shanghai. 1928 北新書局

Diary (April 25th — Dec. 7th 1919) of a Russian girl. It deals with the famine in Petrograd. She relates mostly family events and especially her feelings towards her father who is an egoist. She hates him, but seeing him starve moves her to pity.

Realistic, simple and dignified. *For all.*

1169. 日日夜夜 *DAYS AND NIGHTS*   1 vol. 340 p. by *Constantine Simenov.*
2nd edition 1947 上海時代書報出版社

A very good and interesting book. The author describes the brilliant deeds of a Russian regiment which held out in a block of houses in Stalingrad. A well written book. *For everyone.*

1170. 日內瓦的木刻家   1 vol. 184 p. by *Grace Sinclair.*
1939. Christ. Lit. Soc.

Protestant publication on the subject of the religious struggles at Geneva between the Huguenots and the local bishop. In the preface we are told that it is not desired that any sentiments hostile to catholics should be expressed, but this story leaves, nevertheless, the impression that priests and monks are unjust, intriguing, and animated by sentiments that are far from noble. Moreover, catholic doctrine is attacked in this book in regard to indulgences, the cult of saints and that of the sacred sacrifice. *Proscribed.*

1171. 金錢？愛情? *"LOVE OR MONEY"*   1 vol. 377 p. by *Annie S. Swan.*
2nd. edit. 1937

On the cover of the book is inscribed: "A story of adventure and of the love of youth, sore tried but triumphant in the end. A moving and thrilling tale well translated, which will appeal to all young readers." *For everyone.*

1172. 戰爭 *WAR*　　　　　　　　　　　　　　1 vol. 180 p. by *N. S. Tikhonov.*
　　　　　　　　　　　　translated by 茅盾 1936 文化生活出版社

Very vivid account of war. We are made to take part in battles. We are told about the use of poison gas bombs, and of their manufacture. *For everyone.*

1173. 初戀 *FIRST LOVE*　　　　　　　　　　247 p. by *Turganyev.*
　　　　　　Translated and Annotated by *T. K. Feng* 豐子愷 上海開明書店

The aim of the author is clearly expressed in chapter 22, No. 7.

"O youth, youth! little dost thou care for anything; thou art master, as it were, of all the treasures of the universe — even sorrow gives thee pleasure, even grief thou canst turn to thy profit; thou art self-confident and insolent; thou sayest, "I alone am living — see!" — but thy days fly by all the while, and vanish without trace or reckoning; and everything in thee vanishes, like wax in the sun, like snow. . .And, perhaps, the whole secret of thy charm lies in they being unable to do anything; in thy throwing to the aims, forces of which thou couldst not make other use; lies in each of us gravely regarding himself as a prodigal, gravely supposing that he is justified in saying, "Oh, what might I not have done if I had not wasted my time!" *For enlightened people.*

1174. 湯姆沙亞 *"ADVENTURES BY TOM SAWYER"*　1 vol. 244 p. by *Mark Twain.*
The adventures of Tom Sawyer. *For all.*

1175. 青年成功小傳 *"BOYS WHO MADE GOOD"*　　　　by *Archer Wallace.*
　　　　　　　　　　　　　　　3rd. edit. 1940. Christ Lit. Soc.

On the cover of the book is inscribed : "Archer Wallace, whose books are so popular among young people, has here prepared sketches of fifteen characters, emphasising the secret that has made their lives successful. The central theme which runs through the book is the possibility of overcoming adverse circumstances and turning them to good account. All boys in their teens should read this book." *For all readers.*

1176. 點滴 *RAIN DROPS*　　　　　　　2 vol. 370 p. by 周作人
　　　　　　　　　　　　　　　　　1920 中華書局

A selection of short narratives translated from Russian, Polish, and other authors . . . Chou Tso-jen chose these pieces with a view to propagating humanitarianism. 人道主義 as it is found in the works of Tolstoy, Kuprin, Andreyev, and others. . . From time to time there is felt a sour and pessimistic scent of Communism. . .sometimes a vague religiosity, sentimental, somewhat mystical.

This choice helps us to understand the mentality of the compiler.

This book is one of the first published in the new literary language. It can be recommended to students of higher education after having shown them the dangers to avoid. *Not for everyone.*

1177. 燹娜　　　　　　　　　　　　1 vol. 295 p. by 高葛大將
　　　　　　　　　　　　　　　　　1940 華斌閣印刷局

For those who wish to get acquainted with arctic regions. *For all.*

1178. 寒鴉集 *CROWS FLY*　　　　　　1 vol. 254 p. 劉大杰編
　　　　　　　　　　　　　　　　3rd. edit. 1934 啓智書局

This book contains a number of literary studies and a piece entitled 惡魔的宗教, which is a regular indictment against religions.

The accusation is levelled against religion of approving wars with its authority. (Egypt, Japan, etc.). Then we are accused of abusing women. In passing, the virginity of the Virgin Mary is ridiculed, and woman is presented as possessed by a devil who works through the fire of concupiscence. Original sin is badly interpreted by religions which, moreover, approve of all deviations from normal and proper sexual relations. The author of this indictment also accuses religion of covering the acts of warlords and capitalists.

The strongest expressions are passed over by the reviewer from modesty. *Proscribed.*

1179. 神秘的大衞   1 vol. 273 p.

A book for children. *For everyone.*

1180. 怪飛機 *A STRANGE AIRPLANE*   1 vol. 116 p. transl. by **武承揚選**
                                                                        1946   **美華書局**

Translation of an English book.
Seven detective stories that would lose interest if they were divulged in a synopsis.
For everyone.

1181. 吸血鬼 *VAMPIRES*   1 vol. 122 p. transl. by **武承揚選**
                                                                        1946   **美華書局**

Translation of an English book.
Six detective stories, which equally with those mentioned in the preceding review would lose interest if their plots were divulged. *For everyone.*

1182. 神秘刀 *A MYSTERIOUS SWORD*   1 vol. 102 p. transl. by **武承揚選**
                                                                        1946   **美華書局**

Translation of an English book.
Six crimes resolved by famous detectives. *For everyone.*

1183. 幾個偉大的作家 *SOME GREAT WRITERS*   1 vol. 277 p.
                                            translated by **郁達夫**, 1934 **中華書局**

Extracts from foreign authors, especially from Russian writers. Their ideas do not agree at all with ours. Certain reservations must be made on this book, besides which, it is not attractive reading. *For mature people.*

1184. 戀愛與義務 *"LOVE AND DUTY"*   1 vol. 168 p.
                                                            Commercial Press.

A boy and a girl go to the same school, make each other's acquaintance and fall in love. The heroine, however, is promised to someone else, and her parents force her to marry the other person. Later she meets her childhood friend again, when she abandons her own household and her children to be with him. Her whole life is a series of vexations and miseries. Her friend dies and she herself ends in committing suicide.

A very moving and pathetic book, in which the author condemns free love. *For everyone.*

1185. 福爾摩斯之復活 *RESURRECTION OF HOLMES*   1 vol. 155 p.
                                                        1946   **國民圖書公司**

Resurrection of Sherlock Holmes.
Five detective stories, a synopsis of which would spoil the pleasure of the reader. *For everyone.*

1186. 天方夜譚 *STORIES FROM THE ARABIAN NIGHTS*   1 vol. 478 p.
                                                   1941   啓明書局

Thirteen tales from the "Thousand and One Nights". *For everyone.*

1187. 夢   1 vol. 144 p. translated by *G. F.* 女士
                                        2nd. edit. 1938   北新書局

Allegories, fantasies, dreams. *For everyone.*

1188. 法國短篇小說選第一集   *SELECTED FRENCH SHORT STORIES*
                                      (Vol. I) 1 vol. 166 p.
                                            1939   天津崇德堂

Extracts from books written by French authors. *For everyone.*

1189. 女鋒小說集 *"SHORT STORIES FOR YOUNG PEOPLE"*   2 vol. 128 p. 155 p.
                                      4th. edit. 1941. Christ. Lit. Soc.

On the cover of the book is inscribed: "The book consists of short stories. It is interesting to those who like to read stories. ." *For all readers.*

1190. 福爾摩斯新探案大集成   12 vol.
                                   3rd edit. 1938   上海武林書店

Adventures of Sherlock Holmes. *For all.*

1191. 魔術殺人   1 vol. 159 p.
                                     1940   大連實業印書舘

A rather incoherent detective story. In the second part a clue followed up in the first part is simply dropped and never mentioned any more. *For all.*

1192. 康小姐   1 vol. 172 p.
                                     1940   廣學會

A young girl, whose only sin is illegal traffic in precious stones between Hongkong and Shanghai, is converted by reading a passage from the Gospel. *For all.*

1193. 無敵水手 *"A SAILOR WHO HAS NO RIVALS"*
                                                       新文書局

A girl has an uncle in Africa who presents her with a small animal called "Chi-pu", looking like a cat. A rich man, having read somewhere that the animal possesses mysterious qualities, wants to buy it and offers one hundred thousand dollars. Having his own idea about the value of the animal, a sailor, related to the girl, opposes the transaction. The rich man arranges to have the animal stolen, but it escapes and returns home. Then he tries to beat the sailor at boxing, but is beaten. The same sailor, taken ill, was to be operated upon but the operating knife breaks on his skin! . . He is carried to the ring and, ill though he is, beats the most famous fighter of the world! *For all.*

1194. 銀盒   1 vol. 110 p.
                                    translated by 郭沫若, 1937

A young man comes home dead-drunk and is helped into bed by the maid's husband. The young man has stolen the purse of a young lady. While he is sleeping this purse together with a silver cigarette-case vanishes from his room. He suspects the maid. The cigarette-case is, in fact, found in her room. She is arrested with her husband. When the latter confesses he also mentions the purse, but the parents of the young man manage to keep that affair quiet. He then raves against society that punishes the little man and protects the criminal rich. *For informed readers.*

1195. 虎齒記 *"ARSENE LUPIN"* (Adventures of. .)

1 vol 175 p.   文藝書局

A rich man is murdered. His testament leaves everything to his nearest relation. Nobody puts in a claim.

Pi-li-na, a detective, is put in charge of the case. After no end of adventures, having suspected several persons and again acquitted them, he finally succeeds in arresting the murderer.

The book ends with the marriage of the detective to his secretary who, in the long run, proves to be the nearest relation of the murdered man. *For all.*

1196. 俘虜 *CAPTIVES*   1 vol. 228 p. by *various authors.*
                                            1932   開明書店

An account of episodes of the Franco-German war of 1870. Stories of the heroic deeds that occurred in France and told by famous writers, Daudet, Maupassant, and Zola.

These tales are not unknown to foreign readers. To the Chinese they show the courage of all strata of society in France during this war.

There is nothing to offend good morals in the stories themselves, but the design of the cover of the book is, to say the least, risky. *For everyone.*

Ancient Fiction(¹)

1197. 綠牡丹 *GREEN PEONY*
1 vol. 170 p. by 趙 溢
1928 上海錦章書店

The action takes place at the time of the Tang dynasty. A functionary was ruined by one of his colleagues, who moreover seduced his wife. The functionary made up his mind to revenge himself; in this he was helped by some of his friends; he punished the two culprits. The story, as well as the marriage of a scholar, the functionary's friend, form the main plot of the novel. Naturally the author lingers on "the deeds and gestures" of his heroes.

Here and there are a few unbecoming passages, especially at the beginning, where the author describes how the functionary's wife permitted herself to be seduced. That is why this book *cannot be placed in he hands of all readers.*

1198. 燕山外史
by 陳 球

"During the reign of Yung-lo, there lives in Peking a young man called Tou Sheng-tsu. He picks up an acquaintance with a girl called Li Ai-ku and lives with her. Because his father wants him to marry a Szechwan girl, he parts with Ai-ku who becomes a sing-song girl. A certain Ma-lin helps her find her lover whose wife is very jealous. Taking Ai-ku with him, Tou Sheng-tsu leaves his home. "During a troubled period of civil war" Tou and Li are once more separated. Completely broke, Tou returns home . . . but his wife leaves him. . One day Li Ai-ku comes back; her return inspires Tou and he starts working... until he is appointed inspector of Shantung. He then sends for Li Ai-ku whom he recognizes as his lawful wife. A son is born, and, being in need of a wet-nurse, they engage Tou's former wife, who, after remarrying, has been left a widow. Although Tou receives her in his home, she plans revenge and also tries to injure Ma-lin who kills her. Tou is suspected of the crime but succeeds in proving his innocense, whereupon he is reinstated. In the end he, together with his wife, become one of the immortals".
(Wu I-t'ai, Le Roman Chinois, pp. 110-111).

The book is rather difficult to read, being written in symmetrical lines of from 4 to 6 characters. *For informed readers.*

1199. 品花寶鑑
by 陳森書

The plot of the book is very thin. It merely describes the life of actors and their fans. The characteristic feature of the book is that it is written as if it were a love story: the characters act and talk like lovers, although the book features only men. This had not been the case with any book written before. All the characters in the book actually existed. *Proscribed.*

---

(1) Included in this work are reviews of some famous ancient Chinese stories to give the readers just an idea of the fiction of previous dynasties.

1200. 閱微草堂筆記   Edited from 1789 to 1798 by 紀　昀

"Chi-yün is the only writer who criticised the "Liao Chai Chih Yi" (nr. 1213) . . . In order to illustrate his conception of a good collection of short stories, he wrote this . . . Although the writing of the book was, according to the author "only a pastime" the author adheres strictly to his rules of composition: his style is polished, direct and free of superfluous elegance. Chi Yün read many books unknown to the ordinary public and had an open mind; so his material, and his own ideas, which he sometimes attributes to ghosts, as well as what he ascribes to human beings, is witty and sometimes amusing. Moreover he looked upon human weakness with indulgence." (Wu I-t'ai, Le Roman Chinois, pp. 148, 149, passim). *For informed readers.*

1201. 說岳全傳 *STORY OF GENERAL YUI FEI*   2 vol. 488 p. by 淸錢彩
                                                                    1937　會文堂新記書局

A romanticised biography of Yueh Fei. The second part especially is full of buddhistic revelations, diabolic apparitions etc. The combats between Yueh Fei and the pretenders to the imperial throne during the captivity of the emperors at the Chin court are described in a fantastic manner.

The historical thread is fairly well kept, and the work is innocent from the moral point of view. It is a bad imitation of the San Kuo Chih. The style is that of popular tales told as fairs, vulgar and without literary value.

One will not lightly place this book in the hands of the young because of its mediocre value, and because the supernatural events and the warriors it is about, are described in too disorderly a fashion. *Not for everyone.*

1202. 海上花列傳   64 episodes; edited about 1892 by 韓子雲

"At the age of seventeen the hero of the novel, Chao P'ao-chai, visits his uncle in Shanghai and visits the tea-houses. Being young and inexperienced he falls under the spell of the gay life and soon goes broke. His uncle sends him home but he returns in secret, falls from bad to worse and ends up as a rickshaw-coolie. . . .The 29th to 60th chapters were edited in the 20th year of Kuang-hsü. In this part Hung Shan-ching one day sees his nephew pulling a rickshaw, and immediately sends word to his sister (P'ao-chai's mother). She does not know what should be done but her daughter, an intelligent girl, persuades her to go in search of P'ao-chai. They find him, but have in the meantime become so completely swallowed up in the new life that they forget to return home. . . .Erh-pao, the hero's sister, becomes a sing-song girl. . . .One day she meets the son of a well-to-do family by name of Shih, who promises to marry her". He fails to keep his promise, though, and Erh-pao learns shortly afterwards "that he has gone to Yang-chow-fu and married. Being very deep in debt, she finds no other way out than to resume her former profession. The book ends at this juncture". (Le roman chinois, Wu I-t'ai, p. 90-91 passim). "The characters in the book are such as are met with everyday . . . The style is spontaneous, the descriptions accurate. . . " (ibid p. 93). *To be banned.*

1203. 野叟曝言   Edited about 1880 by 夏敬渠

"Yeh-sou-p'u yen is an impressive work made up of one hundred and fifty four episodes, divided over twenty volumes. These are not numbered as usual, but classified by means of the twenty characters composing two symmetrical lines which, in a certain way, summarize the whole book. It is natural for an honest man of letters who has no rival under the sun, to develop military talent and to fathom literature. Harmonizing the

Canonical books, summarizing the Annals, this is the first extraordinary book among men.

The book nearly comprises the sum of knowledge of the Chinese at the time of its appearance: stories, dissertations, discussions of the Canonical books, interpretations of the Annals, examples of filial piety, exhortations to loyalty towards the prince, the arts: poetry, medicine, strategy and calculus, emotions: joy, anger, melancholy and fear all this can be found in it. Wen-po, also known as Su-ch'en, the hero of the book, possesses every virtue and talent". (Wu I-t'ai, Le Roman Chinois p. 98).

"Yeh-sou-pu-yen" undoubtedly deserves to be qualified as "fiction", its principal character being much too unreal . . . Moreover, it should be understood that the success of "Yeh-sou-pu-yen" is mostly due to curiosity "(Wu I-t'ai, Le Roman Chinois p. 101)."

1204. 鏡花緣 *MIRAGE*　　　　　　　2 vol. 372 & 396 p. by 許嘯天
　　　　　　　　　　　　　　　　　5th edition 1912 上海群學社

Curious stories of "child-heroines" who practise "Kuo Shou" and other sports. *For everybody.*

1205. 鏡花緣 *FLOWERS SEEN IN A MIRROR*　　　　　(1763-1830) by 李汝珍

"One winter day, empress Wu, of the T'ang dynasty, wanted to see the flowers of her garden bloom. Her wish was granted, but the flower fairies were punished by the gods . . . At the same time there lived a bachelor, named T'ang Ao, who obtained a 3rd place in the examinations but was afterwards deprived of his grade. In disgust he follows his brother abroad, trading with foreign countries. One day, during his journeys, he finds a magic herb which confers immortality and the power to lift oneself into the air; he does not tarry to eat the plant and, little later, he leaves his brother, never to return. Afterwards his daughter, T'ang Hsiao-shan, goes in search of her father, without success. However, a woodman hands her an autograph letter of T'ang Ao, in which he gives her the name of Kuei Ch'en, and advises her to go in for imperial examinations. She presents herself for examination, succeeds, and, after a civil war has given the country a new emperor, she is invited to the banquet of the "Red Literature". (Wu I-t'ai, Le Roman Chinois pp. 104-105). *For all.*

1206. 京本通俗小說 *"SOME POPULAR TALES"*　　　by 黎烈文標點
　　　　　　　　　　　　2nd. edit. 1935 商務印書館 *See Biogr. 104*

Collection of stories of olden days, with curious and involved situations that resolve themselves in a comic and agreeable fashion.

Adventures to be told to the people by popular story tellers. *For everyone.*

1207. 官塲現形記 *CHINESE OFFICIALDOM*　　　(1867-1906) by 李寶嘉

"Owing to the untimely death of the author, the book comprises only the first five parts, sixty chapters in all. The third part was edited with a preface by Li Pao-chia himself, in which he says: "I have had the opportunity to watch mandarins. All they do is meet visitors at the gate, and see them off; all their talent consists in collecting the taxes imposed on their district. They suffer hunger and thirst, face heat and cold going on official visits and return only at night from audiences with their superiors. In the end, however, no one understands what all their coming and going is about."

When crops are bad and the government distributes aid "everyone of them, according to the pattern followed in previous distributions, is awarded distinctions and remunerations; therefore, the number of those elevated to the rank of mandarin grows daily, and nobody foresees where it will stop". When the government decides on a purge "major and minor mandarins unite in fraud and corrupt practices increase instead of diminishing". The mandarins scrape up money, the people suffer and become poor while they get steadily bolder as nobody dares utter a protest. . .The book, therefore, contains nothing but· neglect of duty, meanness, embezzlement of public funds, underhand dealings and also a few glimpses of their private life." (Wu I-t'ai, Le Roman Chinois pp. 119-121). *For all.*

1208. 浮生六記 *SIX CHAPTERS OF A FLOATING LIFE*

Chinese text with Engl. transl. by 林語堂
1 vol. 320 p. 西風社印行 *See Biogr. 106*

Memoir written by Shen Fu, a little-known painter, about his life with Yün, his wife. They have ingenuous, poetical minds, and enjoy the simple happines which life gives them. The greatness of nature fills their spiritual beings. . . . .They love each other, have a few dear friends; yet their life is a tragedy.

Yün must take care of the affairs of her in-laws, which makes her unpopular with them. She gets mixed in several fishy affairs and loves a public woman. The author defends her and asks: Is it wrong for a woman to dress as a man and make love to a beautiful courtesan? Neither her artistic aspiration nor her love bring much gratification. . .The prostitute elopes with a rich man. This so grieves Yün that she dies.

Lin Yu-t'ang becomes lyrical when he thinks of these simple, artistic souls! He would like to find their graves, offer fruits and incense, whistle to them a melody of Ravel or Massenet. . . for in presence of such beauty one feels oneself humble. . . . The greatest beauty in the whole universe, according to the author, is a simple, humble life.

The painter cannot forget his sorrow caused by Yün's death; he is poor and forsaken by his family. He contemplates entering a Taoist monastery. . .but, listening to his friends, he looks for solace in the company of women. . . .

It is understood that we do not pronounce judgement on the artistic or literary value of the book. From the moral point of view it is a *dangerous book.* Its religion, if any, is pantheistic and superstitious.

1209. 何典 *THE GHOST'S WORLD*   1 vol. 188 p. by 劉 復

1st edition 1870 2nd edition 1926 *See Biogr. 109*

A caricature on the old Chinese society with its injustices, superstitions and legendary heroes. It contains the story of a young hero, who was first a spirit and later on took a form of a young man.

The action takes place in the world of spirits. The author's contemporaries must have been very pleased with this caricature.

The story itself is harmless, but full of coarse scenes. The book should *not to* be given to *the young folks.*

1210. 老殘遊記 *THE TRAVELS OF LAO TS'AN*   (1850-1910) by 劉 鶚

"It is impossible to summarize this book, as is the case with all other books of this kind. It relates the travels of T'ieh-ying under the name of Lao Ts'an. It deals with what he did, saw and heard. The author's hopes and aspiration can be found in it, as well as a goodly number of sallies against the mandarins". (Wu I-t'ai, Le Roman Chinois, p. 122). *For all.*

1211. 三國志演義 *THE ROMANCE OF THE THREE KINGDOMS*   by 羅貫中

"The San-kuo-chih-yen-yi", attributed to one Lo Kuan-Chung, a historical novel based upon the wars of the Three Kingdoms which fought for supremacy at the beginning of the third century A.D. It consists mainly of stirring scenes of warfare, of cunning plans by skilful generals and of doughty deeds by blood-stained warrior. Armies and fleets of countless myriads are from time to time annihilated by one side or another, all this in an easy and fascinating style, which makes the book an endless joy to old and young alike. If a vote were taken among the people of China as to the greatest among their countless novels, the story of the Three Kingdoms would indubitably come out first." (A History of Chinese Literature, H.A. Giles, p. 277).

"The "San-kuo-chih-yen-yi" is a book that every Chinese read, reads, and will read as long as China exists". (Maspero, La Chine vol. I. p. 29). It is based on the civil war which lasted nearly a century from A.D. 168 to 265". (Bazin, Le siècle de Youen, p. 107).

A few lines in chapter XVI are unbecoming; still the book may be read *by all*.

In English "San Kuo or Romance of the Three Kingdoms" by C.H. Brewitt-Taylor. 2 vol.

1212. 西洋記 *TRAVELS IN THE WESTERN SEAS*

In 100 Chapters, edited in 1597 by 羅懋登

"Popular narrative of the travels of San-pao, the eunuch, in the Western seas."

"The author tells of the expedition of the eunuch San-pao — his real name is Cheng Ho — who is not an imaginary character; ... he served under three emperors and made seven voyages in which he visited more than thirty countries ... He brought back invaluable treasure.

"Chapters 1 to 7 tell how P'i-feng-chang-lao is born, flees the world and overcomes the devil's temptations. Chapters 8 to 14 record the contest in magic art between P'i-feng and Chang T'ien-shih, high-priest of Taoism. Then begins the story of Cheng-Ho: his nomination as Commander-in-chief, his expedition with the aid of P'i-feng and Chang, the heavenly teacher, his struggles against and victories over the magicians he runs into, the submission of many countries and finally his return. In reward of services rendered, a temple is built where sacrifices will be offered to him, although he is still among the living.

"The feats described in this book are for the greater part imitations of those found in "Hsi-yu-chi" and "Feng-shen-chuan". The style is slipshod and often tedious. One point of interest, if not of merit, is that this book is the source of many present-day legends such as the dispute of the Five Spirits with the P'an-kuan, the revolt of the Five Rats in the eastern capital, etc. ..." (Wu I-t'ai, Le Roman Chinois, pp. 42-44 passim). *For informed readers.*

1213. 聊齋誌異 *STRANGE STORIES FROM A CHINESE STUDIO*

(1931-1715) by 蒲松齡

"The collection of stories which is most widely known and enjoyed by lovers of romantic literature is the "Liao-chai-chih-yi" (Strange stories from a Chinese studio). The stories are very short, the longest not comprising more than two pages of Chinese print and many only a few lines; they deal with ghosts, personified foxes, and more such strange and fantastic concoctions after the pattern of the stories from the T'ang era."

Very objectionable because of many immodest passages.

1214. 水滸傳 *ALL MEN ARE BROTHERS* by 施耐庵

"The story is based upon the doings of a historical band of brigands, who had actually terrorized a couple of provinces, until they were finally put down, early in the twelfth century. Some of it is very laughable, and all of it is valuable for the insight given into Chinese manners and customs." (A History of Chinese Literature, H.A. Giles pp. 280,281).

According to Hu Shih this book "gives vent to grievances of the common people and scholars against the government".

The book "goes back to the twelfth century when Sung Chiang and his thirty six confederates, suffering from the iniquities of government officers, formed a much-feared band of robbers. They were killed in their fight against the Tartars invading their country. The first outline of this story can be found in the book "Hsiuan-ho-i-shih". The legion grew and the confederates became one hundred and eight in number. Various episodes were arranged for the stage during the Yuan period. It is probably during the Ming dynasty that the first redaction in one hundred chapters was written. About 1500, an unknown master, afterwards commonly designed as Shih Nai-an, wrote the story in seventy chapters. It so far excells all earlier versions that it constitutes the core of all subsequent redactions. The last few hundred years the book went through a lot of vicissitudes: it was augmented and again critically reedited. It is the classic of moral uplifting, its main argument being that banditry is born of bad government and that a good bandit is better than a corrupt public servant." (Die Chinesiche Literatur, von Richard Wilhelm pp. 182,183).

It is difficult to pronounce judgment on the contents of the book. The great majority of chapters contain nothing objectionable. Passages of ch. 20 are immodest; ch. 23, 24, 25 and 44, 45 still more so. Yet it would shock most Chinese literati to pronounce the book unsuitable for all readers. It may suffice to say that it calls for *some reserve*.

In English "All Men are Brothers" by Pearl S. Buck.

1215. 三俠五義   Edited in 1879 by 石玉崑

The model of all romances of chivalry.

"Emperor Chen Tsung, having no heir to the throne, promises two of his concubines, Li and Liu, who are with child, that he will make empress the one who gives birth to a son. Liu conspires with a eunuch Kuo Huai. As soon as Li gives birth to a son, Kuo-Huai is to take the child away and hand it to K'u Chu, a maid in the palace, to be drowned. Kuo-huai is then to put a skinned cat in the baby's place.

In due time a boy is born, but K'u Chu has not the heart to kill him, so she gives the child to Chen Lin, another eunuch, who hides the boy in the home of the Emperor's eighth brother, where he is educated as if he were the latter's third son. In the meantime Li is accused of giving birth to a freak and relegated to a far-off palace, whence she escapes.

The emperor dies heirless and the third son of the emperor's eighth brother succeeds to the throne. His title is Jen Tsung.

The book then relates the birth of Pao Ch'eng, his marriage, and the first cases brought before his tribunal. When he is prefect of K'ai-feng-fu he meets Li, the former concubine, and hears of her experience. Thereupon Pao Ch'eng institutes the substitution case (Li mao huan t'ai-tzu).

On being informed of the identity of his mother, the emperor introduces her with great pomp into the palace.

By his integrity Pao Ch'eng wins over several errant knights — who give the title to the book —: the three Knights and the five Rats.

It is then reported that the prince of Hsiang Yang, Chao Chiao, plans a revolution. The list with the names of his accomplices is hidden in a pavilion called Ch'ung Hsiu Lu. The Five Rats are brought under the jurisdiction of Yen Ch'a-san, governor of the province, and start investigating. Po Yü-t'ang, the Rat with the brocade pelt, tries to get into the pavilion but walks into a trap and is killed.

The book ends at this juncture." (Le roman chinois, Wu I-t'ai, pp. 159-162). *For informed readers.*

1216. 曼殊小說集 *STORIES BY MAN-SHU* 1 vol. 128 p. by 蘇曼殊
1944 惠迪吉書局 *See Biogr. 140*

An "old style" story. The style is rather difficult. This book presents old-time conditions with a little renovation. It presents a free morality. *For informed people only.*

1217. 紅樓夢 *DREAM OF THE RED CHAMBER* by 曹雪芹

"The book contains 120 chapters, 235 male and 213 female characters. According to the Chinese critics it is unique of its kind. The plot is perfect, the style is finished. It is written in the language of the better classes of Peking at the time of its appearance. Also in this novel, according to the same critics, love is expressed in the most perfect way. Who knows how many readers, men as well as women, have been moved to tears by the death of Ch'ing Wen and Tai Yü. Every feeling, every gesture in the book is natural". (Wu I-t'ai, Le Roman Chinois pp. 63 ff).

"The author was of a very wealthy and over-refined family that fell into poverty in a very short time. Ts'ao-chan took to drinking and died young. In his book he describes the glory of bygone days. We see how Chia Pao-yü grows up in the midst of the girls of the family, which brings about a great number of love-tangles and tragedies. The most pathetic is Pao-yü's love for Lin Tai-yü who dies of love-sickness after Pao-yu's parents have tricked him into a marriage with another girl. Pao-yü leaves home and meets his father when, many years later, he has died to the world and became a monk". (Richard Wilhelm, Die Chinesische Literatur p. 184).

The book is an interesting social, psychological and emotional study.

It is *very objectionable* because of the sentimental atmosphere, and must not be read by younger people.

1218. 兒女英雄傳 *THE HEROIC CHILDREN* Edited about 1770 by 文 康

"Ho Yu-feng, the heroine of the book, is a courageous and intelligent girl, who handles weapons with proficient skill. Her father died in prison, a victim of court intrigue. Yu-feng-nick-named Shih-san-mei—, taking her mother with her, flees to the country and awaits the opportunity to retaliate. To kill time, she travels all over the country righting wrongs, protecting the weak, punishing criminals. One day she runs into a young man, An-chi, who carries a huge sum of money with which to ransom his father who is unjustly put in prison. First his own muleteers, then some monks, plan to kill him, but each time he is saved by Shih san-mei. Later the enemy of her family is sentenced to death for his exactions. Yu-feng, appeased and having lost her mother, decides to leave the world and enter a nunnery. Fortunately An-chi's father, set free, arrives in time. . .and Yu-feng is married to An-chi. The fact that he already has a wife does not impair his domestic peace. After a year An-chi comes out third in the examinations and is appointed to very important posts. He judges a few cases, captures several big bandits. . .often thanks to his wife's help" (Wu I-t'ai, Le Roman Chinois pp. 154-155).

Hu Shih, (Wen ts'uen, 2nd series, vol. 2 p. 168,) writes "The ideas expressed in "Erh-niü-ying-hsiung-chuan" have no value whatever; the only assets of the book are its elegance, its humour and its pithiness." This is considered by many to be too severe a judgement.

It is a valuable book as it is the only one written in everyday Pekinese dialect. *For all.*

1219. 西遊記 *RECORD OF TRAVELS IN THE WEST* by 吳承恩

"The Hsi Yu Chi or Record of Travels in the West is a favourite novel written in a popular and easy style. It is based upon the journey of Hsuan Tsang to India in search of books, images, and relics to illustrate the Buddhist religion". (H.A. Giles, A History of Chinese Literature, p. 281).

"The author has added to the record a great number of adventures, each more fantastic than the other". (Wu I-t'ai, Le Roman Chinois p. 31).

"In its present form the book is an Allegory of the deliverance of man from the visible world and in so far it possesses a remote but unmistakable resemblance to "The Pilgrim's Progress". The dissolute monkey Sun Wu-k'ung represents the human heart that, restless and ever dissatisfied, always strives onward until it finally, in supreme pride, challenges God's throne in heaven. All gods are powerless against this titan; only Lao-tzu manages to throw over him the magic ring which gently encloses when the monkey is quiet, but cuts deep into the flesh when he tries to rise. In the end he is subdued and converted by Buddha. Having accepted the true faith, he joins the monk Hsuan Tsang in his pilgrimage. He overcomes the pig Chu Pa Chieh which represents the animal aspect of human nature, and, together with some shell-arched animals representing the passive side of man's nature, he accompanies the monk on his journey.

Many adventures lie in store for them, among which the most dangerous is the crossing of a turbulent stream. Only a plank spans the stream so that only the monkey ventures to go across. After a while the vessel arrives which serves as the ferry to heaven. As it has no bottom Hsuan Tsang falls into the water upon embarking, but is rescued. When they have reached the middle of the stream they see a body floating by, which Hsuan Tsang learns to be his earthly body. His fellowtravellers congratulate him on his salvation. The ferry-man vanishes as soon as they reach the opposite bank, and thus, the end is reached. (Richard Wilhelm, Die Chinesiche Literatur, p. 182). *For all.*

1220. 儒林外史 *(1701-1754)*   by 吳敬梓

"This book was finished towards the end of the Yung-Cheng reign (1730). Separated from the Ming period by scarcely one century, the literati still clung to the customs of that time. Their only interest lay in their literary lucubrations. . .Wu Chin-tzu describes this kind of man of letters. . .from what he had personally heard and seen. . .no plot unites the various episodes. . .told directly from every day life. . .

The personages in the book actually existed." (Wu I-t'ai, Le Roman Chinois pp. 114-115). *For all.*

1221. 二十年目睹之怪現狀   2 vol. 344 & 320 pp. by 吳沃堯
                                                                     廣益書局

The author relates some extraordinary things and events that he witnessed during twenty years. It is a satirical novel written by Wu Wu Yao (1867-1910).

Here the author describes the morals, customs and traditions of the officials during the reign of Kuang-Hsü. *For everyone.*

1222. 青樓夢   by 俞 達

This book describes the loves of Chin Yi-hsiang and his friends Chih Pai-ling, Yao and Yeh. They are regular customers of the brothels where they pick up acquaintance with thirty six women. The book deals chiefly with their visits there. No objectionable descriptions; they hold hands and snivel over trifles. Fervent admirers of "Hung lou meng" they make believe to live through the scenes of that novel.

One day Yi-hsiang is taken ill, on one of his visits; he is believed dead but — the errand boy from Hades get the name and address wrong — returns to life and tells his experiences in the underworld.

Having passed his examinations, he starts on his career. He chooses Niu Ai-ching, his favourite prostitute, to be his wife. Afterwards he takes four concubines: two prostitutes and two illiterate women. Gradually his family grows: three sons are born and a daughter. Not the slightest quarrel whatever ruffles the harmony of the home. Even Yi-hsiang's visits to the brothel fail to raise as much as a suspicion of jealousy at home. But for an occasional set-back when one of the girls marries or becomes a nun, it would be a real heaven!

Chih Pai-ling also marries and takes several concubines. His children marry his friend's children.

Yi-hsiang is appointed mandarin and works wonders. After a few years he retires in order to be able to look after his old parents. The latter fly off to heaven without dying. Yi-hsiang plans to leave the world and enter a monastery. During his absence his son passes his examination and enters public service. Coming home, Yi-hsiang finds his family well looked after, so he takes off to heaven with his wife and his favourite concubine. There he finds the group of thirty six reunited. Soon his friends follow with their wives and everybody settles down for a blissful eternity.

The book contains no unbecoming descriptions but *is immoral* because it describes the pagan ideal of a voluptuous life.

1223. 七俠五義   by 俞樾 (died in 1906)

"The book "San-hsia-wu-yi" was reedited by Yü Yüeh with a preface in which he says that he saw the "San-hsia-wu-yi" brought from the capital by one of his friends. At first he thought it was an ordinary novel, but, reading it, he realized that the adventures were unedited and unusual; that the style was natural and fluent, the descriptions accurate, finished, colourful and lively. . .He found the opening chapter, the substitution of the heir to the throne (see 三俠五義), too far-fetched and improbable and wrote a new one. Moreover, the heroes of the book: The Nothern Knight, the Southern Knight and the Twin-Knights were four in number, while the title only mentioned three, so he added three more, who were only secondary characters in the original story and changed the title into "Ch'i-hsia-wu-yi". The first edition was published in 1899, the 25th year of Kuang Hsü. It is so widely read that it has almost ousted the original novel from the market". (Wu I-t'ai, Le Roman Chinois, p. 164). *For informed readers.*

1224 a. 滕大尹鬼斷家私 *MARVELLOUS TALES, ANCIENT & MODERN*
    THE ANCESTRAL PORTRAIT   3rd story from the 今古奇觀

At the age of seventy nine a certain governor marries a young girl. This second marriage is looked upon with ill will by the old man's son who does not want the heritage to be divided. A son is born. Shortly afterwards the old man dies, leaving his elder son sole heir to the estate. He leaves his wife a portrait and advises her to take it to an honest officer when the second boy comes of age.

During many years the woman and her son live in a tumbledown part of the mansion. Later on they go to live on a poor farm which is their only possession. When the boy has grown up his mother take the painting to an honest mandarin who finds a more recent testament glued to the back. In this testament the old man leaves them a sum of money equal to the value of the estate inherited by the elder son. They find the treasure buried under the cottage where they had been living. The old man had not revealed his secret at the time of his death lest the older son should kill his brother.

In German: "Das Geheimnisvolle Bild" included in "Chinesische Meisternovellen" by Franz Kuhn. *For all.*

1224 b. 杜十娘怒沉百寶箱   *FULL FATHOM FIVE*   5th story from the 今古奇觀

Li, an officer's son, goes to Peking to pass his examination. There he spends all his money on women, among whom the famous Tu-shih. She saves him from utter dejection, and, because she really loves him, she buys her own freedom and goes South with Li. Tu-shih carries with her a box, the contents of which are unknown to Li. On the way home, Li anticipates trouble when he returns home with his prostitute and fears to be disherited by his parents. He picks up a friend who proposes to strike a bargain: Li would sell Tu-shih to him for 1000 ounces of silver. He would return home and tell his parents he earned the silver in Peking. Li accepts and advises Tu-shih of his scheme. She consents and Li is handed the money. Then, in presence of the two friends, Tu-shih opens the box, revealing 10,000 ounces worth of jewels. She throws her treasure into the river, cursing the two men but particularly Li. Then she jumps into the river. Li is infinitely sorry; his friend dies tormented by the "spirit of the river".

In German: Das Juwelen Kästchen, by Franz Kuhn. *For all.*

1224 c. 李謫仙醉草嚇蠻書 *MIGHTIER THAN THE SWORD*

6th story from the **今古奇觀**

Li T'ai-peh is a great poet and drinker. He goes in for literary examinations but, having no money to bribe the officers of the Board of Examinations, he does not pass. One day the kingdom of Korea sends a threatening letter to the emperor. Our poet is the only one in the whole empire who understands the idiom in which the letter is written, but, as he has no official standing, he cannot be consulted. On hearing this, the emperor, cutting all red tape, promotes him doctor. After reading the letter Li writes an answer that not only conjures the threatening danger but even makes the Koreans vassals of the Chinese Empire.

The emperor wishes to keep the poet in his service, but he prefers wine and liberty. He continues writing poems and even ridicules the empress. His enemies, his former examiners, try to profit from this opportunity to work his downfall. Li T'ai-peh escapes from the capital and drinks to his heart's content till it brings him death. *For all.*

1224 d. 賣油郎獨佔花魁女 *HIS TO HOLD*   7th story from the **今古奇觀**

War scatters all the members of a family. Yao Ching, the daughter, still very young, is left alone in a strange country. By chance she meets a man from her home-town who, pretending to bring her back home, sells her to a brothel. First the young girl resists all temptation. Later on, in order to find herself a husband, she consents to receiving visitors. She picks her choice in the person of a poor oil-dealer. As she has grown very rich in her profession, she buys her own freedom and marries the man who loves her deeply. At her husband's home she finds that his servants are her own parents. In the end the husband also finds his father in a monastery. Thus the couple live in complete happiness.

Although the book points a good moral, *some reserve* should be made on account of a few immodest passages which make it unsuitable for younger people.

In German: Der Olhandler und die Blumenkonigin by Walter Strzoda.

1224 e. 盧太學詩酒傲公侯 *BUT ART IS IMMORTAL* 15th story from the **今古奇觀**

Lu Nan lives in a grand style. The local magistrate often plans to pay him a visit, but each time something happens to prevent him. One day he has some leisure, but, as he starts rather late, he finds the host already stone drunk. The magistrate considers this a personal affront and avenges himself by ransacking the residence and convicting Lu Nan of murder. Lu Nan is in prison until, ten years later, an honest officer revises the sentence. Lu Nan returns to his former style of living but soon goes broke; he then continues to enjoy life as a tramp.

In German: Die Rache des Dschih-hsien by Walter Strzoda. *For all.*

1224 f. 蘇小妹三難新郎 *THREE FINAL BARRIERS* 17th story from the 今古奇觀

Su Hsiao-mei is a very learned young lady. Before she allows anyone to ask for her hand, her father subjects the candidates to a very stiff literary examination. On his wedding day, the bridegroom finds the bridal chamber locked. His bride wants him to pass three more exams before she will let him in. He takes the hurdles in great style and enjoys undisturbed happiness ever after.

In German: Die drei Hochzeitsprüfungen by Walter Strzoda. *For all.*

1224 g. 莊子休鼓盆成大道 *FAITHFUL TO THE WORD*

20th story from the 今古奇觀

Chuang-tzu, disciple of Lao-tzu, marries three times in spite of his having attained "perfection". One day, going for a walk into the country, he sees a young widow fanning the burial mound over her recently deceased husband's grave. The quicker it dries the quicker she can get married without being gossiped about. On his return Chuang-tzu comments on what he saw saying that all women are changeable. His wife protests loudly that she will never remarry! The philosopher dies and after no more than twenty days his widow marries a prince. On his very wedding day the latter is taken ill; the only remedy for his ailment is eating the brains of a man. The bride goes out to find some; she opens her former husband's casket and as she aims the blow Chuang-tzu rises from his coffin.

Having thus lost face, she hangs herself. Chuang-tzu does not remarry any more.

In German: Die Probe auf's Exempel by Walter Strzoda. *For all.*

1224 h. 蔣興哥重會珍珠衫 *STORY OF A PEARL-STRINGED SHIRT*

23rd story from the 今古奇觀

Hsing Ko, a rich businessman, marries a beautiful and educated girl. They are so engrossed in each other that, for several years, the husband forgets to travel for his business. His affairs becoming more urgent, he finally decides to depart. On going away he gives his wife a shirt made of pearls and asks her to wear it in remembrance of him. At the fixed time he fails to return and his wife starts languishing. A certain Ch'en notices this and desires to get in touch with her. A certain woman by name of Pi, having had her palm well greased, promises to bring them together. After six months her wiles conquer the lady's opposition and Ch'en's desire is fulfilled.

After a month he is obliged to resume his travels, so his mistress gives him her pearl shirt as a souvenir to remember her by.

On his return Hsing Ko learns about his wife's conduct and repudiates her without, however, letting the affair be talked about because he still loves her. She then becomes a magistrate's concubine.

Ch'en, back at his own home, is unhappy, thinking of his mistress of whom the pearl shirt constantly reminds him. In the long run neither the shirt nor his worrying escape his wife's notice. So she steals the shirt. After some time Ch'en sets out in search of his mistress and, finding out about her, is taken ill and dies. His wife comes over for the funeral; the expense runs so high that she finds no other way to cover it but remarry. The bridegroom is Hsing Ko. He finds the shirt among his brides's belongings and in that way learns that she is Ch'en's widow.

Later on, during one of his business trips, Hsing Ko kills a man by accident. The magistrate, who hears his case, is the one who took his repudiated wife as a concubine. When Hsing Ko's ex-wife hears about the case, she tells the magistrate that he is her brother and so saves his life. It does not take the magistrate long to perceive that they are not just sister and brother, for they still love each other. When they confess all to the magistrate he generously returns the woman to Hsing Ko.

This way Hsing Ko is in possession of two wives. But that is also amicably settled. Ch'en's widow being the elder, she is pronounced the lawful spouse; the other concubine. Thus everybody is happy.

In German: Das Perlenhemd by Franz Kuhn.

The ideas of the story being misleading, the book must be reserved *for well informed readers.*

1224 i. 蔡小姐忍辱報仇   *VENGEANCE IS SWEET*   26th story from the   今古奇觀

An officer, on his way to his post with his whole family, is killed by the boatmen who divide his belongings among them. The captain lays hands on the daughter. She swears to have her revenge.   In the meantime she experiences no end of misery and often changes owner. In the end she runs into a husband who is really compassionate and avenges her parents. Although satisfied on that point, she thinks her lot too miserable and commits suicide.

Suicide and revenge cannot be approved of. *For informed readers.*

1224 j. 錢秀才錯占鳳凰儔   *MARRIED BY CHANCE*   27th story from the   今古奇觀

The father of an exquisitely beautiful daughter will only accept as his son-in-law a youth of comparable beauty. An Adonis proving hard to find, his friends resort to ruse. They send a good looking but poor young man to go through the marriage ceremonies.   On the night of the marriage he is to stand aside for the real bridegroom, who has money but no looks, to enter the bridal chamber. Somehow the trick does not work. The father discovers the ruse and brings an action against the Adonis.

The magistrate sees that the girl loves the poor boy, so he decides that they are to be married.

With the exception of the rich boy, everybody is of course satisfied with the solution. *For all.*

1224 k. 喬太守亂點鴛鴦譜   *ARBITRARILY MATCHED*   28th story from the   今古奇觀

Miss Sun is engaged to be married to a certain Liu. When the boy falls ill Mrs. Sun wants to put off the marriage. As Liu's family insist, Mrs. Sun, who does not want to expose her daughter to infection, devises a ruse. On the wedding day her young son, dressed as a girl, takes place in the bridal palanquin. The plan succeeds to perfection. In the evening Liu's illness gets worse, so it is decided to let the bride (?) sleep with the daughter of the house. These two make love to each other; after a few days the fraud becomes known. After a lot of tears and cries the issue is favourably settled: Liu gets well and marries Miss Sun; the two lovers also marry. *Some reserve* because of immodest passages.

1224 l. 金玉奴棒打薄情郎   *DAUGHTER OF THE KING-BEGGAR*
32nd story from the   今古奇觀

A young man of noble birth, Mo Chi, marries a common girl for her money. The money provides her with connections in high places, so that her husband can pass his examinations and receive his title. Having reached that height, Mo Chi is ashamed of the low birth of his wife and throws her into the water. The governor of the province, who happens to sail by, saves her and adopts her as his daughter. After some time his fellow magistrates suggest to marry the girl to a distinguished young magistrate. The bridegroom they have picked happens to be Mo Chi. The governor, who knows all about the girl's adventures, consents and the marriage takes place. On the evening of the wedding day, Mo Chi is given a sound flogging by the maids at the entrance of the bridal chamber. Then he is scolded by both the governor and his bride, after which the union is put off till the next day. Repentant, he finds happiness with his wife who, by her adoption, has after all been ennobled.

In German "Die Tochter des Bettlerkönigs", by Franz Kuhn, included in "Chinesische Meisternovellen". *For all*.

1224 m. 趙縣君喬送黃柑子 *YELLOW CRANGES OF A PRINCESS*

38th story from the 今古奇觀

Wu-yueh goes to the capital to compete for a post. When he comes to a certain town where he wishes to stay for a few days, he takes a room in a hotel. One day while buying oranges at the door, he sees a nice woman in the house opposite. This sight so troubles him that he cannot decide to buy any oranges. Fortunately the lady noticed his embarrassment and sends him some beautiful oranges. He tries to find out who she is and is told that she is princess Chao, wife of one of the ministers of the empire, away at the capital. To thank her for her kind attention Wu-yueh repeatedly sends her magnificent presents, in that way trying to get better acquainted.

After some time he is granted a more intimate interview. Just as he enters her room, the minister's return is announced. Our hero hides under the bed but is soon discovered. The minister makes a scene over the disgrace, yet, when Wu-yueh mentions a big sum, the affair is easily settled. Given his liberty, Wu-Yueh pays and finds the house empty the next day. On further information he realizes that he has been imposed upon by two swindlers.

Immodest details make the book *unsuitable for young people*.

In German: Die Gelben Orangen der Prinzessin Tchao by Walter Strzoda.

1224 n. 誇妙術丹客提金 *THE ALCHEMIST*   39th story from the 今古奇觀

An alchemist, P'an, is after the great secret. After many disappointments he meets a rich man who claims to be able to make gold. He is willing to work for P'an and receives two thousand tael to be converted into gold. When the operation has already started, it is announced that the rich man's mother has died. He parts in a hurry leaving one of his concubines behind to look after the furnace. P'an makes love to her and, on the other's return, has to pay a large sum to keep the affair quiet. And then, the process does not work.

Although cheated once, P'an does not give up his dream and is bled white by another gang.

In German: Der Alchimist by Walter Strzoda.

Unsuitable for younger readers.

1225. 金瓶梅 *THE GOLD-VASE-PLUM*

The loves of Hsi-men Ch'ing are told here in full detail. Modern critics, Chinese as well as foreign, assure us that the book gives an accurate description of life in the "better" families of that time, so that it can no longer be said to be mere pornography.

Still, it has always been classified as such, and with plenty of reason. At one time the government banned it, and no Catholic reader, whosoever, can be permitted to read it. *To be proscribed*.

1226. 二度梅 *TWICE FLOWERING PLUM-TREES*

The author describes the corruption of the chancellor Lu Chi and his minister who profit of their position to enrich themselves. Mei, an honest officer, is appointed censor and wants to expose them but pays heavily for his integrity. After that the story deals with Mr. Mei's son, another family by name of Ch'en, the engagement of Mei jr. to Miss. Ch'en, and of Ch'en jr. to a lady of noble birth.

Towards the end Mei jr. and Ch'en jr. are promoted doctor; the chancellor loses his position and is replaced by Mei; a marriage at the court of the emperor ends the book.

In German: "Die Rache des jungen Meh" by Franz Kuhn.

1227. 封神傳演義

"The novel begins with the pilgrimage of Chou Hsin to the Temple of Niü Kwa. When he sees the image of the goddess he writes a disrespectful poem on the wall of the temple. Incensed, the goddess orders three evil genii: a fox, a scorpion and a pheasant, disguised as women, to go and work his undoing. Chapters 2 to 3 tell of Chou Hsin's cruelty and the revolt of his vassals. Then follows the story of the battles between the emperor's armies and the rebels in which the imperial troops are beaten. Chou-Hsin dies.

Emperor Wu, of the Chou dynasty, enters the capital; the commander-in-chief of his army promotes the dead warriors to celestial posts, while Wu distributes feudal estates among the living. This book was and still is eagerly read by many, especially children". (Wu I-t'ai, Le Roman Chinois, p. 41). *For informed readers.*

1228. 好逑傳   by an unknown author of Ming epoch.

Chung Yü is preparing for his examinations. He is very chivalrous and fears nobody. He shows this by rescuing a girl who has been abducted by a minister and by energetic steps in favour of a disgraced officer.

Ping Hsin, the daughter of a minister, also has outstanding qualities: she is wise, beautiful and chaste.

The son of the secretary Kuo wants to marry her, but the girl is clever enough to shake him off. Whatever trick he tries in the absence of her father Ping Hsin is always more clever than he. Ping Hsin's uncle helps Kuo in his plans, hoping to get his part of the family's possessions. One day they try taking Ping Hsin by force but Chung Yü happens to pass by and rescues her. Kuo turns against Chung Yü and tries to imprison him. The girl learns about it, takes him into her house and nurses him. Every precaution is taken to protect their good name while they live under one roof. Well again, Chuang Yü goes to the capital to pass his examination. There his complicity in a fishy affair results in the punishment of the culprits; he thereby unknowingly effects the rehabilitation of Ping Hsin's father. When he returns to his post as minister he wants to give his daughter to Chung Yü to show his gratitude. Although the young man loves the girl he declines the offer. Ping Hsin also declines the proposal; both give the same reason: having lived under the same roof for some time, they would give rise to suspicion if they married.

Further events oblige the parents to insist on the marriage; the young people obey, but they only go through the formalities and do not live together. As many candidates try to get married to Ping Hsin, the situation grows so complicated that the emperor himself must intervene. Having investigated the case, the emperor highly praises the virtue and intelligence of the two heroes and heaps honours on their parents. Henceforth the couple, who loved each other from the first time they met, live in perfect happiness.

There is nothing offensive in this book, yet we deem it *unsuitable for young people* because it will upset their imagination.

In German: "Eisherz und Edeljaspis" by Franz Kuhn.

In French: "La femme accomplie" and "L'heureuse union."

1229. 新編白話聊齋誌異

上海中華書局

One hundred and fifty eight stories and anecdotes: part of them in ordinary language, part in literary style.

Many unbecoming passages. *For informed readers.*

1230. 繪圖兒女英雄傳 *ADVENTURES OF A MAN OF LETTERS — ILLUSTRATED*

4 vol. 145, 161, 169, 136 pp. 廣益書局

Relates the feats of ancient child-heroes who interfere in people's lives. This book is read by everybody and constantly drawn upon by the "Shuo Shu ti".

Objectionable because of improprieties. *For informed readers.*

1231. 施公案

Edited in 1838 by an unknown author.

"This is the first Romance of chivalry. It was edited in 1838. Its title is Shih-Kung-An, for in all the romances of that kind there is a central figure around which the heroes revolve. The novel comprises eighty chapters. It is probably the work of a storyteller whose name has not come down to us. It tells the adventures of Shih Luen (who lived at the time of K'ang Hsi) who started as sub-prefect of T'aichow and ended up as Superintendent General of grain-transport. Besides the cases he judges, the book deals with the capture of highway-robbers, the kidnapping of Shih Luen and his deliverance by his satellites, skirmishes with the "Knights of the Green Forest" etc." (Wu I-t'ai, Le Roman Chinois, p. 153.) *For all.*

1232. 玉嬌梨(雙美奇緣)

1 vol. 87 p.

A young man, Ssu, extremely well gifted and good looking, receives the highest honours. After much bad luck, he marries two cousins with the consent of both. As the two girls dearly love each other, they constitute "one heart" and so, without the slightest difficulty, marry the same man. That is the way in which the author explains that kind of marriage that is very common in Chinese literature.

It is a very interesting book, without the slightest unbecoming detail. The outcome may shock us; it certainly did not shock contemporary readers.

May be read by all provided one rectifies the erroneous idea about marriage.

In French: "Les deux cousines".

1233. 玉蜻蜓

Sun, unfaithful to his wife, lives a gay life together with his friend Ch'en. He has intercourse with a Buddhist nun, who is with child when he dies. On his deathbed he gives the mother a jade jewel shaped like a dragon-fly. He also instructs her to give the jade to the child so that it may prove its noble origin.

When the child is born, the nun cannot keep him; so she pins the jade to his diapers and deposits him at the gate of the local mandarin's residence. The latter adopts the child.

Growing up, the young man passes his examination successfully and goes in search of his parents. His adopted parents know Mrs. Sun. One day when the young man is on a visit at Mrs. Sun's, she notices the dragon-fly which she remembers having given to her husband. Thus the child's identity is established. When Mrs. Sun starts reviling the nun the mandarin intervenes. He reconciles the two women who henceforth live together in peace at the young man's house.

It is a very interesting book. The atmosphere is not any too healthy. *For well informed readers.*

In German: Die Jadelibelle.

PRESENT DAY DRAMA

1234. 群鶯亂飛 *ORIOLS EVERYWHERE* 1 vol. 145 p. by **阿英（錢杏邨）**
1942 國民書店 *See Biogr. 34*

Play in one act.

This book presents a big family consisting of three sons ... two of whom are married-and two daughters. The parents are dead. A succession of disasters fell on the said family. The elder brother retired from his business; the second, owing to his infidelity, was left by his wife, while the younger daughter was seduced by a scamp. In the meantime the eldest sister-in-law scattered the family's wealth. The younger son, who was a student, made valiant but unsuccessful efforts to restore the family. The second brother's wife, unable to bear the disasters, drowned herself. The elder brother, after killing his wife, committed suicide.

As this tragedy contains a lot of cursing, as well as murders and suicides, it presents an unhealthy atmosphere.

May be read *only by informed readers*.

1235. 不夜城 *CITY OF NO NIGHT* 1 vol. 110 p. by **阿英**
1940 潮鋒出版社

A social drama in three acts describing the vices of Shanghai capitalists.

Communist propaganda, without interest and insipid, with long demagogic tirades.

Practically no literary value. *To be condemned.*

1236. 嫦娥 *FLED TO THE MOON: CH'ANG-E* by **張眞**

A play in 4 acts.

The king 后羿 is a cruel man, hated by the people whom he exploits; but he is a skilful hunter and archer. To assist him, he has many slaves whom he treats as brutes and kills at will.

During a hunting party, he meets 嫦娥; she is a beauty, the only child of an old fisher. 逄蒙, the man who by order of the king supervises the work of the slaves, is a friend of hers. The king becomes enamoured of the girl and takes her with him. The father first intercedes but in vain; finally the king puts him in irons and he becomes one of the many slaves.

The heroine, living now in the king's palace, is bored with everything and is still thinking of her old friend. Once, her father visits the king and tries to insist on getting back his child; but he is beaten and had Hsi Wang Mu (西王母) not arrived he would have died. The old Hsi Wang Mu, during the same visit to the monarch, gives him a long life elixir.

The king orders 嫦娥 to hide the liquid, saying the bottle contains poison.

The heroine's father, having fled, is shot by the king, who is so skilful with the bow that he can hit his target from a distance of hundreds of miles.

But 嫦娥 still languishes and suggests to her friend that they make an escape together. Their plans being frustrated, the friend can only flee. 嫦娥 breaks her husband's bow so that he is unable to kill the fugitive. The heroine now kills her guard, and, having taken the poison, she flees with her two servants.

When they reach the mountains covered with snow, one of the servants dies of exhaustion, the other one is captured and killed by the king.

Follows now a scene of the highest tragedy. 嫦娥 curses her husband, and announces to him the coming of her friend as a leader of the slaves to carry out their revenge and to kill the king. Those words make the king wild; He runs after her, but she jumps into the abyss. Instead of perishing like other mortals, having already drunk the elixir, she is received in the moon. The dark spots we now admire on that body are the image of 嫦娥. During this final action, one hears the tumult and cries of the slaves. As an army under the command of 逢蒙 they come along to the place of the crime. The king falls dead struck by an arrow.

For informed persons.

1237. 夜 *NIGHT*   1 vol. 195 p. by 章　泯
1947 大東書局 *See Biogr.* 7

A play in five acts.
Very patriotic play. Of a divided family. The father loves his country and sacrifices his fortune. The eldest son flirts with the enemy, while the second son gives his life for China. The daughter joins the guerillas.
A very simple play suitable for our schools. *For everyone.*

1238. 自求 *YOURSELF TO BLAME*   1 vol. 340 p. by 張 道藩
1935 正中書局 *See Biogr.* 9

1. 自求 p. 1-90. A play in four acts.
A young Chinese, artist by profession, and living in France, repudiates by letter the fiancee chosen for him by his family in China. The father of the girl in question is angry, but the daughter is more intelligent. She employs a stratagem and goes to reside in France. There she meets her fiance, who does not know who she is, who falls in love with her. Soon after, he proposes to her, and only then does she reveal her true identity. *For everyone.*

2. 第一次的雲霧 p. 299-339. A translation of "Premiers Nuages" of Jose Germain. One act.
A quarrel between a young couple on their return from their honeymoon. Everything is made up.
These plays contain too many sentimental demonstrations for Chinese readers but *may be read by anyone.*
The rest of the book consists of criticisms on these two plays and instructions on how they should be presented.

1239. 狄四娘   1 vol. 39 p. by 張 道藩
1940 中國圖書雜誌公司

Tragedy in 4 acts.
The governor of a certain province loves the actress "Ti Ssu-niang". The actress does not reciprocate his feelings but loves a certain Lo. Lo loves the governor's wife. The actress plans the undoing of the governor and his wife, but does not execute her plans because of her mother's cross found in the room of the governor's wife. Sparing their

lives, she herself dies at the hand of Lo who believes that she poisoned the woman he loves. *For informed readers.*

1240. 瀟湘淑女(又名忠義千秋) *FAITHFUL ETERNALLY*

1 vol. 83 p. by 趙淸閣[1]
1944 Chungking, 1947 Shanghai, Commercial Press.

Patriotic play in four acts.

A Chinese family during Japanese occupation. The father is an all-out patriot; the mother lacks all elevation of character, seeing but her own interests. The son is much like his father and discontinues his studies to be a soldier. The chief character though is the adopted daughter, being sought both by her adopted brother and by the chief of police in enemy service. Hating to live with her unworthy mother and very fond of her adopted father she promises to marry the chief of police, to keep her father from jail.

The betrothal is used as an excuse to impart important informations to the guerillas. The son of the chief of police heads the guerillas and he is also in love with the daughter, who prefers him to all her other lovers.

The play ends with the victorious entry of the Chinese Army into the place. The chief of police wants to flee with his betrothed, but rebuked by her, he is killed. All the actors are again together and the adopted daughter gives her promise of marriage to the son of the chief of police. The son of the family returns with the victorious armies and is proud of his officer's rank, but thwarted in his hopes, he gets a transfer from his superiors and accepts to go out on a dangerous mission.

The lovers also intend to carry on their battle for the country. *For everyone.*

---

(1) Chao Ch'ing-ko 趙淸閣.
Playwright, novelist, and short-story writer. Born in Sinyang, Honan. After graduating from the Shanghai College of Fine Arts 上海美術專科學校 she became the editor of the magazine *Nü Tzu Yüeh K'an* 女子月刊 (Women's Monthly), published by the bookstore Nü Tzu Shu Tien 女子書店. During the Sino-Japanese War, she was in the Interior, and worked in the T'ien I Motion Picture Co. 天一影片公司, and the Central Motion Picture Co. 中央電影攝製廠. After the Victory over Japan, she returned to Shanghai. She is now the editor of the monthly magazine *Wên Ch'ao* 文潮 (Literary Current), published by the Chêng Chung Book Co. 正中書局, Shanghai.
Before the War, she wrote only short stories, which she collected into two volumes, entitled *Han* 旱 (Drought, 女子書店); and *Hua Pei Chih Ch'iu* 華北之秋 (Autumn in North China, 鐵流). During the War, she devoted herself completely to play-writing. Up to the August of 1945, she had produced more than twenty volumes altogether. Ther are: *Fan Kung Shêng Li* 反攻膡利 (in 3 acts, 正中); *Nü Chieh* 女傑 (in 5 acts, 華中圖書公司); *Shêng Ssu Lüan* 生死戀 (in 5 acts, 商務); *Kuan Yü* 關羽 (in 4 acts, 正中) *Mu Lan Ts'ung Chün* 木蘭從軍 (in 3 acts, 婦女月刊社); *Tz'u Hên Mien Mien* 此恨綿綿 (in 5 acts, 正言出版社); *T'ao Li Ch'un Feng* 桃李春風 (in 4 acts, also called *Chin Shêng Yü Chên* 金聲玉振, written in collaboration with Lao Shê 老舍. It has been translated into English. 中西): *Hsiao Hsiang Shu Nü* 瀟湘淑女* (in 4 acts, 商務); *Ch'ing Fêng Ming Yüeh* 淸風明月 (in 3 acts, 華中圖書公司); *Hu Hsiao* 虎嘯 (in 3 acts, 黃河出版社); *Hua Ying Lei* 花影淚 (天地出版社): *Yü Kuo T'ien Ch'ing* 雨過天青 (獨立出版社); *Li Hun* 離婚 (商務); *Lu Lin Hao Nü Erh* 綠林好女兒 (獨立出版社); *Ch'ing Ko Tu Mu Chü* 淸閣獨幕劇 (collection of one act plays, 獨立出版社); *Hsüeh Chai* 血債 (collection of one act plays, 獨立出版社); *Kuo Nien* 過年 (collection of one act plays, 獨立出版社); *Chung Hsin Ai Kuo* 忠心愛國 (in 3 acts, 教育部); *Wang Ching Wei Mai Kuo Ch'iu Jung* 汪精衛賣國求榮 (教育部): *Kuang Jung Ti Chan Tou* 光榮的戰鬥 (中國文化服務社); *Shih Hun Lêng Yüeh* 詩魂冷月; *Hsüeh Chien Yuan Yang* 雪劍鴛鴦; *Liu Shui Fei Hua* 流水飛花; *Ch'an Lin Kuei Niao* 禪林歸鳥: etc.
After the Victory, she wrote the following novels: *Yüeh Shang Liu Shao T'ou* 月上柳梢頭 (1947, 大東); *I Ling Hun* 藝靈魂 (藝海書局); *Shuang Su Shuang Fei* 雙宿雙飛; *Chiang Shang Yên* 江上烟; *Feng* 鳳 (獨立出版社): etc.
Critical works: *Pien Chü Fang Fa Lun* 編劇方法論 (How to Write Play? 獨立出版社); *K'ang Chan Wên I Kai Lun* 抗戰文藝概論 (Wartime Literature, 上海雜誌公司); *K'ang Chan Hsi Chü Kai Lun* 抗戰戲劇概論 (Wartime Drama, 上海雜誌公司); etc.

1241. 民族正氣 *SPIRIT OF THE NATION*   1 vol. 102 p. by 趙循伯
1946 Shanghai, The Commercial Press.

A historical drama in five acts.

A beautiful and patriotic play laid in the background of the eighth century, during the reign of the Emperor Hsuen Tsung of the T'ang Dynasty (唐玄宗).

We are given a portrait of the famous Chang Hsun (張巡) who, during the revolt of An Lu Shan, animated the resistance through his great courage. In spite of his feeble resources in men and provisions, he refused to surrender, and sacrificed his men, his favourite concubine, and even his own life, for the sake of his emperor, thus raising the dynasty to glory again. *For everyone.*

1242. 金絲籠 *A GOLDEN CAGE*   1 vol. 274 p. by 陳楚淮
2nd. edit. 1933 中華書局

Four plays.

金絲籠 The son of a mandarin is progressive in his ideas and member of a revolutionary club. His matrimonial projects are opposed. The other members of the club are arrested but he manages to escape with a large sum of money that he has appropriated, and after having freed the parrot from its "golden cage."

樂 Two women out of work talk together on how to ameliorate their situation. That night they learn that their husbands have killed a man to rob him.

韋菲君 A teacher, of good behavior until now, wishes to act for the cinema upon the bad advice of her friends. Her father and another friend try to turn her from this resolution, but without success. She even falls in love with the director of the film who, when she becomes pregnant, refuses to marry her. She then revenges herself by killing him and a friend. *Not for everyone.*

幸福的欄杆 A painter, who lives on the charity of a friend, finds himself shown the door. The friend's wife, however, has compassion of him and threatens to leave too, if he has to go. The artist advises her not to leave at the same time, in order to avoid false suspicions. Furious, she goes alone. *Not for everyone.*

1243. 野玫瑰 *WILD ROSE*   1 vol. 95 p. by 陳 銓
3rd. edit. 1947 商務印書館 *See Biogr. 19*

A play in four acts.

Wang Li-ming (王立民) is in high office under the Japanese occupation. He is intoxicated with power, and therefore excuses his collaboration with the enemy by persuading himself that it is only negative.

His second wife, Hsia Yen-hua (夏艷華), a former dancer, lives with him, but does not love her husband, seeming to have married uniquely for the material benefits of his position. Wang also has a daughter, the issue of his former marriage. Her name is Man-li (曼麗), and she enjoys a good character. The family also has a domestic named Wang An (王安) who is more intelligent than one would suppose him to be in his position.

There is also a certain chief of police (廳長) who frequents the house and who submits himself to Yen-hua for whom he has a pronounced liking.

One day Liu, the nephew of Wang Li-ming, arrives who falls in love with his young cousin, Man-li, who is not indifferent to him. Now Liu is not a stranger to Yen-hua, for he had been her lover in Shanghai when she had been engaged in her profession of dancer there. For him, Yen-hua had been a "wild rose" who attracted him but that love is dead now that his affections are concentrated on a "domestic rose" by which he designates Man-li. Yen-hua, however, does not want to give him up, and tries to exercise on him her charms of a "wild rose".

It is noticed that since Liu's arrival important political secrets have been divulged, and soon both Yen-hua and Wang An are convinced that the nephew is a spy in the service of the Chinese government. Thus Liu's fate rests with Yen-hua who wishes to profit from the fact. Our hero, however, resists her charms and reveals to her that after his mission has been accomplished he intends to run away with his cousin, Man-li. Help comes from an unexpected quarter, for it is Wang An who rescues him from danger. The good domestic is, in fact, also a spy, and one of higher standing than the nephew.

When the chief of police learns of the significance of Liu's activities, he has the house surrounded with the intention of seizing him. Yen-hua, however, intervenes, and promises to marry the police chief if he will allow the nephew and his cousin to escape. Vanquished by these promises, the police chief consents and even offers his own car to facilitate their escape.

In a last interview with Liu, Yen-hua reveals her secret, and we discover that the "wild rose" is also a spy and of a higher grade than either of the two others.

The chief of police then comes for his reward. Yen-hua, however, has told her husband of his intentions, and Li-ming is concealed in the room and a witness of the tender conversation of the police chief. He suddenly comes out of hiding and kills the other with a shot from a revolver. Yen-hua then makes a clean breast of things and tells her husband of her mission as a spy. The latter, under the influence of emotion, loses his sight. Not wishing to survive miserably, he takes poison, but without repenting of his treason to his country.

Once her mission has been accomplished, the "wild rose" gives orders to Wang An to get ready, and together they depart on new assignments.

A very patriotic play. *For mature people.*

1244. 半夜 *IN THE MIDST OF NIGHT*　　　　　1 vol. 198 p. by 陳　綿
　　　　　　　　　　　　　　　　　　　　　　　1944 華北文化書局 *See Biogr. 22*

Two plays.

1) 天羅地網 in three acts; adapted from the play "Payment deferred" by C. S. Forester.

A bank employee poisoned his nephew in order to rob him. He also had illicit relations with a neighbouring woman. His wife, after catching them red-handed, took poison and thus died. The hero was condemned for his wife's suicide. *For grown up people.*

2) 半夜 in five acts, adapted from the Hungarian play "Tuzmadar" by Lajos Zilahy.

A noble and ancient family lived in an apartment. The family consisted of the father, the mother and a young daughter. A cinema "star" who lived on the third floor of the same boardinghouse was found dead with a revolver at his side in his room. The magistrate held an inquest but could not find the guilty one. A love affair was suspected to be at the bottom of his crime.

One of the boarders testified that he saw a person come out of the noble family's apartment, enter the victims room and stay for the night. The clerk's wife confessed to being guilty of the crime, but the magistrate did not believe her as he suspected her of shielding her daughter's honour. The latter was sentenced, but owing to her young age the sentence was light. *For grown up people.*

1245. 太平天國 *THE TAIPING REBELLION*　　　　1 vol. 246 p. by 陳白塵
　　　　　　　　　　　　　　　　　　　　　　　1937 生活書店 *See Biogr. 23*

Play in 7 acts.

A historical play. It is the first part of a trilogy promised by the author. He has selected Chinese history as a subject of his trilogy.

The theme of the first part is the foundation and progress of 太平天國 in the years 1850-52 (this kingdom lasted 12 years). The reason for establishing this kingdom was, the suffering of the people under the Ch'ing dynasty misrule and because of the brigandage the court was unable to prevent. The T'ai p'ing's idea was to set up the kingdom of Shang-ti and to wipe out superstitions. The founder and the first king was 洪秀全 known as 天王 who pretended to be the son of Shang ti. The first successful exploits of the kingdom were important, but unfortunately were mixed with murder and plunder. Soon the leaders began to quarrel among themselves.

In this play there are many coarse expressions.

For all.

1246. 亂世男女　*WARTIME MEN & WOMEN*　　1 vol. 168 p. by　**陳白塵**
2nd. edit. 1946　上海雜誌公司

A comedy in three acts.

A train full of refugees and these same people in the interior of China during the Sino-Japanese war. The author paints some humorous pictures in bringing into relief cross-sections of these personages.

Without great interest. *For mature people.*

1247. 結婚進行曲　*WEDDING MARCH*　　1 vol. 197 p. by　**陳白塵**
2nd. edit. 1947　聯營書店

A melodrama in five acts.

The author wishes to show up the ridiculous and sad situation of young people who wish for the liberty and equality of the sexes in the matter of marriage. According to him, these modern ideas lack sense. The husband ought to be the head of the family, and the wife should occupy herself with the housekeeping and the education of the children. *Not for the young.*

1248. 大渡河　*BIG FERRY RIVER*　　1 vol. 219 p. by　**陳白塵**
1946　群益出版社

Episodes in the Taiping Rebellion. We are presented especially with the exploits of 石翼王 and 韓寶英, ending in the failure of their enterprise.

Readers should be put on their guard against the spirit of vengeance animating the characters and their easy resort to suicide. *May be read by anyone.*

1249. 陞官圖　*THE CHART OF OFFICIAL PROMOTION*　1 vol. 169 p. by　**陳白塵**
1946　群益出版社　群益現代戲劇叢書之三

A prelude, three acts and an epilogue. Two thieves make their way into a yamen, and here is the dream that they have:

They kill the prefect (知縣) and his secretary and usurp their place. Being in accord with the head of bureaux (局長), they make grand plans to augment their personal fortune through bleeding the people. When the plans have been made, however, the visit of the governor (省長) is announced. Great consternation in the yamen! When the governor arrives, the others fall over each other in offering him gifts, one of which is quite original, consisting of the wife of the late prefect! During the marriage ceremonies, however, the people rise against the unscrupulous officials, and come in a body to wreak their vengeance.

At this moment the two thieves wake up!

A play full of good sense and comic situations. As it is meant farcically, the marriage is not to be taken too seriously. *May be read by anyone.*

1250. 後方小喜劇 *COMEDY BEHIND THE FRONTLINE* 1 vol. 179 p. by 陳白塵
2nd edit. 1947 生活書店

Five one act plays.

1) 未婚夫婦 A man and a girl who are engaged rent a room. Tragi-comic situations arise from the fact of the girl not wishing to pass for a married woman. She ends up in losing both the room and her job. *Not for everyone.*

2) 禁上小便 What they do in government offices. The frivolous occupations and ridiculousness of the officials is made fun of.
A very witty comedy but too full of bitterness. *For everyone.*

3) 封鎖線 Of heroic acts during the resistance against Japan. Also full of curses. *For everyone.*

4) 羅國富 Idem. *For everyone.*

5) 火燄 Idem. *For everyone.*

1251. 賣油郎 *THE OIL PEDDLAR* 1 vol. by 陳白塵

A play in 3 acts.
Adaptation of a tragedy written by the Russian author Ostrowsky. The original title of this tragedy is 懸崖之戀.

It is the story of a rich merchant 余友楠 who was a healthy and heartless man. He fell in love with a young student 范嬋 The latter was deceived by the hero's promises, but during his absence she became engaged to a young official 孫克歐. She did not love her new fiancé and when the merchant returned she eloped with him. But in the near future she realized that the merchant was only using her as a plaything, as he was already married.

In the final scene, which is very dramatic, she reproached young men in general for deceiving girls and then rejecting them as if they were common things. After this tirade, the heroine committed suicide.

It shows clearly the author's intention: he wishes to warn modern girls against the dangers they are "likely to meet"; but we do not admit that suicide is a solution for these difficulties. *For enlightened people.*

1252. 秋海棠 *CH'IU HAI T'ANG* 1 vol. 220 p. by 秦瘦鷗
1936 百新書店

A tragedy in five acts.
Cfr. No. 203. The same story.
A good play but to be reserved for adults because of the nature of the subject and some risky details. *Not for everyone.*

1253. 生路 *THE ONE CHANCE* 1 vol. 115 p. by 蔣旂
1940 光明書局

The story of a girl who has two lovers. One is rich but dastardly and a traitor to his country. The other is poor but sincere and sacrifices himself for his people.

She chooses the first who soon begins to maltreat her, and she is soon disgusted with his treatment of her.

The death of the good-for-nothing follows. And now she is free, the heroine joins the other young man, who is poor, in his activities for the country in danger.

Unsuitable for acting in our schools. *For everyone.*

1254. 家 *HOME*   1 vol. 219 p. 敬樂然編選
益智書店

A play in five acts, adapted from the celebrated master-piece of Pa Chin (巴金) "Home" (家).

The celebrated novel "Home" is too well known to need a resumé here. The general theme that runs through the whole book is the cleavage between the older and the younger generations and the reactions that result from this opposition. The older people are against the free choice of the young in their own matrimonial affairs and are also against the young pursuing their studies. *For mature people.*

1255. 梁紅玉 *LIANG HUNG-YU* (The lady commanding an army) 1 vol. 129 p. by 周劍塵
1940   新藝書店

A historical drama in four acts laid in the Sung Dynasty.

1st. act: the post of the Han general is taken in spite of the valiant behaviour of the commander and his wife.

2nd. act: this is laid in the capital attacked by the Ch'ins.

3rd. act: the Han general and his family defend their new post.

4th. act: victory of the general over the Ch'in. *For everyone.*

1256. 北地王 *RULER OF THE NORTH*   1 vol. 125 p. by 周貽白
1940   潮鋒出版社 *See Biogr.* 38

Historical drama in four acts.

The plot is taken from the San Kuo Chih. The kingdom of Hsi Shu is conquered by Wei, due to the perfidy of her supporters and functionaries. The faithful generals together with their families commit suicide.

The play contains magnificent patriotism although the suicides are to be reprehended. *For everyone.*

1257. 花木蘭 *HUA MU-LAN* (the lady that fought in the army) 1 vol. 132 p. by 周貽白
1941   明明書店

When his fatherland was invaded by the enemy, 花弧 an old soldier was mobilized. His daughter 木蘭 begged him not to go because of his advanced age and weak health. She put on men's clothes, and took her father's place in the army. During twelve or more years she was leading a soldier's life, and after her commander's death she led the troops to victory. Her soldiers never knew that she was not a man! When the emperor had learned about her brilliant exploits, he summoned her to the court and wanted to confer honours upon her. She refused all rewards, but at the end of her interview, harried by questions, she confessed that she was a girl. The emperor then wanted her to be his imperial concubine. Mu-lan refused, and so was punished by the emperor. But as the enemy again drew near the capital, she was recalled and led the army to new victories. *For all.*

1258. 金絲雀 *CANARY*   1 vol. 172 p. by 周貽白
1944   世界書局

Play in five acts.

A comedienne, 金絲雀 by name, lives with her younger sister. Several habitués of the theatre aspire to her hand, among others, a rake, 國元, a good liver, 德標, and a young professor, 文華. The last is simple in demeanour but not lacking in character. The whole play unrolls around these candidatures for marriage, and the action drags somewhat.

The heroine wishes to escape from these people but she does not succeed. She manages, however, to accomplish a good act in bringing together her sister and the professor.

In a final scene, 金絲雀 decides to go away by herself, but the good liver, in trying to recover the revolver in her hand, pulls the trigger and wounds her mortally. Upon this, the rake kills him with the same weapon.

At the same moment, a stage manager 小堂 runs in and accuses the rake of being the assassin of the girl. *For adults.*

1259. 綠窗紅淚 *HER TEARS ARE FALLING*   1 vol. 157 p. by 周貽白
1944 世界書局

A play in four acts.

A brother and his elder sister plan to drive away a so-called maternal uncle who manages the family fortune for his own benefit. Their mother opposes their plans but they succeed in carrying them through.

The uncle does not remain inactive but uses his son-in-law to circumvent the heroine, and create trouble between her and her brother. This is done so successfully that the brother and sister separate after dividing the family fortune.

Finally the girl discovers that her tempter is already married and she seeks death after admitting her error in a letter written before she dies.

Her suicide is to be deplored from the moral point of view, but as the author does not plainly approve of it, we do not see why this book should not be read by anyone who is interested. *May be read by anyone.*

1260. 陽關三疊 *ADIEU*   1 vol. 161 p. by 周貽白
1944 世界書局

A play in four acts.

李伯年 is guilty of misconduct and his wife demands a divorce. His younger brother, 仲華, on the contrary, is a serious young man and in love with 汪月秋.

In order to rise in the world, 伯年 wishes to give his sister to 賈, a most despicable man, who has sent his wife and daughter away, and lives with his concubine.

孝庵 is the go-between in these plans. He is a person deprived of all morals.

The younger generation has saner ideas, for it opposes there vicious bargains. The story ends with the marriage of 仲華 with 月秋 (who is, in fact, the daughter of 賈 who has taken the name of her mother), and with that of 伯年's sister to 元超, the son of the go-between.

The aim of the play is good, but although the author does not approve of divorce, he seems to speak of it too lightly. Reference also is made too often to the misconduct of the older people, and the opposition of the younger people to their parents is too violent. *For those aware of the dangers.*

1261. 連環計 *TRICK WITHIN A TRICK*   1 vol. 140 p. by 周貽白
1945 世界書局

A historical drama in five acts.

董卓, a cruel potentate dreams of raising himself to the throne. His adopted son, 呂布, is also a bold warrior who covers himself with glory.

In order to frustrate their conspiracy and lay low his adversary, the general, 王允, gives one of his singers to the son to wife, passing her off as his own daughter. He gives the same person to the father as a concubine, and 董卓 takes her away in his suite.

When the son learns of this abduction, and being ignorant of the machinations of the general, he slays his father in a rage. Thus the danger to the throne is averted.

We reprove the theory admitted by the author that a woman may prostitute herself to save the state. *For adults.*

1262. 亡蜀遺恨 *SORROWS OF A TRAMPLED NATION*   1 vol. 125 p. by   周貽白
(一名北地王)   1946   潮鋒出版社

A historical drama in four acts.
Cfr. with review No. 1256. *For everyone.*

1263. 鋼盔 *THE STEEL HELMET*   1 vol. 148 p. by   周尙文
                                           1945   獨立出版社

A play in four acts.
This play describes the disposition of certain people in a particular locality when mobilisation is ordered during the war. When the young people are called to arms, most respond with enthusiasm while a few sons of rich families continue their lazy and useless way of life, becoming objects at which the population points fingers of scorn. *For everyone.*

1264. 桃花扇 *THE PEACH BLOSSOM FAN*   1 vol. 133 p. by   周　彥
                                           1946   建國書店當今戲劇叢書

A play in three acts and two supplementary parts.
Cfr. No. 1493. The same theme, with a few retouches concerning Hou Fang-yu. *For mature people.*

1265. 近代獨幕劇選 *ONE ACT PLAYS*   1 vol. 460 p. by   朱肇洛
                             1941   北京文化學社 *See Biogr. 42*

Fourteen one-act plays. Some are originally written in Chinese, some are translations from Japanese, English, Russian.

The first is objectionable because it represents and approves of suicide; the fifth and eighth contain a light scene. Several plays are very good.

Inoffensive *for informed readers.*

1266. 晚禱 *EVENING PRAYER*   1 vol. 84 p. by   朱　雷
                                           1941   光明書局

Several one-act plays.
1) 馬兜鈴先生課上   Model classes and teachers!
2) 晚禱   The sacrifices of a woman.
3) 米潮   A family portrait.
4) 紅樓二尤   *A* retouched memory of the   紅樓夢.
May be read *by anyone,* but not suitable for our schools.

1267. 獨幕劇新集 *COLLECTION OF ONE ACT PLAYS* 1 vol. 240 — 7 p. by   朱　雷
                                           1946   光明書局

1) 藝術與愛情   If you do me in the eye, I'll go one better!   A comedienne falls into a trap.
2) 爲祖國飛行   An episode in the Spanish War.

3) 晚禱 The war in Poland. The suicide in the story is to be reproved.

4) 佳偶天成 An original way of concluding a betrothal.

5) 茶宴 A reunion of old students. Memories of old days and various happenings.

6) 監驕 An exploit of the resistance.

7) 縣官坐堂 An original official.

8) 出路問題 Of girl students who have arrived at the end of their studies. They are wondering what to do. The advice of an old man.

May be read by anyone.

1268. 圓謊記 *A LIE COVERED*　　　　1 vol. 129 p. by 朱端鈞
　　　　　　　　　　　　　　　　　　　1944　世界書局

A comedy in four acts.

Lien (蓮), the wife of Meng (孟), flirts a little with a certain Ching (景). It is partly the fault of her husband who is too severe and never relaxes. One day, while he is absent, Lien and Ching have a rendezvous for dinner. The dinner, however, misses fire, because of the inopportune arrival of Lien's sister and cousin. The husband gets wind of the affair. In order to throw sand into his eyes, the female members of the family, and a few others who are willing to help, plan an expedient which they hope will induce Meng to think that his wife and Ching have met by accident. But the truth of the matter is revealed when Ching arrives rather late.

The guilty wife then decides on a drastic course, to wit, to go off with Ching. A common friend, however, manages to prevent her, and in addition, he employs all his eloquence to persuade the husband to treat his wife better and to go out more often in her company. Upon this, the husband realizes that his too great reserve has been partly at fault. He changes his attitude, and henceforth his wife lives happily with him.

The author wishes to show in this piece how women's deceptions complicate life. It is not suitable for very young people because of the nature of the subject itself. *Not for everyone.*

1269. 試金石 *TOUCHSTONE*　　　　　1 vol. 106 p. by 朱應之
　　　　　　　　　　　　　　　　　　　1947　燕都印書館

Tragedy in 4 acts.

A tragedy with patriotic subject, which took place during the Japanese occupation. A university professor sacrificed his life and his family for the benefit of his country. During his history lectures he accused with scorn, before his numerous audience, the enemy and their cooperators. He was offered a position by the new government. He replied in his usual way, which was rather realistic. His two sons established an anti-Japanese society and acted accordingly. The whole family was sentenced to death by the enemy.

A remarkable expression was used by the head of this noble family: "When the enemy occupies the country, that is the time for every Chinese to show his patriotism", "that is the time to recognize who are the true patriots". *For everyone.*

1270. 銀星夢 *STAR SPANGLED SKY*　　　1 vol. 172 p. by 方君逸
　　　　　　　　　　　　　　　　　　　1944　世界書局

A play in which two friends are represented in miserable circumstances. Two young men visit them frequently and a real friendship grows up between the four.

鶯　dreams of the cinema and is soon caught up in the turmoil of the life of a "star". Her friend, seeing that she is adulated and rich, leaves her.

A good, liver, 馬, abuses the "star" who soon comes to realize the emptiness of the whirl in which she is involved. And her fortune begins to decline because she refuses to act immoral roles.

Rendered pregnant through her relations with 馬, she finds herself abandoned by everyone. She turns to her old friend, 堅, who gives her the cold shoulder, so that driven to the extreme of misery, she surrenders herself to her only refuge, death.

The author has presented us with a good play and we are glad to find his condemning those very same books that we have condemned ourselves. Moreover, his principal characters are admirable people in spite of their weaknesses

We are also glad to see him ridiculing the idiotic cinema people who think that they can create whatever atmosphere they please, and who never realize the wrong they are guilty of in depicting the immoralities they so often present to us.

We should, however, warn the heads of establishments that they should not be in too great hurry to produce this play for the benefit of very young people, as it contains details that might be shocking to an immature audience. *Not for everyone.*

1271. 滿庭芳 *LITTERED WITH BEAUTIES*   1 vol. 224 p. by **方君逸**
                                                        1944   世界書局

A play in one act.

A charitable society is giving a performance for the benefit of an orphanage. We are presented at too great length with what happens in the corridors of the theatre before and during the performance.

The committee of the society is composed of some ladies of mature age, some young ladies, and a few men. The older ladies take a fancy to the young men who naturally prefer the younger women.

The whole play is a satire revealing these flutterings, rivalries, and jealousies, which are covered by a benefit performance for charitable purposes. In the actual happenings all charity is conspicuously absent.

The play is too long drawn out, especially so as it consists of only a single act.

It is suitable *only for mature people* because of the subject it deals with.

1272. 花弄影 *EVEN THE SHADOWS ARE CHARMING*   1 vol. 140 p. by **方君逸**
                                                              1944   世界書局

A play in five acts.

The young wife of a manufacturer engages a tutor for her children. As he lives in the house, both she and her step-daughter fall in love with him. The tutor loves the young wife and declares that he is not interested in the girl, who then chooses a man of mature age for herself. And the tutor leaves to avoid scandal. *For mature people*

1273. 離恨天 *UNMENDABLE SORROW*   1 vol. 188 p. by **方君逸**
                                                       1944   世界書局

Ying (英), the daughter of a rich family, makes her parents give their consent that she goes to continue her studies in Hangchow. The parents are very much opposed to the plan at first, but end up by giving their consent. Ying then goes disguised as a man (for it all happened at a time when the weaker sex was not as emancipated as nowadays), and she works hard for three years.

Shan (山), a student who is not so wealthy, becomes the friend of Ying for whom he has a great affection. Now a day comes when doubts occur regarding the sex of the heroine, and for this reason, she decides to leave the school. Shan accompanies her, and during the journey the two young people discover that they are in love with each other. Ying, however, still refrains from revealing her true identity and sex, but arranges for a meeting with her friend for the following year.

Her friend is faithful, but on the very day of the meeting, Ying's father promises her in marriage to one of the Wang family. The friends, however, manage to meet, and Ying promises her Prince Charming that she will not marry anyone except him.

When Shan learns of Ying's marriage with another, he falls grievously ill, but in the last scene, here is Ying, dressed as a bride, seated by his bed, swearing that she will never leave him again. *For mature people.*

1274. 四姊妹 *THE FOUR SISTERS*   1 vol. 96 p. by   方君逸
         2nd. edit. 1945   光明書局

A play in five acts.

The interest is centred around a family consisting of the father, a good man of strong family affection, the mother, who is vain but nevertheless has a good heart, and their four daughters. The elder is serious minded and takes to heart the education of her younger sisters, who are not of strong character but nice girls all the same.

All four sisters adore their father and prove their affection by sacrificing what they like the most, in order to raise a sum of money needed for a journey.

During the course of the play we become acquainted with the suitors of these four girls of little fortune, and the various reactions of their keeping company together.

Two of the sisters become definitely engaged, and in a final scene, emphasis is again laid upon the great love that unites the members of this family.

As the play is about nothing but love and offers of marriage, it is not suitable for our institutions. Nevertheless, it contains nothing contrary to good morals. and on the whole, is a beautiful piece. *For everyone.*

1275. 紅豆曲 *LONGING FOR EACH OTHER*   1 vol. 151 p. by   方君逸
         1945   世界書局

A play in four acts.

It begins with a happy household. But the husband is a musician and lives only for his art. Unfortunately, his good taste does not find favour with the public, as modern music is the order of the day. He becomes poorer and poorer, as he refuses to prostitute his art and put it at the service of modern popular songs. Conquered by his material difficulties, he is driven to despair and disappears. He is believed to have committed suicide.

His wife, who loves him, is a very brave woman, and struggles against circumstances for her livelihood. And she manages to give a fairly good education to their son who, like his father, has a astonishingly marked disposition for music, which peeves the mother in no small measure.

Six years after his disappearance, the musician returns dressed as a beggar. Knowing that his wife is out, he pays a secret visit to his son who does not recognize his father. The latter, however, reveals his identity, and gives his son a red bean (symbol of love) to be passed on to his mother.

After this, he goes away, and throws himself in front of a tram not far from the house. He is taken to his former home in a dying condition, and thus the husband and wife are re-united.

This book may be read *by anyone* as the author himself condemns the suicide.

1276. 蝴蝶夫人 *MADAME BUTTERFLY* 1 vol. 124 p. by 方君逸
1946 永祥印書館

A play in three acts.

A Chinese revolutionary goes to Malaya, and there he marries a former courtisan of great beauty, named Butterfly (蝴蝶). The newly-wed husband and wife love each other very much, and the wife demonstrates a most disinterested devotion. She proves her love thoroughly, for after her husband leaves after only three months of wedded bliss, she is faithful to him for five long years.

A child is born of their union, and the mother and child dream of nothing but the return of the father. He however, has not remained faithful, for five years after his return to his own country, he decides to marry again.

He comes to Malaya again on his honeymoon. Butterfly's friends wish to tell her of the fact, but her love refuses to admit the possibility of her husband's infidelity.

The husband tries to avoid an encounter with his first wife, but his bride is more courageous. She meets Butterfly and soon entertains a warm affection for her. During a conversation, Butterfly learns the identity of her visitor — that she is her husband's new wife. She has a moment of weakness from which she recovers quickly. Entrusting her child to the other she makes an end to herself.

This play gives us the impression of being a beautiful piece and depicts a great love. The only thing to regret about it is the suicide with which it ends. *For mature people.*

1277. 賭徒別傳 *A GAMBLER* 1 vol. 126 p. by 錫 金
1945 世界書局

A play in five acts.

There are two principal characters. One is a teacher who is an inveterate gambler. The other is a girl who also loves gambling and who urges on the man in his vice.

Ordinarily these two lose, but one day, the teacher wins a large sum and goes away to live with a lady friend.

When his money is spent, he returns to find his gambling partner settled down and married. She wants to put him on the right path, but is unsuccessful, for he leaves her after extorting some money, which will enable him to continue his life as a gambler. *For adults.*

1278. 上海屋簷下 *IN SHANGHAI* 1 vol. 121 p. by 夏衍 (沈端先)
1946 國民書店 *See Biogr.* 132

Tragedy in 3 acts.

In this play the author presents to us in his own simple style, the daily events in the lives of ordinary people in Shanghai. The scene is in a courtyard occupied by five families. Each has its story and these stories show us the sufferings endured by the middle classes. A teacher's family: the teacher had an optimistic temperament, but life was hard for these good-natured people, as they could not earn enough for their daily needs. The second consisted of a young married couple: the husband, whose health was weak, was obliged to give up his position, and both were struggling in poverty. Their old father came on a visit and received a hearty welcome, for which purpose the young couple sold the wife's clothes in order to pay the expenses. However the old man noticed this good act and left his last penny with them. Besides these two families, there was an old man, whose son went to fight the enemy. This old man went daily to see whether his son had reached the rank of a general. There was still another family, in which the husband was in a foreign country; his young wife was alone and had to become a prostitute in order to live. She lived in fear, fearing the return of her husband. At the end the author presents us with a big drama, which took place in the fifth family. Here the author gave free course to his great dramatic power. He introduces us to a small family the head of which was a revolutionist, but with a good heart and very modest. He had left his house for over eight years and become a partisan of the "Resistance" and was arrested by the Japanese. After his release he went to inquire from his bosom friend about his wife's dwelling.

Now this friend, having the duty to care for and protect the woman, came to love her, and finally married her. He was surprised to see his visitor, whom he believed to be dead, and he could not find words to explain the situation. At the end, the husband understood and, as he was of a good character, forgave the other. At this time his wife entered and explained what had happened, and wanted to return to her former husband. All this took place in a dramatic atmosphere. The husband misjudged her motives and wanted to give her up. Their daughter, aged 14, of good up-bringing, arrived. When she learned what was the matter she exclaimed "papa"; this word was the reward for his many terrible sufferings. The disloyal friend, who came to witness the scene, resolved to leave the house but the woman stopped him and wept on his breast. When her husband saw this, he understood the real feelings of his wife and, after a tender look at his daughter, he left them, in great dignity.

Of course we cannot approve of several of the situations nor of the last scene; the author too seems to disapprove, but merely wants to paint the hidden scenes in the lives of ordinary people. *For enlightened people.*

1279. 都會的一夜 *A METROPOLITAN NIGHT*   1 vol. 226 p. by 夏衍 等
1940 天下書店

A collection of nine pieces.
都會的一夜 tells of revolutionary activities and their repression by the police about the year 1930.
黎明: the miserable life of workers.
舞女淚: sadness of a dancer.
劉三爺: fanaticism of a father who slays his son to punish him for a misdeed.
放棄; story of a lost girl.
All these miseries are caused by the evils of contemporary society. *Not to be recommended to anyone.*

1280. 愁城記 *THE CITY OF SORROWS*   1 vol. 102 p. by 夏衍
1946 開明書店

A play in four acts.
A member of the Chao (趙) family of Shanghai has died. The brother of the dead man seizes his fortune and with it engages in business of a doubtful nature, speculating the rise of prices and helping thus to add to the misery of the people. His niece, Chao Wan (趙婉), who has recently married, passes her days happily with her husband, until one fine day, she finds herself driven out by her uncle who has been pushed to this measure through avarice.

The young couple is soon reduced to miserable circumstances. A family friend, who bears a grudge against the uncle, then comes to Chao Wan and tells her that by right a part of the fortune that her uncle has unjustly appropriated belongs to her. A law case follows which ends in the ruin of the family and the suicide of the uncle.

The young couple, together with some friends, then decides to leave for the interior there to devote themselves to patriotic work. *May be read by anyone.*

1281. 心防 *FORTRESS OF THE HEART*   1 vol. 109 p. by 夏 衍
1946   開明書店

A play in four acts.

An episode of the Sino-Japanese war. We are presented with the activities of a group of intellectuals. A journalist and several artists sponsor the good cause through the diffusion of ideas. The principal hero, Hao-ju (浩如), is in the forefront of the struggle through the channel of his newspaper, and pays with his life for indulging in his patriotic feelings. *For everyone.*

1282. 法西斯細菌 *FASCIST INFECTION*   1 vol. 142 p. by 夏 衍
2nd. edit. 1946   開明書店

A play in five acts.

We are presented with the Yu (俞) family at different stages of the Sino-Japanese "incident." The husband who is a doctor with sound knowledge and married to a Japanese woman, is making researches in typhus. He is presented first with his friends in Tokyo, then in Shanghai and in Hongkong, and eventually during the war in Kueiling. After having witnessed the atrocities of her compatriots, his wife hopes for a Chinese victory at heart.

A patriotic story but it does not carry you away. *For everyone.*

1283. 復活 *RESURRECTION* (adapted)   1 vol. 137 p. 夏衍改編
3rd. edit.   美學出版社

A play in six acts adapted from "Resurrection" by Tolstoy.

A girl is betrayed and abandoned by an officer, a member of the nobility, who seeks consolation with other women. The poor girl is driven out of the house by the mother of her tempter who happens to be her own aunt with whom she had sought refuge. She then sinks very low, cursing God and society.

Ten years after, the officer has to judge a case at the assizes, and he discovers his old friend in the person of the accused. From a prostitute she has become a murderer. The judge is seized with remorse, and forsakes his fiancee, deciding to link up his lot with the accused in the hope of resuscitating her morally. He takes care of her while she is in prison, and subsequently he accompanies her to Siberia. He even proposes marriage to quieten his scruples of conscience. The heroine changes completely and in common with her co-prisoners, she becomes an example of virtue and charity.

Another prisoner who is as noble and virtuous as herself loves her with all his heart and the girl, touched by his love, also loves this young man.

The officer manages to obtain the release of his friend, but she refuses to accompany him back to Russia and wishes to remain with the other prisoners, because it is with them that she has found real happiness and the real path to resurrection.

Tolstoy, because of his false mysticism, his rationalism, nihilism and atheism, was excommunicated from the Orthodox Church. He is overcome with pity for those who suffer and his sympathy goes especially towards the depraved. "He melts the hearts of his readers almost exclusively over the miseries of the prison house and other such places as though unhappiness was not moving except in crime and abjection." (Bethléem, "Stories to Read" . . . p. 117).

An example of this is given in Maleswa in "Resurrection", which does not, however, prevent it from being a masterpiece of art and literature.

In his adaptation, Hsia Yen (夏衍) has not insisted on the ideas of atheism and nihilism. He has, nevertheless, remained faithful to the original in making the convicts and fallen miserables depicted paragons of virtue and charity.

This book is *not to be recommended to anyone* because of the subversive morals of the author.

1284. 寒夜曲 *NOCTURNE FRIGIDAIRE*   by 吳 琛

A Tragedy in three acts.

The story is about a newly-wed couple much in love with one another. However, the mother of the husband was of very bad temper and pervertly jealous. One day a boy friend came to see the young wife and was caught by the old woman. Scared out of her wits, the young wife fled back to her father's home.

It happened that the old woman had a daughter, with whom the severe old dame had a most serious quarrel. The daughter escaped from home and went to the young wife's house, where the husband also came to visit his sister. Unfortunately the unhappy trio were found by the old woman in pursuit of the fugitive daughter. Placing entirely the blame upon the young wife, the old woman diluged her with terrible reproaches. Frightened and enraged the young wife plunged into a river. Her husband also committed suicide.

The final tableau shows the old woman standing by the river, reproached by the ghosts of the couple who accused her of being guilty for their death. The despaired old dame also drowned herself.

For enlightened people only, on account of the many suicides. (N.B. Through the inattention of the compiler, this review is not proper inserted in the index according to the transliteration of the name of the author).

1285. 不忠實的愛情 *UNFAITHFUL LOVE*   1 vol. 196 p. by 向培良
                                        1929 啓智書局 *See Biogr. 64*

Two plays: the first is in three acts, the second in four.

1) A youth who married a worldly and capricious girl, neglected her and she flirted with a young writer. Her husband caught her and as he thought that it was due to his neglect he committed suicide. *Everyone should be advised against reading it.*

2) A student of a Peiping university who was married to a girl from his native town, fell in love with another student. All his friends advised him to secure a divorce. In the meantime the girl-student was informed about his marriage and she considered herself insulted. Although the young man wanted to divorce his wife, the arrival of his uncle made him change his mind.

As this book seems to approve of divorce it can be read *only by informed readers.*

1286. 佛西戲劇第一集   *PLAYS BY HSIUNG FUO-HSI* (Vol. I)
                                      1 vol. 284 p. by 熊佛西
                                      1934 商務印書舘 *See Biogr. 70*

蟋蟀 A drama in four acts. Three brothers, who up to now have been very united, fight and kill each other because they are all three in love with the same princess. Impossible to be acted in our schools.

一片愛國心 A tragedy in three acts. A Chinese child offends her mother who is Japanese. She repents subsequently and becomes mad. Can be acted in our schools.

洋狀元 A comedy in three acts. A satire on students returned from abroad. Proud and disdainful, they are good for nothing. Unsuitable for acting in our schools.

神童 A satire in two acts, directed against parents and teachers who should educate but who only spoil those in their charge. Unsuitable for acting in our schools.
For everyone.

1287. 佛西戲劇第二集 *PLAYS BY HSIUNG FOU-HSI* (Vol. II)

1 vol. 152 p. by 熊佛西
1935 商務印書館

王三 A drama in one act. About a poor man who is an executioner to gain his livelihood. Can be acted in our schools.

藝術家 A comedy in one act. Since an artist has to be dead before his works are of value, the hero pretends to be dead and his pictures are sold for a high price. Good for acting in our schools.

蘭芝與仲卿 A drama in one act. Disagreement between mother-in-law and daughter-in-law. Suitable for girl schools.

詩人的悲劇 A comedy in one act. Man in search of love.

喇叭 A young girl is hypnotised by a trumpet-blower, and abandons her fiancé. She repents of her act too late, alas! Suitable for girls schools.
For everyone.

1288. 佛西戲劇第三集 *PLAYS OF HSIUNG FOU-HSI* (Vol. III)

1 vol. 207 p. by 熊佛西
1935 商務印書館

愛情的結晶 A drama in three acts. A couple has an illigitimate child whom they abandon. Twenty years later they wish to adopt it, but the young man refuses. *For everyone.*

模特兒 A comedy in one act. A model is surprised by her father. There is a violent scene. *Not for everyone.*

裸體 A comedy in one act. A father forbids his children to look at the naked statue of Kuanyin, but they discover him looking at it. *Not for everyone.*

一對近視眼 A comedy in one act. Two friends who cannot see without glasses believe that they have seen a ghost. It is actually a gleaming mirror.

Can be acted in our schools. *For everyone.*

偶像 A comedy in one act. Two buddhist priests destroy their idols in order to obtain food. They are deceived. *For everyone.*

蒼蠅世界 A comedy in three acts. About the movement for extinguishing flies. Suitable for our schools. *For everyone.*

1289. 王三 *WANG SAN*

by 熊佛西
Com. Press 1930-1932.

During a famine year the Wang family was without bread. Their buffalo also cried out with hunger so pitifully that it melted the hearts of humans. And in spite of this the landlords insisted on what was due to them, and other individual came to exact taxes on the animals. Misery reigned, great misery.

A well-to-do relative came on a visit and he engaged Wang to exercise the same lucrative profession as himself, and Wang not knowing the real nature of the offer, accepted. Now this relative happened to be a bandit! Wang refused to take life and ran away, but the police were on his tracks, who caught him, after which he was condemned. Meanwhile the old mother had died, his wife had been seduced by the landlord, and the buffalo had died also. Nothing but misery, misery. *For everyone.*

1290. 鋤頭健兒 *A COUNTRY HERO*   by 熊佛西

Com. Press 1930—1932.

Struggle of the older generation against a brave young man named Chien-erh on the subject of superstitions. All the inhabitants believed in the tiger-spirit, and regilded the temple to avert his wrath. Only Chien-erh was against it and did not believe in these superstitious acts. He burnt the temple and thus excited the anger of the older generation who wished to kill him. His friend rescued him and he made good his escape, after which he met the tiger and slew it. From a "criminel" he had become a "hero". *Very anti-superstitious story. For everyone.*

1291. 屠夫 *THE BUTCHER*   by 熊佛西

A certain K'ung-money-lender by profession, and a fisher in troubled water — tried to stir up trouble between the two Wang brothers, who disagreed about some details in the testament of their parents. K'ung's object was to lend them money, in order that they would go to law, and then to mortgage their property. He had some success, but his game was uncovered by several of his former victims. They united against him and brought him to the court, where he was severely punished. *A very good play.*

1292. 卞昆岡 *THE PIEN K'UN RIDGE*   新月 vol. 1. No. 2 & 3, 57 p.

(5 scenes) by 徐志摩, 陸小曼

See Biogr. 72

The play is about a widower who was a stone-cutter by trade. He lived with his little son and mother. He loved his child very much as the latter had the eyes of his wife. His old mother wanted him to marry again and tried hard to find a suitable wife... After some time he married, but the new wife hated his son, as his eyes reminded the widower of his deceased wife. As the time passed she began to lead a bad life, and the boy's eyes were the only witness, hence she made the boy blind. But the child remained a ear-witness; hence arose quarrels between the boy and the new lover of his foster mother. In his rage the lover killed the boy, and fled with his accomplice. When the father returned he found his son and a stranger's coat; he understood and killed himself. *Very objectionable* because of lewd scenes.

1293. 阿 Q 正傳 *THE TRUE STORY OF AH-Q,* for the stage   by 許幸之

3rd edition 1942 光明書店

See Lu Hsün's novel on which this play is based (Nr. 635).

The play follows the novel very closely; the general theme and the chief motives are kept. A few characters were added in the play. Some points differ, though slightly.

1) Regarding the subject-matter: the original is a satire about the shortcomings of the Chinese people; the object of the satire is to compel the young generation to acknowledge these and to correct them. In the play, the satire passes lightly over the rest, and concentrates on the idea of "revolution". The revolution was a failure as far as all social classes: officials, literati, landlords, and common people were concerned. No one seemed to understand that the revolution should have been a "deep-seated" and real renewal. Everyone saw in it a mere opportunity to enrich or to avenge himself. This idea is brought out very strongly in the play.

2) Regarding the form: the novel could be read by everyone, but the play is rather coarse and oversteps the limits of decency; it presents two adulterous acts which are not mentioned in the novel. A person could not call this book an immoral one, but the atmosphere is

worse than vulgar, and the language is coarse. The book can *be read by grown up people* such as professors and teachers. It should not be placed in the school libraries and must not be given to students. Any modest girl could not refrain from blushing while reading this novel. Let us, then, keep this book away from her.

1294. 何洛甫之死 *KILLED IN REVOLUTION*   1 vol. 148 p. by 徐 訏
1940 夜窗書屋 *See Biogr. 74*

Tragedy in five acts.

Subject: during the national revolution against the militarists of the north, two brothers, who have always been very united, find themselves in different camps. The one in the military party captures the other and after a number of denouements, has him executed for fidelity to his convictions.

Too much fanatic support of revolutionary ideology. Could be retouched for our schools. *For grown-up people.*

1295. 生與死 *LIFE & DEATH*   1 vol. 147 p. by 徐 訏
1941 夜窗書屋

A tragedy in four acts.

This play is very well constructed but its atmosphere is not wholesome. It has, for instance too many murders. *For mature people.*

1296. 孤島的狂笑 *LAUGHTER OF AN ISLAND*   1 vol. 98 p. by 徐 訏
1941 夜窗書屋

1) 租押頂賣 One act. The story of a coat and of the suitor of the daughter of the proprietor of a house to let. *For everyone.*

2) 男婚女嫁 Two acts. A comedy with the aim of ridiculing those who marry for money, and those who marry for beauty. *For mature people.*

1297. 母親的肖像 *MOTHER'S PORTRAIT*   1 vol. 102 p. by 徐 訏
1941 夜窗書屋

A play in three acts.

Wang Po-yu, a painter, loves his cousin who however, since her family is ruined, has been given in marriage to a rich man named Li Mo-ching. The last is a pearl dealer and is often abroad. Now Po-yu profits from his absence and lives with his beloved cousin. Four sons are the fruit of their co-habitation.

The cousin dies, and her husband, Li Mo-ching, ignorant of the whole affair, marries Miss Yao-ching who has relations with the eldest of his sons, Li Cho-yu, thereby becoming pregnant. Her lover is also a painter. He abandons his mistress and goes to live in Paris. Upon his return he takes up his relations with her again. One fine day Mo-ching discovers them in the act, and Cho-yu takes to flight. The husband wishes to obtain a divorce but the wife refuses. He then falls grievously ill and, calling his children to him, he reveals to them their paternity. He dies regarding a "portrait of his mother" which he considers his masterpiece.

Very licentious subject. Extra-conjugal relations that should be condemned. Divorce approved of by the author, etc. *Not to be recommended to anyone.*

1298. 兒女風雲 *"LE DÉPIT AMOUREUX"* (Adaptation)

1 vol. by **胡春冰** and **龔家寶**

1943 光明書局

A free adaptation of the play, "Le dépit amoureux" of Molière.

A lover mistakes his fiancee, but ends by discovering the real one and marries her. *For everyone*, but not to be acted in our schools.

1299. 當兵去 *LET'S ENLIST*   by **胡紹軒**[1]

Théâtre ambulant.

When the war of resistance against the Japanese began, "théâtre ambulant" was extensively employed. This play "Let's Enlist" by Hu Shao-hsuan was the first of its kind written by a Chinese. The play depicts a scene in a country highway where people who were bereft in one way or other met and discussed their different views on conscription. Among the characters were a young lad whose whole family were killed by Jap bombing rushing to join the army, an old man who bid his son in the city to evade drafting, a peasant woman who had just seen her husband entering camp. Another air raid on the city which killed his son changed the old man's attitude. The play ended with the group marching and singing the song "Let's Enlist". *For everyone*.

1300. 我們不做亡國奴 *WE WOULD RATHER DIE*   by **胡紹軒**

A Play in one scene, three acts.

Suitable for a village stage.

Before each of the three acts begins explanations on the importance of liberty. The play depicts the oppression on the people by the Japs, which is much more unbearable than suffering poverty. The method is valuable for propaganda. *For everyone*.

1301. 鐵砂 *IRON ORE*   by **胡紹軒**

A play in four scenes.

It depicts the life of the iron miners at Ta Jeh during the war. The Japs coerced the miners to build the railway for the transportation of the thirty million tons of ore stored up, and forced children to give blood for transfusion. But the miners finally revolted, killed some fifty Japs, and dumped the iron ore into the river and joined the guerrillas. Interwoven into the story of blood and fire is a touching tale of love about a leader of the miners and the patriotic daughter of a traitor. *For everyone*.

---

(1) Hu Shao-hsüan 胡紹軒.

Playwright. Born in Tayeh, Hupeh. Before the Sino-Japanese War, he edited the magazine *Wên I* 文藝 (Literature) at Wuchang. After the Victory over Japan, he resumed the publication of the said magazine. Its contributors are: Lao Shê 老舍 Yü Shang-yuan 余上沅, Wang P'ing-ling 王平陵, Chao Ching-shên 趙景深, Hsiung Fo-hsi 熊佛西, Ku Chung-i 顧仲彝, Mu Mu-t'ien 穆木天, Ma Yen-hsiang 馬彥祥, Liu Wu-chi 柳無忌, and other famous writers.

He wrote the following plays: *Tou Chêng* 鬥爭 (also called *Sha Shang Ch'ien Ch'ü* 殺上前去); *Tang Ping Ch'ü* 當兵去* (in *Chieh T'ou Chü Hsüan* 街頭劇選, edited by Chou P'ing 周平, Shanghai, 金湯); *Wo Mên Pu Tso Wang Kuo Nu* 我們不作亡國奴 *; *Ti Ch'i Hao Jên T'ou* 第七號人頭; *Ping Yuan Ch'iang Sheng* 病院槍聲; *Lu Kou Ch'iao* 蘆溝橋; *Han Chien Tao Yen* 漢奸導演; *Hsiang Kang I Fu Jên* 香港一婦人; *Wai Kuo Chi Chê Tso Fei Chi* 外國記者坐飛機; *Shan Ch'eng Chih Huo* 山城之火; *Ch'ang Chiang Hsüeh* 長江血; *Mu Ch'i Chih Chien* 母妻之間; *Mên Wai* 門外; *Hang Hsien Shang* 航線上, *Fang K'ung Tung* 防空洞; *Tieh Sha* 鐵砂* (in 4 acts, 獨立出版社); *Yen Ch'ang* 鹽場; (in 4 acts); *P'i Chi T'ai Lai* 否極泰來* (in 4 acts, 獨立出版社); *Mei K'eng* 煤坑 (in 3 acts, 文通); etc.

Critical works: *Chung Kuo Hsin Wên Hsüeh Chiao Ch'eng* 中國新文學教程 (Modern Chinese Literature, 文通); *Chan Shih Hsi Chü Lun* 戰時戲劇論 (Wartime Drama, 獨立出版社); etc.

1302. 否極泰來 *'TIS DARKEST BEFORE DAWN*   by 胡紹軒

A play in four scenes.
Awarded by the CMI, the play is based on a passage written by President Chiang Kai-shek in his book "China's Destiny", admonishing the youth of China that they should take up constructive jobs such as engineers, aviators, school teachers, border pioneers etc. The story tells about how two young men from wealthy families refusing the temptation of wealth and comfort to brave poverty and opposition in working in the country, and how stubborn reactionaires and pleasure-seeking people moved and convinced by their sincerity came to join their work. *For everyone.*

1303. 眼兒媚 *FLIRTING EYES*   1 vol. 145 p. by 胡 導
                                        1944 世界書局

A Play in four acts.
        An unmarried banker, forty years of age, has adopted two girls, Mei and Hua. They are both very beautiful, and the former especially, fascinates others by the light in her eyes.
        According to the terms of a will, Mei has to choose a husband after two months. Now a certain Cho whom Mei wishes to marry has to go to Mongolia and can return only at the end of six months. In order to arrange matters, Mei proposes to the banker that he marries her for form's sake only, and divorces her after six months when her friend returns. The banker consents to this ruse, but finding that he has fallen in love with Mei, he proposes divorcing her after only one month, being afraid that he will succumb to temptation. His so-called "wife" however, manages to dissuade him and even succeeds in making him consent to prolonging the agreement to ten years, as she has learnt in the meantime that her fiancé will not return until after that lapse of time. Upon this, the banker, not being able to hold himself back, confesses his love for Mei who is so touched that she begins to love him in return. After this avowal, the couple behave as though they were married for good.
        In the meantime, a friend of the banker has been entrusted with the care of Hua, and he in his turn falls in love so that another couple is united.
        Upon all this Cho returns from Mongolia to everyone's consternation. All ends happily however, for he also has been unfaithful to his first love and married a native of the faraway country he has visited.
        The book ends with three couples happily united.
        There are some crude details in this book, and the marriage tie is made fun of to a certain extent. *For mature people.*

1304. 潘巧雲 *LIFE OF A VIRAGO*   1 vol. 108 p. by 黃 鶴
                                        1945 世界書局

        A play in five acts.
        The author presents in his own manner the well-known story of 潘金蓮 in the 水滸 The names have been changed but the story remains the same.
        It must be admitted that this version has not gained in morality. Here also it is only a vulgar exhibition, where we are presented with the relations of the heroine with a buddhist monk, which are anything but edifying.
        The play ends with the murder of the heroine and her woman servant, and the flight of the guilty husband in company with his accomplice. They both enrol in the famous band of gentlemen of fortune, 宋明公. *Not to be recommended to anyone.*

1305. 大團圓 *REUNITED* by 黃宗江

A play in 4 acts.

The author presents a Pekinese family whose chief was an old official. His wife struggles with financial difficulties in nourishing all the family of four sons and three daughters; she has in her service an old servant, quite sympathetic and full of solicitude for all.

We assist at the disintegration of the said family. The elder son, a teacher in a school of the town, is not realistic enough to be of any help. Another son is somewhat silly, and attached to the old traditions. The third one is a great dreamer living for poetry. The youngest boy and the youngest of the girls are Catholics, who look for aid and advice in praying. The oldest of the girls rushed full of conviction into the revolution, and with the help of a revolutionist friend, she greatly helped her country. After some time, the boys (with the exception of the oldest) and the youngest of the girls, all engaged themselves in the resistance too.

When the war is over, the members, who on advice of the son-in-law stayed home, have already taken all their belongings to the pawn-shop, and it is only because of the resistance of the mother that the house itself has not been sold.

Now after the war, the characters have changed not a little. The dreamer has become a man, but his manners are too bold. The oldest girl has lost her revolutionary ideal. The youngest son and daughter have renounced their faith. The mother exhorts them to be "good", but she too finds the times have changed, that there is something wrong with modern society, and that to remain good according to the old conventions is a difficult thing.

The play ends with the selling of the paternal house and the dispersion of the family. The very meaning of the title is not realized: it is not a happy ending, not a union, but a disintegration, a disunion. *For informed readers.*

1306. 闔第光臨 *"...THE PLEASURE OF YOUR COMPANY"* 1 vol. 155 p. by 洪謨
1944 世界書局 *See Biogr. 86*

A play in three acts.

A good man who loves a peaceful life and is somewhat indolent, has his house turned upside down by the unexpected arrival of his mother-in-law and a whole following in attendance on her.

Seeing that he is exasperated by the upheaval of his household, two friends play a practical joke on the visitors by pretending that they are ghosts. The ruse is successful for the guests are put to flight, and life resumes its even course. *For everyone.*

1307. 洪深戲曲集 *THE COLLECTED DRAMAS OF HUNG SHEN*
1 vol. 163 p. by 洪深
1937 *See Biogr. 87*

The author of this book presents his own opinions and ideas on theatre, he even introduces two plays of his own composition. He describes the struggles of the poor in the first, and in the second life in the Chinese army.

Except for frequent cursing the book contains nothing immoral or corrupt. *For everyone.*

1308. 夢裏乾坤 *AN ENTIRELY DIFFERENT WORLD* 1 vol. 96 p. by 洪深
1940 益智書局

It helps to sleep over it, it helps even to dream! In this play, the author presents to us a family before and after a dream. The latter has put a few sound ideas into the head of the eldest son who wanted to get a divorce. *May be read.*

1309. 人之初　　　　　　　　　　　　　1 vol. 95 p. by 洪　深
　　　　　　　　　　　　　　　　　　　　　1947　正中書局

Three acts with a prologue and an epilogue.

A certain Ch'en Pin-sheng (陳炳生) is ill and his wife is also in the same condition. The reason is because of the lack of hygiene in their household and the dirty conditions in which they live. Cleanliness is recommended to them but in vain. In spite of the devotion of his friends the hero becomes a thief and extorts a large quantity of merchandise from one of his relatives. His wife prays him not to commit this crime but he does not listen to her. Although he is discovered while committing the theft he is treated with the greatest leniency.

In the final scene he appears a reformed man and even refuses to drink water that has not been boiled. *For everyone.*

1310. 女人，女人　*WOMEN! WOMEN!*　　1 vol. 194 p. by 洪　深
（一名多福多壽多男子）　　　　　　　2nd edition 1946　華中圖書公司

A comedy in three acts.

A very interesting comedy that presents ideas that are prevalent at the moment in the world and upon which are founded the relations between men and women, and between married people and society.

Under the form of gatherings of women, the author treats of such subjects as divorce, birth-control, abortion, girl mothers, triangular love affairs etc.

The author is to be congratulated on not being the dupe of erroneous notions that are current in the present day world and which are the cause of the dislocation of society. In this play, he presents us with concrete cases and resolves them in a satisfactory manner.

Abortion is condemned by conscience and the law, divorce because of the unhappiness that goes in its train, birth-control because it is against Chinese tradition, and triangular love affairs because of the family conflicts that they occasion.

We are glad to come across an author who sponsors sane ideas. His play would be even more valuable if it went more to the bottom of things.
For mature people only because of the special nature of the subjects treated.

1311. 寄生草　　　　　　　　　　　　　1 vol. 114 p. 洪　深
　　　　　　　　　　　　　　　　　2nd. edit. 1947　上海雜誌公司

A comedy in three acts.

The subject is exactly the same as that reviewed as No. 1443, except that a few names have been changed.

Hung Sheng (洪深) has presented it in so natural and innocuous a manner that we see no reason to pass reserves on his adaptation. For everyone.

1312. 女性的解放　*EMANCIPATED WOMEN*　1 vol. 123 p. by 易　喬
　　　　　　　　　　　　　　　　　　　　1946　潮鋒出版社

A play in three acts based upon "A Doll's House" by Henrik Ibsen.

Chuang (莊) and An-na (安娜) who are married love each other very much, but their home seems to be that of two children who play at being in love, because Chuang treats his wife as though she was a child.

Soon after they were married, An-na had committed a fault to save her husband from difficulties and forged the signature of her father to a cheque. A certain Chiang (姜) a man of doubtful character, had lent the money which had been repaid by the cheque. Chiang happens to be a clerk in the bank to which Chuang has been appointed as manager.

Chiang now threatens An-na that he will reveal the secret if she does not help with her influence to have him retained in his old job at the bank.

An-na, however, is not in a position to save Chiang from dismissal and scandal flares up. In a stormy interview with her husband, An-na realizes that her husband's love for her is completely egoistical. She admits to herself that she committed a fault in signing the cheque but she did it entirely for her husband. She finds that her love for her husband has been extinguished now that she understands his selfishness.

There is a friend of An-na's who is willing to marry Chiang, and she has such a softening influence on him that he gives up his persecution of An-na. When Chiang hears of this, he is so relieved that the scandal is going no further and his own honour will be saved, that he asks his wife to pardon him for his hastiness, thinking that they can continue as before. An-na, however, has seen his real nature and also learnt of the doubtfulness of some of his financial transactions. Therefore she decides to leave him and for the future to devote herself to the welfare of the country.

Her departure is to be reproved because it means also the abandonment of her child which can have only unhappy consequences. *For mature people.*

1313. 最佳劇選 *COLLECTION OF BEST PLAYS* 1 vol. 234 p. **易喬編選**
1947 潮鋒出版社

1) 女記者 by 田漢 p. 1-46. A journalist suffering from despair has the intention of drowning himself, but he recovers to offer his life for the country. The author admits divorce. *Not for everyone.*

2) 一袋米 by 尤兢 p. 47-94. A family tragedy during a year of famine. *For everyone.*

3) 同胞姊妹 by 顧仲彝 p. 95-130. Cfr. No. 1321. *For everyone.*

4) 饑餓 by Semenov, p. 131-165. The same subject as 2). *For everyone.*

5) 保祿摩萊爾 bl 拉里阿甫 p. 166-185. Death of a revolutionary. *For everyone.*

6) 都會流行症 by 莫利哀原著 p. 187-234. Two ladies who dream of modern lovers fall into a trap. *For everyone.*

1314. 香妃 *THE FRAGRANT LADY* 2 vol. 309 & 324 p. by **顧青海**
1934

Play in 3 acts.

This play presents the Emperor of China at war with the king of the desert; the war was about Hsiang Fei, the king's wife, whose beauty attracted the Emperor. After the victory the emperor carried off Hsiang Fei, who became home-sick for the desert and turned down his advances. The Empress Dowager helped her to commit suicide. *For informed readers.*

1315. 重見光明 *RETURN TO LIGHT* 1 vol. 103 p. by **顧仲彝**
1944 世界書局 *See Biogr. 91*

A play in four acts.

Wei Jui kuang, a husband who is very docile to his wife in spite of difficult temperament, adopted a blind girl. The latter was very beautiful, and possessed great talents. Jui kuang fell in love with her but could not admit this fact to himself. The girl also fell in love with her benefactor. But Jui kuang was not the only man who fell in love with his adopted child; his own son fell in love with her but the latter's love was not answered.

One day a famous doctor performed an operation on the girl's eyes and she recovered her sight. On finding out that her benefactor was an old man she lost her love for him and began to love his son. *For everyone.*

1316.   三千金   *THREE DAUGHTERS*   1 vol. 149 p. by   **顧仲彞**
                                        1944   世界書局

A play in four acts.

A retired official who is very rich and seventy years of age, wishes to divide his fortune between his three daughters. Two of them are married and are of doubtful conduct, while the youngest is of good character and lives with her father.

On the day that the fortune is divided, the two elder sisters protest in flowery language their attachment to their father, while the younger is more reserved and says nothing. This attitude renders the father indignant so that he gives his whole fortune to the two eldest, after which the younger sister leaves with a young man of modest fortune who, however, promises to make her happy.

The old father who has reserved to himself the right of living with his two elder daughters, soon finds out that they do not love him. And they end up, in fact, by throwing him out. He then goes to his youngest daughter who receives him very kindly.

There he is pursued by his other two daughters who are afraid that their father will bring a lawsuit against them, and they try to bring him back by force.

The eldest arrives with her lover and the second sister appears with her husband who slays his brother-in-law in self-defence.

In a pathetic interview, the eldest sister calls upon her father to return with her. At this moment the masks fall from the faces of the characters and their true natures are revealed. The eldest ends by killing her lover after which she takes poison herself. The second, moved by the sight of her father, asks his pardon. And the old father forgives everyone while his eldest daughter dies in the arms of her two sisters. *For adults.*

1317.   新婦   *THE BRIDE*   1 vol. 152 p. by   **顧仲彞**
                                        1944   世界書局

A widow has two sons. The younger lives at home with his fiancee, while the other, who has been away for several years, sends word to his mother that he is on the point of returning with his newly married wife.

The mother is unbalanced in her love for her sons. Being afraid that her younger son's affections will be stolen from her by his fiancée, she makes him break his engagement. And when the elder son arrives with his wife, who is a medical doctor and a very intelligent woman, she devotes herself to destroying their happiness and alienating her son from his wife. The latter, being understanding and fearless, resists her mother-in-law, and struggles for her happiness; but her husband is more feeble and listens to the perverse advice of his mother, and refuses to leave for Shanghai with his wife, where she intends to continue her scientific researches. The intelligent daughter-in-law, however, is on the alert, and she openly attacks the mother and her two sons in a long tirade in which she reproaches her mother-in-law with her bad acts.

In fact, the fiancée of the younger son had attempted suicide because of her dismissal. Now, the elder daughter-in-law, after giving the others a piece of her mind, takes up her trunks and goes, taking the younger girl (the dismissed fiancée) with her.

Her husband then goes after her, convinced that she is thoroughly in the right. But the younger brother, who has a weaker character, decides to remain at home with his mother.

The aim of the author in this play is to show the harm that can be done by an unreasonable mother-in-law. Such women marry their sons for their own selfish reasons, and the daughters-in-law are merely their servants.

Obviously such egoistic creatures do exist, but neverthless the author generalises too much and his attacks are too violent. *For mature people*.

1318. 野火花 *LA MALQUERIDA* (adapted) 1 vol. 83 p. by 顧仲彝
1944 世界書局

A tragedy in three acts. An adaptation of the play "La Malquerida" by Joacinto Bonavente.

The betrothal of Chin-sheng and Hui-ku is being celebrated. Returning home in the evening, the young man is shot at and killed. Rumour accuses Li of this crime because he also loves Hui-ku.

Her mother, by the way, remarried several years ago, and is passionately in love with her second husband.

It transpires that the murderer is Hui-ku's step-father, who loves her and has sworn to kill anyone who comes near her.

Hui-ku wishes to deliver him to justice, hoping that afterwards her mother's love will return to her, but her mother wants to save her husband at all costs, and decides to send her daughter away to some distant relatives.

In a very dramatic scene, Hui-ku is on the point of delivering her step-father to the police, but to the stupefaction of everyone, reveals her secret instead, that she is passionately in love with this man, and proposes to escape with him. He agrees readily as he also is in love with her. And he threatens to kill anyone who prevents their flight together.

His wife (Hui-ku's mother) opposes his plan in a paroxysm of passion, and she is mortally wounded by her enraged husband. He is then delivered to the police by those present who are indignant at his conduct, while the daughter returns to the arms of her dying mother.

This play *cannot be recommended to anyone* because of the incestuous love affairs presented, and the crimes depicted.

1319. 殉情 *KABALE UND LIEBE* (adapted) 1 vol. 132 p. 顧仲彝改編
（一名戀愛與陰謀） 4th. edit. 1945 光明書局

Tragedy in five acts adapted and copied servilely from the "Kabale und Liebe" of Schiller.

Ting Nan, the son of a minister, falls in love with the daughter of a teacher. His father is opposed to this marriage and wishes him to marry a girl of his own position. Ting Nan refuses this other girl.

The minister takes it out on the parents of the girl student. The mother dies of grief and the father is imprisoned. The heroine, in order to liberate her father, writes a compromising letter that is bound to provoke the jealousy of Ting Nan who is resolved to endure his father's anger, but after reading the letter, he gives a poisoned drink to his girl friend which he also drinks himself, and both of them die just at the moment the minister comes, bringing his consent to their marriage.

This play is dramatically poignant but it is *not to be recommended to anyone*:
1. because of the extreme pessimism that it contains,
2. because of the opposition to parents demonstrated in a brutal fashion,
3. because of the murders and suicides.

1320. 八仙外傳 *UNUSUAL LIFES* 1 vol. 99 p. by 顧仲彝
1945 世界書局

A play in four acts.
A story of seven immortals who come to ask for a young girl in marriage. Being

refused, they return under the guise of ordinary men. And still not being able to obtain the consent of the heroine, they reveal to her their real identity as immortals, and take her away to make her the eighth immortal.

This play runs the danger of distracting the imagination of young people. *Not for everyone.*

1321. 同胞姊妹 *THE DEAR DEPARTED* (adapted)   1 vol. 127 p. by   顧仲彜
                                                              1946   世界書局

　　Five one-act plays.

1) 同胞姊妹 : Adaptation of "The Dear Departed" by Houghton. *For everyone.*

2) 劉三爺 : The son of 劉三爺 betrays a friend of his father who has sought refuge with him after committing a murder. When the father learns of it, he kills his son. *Not for everyone.*

3) 駕鴦刼 : An adaptation of "The First and Last" by Galsworthy. A young man kills the so-called husband of a prostitute with whom he is in love, and who loves him in return. The brother of the murderer, a well-known barrister, arranges the evidence so that the family honour is preserved. He is not moved by the fact that an innocent man is condemned to death for the murder that his brother has committed. The latter, however, has more conscience. Disgusted with the false world of his elder brother, he and the woman he lives with take poison together. *Not for everyone.*

4) 夫婦之間 : Adaptation of "Winners All" by Ida Lubleski Ehrlich. A very witty comedy, demonstrating that it is just as well married people quarrel from time to time. *For everyone.*

5) 結婚的一天 : Adaptation of "A Good Woman" by Bennett. On the day of the wedding, an old admirer appears before the bride and groom. *For everyone.*

1322. 上海男女 *SHANGHAI PEOPLE*   1 vol. 114 p. by   顧仲彜
                                                              1946   世界書局

　　A play in three acts.

　　In this play the author describes the "modern world" of the big city of Shanghai.

　　It is about the family of a business man. The husband thinks of nothing but how to enrich himself, by any means, the opening of a gambling den, a dance hall, through speculations, etc. The wife who is a superstitious and limited woman passes her time quarreling with her husband's concubine and neglects the education of her children. The poor cast-offs go their own way, that is, to the bad. The concubine flirts with whoever comes along.

　　The intimate counsellors of the head of the family are of the same calibre as himself. The servants are not respected. The amahs are abused and are packed off whenever an "accident" occurs. All this is supposed to be "modern life" in Shanghai!

　　Misfortune, however, is not long in coming. Money losses, suicides, and revolts are depicted. *For mature people.*

1323. 黃金迷 *L'AVARE* (adapted)   1 vol. 104 p. by   顧仲彜
                                                              1946   世界書局

　　A comedy in five acts, adapted from "L'Avare" by Molière.

　　According to our point of view this version of Molière's famous comedy in Chinese dress still remains too French.

　　As everyone knows, a miser is portrayed in this play, and there is an intrigue consisting of a double matrimonial affair. *For everyone.*

1324. 梅蘿香 *THE EASIEST WAY* (adapted)   1 vol. 132 p. by **顧仲彝**

1946 世界書局

A play in four acts, adapted from "The Easiest Way" by E. Walter.

A lady of easy morals makes the acquaintance of a young man of no fortune named Tzu-ying (子英), and falls in love with him. On his part, he falls in love with her, and makes her promise that she will change her way of life and wait until he can marry her. Upon this, he takes his leave to make a fortune which he hopes to offer her.

During his absence the young lady lives in poverty but she gets tired of it after a few months, and although she is really in love with the young man, returns to her old way of life with another friend.

Tzu-ying comes eventually with a fortune that he has made and wants to marry the heroine, who however, hides her infidelity from him. When he learns of it from a friend, he abandons her. The heroine, in despair, returns to her old associates. *For mature people.*

1325. 人之初 *TOPAZE* (adapted)   1 vol. 146 p. by **顧仲彝**

1946 世界書局

A play in four acts, adapted from "Topaze" by M. Pagnol.

A poor and credulous teacher named Po-nan (伯南) is dismissed from his job. Because in his simplicity, he treads on the toes of well-placed people, and does not know how to adapt himself to the ways of the world.

The mistress of a manipulator of shady affairs inveigles him into their "combine". In his natural honesty, Po-nan protests at first, but the lady in question manages to muzzle him by feminine artifices. In spite of severe heart-searchings, the hero remains in the "combine", and plays his part so well, that he even succeeds in surpassing the leader of the group, and in taking his mistress from him!

The play ends with this singular development, and the warnings of an old friend who talks the language of the conscience.

This play is *not to be recommended to young people.*

1326. 嫦娥 *FLED TO THE MOON: CH'ANG-E*   1 vol. 131 p. by **顧仲彝**

2nd. edit. 1946 永祥印書館

A play in five acts.

Why do we see the images of 后羿 and 嫦娥 in the moon? Here is the answer.

King 后羿, whose armies were no longer what they were, found himself besieged by his own wife. Being victorious, she imposed very hard conditions on him. One of them was that he would not take any new concubines without her approval. If he broke this stipulation, then he ran the danger of having the new addition to his harem put to death on the third day after her entry.

Now the most beautiful girl in the world happened to be brought to the King. Her name was 嫦娥. The King fell in love with her at sight, and she returned his love. Three days after their union, however, the Queen exacted the accepted conditions. But arrived on the scaffold, 嫦娥 suddenly flew into the air and darted into the moon. The King, who could not bear to be parted from her, then took a magic pill which enabled him also to fly to the moon.

But when 嫦娥 arrived in the moon, she was made to take a vow of chastity, swearing that she would never again cast her eyes upon men. It so happened that the very moment she was taking this vow, her husband arrived on the scene and they had an interview together, for which they were punished.

During the absence of the Sovereign of the Moon, which occurs on the fifteenth of the eighth moon, the inhabitants of that planet unite together, and 后羿 and 嫦娥 took advantage of the situation to fall into each other's arms. The King of the Moon, however, surprised them in their embrace, and as punishment, they were sentenced to a further sojourn in the moon for 3,000 years.

That is why we see their images in the moon. *For mature people.*

1327. 大地之愛 *BEYOND THE HORIZON* (adapted)   1 vol. 108 p. by **顧 仲 彝**
1946 上海永祥印書舘

A play in three acts adpted from "Beyond the Horizon" by Eugene O'Neill.
Act. I. Two brothers, An-jung (安榮) and An-hua (安華), who are very united, love the same girl, Li-chin (麗金). The elder is very attached to the land, while his younger brother dreams of crossing the seas. Li-chin chooses the latter and asks him not to leave his native country. An-hua consents and his elder brother, cursed by their father, leaves in his place. An-jung is glad to go because he cannot bear to be near the girl whom he loves, knowing that she belongs to another.
Act. II. Three years after. The husband and wife are living in poverty and discord. An-hua knows nothing of farming, and there is coolness between him and his wife who dreams of her brother-in-law who is far away. The father has died, and the elder brother makes a short appearance only to go away again.
Act. III. Five years after. The husband and wife are beginning to founder in misery. Their little daughter is dead and An-hua is seriously ill. His wife detests him and is continually thinking of the absent one. Recalled by a telegram, the elder brother returns after having lost a fortune in speculations. There is a medical specialist who comes with him, and this man, after examining the younger brother announces that he is approaching his end. This puts An-jung into despair, but gives hope to Li-chin! An-hua is horrified when he realizes that his sister-in-law has designs on him.

An-hua dies full of grand dreams that call to him from afar just the same as when he was young.

In this play, the author describes a touching love between the brothers. At the same time he gives a magnificent portrait of two failures. The one who should have remained at home, went away, while the other who should have gone, stayed at home. Both are conquered by life. Li-chin is to blame for not encouraging her husband, and for having neglected her little girl. *May be read by anyone.*

1328. 衣冠禽獸 *BEASTS IN HUMAN APPARELS*   ...1 vol. 125 p. by **顧 仲 彝**
1946 永祥印書舘

A play in four acts.
It is about a very united family. The parents, from being poor, have become extremely rich. They have three daughters. The youngest is engaged and on the point of marrying.

Then the father dies and the four women who are left do not know how to regulate their finances. Old friends of the father exploit the situation, and soon the family is reduced to poverty again. To cap it all, the suitor of the youngest daughter retires from his suit which drives her out of her mind. The second daughter then decides to sacrifice herself and promises to marry one of those who have robbed the family.

In a final scene, her future husband gives her a lesson on how one dismisses robber creditors! *May be read by anyone.*

1329. 水仙花 *NARCISSUS*　　　　　1 vol. 125 p. by **顧 仲 彝**
3rd. edit. 1947　光明書局

A play in four acts adapted from the story of "Jane Eyre" by Charlotte Bronte.

Hsien (憲) has a wife who has become mad and whom he keeps in secret. He wishes to become engaged to a rich girl who does not know of his previous marriage. And he would divorce his wife if it were not for the fact that he is prevented by her brother, a truculent lawyer.

On the day that they are engaged, the rich girl reveals herself under her real colour. It seems that she is not in love but only wants to make a good marriage. The contract is dissolved.

It happens that Hsien is in love with a young orphan (who is particularly fond of narcissi) who gives lessons to his little daughter. This girl loves him in return, and so their engagement is celebrated after the other one is called off.

At this moment, however, Ying-hsien (瑩仙), which is the name of the orphan, learns that her fiance's wife is still alive and she flees into the night.

After three days of painful walking, she arrives at the house of a cousin who is a kind of protestant pastor. The latter, being a young man who is full of grand altruistic plans, breaks his relations with a rich girl, and asks Ying-hsien to go with him to Tibet where they will propagate the Christian religion.

Ying-hsien refuses because she is haunted by the memory of her fiance. And after a month in her cousin's house, where she inherits a large fortune, she returns to Hsien.

She finds him completely ruined having become blind in attempting to save his wife, during a fire that broke out in his house. The wife having died in the fire in spite of the efforts of Hsien, Ying-hsien now feels free to stay with him to look after him. Overcome with joy, the hero dies just as he is about to become engaged to the girl of his heart.

The divorce envisaged it to be reprehended, and the character of the pastor is rather caricatured. Apart from these defects there is nothing objectionable in the play. *May be read by anyone.*

1330. 西 施 及 其 他 *HSI SHIH* (A renowned beauty) 1 vol. 142 p. by **顧 一 樵** and **顧 青 海**
1947　商務印書館

1. 西施 4 acts. pp. 1-76. Story of the very sympathetic heroine Hsi Shih, who sacrificed her love on the altar of patriotism. The author is rather free with historical truth and makes the heroine die though she fell in love with her new admirer.
2. 昭君 3 acts, pp. 77-142. A Chinese princess was given in marriage to a Mongolian king in order to save the country from danger of invasion. She fell in love with her husband, but died young and came back as a "spirit" to exhort the Chinese emperor to be on the look-out for danger.
For grown up people.

1331. 李 太 白 *LI PO*　　　　　1 vol. 107 p. by **孔 另 境**
1944　世界書局 *See Biogr. 94*

A historical drama in five acts with a prologue. A play with a moral describing the bad influence of Yang Kuei-fei and Chang Hu-fei and their clique with the eunuchs. These reject the poet and treat him shamefully on two different occasions. At the last moment, instead of allowing himself to be taken by soldiers, he prefers death, and throws himself into the river. *For everyone.*

1332. 沉箱記　*SUNKEN TREASURE*　　　1 vol. 116 p. by　**孔另境**

1944　世界書局

A play in four acts.

In this play the celebrated courtisan, Tu Shih-niang (杜十娘) is glorified.

A certain 于先, the son of an official, arrives in Peking with a fortune in his pocket. During a whole year he frequents the society of 杜微 and falls in love with her. The courtisan returns the love of the young man. When he comes to the end of his money, however, 杜微's mother does not wish to receive him any longer. But the heroine procures the sum necessary for her redemption, and the two lovers decide to present themselves to the parents of the young man, to ask for their consent to their marriage.

杜微 however, finds her lover undecided, for knowing the strictness' of his father, he realizes that he will never obtain his consent to such a marriage.

A rake, who is fascinated by 于先, wishes to take advantage of the situation, and offers 于先 1000 ounces of silver for the favours of the courtisan. The young man accepts the offer, and with the money, he hopes to obtain the good will of his father.

When the heroine realizes the infidelity of her lover, she feigns consent to his act, and accompanies the young men on a journey to the south under the pretext that before her marriage, she must first sacrifice at the tomb of her mother.

When they are all aboard the boat, 杜微 opens a box containing a great treasure, which she shows to the bewildered young men. This treasure is the fruit of her long life as a courtisan. While she reviles the two spectators, she avows that she had intended to put this at the disposal of 于先 who, furnished with such a fabulous sum, would have obtained the consent of his father to his marriage. Confronted with his infidelity, however, she curses him, and throws the precious pearls into the river, one by one. Finally, she throws herself into the water. *May be read by anyone.*

1333. 春秋怨　*CAN ONE FORGET?*　　　1 vol. 106 p. by　**孔另境**

1944　世界書局

A historical tragedy in four acts.

The ruling house of 魯 is forced to conclude a treaty of alliance with 晉 whose ruling house is more powerful. A minister of the latter state demands the hand of 孝姬, the beautiful young wife of 孝叔. 魯 dare not refuse for it would mean the fall of the dynasty. 孝姬 is sacrificed even though she loves her husband tenderly, and she goes to live in the court of 晉.

There she becomes the mother of two children who are very attached to their father, who after six years of marriage with 孝姬, falls out of royal favour and is condemned to death together with his two brothers.

His wife and children, through the mercy of the queen, return to 魯. And the heroine is very happy to be able to return to her first husband. He, however, is madly jealous. He seizes the two children and throws them into the river to revenge himself upon his rival.

孝姬, in a paroxysm of anguish, curses her husband, and delivers him to justice in order to revenge the death of her children, after which she throws herself into the river. *For mature people.*

1334. 鳳還巢　*THE "PRODIGAL" HUSBAND*　　　1 vol. 123 p. by　**孔另境**

1944　世界書局

A play in three acts.

A husband and his wife have been separated for over a year, when the man's father announces that he is coming on a visit. Not wanting him to learn of their divorce, they agree to stay together for a short time and act as though they were a harmonious couple.

The father arrives, and the young people act their part, but it transpires that the father has known all about them for a long time, and he creats a scene with a very salutary effect, for the husband and wife are reconciled to each other and decide that they will continue living together.

A good play. The author condemns divorce, but admits it, nevertheless, in certain circumstances which is contrary to good morals. *For adults.*

1335. 蠱惑 *ENTICED*   1 vol. 94 p. by   孔另境
                                          1945   世界書局

A tragedy in four acts.

An officer of the revolutionary army has to leave on a special mission three days after his wedding. When he is bidding his wife goodbye, she makes him promise that he will not seek the company of an actress with whom he has been connected previously. He promises, but he has hardly arrived in Shanghai, when he hurries to his former mistress.

Now for some time already, she has been connected with a terrorist group that are enemies of the party to which her lover belongs. She succeeds in lulling him into a feeling of security, and, after several weeks of intimacy, manages to steal from him military secrets of great value.

Just at the moment when she is doing this, P'ei-shan, the wife, arrives on the scene in search of her husband, and she surprises the female criminal. She tries to prevent her, but is confronted with a gun which the other fires at her with fatal effect. The officer also arrives on the scene, and, seeing that his dear wife has been slain, he goes in pursuit of his mistress who has darted off with the documents to give them to the leader of the group. When the latter sees the officer arrive, he wants to give fight, but is prevented by one of the group who kills his chief. Our hero then secures the gun and shoots his mistress in revenge for the death of his wife.

The author wishes to show in this play that in order to accomplish special missions, experience and a knowledge of mankind is necessary.

It is *suitable for adults only,* because of the murders that it contains that are to be deplored.

1336. 屈原 *CH'U YUAN*   1 vol. 144 p. by   郭沫若
                                          1946   群益 *See Biogr.* 96

The story took place in the "Warring States period" about the year 313 B.C. Ch'ü Yüan, celebrated poet and minister possessed so much influence over the king of Chin that the queen was suspicious, especially when the king began to favour a foreign policy which was opposed to her own. So she tried to poison the king's opinion against Ch'ü Yüan. She arranged for the performance of a ballet with music; in the midst of this ballet she pretended to fall ill and fell into the arms of Ch'ü Yüan as the king entered; this action gave her a pretext for accusing him of brutal assault. The king fell into this trap and dismissed his minister and friend. But the dancers understood the true motive and from them Ch'ü Yüan's adopted daughter learned about the queen's crime. From this time the girl resolved to clear the name of her adopted father. One day she dared to accuse the queen of her crime in public. For this act she was cast into prison and severely whipped. She was rescued from prison during the night and met Ch'ü Yüan who took pity on her and had brought her a drink of some wine given to him as a present. Scarcely had the girl tasted the wine when she felt a terrible pain in her stomach, and she exclaimed "It is poisoned wine! But I shall die happy, for I have saved your life; the queen intended to poison you." Ch'ü Yüan was struck with grief and decided to leave Chin, and to take refuge in a more hospitable country. *For everyone.*

1337. 虎符 *THE MARSHAL'S CREDENTIALS*   1 vol. 190 p. by 郭沫若
1946 群益

A historical play in 5 acts.

This scene takes place in the "Warring States period", 257 B.C. It is a story of a Prince Hsin Ling, who saved the kingdom of Chao by means of the "Hu Fu", a staff used by the kings to call out their troops. Prince Hsin Ling extracted permission from his master, the king of Wei, to go to the help of Chao against the encroachments of the kings of Chin. By this deed he protected his own country against the greed of the invader. Unfortunately he could raise only 3000 men in his own domain and this was not enough to decide the issue of the war. Then someone suggested to him to steal the "Hu Fu". The person who undertook to commit the theft was a royal concubine, and a deadly enemy of her husband who had murdered her father. Prince Hsin Ling, with the possession of the priceless talisman, gathered 20,000 men and went at their head to liberate the beseiged capital. In order to succeed, Hsin Ling was obligd to kill the commander-in-chief of the Wei forces. The king of Wei, suspicious about the fraud, and angry at the killing of his general, swore to be avenged. Hsin Ling's mother, out of self-sacrifice, confessed to be the guilty one and was commanded to stab herself. The real culprit, the king's concubine and Hsin Ling's lover, stabbed herself over her father's grave. Hsin Ling's house was razed to the ground, but the prince of Chao's territory could not be touched. *For everyone.*

1338. 棠棣之花 *BROTHERS*   155 p. by 郭沫若
1946 群益出版社

Tragedy in 5 acts.

The story takes place about the year 371 B.C. at the time of the "Warring States". To the East of Tung Kuan (Shensi) there were six kingdoms: Han, Wei, Yen, Ch'i, Ch'u, and Chao. To the West there was only the Ch'in dynasty, which was very powerful. Han, Chao and Wei were descendants of the ancient Tsin family, but were at that time divided: some wanted to join the Ch'in family, others were against it. Hsia Lei, Minister of State in Han, was for it, but was opposed by Yen Chung-tzu. Yen was obliged to flee and blamed Hsia-lei. In the house of Ch'i there was a very brave young man, Nie-sheng, who was anti-Ch'in. He was living with his old mother and his sister, Nie-wen. Yen Chung-tzu paid him a visit and tried to win him over to his side (to suppress Hsia-lei). Nie refused, for he wanted to stay with his mother. After her death and when the funeral was over, our hero went in search of Yen. He found him in a hotel at P'u-Yang in the company of his friend, Han Shan-chien. Yen told Nie-sheng about the sinister plans and ambitions of Hsia-lei, who wanted to become king of Wei. It was Shan chien who had learned about these plans, for he was in Han's service.

Nie-sheng, on hearing about these plans, decided to go to Tung-Meng, where Hsia lei was living, and kill him. In order to conceal his identity he pretended to be an officer in the service of Chin, and induced Shan chien to introduce him. When he was just about to leave, he received a twig of a peach-tree from the hotel-keeper's daughter, by which she let him know that she loved him. Her name was Ch'uen Ku.

Our hero's plans were very successful. Hsialei and Han king were killed. Shan chien lost his life in the flight. Nie sheng committed suicide, previously mutilating his face, so not to be recognised as the brother of his sister, to whom he bore a strong resemblance.

Nie sheng's dead body was exposed on a highway, and a big reward was promised to any one who could identify him. Nie-wen, dressed in man's clothes, also set out after her brother had departed, and, having reached the hotel at P'u yang, learned from an elderly blind man, who came from Tung Meng, what had just happened. Ch'uen Ku was also informed. Our two heroines, both in men's clothes, immediately set out for Tung Meng where they recognized the corpse of their beloved one, wept over him, and, praising his great courage, gave up the ghost at his side. *For all.*

1339. 孔雀胆 *THE PEACOCK'S GALL-BLADDER*   1 vol. 202 p. by 郭沫若
1946 群益

Historical play in 4 acts.
The incident took place at the end of the Mongolian dynasty "Yuan" at Kunming in the year 1362.
A Chinese general Ying Kung, who had the king's confidence, aroused the jealousy of the king's concubine, and the latter, helped by other Mongolian officials, set out to shake Ying Kung's position.
However Ah-Kai, the king's daughter from this Mongolian concubine, was given in marriage to Ying Kung and took her husband's side against her own mother. By a clever trick, the concubine persuaded the king to believe that Ying Kung was the one who had poisoned the king's son, although in reality she was the guilty one.
After a number of incidents, the concubine's chief abettor succeeded in killing Ying Kung with poisoned arrows, and poisoned his fellow-assassins in order to secure their silence. Ah-Kai, who was unable to prevent the murder in spite of all her efforts, expressed her grief in a tragic scene. She hid the two sons of Ying Kung, in order that they would avenge the death of their father; after this she drunk the poisoned liquid of "peacock's liver", which had been the cause of all the other deaths. *For everyone.*

1340. 筑 *THE HARP*   1 vol. 188 p. by 郭沫若
1946 群益

Historical play in 5 acts.
Another episode of the "Warring States period", taking place in the 28th year of Shih Huang-ti.
Worn out with the tyranny and cruelty of the emperor, one of the victim's friends swore to take revenge on the tyrant. But his intention was found out and he was arrested before he could accomplish his plan. In the meantime, other conspirators determined to organize a dancing party in the course of which the murderer had to stab the king with his dagger, which was hidden in the bamboo used to scrape his guitar.
The king, completely absorbed by the music, was persuaded to dance, and thus gave a good opportunity for the murderer to stab him, but the latter missed his stroke. The king ordered the assassin with his wife to be whipped and then to be crucified at the palace gates, where they had to die of hunger and cold. *For everyone save children.*

1341. 南冠草 *POEM FROM A PRISON HOUSE*   1 vol. 197 p. by 郭沫若
1946 群益出版社

Historical play in 5 acts.
After the overthrow of the Ming, the Manchu dynasty Ch'ing was far from rallying all the people to their banner. Under the reign of the emperor Shun Chih, Ming partisans

were still active and wanted to restore the old dynasty. The main plotters, who were in the Shanghai — Sungchiang territory, were arrested and sentenced to death; the last of these — a young man of 17 named Hsia Yuen shuen — was also betrayed and arrested. In the course of his slow journey from Sungchiang to Nanking, his friends tried to rescue him. They succeeded in releasing him from his guards, but he was unwilling to break his word, refused to take the opportunity of escape and continued his journey.

Thrown into prison in Nanking, he got a public trial and was finally sentenced to death with one of his faithful followers. During the trial he met a former friend, who was now a supporter of the new regime; he did not hesitate to reproach him for his treachery. Neither his age nor his courage stirred pity in the hearts of men. On his way to the execution plot, he recited an unfinished poem which had the title "Nan Kuan Ts'ao" (Same with the name of the play) which served him as a spiritual testament. He was beheaded in Nanking, facing the Purple Mountain and shouting "Long live China". *For everyone.*

1342. 歸去來兮 *RETURNING*
by 老 舍
1946 *See Biogr. 137*

Drama in 5 acts.

Another patriotic war-time play, in which the author brings into contrast a poor family of idealist artists, and a certain Chiao, who has a passion for money and forgets all his duties, in order to enrich himself a little more every day. This Chiao thought he held the artist Liu in his claws, because he had given him some money, and wanted to force him to give his daughter in marriage to his son Chiao Jen-sheng, described as a useless creature. Liu was against it and his daughter also. Chiao prepared another marriage, that of his daughter Chiao Li-hsiang, with a rake. Luckily, none of Chiao's plans succeeded. The Liu's fled to Chungking in order to devote themselves there to patriotic work; and at their instigation, the young Chiao's, in order to expiate their faults, as well as those of their father, finally engaged themselves in the service of their native land. In a pathetic monologue, Mrs. Chiao cursed her husband for having ruined her family by his passion: his worship of the golden calf. "Your daughter-in-law became crazy, your eldest daughter ran away because you wanted to give her to a rake, your younger daughter became corrupted because you prevented from guiding her, your son Jen-sheng has fled because he is ashamed of your behavior . . . . . He fled to expiate your errors." Finally the madwoman appeared, and expressed her joy on seeing her brother-in-law depart to the battle front avenge the death of her husband. *For all.*

1343. 國家至上 *ABOVE ALL THE FATHERLAND* 1 vol. 150 p. by 老 舍 and 宋之的
1945   新豐出版公司

Patriotic play in 4 acts.

A play composed at the request of the Mohammedans themselves for the sake of strengthening the union between Mohammedans and non-Mohammedans in China. The first two acts are written by 老舍 and the last two by 宋之的. It is the story of two notable Mohammedans who were reconciled in order to face the Japanese, and made efforts to co-operate with the Chinese. Naturally a traitor came to interfere, sowed discord, and prepared for himself a good situation as a Japanese collaborator. He instigated the death of the chief heroes; the latter, before he died, acquainted himself with the underhand dealings of the traitor and killed him. *For all.*

1344. 這不過是春天 *THIS IS ONLY SPRING*
1 vol. by 李健吾
1934 *See Biogr. 98*

A play in 3 acts.

The story takes place in the family of a police inspector. His wife was visited by a relative, whom she once loved; the meeting brought back the old love as she has ceased to love her husband.

This relative was sought by the police, as he was travelling under an assumed name and was a revolutionist; although he did not return the woman's love, she helped him to escape from the hands of the police when his identity was discovered. She hated to part with him.

Nothing obscene is written in this book, but as it deals with illicit love, it is permissible *only to experienced readers*.

1345. 梁允達 *LIANG YUN-TA*   1 vol. 244 p. by 李健吾
1934 生活書店

1. 梁允達 p. 1-116. Three acts.

Mr. Liang has a son who misconducts himself and who is a gambler. His daughter-in-law also cannot be cited as an example of virtue. An old friend comes to see him and reminds him of a murder they committed in common twenty years ago (the murder of the father of Mr. Liang). This friend causes disagreement in the household, gives bad advice, flirts with the daughter-in-law, and blackmail Mr. Liang who, driven to the extreme, kills the other, just at the moment his daughter-in-law commits suicide by drowning herself.

2. 村長之家 p. 117-244. Three acts.

Portrait of a village elder who is concerned only with the affairs of the village and completely neglects his wife and daughter. He refuses to allow his own mother to enter the house because she had abandoned him when he was a child and remarried. Only when his daughter drowns herself, does he understand the real situation, but his regrets come too late. *For everyone.*

1346. 以身作則 *TO TAKE AS MODEL*   1 vol. 149 p. by 李健吾
7th edition, 1946 文化生活出版社

A comedy in three acts.

徐守淸, an old style scholar, is depicted as a typical example of his kind. He is a great stickler for formality, and he preaches at random the moral teachings of the old sages, which does not prevent him from being endowed with a fair amount of hypocrisy. No weakness is admitted when the weak sex is concerned, but he nevertheless takes certain liberties himself!

His daughter, having been inculcated to satiety on these doctrines, pays no heed to all the austere advice. She dreams of a "Prince Charming" who has appeared in the guise of an old style physician, having chosen to act this comedy in order to approach his lady-love.

The scholar's servants are all deceiving him, and there is only one old servant who has some good sense.

Synopsis of the play: 方, an officer who has risen from the ranks, is engaged to 徐玉貞 without knowing her. He introduces himself, disguised as a physician, deceiving thus the old 徐 scholar. Being, however, too free and easy when examining the young lady who is only pretending to be sick, he is shown the door. The scholar, who is a widower, engages a new maid, and takes liberties with her, in spite of his rigid principles. The officer's orderly also introduces himself into the house and makes love to the maid who is on friendly term with the master.

Soon after, however, it is discovered that 方 is, in fact, the fiancé of 玉貞, and he comes to claim her. 徐 finally gives his consent to the marriage, on the condition that the orderly who has snatched his girl-friend away from him, be given a good flogging.

The performance of this play is *not to be recommended* as there is too much emphasis on details of love-making and on the hypocrisy of the moralists.

It seems to be the aim of the author to demonstrate that "old style" education is outdated and does not bring good results. This may be so at the present time, but the author forgets that for thousands of years it has borne good fruit, and not all the teachings of the ancient sages should now be discarded. And it cannot be said that present-day youth are so full of virtue from all points of view. . .

1347. 撒謊世家　*A FAMILY OF LIARS*　　1 vol. 202 p. by 李健吾
1939 文化生活出版社

Drama in four acts.

A young wife has the fault of always telling lies. Moreover, she frequents the society of a friend of her husband, but without any real harm ensuing. Her husband, however, learns of it and she explains herself away by telling any lies that come into her head. Her husband loses confidence in her and abandons her, after which the heroine is seized with repentance and reforms, so hat in the end she is reconciled with her husband.

Difficult to act in our schools. *For everyone.*

1348. 母親的夢　*MOTHER'S DREAM*　　1 vol. 109 p. by 李健吾
4th. edit. 1939 文化生活

1. 老王和他的同志們 p. 1-80. Four tableaux.

The author tells of an incident that happens during a foreign invasion. He describes the state of mind of students, the police, civilians, soldiers, and particularly, of 老王 *For everyone.*

2. 母親的夢 p. 80-109. One act.

Of a poor family. The second son is a soldier, the third a rickshaw coolie, while the daughter helps the old mother, who has a dream of her absent son. The dream fades and calamities descend upon the family.

A very beautiful play containing admirable characters. *For everyone.*

1349. 黃花　*A SHORT-LIVED FLOWER*　　1 vol. 114 p. by 李健吾
2nd. edit. 1947 文化生活出版社

A play in three acts.

A celebrated dancer, going under the name of Yao (姚), engages in this occupation to obtain the wherewithal to keep a child whom she is bringing up in secret. The child is the issue of an illicite affair that she had with an aviator who subsequently died for the country.

Her sister, Madame Liu, happens to flirt with the same men who frequent the dancer. And one day the sisters meet in a hotel. Madame Liu, who is the elder sister, thinks that she has seen a ghost when she recognises the sister she believed dead.

Another day when they meet again, she reproaches her sister for being a dancer. Yao answers her sharply, accusing the other of being as guilty as herself, and also excusing herself for choosing such a profession because she did it only for the good of her child.

Now he is dead, she announces the resolution she has made to change her way of life. And in fact, the next day she leaves the hotel and becomes a nurse in a military hospital.

"Let he who has no sin cast the first stone" quotes the author in the preface, and through that he wishes to absolve his heroine and cover the shame of the sister. *For mature people.*

1350. 風流債 *UNTELLABLE DEBTS*   1 vol. 177 p. by 李健吾
1944 世界書局

A comedy in five acts.

In this play the author presents us with a family where the mother alienates all the people around her, makes her nearest relatives unhappy, and hides the faults she committed formerly — all under cover of the Catholic religion.

We do not know the real intentions of the author. And we admit there are scabby sheep among the Catholics just as there are among the members of any religion. The author, Mr. Li Chien-wu, may, however, be reproached for not seeming to understand anything about the Catholic religion, and for having rendered it a bad service in writing this parody.

The family that he describes is, in fact, not Catholic at all, although masquerading under that name. And the portrait of a Catholic priest that the author throws in for good measure cannot be considered as anything but an insult.

The author is altogether too flippant, and he seems to have forgotten that crass ignorance is reprehensible, and that for an uninformed audience, the principle "ab uno disce omnes" always holds good. *Not to be recommended to anyone.*

1351. 喜相逢 *GLAD TO HAVE MET*   1 vol. 124 p. by 李健吾
1944 世界書局

Adaptation of a play "Fedora" by Victorien Sardou produced in 1882. A tragedy in which a great quantity of blood was shed in the violent deaths of several characters. At the beginning a young man died in the arms of his fiancée through loss of blood. The latter resolved to avenge his death. It was believed to be a murder for political motives, and a young fanatic of the Kuomintang was suspected. Miss Ch'u, the victim's fiancée, and Ch'in the suspected one left Peiping and came to live in Shanghai, where they had a rendez-vous. The girl, strange to say, felt no abhorrence at his presence. She received a complete confession from the young man and informed the police, but too soon, for later on she learned that it had been a case of lawful self-defence. The victim had been caught redhanded in adultery with Mrs. Ch'in and had shot at Ch'in who returned the shot. Thus it was a "passion" crime and not a political one. The story opened Miss Ch'u's eyes with regard to her former fiancé. From that time she began to have a great admiration for Ch'in, whose wife died soon after the murder. She explained to her new lover the trap she had prepared for him, and she saw that he escaped from it. They married and departed for their honeymoon to the Shiu-San islands. On their return to Shanghai, they learned the news that Ch'in's brothers had been murdered in Peiping as a punishment for belonging to the Kuomintang. His mother had died of chagrin. Miss Ch'u blamed herself for these two deaths as it was she who informed the police about the young man's existence, in order to avenge her fiancé. Overwhelmed with grief and seeing that she could not prevent these deaths, she committed suicide so that the shadow of the dead persons would not stand between her and her husband. The latter in a final embrace forgave her. *For enlightened people.*

1352. 花信風 *APRIL BREEZE*　　1 vol. 175 p. by 李健吾
1944　世界書局

Adaptation of another of Sardou's plays "Fernande", produced in 1870. It is a satirical melodrama about society. In the Chinese play, the tenant of a gambling den was thrown into prison by the police; in order to release him, his daughter, Hsiao-lien, sold herself to a cabaret proprietor. Her mother's friend and her own succeeded in rescuing her from this wretched situation. Mrs. Ho took them to her house and gave them a new name so that their past should not be known. Mr. Fang, who was Mrs. Ho's lover, fell in love with Hsiao-lien (whose name was then "Ai Yü"). When Ho noticed this, she was deeply grieved but pretended to be indifferent. However she left no stone unturned in order to prevent this marriage. She stole the letter in which Hsiao-lien told her fiancé what had happened to her in the past. The marriage took place and Hsiao-lien believed that her husband knew all and forgave her. After their honey-moon Ho hastened to visit them and revealed the guilty secret. Fang was so angry that he bullied her and dismissed her, not believing that she had written a letter. Hsiao-lien asked for a divorce. Luckily a good fairy knew about Ho's plotting, and endeavored to settle the dispute by explaining to Fang that Hsiao-lien was speaking the truth and pointed out Ho's treachery. Fang asked his wife's forgiveness and all was settled. Thus the marriage was not broken. *For enlightened people.*

1353. 秋 *AUTUMN*　　1 vol. 174 p. by 李健吾
1946　文化生活出版社

A play in three acts adapted from 秋 "Autumn" by Pa Chin (巴金).

The big Kao family is nearing its ruin. K'o-ming (克明), the chief of the clan, is well-intentioned, but is incapable of opposing effectively the heedlessness of his younger brothers.

Among the younger generation, Chueh-ch'in (覺親) is good but weak and cannot go against the current; Chueh-min (覺民) is more energetic but has no real authority. The one with the best character is their sister, Shu-hua (淑華), who dares to affront the older people and indicate to them their faults.

The play also presents us with a succession of quarrels between the two generations, caused by the follies of the women and the frivolous life of K'o-ting (克定).

The drama ends with the material and moral ruin of the clan.

At the end, however, courage comes to Chueh-hsin (覺新) who reproaches his uncles (the third one is dying) for their bad lives. He shows them the door and decides to join his younger brother. He plans to sell his house and to go away, taking the younger members of the family to a more salutary environment. *For everyone.*

1354. 沉淵 *THE ABYSS*　　1 vol. 225 p. by 林　柯
1940　文化生活

A very moving tragedy.

Chao has a second wife, Mei.

He has a son named Fan by his first wife and a daughter named Tse by his second wife.

Chao kills his father-in-law and puts his brother-in-law, Fang, into an orphanage.

Seventeen years later he regrets his action and, driven by remorse, takes out the boy and makes him tutor to his son, Fan.

Now Tse is in love with Fang, and Mei also. Mei kills Fang from jealousy, and Fan, who defends Fang, is also killed. Mei goes out of her mind. *For enlightened readers only.*

1355. 春 *SPRING*   1 vol. 322 p. by 林 柯
1947 文化生活出版社

A drama in four acts adapted from "Spring" (春) by Pa Chin (巴金).

We are presented with the Kao (高) family in process of disintegration. The author shows us the tragic abyss that separates the older from the younger generation. The older people are penetrated with the spirit of the old tradition, passing their days in vain disputes and other less innocent occupations. They are the absolute masters of their families and dispose of their children as they wish. The injustice of this is especially evident in the lack of liberty on the part of the younger generation in the choosing of their mates, and also in the refusal of the older people to allow the younger ones to pursue their studies. Thus Hui (蕙), a girl with a good character is forced to marry a good-for-nothing, and she dies soon after in her new family. And Ying (英) is not allowed to study while she too is threatened with a forced marriage.

The younger generation revolts. Chueh-hsin (覺新) wants to oppose the elders but he does not have enough courage. Chueh-min (覺民) preaches rebellion openly and explains to his sisters and girl cousins that their lives are not ruled by Fate, and that they are responsible themselves for their futures. Ying also revolts against the will of her father and she resolves to go away in search of a cousin who has escaped to Shanghai. All the members of the younger generation approve of Ying's decision.

Although the author attacks real situations that exist in China and he has good reason for most of his grievances, nevertheless the readers should be warned that he is too violent in his attacks, and moreover, he offers no remedy for what he criticizes. *Not for everyone.*

1356. 十字街頭 *CROSSWAY*   1 vol. 126 p. by 魯 思
1944 世界書局

Four young men, who have finished their university studies, find themselves in Shanghai where they are without employment. We are given their reactions to this sad situation. One of them finally obtains a position as a clerk but he soon finds himself dismissed.

Two young girls, who also have achieved their studies, come to the same city where they are employed in a factory. It is not long, however, before the factory closes down and the two girls are thrown out.

The aim of the play is to show the reactions of young people to such difficult situations. Some are discouraged, while others find themselves at the crossroads. *For mature people.*

1357. 狂歡之夜 *THE REVISER* (adapted)   1 vol. 139 p. by 魯 思
1944 世界書局

An adaptation of the comedy, "The Reviser" by N. N. V. Gogol.

The scene is laid in a little sub-prefecture. The administration, the hospital, the police-station, the school, the post-office — all the local services are of an "exemplary" slackness. Those responsible have only one thought in their minds — how to get rich.

These people learn that they are about to be submitted to an official inspection. Their carelessness then changes into fear.

In a hotel of the city there is a young man who is short of cash. Some simple spirits find in him the expected inspector. The frightened sub-prefect and the officials fall over each other in their eagerness to invite him to stay in the prefecture, and those with guilty consciences bring him gifts to make him favourably disposed towards them.

The young man allows them to make a fuss over him, and he takes advantage of his sojourn in the prefecture to flirt with his hostess, and even obtains the promise of the hand of the daughter of the house. He has, in fact, boasted of his grand position and his wonderful relatives.

Nevertheless he is afraid of being discovered as an impostor and makes haste to pack his bags, not forgetting to wrap up all the presents he has received.

He leaves, promising to return the following day with his uncle when the official celebration of his engagement will be celebrated.

On the following day the sub-prefecture is decorated for a celebration. Everyone is waiting for the future son-in-law, but instead of him, the chief of the local post office arrives with a letter that has been posted by the young man, and in which he has described the whole comedy for the benefit of a newspaper. In his article, he has ridiculed all the officials of the place.

The anger of these latter flares up, and to complete their discomfiture, they hear of the arrival of the real inspector at the city gate. *May be read by anyone.*

1358. 藍天使 *ANGEL IN BLUE*　　　　　　1 vol. p. by 魯　思
　　　　　　　　　　　　　　　　　　　　　　1944　世界書局

A comedy in five acts.

Both the students and their professor of philosophy, a bachelor of ripe age, are carried off their feet by a courtesan called "the blue angel". The latter worms out of the professor everything that she wants. And in the meantime, the university, hearing of the scandal, dispenses with his services.

"The blue angel" continues to flirt with her admirers, and the impoverished professor sees himself neglected for younger rivals. And in the end, the heroine decamps with one of them.

This play contains many crude details, and has an atmosphere troubling to the reader. *Not to be recommended to anyone.*

1359. 愛戀 *LOVE*　　　　　　　　　　　1 vol. 144 p. by 魯　思
　　　　　　　　　　　　　　　　　　　　　　1945　世界書局

A play in three acts.

A widow has a son whom she loves very much. Her son is married to a very modern girl who, however, is a good sort. She regards with a jaundiced eye the love between the young people. She is very jealous even though her son, on his part, is very fond of her. This situation is the source of endless disputes between the young ones.

One day the mother overhears an interview in which her daughter-in-law sends an admirer packing, and she twists this scene, accusing her daughter of infidelity to her son. A violent quarrel ensues between the young people, after which the young wife leaves the house under the pretext of going to look for her lover.

Her husband suffers greatly from her absence, and his mother cannot take the place of his wife. When his mother realizes this, she becomes ill.

Actually the young wife is not far away, having spent fifteen days in a boarding house, after which she returns home.

The mother realizes at last that she has to sacrifice herself, so she decides to go away on a long journey. Thus the reunited and reconciled couple is enabled to live happily. *May be read by anyone.*

1360. 近代戲劇選 *SELECTED MODERN PLAYS* 1 vol. 326 p. by 歐陽予倩

1942 上海一流書局 *See Biogr. 122*

A collection of seven short plays. Some are well written; others contain less orthodox doctrines, and some rather vulgar songs. *For enlightened people.*

1361. 兩代的愛 *LOVE IN TWO GENERATIONS* 1 vol. 228 p. by 巴人（王任叔）

1947 海燕書店 *See Biogr. 167*

A play in five acts.

In this play the author wishes to depict the love between certain characters, and at the same time, love towards society. It is a pity, however, that he chooses heros that a little cracked. Moreover, there are too many characters in the play, and the intrigue has no interest. *Not for the young.*

1362. 打出幽靈塔 *SHATTERED CAGE* 1 vol. by 白薇女士（黃素如）

2nd edit. 1936 *See Biogr. 83*

Four plays.

1. 打出幽靈塔 p. 1-146. In this play we are presented with a capitalist who has enriched himself by sucking the blood of the poor and in trading in opium. He lives with his seventh concubine, a son and an adopted daughter who is really his natural child, although he is ignorant of the fact himself. Being an accomplished rake, he begins to be tired of his concubine, flirts with his maid, and wants to make his daughter his wife! He kills his son who also loves his sister and shuts up his daughter, who, in the end, is saved by a servant and friends. During this last scene, the father is slain and the daughter discovers her real mother and dies in her arms.

The play aims at showing us the hypocrisy of capitalists and the necessity for revolution. This book however, *is not to be recommended to anyone* because of the passions described and the immoral scenes and crimes that it contains.

2. 娘娘 p. 1-34. A social drama and satire against the Christian religion. In it is described the devotion of revolutionaries and the falseness of those who believe in God. The picture it presents of Christians is an absurd parody. *To be proscribed.*

3. 假洋人 p. 1-34. The inhabitants of Formosa pass themselves off as Japanese to exploit the Chinese, and in turn, they are exploited by the Japanese. *Some incongruities.*

4. 樂土 p. 1-72. In this play the author gives us the portrait of a general who possesses a mass of concubines whom he abandons when danger threatens in order to take another one. And he stops at nothing in order to achieve this end, not even at murder. The author causes the meaning of real revolution to come from the mouth of the father of the victim. This is a play that *everyone should be dissuaded from reading.*

1363. 街燈下 *UNDER THE STREET LIGHT* 1 vol. 218 p. by 白薇．瘋子等

1940 上海國風書店

1) 夜深曲 The mother of a family who is a refugee succumbs to her suffering. *For everyone.*

2) 街下燈 A street scene in Shanghai. The misfortunes of refugees. *For everyone.*

3) 傷寒線 The injustice of business men and the reaction of their clients. *For everyone.*

4) 別有天地 Exploiters of the people. Contains risky details. *Not for everyone.*

5) 南面王 How the directors of a work of charity exploit the refugees. *For everyone.*

6) 魔 Monologue of a desperate person. *Not for everyone.*

7) 導師　A married man with new matrimonial projects falls into a trap. *Not for everyone.* These pieces are without interest.

1364. 賽金花 *LIFE OF AN UNUSUAL COURTESAN*　1 vol. 94 p. by 鮑　雨
1946　潮鋒出版社

1) 賽金花　One act. An episode of the resistance containing a few crude details.
2) 克復　Three acts. Another story of the resistance.
These two plays are of no special interest and moreover, are *not for the young.*

1365. 春常在 *SPRING IS ALWAYS HERE*　1 vol. 209 p. by 沈蔚德
1946　商務印書館

A Play in five acts.

Scene: a rural town in China. Social conditions are very bad, due to the chicaneries of a big landowner of the name of 夏. Life for the small farmers is very hard. A teacher, 方, settles in the place, and being a very kind man, he succeeds in winning the love of all the children, guiding them on the right road. He then devotes his energies to the improvement of social conditions of the small people, by establishing a kind of bank where they can borrow money at low interest — very much to the annoyance of 夏. The latter thinks of nothing but enriching himself more and more, and to make things worse, he promises his daughter, who is a very good girl, to his compradore, a man without any conscience.

方 also has a daughter, a girl who has all the virtues. It appears, however, that she is only his adopted child, and that her mother intends to take her back.

These two girls, and a third one whose father, 趙, is in discord with his brother, are presented to us by the author as models of virtue whom our modern dolls should try to emulate.

方's social activities grow wider in scope as time goes on: he helps the poor and the children, takes care of the sick, settles people's differences, and all this "for the love of our neighbours" as he explains to his daughter. 夏, on his part, is unrelenting. Without heeding Heaven's punishment — his wife has eloped with the compradore, his daughter has run away to the town in order to continue her studies, and his farm has burnt down — he continues to wrong 方. At a time when the latter is seriously ill, he does not shrink from wanting to hand him over to the soldiers to put into prison.

In a final scene, in which 方's character shows up in all its beauty, the big landowner cannot help being touched, and he avows to have been won over by his adversary's generosity. In this scene, the author groups together all the actors, including 夏's daughter and 方's adopted daughter. 方 dies a victim of his great charity.

This is a beautiful play of high moral quality. Though no mention is made of religion, we may venture to affirm that 方's noble actions and noble character can only be explained by his being animated by true Christian spirit. Any Catholic would be proud to have written a play of such high moral value.

We think, however, that on account of the great number of actors of both sexes necessary, it would be difficult to produce this play in our establishments. *For everyone.*

1366. 孔雀屏 *LE VOYAGE DE MR PERRICHON* (adapted) 1 vol. 100 p. by 石華父
1944　世界書局

A comedy in four acts, adapted from "Le Voyage de Mr. Perrichon" by Labiche.

Mr. 百里響 goes into the country with his wife and his daughter. Two suitors of the young lady accompany them. We are entertained with the exploits of the suitors and in the end, the young lady chooses between them.

The whole play is seasoned with plenty of humour. *For everyone.*

1367. 晚晏 *ONCE IN A LIFETIME* (adapted)   1 vol. 130 p. by   **石華父**

1944   世界書局

An adaptation of the play "Once in a Lifetime" by George S. Kaufman and Edna Ferber.

The author has made of it a drama in six acts in which he has added in the last act, the suicide of the lover of the daughter of the principal characters.

The plot develops from an invitation to dinner sent out by a rich man who faces ruin. The principal guest slips away, and the guests on the whole are linked together by ties that do not conform to good morals. *Not to be recommended to anyone.*

1368. 雁來紅 *THE MAGISTRATE* (adapted)   1 vol. 125 p. by   **石華父**

1944   世界書局

A play in three acts.

An adaptation of "The Magistrate" by A. W. Pinero.

A widow, who has a son, receives an offer of marriage. She deceives her admirer regarding her age, giving it as five years less than what it really is. It has not occurred to the good woman that her son will have to become younger accordingly.

Now this young fellow who is only fifteen, already gives indications of having the instincts of a grown man, and the step-father is rather surprised at his precociousness.

Now one fine day when they are ignorant of each other's presence, they are all compromised in a scuffle in a hotel. Madame is taken in the very act of transgressing hotel regulations, while her husband and the son take to their heels.

The husband happens to be a magistrate, and passes judgment on his wife in absentia. Not knowing her real identity, he sentences her to seven days. When he returns home, his wife arrives in a fury, having in the meantime, been released by the chief magistrate who knows who she is.

In a final scene everything is explained and the wife is obliged to reveal her real age and that of her son. The latter becomes engaged to a cousin, and order is restored.

The play is much more complicated than this synopsis, and the tragi-comic situations tumble over each other.

The tone of the play is flippant, and the perverse precocity of the young man is not suitable for acting before a very young audience. *For adults.*

1369 職業婦女 *WOMEN IN PROFESSION*   1 vol. 84 p. by   **石華父**

1947   萬葉書店

Play in four acts.

A magistrate's office. A resident magistrate, a man of middle age and apparently settled in 'life'! He dismissed all married officials, and exacted great simplicity from those who remained.

For his private office he kept an "up-to-date" girl who ridiculed his recommendations. Her boss tolerated those flapper manners, for, in spite of his external severity and stiffness regarding his daughter who wanted to have her future husband after her own choice, the magistrate was infatuated with his secretary. In order to please her, he was even unjust in his administration of public affairs.

When the dismissed employees accused him, the central office sent an inspector. This inspection brought about the end of the play. The magistrate was scared and decided to escape in company with his secretary. The latter made an appointment where there assembled accidentally(?) the magistrate and his wife, who thus took him red-handed. There also came

the magistrate's daughter and her friend, who happened to be the inspector's brother! Others too, found their way to the place of meeting; among them was the secretary's husband!!..She was married, but had kept it secret in order to keep her situation.
The play ends by an arrangement which puts everyone at ease, and proves that women are not inferior to men. *For all.*

1370. 枉費心機 *FRUSTRATED*   1 vol. 175 p. by 石　靈
1941　光明文藝叢書

A comedy in five acts.
A young man, who is an abject flatterer, manages to make himself agreeable to a rich man who promises to give him his daughter in marriage. The imposture, however, is soon discovered and the girl is given to another suitor who has been in love with her for a long time.
Not suitable for acting in our schools. *For everyone.*

1371. 精忠報國 *"HERO NATIONAL": GENERAL YUI-FEI* 1 vol. 159 p. by 舒　湮
1947　光明書局 *See Biogr. 138*

A play in five acts.
The action is laid at the end of the Sung Dynasty. We are presented with the life of the great general Yueh Fei (岳飛) the national hero who led the resistance to the invaders. Here are depicted his victories, the attachment of the people to him, his sentence and death. *For everyone.*

1372. 董小宛 *THE EMPEROR'S MISTRESS*   1 vol. 193 p. by 舒　湮
1941　光明書局

A historical tragedy dealing with the Manchou invasion and the fall of the Mings.
It is written on a patriotic note castigating traitors who sell their country in co operating with the enemy, and glorifying heros who die for their fatherland.
It is however, too complicated to be acted. *For everyone.*

1373. 浪淘沙 *BROKEN SURF*   1 vol. 220 p. by 舒　湮
1947　萬葉書店

A play in six acts, being the first part of a trilogy of patriotic and historical drama.
We are presented with the actions of different members of the same family, at the time of Yuan Shih-k'ai and the Boxer Rebellion. The older people are for traditional ideas and support the Empress Dowager, while the young are for the revolution and K'ang Yu-wei.
There is not enough action and therefore the play drags. History is mixed with a love story. There are some improper details. *Not to be recommended to the young.*

1374. 鳩那羅的眼睛 *THE EYES OF KUNALA*   1 vol. 92 p. by 蘇雪林(蘇梅)
1946　商務印書館 *See Biogr. 141*

1) *The Eyes of Kunala.* Tragedy in three acts, p. 1-66.
This first play of the authoress presents a story acting at the time of the Indian King Asoka, who is known in history for his fervour to propagate Buddhism. The real center of the play yet is not the son of Asoka, Kunala, although he gives his name for the title of this play, but his step mother, the Queen. On her, the vigourous acting of the play, and the poetic dramatisation by the authoress concentrates. It is she who by her woman love and hating inspirates the whole play.

The acting of the play is in rough lines as this: the Queen falls in love with her step son, the prince Kunala, who is already married and who in no way consents to the unmoral feelings of his step mother. In a last attack-dramatisised in the first act of the play — she tries to persuade the prince. Called to reason by the cold attitude of the prince, she changes from love to hatred. Instrument to realise her plans is the first minister of state, who burns in love to the Queen. First rejected by her, he gets some hope under the condition to help extinguish Kunala.

The second act puts us on the side of the sick King. In vain he called for the skillest physician of his kingdom. This is the favourable moment for the Queen's revenge. By her medical knowledge she relieves the pains of the King, but in reward gets royal power for a week in the kingdom. She does not hesitate to fill a royal order to the prince, depriving him of the lights of his eyes, and chasing him from court and the office he holds in a far province. The bearer and executioner of this order is nobody else than the first minister himself.

At the beginning of the third act the King, unaware of the machinations of his wife, is wondering about the long time his son the prince has let him without any report. In a following scene the first minister calls the attention of the Queen at the danger which arised when two people, a man and a wife, wanted to enter the court. To late! The King hears these people outside singing an air nobody but his son would know. Against the will of the Queen and the minister, he makes the two enter the room and recognises in the blind man his son. The following scene brings the manifestation of the machinations of the Queen, and accusation of the crime by the King. The play ends with the report of the death of the Queen, who, fleeing from the aspect of the King, put an end to her life at the feet of the statue of a god she implored when she decided her revenge.

There is no doubt that a play like this would give an opportunity to show the literary hability of the authoress. Really she shows herself at the top of the task. The description of love and woman hating demonstrates her poetic talent. There would be very few people who would not be touched by her expressions. But ordinary people — and it may be even students of middle school education — would more easily be harmed by the vivid picture of forbidden love. It is therefore the play *cannot be given in the hand of everybody.*

2) 玫瑰與春 *The Rose-tree and the Spring* p. 67-92.
Allegory in one act.
The author describes the different kinds of love struggling in the human heart in an allegory full of poetical feeling, and in the end the nobler feelings triumph.
The hero, 玫瑰, the lover of 春 only thinks of himself; he loves his betrothed, but in a selfish way: he wants her all to himself, and to himself alone.
春 is in love with 玫瑰, but this love is not enough for her. She also loves the weak and suffering. This love ennobles and enriches the first. Inspired by 春寒, selfishness itself, she sways a moment. . .but the plaintive sighs of suffering mankind bring her back to her right feelings. Forced to the choice between her lover and this love ennobled by pity, she decides, though torn by the sacrifice, to quit her lover.
Written in a rather difficult, though polished style, this play seems to us one of the best of nowadays literature. *For everyone.*

1375. 復國 *REBUILD THE NATION*   1 vol. 165 p. by 孫家琇
                                              1946 商務印書館 *See Biogr. 142*

A play in four acts.
The author brings before us two historical personages, 西施 and 范蠡. He admits himself that he has altered history a little to suit his purpose.

西施 is a poor girl but beautiful and she has been noticed by the statesman Fan, who asks for her hand in marriage. But in the midst of the matrimonial ceremonies, he is recalled by his sovereign, due to imminent war with a neighbouring state.

After three years of war, the sovereign is vanquished and has to make his submission. His officials advise him to send a number of beautiful women to the conquerer to enfeeble him by this means so that later, they can obtain their revenge.

In his quest for beautiful women Fan asks his betrothed to make a great sacrifice for the sake of her country. Through love for him, the girl consents and goes to live in the court of the conqueror.

After ten years of sojourn there, a new war breaks out between this sovereign and a third state. The prince of the state with which the story begins takes advantage of the turn of affairs and thereby retrieves his fortunes. The girl is rescued by her original lover whom she has always loved and who has remained faithful to her, and who, after his marriage, resigns from affairs of state to live peacefully with the heroine.

The play gives us portraits of characters of really heroic stature, and tells of a great love. There is no reason why it should not be read by anyone, but its acting might lend itself to sentimental exhibitions not *suitable for those who are too young.*

1376. 凱歌 *SONG OF TRIUMPH*   1 vol. 236 p. by 宋之的

1946   上海雜誌公司 *See Biogr. 146*

Six one act plays, describing the patriotic spirit of the Chinese in their struggle with Japan.

They contain certain trivial expressions and some risky allusions. *For everyone.*

1377. 春寒 *SPRING CHILL*   by 宋之的

Tragedy in 5 acts.

The title contains the meaning of this play. The first words means "Springtime"; the second qualifies it and lets us understand that the season has not reached its zenith, but is still at the time when the air is cold and the sky clouded over.

In this way the author wants to convey the idea that his native land is occupied by Japanese, (the play was written at that time), and furthermore, he wants, like a prophet, to to point out that after their victory heavy clouds will darken the Chinese landscape.

To attain this end the dramatist takes one concrete example. He describes a critical situation in a Chinese sub-prefecture. Three groups of people come upon the stage. Honest people of whom China can be proud, like Dr. Shu who devoted himself to the service of his fellow countrymen, by carrying on a relentless struggle against certain microbes, which caused a sickness frequent among Chinese. The courageous doctor continued to work, was honest, and wanted to perform great things, but was frustrated in his efforts by his enemies in the house. The latter are the second category of people whom the author describes: he gives us one concrete example in Ho Chih-yuen and his party. They diverted benefits which were meant for the people as a whole to their personal advantage, and prevented China from enjoying the "Springtime".

The third category are hesitating people: they ride two horses, are neither good nor bad, but are the clouds that darken a springtide sky. The author gives us the example of Fang, a lady doctor.

The story of the lives of these people is far from being pleasant to read. It is its deep meaning that we must understand.

This play reminds us of Lu Hsün who so often gave warning to his countrymen.

At the end we find Dr. Shu's phrase addressed to a journalist Wu Ch'i: "You are leaving for the front", he said, handing him a picture of the Blessed Virgin, "when you strike at the enemy, strike at a vital place"! The big clouds which darkened the sky would be scattered! "Clouds" prevent "Springtime" from reaching its splendour. It is only by our courage and strength that we can make the sun shine brightly again, and ensure that China will know a true Springtime. *For all.*

1378. 宋春舫戲曲集 *PLAYS BY SUNG CH'UN-FANG*   1 vol. 112 p. by 宋春舫
1937　商務印書館　*See Biogr. 147*

1) 五里霧中　Three acts. Of a man overcome by his fate.
2) 一幅喜神　One act. A bored collector.
3) 原來是夢　Two scenes. "Only a Beautiful Dream".
For everyone.

1379. 恨海 *REGRET TO NO END*   1 vol. 90 p. by 宋　約
1945　文章書房

A tragedy in four acts. The aim of the author is to show how easily the young are perverted.

Two couples are dealt with. The first is disunited because of the bad conduct of the male, who gives himself up to vice and dies abandoned.

The other couple is equally disunited but this time it is due to the fault of the girl.

This play contains a good moral and should make parents reflect on the consequences, all too often disastrous, of very early betrothals. *For everyone.*

1380. 田漢戲曲集 *3. AN ANTHOLOGY OF PLAYS BY T'IEN-HAN*   vol. 3
1931　上海現代書局　*See Biogr. 152*

Seven plays.
1. 咖啡店之夜　A night in a restaurant. The play describes an unhappy love.
2. 午飯之前　Before breakfast. A poor family: An ailing mother with three daughters. The eldest girl is a protestant. She appeals to the pastor for help and is deceived by him. The play ends in a spirit hostile towards religion.
3. 鄉愁　Homesickness. A family emigrates to Japan but returns to China because everything is better in the home country.
4　搜虎之夜　Describes love stronger than threats or blows. It ends in suicide.
5. 落花時節　The unrequited love of a student.
6. 一致　Wants to prove that all men are equal.
7. 林沖　Shows a buddhist monk who saves a woman from great moral danger.
Very objectionable.

1381. 田漢戲曲集 *4. AN ANTHOLOGY OF PLAYS BY T'IEN-HAN*   vol. 4
1931　上海現代書局

1. 蘇州夜話　Nightly talk at Suchow. Having lost his family in the turmoil of war, a professor from Peiping goes to the south. There he meets his daughter selling flowers.

2 湖上的悲劇 Drama at sea. A girl refuses the match arranged for her by her parents. She simulates a suicide at sea, but, secretly, lives at the home of her parents, where she appears as a ghost. The boy she loves comes and lives in the same house. In a talk with the sister of her beloved, she learns that he is married. In anger she commits suicide, this time in earnest. Her lover dies of a stroke at her side.

3. 江村小景 Tragedy near the river. In the war of 1937 two brothers join the southern and northern armies respectively. On their way home they meet, and, unaware of their identity, kill each other.

4. 生之意志 The will to live. A father drives his son out of the house because he has got mixed in a love affair. One day his daughter, a student at some university, gives up her studies and returns home. When her father asks for the reasons why she stopped her studies, the baby she has kept hidden on her breast starts crying. The only explanation for her conduct which she gives is: "My will to live was too strong". The cries of the baby soften the father who has wanted to strike his daughter; he takes the baby in his arms. . .and calls back his son.

5. 垃圾桶 A girl throws her baby on the refuse-bin. Beggars come to look for things they can still use, find the child, and quarrel over who is going to keep it.

6. Piano 之鬼 The Ghosts of the piano. Three rich girls, sympathizing with the hardships of working girls, decide to sell their belongings and live as they do. The youngest of the three wishes to keep their piano. The other two tell her how three girls died of consumption making that piano; their ghosts still haunt the rooms in which they died. . .In the end the piano is also sold.

7. 名優之死 The death of a great actor. The leader of a troupe falls in love with an actress who loves another actor. While on the stage, acting an important part, the leader of the troupe thinks of the girl who is probably flirting at that time in the wings. He strains himself so much that he drops dead in the middle of his acting. When she witnesses his great love the actress regrets her refusal and hates her flirt.
Very objectionable.

1382. 現代創作文庫 *AN ANTHOLOGY OF MODERN WRITING* 262 p. by 田　漢
1936　上海萬象書屋

Selection of plays by T'ien Han. Almost identical to the 11th volume of the collection edited by the 三通書局 (cfr. nr. 1384).

As this book was edited before the incident, two patriotic plays are included. *For all.*

1383. 麗人行 *BALLADE OF FAIR WOMEN* by 田　漢

Tragedy in 21 acts.

Portrait and psychological analysis of three modern women. The first, Jo-Ying, was well educated and wanted to succeed in life, but was of weak character and too fond of pleasure. Seven years ago she got married and had a child called "Baby". Her husband left for the interior some years ago, to fight the invading Japanese. Jo-Ying was struggling with material difficulties, and being weak went to live with Wang Chung-yuen, a bank official. In spite of this, she was sad, and was often thinking of her husband. The second heroine, Li Hsing-ch'iun, to whom the author introduces us, was Jo-Ying's friend. Hsing ch'iun was an energetic person; in concert with Meng nan, her husband, she was director of a school. In addition, her husband was publishing an anti-Japanese magazine. To complete his work, the author introduces Chin Mei, a young working girl who, inspite of her resistance, was raped by Japanese soldiers. In her shame she wanted to kill herself, but Jo-Ying and Hsing Ch'iun saved her. When her husband heard what had happened he became very angry, but after Meng nan explained the incident, he forgave her.

At this time Yu liang, Jo Ying's husband, came back to Shanghai with the intention of fighting against the army of occupation. He came to know about his wife's misconduct. After explanations on his friend's part, he arranged to meet his wife in Hsing ch'iun's house. When he arrived there the Japanese police burst in, in order to arrest Meng nan; the latter took to flight. Yu liang, pretending to be Meng nan, was arrested together with his wife. In prison, Jo Ying asked Chung-yuen to intercede for them with the Japanese, but being infatuated with a dancing girl, he paid no attention to their request.

Japanese police discovered that Yu liang had assumed Meng nan's name, and released him and his wife in the hope of arresting, through them, their friend Meng nan. Thus they were secretly watched.

Jo Ying, being no longer in love with her husband, returned to Chung-yuen, but the latter did not love her any more and our heroine left Wang's house. Her child had been given long before to Hsing ch'iun.

The latter, her husband having gone to the interior, undertook alone the direction of the school, and continued anti-Japanese propaganda with the help of her friend, Liu Ta ko. The Japanese paid her a surprise visit, but found nothing in her house thanks to the great calmness of our heroine. She had sent "Baby" to the interior in order that he would have a better education than was possible in a city occupied by the enemy. Chin mei on her part was despised, owing to her trouble with the soldiers. This was the cause of a quarrel between her husband and a calumniator, the result of which was that the husband became blind through an act of treachery. The unfortunate wife, left without work in spite of her various attempts, was obliged to sell her virtue in order to have the necessaries of life. She was suffering on account of this, and her husband became suspicious.

One day a creditor appeared and was reproaching the blind man; this brought on a fight. Just at that moment American planes dropped bombs; the creditor took to flight and the blind man overpowered his wife; the latter ran away and wanted to throw herself into the river. Her two friends, Jo ying and Hsing Ch'iun, passing by at that moment, saved her life.

The play ends by a description of grief of the three modern women, who were consoling each other, telling each other how hard life was and hoping for victory which would bring them happiness. This confidence made them forget their sufferings. *For enlightened people.*

1384. 現代作家選集 *AN ANTHOLOGY OF MODERN WRITERS*

11th vol. by 田 漢
三通書局

Eleven one-act plays, followed by short essays and a few pieces of verse.

The main subject is love. The author offers a few very good plays where fidelity is pictured between engaged couples, (engaged without pressure by the parents). In very simple language he expresses deep emotions. In one of the plays there is a suicide. As a rule, the passages treating about love are too langourous, but quite inoffensive. *For all.*

1385. 妻 *THE BETTER-HALF*

1 vol. 144 p. by 鄧昭暉
1944 世界書局

A play in five acts.

楊柔 is a widower who lives with his sister, 蓓. The latter wishes to enter into relations with a young man, named 王. 楊 is jealous and opposes their intimacy. He goes so far as to send a menacing letter to 王.

Now a friend of the family, 趙, knows the great secret that weighs upon the household. He knows that 楊 killed his wife in an access of jealousy, and that he loves 蓓, who is not his sister but the sister of his dead wife. 趙 tries to turn 楊 from this dangerous path, threatening him with revealing everything if he does not consent. As 楊 refuses to listen to his friend, the latter proceeds to put his threats into execution, and 醴 revolts against her so-called brother. The latter, driven to desperation by her behaviour, shoots himself. *For adults.*

1386. 丈夫 *HUSBAND*   1 vol. 139 p. by 鄧昭暉
1945 世界書局

A play in five acts.

A rich family named Yao is depicted. War breaks out and other families come to refugee with them. The son, Yao Chih, goes away, leaving his young wife, Chang, with her mother.

Misery soon overtakes them and life becomes very difficult. Chang, however, retains her energy for seven years and works hard to keep her mother and child. Then she also is engulfed in discouragement. Not being sure whether her husband is still alive, she cedes to the solicitations of a man who has no conscience, and marries him.

At the moment she decides definitely to go with this man, her husband re-appears. Flabbergasted, the heroine announces that she has re-married, and the curtain falls on this scene.

For adults because the second marriage is to be reproved. *Not for everyone.*

1387. 妙峰山 *MIAO FENG SHAN*   1 vol. 200 p. by 丁西林
1945 文化生活出版社 *See Biogr. 154*

A comedy in four acts.

A bandit chief who at one time was a university professor, now named Tiger Wang (王老虎), has been arrested and at the moment is under surveillance of the police at the village inn. Several professors and students on holiday are in the same inn.

The next day, the whole situation is changed. Wang is delivered, and he and his men seize the chief of the local police and the excursionists. Among the latter is a fine slip of a girl named Hua (華) who has helped in securing the release of the bandit chief. He, by the way, is not indifferent to her charms, and she, on her side, has been equally smitten by him.

The prisoners are conducted to Miao Feng Shan (妙峰山) in which district the bandit band operates. When they arrive there they all decide to remain with the group and help in the resistance against Japan.

The terrible Tiger Wang is softened under the influence of Hua and the story ends with their marriage.

The play is full of humour and picturesque details, but nevertheless, the action drags somewhat. *May be read by anyone.*

1388. 西林獨幕劇集 *ONE ACT PLAYS OF TING HSI-LING*
1 vol. 186 p. by 丁西林
1947 文化生活出版社

Seven one act plays.
1) 一隻馬蜂 An engagement concluded in a gay and original manner.
2) 親愛的丈夫 The ideal young wife — but it happens to be a man!
3) 酒後 Adaptation of a novel of 凌叔華 A strange desire.
4) 北京的空氣 Peking boys.
5) 瞎了一隻眼 A conjugal comedy.
6) 壓迫 Another original betrothal.

7) 三塊錢國幣   A quarrel over nothing.
A lot of wit and humour; *for everybody, except No.2.*

1389. 雷雨 *THUNDERSTORM*   1 vol. 532 p. by 曹禺 (萬家寶)
9th edition 1945   文化生活出版社   *See Biogr. 161*

As the title shows, the play is vehement. The storm out-of-doors takes the place of the scenery, and is "deus ex machina" of the tragedy when tension is at highest. Uneasiness in-doors, when the weather is oppressive, and a storm in his heart, let loose the evil passions of Chou Fan-yi, the principal character of the play.

Fan-yi is the wife of Chou P'u-yüan; from whom she has a son, Chou Ch'ung, a poet and idealist, an humanitarian dreamer wandering in an ultra-realistic world. By contrast with the others, he brings into relief the rugged clarity of this sensual and materialistic environment.

Chou P'ing, his half-brother and more advanced in years, is of a completely different disposition. Natural son of P'u-yüan and a servant girl, his heredity weighs heavily on his body and soul. He goes so far as to commit sin with Fan-yi. Lu, the mother of Chou P'ing, having been abandoned by Pu-yüan took to flight with her second son, to whom she had just given birth, and whom P'u-yüan refused to acknowledge. It was believed that she died with her child. In reality she married a certain Lu Kuei, a greedy man whose throat was always dry, and whose purse was always empty. From this marriage they had a daughter, Shih-Feng. Like her father, she was in domestic service in the house of Chou: an accident pure and simple — as the author would like us to think!

Furthermore, all these characters were unaware of their relationship.

P'u-yüan, soon after his marriage to Fan-yi, went to the North. He became a rich coal-mine-owner. Lu Ta-hai, the second son of P'u-yüan and Lu, who was thought to have been drowned with his mother, was the leader of a group of strikers in P'u-yüan's mine. This incident caused him to return home in order to make complaints to the owner; he was thus, on this occasion, fighting with Chou P'ing, whom he did not know to be his brother.

Chou P'ing, after his adultery, followed in the footsteps of his father. He fell in love with Shih-Feng, with whom Chou Ch'ung also maintained a platonic love. Fan-yi was much grieved by this situation; she was so jealous that she fell ill.

At this time, Lu, the former mistress of P'u-yüan, mother of Chou P'ing and Lu Ta-hai, wife of Lu Kuei, and mother of Shih-Feng, returned home. Fan-yi brought her to her house in order that she should take back Shih-Feng. Lu found her photo in a sideboard in the parlor, and understood the situation.

Chou P'ing, who had to go the following day to the mines, arranged to meet Shih Feng in the evening in her room. Shih Feng had sworn to her mother that she would have nothing more to do with the Chou, and refused to let him in. He entered through the window, thus taking her by surprise. Fan-yi suspected the meeting and was on the watch. She shut the window from the outside and the two lovers were locked up in the closed room. In the meantime Lu Ta-hai arrived and wanted to kill Chou P'ing. Lu held him back, while Chou P'ing and Shih Feng fled in different directions.

All the characters of the play were finally brought together in Chou's residence. Shih Feng confessed she was pregnant, and got her mother's permission to leave with Chou P'ing. But Fan-yi appeared. As she was not a real mother, she called Chou Ch'ung to enjoy the scene. Then she called P'u-yüan who acknowledged Lu, and introduced her to Chou P'ing as his mother! Shih Feng ran away; Chou Ch'ung followed in order to save her: both perished, electrocuted by a wire which had broken loose during the storm. Chou P'ing commited suicide; Fan-yi and Lu became crazy. Such is the late poignant scene, dominated by Fate, worthy of Greek tragedians.

(See Coll. Com. Syn. 1944, p. 177 "L'Univers de Ts'ao Yü" by Gérard de Boll).

Not to be recommended to anyone.

N. B. "It is clear, that Ts'ao Yü's works should not be put into the hands of everyone. The author is ignorant of Christian morals, and his plays unfold themselves in the atmosphere of sin. On the other hand, we must not shut our eyes to the influence this author has on the present-day youth of China. In Catholic universities and colleges, many of the pagan students, and the best among them, have read nearly all his works. We cannot prevent these books from being read, but we can take advantage of the opportunity and point out where he sins against morality in his plays, sound the alarm, and at times indicate the "Light" that shines through darkness.

Furthermore, this article will show all our readers the impression made on youth, now-a-days, by the stage. May it encourage Catholics to compose and translate dramatic works, of equal or superior literary value, capable of counterbalancing this poisonous influence, and acting as an inspiration to pagan authors of good will."

(See Coll. Com. Syn. 1944, p. 177 "L'Univers de Ts'ao Yü" by Gérard de Boll).

1390. 日出 *SUNRISE*   1 vol. 332 p. by 曹　禺
22nd edition 1947   文化生活出版社

In Jih Ch'u, the principal character is a young girl of 23. Her name is Ch'en Pai-lu, a modern girl from a good family. After her father's death she tasted the bitterness of poverty: later she became a movie-star and a well-known dancer. At that time she was living in a hotel, her expenses being paid by her admirers, and she had given up her freedom. Still young, she knew what life was, and had experienced love adventures. She was living for some time with an ideal young man, but he left her taking away her child. She came back to her sad imprisonment.

In the 1st act, Fang, a friend of her childhood days, a simple country fellow, invited her to go into the country with him, and, with a rather comical abruptness, proposed to her. Ch'en persuaded him to stay a few days at the hotel, in order to have an idea of the way of living of the people who surrounded her.

Just at the time when Ch'en was alone in the drawing-room and the lights were out, a little girl bursted into the room. She begged Ch'en to save her. It was a child of 14 or 15 years, Hsiao Tung-hsi. She had been the victim of an attempted rape by Chin Pa, a bulky fellow and powerful speculator; but she had given him a slap in the face and escaped.

Ch'en took her in and was protecting her. However, the little girl, having left her hiding-place, was taken unawares and carried away. A brothel where the little girl was put is the scene of the 3rd act. Fang was looking for her without success. Exhausted by ill-treatment, she finally hanged herself. The 2nd act introduces us to another society. P'an, a bank manager and one of Ch'en's admirers, was obliged to dismiss some twenty employees in order to find a position for a lady-customer's friend. Among those dismissed was Huang, the bank messenger. Out of a job, he could not support any longer his wife and his three childern. His small wages — 12 dollars and a few cents a month — did not allow any saving. He went to ask help from the manager; but the latter's servant jeered at him and put him out. Later he asked Li, the bank secretary, to take him back. The latter, who was ambitious and hardhearted, upbraided him for having so many childern, and advised him to steal or commit suicide. Huang had no more success in his appeal to the bank-manager. The latter knocked him down with his fist during a dispute, thinking that the other was going to attack him. Then he gave him three dollars and had him carried out.

With this money Huang bought some opium, which he made his children eat. He himself, taking Li's advice, threw himself from a tower but was not killed. Going mad, he went to Li and P'an, and upbraided them for their injustice. A pathetic scene of great social import.

In the 3rd act, misfortunes befell the rich men too. After some speculations of Chin Pa, who remained in the back-ground but whose influence was felt, P'an's bank got in trouble. P'an was obliged to take out a mortgage. Li found this out when rummaging in his desk, and, by threatening blackmail, got himself appointed vice-manager. Immediately he began to strut about in society, although people were sneering at him behind his back. With his manager's consent he bought stock-shares which save the bank from bankruptcy. P'an, thinking the situation was saved, jeered at his former secretary, reproached him for his blackmail, and dismissed him with the 25 dollars which remained from his monthly salary. At this moment Li learned that his son was ill; but he gave no heed to the fact until it was too late, for he was thinking of nothing else but the insult he had received, and the revenge he was plotting.

In fact the shares went down: the speculator was spreading about false news in order to ruin the bank. Li, by telling P'an this news, was tasting his revenge. Ch'en, at this time, had large bills to pay. As P'an was ruined, he was unable to help her. In order to "borrow" 3000 dollars, she went to another "friend", George; he was a "returned student", a type at whom the author sneers both here and in his play "Peiching Jen", in a cruel way. . . He had proposed marriage, now he stepped aside politely. Ch'en locked the door of her room, counted out ten tablets of sleeping drug, crushed them and drank the poison. She looked out through the window: "The sun is appearing above the horizon, darkness is left behind". She inhaled the fresh air, yawned, and turned away from the window. "But it is not our sun, we are going to sleep"! She pulled down the blinds, stretched herself on the couch and awaited the sleep of death. . .

Just then, Fang entered the drawing-room, and pulled back the window-curtains. "Now that is funny, why not let the sunshine in? Listen to me. If you continue to act this way you are going to certain death. Listen to me; come with me; don't let them lead you astray any longer. Look, the sun is outside, it is spring-time"!

From a neighbouring yard the workmen's song arose! "The sun is outside" said Fang, "the sun is theirs. . .let us go and tackle Chin Pa."

The play ends on this contrast.

(See Coll. Com. Syn. 1944, p. 178 "L'Univers de Ts'ao Yü" by Gérard de Boll).

Not to be recommended to anyone.

1391. 原野 *THE WILD*　　　　　　　　　1 vol. 330 p. by 曹 禺

　　　　　　　　　　　　　　　　12th edition 1946 文化生活出版社

Yüän Yeh is a revenge and a love drama. Revenge for lost love, revenge for recovered love. Wild love and ferocious revenge.

Ch'ou Hu, adopted by the Chiao family, was promised in marriage to a girl by the name of Chin-tzu. By low scheming, Chiao Yen-wang and his wife thrust aside the adopted son, and married their own son, Ta-Hsing, to Chin-tzu instead. Ch'ou Hu was falsely put into prison, and, owing to ill-treatment, became lame.

But the lame man escaped from prison and returned to the Chiao's residence. Vengeance was ready. Ch'ou Hu had learned that Chiao Yen-wang was dead, and that his wife, "the Mother", had become blind. He would take his revenge on her, reaching at her through her son and her grandson, Hei-Tzu, the child of Ta-Hsing and some other woman. Ch'ou Hu would find in his former fiancée an abettor easy to win over, and to dazzle by promise of a rich marriage and travel in legendary countries. Chin-tzu hated her mother-in-law, who forced her to lead a dog's life; she was aware that her husband did not sufficiently protect her, owing to his weak character.   In a revolting scene, Chin-tzu asked her husband if he loved her more than his mother; if both were drowning, who would he save? She insisted on the answer until he replied: "let mother. . .drown"!

The mother being blind and Ta-Hsing absent, Chin-tzu consented to give Ch'ou Hu food and lodging. But the mother suspected that Ch'ou Hu had come back and was living in the house. She sent Ch'ang Wu, the father's former friend, to spy on them; then she herself came to them without being announced. Ch'ou Hu concealed himself in Chin-tzu's room. Pai Sha-tzu, a silly fellow working for the Chiao family, was present. The mother made him go into Chin-tzu's room, and went with him herself armed with an iron bar; but Ch'ou Hu knocked her down and escaped through the window. Chin-tzu made Pai Sha-tzu promise not to disclose the identity of the unknown man.

Ta-Hsing was recalled and came back at once. In his presence, the mother accused Chin-tzu of adultery. At the end, Chin-tzu admitted and was boasting of it. She screamed out her hatred for the mother, who made use of witchcraft in order to bring about the death of her daughter-in-law. The mother wanted Ta-hsing to administer the lash to his wife. Ta-Hsing, consumed with jealousy, wept but hesitated. . .Ch'ou Hu reappeared! Ta-Hsing, passing over what had happened formerly, only saw in him his former friend of childhood, and invited him to stay in his house. The mother, alarmed, advised her son to send away his wife. She succeeded in provoking Ta-Hsing, who left the house in search of a dagger. Then, by promises and threats, she tried to prevail on Ch'ou Hu to run away with Chin-tzu; but Ch'ou Hu was bent on having revenge.

Coming back that evening, Ta-Hsing sat down with Ch'ou Hu to have a drink. Ch'ou Hu, who had not the courage to strike a first blow against his childhood's companion, was gradually revealing the enmity which was dividing the two, and told Ta-Hsing what had happened recently. Ta-Hsing questioned Chin-tzu, who confessed her sin and declared that she was ready to go with Ch'ou Hu. Ta-Hsing, overwhelmed with grief, fell on his knees before his wife and was beseeching her to remain; the latter treated him as a coward. Exasperated, Ta-Hsing told them that he had called in the police.

In the night, Chin-tzu awaked Ch'ou Hu; the latter killed his friend; the mother, by mistake, killed her grandson who was sleeping in Ch'ou Hu's bed.

At this moment, the police, summoned by Ch'ang Wu, arrived and surrounded the house. But Ch'ou Hu took Ch'ang Wu as a hostage, and succeeded in reaching the woods. He sent Ch'ang Wu back and proceeded on foot, but got lost. The lonely woods, the darkness of the night, the whistling and soughing of the wind, the mournful cries of the birds and the moans of his mother who was pursuing, all this filled him with terror, now that his crime was committed and his revenge satisfied. Ta-Hsing's shadow was haunting him, and his mind was troubled. He could no go on, he felt himself surrounded. Chin-tzu had to leave him; the son she was bearing would continue the family.

There were still two bullets in his revolver. In order to make Chin-tzu leave him, he shot once in the air; immediately a volley from detectives answered him. Chin-tzu consented to leave and then he killed himself.

(See Coll. Com. Syn. 1944, p. 179 "L'Univers de Ts'ao Yü" by Gérard de Boll).

Not to be recommended to anyone.

1392. 北京人 *PEKING MAN*   1 vol. 326 p. by 曹 禺
                                  7th edition 1947 文化生活出版社

In the first years of the Republic there lives in Peking an old man named Tseng Hao. He has one preoccupation: his death! His coffin has long been ready and is given every year a new coating of paint. It is all that is left of the once considerable family belongings. Tseng Ssu-yi, his daughter-in-law, has constantly to find new ways of making money. She lets part of their house to Yuan Jen-kan, an anthropologist, and his daughter, Yuan Yuan. She plans to marry Su-fang, her niece, an adopted daughter of Tseng Hao, to the anthropologist. She pressed her husband, Wen-ch'ing, to look for a job, and she has even delicately suggested selling the old man's coffin, which Mr. Fu, to whom they owe money, would like to possess.

Lack of money is not the only trouble. Tseng Hao has married his daughter, Wen-ts'ai, to Chiang T'ai, who studied abroad but has since failed in all his enterprises. Wen-ch'ing and Ssu-yi have a grandson, Tseng T'ing, who at the age of fifteen was married to a girl of sixteen. An unhappy marriage, which the birth of a child, now imminent, will not, it seems, make any happier.

The whole clan is heading for disaster: egoism and laziness undermine its shaking frame. The old man has no faith in his sons or grandsons; he himself has, after all, done nothing but eat his capital and bully his children.

The presence of Jen-kan who is engaged in research on the Peking Man, and Yuan Yuan suggests a deeper conflict. Their unsophisticated nature contrasts vividly with the overrefined tradition of the Tseng's. Free instincts, primitive feelings, exuberant life on the one hand; on the other hypocrisy, sophistication, endless quarrels: the case against civilization in a nutshell!

(See "Bulletin de l'Aurore" 1944, p. 417: "Procès de la civilisation" by Jean Monsterleet, S.J.) *Not to be recommended to anyone.*

1393. 家 *HOME*　　　　1 vol. 370 p. by 曹 禺
　　　　　　　　2nd edition 1946 文化生活出版社

A tragedy in 4 acts.

Pa Chin's masterpiece arranged for the stage. The author faithfully describes the characters of the book; the play makes the story more vivid, realistic and characteristic.

As for the story behind the play cf. No. 707.

This tragedy is very pathetic. It paints a vivid picture of old China and the dying generation. From the beginning to the end these two philosophies of life clash, and it is clear that the author favours the new generation.

We must admit that the author has succeeded very well, and the "young members" of the audience are only too eager to show their appreciation when the story is presented on the stage.

There is some danger in performing this play on the stage. The author gives a vivid picture of Chüeh Hsin's character; but as this individual holds the principal role, his indecision is likely to tire the audience unless it is played by a skilful actor. *For enlightened people only.*

1394. 蛻變 *METAMORPHOSIS or THE LADY IN WHITE* 1 vol. 404 p. by 曹 禺
　　　　　　　　3rd edition 1946 文化生活出版社

A play in 4 acts.

A play written by the well-known author who for many years, and, we should add, rightly, was approved by his audience. In his commentary on this play Pa-Chin admits that tears were in his eyes when he read it. We think that many others from the audience showed the same weakness.

The author describes conditions in a hospital behind the fighting lines. The director of the hospital and his clan of servants took no care of the wounded soldiers, who were arriving there in great numbers. For them the hospital was a fair field to fill their pockets and pass their time pleasantly with girls.

But the Government was keeping an eye upon them and sent an inspector. The inspector found out that medicine was wanting, that bandages and furnitures were taken to girl's quarters. Protests from these ladies add some gaiety to the play.

A solitary voice dared to protest against this state of affairs. It was a woman-doctor by the name Ting. She was a true national heroine, who had sacrificed everything for her country's sake; she had given her only son, who joined the Resistance.

After the inspection, the Government-inspector dismissed all those parasites and the hospital took on a new appearance. The soul of the institution was Dr. Ting. From morning till night she was going from one sick person to another, and was performing many operations. Of a rather cold nature, she nevertheless was generous, and the soldiers worshipped her. During bombardments, and even when her son arrived seriously wounded, she continued to work. At this point in the play the author reaches the sublime.

While being visited by her former enemies and performing her ordinary duties, she continued to sacrifice herself in spite of the fact that her boy's life was in danger near by. At this tragic moment, soldiers she had cured and who were returning to the front, bringing with them into the trenches the memory of her kindness, came to bid her goodbye. . . . . And it was at this moment her son underwent an operation. Her heart was rent with two loves: love for her country, and maternal love. A truly tragic moment.

The operation on her son was successful, and Dr. Ting made a speech to the soldiers who were going to what might be their deaths. She told them that they all wanted their China to be "strong and clean".

We can only congratulate this great playwright on this masterpiece. It is by far the most serious book among war-time literary work. The picture of Dr. Ting represents the soul of China at war. *For all*.

1395. 正在想 *AM TILL THINKING*   1 vol. 82 p. by 曹　禺
1940　文化生活出版社

A story teller sees that his profession has fallen upon evil days, but hopes to restore his fortunes by composing a play to be acted in a theatre. He succeeds only in producing a farcical piece.

It consists in showing at the same time both the actors and the spectators at the first night of a play.

First we are presented with the quarrels between Mr. Wo Kua and his wife concerning the preparations and other details of the production, then the guests arrive among whom are the sweetheart of the Wo's son, and the Li family. At last the play begins, is interrupted, begins again. The actors do not know their parts and even sometimes forget the names of their assumed roles. They hesitate, stumble, make mistakes, ask what they should do, correct themselves, correct each other, and the performance ends in a catastrophe in which actors and spectators use bad language against each other.

Good actors could obtain a really comic effect from this play.

It contains, however, a number of trivial expressions and some allusions that oblige us to put it in the category of books against which a warning is necessary. *Not for everyone*.

1396. 樑上君子 *A DOCTOR UR* (adapted)   1 vol. 114 p. by 佐臨 (黃佐臨)
1944　世界書局　*See Biogr. 84*

A play in three acts, adapted from "A Doctor Ur" by Molnar.

The central figure is a gentlemanburglar who is on terms of equality with a lawyer, whom he supplies with legal cases and who, in return, obtains his acquittal every time he is caught.

One day, the burglar, whose name is Pao San, takes the place of the lawyer, and the latter, being taken for a thief, passes the night under arrest. His wife in the meantime flirts with the police inspector, while his deputy is engaged in the same pastime with the wife's sister, and the burglar lords it in the lawyer's place, in the midst of a reunion of old students. During the celebration, while everybody is drinking, the burglar steals three watches from his friends.

On the following morning, the master of the house returns home and delivers a sermon to his wife. Pao San, however, clears her from suspicion, while the deputy obtains the hand of the object of his dreams.

The story ends badly for the burglar, for he is caught in the act of stealing and is taken off to prison.

The play contains many flippant allusions. *For adults only.*

1397. 荒島英雄 *THE ADMIRABLE CHRICHTON* (adapted) 1 vol. 98 p. by 佐　臨
　　　　　　　　　　　　　　　　　　　　　　　　　1945　世界書局

A comedy in four acts.

An adaptation of the play "The Admirable Crichton" by J.M. Barrie.

A family of which the head makes much of the equality between masters and servants, is isolated for two years on a desert island. There, the servant reveals himself the master! When they return home an account is rendered of the utopia of this kind of equality. *For everyone.*

1398. 天下太平 *THE WORLD IS PEACEFUL*　　　　1 vol. 386 p. by 左　兵
　　　　　　　　　　　　　　　　　　　　　　　　　1937　戞友圖書公司

Dramatised history of the Kuomintang in a certain spot in the environs of Shanghai in the years 1924-27.

First there is a description of a village with the rich residents and the oppressed. One of the latter sends his son to school. Later the young man leaves to found a school in his native village, but it is boycotted, and the father has to bleed himself white to keep his son who becomes exasperated and joins the party in power, taking part in its struggle against its adversaries. In time he obtains a good appointment but fresh misfortunes arise.

The book contains a number of execrations and obscene expressions. *For mature people.*

1399. 楊貴妃之死 *THE DEATH OF YANG KUEI-FEI*　　1 vol. 77 p. by 王獨清
　　　　　　　　　　　　3rd edition 1930　樂華圖書公司　*See Biogr. 170*

A play in 6 acts.

Yang Kuei-fei, Emperor Huan-Tsung's famous concubine, did great harm to the Chinese people by her loose conduct. They demanded her death. She accepted this punishment in expiation of the harm she had done. This play is *not suitable for young people.*

1400. 夢裏京華 *CAPITAL IN THE DREAM*　　　　1 vol. 114 p. by 王文顯
　　　　　　　　　　　　　　　　　　　1944　世界書局　*See Biogr. 172*

This play appeared originally in English under the title of "Peking Politics". The translation has been made by 李健吾.

It is a satire on a historical event that occurred after the collapse of the empire. The name of the personage depicted is not cited, but everyone knows the general who attempted to restore the empire after the end of the Ch'ing Dynasty.

In this play, the plans made by certain high personages to prevent the restoration are revealed. A number of good scenes are presented, including that depicting the haste of the concubines and other women to assume their new role. They are doomed to disappointment, however, as the attempt fails. *For everyone.*

1401. 桃花源 *THE PEACH FOUNTAIN*   1 vol. 97 p. by 魏如晦 (錢杏邨)
1940   潮鋒出版社 *See Biogr. 34*

A play.

A young woman is pursued in the fairy land of peach trees. Nevertheless, her lover succeeds in hiding her. The pursuers are furious and set fire to the place. But the year after, when the peach trees are in bloom again, the two lovers marry. *For everyone.*

1402. 洪宣嬌 *HUNG HSUAN-CHIAO* (A woman in revolution) 1 vol. 126 p. by 魏如晦
1941   國民書店

A historical drama in five acts dealing with the suppression of the T'ai P'ing Rebellion. *For everyone.*

1403. 碧血花 *LAMENT FOR THE FALL OF THE MING'S* 1 vol. 183 p. by 魏如晦
(一名明末遺恨)(又名葛嫩娘)
1946   國民書店

A historical drama in four acts.

The events occur at the end of the Ming Dynasty when the Ch'ings are invading the country. The heroine, 葛嫩娘, is the daughter of a good family but has been sold into a house of courtisans. She persuades her lover, 孫克咸, a high official, to devote himself to the defence of the country, and to go with her to join in the resistance to the invaders.

The enemy is approaching the capital (Nanking) when these two take to flight accompanied by a maid named 美娘. In spite of the fact that the majority of the officials go over to the new regime, these three retain their confidence in the future and resist the Ch'ings for several years. Friends advise them to surrender, but they continue the struggle.

In the end they are made prisoner and executed because they refuse to recognize the legitimate claim of the invaders.

The hero and heroine are beautifully depicted and the play is animated throughout with patriotic fervour. The first act, however, contains some levities where the scene is laid in the house of courtisans. *May be read by anyone.*

1404. 五姊妹 *FIVE SISTERS*   1 vol. 58 p. by 魏如晦
2nd. edit. 1946   潮鋒出版社

A play in three acts.
Very patriotic in atmosphere.
A family composed of a father with five daughters has to put up a hard struggle with material difficulties. The elder sister, who has the responsibility of the household on her shoulders, wishes to bring about an increase in the family revenues. She therefore persuades her father to take service with the enemy. From this arises a difference of opinion between the father and the younger daughters on the one hand, and the elder daughter with her sisters on the other. The younger girls have admirable patriotic sentiments.

The play ends with the assassination of the "collaborator" father and the lesson to be derived from it by his daughters. *For everyone.*

1405. 釵頭鳳 *IN LOVING MEMORY* 1 vol. 164 p. by 魏于潛
1944 世界書局

A play in four acts.

Yu (游) has lived since an early age with his cousin, Hsün (齋). The two young people love each other tenderly, and Yu's mother crowns their happiness by announcing their betrothal. In order to celebrate this event, Yu gives a precious hairpin to his fiancée, and she gives him a gift in return.

Their happiness, however, is of short duration, for the mother, who is extremely superstitious, finds out from two soothsayers that their horoscopes do not agree with each other, and their marriage, therefore, will be unlucky. Because of this, the mother separates them, and makes Hsün enter a convent.

Hsün comes out soon after, but not until after she has been subjected to the assault of a young rake.

Upon coming out of the convent, Hsün has a last interview with her lover who has passed first in the imperial examinations.

In the last act, the two principal characters, each married to someone else, meet after a lapse of years. This meeting occurs at a certain place that Yu visits frequently because it reminds him of his old friend.

This meeting is touchingly poignant and reveals to us the sentiments of the separated lovers, who both live in the memory of their great love. *May be read by anyone.*

1406. 甜姐兒 *LA PETITE CHOCOLATIERE* (adapted) 1 vol. 164 p. by 魏于潛
1945 世界書局

A comedy in four acts, adapted from "La petite chocolatière" by Paul Gavault. 小玉 nicknamed 甜姐兒, is engaged to be married. Going through an abandoned village one evening, she is delayed by a breakdown to her car, and is forced to lodge for the night with a young man, 君慎, who is also engaged to be married. The latter is expecting his fiancée to arrive on the following day.

Although they are lodged in separate rooms and there are other people in the house, 小玉's fiancé is angry when he hears of this escapade. The father of 君慎's fiancée also takes exception, and he goes as far as to break the engagement of the young people. And 小玉 is dismissed from her job on account of another blunder of 君慎.

The conversations between the hero and heroine are nothing but avalanches of bad language, but soon they find out that this is just a way of saying that they love each other. At the end of the play, therefore, we have the happiness of learning of their betrothal.

The story is complicated with love affairs between the servants and other flippancies. In spite of her faults, however, the "sugar queen" is a very sympathetic person. *Not to be recommended to anyone.*

1407. 贓吻記 *A KISS EMBEZZLED* 1 vol. 106 p. by 吳伣之
1945 世界書局 *See Biogr. 177*

A comedy in three acts.

During a charity bazar, a saloon lizard succeeds in imposing himself upon the gathered company, and puts the kiss of a young lady up for auction. Without having a penny, he himself makes an enormous bid which gains for him the kiss. He however, contents himself with merely kissing the young lady's hand. The latter falls in love with him. He, on his part, manages to circumvent a rich man and to extort from him a large sum of money. Due to this, he is able to pay for the kiss and has the hand of the heroine thrown into the bargain. *May be read by anyone.*

1408. 紅樓夢 *DREAM OF THE RED CHAMBER*   1 vol. 219 p. by 吳 天

1946   永祥印書館   *See Biogr. 178*

A play in five acts.

A faithful dramatic version of the love story in the celebrated romance of the "Dream of the Red Chamber". Cfr. Review No. 1217. *Not to be recommended to the young.*

1409. 子夜 *MIDNIGHT*   1 vol. 175 p. by 吳 天

2nd. edit. 1947   永祥印書館

An adaptation of the novel, 子夜, the masterpiece of Mao Tun (茅盾

This romance describes the industrial and financial society in Shanghai in 1930 in relation with the advance of the communist armies that have taken Changsha and are menacing Wu-han, while Yen Hsi-shan and Feng Yu-hsiang are agitating in the north, rebelling against the Nanking government.

The story abounds in details, facts and characters, to such an extent that it is difficult to keep track of them all. The minor events and characters run the risk of submerging the main intrigue.

Wu Sun-fu (吳蓀甫) is a big business man endowed with a strong will and large financial interests. He wishes to give work to the people and at the same time acquire for himself influence and fame, with the ultimate end of bringing about the industrial, economic and social rise of his country. To realize this programme, he sacrifices his family joys, his other pleasures, and even his sleep.

His first dream, to create a modern industrial village, is soon reduced to smoke through communist troubles, the carrying off of peasants, massacres, fires and other acts of violence. And in Shanghai itself he is involved in a mass of difficulties against which he struggles, and in which he shows his "hand of iron". He also meets with foreign competition, difficulties of transport because of the civil war, and the rivalry of a powerful financier who has no scruples. He has to impose a reduction of salaries on his employees which leads to a strike and much agitation.

In the end he is ruined by the intrigues of his enemies. After wishing to commit suicide, he gives in to the persuasion of those around him, and retires.

In this romance, Wu's friends discuss the political and economic questions of the day, and military events that have an influence on their daily life. Love intrigues also are numerous.

Mao Tun wishes to show that under present circumstances, the economic and industrial rise of China is impossible. He also reveals a socialistic point of view in describing the wealthy class as absolutely materialist and self-indulgent.

(An extract from "Mao Tun, A Painter of His Time", by P.O. Brière, Bull. Aurore, 1943, T. 4, No. 1).

Not to be recommended to anyone.

1410. 春雷 *THE FIRST THUNDER IS HEARD*   1 vol. 172 p. by 吳 天

2nd. edit. 1946   開明書店

Wang Tien-hu (王殿虎) lives with his concubine, a former dancer named Fei-li (菲莉), and they have a son, Shu-pen (樹本).

Wang, the head of the family, is a general of the old regime, a man without a conscience. He is responsible for the death of an old servant and of the wife of the latter. Before coming to live with the general, Fei-li already had two children who are now with a friend, as the general does not want to have them in the house. One of them is called Ho Cheng-ming (何正明), a boy of revolutionary spirit, while the other, a girl, named Chao-ti (招弟) works for her living. They are both loved by their mother, Fei-li, to distraction, although she will not reveal to them her relationship to them.

One day Shu-pen learns that he is not the son of the general but that he is the issue of two servants. He also discovers that his so-called father was the murderer of his real parents. Shocked at his discovery, he resolves to take vengeance and kill his adopted father. Being however, a versatile character lacking in perseverance, he fails to execute his project.

Now Cheng-ming, on his part, in an encounter with Fei-li, discovers that she loves him excessively, and therefore he decides to avoid her, and he even abuses her on several occasions.

The drama develops with the arrival of the revolutionary army. Seized with remorse, the general goes, one night, to the pit in which his victims have been drowned. There he sees a spectre at which he shoots. It happens that the spectre is his adopted son, Shu-pen, who thus dies by the same hand as his parents.

Cheng-ming is accused of the murder and the general wishes to execute him, but is preventd by Fei-li. The latter, not knowing the identity of his saviour, curses Fei-li and inflicts a moral wound on her.

In the meantime, the real murderer is drawn to the scene of one of his greatest crimes to which he is also driven by remorse. There he falls into the pit in which many of his victims were drowned, and thus meets his death.

Cheng-ming finds out the identity of his victim. Consternation ensues. He gathers her up in his arms, implores her pardon, and takes his precious burden to an infirmary. On the way, he meets his sister, Chao-ti, enroled in the revolutionary army. Together, they see to the funeral rites of their mother while a "new Spring comes into the world".

A play with dramatic force but breathing too much vengeance and too full of crimes. *For mature people.*

1411. 牛郎織女 *THE COWHERD AND THE WEDDING MAID*
1 vol. 170 p. by 吳祖光
1946 開明書店 *See Biogr. 180*

A play in four acts.

牛郎, dissatisfied with life that has frustrated him, dreams of leaving his family and the earth and of going to heaven. 織女, on her part, feels the emptiness of existence in heaven and yearns to pass her life in the company of a human being.

The wishes of both our heroes are fulfilled by their union in heaven. After it has been consummated, 牛郎, however, feels as frustrated as before and longs for his beloved family. He plans secretly to return to earth in the company of his wife whom he loves. But the Goddess 王母娘娘 surprises and stops them. Taking pity on them, she partly fulfills their wishes, allowing 牛郎 to return to his family, and to come back to heaven every year on the 7th day of the 7th moon.

A play full of poetic spirit that pervades it from beginning to end. *May be read by everyone.*

1412. 風雪夜歸人 *RETURN ON A STORMY NIGHT*
1 vol. 202 p. by 吳祖光
2nd. edit. 1946 開明書店

A play with a prologue, three acts and an epilogue.

A famous actor whose aspirations have not been fulfilled finds the same state of mind in the concubine of a man of the world. They plan to leave their present surroundings together and go somewhere else where they will live poor but happy. When, however their intention is known, they are prevented from putting it into execution. Forced to separate, one leaves the stage while the other goes off with another companion.

Twenty years after, their tragic fate unrolls in a still sadder fashion. *For mature people.*

1413. 少年遊 *WANDERINGS OF THE YOUNG*   1 vol. 182 p. by 吳祖光
4th. edit. 1946   開明書店

A play in three acts.

A group of girl students have finished their studies in a university in Peking under the Japanese occupation. None of them has any future. The war prevents them from returning to their families and in the upheaval of the war it is impossible to find a job.

Four of them arrange to live together in a furnished room and soon they suffer from great poverty. One of them is married but cannot return to her husband because of the opposition of his parents. Her husband, however, makes a short appearance when he shows that he has a good and unselfish character.

These girls, in the midst of their poverty, engage in espionage work with a hero of the resistance, and due to their efforts several important Japanese are made to disappear.

Eventually, when their activities are discovered, the husband offers himself as the victim while the rest of the group joins the army.

The author gives us a good dose of psychology in describing characters so diverse and life-like.

There is only one word to add, and that is that these girl graduates do not all remain faithful to their ideals. There are also a few defections.

This play may be read by anyone but is not suitable for acting in our schools. *For everyone.*

1414. 正氣歌 *SONG OF THE EVERLASTING SPIRIT*   1 vol. 199 p. by 吳祖光
3rd. edit.   開明書店

A play in five acts.

The Sung Dynasty is on the point of being annihilated by the Yuan. The chief cause for its fall is the lack of conscience of the officials who think of nothing but how to amuse themselves and who do nothing to rescue the reigning house. There are a few energetic men who wish to remedy this state of affairs but their efforts have no chance of success.

The hero of the drama is the great Wen T'ien-hsiang (文天祥), the patriot who struggled with the invaders to the bitter end. An admirable figure of a historical hero, courageous and full of integrity, he is forced to succumb to the power of the Yuans in the end. *May be read by anyone.*

1415. 捉鬼傳 *LAYING DEVILS*   1 vol. 149 p. by 吳祖光
1947   開明書店

A play in three acts.

鍾馗, who is of a repulsive ugliness, is not received kindly as a doctor in spite of his capacities. The emperor punishes him and advises him to become a devil catcher after he has committed suicide. After he has been executed, he becomes a fossil. After a million years he wakes up again, and finds the world even worse than before. He runs away from the sad spectacle.

The author uses this story to decry the deceits practiced by officials both ancient and modern. *For mature people.*

1416. 稱心如意 *AS YOU DESIRE*   1 vol. 143 p. by 楊 絳
1944 世界書局

A poor girl student who is an orphan, named Chün-yü (君玉) is invited by rich relatives who wish to offer her a roof over her head. But when she arrives, she is sent to some other relatives, because she is so beautiful that she threatens the peace of mind of the husband. She does not succeed any better with these other people who discover many faults in her.

The poor heroine is really a good girl, although rather impulsive. She finds herself forced to move again to still other relatives, and there, in the new household, she provokes the jealousy of the lady of the house.

Finally she manages to find refuge with an old uncle, who is an original character but of good heart, who soon develops an affection for his young relative and gives her in marriage to a poor student who has been pursuing her for a long time.

In this four act comedy, the defects and eccentricities of the various families brought in are presented with a great deal of humour. *For everyone.*

1417. 弄假成眞 *UNFORESEEN CONSEQUENCES*   1 vol. 120 p. by 楊 絳
1945 世界書局

A comedy in five acts.

A girl escapes from the clutches of a young man who is poor and a braggart. The latter consoles himself very soon after, and goes off with a relative less wealthy than the first girl.

Upon their return from their escapade, they find everything prepared for their wedding. And the bride, seeing the poverty of her new house, is well punished for her jealousy and coquetry. *May be read by anyone.*

1418. 光緒親政記, 清宮外史 *INTIMATE HISTORY OF THE IMPERIAL PALACE OF THE CHING'S*   1° vol. 264 p. by 楊村彬
1946 國訊書店 *See Biogr. 185*

A play in five acts.

The historical period depicted is the reign of Kuang Hsü (1894-95). History, however, has been somewhat retouched by the author in this play.

The events depicted are so well known that it is not necessary to describe them in detail. We have the following characters; Kuang Hsü deprived of all power, the Empress Dowager jealous of her authority, the Grand Eunuch who intervenes in state affairs, the Empress, the imperial concubines, and a few other historical personages.

All this is without great interest because real drama is lacking in this play. *For mature people.*

1419. 光緒變政記, 清宮外史   2° vol. 165 p. by 楊村彬
1946 國訊書店

A play in four acts.

The Empress Dowager, Ts'i Hsi, and the Grand Eunuch pass their days agreeably in the Summer Palace, while Kuang Hsü and his concubine remain in Peking. The Emperor, under the guidance of K'ang Yu-wei, is preparing to introduce salutary reforms. And in secret, they are plotting to take the power into their hands and imprison Ts'i Hsi. Yuan Shih-k'ai, however, betrays the Emperor, and tells Jung Lo of the plot, and the latter goes to the rescue of the old Empress Dowager.

This is another play which lacks dramatic interest. *For mature people.*

1420. 少年英雄 *YOUNG HEROES*   1 vol. 78 p. by 楊蔭深
1933 開明書店 *See Biogr. 187*

A collection of four short plays dealing with filial piety and patriotism.
Can be acted in our schools. *For everyone.*

1421. 楚霸王 *DEFEATED: CH'U PA-WANG*   1 vol. 143 p. by 姚 克
1944 世界書局 *Sec Biogr. 188*

A play in four acts.
The Prince of Ch'u (楚) allows his rival to escape. The latter takes advantage of the situation to reorganise his forces and renews his attack on his adversary. The Prince of Ch'u, in spite of his great courage, sees himself defeated and is obliged to conclude a truce. Then, his enemy, reinforced by still more allies, again attacks him and forces him to retreat.

Now the Prince who loves his wife very much, has to separate from her. He agrees to meet her by the river. He accomplishes an orderly retreat and arrives at the rendezvous. But his wife dies owing to the treachery of the general into whose care she has been entrusted. When the Prince hears of this, he makes his army cross the river but he himself seeks death. *For everyone.*

1422. 清宮怨 *UNHAPPY LIFE IN THE MANCHU PALACE*   1 vol. 167 p. by 姚 克
1944 世界書局

A play in four acts with a prologue.
This play presents an episode in the agitated life of the Empress Dowager (西太后). It occurs at the time when the Emperor Kuang Hsü wished to introduce much needed reforms into the empire and was strongly opposed by the Empress Dowager.

The story is rendered extremely poignant by the introduction of the figure of the Pearl Concubine, the Emperor's favourite. She is represented as a superior woman, very much in love with her lord and the inspirer of his liberal ideas.

The jealous old Empress finally deprives them of all power and puts them into prison. The play ends with the death of the Pearl Concubine when she is flung into a well upon the flight of the imperial court.

The author has taken some liberties with history and it is obvious that his sympathy is with the imperial couple, and especially with the beautiful concubine. *For everyone.*

1423. 銀海滄桑 *IN THE SPOT LIGHT*   1 vol. 169 p. by 姚 克
1945 世界書局

A play in four acts.
A young woman, Lin Yin, leaves Peking secretly to go to Shanghai, with the intention of acting in a film of which she has written the scenario. In Shanghai, she finds K'ao who has formerly been her admirer.

Her husband, Hsiao, follows her, taking with him their little daughter, Yün. He hopes to bring her back to Peking. But although she loves her husband, he does not succeed in persuading her to return home.

During three years Lin Yin leads the life of a celebrated star, but as she does not respond to his advances, the director of the company is looking around for someone to replace her who will be easier to deceive. This happens just at the moment when the heroine has had enough of the kind of life she is leading, and longs for her husband and child.

One day, she learns that her husband is in Shanghai, where he is in miserable circumstances. He has, in fact, become blind and is earning his living as a soothsayer. Kao discovers him with his daughter and tries to persuade him to resume his life with his wife. Hsiao, however, refuses, and is adamant in his decision. Nevertheless, he allows his daughter to go to her mother so that she may obtain a suitable education.

His wife manages finally to discover her husband's retreat and comes to see him. But she arrives too late, just at the moment when he is swallowing a dose of poison. He dies before her very eyes.

The aim of the author is excellent — to show how false the life of a star is, how empty and deceptive. The suicide that ends the play is, however, to be reproved. *Not for everyone.*

1424. 美人計 *BEAUTY IS THE BAIT*   1 vol. 142 p. by 姚　克
                                                                    1945　世界書局

A play in four acts.

In view of an alliance with 劉備, 吳國太 consents to give him her daughter in marriage, but only on condition that her daughter and son-in-law remain with her after the wedding.

Once the wedding is over, the young couple flee and wish to enter the state of the young husband, under the pretext that the enemy is advancing to attack it.

吳國太, indignant at the flight of the young couple, pursues them, and comes up with them at the moment they are crossing the river. There she curses her daughter and refuses to pardon her. And in despair, the latter crosses the river. *For everyone.*

1425. 春花怒放 *WHEN THE FLOWERS ARE IN FULL BLOOM*
                                                    1 vol. 140 p. by 姚亞影
                                                                    1946　建國書店

A play depicting a family of rich people who engage in illicit trade during the war and whose children think of nothing but how to amuse themselves. There are also some poor people who contribute from their slender means for the good of the country.

After the bombardment of Hongkong, and other Japanese atrocities, in which several of the characters concerned, find their death, the youth depicted in the play is reduced to order, and decide to devote themselves to the service of the country, to deliver her from danger. *May be read by anyone.*

1426. 沒有男子的戲劇 *A PLAY WITH NO GENTLEMEN* 1 vol. 251 p. by 葉　尼
                                                    3rd. edit. 1940　潮鋒出版社

A series of five one-act plays, and two *chieh-t'ou chü* (street plays) 街頭劇.

The whole series deals with the war, of the armed resistance to Japan, of the disgusting dealings of certain capitalists and of their exploitation of the working class.

The language is very simple but expressive. Most of these plays are suitable for acting in our schools. *For everyone.*

1427. 夜光杯 *CUPS OF NIGHT RADIANCE*　　1 vol. 237 p. by **尤兢（于伶）**
1937　上海一般書店 *See Biogr. 193*

A play in five acts.

郁, a well-known lady dancer, is married to 湯. In concert with her husband, she decides to simulate a divorce in order to enter into relations with a retired dancer of the male sex. The latter has climbed to a high estate through collaboration with the enemy during the late war. The idea of the heroine is to profit from her old relations with this man to assassinate him.

Having gone north, 郁 succeeds in her plans, and plots with the adjutant of 郭 to kill 應,郁 and 郭 are, however, betrayed by the mother of the adjutant who hopes thus to save the life of her son. 郭 is shot and to avoid the same fate, 郁 takes poison. Her husband, 湯, had been shot several days earlier, after having been arrested by the police as a suspicious character. When the mother of 郭 learns of what has happened, she becomes almost mad and decides to avenge the death of her son.

The aim of the author in this play is to show the heinous nature of the crime of collaborating with the enemy. *For mature people.*

1428. 女子公寓 *WOMEN'S HOSTEL*　　1 vol. 178 p. by **于伶**
1941　國民書店

A play in five acts.

The intrigue is built around a hostel for young ladies, where men are not allowed. Owing to this rule, the reputation of the inmates is preserved, but in reality, they do nothing but flirt — to use a modest word — when they are out of the hostel. From this arise gallantries, jealousies, and even dramas without end.

Finally one learns that the lady director herself has been submitted to the same fate as her protegees, and that one of the tempters of the young ladies is no other than her former husband, although in justice it may be added that he had indulged in his carryings-on without her knowledge.

Most of the inmates of the hostel go to the bad. *For mature people only.*

1429. 大明英烈傳 *BUILDERS OF A DYNASTY*　　1 vol. 268 p. by **于伶**
1941　雜誌公司

A historical drama describing the struggle of certain heros under the Yuan. They finally establish the Ming Dynasty.

Exaltation of national sentiment and patriotism is contained in this play. Revolt against foreign oppressors is described.

Can be acted with some modifications. *For everyone.*

1430. 長夜行 *LONG NIGHT JOURNEY*　　1 vol. 179 p. by **于伶**
1946　上海新知書店

A play in four acts.

Several families are residing in the same house during the war. These people, however are not animated by the same spirit. One plans to enrich himself, another cares only about drink, and still others hope to devote themselves to the service of the country. But they share one common fate in that everyone is unhappy.

The play ends with the American declaration of war, which inspires several of the characters depicted to decide to work more efficaciously for the good of China.

No connected narrative, and a lack of real tragedy. *May be read by anyone.*

1431. 上沅劇本甲集 *PLAYS BY SHANG YUAN* (1)　　1° vol. 158 p. by 余上沅
1934　商務印書館　*See Biogr. 195*

1) 回家　p. 1-27. One act. A soldier who has been in the army for ten years returns home full of joy only to find his wife married to his own father. *Not for everyone.*

2) 塑像　p. 29-115. Four acts. A dramatic and pathetic meeting between an artist and his mistress. *Not for everyone.*

3) 兵變　p. 115-157. One act. A comic scene from which two lovers profit. *For everyone.*

1432. 鐘樓怪人　*NOTRE DAME DE PARIS*　　1 vol. 118 p. by 袁牧之
1944　世界書局　*See Biogr. 200*

A play adapted from the romance of Victor Hugo that has for chief characters, the monster Quasimodo, and Esmeralda.

Hugo gives to his monsters the noblest of sentiments and to priests the most miserable roles. This antithesis is faithfully reproduced in the present volume, where calumnies and blasphemies tumble over each other. *Proscribed.*

1433. 山城故事　*TALE OF A SMALL TOWN*　　1 vol. 132 p. by 袁俊(張駿祥)
1941　文化生活出版社　*See Biogr. 12*

A woman no longer young, marries, after her first lover, who kept her in luxury, abandons her.

Meanwhile she discovers that her husband is not rich. In order to escape this embarrassment, she suggests to another young man that he should go and live with her in Shanghai. He however, quickly sees through her game and leaves her.

Thus the heroine is forced to be contented with her poor husband. *For everyone.*

1434. 山城故事　*TALE OF A MOUNTAIN CITY*　　1 vol. 210 p. by 袁俊
2nd. edit. 1946　文化生活出版社

A play in three acts.

It is of the Hsiang (向) family. The mother is an excellent person of honest character but with a great weakness for her two sons, Ho (鶴) and P'eng (鵬). The elder has a good heart and suffers from the poverty in which they live, and especially dislikes to see his mother doing all the work of the household. The younger is an emancipated young man, but nevertheless is a good son.

Ho is engaged in the service of an unscrupulous man, and the mother refuses to accept the money that he brings home, being suspicious of the source it comes from. Soon Ho falls in love with his employer's wife, a former dancer who, on her part, also feels drawn to him. Ho, however, gets to know of the illegal affairs of his employer and with a heavy heart, he leaves both his employer and his wife. His employer, however, having surprised him making advances to his wife, decides to deliver him into the hands of his enemies.

Without suspecting any danger, Ho falls into the trap. His mistress (i.e. his employer's wife) hastens after him to warn him, but does not succeed in reaching him in time. In the final scene, Ho kills his employer and also puts an end to himself.

When the mother hears of the affair, she hurries off in the utmost consternation to search for the body of her dear son. *For mature people.*

1435. 邊城故事　*TALE OF A BORDER CITY*　　1 vol. 197 p. by 袁俊
1941　文化生活出版社

Melodrama in five acts.

The workers in a gold mine, instigated by corrupt officials, rebel against the industrialisation of their concern by the central government. After a good number of denouements, the traitors are discovered and punished, and the workers converted. The government has gained a victory — but several innocent victims have been made to suffer.

There is one feminine role and two feminine supernumeries. *For everyone.*

1436. 萬 世 師 表 *MODEL FOR TEN THOUSAND GENERATIONS*

1 vol. 280 p. by 袁　俊
2nd. edit. 1946　文化生活出版社

A play in four acts.

The drama is built around the disinterested life of a university professor and his wife. They sacrifice themselves in a really heroic fashion for the country and their school.

There is a scene in which a revolution is organised by the hero among his students. His anti-government act costs him fifty days in prison. *For everyone.*

1437. 美 國 總 統 號 *PRESIDENT LINER*

1 vol. 161 p. by 袁　俊
1946　文化生活出版社

A play in three acts.

There are several Chinese passengers returning home on a President liner. The life aboard is presented. There are many jealousies and the less enviable aspects of these people is brought before our eyes.

Contains some levities. The play is fairly interesting as a whole but the real comic spirit is lacking. *May be read by anyone.*

1438. 富 貴 浮 雲 *YOU CAN'T TAKE IT WITH YOU* (adapted)

1 vol. 125 p. by 袁　俊
1944　世界書局

A comedy in five acts.

An adaptation of the comedy of Georges S. Kaufman and Moss Hart, "You can't take it with you".

It is about an original family. A rich young man is in love with one of the daughters. The parents of the young man come on a visit which ends in a fiasco, but everything comes to a happy conclusion in the last act.

It is a very original play but difficult to understand. *For everyone.*

1439. 現 代 最 佳 劇 選 *A SELECTION OF BEST MODERN DRAMAS* 5th vol. 275 p.

1942　光明書店

Eight plays by different authors.

On account of their frivolity, unhealthy surroundings and tendency, *the first four must be reserved for informed readers. The last four may be read by all.*

Drama Translated

1440. 大學教授 *"PROFESSOR STORIZIN"* 1 vol. 129 p. by *Leonide Andrajeff.*
Translated by 芳信 1944 世界書局 *See Biogr. 50*

A tragedy in four acts.

The drama consists of the life of a university professor. He is unhappily married. His wife is unfaithful and his children rather queer. One of his friends is his wife's lover, a vile person. Another is a young student who is infatuated with him. He himself is an admirable character.

The drama develops through a murder, and abnormal situations, ending in the death of the hero.

There is not a normal person in the whole of the book and moral sense is conspicuous by its absence. *Not to be recommended to anyone.*

1441. 婚禮進行曲 *"LA MARCHE NUPTIALE"* 1 vol. 222 p. by *Henri Bataille.*
translated by 王了一 1934 商務印書舘

A play in four acts.

Grace de Plessans, a girl with mystic inclinations and passionately fond of music, falls in love with her piano instructor and goes off with him. Later she realizes that she has mistaken her real feelings but considering the gift of herself, once made, as irrevocable, she seeks release in death. *Proscribed.*

1442. 紅袍 *"LA ROBE ROUGE"* by *Eugène Brieux.*
Com. Press 商務印書舘

A tragedy in four acts. The piece consists of domestic palavers between barristers, and judges, and the judgment of a murderess. *For adults.*

1443. 寄生草 1 vol. 114 p. by *A. H. Davis.*
1930 上海光華書局

Play in 3 acts.

An earnest and attractive young orphan, Chou Hsin-yun, is a governess. She is treated as one of the family. Mrs. Wu, a nervous wreck, neglects her husband and transfers all her responsibilities on Miss Chou, who serves her faithfully and even manages to bring a little joy to the household. Mr. Pao, Mrs. Wu's brother, visits the family in a fruitless attempt to cure his sister. The young governess makes a deep impression on him and he advises Mr. Wu of the fact. Anticipating the possible departure of Miss Chou, Mr. Wu all of a sudden awakes to the fact that he cannot live without her. Mr. Pao takes advantage of this to make Mrs. Wu suspicious of her husband's conduct. This forces Mrs. Wu to energetic action, which works a quick cure. The marriage of Mr. Pao and Miss Chou brings the play to an end. *For informed readers.*

1444. 茶花女 *LA DAME AUX CAMELIAS*   1 vol. 390 p. by *Alexandre Dumas.*

A courtisan, Marguerite Gautier, has as her lover a young man named Armand Duval. . . At the urgent prayer of the latter, she abandons him but not without having seen for an instant her Armand."

On the Index. Cfr. Bethleem, Novels to read. . .p. 32. On the Index: "Omnes fabulae amatoriae" of this author. *Condemnatus ab Ecclesia.*

1445. 半上流社會 *LE DEMI-MONDE*   1 vol. 230 p. by *A. Dumas Fils.*
translated by 王了一 商務印書館

Suzane, Baronne d'Ange, is an ambitious courtisan who dreams of marrying M. de Nanjac, a rich gentleman. She succeeds in spite of the ingenuity of Olivier de Jalin who tries to baffle all her projects. *Proscribed.*

1446. 正義 *JUSTICE*   1 vol. 142 p. by *John Galsworthy.*
1936 商務印書館

An employee forges a cheque and runs away with his mistress to free her from the cruelty of her husband. The crime is discovered and the young man is condemned to three years in prison. When he is set free he is again engaged by his former employer on condition that he separate from the lady in question until she obtains her divorce.

With justice again on his tracks, the young man tries to save himself by jumping through a window, and kills himself. *For grown-up people.*

1447. 三姊妹   162 p. by *John Galsworthy.*

Play in 4 acts.

Pessimistic description of a family of Russian intellectuals. One of the three sisters described is unhappily married; she pursues a married man. Another is going to be married, not because she loves but to have more freedom. Her fiancé is killed in a duel. *For informed readers.*

1448. 群衆 *THE MOB*   1 vol. 110 p. by *Galsworthy.*
translated by 朱復 1930 商務印書館

Tragedy in four acts recounting the story of an English anti-militarist. Moved by a sentiment of universal humanitarianism, he opposes the war that his country has declared against a feebler country.

His activities meet complete frustration and he pays with his life.
Difficult to present. *For everyone.*

1449. 愛 *AIMER*   by *Paul Geraldy.*
Translated by 王了一 1934 商務印書館

Act. I. A couple who have been married for several years already, love each other as on their wedding day, when a friend visits them and the wife realises that she has been noticed by him.

Act. II. The friend bewitches the wife to such an extent that she avows her love for him and resolves to leave her husband to go with him.

Act. III. At the last moment she hesitates. In a last interview with her husband, she confesses that she cannot leave him afer all, and it is he that she really loves.

The moral of the book is good, but it would be better not to act this play before our students, because it deals too squarely with the problem of divorce. For adults, however, the book may have good effects. *For adults.*

1450. 欽差大臣 *THE REVISER*   1 vol. 148 p. by *N. Gogol.*
                                    Translated by 芳信 1944 世界書局

A comedy in five acts.

A good comedy based upon a misunderstanding — a young man without resources being mistaken for the inspector that everyone is expecting. *For everyone.*

1451. 女店主 *LA LACONDIERA*   1 vol. 118 p. by *Goldoni*
                                    1929 北新書局

The heroine, the daughter of an inn keeper, is betrothed by her father to a domestic. She is the object of amorous tentatives on the part of two functionaries who lodge in the inn. The police inspector uses his influence to get her, and the tax collector his riches.

A misanthrope, who tries to dissuade these two personages from their project, attracts to himself the attention of the girl, who soon gives evidence that she loves him. The jealousy of the two others is aroused.

The domestic, who is the official fiancé, demands explanations when he discovers the intrigue. Faithful to the intentions of her father, the girl marries him to the joy of the unsuccessful suitors.

An innocent piece but not very profound. *For everyone.*

1452. 夜店   1 vol. 120 p. by *Maxim Gorki.*
                                    translated by 胡明 2nd. edit. 1947 光華出版社

"Gorki deals particularly in vagabonds; his characters are devoid of all moral sense and his doctrine is revolutionary." Stories to Read and Stories to Proscribe, Bethléem, p. 174.

His drama and especially "L'albego dei poveri", is "d'ambiente russo e dei bassifonti." Manuale di Letture, Gasati, p. 83.

This play is an illustration of what Bethléem says above. In presenting to us the inhabitants of this inn, the author occasionally arouses our sympathies, but nevertheless, from the moral point of view, the play ought to be proscribed. *Condemned.*

1453. 沙杜南 *SATURNIN*   by *Henry Grall.*
                                    1941 工商學院工教出版社

Shows how the J.O.C. (Catholic Young Workers) methods can give an apostle strong influence in a Communist environment.

The play is easy to stage and *can be warmly recommended.*

1454. 海上夫人 *THE LADY FROM THE SEA*   194 p. by *H. Ibsen.*
                                    4th edit. 1926 商務印書館

This play touches on three marriage questions:
1. In marriage both partners must strive for their common happiness.
2. Marriage is contracted only with the free consent of both parties.
3 Both partners have their share in the responsibilities.

The idea of a second choice for persons already married must be condemned. The author also ignores the divine element in marriage.

Ellida is a young girl without relations. Doctor Wangel, a middle aged widower, asks for her hand. Ellida accepts but without enthusiasm, only in the hope that marriage will give her an easier life. Married, she feels estranged with Wangel's folks and especially with his daughters. She lives alone most of the time and swims a lot. The doctor noticing her desire for solitude, thinks she is ill and treats her as such, which causes still more discomfort to Ellida. One day a friend of her husband daughters recalls to her mind a man who she thinks once loved her; later on, the man comes and asks her to go with him. She tells her husband of her feelings and asks to be allowed to choose freely. Dr. Wangel generously consents. When the other comes back for an answer she chooses her husband whom she loves, having recognized his kindheartedness. *For informed readers.*

1455. 社會棟樑   *PILLARS OF SOCIETY*   1 vol. 204 p. by *H. Ibsen.*
                                                    1938 Com. Press   商務印書館

A play in four acts. The plot revolves around a rich merchant. A great many affairs pass through his hands and he is the object of much flattery, and he has many visitors.

One day, a friend, who went to America fifteen years before, returns on a visit to his native town. He had to go abroad because he was thought to have committed a theft. But in reality, it was the merchant who was guilty, and his friend offered to save him from dishonour in order to spare his wife.

During his stay the friend finds himself forced by certain grave reasons to reveal the truth. The merchant, however, succeeds in preventing him, and in making him leave in a ship in company with a girl, who wishes to escape from hypocritical society.

After the friend has gone, the hero proclaims before the whole town that he is the guilty one, and from henceforth he will work only for the good of the people. *For everyone.*

1456. 伯遴賚侯爵   *LE MARQUIS DE PRIOLA*   1 vol. 157 p. by *H. Lavedan.*
                                      translated by 王了一 1934 商務印書館

A new study of the character of Don Juan personified by the Marquis de Priola, a cynical seducer. *Proscribed.*

1457. 僞善者   *TARTUFFE*   1 vol. 105 p. by *Molière.*
                              translated by 陳古夫 1936 商務印書館

Yes, there are Tartuffes in the world — that is to say, men who under the cover of virtue commit the vilest acts. But even genius of the quality of Moliere's has no right to generalise in painting such pictures. The effect produced goes a bit too far! *Not to be recommended to anyone.*

1458. 大雷雨   1 vol. 114 p. by *A. Ostrowski.*
                              translated by 芳信 1944 世界書局

A tragedy in five acts.

A young married woman, sensitive and very pious, feels that her piety is leaving her little by little. Moreover, she is no longer happy with her husband who nevertheless, loves her very much. Her mother-in-law is a person with a cold, egoistic nature — a widow — who is jealous and does not want to lose the love of her son.

The younger sister of her husband, a cynical girl of doubtful morality, learns the secret of the young wife who has confessed her love for the nephew of a rich merchant, and who has a horror of her sin but finds it impossible to suppress her feelings.

While the husband is away, the sister-in-law arranges a rendezvous for the guilty lovers and they meet each other several times. When the husband returns, the heroine feels her guilt weigh more and more heavily upon her, and hates herself for having sinned. In spite of everything, however, she consents to a last interview with her lover who is being condemned to go to Siberia by his uncle. After this last meeting, her despair is so great that she drowns herself.

Her husband searches for her, and when he finds the body, throws himself upon it while directing some well-merited reproaches at himself and especially at his mother.

The psychological moments when the heroine explains her feelings and sees the magnitude of her sin are accompanied by thunder. Hence the title of the play. Its aim is to describe the storm that goes on in the heart of a good and pious woman who has a horror of an illicit love that she cannot suppress. *Not for the young.*

1459. 小學教員　*TOPAZE*　　　　　　　　1 vol. 260 p. by *Pagnol.*
　　　　　　　　　　　　　　　　　　　　　　1936　中國書局

This translation of the masterpiece of Marcel Pagnol has been brilliantly done and deserved the literary prize of the Sino-French Association of Friendship of Shanghai. The preface gives an excellent analysis of the play and of the work of Pagnol (cf. Etudes, Dec. 20, 1928 p. 711-715, Une analyse de Topaze).

Told shortly, the story is of a teacher in a lycee, whose naive honesty has caused him to be dismissed. He soon after becomes an intermediary for an official who speculates in supplies destined for the town, and is the one behind whom the other hides. Not long after, however, Topaze becomes less naive in perceiving that it is success and not honesty that assures one of the respect of our fellow citizens in modern materialistic society.

The play condemns plainly the abuses that it describes. Nevertheless it is not for very young readers. *Not for everyone.*

1460. 討厭的社會　*LE MONDE OU L'ON S'ENNUIE*　1 vol. 202 p. by *Ed. Pailleron.*
　　　　　　　　　　　　　　　　　　Commercial Press　商務印書舘

A comedy in five acts laid in a background of 19th. century society.

Two young people love each other but are suspicious of each other. They end up by marrying. *For everyone.*

1461. 愛與死的搏鬥　*THE GAME OF LOVE AND DEATH*
　　　　　　　　　　　　　　　　　1 vol. 172 p. by *Rolland Romain.*
　　　　　　　　　　　translated by 李健吾 1946　文化生活出版社
For mature people.

1462. 西哈諾　*CYRANO DE BERGERAC*　　　　1 vol. 304 p. by *E. Rostand.*
　　　　　　　　　　　translated by 方于 1930　商務印書舘

A play in five acts.

Learning that Roxane whom he adores is in love with Christian, Cyrano promotes his rival's suit. He writes his love letters for him, and makes poetic declarations for him under Roxane's balcony. Christian is slain at the seige of Arras, but Cyrano keeps his secret and does not reveal it until the moment of his death, fifteen years later. *For mature people.*

1463. 羅米歐及朱麗葉　*ROMEO AND JULIET*　1 vol. 181 p. by *Shakespeare.*
　　　　　　　　　　　translated by 曹未風 1946　文化合作公司

The hero and the heroine come of two rival families. Romeo falls in love with Juliet, daughter of the enemy, and adores her to distraction. A priest unites them. Romeo is unhappy enough to kill a cousin of Juliet in a duel and is exiled for it. Through swallowing a narcotic that produces the effect of death, Juliet escapes marrying a man whom she detests. Romeo, when he discovers her, thinks that she is dead, and takes poison. When the heroine wakes from her coma, she sees what has happened, and stabs herself to death falling on Romeo's body.

The denouement is unbelievable but the play is of great beauty. *For mature people.*

1464. 如願 *AS YOU LIKE IT*   1 vol. 133 p. by *Shakespeare.*
translated by 曹未風 1946 文化合作公司

A romantic comedy; one of the most charming of Shakespeare's comedies. *For mature people.*

1465. 仲夏夜之夢 *A MIDSUMMER NIGHT'S DREAM* 1 vol. 124 p. by *Shakespeare.*
translated by 曹未風 1946 文化合作公司

The scene is laid in Athens on the occasion of the marriage of Theseus, the duke, to the amazon, Hippolyta. The action is complicated by a series of love intrigues. Fairies figure largely and the comic element is also important. *Not for those who are too young.*

1466. 漢姆萊特 *HAMLET*   1 vol. 221 p. by *Shakespeare.*
translated by 曹未風 1946 文化合作公司

Through seeing the spectre of his father, Hamlet learns that his father has been killed by Claudius (his father's brother) in connivance with his wife. The young prince then simulates madness and neglects his betrothed, Orphelia, which causes her to lose her wits in her turn, and drown herself.

In a duel with Orphelia's brother, Hamlet is slain with a poisoned sword, but before he dies, he succeeds in slaying Claudius, while the queen, his mother, drinks a poisoned beverage, prepared by Hamlet. *For mature people.*

1467. 安東尼及枯婁范 *ANTONY AND CLEOPATRE* 1 vol 216. p. by *Shakespeare.*
translated by 曹未風 1946 文化合作公司

A picturesque, romantic and poetic evocation of one of the most dramatic episodes of ancient history. *For mature people.*

1468. 凡隆納的二紳士 *TWO GENTLEMEN OF VERONA*
1 vol. 131 p. by *Shakespeare.*
translated by 曹未風 1946 文化合作公司

Silvia, daughter of the Duke of Milan, loves Valentine, a gentleman of Verona. The latter finds himself betrayed by his friend, Proteus, who also loves the same girl. Silvia takes to flight and finds Valentine who is now commanding a band of brigands. Valentine forgives Proteus and leaves him to his fiancée, Julia. *For mature people.*

1469. 馬克白斯 *MACBETH*   1 vol. 144 p. by *Shakespeare.*
translated by 曹未風 1946 文化合作公司

A terrible story. Macbeth is journeying through the country with Banco when he meets three witches who predict that he will become king, and the descendants of Banco will be kings also. Everything comes about as predicted by the witches. Macbeth murders Duncan, his king, and Lady Macbeth makes suspicion to fall upon the retainers of the king. Macbeth also causes Banco's death. Remorse for his crimes never leaves him. Lady Macbeth dies, and Macbeth is slain by his enemies. *For mature people.*

1470. 李耳王 *KING LEAR* 1 vol. 195 p. by *Shakespeare* translated by 曹未風 1946 文化合作公司

King Lear divides his estates between his two elder daughters, and disinherits his youngest daughter, Cordelia. Once they have the property in their hands, he is chased away by his two elder daughters. He however, finds refuge with Cordelia. He becomes mad with his sufferings. Cordelia dies strangled, and her father expires on her body. *For mature people.*

1471. 威尼斯商人 *THE MERCHANT OF VENICE* 1 vol. 151 p. by *Shakespeare*. translated by 曹未風 1946 文化合作公司

A merchant of Venice, Antonio, in order to aid his friend, Bassanio, to obtain the hand of the beautiful Portia, underwrites an agreement in which is a cruel clause — to wit, that a pound of his flesh will be forfeit if he cannot repay the loan at the specified time. He escapes from the clutches of the Jew, Shylock, only through a ruse of Portia's. *For mature people.*

1472. 暴風雨 *THE TEMPEST* 1 vol. 129 p. by *Shakespeare*. translated by 曹未風 1946 文化合作公司

Prospero, Duke of Milan, has been chased away by his brother, Antonio. He lands on a desert island with his daughter, Miranda. Many years later, when Miranda has grown into a beautiful girl, Prospero orders Ariel, a spirit in his power, to create a storm that throws Alonzo, King of Naples, and an ally of Antonio, upon the island. Alonzo's son, Ferdinand, is with him and falls in love with Miranda. In the end Prospero is re-established in his estates. *For mature people.*

1473. 聖女貞德 *"ST. JOAN"* 1 vol. 200 p. by *Bernard Shaw*. translated by 胡仁源 1934 商務印書舘

Story of St. Joan of Arc. *For enlightened people.*

1474. 太戈爾戲曲集(一) *COLLECTED PLAYS OF TAGORE* (Vol. I) 1 vol. 78 p. by *R. Tagore*. 2nd. edit. 1924 商務印書舘

齊德拉 Chitra, who has been brought up as a man, feels his womanly aspect awakened at contact with the god, Madana (Eros). A sensual play *not to be recommended to anyone.*

郵局 A symbolic drama with a pantheistic conception of life and death. *For adults.*

1475. 萬尼亞舅舅 *UNCLE VANIA* 1 vol. 94 p. by *Tchekhof*. translated by 麗尼 1946 文化生活出版社

Of life in the country. Too agitated. *For mature people.*

1476. 海鷗 *THE SEAGULL* 1 vol. 117 p. by *Tchekhof*. translated by 尼 1946 文化生活出版社

For mature people.

1477. 伊凡諾夫 *IVANOV* 1 vol. 134 p. by *Tchekhof*. translated by 麗尼 1946 文化生活出版社

A pessimistic drama containing seductions and a suicide. *Not to be recommended to anyone.*

1478. 櫻桃園 *THE CHERRY ORCHARD*   1 vol. 97 p. by *A. Tchekhov.*

translated by 芳信 1944 世界書局

A play in four acts.

A drama centred around the paternal mansion, containing exaggerated fatalism. *For mature people.*

1479. 櫻桃園   1 vol. 153 p. by *A. Tchekov.*

translated by 滿濤 1940 文化生活出版社

A social drama of Russia at the end of the year 1913.

It is pessimistic and breathes social discontent. Thus it is a breeding ground for revolution.

Should be read *only by advanced students.* And they should be informed of the tendencies of the author.

1480. 黑暗勢力 *THE POWER OF SHADOWS*   1 vol. 164 p. by *Tolstoi.*

translated by 芳信 1944 世界書局

A play in five acts. *Dangerous* because of the subversive ideas propagated in it.

1481. 少奶奶的扇子 *"LADY WINDERMERE'S FAN"* 1 vol. 118 p. by *Oscar Wilde.*

上海大通圖書社

After a short period of married life, a young wife leaves her husband and child and lives a disorderly life. Twenty years later she meets her daughter who has recently married. Unaware of the relationship, the young bride believes slandering reports that her husband loves that dissolute woman (her mother). This shocks her so deeply that she contemplates leaving her home and going away with another man. At the last moment the mother, preserving her incognito, makes her change her mind and restores her to her husband. *For informed readers.*

1482. 少校夫人   1 vol. 132 p. by 斯華金斯基

1944 世界書局

A tragedy in five acts.

The son of a rich family, married to a beautiful woman of good character, has a weakness for an adopted sister, and proves it in an unmistakable fashion one day when she is going away on a journey. The latter realises that their little affair is discovered. Being a cynical woman without a conscience, she marries a retired officer. The officer is in love with his wife who, however, despises him thoroughly. Although she flirts with all the men around her, she is cold towards her adopted brother who understands how the land lies but nevertheless retains a very lively love for her.

One day when she is planning to go to Moscow, he proposes a rendezvous at the scene of their first effusions. She accepts. The hero, overcome with passion, proposes that he accompany her, and exasperated by her refusal, takes her up and throws her into the water.

The wife of the murderer hastens to the scene and implores him to save his victim, who, however, drowns.

The author tries to present to us in the victim, a heroine in the manner of the Greek tragedies, pursued by her fate. There is added a dose of Russian mysticism. *Not for the young.*

1483. 結婚 *"MARRIAGE"*   1 vol. 102 p. by 果戈里

Translated by 馮驥 2nd. edit. 1941 光明書局

Operetta in three acts.

A very grown-up young lady wishes to marry. A go-between brings six candidates for her hand. Five are eliminated and the sixth escapes through the window on the day of the wedding. *For everyone.*

1484. 世界名劇精選 *BEST PLAYS IN THE WORLD* No. 1, 1 vol. 262 p. by 舒　湮
1941 光明書局 *See Biogr. 138*

A collection of pieces translated from American, Russian, and Japanese authors, all dealing with the miseries of the poorer classes.

Some of the scenes are too realistic, and the general tendency is pessimistic. *For grown-up people.*

1485. 世界名劇精選 *AN ANTHOLOGY OF WORLD KNOWN PLAYS*
No. 2, 1 vol. 205 p. 舒　湮編
1941 光明書局

A series of plays translated from Russian, French and English.

They consist of criticisms and satires of contemporary society. Several are suitable for acting in our middle schools. *For everyone.*

1486. 戲曲集 *SELECTED MODERN JAPANESE PLAYS* 1 vol. 219 p.
translated from the Japanese by 崔萬秋
1929 中華書局

1. 父與女 A father of a family does not want any rich sons-in-law for his daughters. A young man of fortune dresses as a poor man and deceives the father. When he discovers the fraud, the father is at first angry, but ends up by blessing the lovers.
2. 野島先生之夢 A poor clerk borrows in order to live. Those who are even poorer do the same from him and moreover, one of these coverts his wife and his cousin.
3. 畫室主人 A painter has killed his wife from jealousy. Then he falls in love with a pupil who comes to him for lessons. She, however, prefers one of his other pupils.
For everyone.

1487. 陰謀與愛情 *KABALE UND LIEBE* 1 vol. 168 p. transl. by 張富歲
2nd edit. 1935 Commercial Press.

Tragedy in five acts.

The son of a mandarin falls in love with a poor girl. His father opposes the marriage and makes his son believe that his betrothed is unfaithful to him. The play ends with the suicide of the engaged couple and the repentance of the father.

The play is too fantastic in conception and the solution unconvincing. *For grown-up people.*

1488. 手巾 1 vol. 123 p.
世界文藝書社

A rather complicated love affair, full of surprises but ending well. Very lively. *For everyone.*

Ancient Drama

1489. 長生殿 *PALACE OF THE IMMORTAL* by 洪 昇
In 50 acts

This play equals in beauty "T'ao Hua Shan" (nr. 1493), of the same period. It deals with the love of the T'ang emperor Ming Huang for Yang Kuei-fei, his favourite. The story is very popular and was sung by Pai Kuei-yi and Ch'eng Hung in their 長生歌 and arranged for the stage in 梧桐雨 by Pai Po during the Yuan dynasty.

Ming Huang and Kuei-fei have pledged fidelity to each other in the Palace of Lasting Life, whence the title. The play opens with a description of the life of Kuei-fei and her surroundings at the court of the T'ang emperor. Follows the revolt of An Lo-shan, formerly the emperor's favourite. The emperor is forced to leave his capital and finds refuge in Szechwan. On the way down the army mutinies, demanding the death of Yang Kuo-chung, prime minister and brother of Kuei-fei, and of Kuei-fei herself who are held responsible for the disaster menacing the empire. Ming Huang is prevailed upon and, although unwilling, grants their demand. To save the life of the emperor Kuei-fei commits suicide. After some time the revolt is repressed and the court returns to the capital. By that time Ming Huang has abdicated, giving all his time to mourning his tragic separation from Kuei-fei. A famous magician brings them together again in one of the Palaces of the Immortal. Following this, he dies, never again to be separated from his love.

Same remarks as for "T'ao Hua Shan"; *more caution is required for this play* because immodest allusions are more numerous and two scenes, 21 and 42, are downright lascivious.

1490. 琵琶記 (三不從) *STORY OF THE GUITAR* by 高 明
Edited in 1367 in 42 acts.

Ts'ai Yung is a young scholar, since two months married to Chao Wu-niang, a model daughter-in-law. His parents are eighty years old.

An imperial decree summons to the capital all candidates for the title of Doctor. Since nobody would look after his parents during his absence, Ts'ai Yung and his wife deem it their duty to ignore the decree. A conflict ensues. Having exhausted all arguments by which to persuade his son, the old man commands him to go. In duty bound, Ts'ai leaves his parents and bride, in quest of honour.

He passes his examination and tops the honourroll. The emperor, in need of incorrupt servants, appoints him censor at the palace. Urged by his filial devotion, the young doctor prefers his duty to his parents to this great distinction. The emperor forces him to stay.

In the meantime his parents experience dire poverty, occasioned by a complete failure of the harvest. Soon they are even short of bread. Their suffering is aggravated by the fact that they think they have been wilfully forsaken by their son. Wuniang sells her gowns, her jewels, all her belongings in order to relieve their plight. She does not shrink from going out to beg for some rice and even eats chaff to save the last mouthful for her parents. In spite of these sacrifices they die of starvation. She sells her hair to buy them a coffin; then, with her own hands, she digs their grave.

Having thus heroically fulfilled her duty to the living, she paints the portrait of the deceased in order to be able to make the annual offerings. Then, dressed as a nun, she starts on her way to the capital, in search of her husband. She goes from village to village playing the lute to cover the expense of her pilgrimage.

The imperial Chancellor, Niu, is the most opulent and influential man in the empire. He has a daughter, of marriageable age, beautiful and virtuous. Overlooking a great number of suitable candidates, he has set his mind on marrying his daughter to Ts'ai Yung. After repeated protests, unable to resist the Chancellor any longer, the latter consents. Although he does not know the fate that has befallen his home, he is so unhappy that the charms and virtues of his second wife cannot make him forget his duties as son and husband. A messenger dispatched by him never reaches his native place, but hands him a faked reply and cheats him out of a lot of money.

For three years he lives a wretched life until he finally tells everything to his wife. She decides to accompany him to his native country, but, again, the Chancellor frustrates their plan. In the long run the Chancellor recognizes his fault and invites the parents and wife of Ts'ai Yung to the capital.

By this time Wu-niang has arrived in the capital where she becomes acquainted with Niu Shih, the second wife of Ts'ai Yung. The tale of her troubles, the infidelity of her husband and the purpose of her journey, and of her heroic devotion to duty endear her to Niu Shih. When the latter discovers that Wu-niang is the wife of her husband, she brings them together in a pathetic scene. Thereafter Wu-niang and Niu Shih, who love each other as two sisters, both serve their beloved husband.

This time the Chancellor is not adamantine and grants a three years' furlough during which the hero, accompanied by his two wives, goes to his home and mourns his parents.

When the time of mourning is over, an imperial messenger arrives with a decree that praises Wu-niang's virtues, ennobles the family and heaps distinctions on Ts'ai Yung.

We must censure the polygamy preconized in the play, although it was prevalent in society at that time.

The play points a good moral and sets a beautiful example of filial devotion; still, we must *caution against some expressions* that are too suggestive for readers familiar with the subtleties of the Chinese language.

1491. 玉鏡臺 *THE JADE MIRROR*   by 關漢卿
6th in the series of 100 Yuan plays.

Ying-ying, daughter of Mrs. Wen, attains a marriageable age. Her mother looks for and finds a suitable match. A certain doctor Chin is chosen. Ying-ying refuses him, but in the end she is prevailed upon and acquiesces. Though married to him, she still does not recognize him as her husband. After some time a messenger brings her a gift presented by the emperor; she can only accept it, if she consents to consider Chin as her husband. Her vanity gets the better of her and she accepts both the gift and the husband. *For all.*

1492. 謝天香   by 關漢卿
9th in the series of 100 Yuan plays.

P'ang, a bachelor, is in love with a prostitute. He must leave her, to go to the capital to pass his examinations. To prevent her from being unfaithful during his absence, he commits her to the care of the local governor. The latter falls in love with her, and, while P'ang slaves away, at his examinations, they have a good time. He marries her but has no intercourse with her. . .After his promotion, P'ang returns to see his beloved married to the governor and does not try to hide his anger. The governor soothes him by giving back the woman whom he had only married to protect her against any possible temptation during her lover's absence. *Unsuitable for younger people.*

1493. 桃花扇   by 孔尙任

In 41 acts.

This is one of the best plays of the Ch'ing period. It describes admirably the troubled times at the end of the Ming period. The characters are historical personages; the love story is the authors's.

Hou Fang-yü, a young man of letters, marries Hsiang Chün, an actress of conspicuous talent and beauty. On their wedding day Fang-yü gives her a fan on which he has written a few lines of poetry. The bride's trousseau is offered by Yüan Ta-yüeh, known playwright, author of the drama 燕子箋. He formerly was a public servant; he has a vile character and is detested by the younger nobility of his time. As Hsiang Chün rejects the present, Ta yüeh broods on vengeance. He falsely accuses Fang-yü of complicity in a certain plot against the emperor; this forces Fang-yü to leave his young wife and flee. Meanwhile the last Ming emperor hangs himself on the Coal-hill. Ta-yüeh's faction place a new emperor on the throne at Nanking. This gives Fang-yü's enemies a chance to give free course to their vengeance. Ta-yüeh gives Hsiang Chün as concubine to one of his friends. She wants to be faithful, so on the night when they come for her, she throws herself down, wounds her forehead and loses consciousness. Blood trickles from her head on the fan, forming a pattern resembling peach flowers; hence the title of the play. In the midst of the disorder Hsiang Chün's foster-mother, also a well known actress, manages to go in her place, thus saving her daughter from unfaithfulness. Then follows a period of unrest; the Ch'ing armies march South. The emperor in Nanking and Ta-yüeh's party perish.

After a lot of vicissitudes Fang-yü and Hsiang Chün finally find each other, to separate again when they enter a Taoist monastery.

Besides the opening of scene 7, which is very immodest, the play contains a number of immodest insinuations, a thing that is common to most Chinese plays. *For informed readers only.*

1494. 黃梁夢   by 馬致遠
                                        45th in the series of 100 Yuan plays.

Bachelor Liu sees his future in a dream: his marriage, the unfaithfulness of his wife, his exile for high-treason, his flight with his children. When he awakes, a monk. who happens to be there, shows him the happiness of those who follow the "Tao". Liu decides not to pass his examinations and to follow the monk.

For informed readers because of an objectionable scene.

1495. 牡丹亭 (還魂記) *PEONY PAVILION*   by 湯顯祖
In 55 acts (1550-1617)

Tu Li-niang, sixteen, daughter of a certain prefect, and a truly ideal girl. She is strikingly beautiful and the joy of her parents. Her father wishes her to become a woman who will be the pride of her future husband. Therefore he engages Ch'en, an old scholar, to perfect her literary education.

She studies the Shih Ching and is so much obsessed by some lines that, one day, while she is strolling in the garden, the lover of her dreams materializes. They are married in the "Peony Pavilion". All this happens in a dream.

The memory of this dream haunts her so that the best care of her parents cannot prevent her from dying of love-sickness.

For three years she dwells in Hades. After that she is pardoned because she only trespassed in a dream, and permitted to return to earth as a spirit.

At this time Liu Meng-mei is on his way to the capital where he will pass his final examination. He falls ill and stays for many months in the native town of Li-niang. He lives in the temple built there in her honour by her parents who have moved to another town. He discovers her portrait and falls violently in love with her. During the night her spirit comes to visit him and they engage themselves to be married. She tells him her story and urges him to unearth her body in order to reunite it to her spirit. On Li-niang's resurrection they marry and take flight lest Meng-mei should be arrested for grave-robbery.

Li-niang's father has in the meantime been engaged in a war to which he gives the whole of his mind in order to forget two deaths: his daughter's and his wife's. A false message made him believe the latter died.

After Meng-mei has passed his examinations, topping the honour roll, his wife persuades him to go in search of her father; when they find him, he not only does not believe his daughter's adventures, but even imprisons his son-in-law for having robbed his daughter's grave.

Finally the emperor himself intervenes, authenticating the resurrection of Li-niang, which puts an end to the family discord. Thereafter, honoured for their virtues and rewarded for their merits, they live in unbroken happiness till the end of their days.

It is one of the best Ming stories. A few pages are rather unbecoming; it should, therefore, *not be given to younger people.*

In German: "Die Ruckkehr der Seele" by *Vinzens Hundhausen.*

1496. 西廂記 *STORY OF THE WESTERN PAVILION*   by 王實甫
This is one of the most celebrated plays in Chinese drama.

On his way to the capital where he will pass examinations, Chang Sheng-yü, a poor scholar, son of an ex-minister, meets the beautiful Ts'ui Ying-ying, daughter of the deceased prime minister. She and her mother are escorting the minister's casket to his native county. Enchanted by the beauty of the girl Sheng-yü decides to stay at the same monastery where the two women occupy the "Western Chamber". With the help of the girl's maid, he succeeds in handing the girl a love poem.

A rebel general, having heard that the girl is staying at the monastery, plans to capture it and the girl. Although Ying-ying is betrothed, her mother promises her daughter to any one who will deliver them from this danger. With the help of a loyal general, Sheng-yü saves them. . .but the mother changes her mind.

In secret Sheng-yü makes love to the girl, who returns his feelings, so that soon they spend the night together. On hearing about this, the mother has no other way to save her daughter's good name but to consent to their marriage. The ceremonies being over, she sends Sheng-yü to the capital to pass his examination. During his absence the ex-fiancé comes to claim his rights; the mother seconds him; but Ying-ying remains faithful. After Sheng-yü's return they live happily for the rest of their lives. (The original story ends with the separation of the heroes).
Proscribed.

1497. 燕子箋 *SWALLOWS DIVE*   2 vol. 162 p. and 188 p. by 阮大鋮
1934 大中書局

A story written at the end of the Ming Dynasty.
The events occur at the time of the Emperor Ming Huang of the T'ang Dynasty.

Huo Tu-liang, a young scholar of great talent, paints his portrait beside that of his beautiful cousin, Hsing Yun, and the two swear eternal fidelity. The picture is then given to a workman to mount.

This craftsman receives at the same time, for mounting, a portrait of Kuan Shih Yin from the beautiful Fei Yun, daughter of a high official. And after the mounting has been finished, the two pictures are interchanged so that Fei Yun receives the portrait of two young lovers whom she does not know. To her great surprise, however, it seems that the girl painted by the side of the handsome young man bears a strange resemblance to herself. Thus she finds herself in love with him.

She pours out her love in verses which she inscribes on a piece of letter paper. This paper is taken by a swallow who lays it at the foot of Tu-liang, who, after he has read it, is overcome, especially as he does not know who has written these verses.

In the meantime the official examinations have become due, and a friend of Tu-liang's succeeds in substituting a mediocre copy written by himself for Tu-liang's paper, thus depriving the latter from first place when the results are declared. Wishing also to deprive him of Hsing Yun, he accuses Tu-liang falsely of having secret relations with Fei Yun and thus forces him to flee.

The revolution of An Lo-shan follows during which all these personages are dispersed. But after a number of denouements, Tu-liang meets the one who wrote the love letter, and marries her.

Soon after, Hsing Yun, who has been reported lost, reappears, and wishes to take Tu-liang away from Fei Yun. After a number of quite lively altercations, an arrangement is come to and both become the wives of Tu-liang.

In the meantime, owing to Hsing Yun's efforts, the fraud committed at the examinations against their husband is admitted, and Tu-liang is made a Doctor.

This story, just as all those of the same kind, contains a certain number of risky allusions. That is why it should be read only by grown-up people. *Not for everyone.*

1498. 鐵拐李 *MANDARIN LU'S METEMPSYCHOSIS.*   by 岳白川
29th in the series of 100 Yuan plays.

Lu, a mandarin, is sentenced to death for his injustice. The god of Hades permits him to come back on earth in the misshapen body of a certain Li, who has recently died. He must promise to abstain from the pleasures of the flesh and become a Taoist monk. On his return on earth his former wife and Mrs. Li both claim him. . .a monk reminds him of his promise. . .Fear of hell makes him say farewell to women and follow the monk. *For all.*

1499. 灰闌記

Theater Play of Yuan Dynasty.

Chang Hai-t'ang becomes the concubine of Mr. Ma. Mrs. Ma accuses her of infidelity while she herself poisons her husband to get off with a certain Chao. She accuses Chang of the murder and also claims Chang's child as her own to get hold of the inheritance.

The tribunal pronounces Chang guilty; she lodges an appeal and also claims the child.

The judge then chalks a circle on the floor and puts the child in the centre. The woman who succeeds in snatching the baby out of the circle will be considered to be the mother. Twice they both get hold of the child and twice Chang Hai-t'ang lets go. So Mrs. Ma is declared to be the mother.

Chang Hai-t'ang still claims the baby, saying she had to let go her hold lest the child should be hurt. These words satisfy the judge; he gives the child to the mother and punishes the culprits. Hai-t'ang inherits the estate and goes to live on it with her child and her brother. This brother was a beggar. Mrs. Ma had given him alms. In fact this was Hai-t'ang's charity, but Mrs. Ma had told the beggar that his sister did not want to help him; on the other hand she told Mr. Ma that Hai-t'ang gave presents to a lover.

In German: "Der Kreidekreis" by Wollheim da Foncesa.

For informed readers. A few unbecoming details.

1500. 鴛鴦被   by an unknown author.
4th in the series of 100 Yuan plays.

Li Jen, a mandarin, must go to the capital to defend himself against accusations. Having no money he borrows from an old usurer who asks not only for the mandarin's signature but also for his daughter's. Li Jen then goes away, promising to return soon.

After one year he does not return. The time of the contract runs out and the old usurer claims the daughter. Misinformed about the age and looks of the man, she is willing to marry him. She even consents to a meeting before the marriage. Fortunately a young bachelor presents himself for the interview instead of the old man who has another engagement. The two young people instantly take to each other. In the end Li returns, blesses the two lovers and punishes the old usurer.

For informed readers because of a few unbecoming details.

— *THE END* —

CONTENTS

Present Day Fiction & Drama in China

Short Biographies of Authors

1500 Modern Chinese Novels & Plays

*All the books reviewed in this volume are classified here into several categories;
each book is followed by one of the following four signs:* **E, R, RR** *and* **P**. *These signs
indicate the categories into which we classify all the books according to their moral value.
Educators interested in the ethical value of a book, will find here a list which is easy to
consult. The signification of these signs is as follows:*

　　E (for everyone) — *meaning that a book thus qualified, has nothing offensive to
morality, nor trespassing against Christian doctrines. At the same time we are not stating
that such a book is necessarily good. The only meaning we give to this qualification is
that it contains nothing bad. It is also evident that many books, but not all of them,
bearing such signs are good in reality.*

　　R (not for everyone) — *we qualify by this sign the books which can be read by
well-informed people (married people, persons with middle-school education, grown-ups
etc.) In this kind of books one can come across some expressions ever so slightly risky
or rather coarse, trifling descriptions, bold sayings, false ideas (divorce, suicide, etc; not
defended by the author) and non-too-pure atmosphere etc.*

　　*In our opinion, these books are simply reserved, and should be excluded from the
pastoral libraries, etc. . In the city where the mind of the people are more world-wise
one can tolerate reading them, while principals of middle schools should give judgments
as they deem wise. As for seminary library, the director should try to examine the books
which we have classified in the above-mentioned categories, and make a judicious choice.*

　　RR. (not to be recommended to anyone) — *books under this qualification are
definitely recommended to be refrained from reading, even for well-informed persons, unless
they are with certain special intentions, as these books contain some much-repeated,
risky passages, disturbing readings, frivolous descriptions. We have also thus qualified
the books opposed to religion; those books containing unhealthy atmosphere dangerous
for the ethical and social education, and the books combatting openly the orthodox ideas
and defending subversive one, (divorce etc.).*

　　P (proscribed) — *these are the books strictly forbidden, to be kept from reading,
excepting by people with motives of importance. We understand by this sign that the
book is of immoral nature or touching upon immorality.*

　　(N.B. For Catholic educators: *Meminerint lectores quosdam libros prohibitos esse
vel ipsa lege naturae vel lege Ecclesiae positivae. C.J.C. c1399).*

*The arabic figures after the above mentioned signs in the following column refer to the
number in the review where the books are discussed.*

3 Strokes

4 Strokes

5 Strokes

474 CONTENTS

10 Strookes

11 Strokes

ERRATA

Page	Line				
X	20	for	"The Crime of Fan Chi" "范集的犯罪"	read	"The Crime of Fan Mou" "范某的犯罪"
XIII	28	for	"雪之除夕"	read	"愛的焦點".
XIII	28	for	"愛的焦點"	read	"雪之除夕".
XX	24	for	"波希米的人們"	read	"婆漢迷".
XXIII	22	for	"小哥倆"	read	"小哥兒倆".
XXIV	4	for	"which has been re-named subsequently as"	read	"Later she wrote".
XXIX	4	for	"徐傑"	read	"許傑".
XXXII	42	for	"who died"	read	"who has fought.
XXXVIII	17	for	"his"	read	"hers".
L	3	for	"風雨夜歸人"	read	"風雪夜歸人".
8	19	for	"張廷謙"	read	"章廷謙".
38	17	for	"夏丏尊"	read	"夏丏尊".
62	24	for	"文季月刊"	read	"文學季刊".
116	37	for	"死生同心"	read	"生死同心".
119	11	for	"Love of Hatred"	read	"Love and Hatred".
136	11	for	"章浪"	read	"章泯".
167	12	for	"海落"	read	"淪落".
178	22	for	"綠綠堂隨筆"	read	"緣緣堂隨筆".
191	12	for	"張又吾"	read	"張又君".
196	4	for	"謝元逸"	read	"謝六逸".
224	first	for	"天堂北獄"	read	"天堂地獄".
247	37	for	"劉黑芷"	read	"羅黑芷".
309	12	for	"鳩線媚"	read	"鳩綠媚".
312	39	for	"寒火集"	read	"寒灰集".
334	17	for	"爾都集"	read	"雨都集".
336	17	for	"海外奇霓君"	read	"海外寄霓君".
336	25	for	"朱光簪"	read	"朱光潛".
338	32	for	"胡適"	read	"胡懷琛".
339	37	for	"偏具集"	read	"偏見集".
382	23	for	"自求"	read	"自救".
383	48	for	"光樂的戰鬥"	read	"光榮的戰鬥".
449	15	for	"山城故事"	read	"小城故事".
449	23	for	"出城故事"	read	"山城故事"
457	37	for	"尼"	read	"麗尼".

SCHEUT EDITIONS （普愛堂出版社）

Series I. Critical & Literary Studies

VOL. I *Romans à lire et romans à proscrire* by Jos. Schyns & others. Peiping 1946
In Chinese: 文藝月旦(甲集) by 善秉仁. Peiping 1947

VOL. II *Histoire de la litterature chinoise moderne* by H. Van Boven. Peiping 1946
English edition in preparation.

VOL. III *1500 Modern Chinese Novels & Plays* by Jos. Schyns & others. Peiping 1948
Sole Distributors: Catholic University Press Peiping-China
In Chinese: 文藝月旦(乙集) by 善秉仁. (in preparation).

VOL. IV *500 Short Biographies of Modern Authors* by Chao Yen-sheng (in preparation).

Series II. Practical Mission Life

VOL. I *Le Savoir-Vivre en Chine* by Jos. Nuyts. Peiping 1947
English edition in preparation.

Series III. History & Geography

世界大事年表 by 夏仰聖 Peiping 1947 (available at Catholic University Press, Sales Office, Peiping-China).

Series IV. Philosophy & Sociology

VOL. I 邊疆公教社會事業 by 王守禮. Peiping 1947
VOL. II *Le Communisme arrive au village chinois* by Fr. Legrand. Peiping 1947
In Chinese: 中共在農村. Catholic Truth Society, Hongkong.

Series V. Religion 少年良友 by 葛立模. Peiping 1948.

Also available at "Scheut editions":

L'Apostolat Intellectuel en Chine by Fr. Legrand. 1948
In Chinese: 文化傳教工作 by 高樂康. 1948
Syntaxis Linguae Latinae by F. Sercu. Peiping 1941
Le Triomphe de la Charité by J. Leyssen. Peiping 1943
The Cross over China's Wall by J. Leyssen. Peiping 1941
Formatio Cleri in Mongolia by J. Leyssen. Peiping 1940
Het Chineesch taaleigen Vol. I by Jos. Mullie Peiping 1930
Het Chineesch taaleigen Vol. II by Jos. Mullie. Peiping 1931
Het Chineesch taaleigen Vol. III by Jos. Mullie. Peiping 1932
The Structural Principles of the Chinese Language Vol. I by Jos. Mullie Peiping 1932
The Structural Principles of the Chinese Language Vol. II, III by Jos. Mullie. Peiping 1937

Scheut editions: Verbist Academy, 2 Niu P'aitze Hutung, Peiping (20) China
懷仁學會　北平 (20) 牛排子胡同二號
Also on sale at Scheut mission, 209 Lin-Sen Road, Tientsin
天津林森路二〇九號　普愛堂
Scheut mission, Hua-Shan-Lu 135 N° 7, Shanghai
上海華山路135弄7號　普愛堂

史地傳記類　PC0146

中國現代小說戲劇一千五百種

主　　編 / 謝泳、蔡登山

數位重製・印刷 / 秀威資訊科技股份有限公司
　　　　　　　http://www.showwe.com.tw
　　　　　　　114 台北市內湖區瑞光路 76 巷 65 號 1 樓
　　　　　　　電話：+886-2-2796-3638
　　　　　　　傳真：+886-2-2796-1377
劃撥帳號 / 19563868　戶名：秀威資訊科技股份有限公司
　　　　　　　讀者服務信箱：service@showwe.com.tw
網路訂購 / 秀威網路書店：https://store.showwe.tw
　　　　　　　網路訂購：order@showwe.com.tw

2011 年 5 月
精裝印製工本費：1650 元

Printed in Taiwan

國家圖書館出版品預行編目

中國現代小說戲劇一千五百種 / 謝泳、蔡登山編.
-- 一版. -- 臺北市 ： 秀威資訊科技, 2011.05
面 ； 公分. -- (史地傳記類；PC0146)
BOD 版
ISBN 978-986-221-737-5(精裝)

1.中國小說 2.現代小說 3.劇本 4.提要

016.857 100005911

讀 者 回 函 卡

感謝您購買本書，為提升服務品質，請填妥以下資料，將讀者回函卡直接寄回或傳真本公司，收到您的寶貴意見後，我們會收藏記錄及檢討，謝謝！
如您需要了解本公司最新出版書目、購書優惠或企劃活動，歡迎您上網查詢或下載相關資料：http:// www.showwe.com.tw

您購買的書名：＿＿＿＿＿＿＿＿＿＿＿＿＿＿＿＿＿＿＿＿＿＿

出生日期：＿＿＿＿＿年＿＿＿＿＿月＿＿＿＿＿日

學歷：□高中 (含) 以下　　□大專　　□研究所 (含) 以上

職業：□製造業　□金融業　□資訊業　□軍警　□傳播業　□自由業
　　　□服務業　□公務員　□教職　　□學生　□家管　　□其它＿＿＿

購書地點：□網路書店　□實體書店　□書展　□郵購　□贈閱　□其他

您從何得知本書的消息？

　　□網路書店　□實體書店　□網路搜尋　□電子報　□書訊　□雜誌
　　□傳播媒體　□親友推薦　□網站推薦　□部落格　□其他＿＿＿＿＿

您對本書的評價：（請填代號　1.非常滿意　2.滿意　3.尚可　4.再改進）

　　封面設計＿＿＿　版面編排＿＿＿　內容＿＿＿　文／譯筆＿＿＿　價格＿＿＿

讀完書後您覺得：

　　□很有收穫　□有收穫　□收穫不多　□沒收穫

對我們的建議：＿＿＿＿＿＿＿＿＿＿＿＿＿＿＿＿＿＿＿＿＿＿

＿＿＿＿＿＿＿＿＿＿＿＿＿＿＿＿＿＿＿＿＿＿＿＿＿＿＿＿＿＿＿

＿＿＿＿＿＿＿＿＿＿＿＿＿＿＿＿＿＿＿＿＿＿＿＿＿＿＿＿＿＿＿

＿＿＿＿＿＿＿＿＿＿＿＿＿＿＿＿＿＿＿＿＿＿＿＿＿＿＿＿＿＿＿

11466

台北市內湖區瑞光路 76 巷 65 號 1 樓

秀威資訊科技股份有限公司　　　收

BOD 數位出版事業部

....

（請沿線對折寄回，謝謝！）

姓　　名：＿＿＿＿＿＿＿＿　　年齡：＿＿＿＿　　性別：□女　□男

郵遞區號：□□□□□

地　　址：＿＿＿＿＿＿＿＿＿＿＿＿＿＿＿＿＿＿＿＿＿＿

聯絡電話：(日) ＿＿＿＿＿＿＿＿＿＿＿　(夜) ＿＿＿＿＿＿＿＿＿＿＿

E-mail：＿＿＿＿＿＿＿＿＿＿＿＿＿＿＿＿＿＿＿＿＿